DHOFAR
MONSOON MOUNTAINS TO SAND SEAS

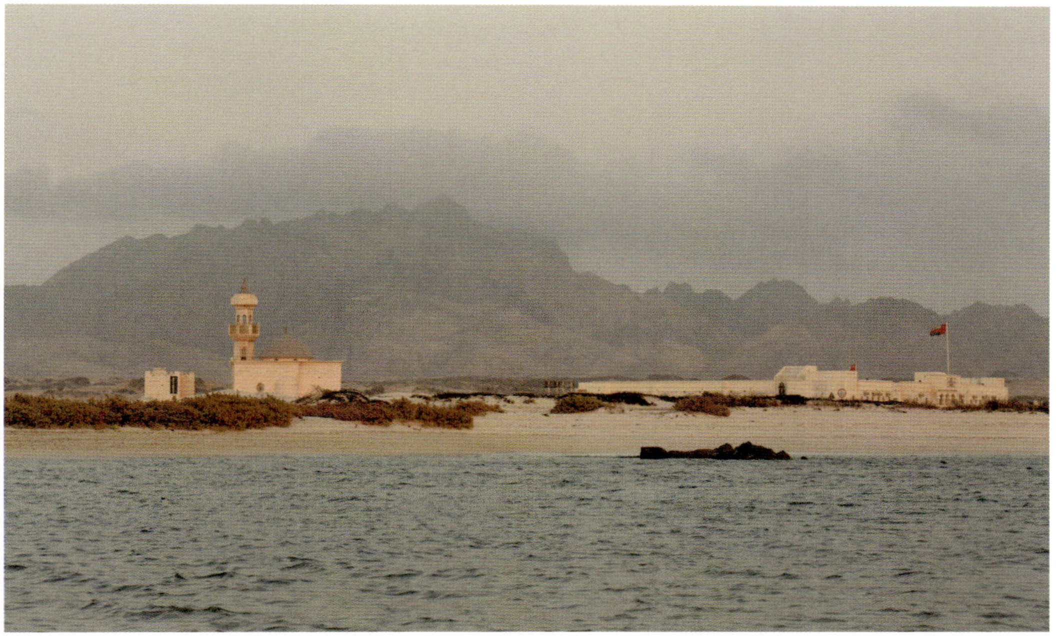

DHOFAR
MONSOON MOUNTAINS TO SAND SEAS

ANDREW SPALTON & HADI AL HIKMANI

GILGAMESH

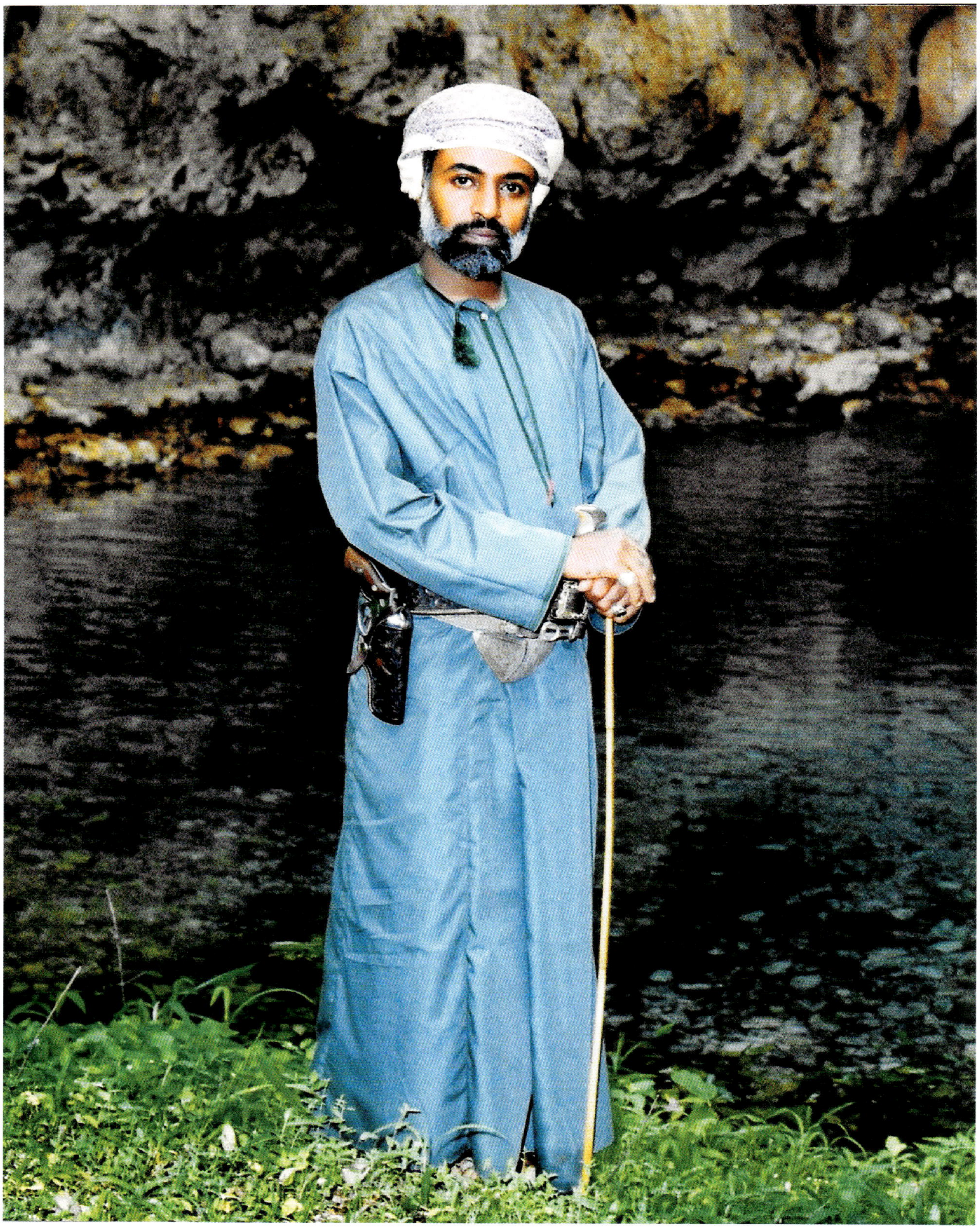

The Late Sultan Qaboos bin Said

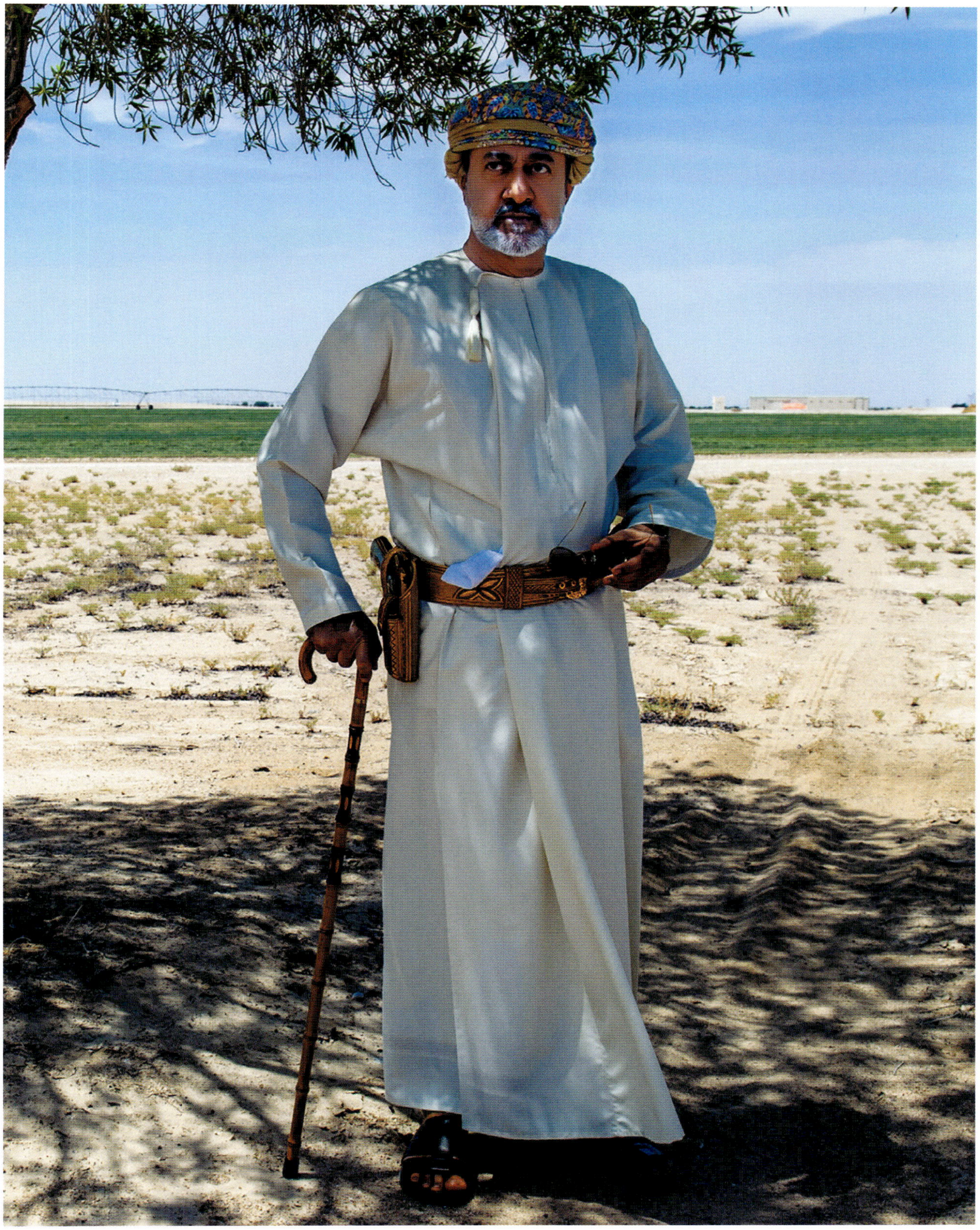

His Majesty Sultan Haitham bin Tarik

DHOFAR
MONSOON MOUNTAINS TO SAND SEAS

Photographic credits;
t=top, b=bottom, l=left, r=right, c=centre
All photographs by **Andrew Spalton**, except: **Hadi Al Hikmani** 135, 147, 149, 150(tl), 151, 152, 154(br) & 175(tr); **Khalid Al Hikmani** 150(tr); **Ahmed Al Touqi** 84, 85, 96; **Robert Baldwin** 161(tr); **Paul Bates** 157(br); **Michael Butler** 227; **ESO (taken by Darryl MacDonald)** 160 & 195(tl); **Hanne & Jens Eriksen** 150(tr), 164, 165(b), 166(br), 167(t & b), 169(t & b) & 197(tr); **Paul Flandinette** 161(tl), 189 & 191(t, bl & br); **Andrew Gardner** 171, & 176(t), 177(tl, bl & r); **Brandon King** 237(t); **Gary Lyon** 190; **Mike McGrady** 195(c); **Tim Michels** 207; **Mohammed Mustafa** iv, v; **Toufic Abou Nader** 55(tl); **PDO / GlassPoint Solar** 239; **Jeffrey Rose** 21(t); **Pipat Soisook** 156; **Mohammed Tabook** 87; **John Ward** 206; **Robert Whitcombe** 94; **Andrew Willson** 179; **Joanna Wong @5OES** 161(b).

Editorial: Henry Harding, Alex Newby
Design: Martin Humphreys
Maps: Terry McCormick

Published in collaboration by Gilgamesh Publishing and
the Diwan of Royal Court of the Sultanate of Oman in 2020
Registered with Ministry of Information, Sultanate of Oman
Email: info@gilgamesh-publishing.co.uk
www.gilgamesh-publishing.co.uk
ISBN 978-1908531-85-8

CIP Data: A catalogue for this book is available from the British Library.

Contents

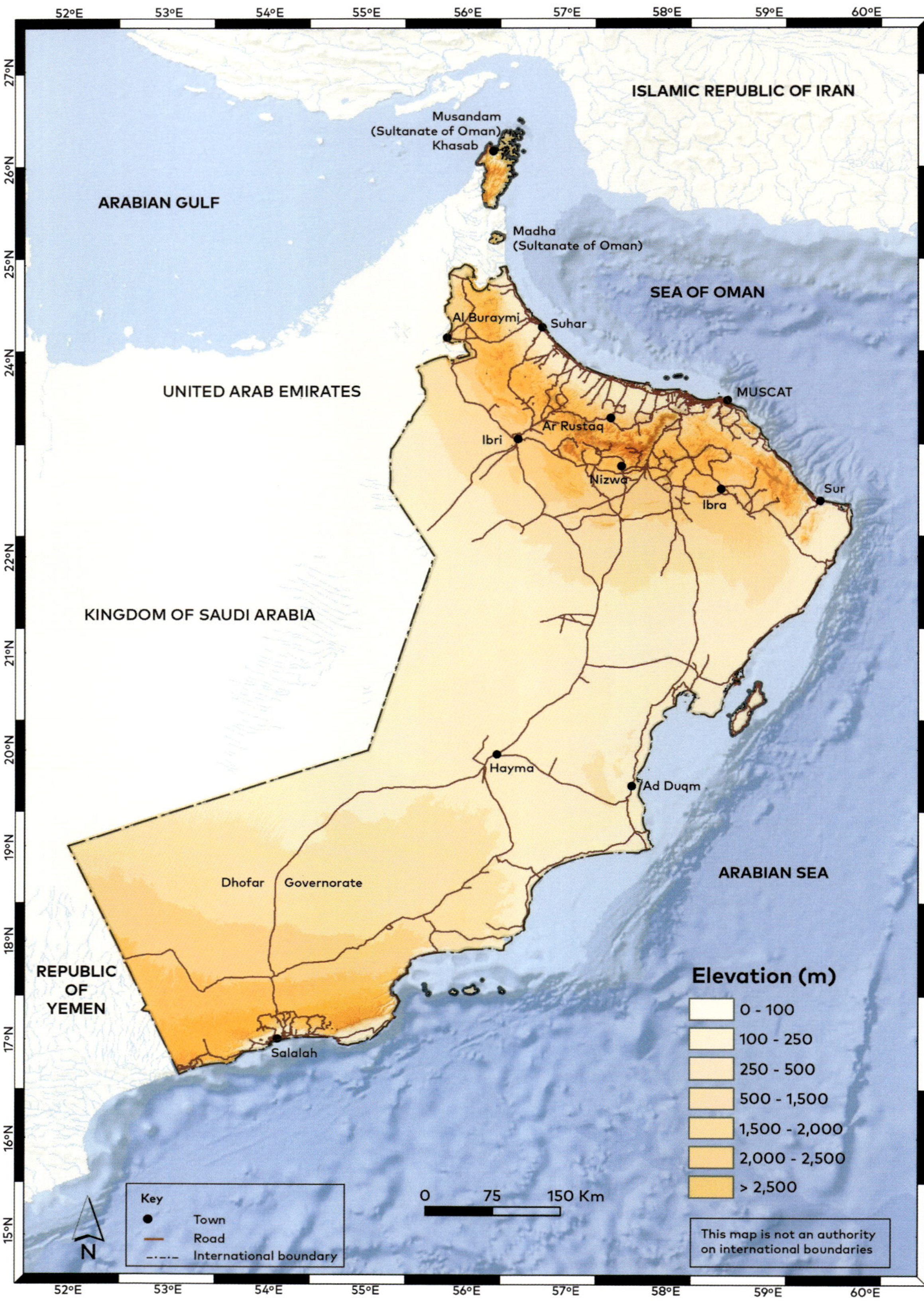

The Sultanate of Oman

Foreword

The Dhofar Governorate of the Sultanate of Oman is blessed with the magical *khareef* season when, during the months of July and August, the Southwest Monsoon sweeps in from the Arabian Sea and transforms the brown mountain landscape to a luscious green. As a result of this extraordinary phenomenon, Dhofar Governorate is blessed with a variety of breathtaking landscapes unlike anything seen anywhere else in the region. To the south are the richly verdant mountains, to the north the reddish-orange sand dunes of the great sand seas of the world famous Empty Quarter, and between lies the vast stony desert of the Najd. Along the shorelines, spectacular seascapes include both wild monsoon-swept rocky shores and pristine sandy beaches, while offshore lie harshly beautiful and remote islands. These unique places are home to a very special biodiversity that includes globally iconic animal and plant species such the Arabian leopard, Arabian Sea humpback whale and the frankincense tree.

The late Sultan Qaboos bin Said's commitment to the conservation and sustainable development of the unique natural environment of Dhofar was clear at the dawn of the Sultanate's modern renaissance. His wise directives led to the preservation and protection of the natural environment, increased environmental awareness among all segments of society and to finding solutions for challenges including desertification, overgrazing and marine pollution. This approach will be complemented by the vision of His Majesty Sultan Haitham bin Tariq whose wise directives will continue to safeguard the natural environment while developing programs, especially for ecotourism, that support sustainable development.

This book shows the wonderful diversity of Dhofar; its natural landscapes, climate, water resources, the wild flora and fauna and also the traditional livelihoods of its people that are deeply rooted and very much part of today's modern society. Above all this book reminds us all that we have a duty to safeguard this magnificent place.

Khalid Bin Hilal bin Saud Al Busaidi
Minister of the Diwan of Royal Court
Sultanate of Oman
December 2020

Introduction

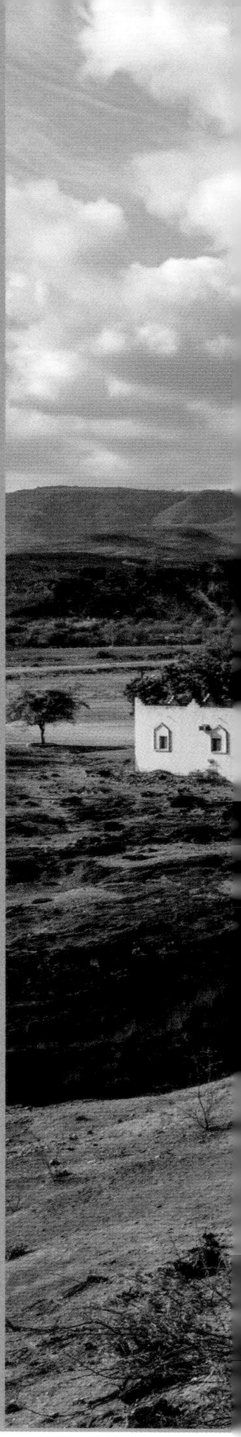

For more than 2,000 years, historians, geographers and travellers have written of the marvels and natural wonders of Dhofar. The Greek writer Herodotus, who lived 2,400 years ago, wrote, 'In Arabia alone of all lands, there grows frankincense', where 'winged snakes, small in size and spotted in appearance, guard these incense-bearing trees.'[1] The Greek geographer Ptolemy produced the first map of Dhofar and wrote of the 'City of the Abyss', referring to the ancient city of Samharam below the great waterfall of Wadi Darbat. Arab travellers including the historian Abu Ubayd Al-Bakri and the scholar Ibn Battuta visited Dhofar and wrote of mighty kings, frankincense, gold, Arabian horses and camels.[2] European travellers were astonished at the rich meadows and woodlands and the diversity of plants and animals of the green mountains; in 1897, after visiting the 'marvel' of Wadi Darbat, the explorers James and Theodore Bent concluded, 'This really is Arabia Felix'.[3]

(Above) The monsoon mountains of Dhofar have sustained life for millennia. Water from the spring of Ayn Razat at the base of the Jabal is distributed by surface channels known as *aflaj*.

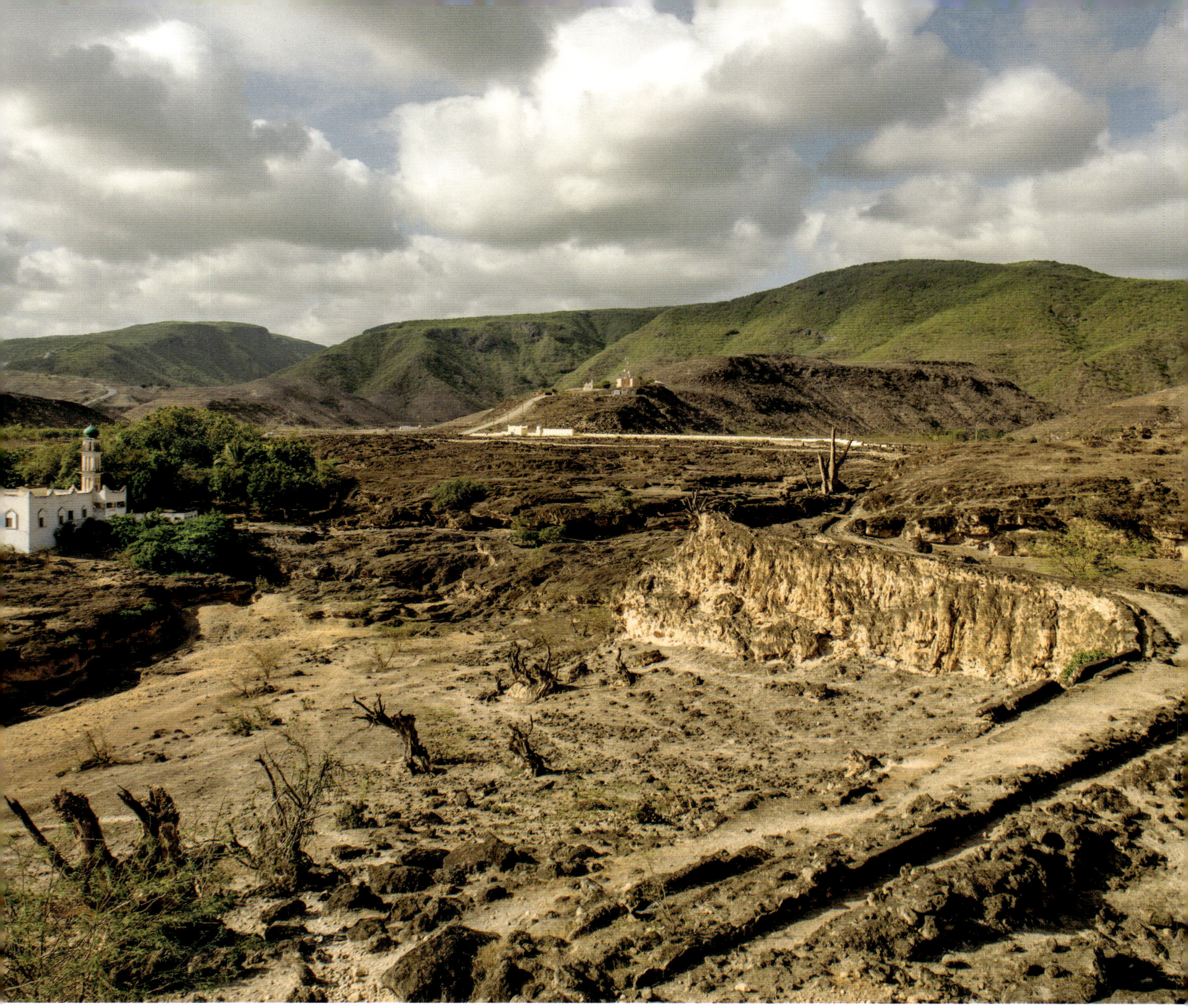

At the heart of Dhofar is the crescent-shaped mountain (commonly known by the Arabic term *Jabal*) that sweeps 250 kilometres west from the Arabian Sea coast to the border with Yemen. It is formed from three adjoining mountains: in the west Jabal Al Qamar that rises from the sea, in the centre Jabal Al Qara that overlooks the coastal plain or *Jarbib* and in the east the mighty Jabal Samhan. To the north of the mountains are the vast waterless plains of the Najd that merge with the great sand-seas of the Empty Quarter or *Ar Rub Al Khali*, the world's largest sand desert.

However, to really know Dhofar one must go back not a mere 2,400 years to the time of Herodotus but 700 million years to when the land was born. This is best understood from atop the high escarpment of the towering Jabal Samhan, overlooking the Salawt Plain several hundred metres below. The scene is breathtaking as the magnificent escarpment runs south-west towards Mirbat and east towards Hasik, but what is most striking is the mass of dark rock below, through which run rust-red veins, broken only by the pale *wadis* that snake towards the distant sea. For Dhofar this is the beginning of time, for here the rocks are around 700 million years old, with some up to 1300 million years old– the oldest rocks known in Oman.[4]

These rocks were formed at a time when the Middle East was part of a supercontinent known

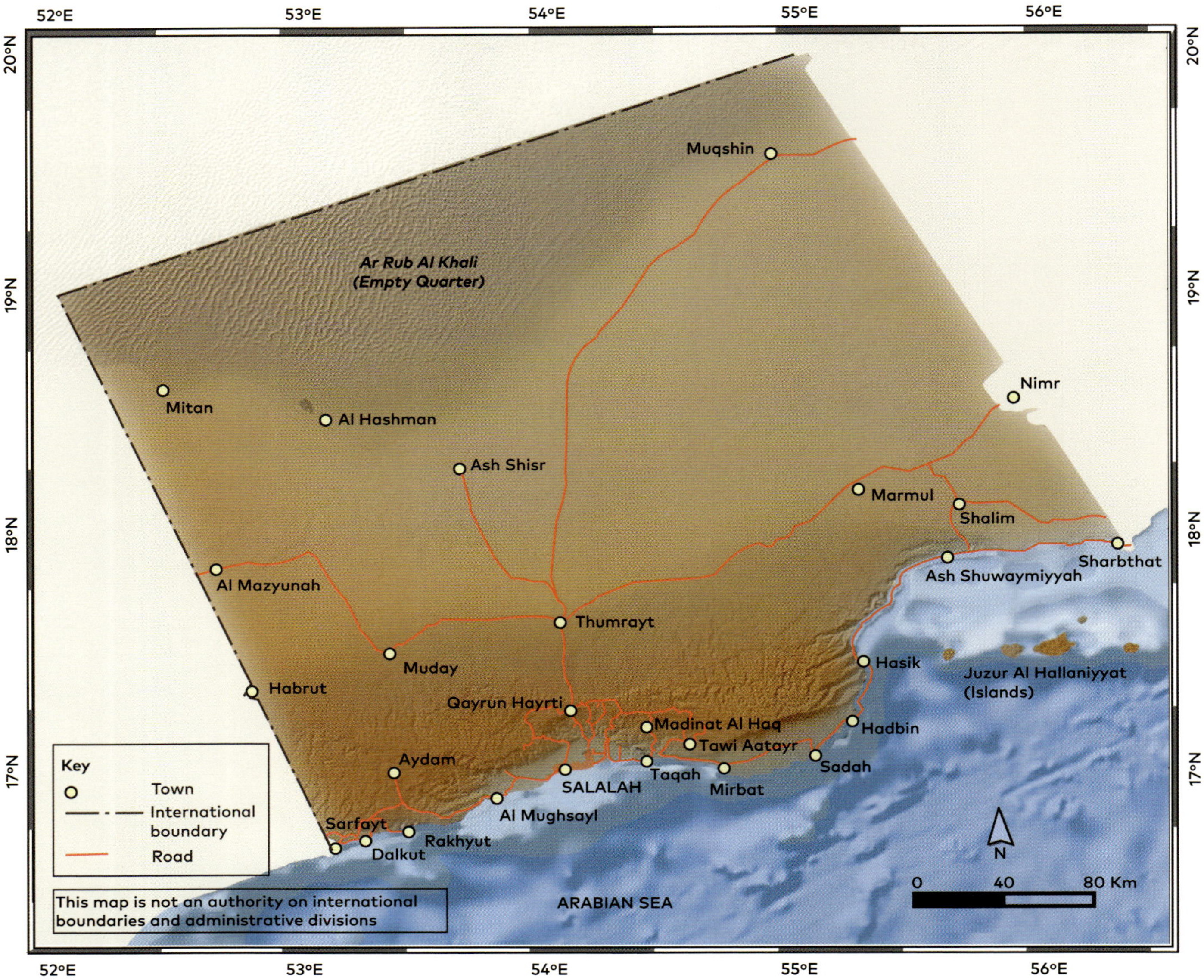

Fig. 1 Map of the Governorate of Dhofar showing major roads and settlements.

as Gondwana, mostly located in the Southern Hemisphere. In the early times of Gondwana there were no plants, no reptiles and no mammals; life as we know it today did not exist. Then very slowly, over hundreds of millions of years, Gondwana moved north, fragmenting into the separate continents that today form the modern world. The igneous and metamorphic rocks of the Salawt Plain tell the story of those very ancient times.

However, most of Dhofar is not quite so old and most rocks are sedimentary, having been formed by deposition in ancient seas. Much of the Jabal and the southern Najd is limestone that formed 35-55 million years ago, while the northern Najd is also limestone but only 5-20 million years old. The youngest areas of Dhofar are the great sand-seas of the Empty Quarter, which are less than 2.5 million years old.[5]

Dhofar's ancient landscapes have not always been as arid as they are today. As recently as 20,000 years ago awesome rivers flowed across the Najd and filled great lakes in what is today the Empty Quarter. In the shallow waters of these lakes hippopotamuses foraged for food while water buffaloes, long-horned cattle and wild asses grazed the verdant plains and came to the lakeshore to drink. This was a time when the Southwest Monsoon, or *Khareef*, as it is known in Dhofar, of the Indian Ocean extended further north and when, much of southern Arabia was like the Dhofar Jabal is today, rich semi-tropical woodlands and grasslands. However, the monsoon weakened and all that remains of the hippos and water buffaloes are their fossilised teeth buried in the orange sands of the Empty Quarter.[6]

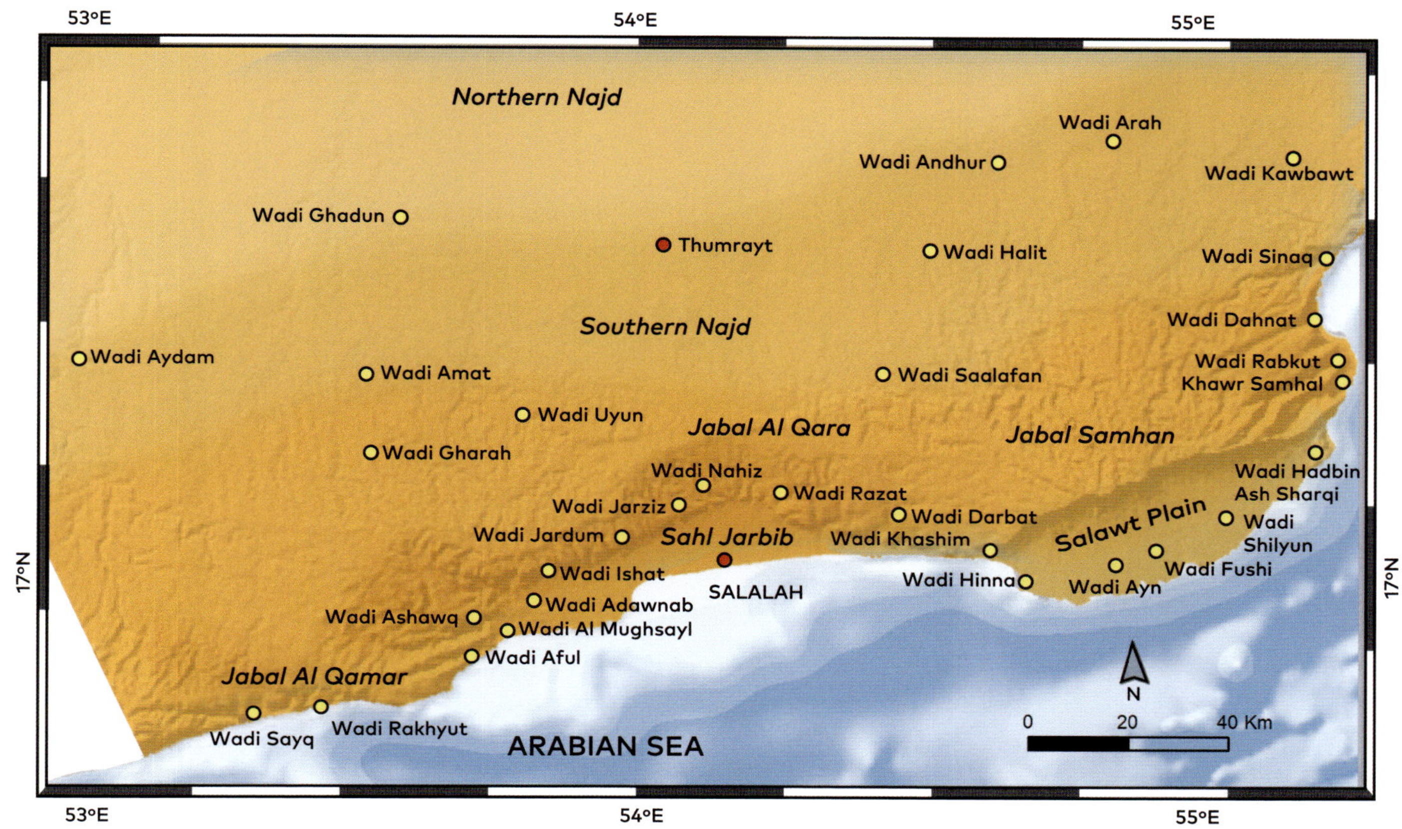

Fig. 2 Map to show the major wadis of the Dhofar mountains and the Najd.

Fortunately the influence of the monsoon did not disappear altogether and it is this that gives Dhofar its unique character. Each year, in late June, the Southwest Monsoon continues to sweep up the Indian Ocean, transforming the mountains of Jabal Al Qara and Jabal Al Qamar from dry brown desert to a verdant green Arcadia. In the east it touches the southern slopes of Jabal Samhan and along the coast it brings relief from the summer heat. However, the fingers of the monsoon don't reach far beyond the mountains and in the summer both the Najd and the great sand-seas of the Empty Quarter endure some of Oman's highest temperatures.

Thanks to the monsoon Dhofar has an extraordinary variety of natural habitats that are home to most of Oman's biodiversity. In the south are the rich Ṣġót (*Anogeissus dhofarica*) forests of Jabal Al Qara and Jabal Al Qamar whose canopies capture precious water from the swirling fogs; water that then travels underground to bring life to the coastal plains. At the height of the monsoon these forests and the grasslands above teem with birdlife; some species like the bright yellow Rüppell's weaver (*Ploceus galbula*) are resident while others, including the striking aquamarine grey-headed kingfisher (*Halcyon leucocephala*), have come from afar to nest and raise their young. In the deserts of Jabal Samhan and the Najd, groups of Nubian ibex (*Capra nubiana*) and Arabian gazelle (*Gazella arabica*) move along the wadi beds, sometimes pursued by the elusive Arabian leopard (*Panthera pardus nimr*), while overhead the majestic Verreaux's eagle (*Aquila verreauxii*) glides in search of the rock hyrax (*Procavia capensis*).

In the more remote corners of the Najd and the Empty Quarter, the desert awakens only in the cool of the night, when the endemic Omani spiny-tailed lizard (*Uromastyx thomasi*) searches for

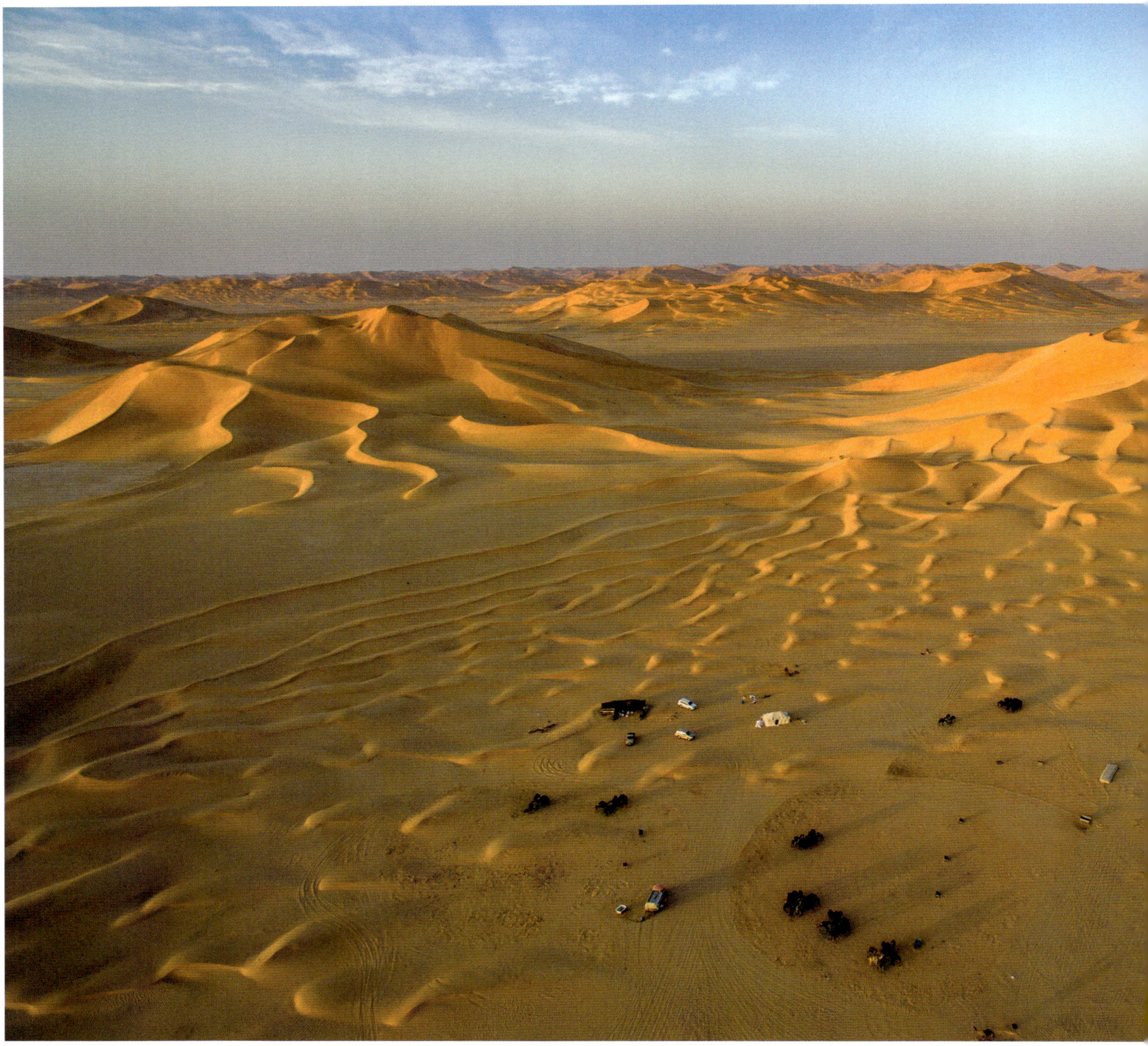

The sand-seas of the Empty Quarter ***(above)***, dominate northern Dhofar and though the environment is harsh they are home to interesting wildlife and to nomadic camel herders.

Just as the fabled riches of Dhofar have drawn explorers and travellers for many centuries, today Dhofar's natural wonders, such as Wadi Darbat ***(top right)***, attract thousands of visitors each year.

plant food and the ghost bat (*Otonycteris hemprichii jin*) pursues insect prey that gather close to precious watering holes.

Meanwhile the great upwelling of the sea brings a richness of wildlife not seen elsewhere in the region. Flocks of up to 10,000 Socotra cormorants (*Phalacrocorax nigrogularis*) search for shoals of sardine, while on the remote Al Hallaniyyat Islands thousands of masked boobies (*Sula dactylatra*), which spend almost their entire life at sea, nest on the islands' barren slopes. On long sandy beaches loggerhead sea turtles (*Caretta caretta*) come to nest, while on the rocky shores lives the highly prized abalone (*Haliotis mariae*) shellfish. Out at sea are pods of dolphins and

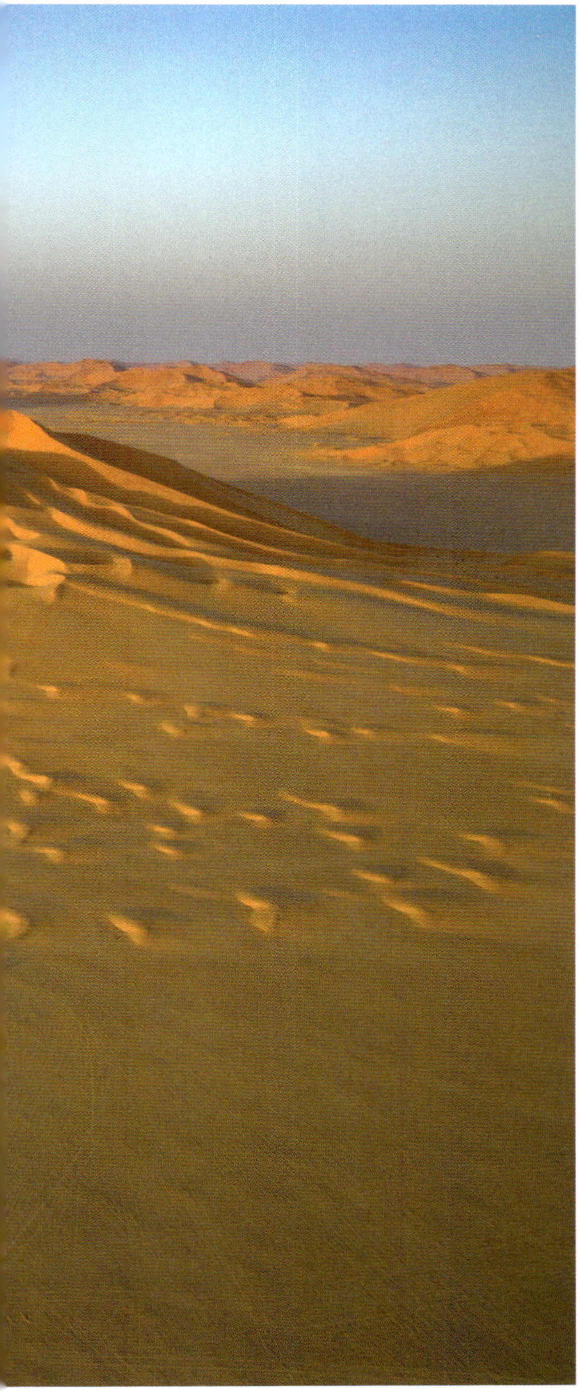

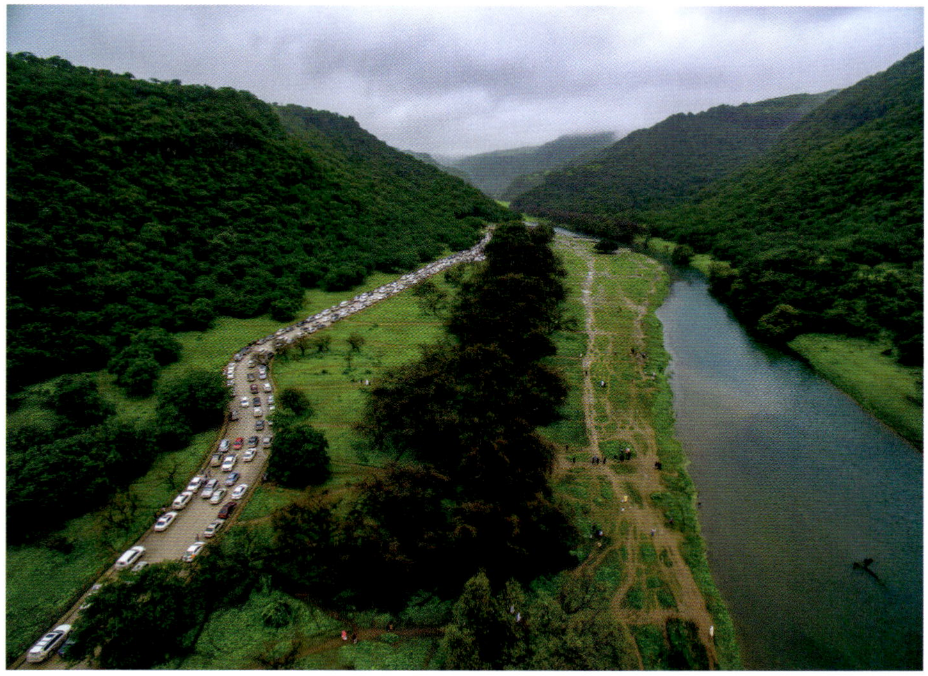

whales including Oman's own Arabian Sea humpback whale (*Megaptera novaeangliae*).

Dhofar is also a land of people, who since at least the Late Stone Age, 13,000 years ago, have made this land their home.[7] From the stone remains scattered over the Jabal and the Najd we know the first people were highly mobile hunters who roamed the mountains and deserts in search of quarry. Later these people started to settle, to keep sheep, goats, cattle and camels. They were also fishing and building settlements on the Jabal and the coast.[8]

Through out their long history the people enjoyed times of great prosperity largely thanks to the resin of the frankincense tree (*Boswellia sacra*) that was so highly prized in distant foreign lands. Great settlements were built on the frankincense trade route; at the coastal ports, such as Samharam and at Ash Shisr, that commanded the overland route to Europe.[9]

Trade in frankincense and other valuable goods linked Dhofar with ports in the Arabian Gulf, Red Sea, East Africa and as far east as China.[10] However, for most Dhofaris of the Jabal and the Najd, life revolved around the herding of livestock supplemented by the hunting of wild animals and the gathering of wild plants. Coastal communities held some livestock but also looked to small farms and to the sea for their livelihoods. These largely subsistence-based systems continued almost unchanged until the 20th century.

In 1970 the late Sultan Qaboos Bin Said acceded to the throne and the period of the Omani Renaissance began bringing prosperity, social and economic progress to all the people of Oman. The largely agriculture and fisheries based economy was replaced by one based on oil revenues and new roads, electric facilities, schools, hospitals and government offices were built across Dhofar.

Today Dhofar is Oman's largest governorate, covering nearly 100,000 square kilometres and is home to about 10% of the nation's population[11]. Its capital is Salalah and its 10 provinces (*wilayats*) are Salalah, Taqah, Mirbat, Sadah, Shalim Wa Juzur Al Hallaniyyat (Islands), Dalkut, Rakhyut, Thumrayt, Muqshin and Al Mazyunah. It is prosperous and developed, and like the rest of Oman its economy is based principally on oil and gas with renewable energy becoming increasingly important; Oman's first solar power, solar energy and wind power projects are in Dhofar. Fisheries and agriculture are the oldest sectors and continue to make critical contributions to development in the areas of employment, trade and food security. Tourism is one of the newest sectors and in the summer, as temperatures reach a blistering 50°C across most of the Arabian Peninsula, increasing numbers of people travel south to Dhofar to enjoy cloudy days, cool refreshing winds and light rains of the *Khareef* season from June to September.

However, while the people of Dhofar have absorbed modern development and prospered, their ancient traditions that revolved around subsistence pastoralism, agriculture and fisheries remain deeply rooted in all aspects of society. The owners of farms in Salalah and Taqah may no longer work the fields themselves but have a deep emotional attachment to the land where their forefathers toiled. The people of the Jabal who no longer depend on the livestock that kept their ancestors alive, still own herds of cattle, camels and goats and take every opportunity to be with them. In the Najd and the Empty Quarter the once nomadic camel farmer is no more a nomad and today owns a pickup yet his camels are his most prized possession. Fisherfolk may increasingly employ others to do the fishing but remain deeply attached to the sea.

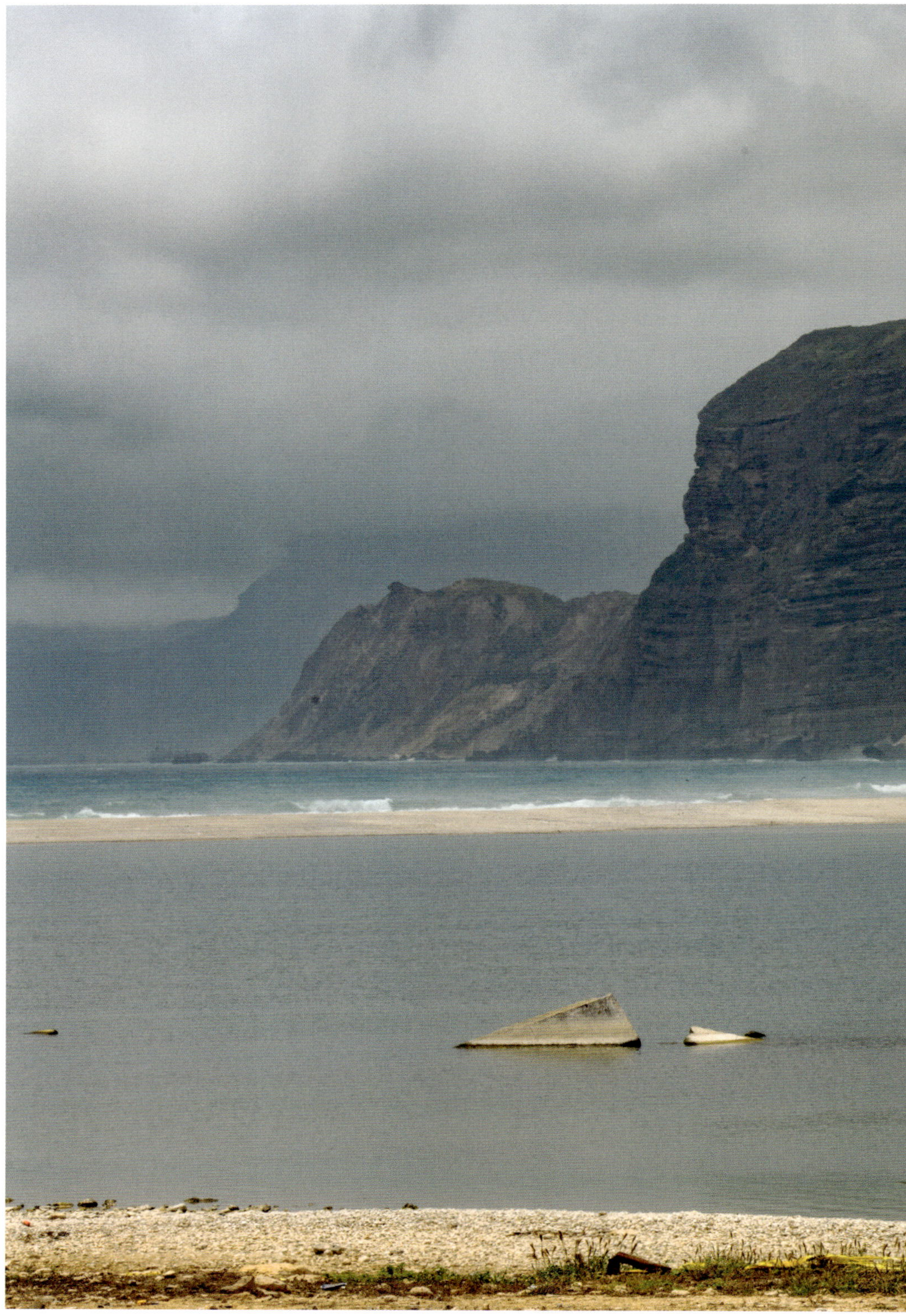

In this book we tell the story of Dhofar, from the verdant mountains in the south to the towering dunes of the Empty Quarter in the north, and from the moonscapes of the Najd in the west to the gravel plains of the Jiddat Arkad in the east. We explore the climate that continues to shape the landscapes; the summer *Khareef*, the winter *shamal*, coastal fogs and tropical cyclones. Water is life and we write of the condition of this most precious of resources. The book also serves as a record of the diversity of Oman's natural flora and fauna, much of it unique to Arabia. We learn about the livelihoods of the people that have shaped the land that shaped them for thousands of years. Finally we consider how we, as custodians of Dhofar's land and water resources, should manage them sustainability for future generations.

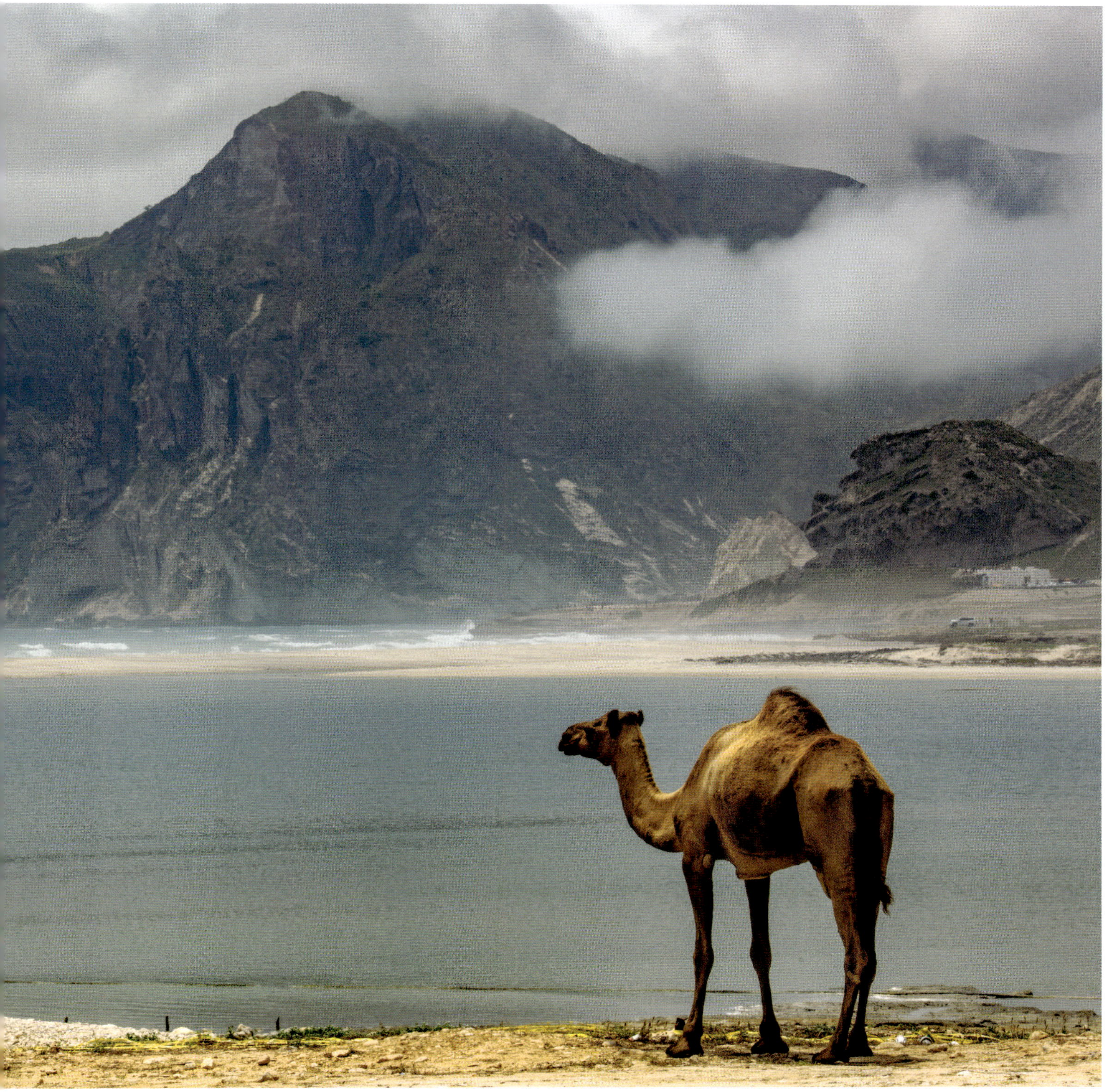

Khawr Al Mughsayl and the sea cliffs of Jabal Al Qamar. Noteworthy for its absence is the coast road that was swept away by Cyclone Mekunu in May 2018– a strong reminder that climate change may lead to more extreme weather events.

1 Dhofar through the Ages

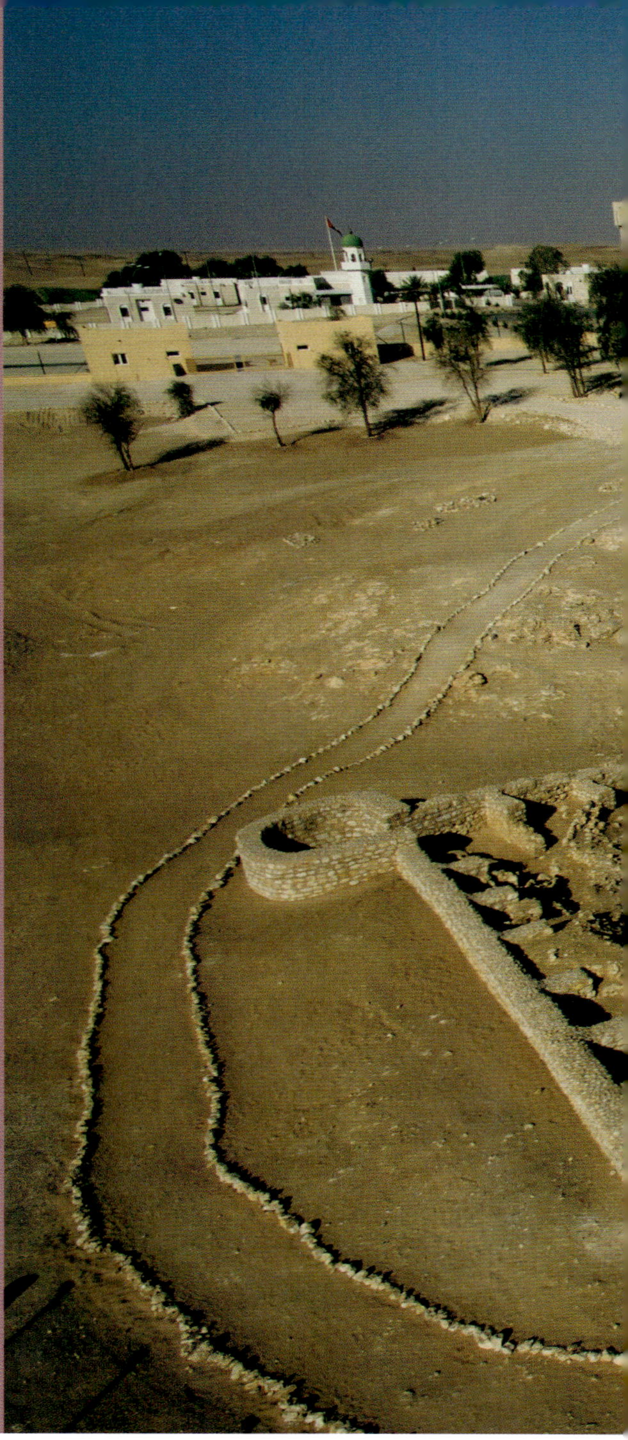

Introduction

Early humans are thought to have migrated from Africa to Eurasia between 130,000 and 70,000 years ago, following either the Levantine corridor of northern Arabia or the Indian Ocean rim route of south Arabia, or both.[12] Archaeological evidence has been found at Stone Age sites in the Najd, concentrated around Muday, that suggest the peopling of southern Arabia took place via the southern route, exiting Africa via the Horn of Africa and travelling across the Red Sea to reach Dhofar approximately 106,000 years ago.[13]

However, gaps in chronology of early human occupation of Arabia remain but there is general agreement that humans have been continuously present in Dhofar since the late Stone Age, approximately 13,000 years ago, while recent evidence suggests as early as between 28,000 and 33,000 years ago.[14] Evidence comes from a number of sites, including the Al Hatab rock shelter in the lower Wadi Dawkah and Matafah in Wadi Ghadun.[15] At this time southern Arabia was wetter

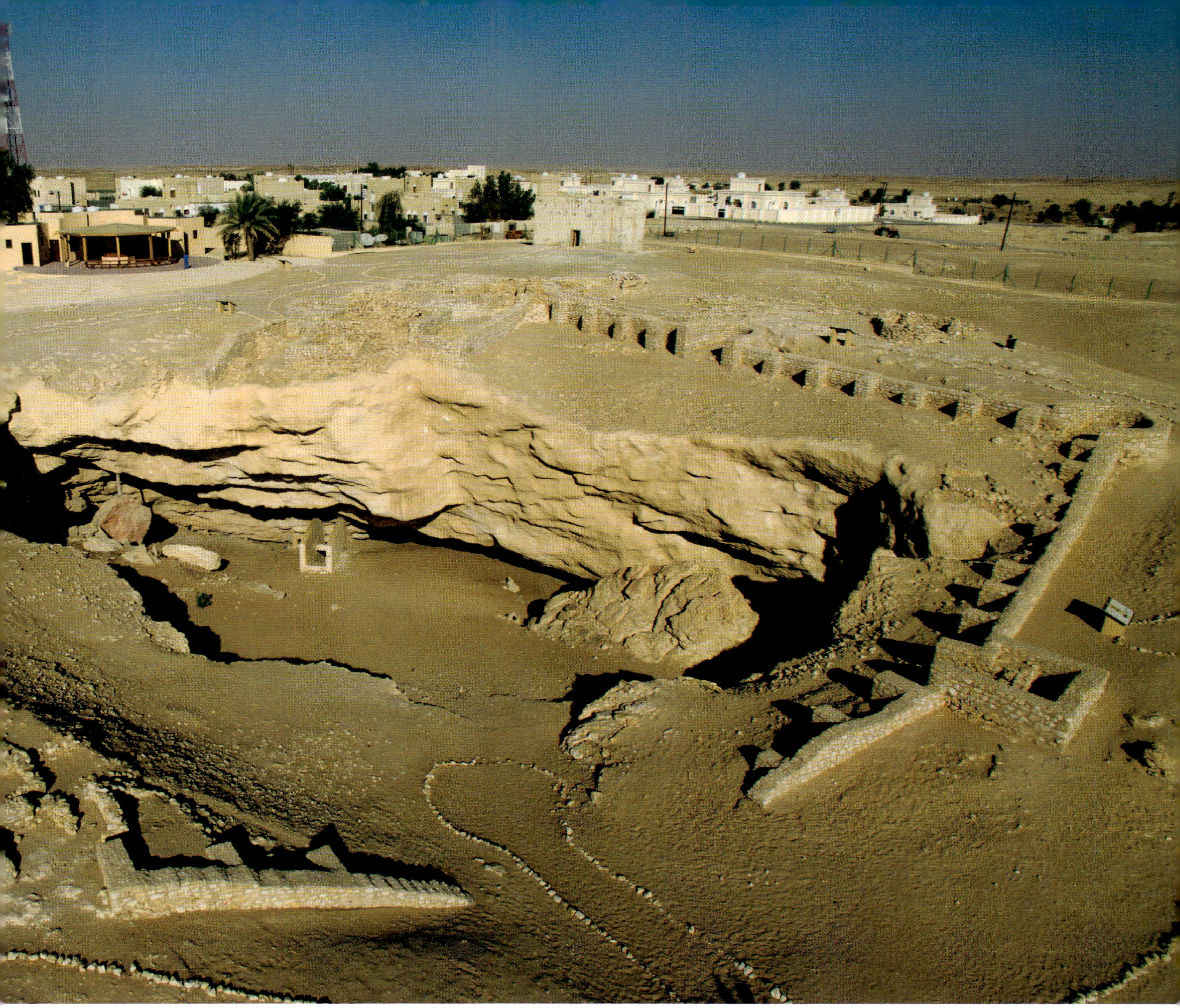

than today, and the monsoon rains extended much further north and lakes formed in what today is the hyper-arid Empty Quarter.[6]

Evidence from Neolithic settlements close to former riverbeds and lakes of the Najd, such as those at Uyun, indicate that by this time people were no longer relying solely on hunting and gathering but had started to keep herds of sheep, goats and cattle, with cattle herders practising transhumance, spending summers in the Empty Quarter and winters in the Najd. The absence of Neolithic settlements on the Jabal suggest that human habitation here was difficult.[8] But by approximately 5,000 years ago the monsoon had weakened and a more arid

(Above) A 1992 expedition to Ash Shisr, based on Ptolemy's map of 150AD, claimed it to be the legendary lost city of Ubar, the so-called 'Atlantis of the Sands'. Ptolemy's map shows a region somewhere in south-east Arabia labelled 'Iobaritae', meaning that it belonged to the Ubarites. The late-medieval version of *One Thousand and One Nights,* in the 14th or 15th century, romanticised Ubar and turned it into a city, rather than a region or a people.[16] Ash Shisr is one destination along the 'The Frankincense Trail' inscribed on the UNESCO World Heritage List, which states 'The Oasis of Ash Shisr and the entrepôts of Khawr Rawri and Al Balid are outstanding examples of medieval fortified settlements.'[17]

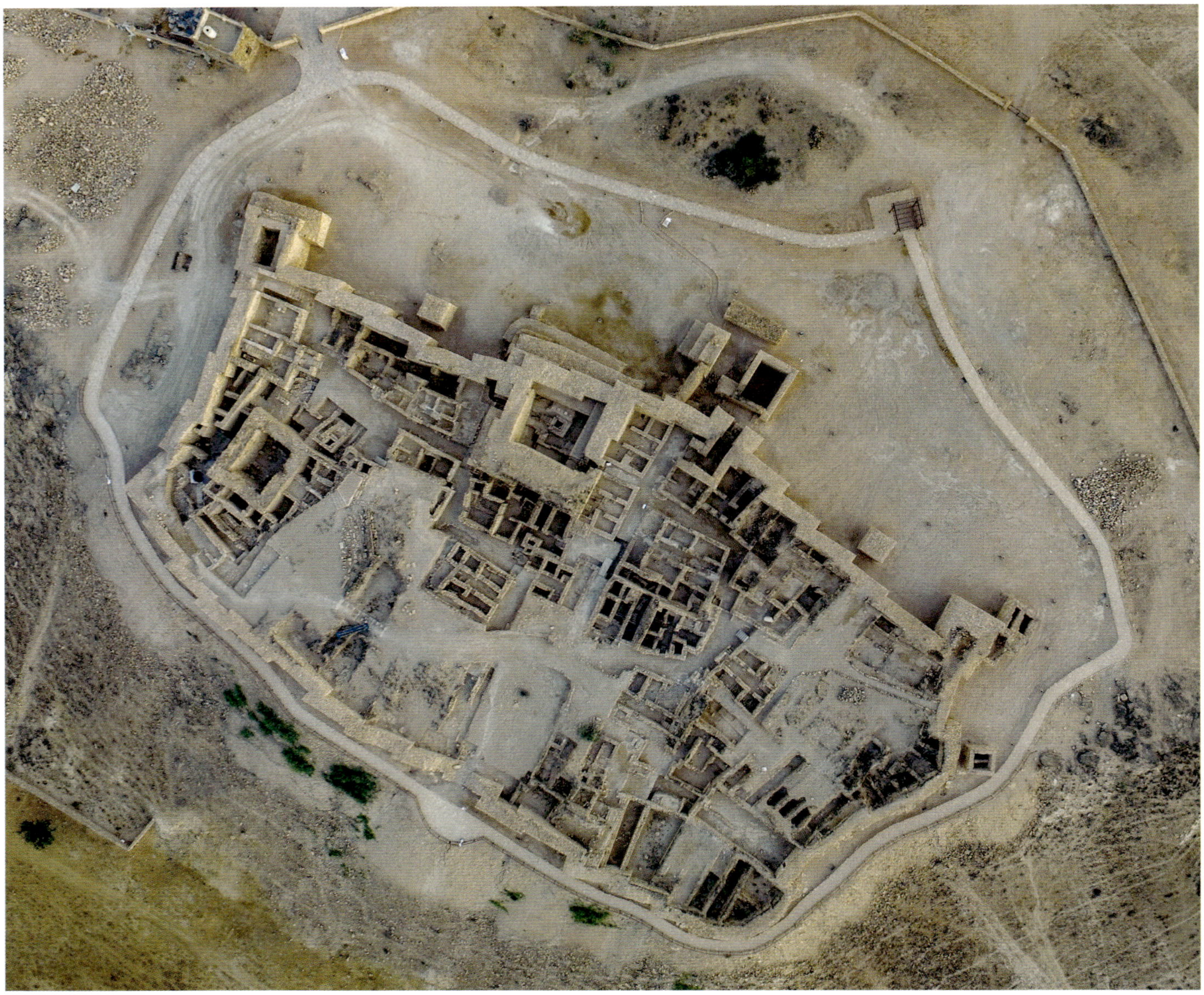

climate forced people south to the southern Najd and the highlands of the Dhofar mountains.[10]

By the Bronze Age (5,000-3,000 years ago) people seem to have left the Najd and moved south, where they built settlements on the north side of the Jabal, for example at Hijayf on Jabal Al Qara, on the Jarbib and at strategic points on the southern coast where they took advantage of the abundant marine resources. This period coincides with the appearance of domesticated camels[18] in the region, joining cattle. The presence of shell middens at coastal settlements might be an indication of an early pattern of transhumance with the highlands, a system that has been followed until today.

Iron Age (3,000-1,600 years ago or 1000 BCE [Before Common Era] to 400 CE) settlements stand out as sites of permanent occupation and include the fortresses at Ayn Hamran, Al Balid and Ash Shisr.[8] These were bustling centres of trade, in particular of frankincense, which was carried to Mesopotamia, Syria, Greece and Italy either overland by camel train via Ash Shisr or by ship to Aden and thence north along the Red Sea. It was frankincense above all that brought Dhofar to the attention of early historians, including the Greeks Herodotus and Ptolemy I and later the Roman Pliny the Elder. All wrote of the trade in this exotic commodity and Ptolemy I produced the first known map of Dhofar.

The Early Medieval (400-1100 CE), or Early Islamic period, is characterised by the development of trading centres, from Al Mughsayl in the west to Hasik in the east, including Sadah, Mirbat and Al Balid.[10] Sea trade linked Dhofar with the Gulf, East

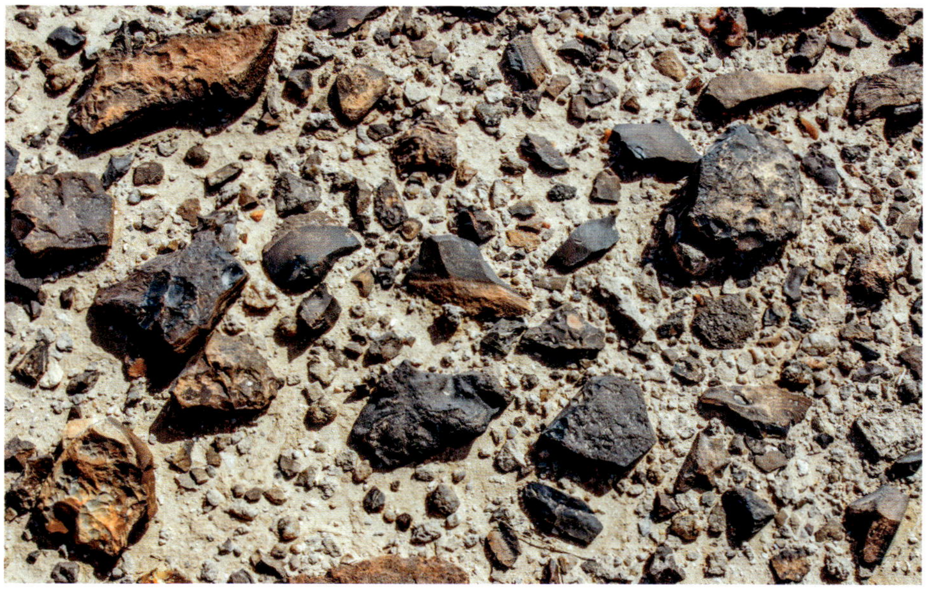

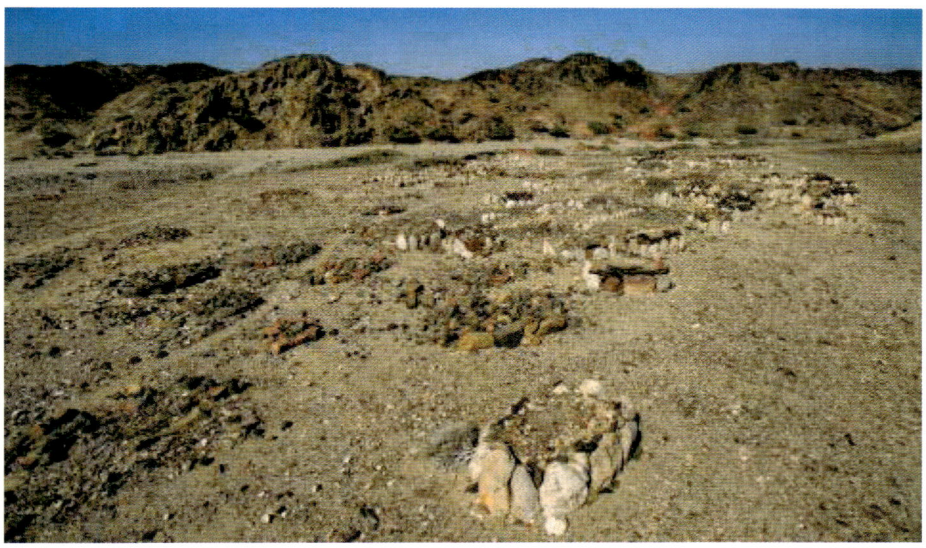

A Middle Paleolithic stone tool workshop ***(left)*** at Muday dates back at least 13,000 years. The ancient city of Samharam ***(far left)*** must have thrived no less than 2,400 years ago and the boat-shaped graves on the Salawt Plain ***(below left)*** date from the Late Iron Age through to the Early Islamic period, 1,400 years ago.[19]

Africa and as far east as China. The Islamic period archaeological sites, such as Al Balid, are marked by an abundance of traded goods, namely Ming porcelain, Rasulid coins, Chinese coins and local ceramics of the period.[8] On the Jabal the pastoralists built stone-walled dwellings for themselves and their animals.Some of the first written reports by travellers come from this period, with Abu Ubayd Al-Bakri writing in about 1080 that Dhofar was home to exalted and mighty kings and where there were camels, Arabian horses, pure gold and other goods and wares.[2]

Modern Times (1100-1900 CE) are marked by four principal activities: livestock-holding on the Jabal and the Najd, agriculture on the Jarbib, fisheries on the coast and prosperous trade. Marco Polo (13th century) remarked on the importance of the frankincense trade while Ibn Battuta (14th century) visited the Sultan in his Salalah palace and even went to the small village of Hasik, where he noted that local homes were made of fishbone and camel skins. He also observed that fish were fed to the livestock, a practice that continues today.[2]

Triliths *(below)*, dating from the Iron Age and found mainly in the southern Najd, may have been associated with the trading of frankincense.

Little is written of the livelihoods of the Dhofari people after the visit of Ibn Battuta although there is an account by two Jesuit priests who stayed on the island of Al Sawda, the second largest of the Al Hallaniyyat Islands, in 1589.[20] They observed of the local people: 'They cover their houses with the weed that the sea throws up on the shore; they live on fish, which is never lacking, but they have no wood with which to boil or roast it, so they eat it raw, first drying it in the wind.'

The next records are those of European explorers in the mid-19th and early 20th centuries. Haines visited Dhofar in 1834 and one of his men travelled extensively across Jabal Al Qara.[21] He was made very welcome and enjoyed great hospitality. Though he visited in February, usually the dry season, he wrote of a coastal plain with 'wild clover growing in abundance and affording pasture for cows and immense flocks of sheep and goats' and of 'numerous clear mountain-streams that were meandering in every, direction'. He also wrote of people descending from the Jabal to trade cattle, butter and frankincense for dates from trading boats along the sea coast. Miles sailed into Salalah in December 1884 and noted that amongst the exports were

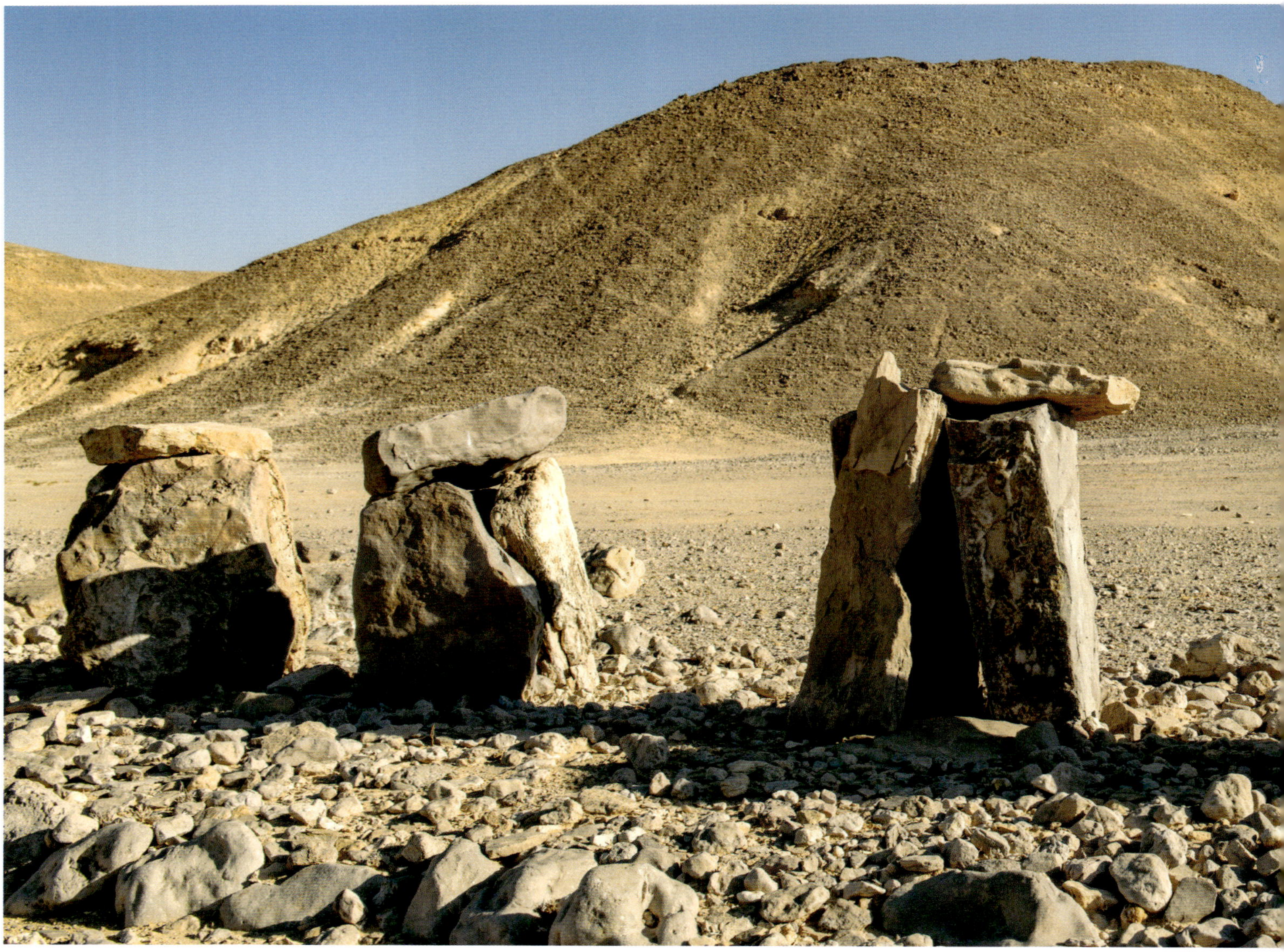

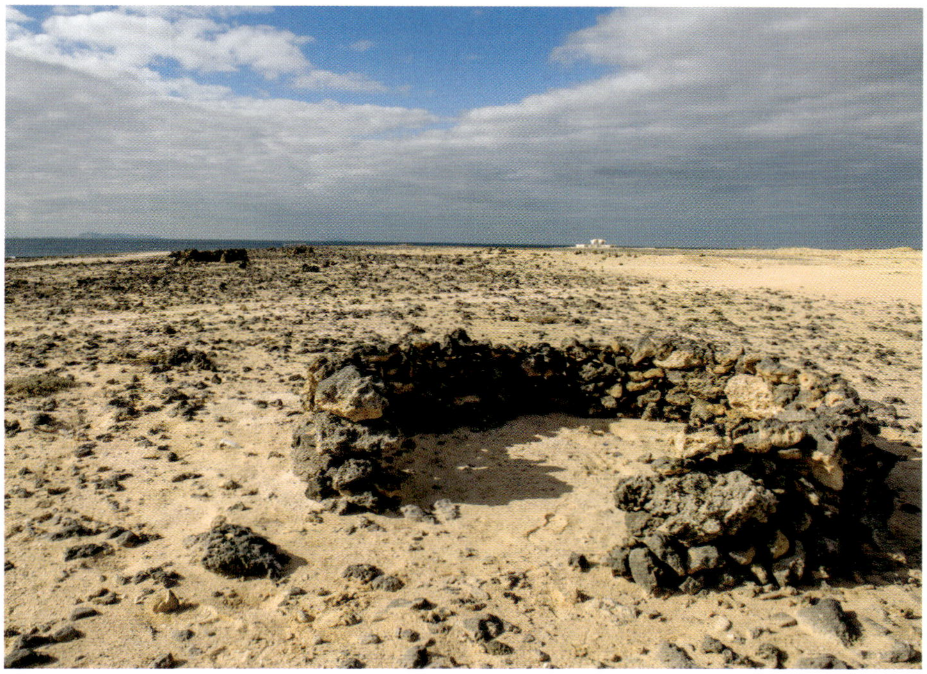

An abandoned coastal settlement at Manji ***(left)*** and Islamic graves built on terraces in Wadi Andhur ***(below)*** are both considered to belong to the Late Islamic period.

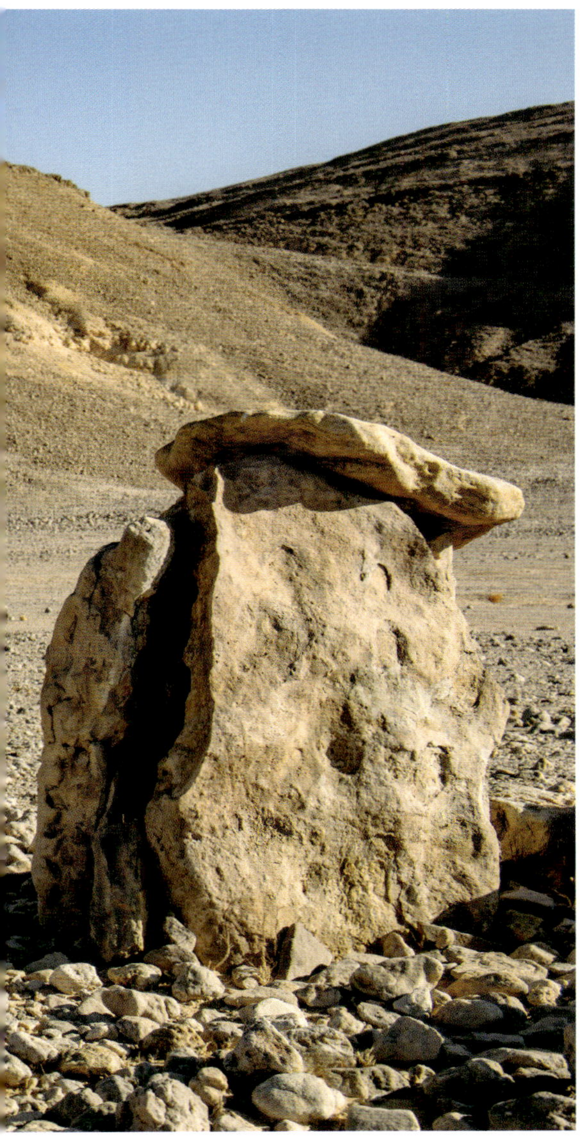

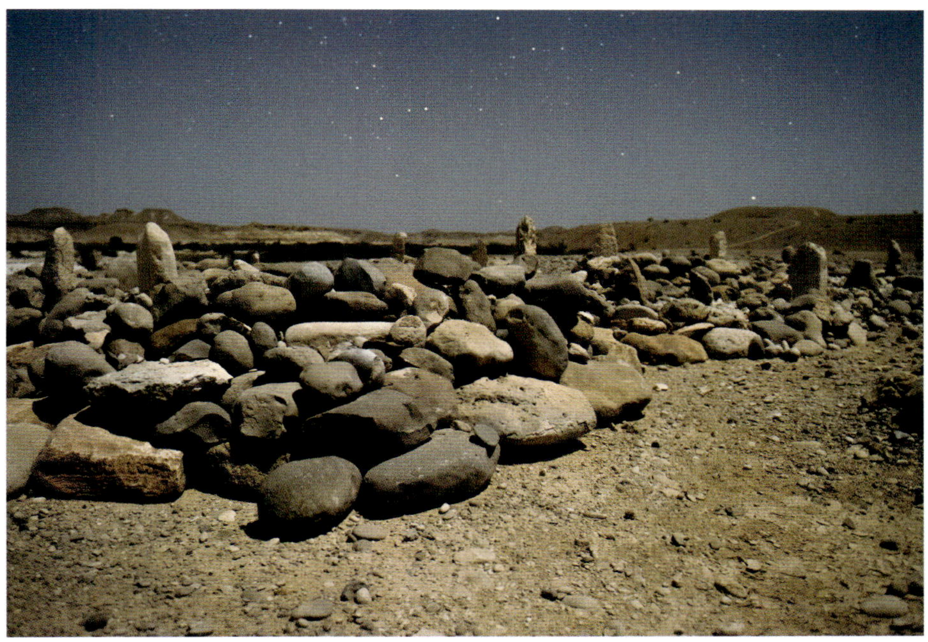

ghee, animal skins, frankincense, sardine oil and shark fins.[22] He also visited herdsmen living in a cave on Jabal Al Qara and on the island of Al Hallaniyyah found 34 people subsisting on a diet of fish and goats' milk and living in very crude habitations made of 'loose stone with a scanty roofing of mats laid over sticks and fish bones'.

By the time James and Theodore Bent visited in the late 1890s the

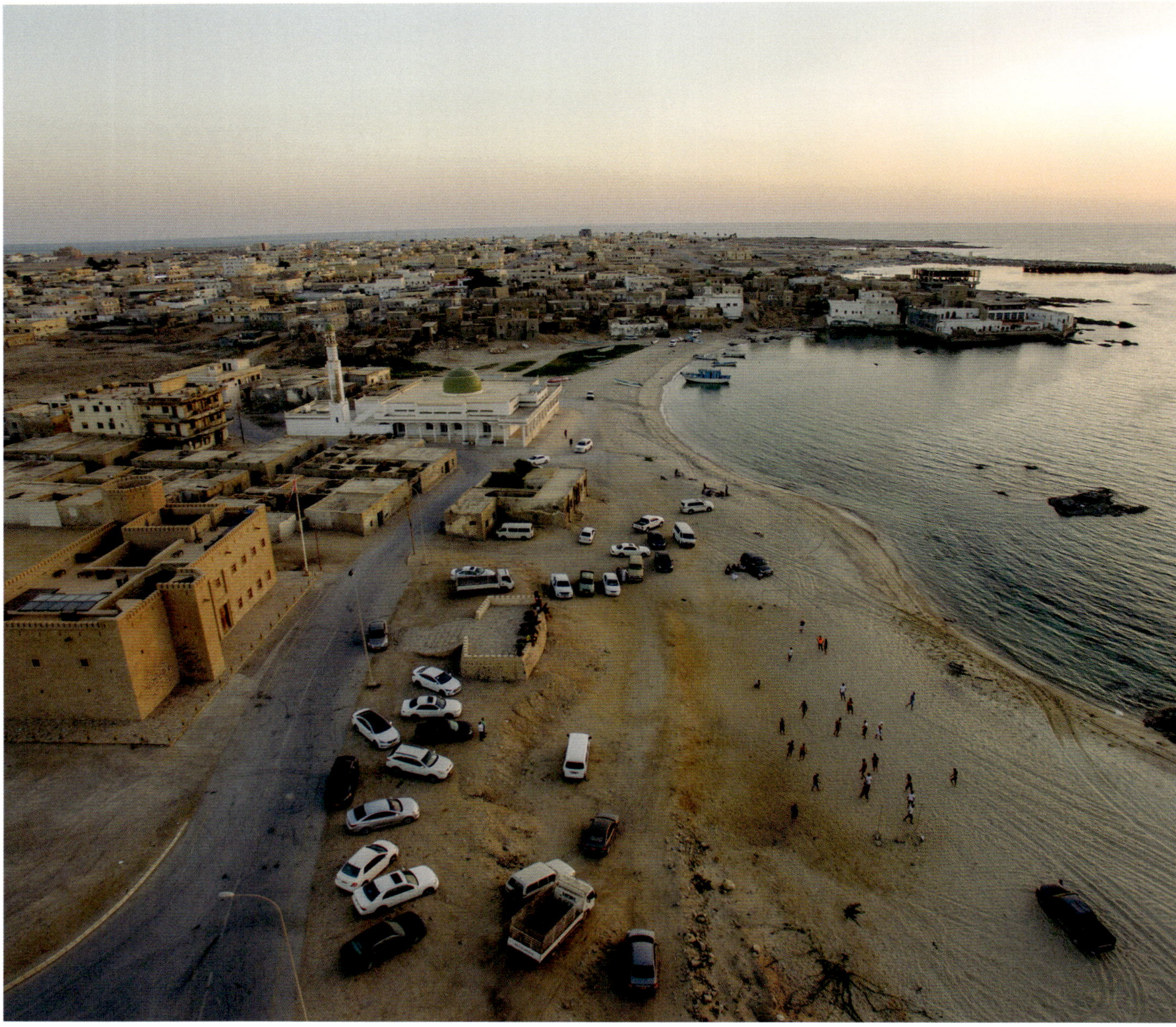

reign of the Al Busaid dynasty had commenced and was to become the longest and most stable in Dhofar's history.[3] The Bents wrote of a fertile coastal plain where coconut, cotton, coffee and other vegetables and fruits were grown. They recorded the ongoing trade in frankincense, which had declined significantly over the years, and by that time the incense was mostly shipped to Bombay. They journeyed up Wadi Jarziz and wrote of people who lived in ancestral caves on the Jabal and during the monsoon moved to the coastal plain where they lived in huts made of reeds.

Bertram Thomas visited northern Dhofar in 1928 and recorded that shark-fishing by swimming on inflated animal skins was the primary occupation of camel-owning communities between Ras Sharbthat and Ras Naws.[23] About two years later Thomas followed a route similar to that of the Bents, climbing Jabal Al Qara via both Wadi Jarziz and Wadi Nahiz. He wrote of herdsmen on the Jabal, and frankincense harvesting in the Najd, before proceeding across the desert, first to Muqshin and later to Ash Shisr before crossing the Empty Quarter.

It seems that by the mid-20th century the lives of the people of Dhofar had remained unchanged for many centuries while much of the world was going through huge economic development and suffering world wars.

Perhaps the first sign of the economic and social changes

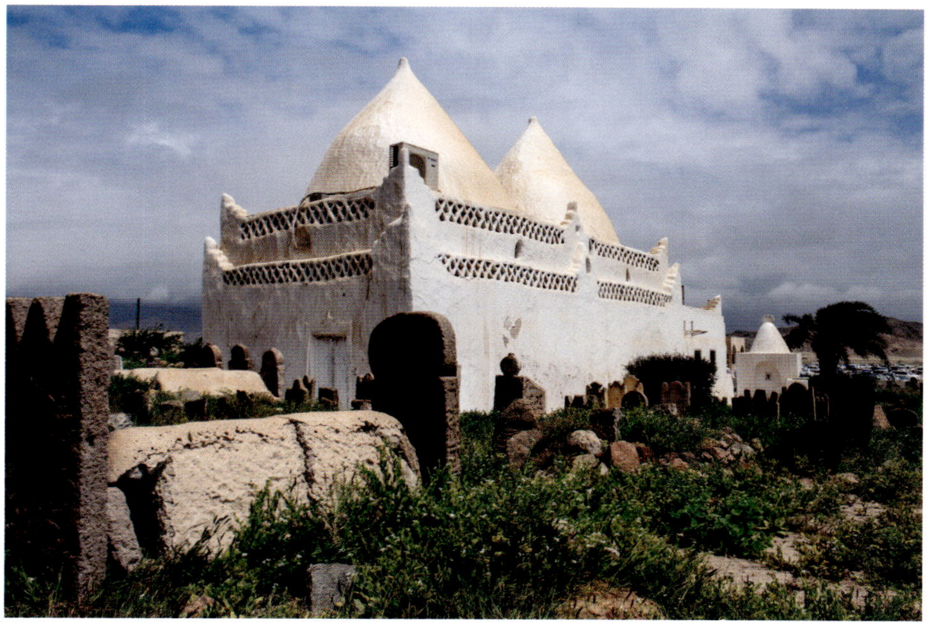

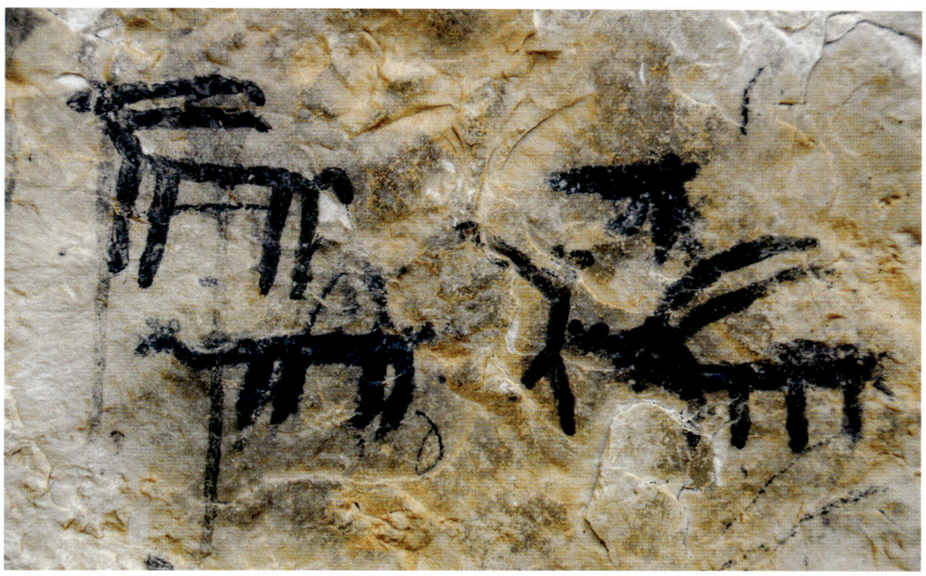

Close to Mirbat is the tomb of Mohammed Bin Ali *(left)*, a respected religious leader who died in 1161. Other tombs in Dhofar include that of Prophet Job on Jabal Al Qara, which overlooks Salalah City, where the tomb of the Prophet Hud is located.

Petroglyphs *(below left)* depict wild animals such as Nubian ibex.

Mirbat *(opposite)* is one of Dhofar's ancient coastal trading centres.

that were to follow was the arrival of oil prospectors in the late 1940s. Their efforts were concentrated in the Najd and in 1957 were rewarded with the discovery of the Marmul oilfield. Other discoveries followed and in the early 1960s an oil-producing nation had been born.

In 1970 the late Sultan Qaboos Bin Said came to power and the lives of his people were changed forever. The government set about a rapid programme of modernization, constructing roads and building schools, hospitals and government centres. A largely subsistence based economy was replaced by a cash economy and the people of Dhofar entered a period of great stability and prosperity.

2 Landscapes

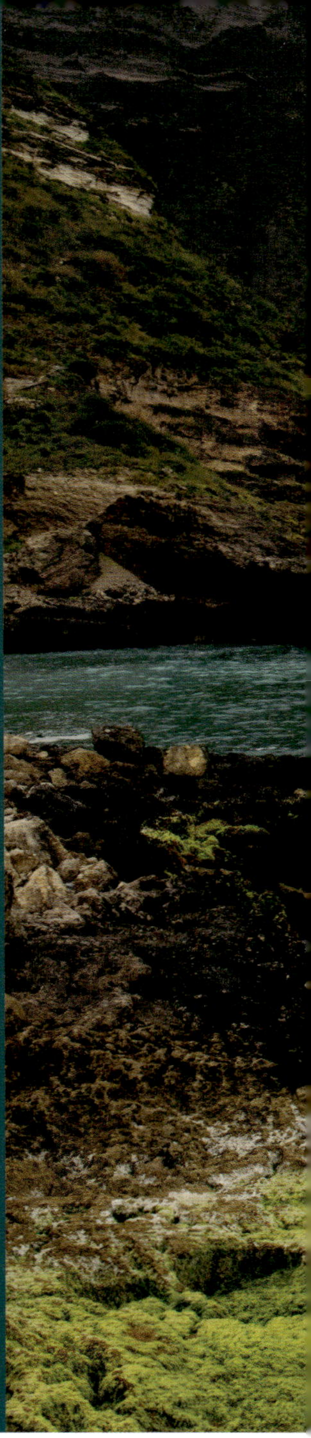

Introduction

In the north of Dhofar lies the seemingly inhospitable sprawling vastness of the Empty Quarter desert, crossed occasionally by a camel or pickup, while to the south, resembling Alpine meadows, are rolling green hills dotted with tiny hamlets and grazing livestock. Dhofar's contrasting and stunning landscapes have been shaped by a geological history going back 1,300 million years and by human occupation from at least 13,000 years ago.

In the far south, Dhofar's magnificent rugged and windswept coastline, coastal plains and offshore islands stretch from the mountain border with Yemen to the deserts of central Oman. But it is the crescent-shaped limestone mountains of the Dhofar mountain chain that dominate the region, separating sea from desert. It comprises three contiguous mountain massifs. In the east, Jabal Samhan rises swiftly to 1,760 metres and towers above the ancient basement rocks

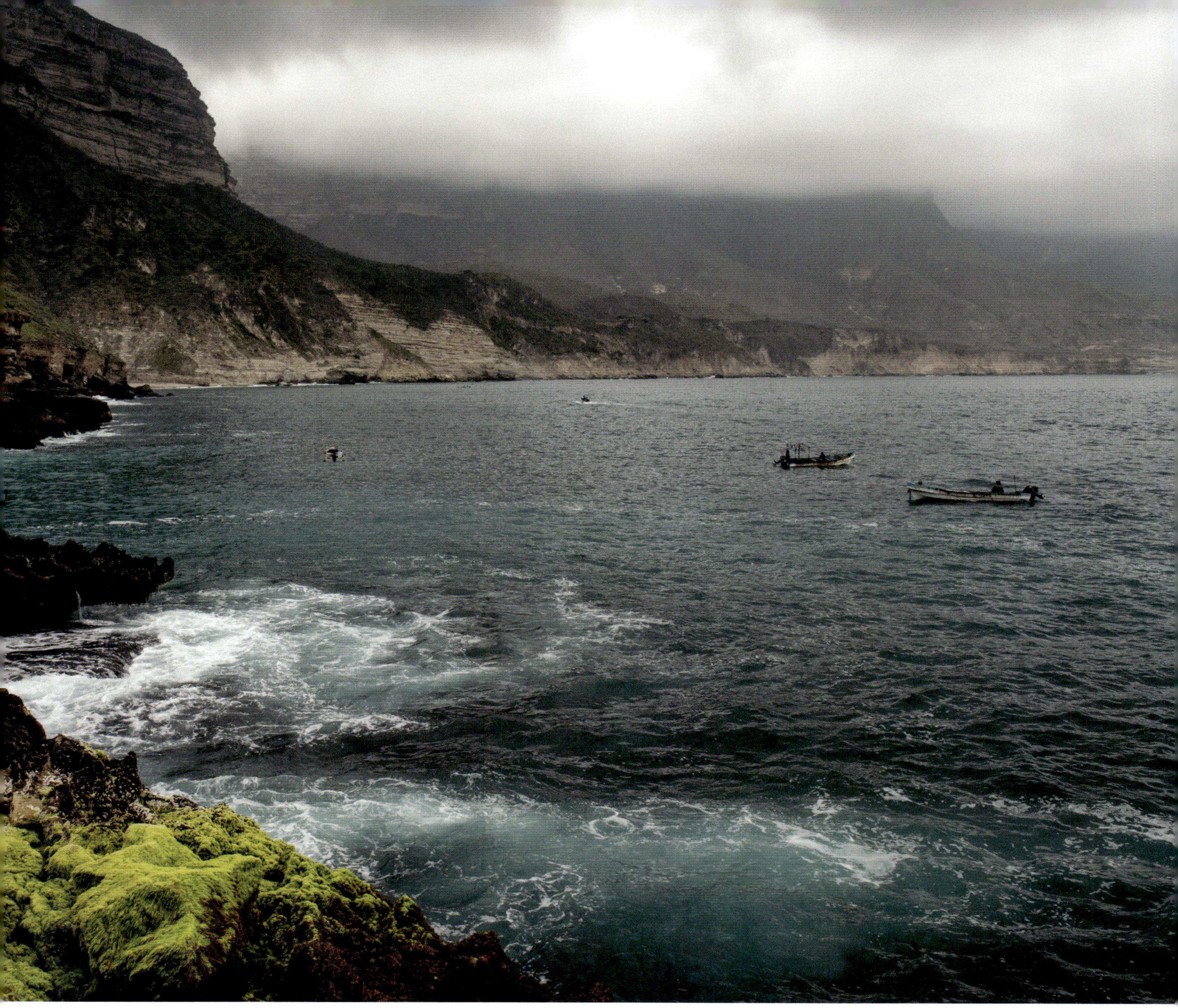

of the Salawt Plain to the south. This is Dhofar's highest mountain but it is also its driest. Its harsh barren plateau slopes north to the desert, meets the sea in the east, and in the west looks down to the thickly wooded escarpments and gently rolling grass-covered hills of Jabal Al Qara. Here, for three months of the year, the swirling fogs of the Southwest Monsoon, or *khareef,* transform the landscape from brown to lush green. Jabal Al Qara forms the central massif of the Dhofar mountains and is separated from the sea by the *Jarbib* plain. In the far west is Jabal Al Qamar, which also comes under the magical influence of the monsoon, but unlike Jabal Al Qara it rises directly from the sea. However the green mountaintops of Jabal Al Qara and Jabal Al Qamar extend no more than 30 kilometres north before the moisture is sucked out of the air by the heat of the desert that lies beyond the watershed. This is the Najd, where the mighty *wadis* rush north before slowing to a gentle meander and finally disappearing in the endless gravel plains that extend north to the great sand-seas of the Empty Quarter, a vast ocean of billowing orange dunes

(Above) Looking east from Shaat on Jabal Al Qamar: the monsoon rainfall transforms the coastal cliffs, and the cool waters below are a haven for fish and other marine wildlife.

Coastline, coastal plains and islands

Dhofar has approximately 500 kilometres of coastline, from the international border with Yemen to just east of Sharbthat, and for much of that distance it runs parallel and to the south of the Dhofar Mountain Chain (the Jabal). In places, the Jabal abuts the sea and elsewhere coastal plains and hills lie between the mountains and the sea.

Salalah dominates a long sandy beach and flat coastal plain but otherwise the coastline is predominantly rocky, with often towering limestone cliffs broken periodically by coves, sandy beaches and occasional coastal lagoons, locally known as *khawr*. In many places the scenery is breathtaking and retains a wild rugged beauty.

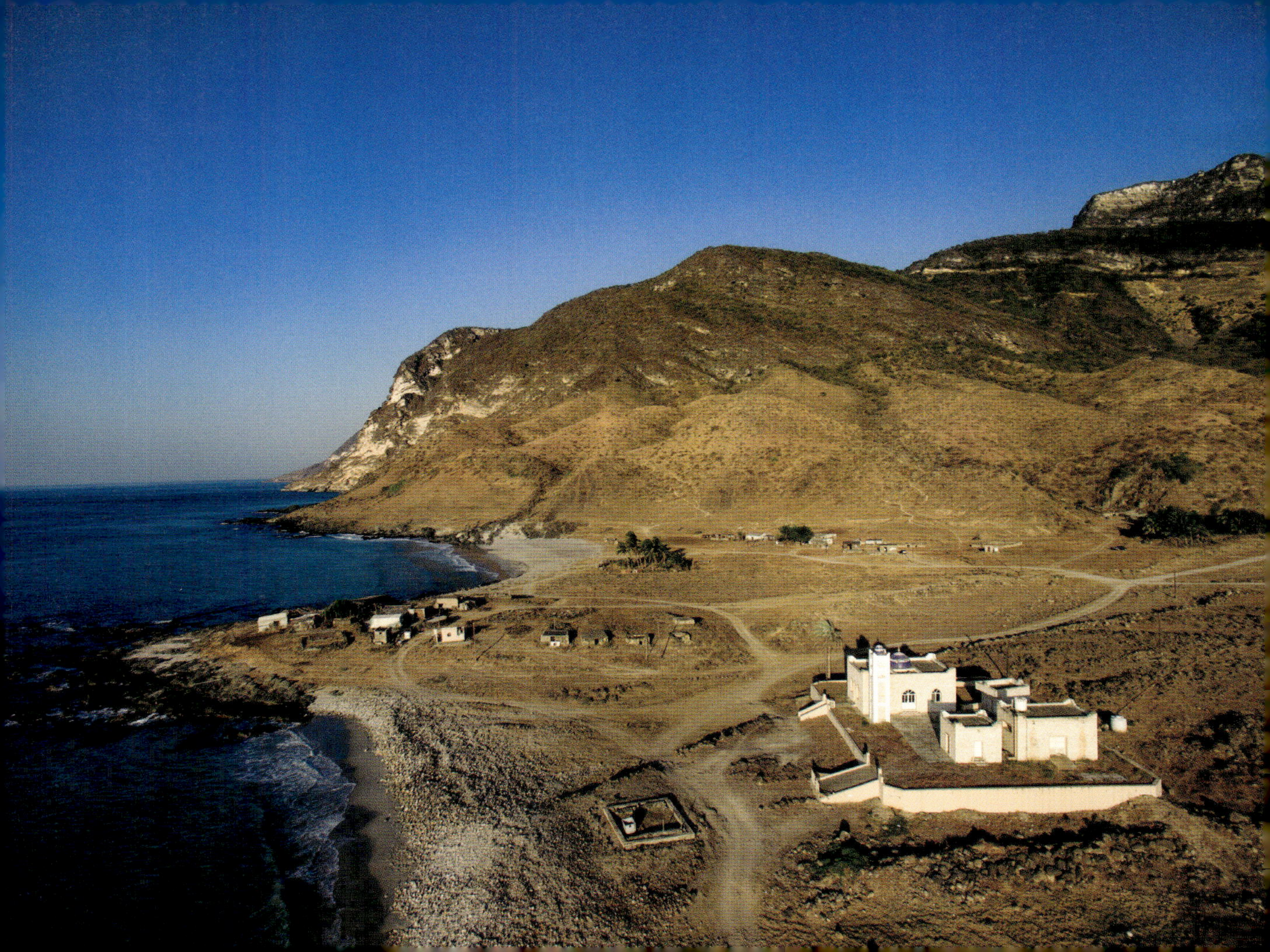

Western Seaboard

Sarfayt to Al Mughsayl

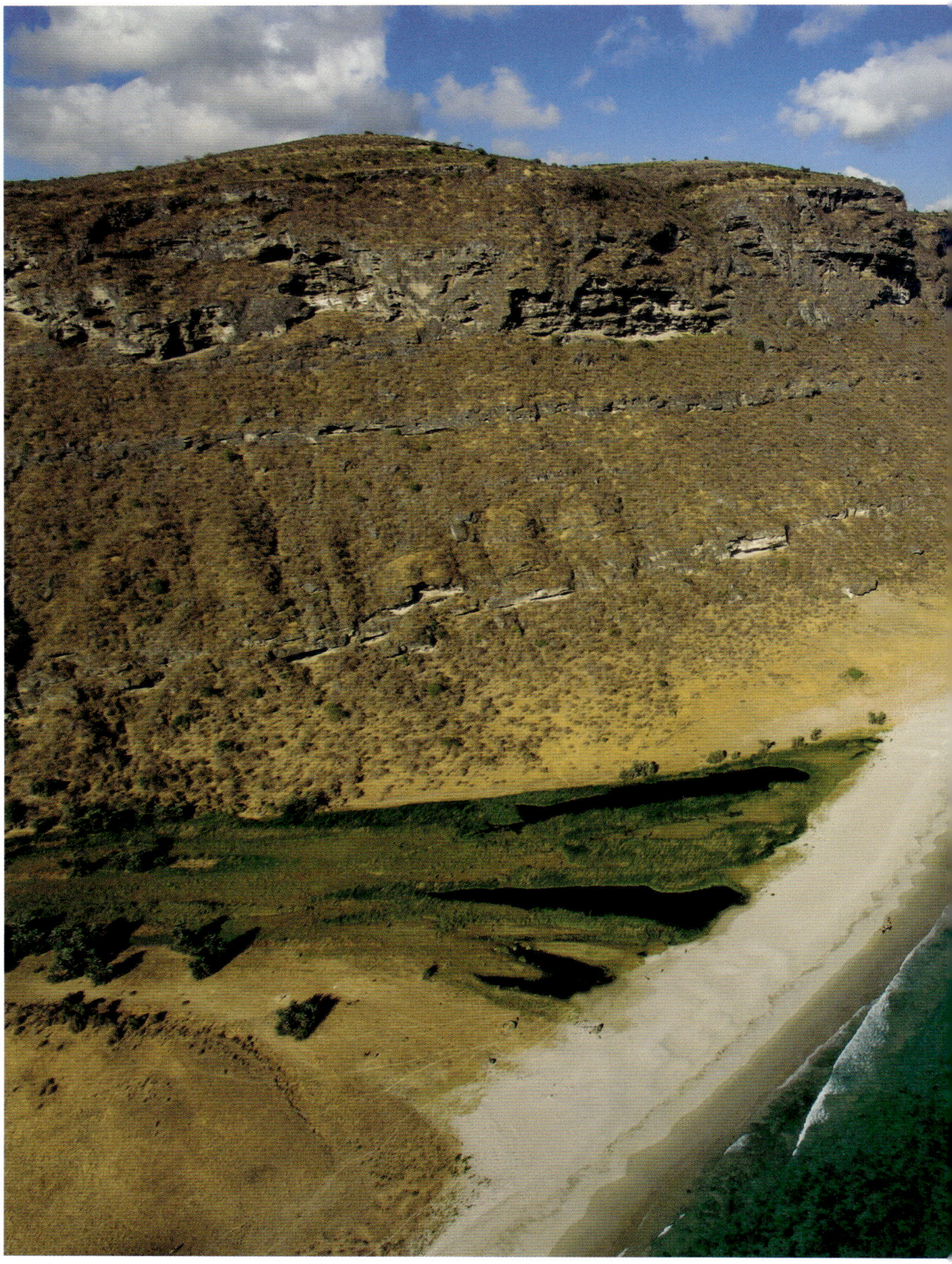

The western seaboard begins on the Oman-Yemen border, on the southern aspect of Jabal Al Qamar. Here the steep wooded slopes, broken occasionally by low cliffs, run down to a largely inaccessible and rock-strewn seashore. In the months following the monsoon this is perhaps the most colourful of Dhofar's coastlands; light-green plateau pastures contrast with the dark-green forests that in turn contrast with the greys and pale creams of the limestone cliffs above and the turquoise blue of the sea below.

About 15 kilometres from the border is the small town of Dalkut, the principal settlement of the western seaboard. Built on a narrow coastal plain, it is dwarfed by the high escarpment behind. Further east and midway between Dalkut and Rakhyut, the gigantic Wadi Sayq descends from the north and meets the sea. Khawr Kharfut, a brackish lagoon, sits at the centre of the wadi mouth, protected from the sea by a narrow sandbar. With its lush vegetation and palm trees, Khawr Kharfut has a tropical feel and is the best known of Dhofar's western *khawrs*.

In places the southward-flowing wadis have created coastal inlets and small raised plains where settlements have been built. The village of Rakhyut, straddling a small and sparsely vegetated *khawr*, sits on an alluvial plain in the mouth of Wadi Rakhyut. Further east is the coastal plain of Al Hawtah, comprising rocks that are the amongst the oldest of the southern coast and which are thought to date back at least 500 million years.[5] At its western end nestles a tiny settlement and at the eastern extreme is a small *khawr*.

Between Al Hawtah and Al Mughsayl the cliffs are spectacular and in places, particularly close to Shaat, rise nearly 400 metres directly from the sea. Elsewhere there are coastal platforms, such as at Al Fazayih, which has fine examples of desolate sandy beaches and sheltered coves. Further east, beyond the *khawr* of Wadi Aful, the coastal cliffs peter out and are replaced by sandy beaches and bays against the backdrop of largely-dry low hills. This is a place of transition as the coastal Jabal Al Qamar ends and the inland Jabal Al Qara begins.

Marking this point of transition are Al Marnif Cave and Al Mughsayl Blowholes where, during the *khareef* season, waves from the rough monsoon sea crash against

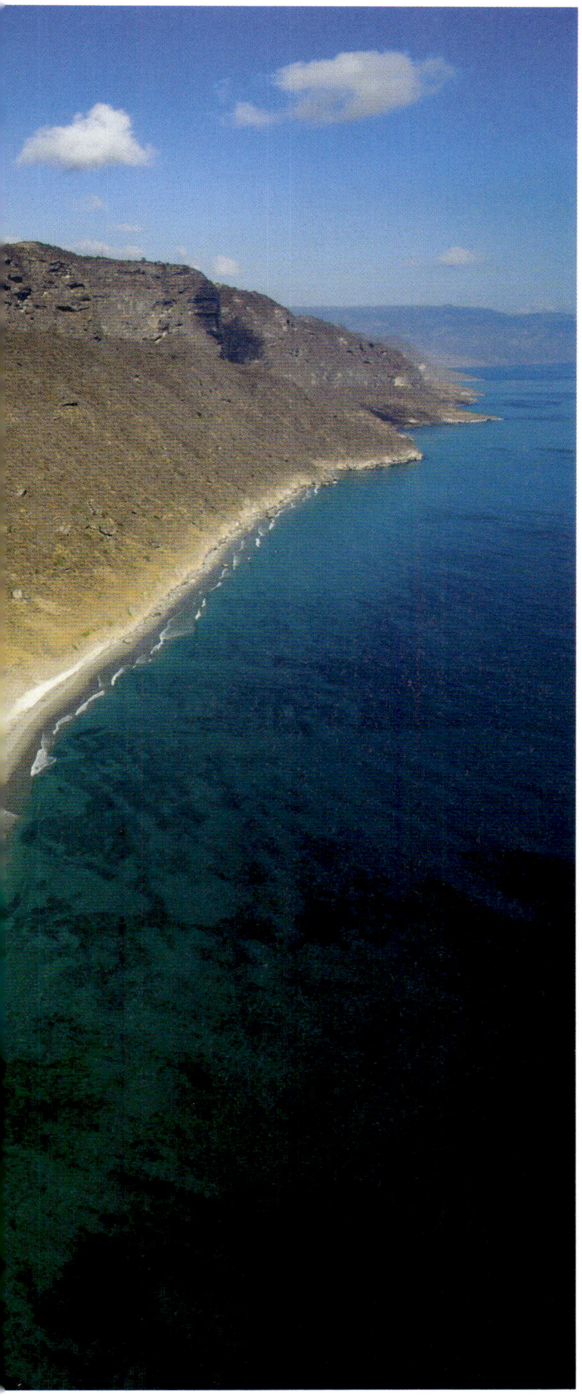

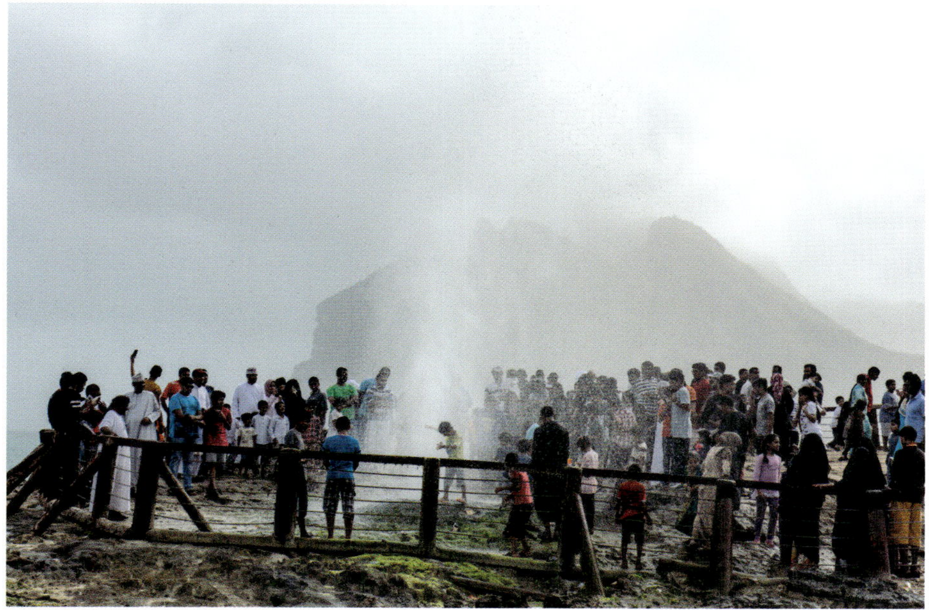

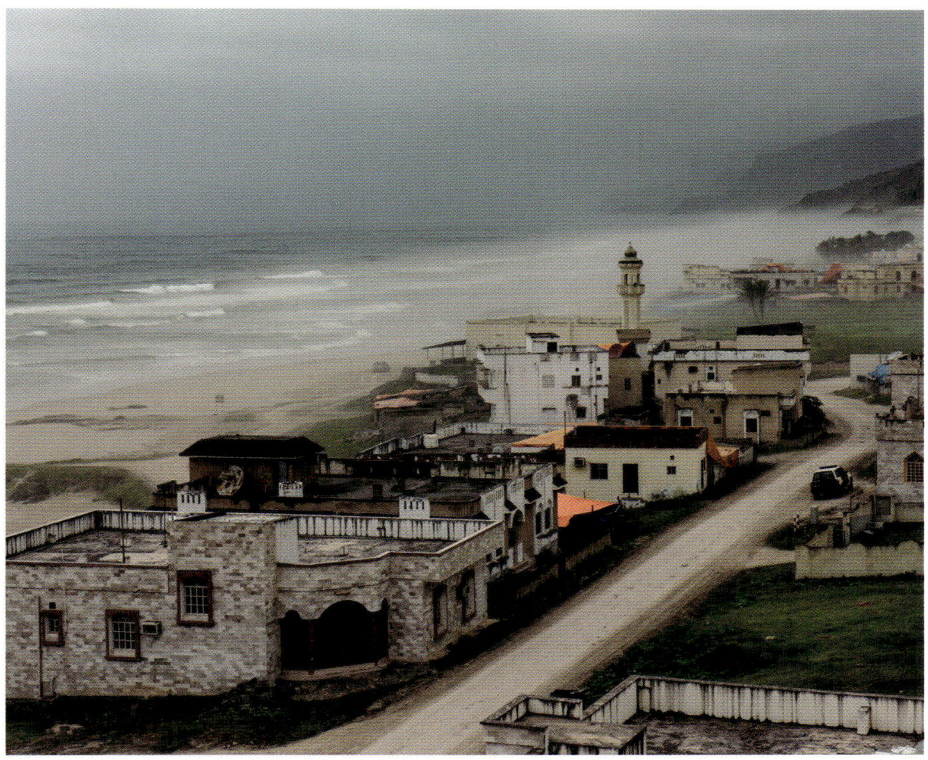

underwater limestone caves, and seawater and air is blown up through vertical shafts, creating water fountains that can reach 30 metres. Beyond the blowholes is the well-vegetated Khawr Al Mughsayl, a protected area that marks the western end of Al Mughsayl beach, which is over six kilometres long and one of Dhofar's most beautiful sandy beaches.

The town of Dalkut ***(above)*** bears the full force of the monsoon, while just to the east lies Wadi Sayq , encompassing the brackish lagoon of Khawr Kharfut ***(above left)***. At the eastern end of Jabal Al Qamar are Al Mughsayl Blowholes ***(above top)***, a popular destination for visitors during the monsoon.

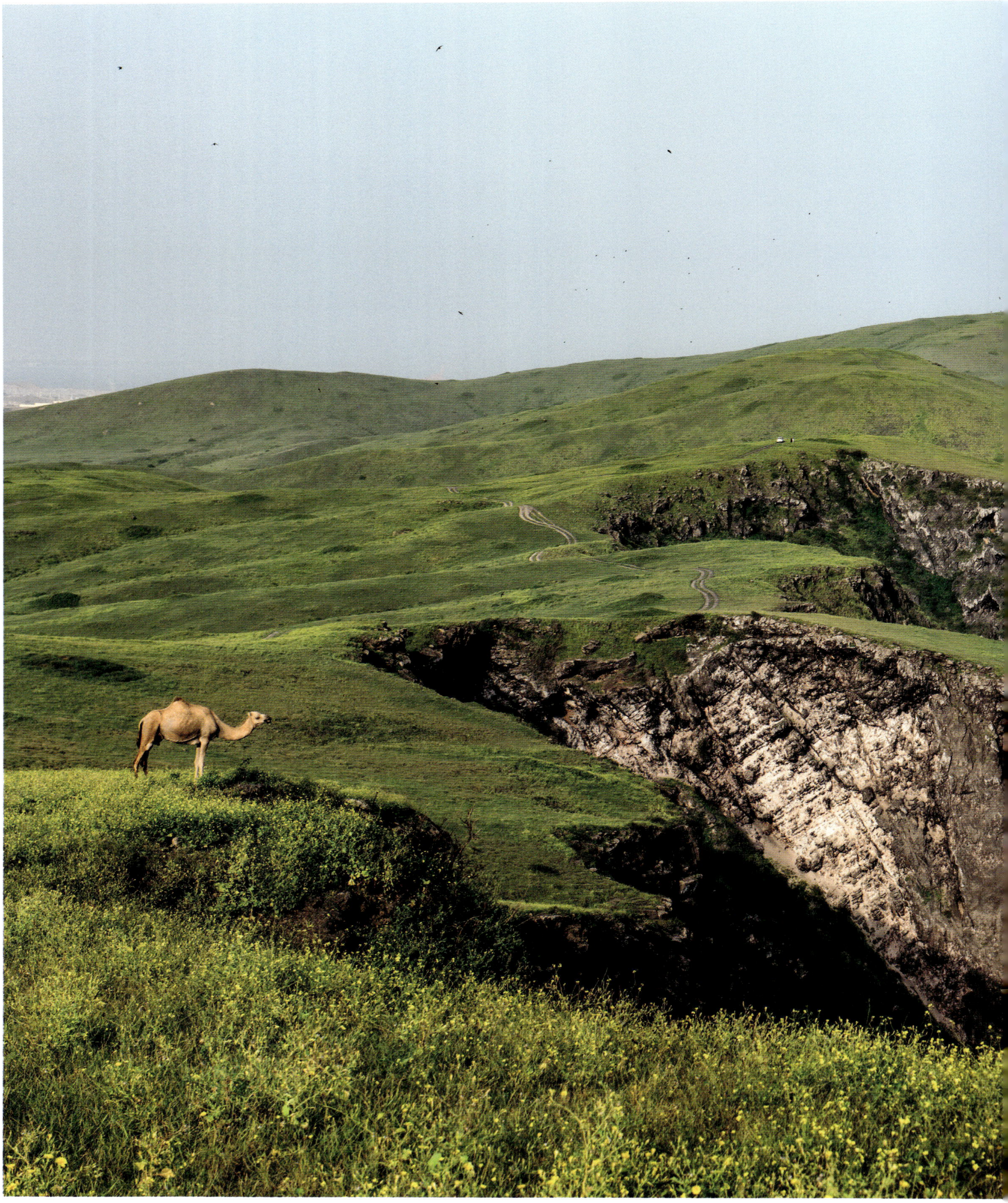

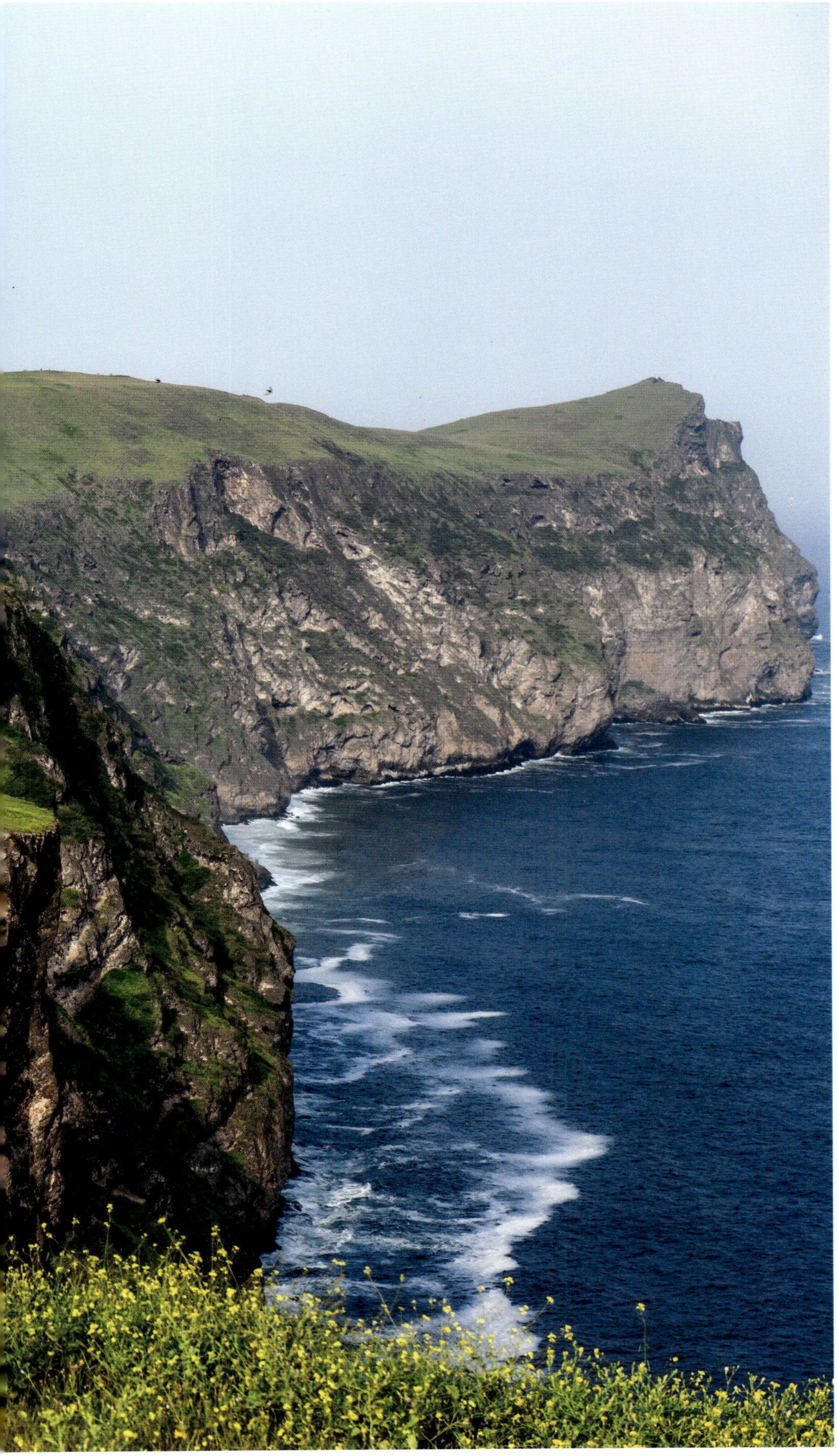

The Jarbib

Jarbib – Al Mughsayl to Salalah

Jarbib is a Jibbali term used to describe the coastal plain and hills that stretch the length of Jabal Al Qara, from Al Mughsayl in the west to Wadi Hinna and Mirbat in the east.

Between Al Mughsayl and Raysut, the Jarbib includes the inland hills of Qardhit in the west and the deeply scoured alluvial plain of Wadi Adawnab in the east. Though the hills capture some of the monsoon fog and rainfall, this area seems to lie in a rain shadow created by local topography. Consequently it is usually very dry, even at the height of the monsoon. However, this is not true for the higher ground to the south that forms the coastal headland, including Ras Hamar, between Al Mughsayl and Raysut port. Here, especially in years with a strong monsoon, the dull and sparse slopes are transformed into a luscious green carpet. Vertical cliffs plummet into the sea and a lone, densely-vegetated sea stack, cut off from the mainland and standing about 100 metres tall, is testament to former times when the entire headland was more richly vegetated.

(Left) In years of a strong monsoon, such as 2016, the usually dry coastal hills of Ras Hamar turn green. The pastures draw livestock and also tourists, who picnic on the high cliffs.

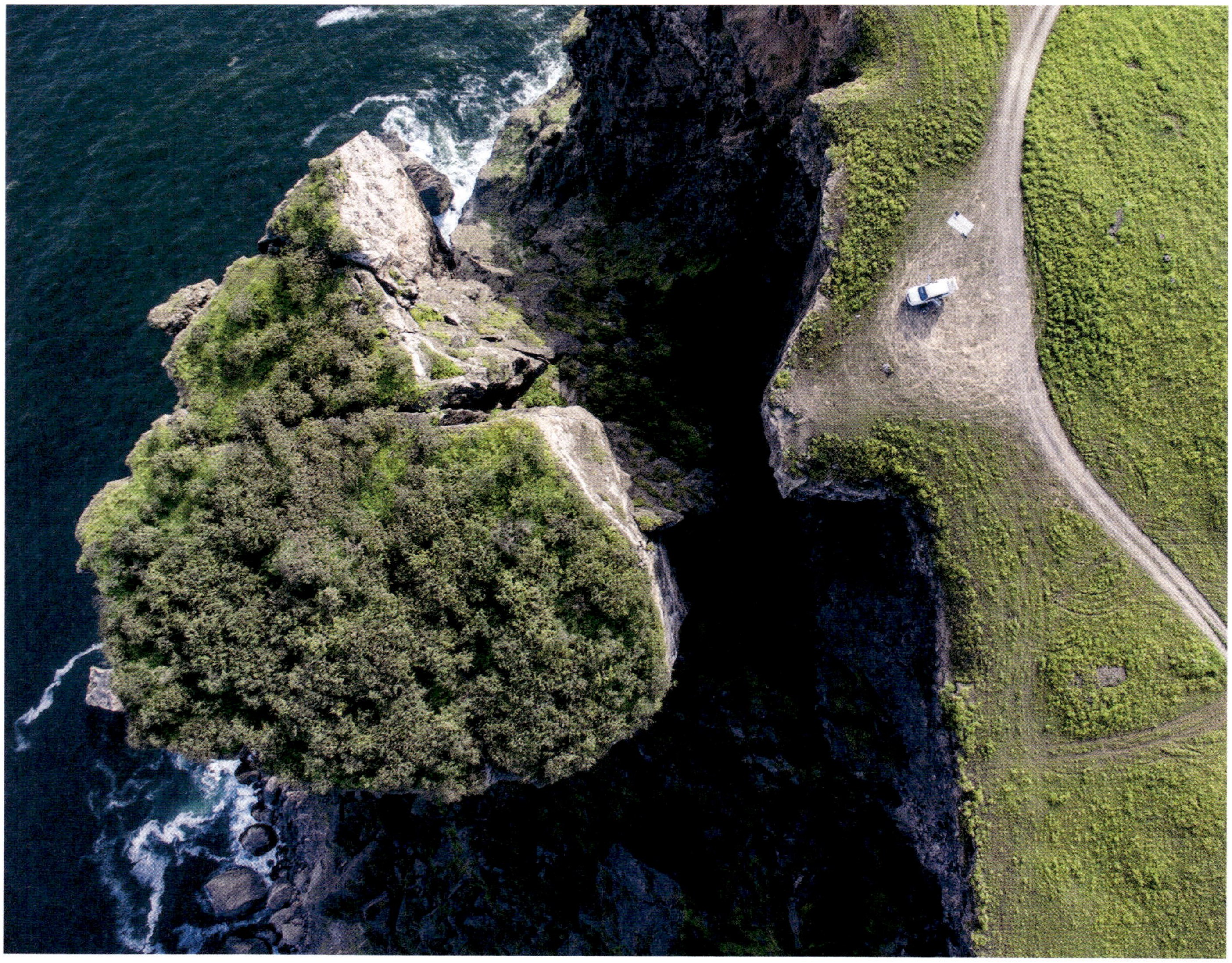

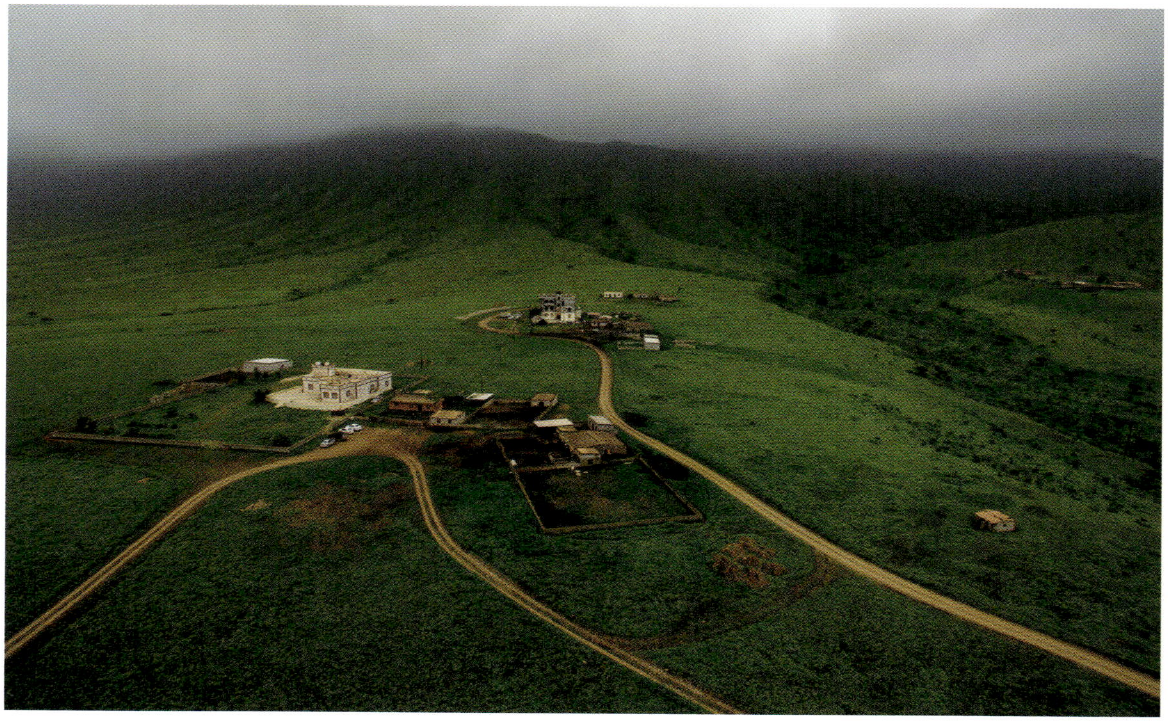

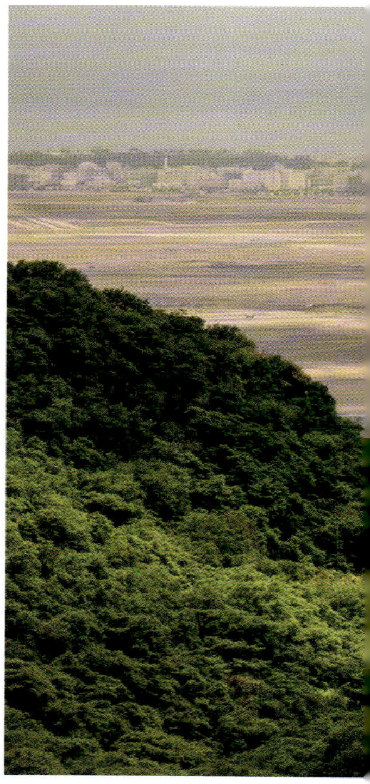

Jarbib – Salalah Bay to Mirbat

The crescent-shaped coastal plain stretches 60 kilometres from Raysut in the west to Taqah in the east, where it narrows. At its widest it extends inland for nearly 15 kilometres to Ayn Sahalnawt. The modern city of Salalah, Dhofar's capital, dominates the coastal plain. Not so long ago the city nestled quietly amongst coconut palms, lush farms and gardens and there was almost a sense of time standing still, a glimpse of a bygone age. Taqah and other towns seemed far away. Today the skyline of the modern and bustling Salalah has grown taller and the city has spread out in many directions. In the west the high cranes of Salalah's port dominate the sunset, while to the north lines of electricity pylons march along the mountain foothills. Roads snake up the Jabal and a four-lane highway connects the city to Taqah and then to Mirbat in the east. But between the city and the sea the farms remain and it is here amongst the coconuts, bananas and rushing water channels that the ancient heart of Salalah lies.

Outside the city the rather featureless coastal plain is changing rapidly and there is little sign of the former woodlands of which local herders talk. Often the only vegetation is the invasive mesquite or *ghaf al bahri* that creeps north towards the Jabal. In places are found the shallow water courses of southward-flowing wadis, and where they meet the sea brackish *khawrs* have formed. There are at least 25 *khawrs* and most are separated from the sea by fragile sandbars that are sometimes broken during heavy rainfall. Some *khawrs* are fringed by mangroves while others are edged with dense stands of reeds. These provide important refuge for coastal wildlife, particularly birds and fish, as well as green spaces in a rapidly developing urban landscape. At least ten *khawrs* are protected areas, including Khawr Salalah, which is a particularly fine example of a wetland reserve, while Khawr

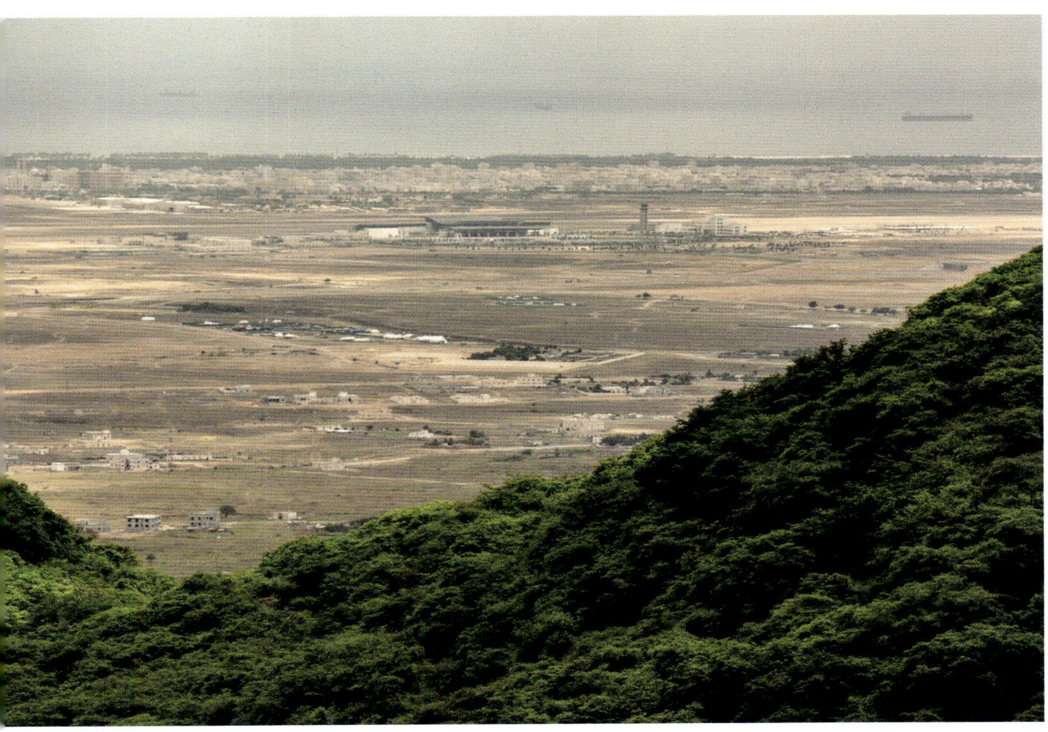

South of Adawnab a thickly-vegetated coastal stack ***(above left)*** contrasts with the heavily grazed pasture of the clifftops.

Salalah City ***(left)***, viewed from atop Jabal Al Qara, dominates the Jarbib. In years of a weak monsoon the Jarbib remains dry but when the monsoon is strong the area is transformed into lush green pastures ***(far left)***.

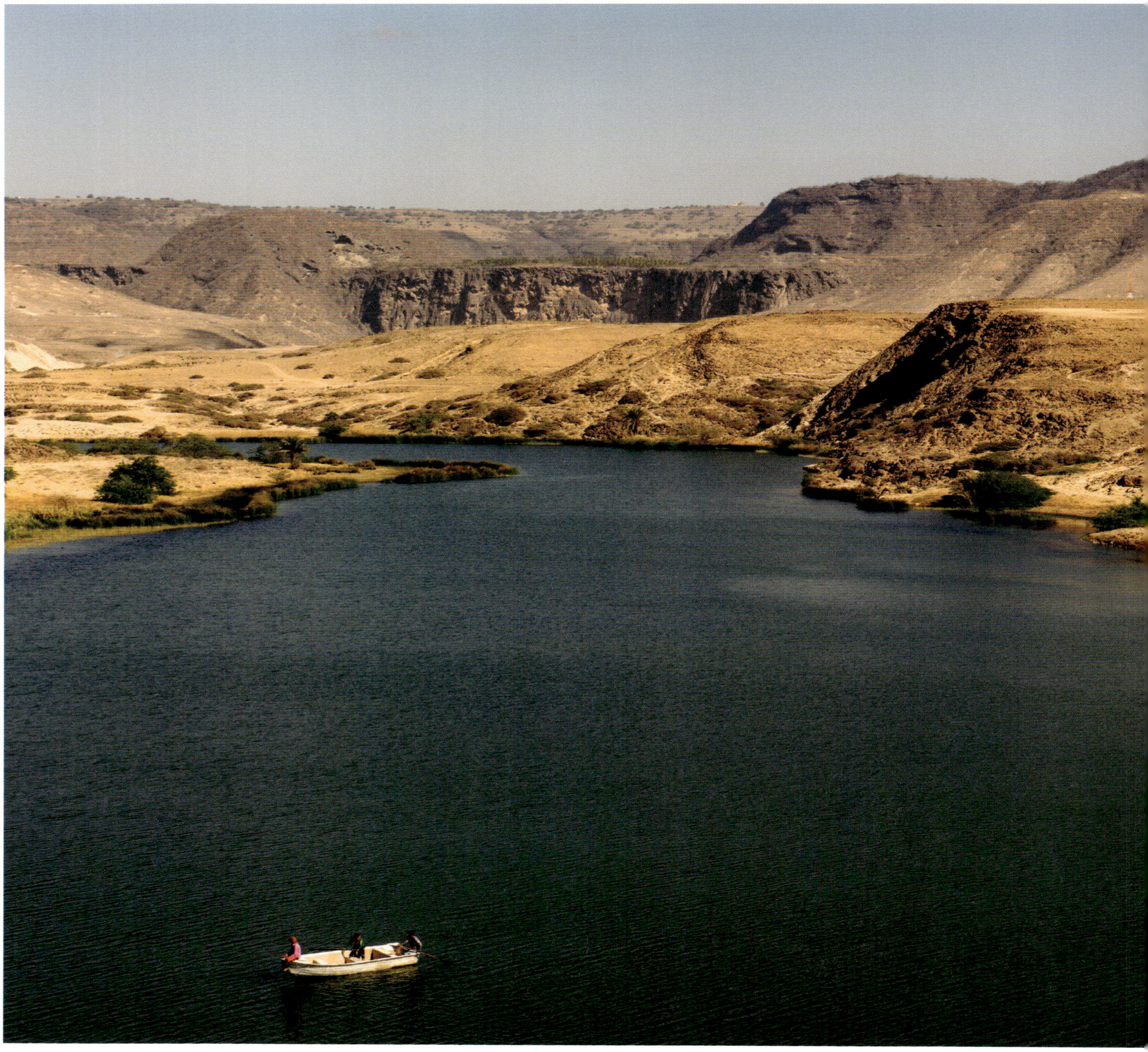

Fringed by mangroves, Khawr Qurm Al Kabir ***(opposite top)*** is one of several *khawrs* that are important green spaces in Salalah City. In the east is the town of Taqah ***(opposite bottom),*** and, more easterly still, lies Khawr Rawri ***(above),*** set against a backdrop of the Darbat Falls and Jabal Al Qara.

Al Balid is part of the 'Land of Frankincense' World Heritage Site. Between the *khawrs* are white beaches backed by a jumble of dunes and high-salinity salt flats, known throughout the region by their Arabic name, *sabkha*.

Taqah sits at the eastern end of the sandy coastline. Its recently restored fort overlooks a growing town, irrigated fields shaded by

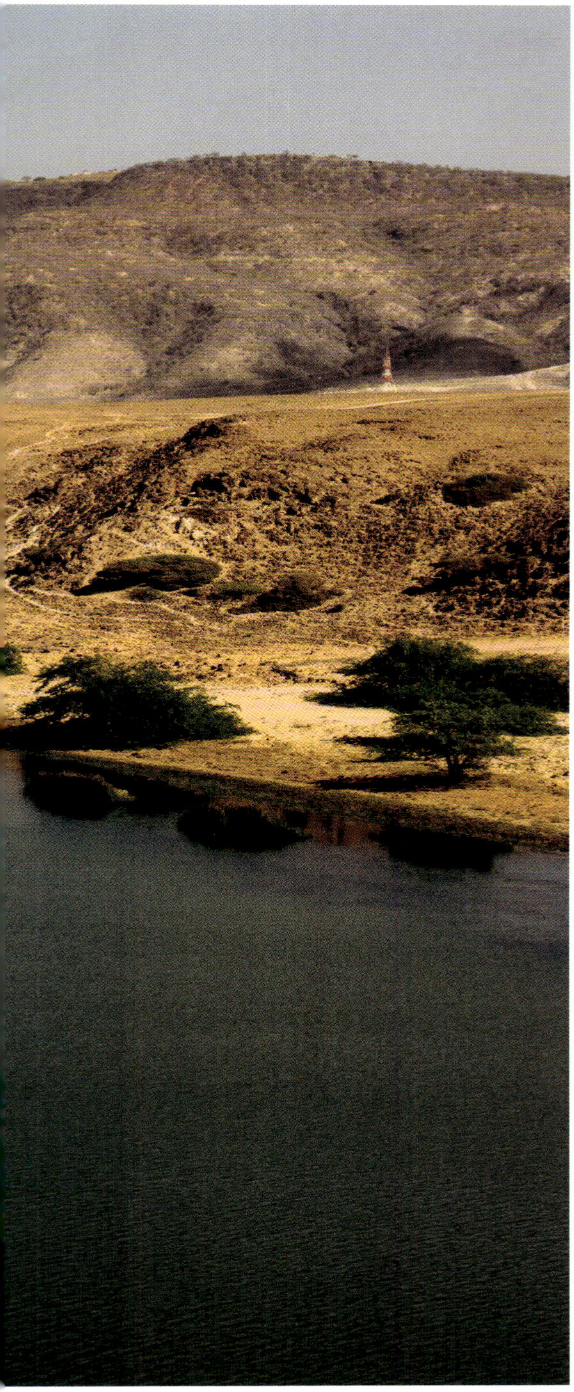

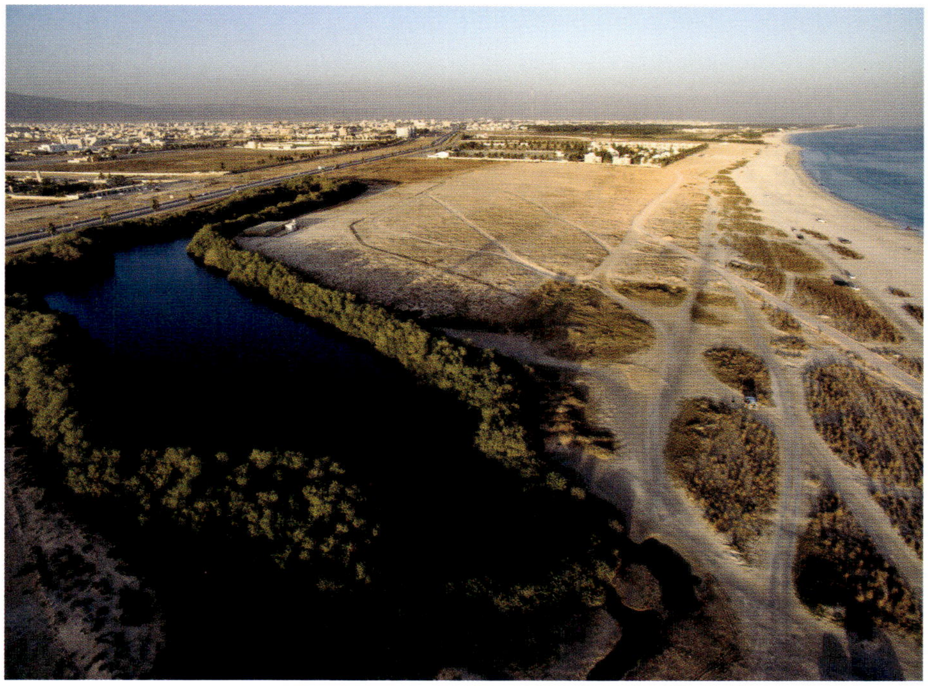

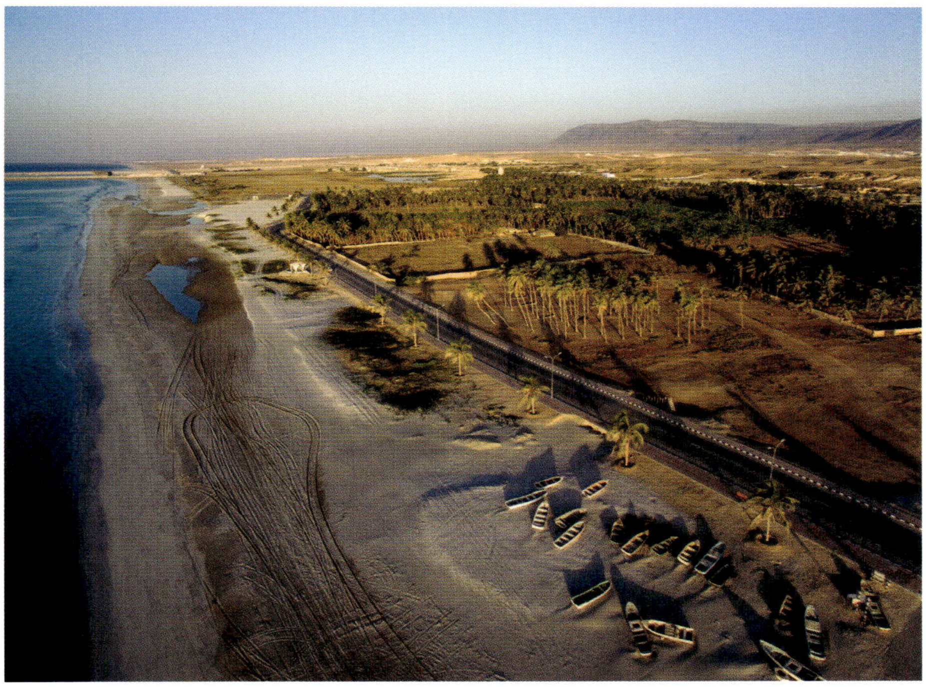

coconut palms, and to the west, Khawr Taqah, a protected area, with, beyond that, a modern fishing harbour. After Taqah the sandy coastline is replaced by low hills and steep coastal cliffs. The landscape is dominated by Khawr Rawri, which sits in the mouth of Wadi Darbat. The brackish lagoon extends over two kilometres and is Dhofar's largest *khawr,* while the ancient settlement of Samharam is arguably its most famous archaeological site and forms part of the 'Land of Frankincense' UNESCO World Heritage Site.

Beyond Khawr Rawri the coastal plain is a narrow raised platform, with modest though steep sea-cliffs, that is interrupted only by seaward-flowing wadis, some of which, including Wadi Sinur, have small *khawrs* where they reach the sea. The tiny island of Ajunut, scattered with medieval remains, is largely hidden from view and just beyond Wadi Hinna the cliffs are replaced by a relatively modest coastal dune field that is nonetheless Dhofar's largest, sweeping east towards Mirbat.

Salawt Plain – Mirbat to Hasik

The ancient town of Mirbat sits on a rocky promontory, with the new, modern town and fishing harbour spreading south. Mirbat marks the westerly extent of the Salawt Plain, which comprises rocks from the time, at least 700 million years ago, when Oman was part of the supercontinent of Gondwana.[4] These are the crystalline basement rocks that underlie most of Oman, and the striking reds and browns of these metamorphic and igneous rocks contrasts with the much younger pale cream limestone massif of Jabal Samhan that forms a stunning backdrop to the north. Viewed from the top of Jabal Samhan or from space, the Salawt Plain appears streaked or striated as rusty-red lines of rock run north-west to south-east. These lines are in fact where molten magma has cooled and solidified within the crust of the planet. With such high geological and landscape value, the Salawt Plain has been proposed as a National GeoPark.[24] The road from Mirbat to Jawfa and on to Sadah cuts through this landscape and the ridges of magma are easily seen.

Unlike most of Dhofar the coast east of Mirbat is craggy and the hard basement rocks extremely jagged, having faced the full might of the monsoon for thousands of millions of years. Small rocky headlands alternate with sandy bays and there are few settlements east of the small island of Hin. Access is difficult and the larger settlements, including Sawb and Jawfa, are closer to the Jabal Samhan foothills and the main road that links Mirbat to the coastal town of Sadah.

(Centre top) Jabal Janjari, just southwest of Sadah, overlooks a long sweeping bay to the south and, to the north, looks on to the ancient igneous and metamorphic basement rocks that run north-west towards the southern escarpment of Jabal Samhan ***(bottom left)***.

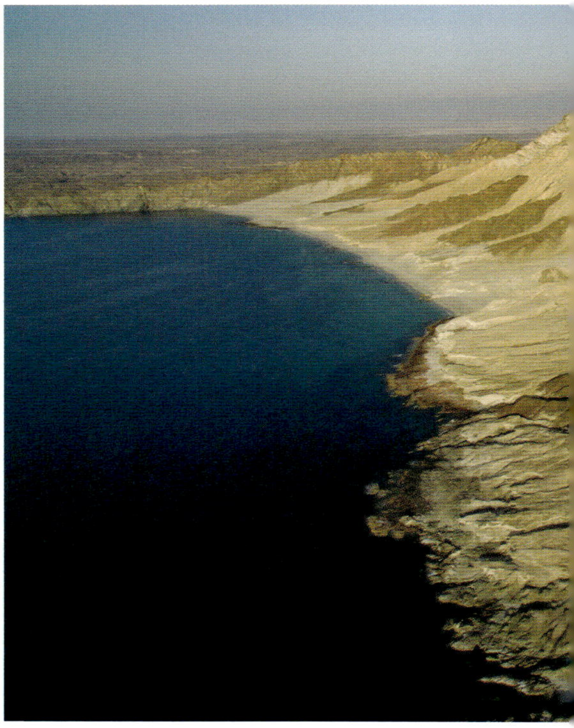

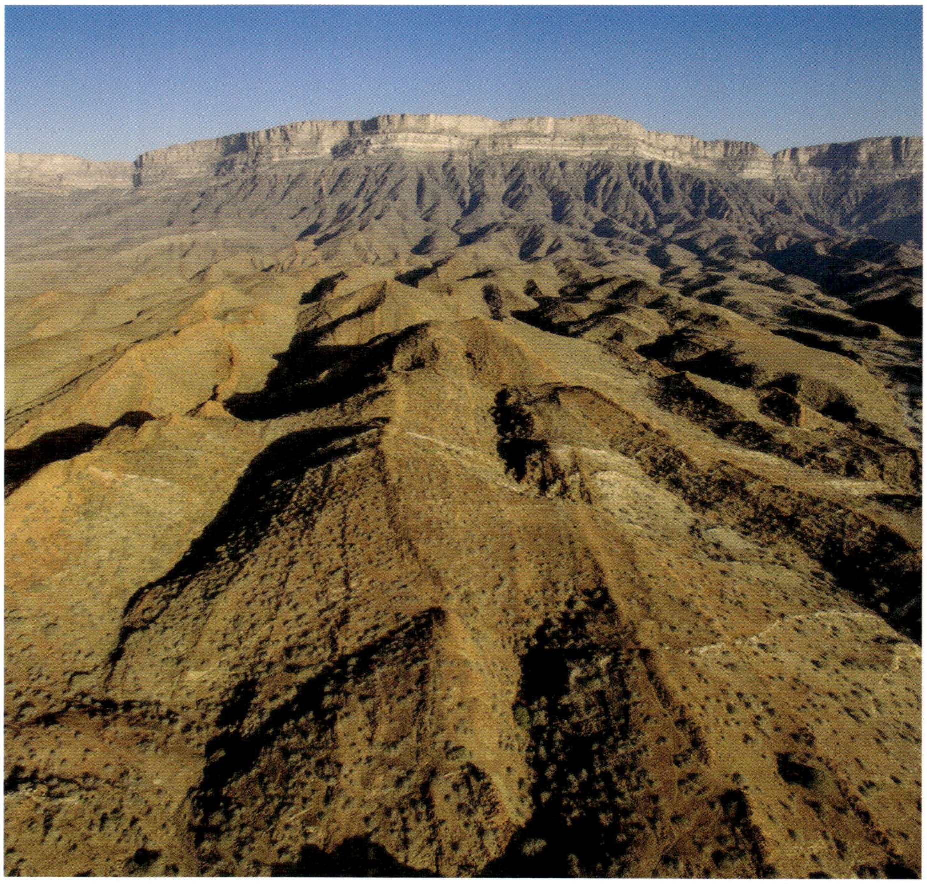

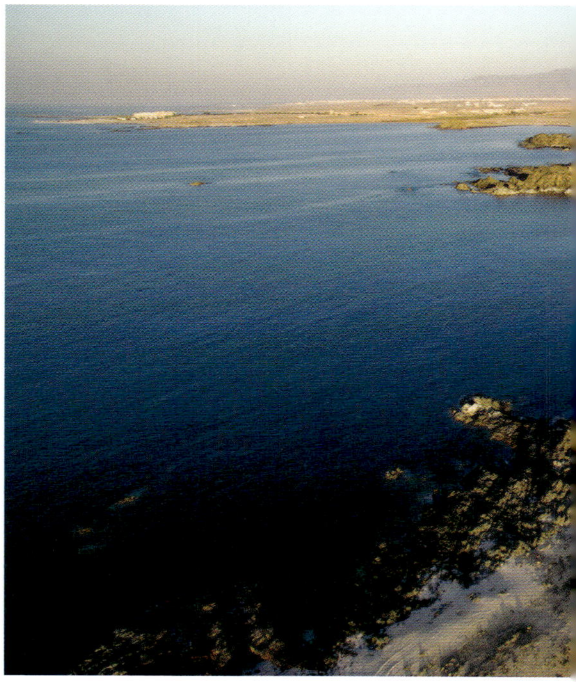

To the west, the Salawt Plain includes rugged coastline extending as far as Mirbat ***(centre bottom)*** while to the east the town of Hadbin ***(bottom right)*** sits below soft limestone cliffs, which are in contrast to a shoreline dominated by ancient granite rock.

Consequently this section of coastline is amongst the most remote of southern Dhofar and is reached only via north-south tracks that follow the wadis that drain from Jabal Samhan to the sea. These include Wadi Ayn, Wadi Fushi and Wadi Shaat and typically there are small *khawrs* where they reach the sea. Just east of Wadi Shaat is Jabal Janjari, an isolated hill rising to over 400 metres and overlooking a magnificent bay to the south.

Just beyond Janjari is the port of Sadah, which came to prominence for its importance in the export of frankincense from Jabal Samhan. East of Sadah the Salawt Plain narrows and the rocky shore is broken by the 600-metre-high Jabal Masirah, where strong onshore winds have led to the formation of extensive coastal sand dunes. The town of Hadbin perches on a coastal terrace, a step-like platform, underneath Jabal Jashim and overlooks a shore dominated by massive bleached granite outcrops.

Beyond Hadbin is Ras Naws, after which the coast is sheltered and escapes the direct impact of the monsoon seas. A small *khawr* marks Wadi Samhal, which drains the south eastern slopes of Jabal Samhan. The shoreline becomes more gentle and the village of Hasik is found on the coastal plain, just north of the mouth of the mighty Wadi Rabkut, the major eastward-flowing wadi of Jabal Samhan. Hasik, a natural harbour, was until relatively recent times one of the most isolated settlements of Dhofar and could only be reached by sea. On a clear day the island of Al Hasikiyyah, the most westerly of the Al Hallaniyyat Islands, can be seen.

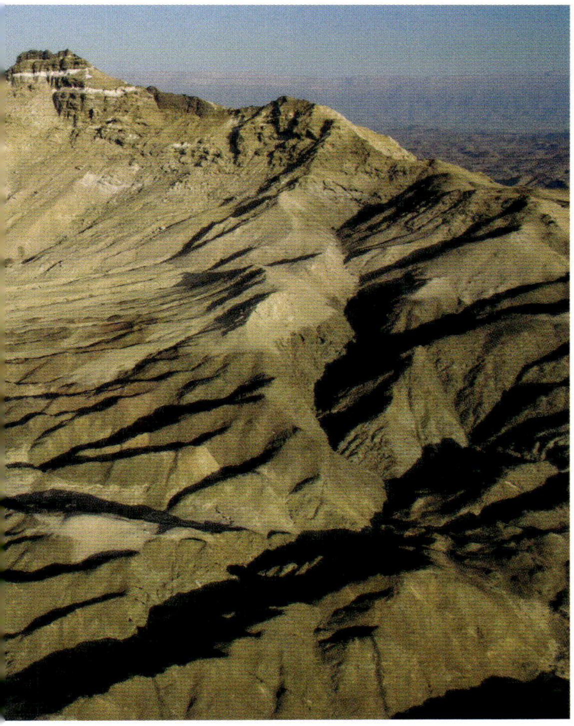

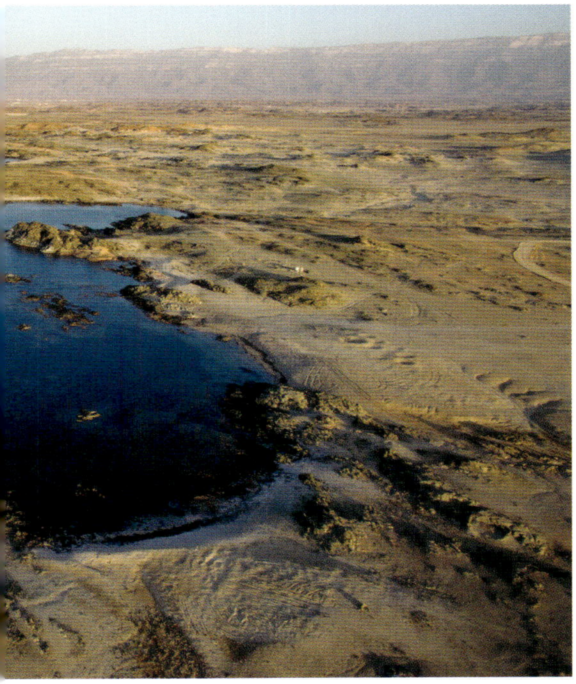

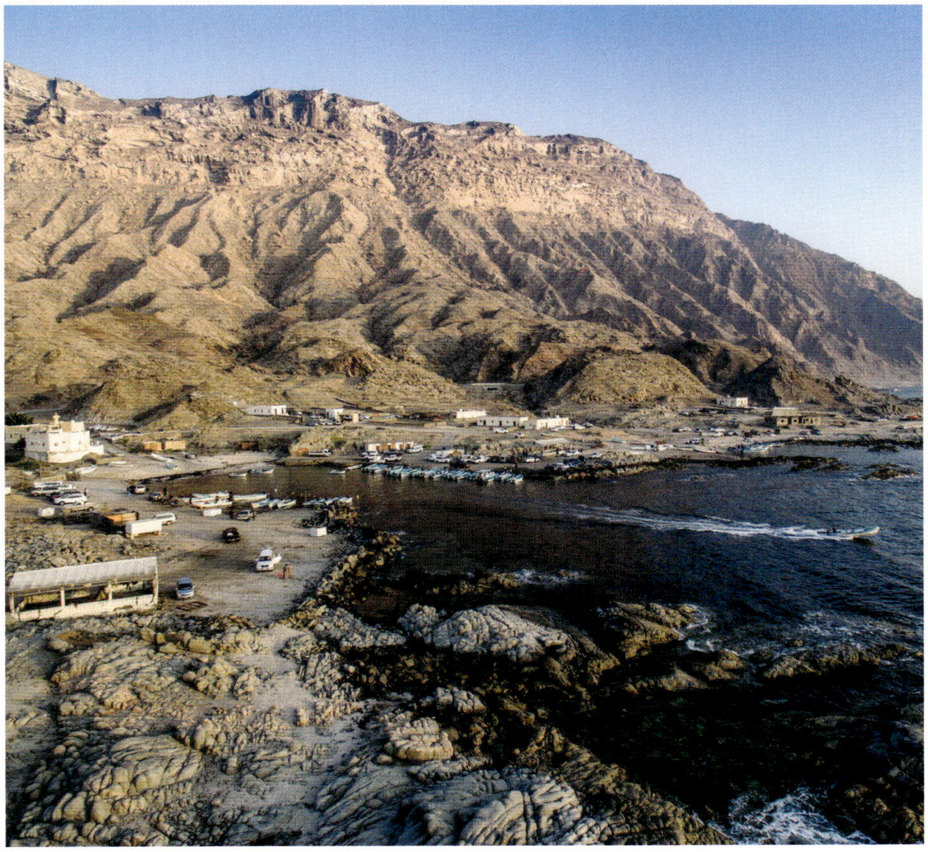

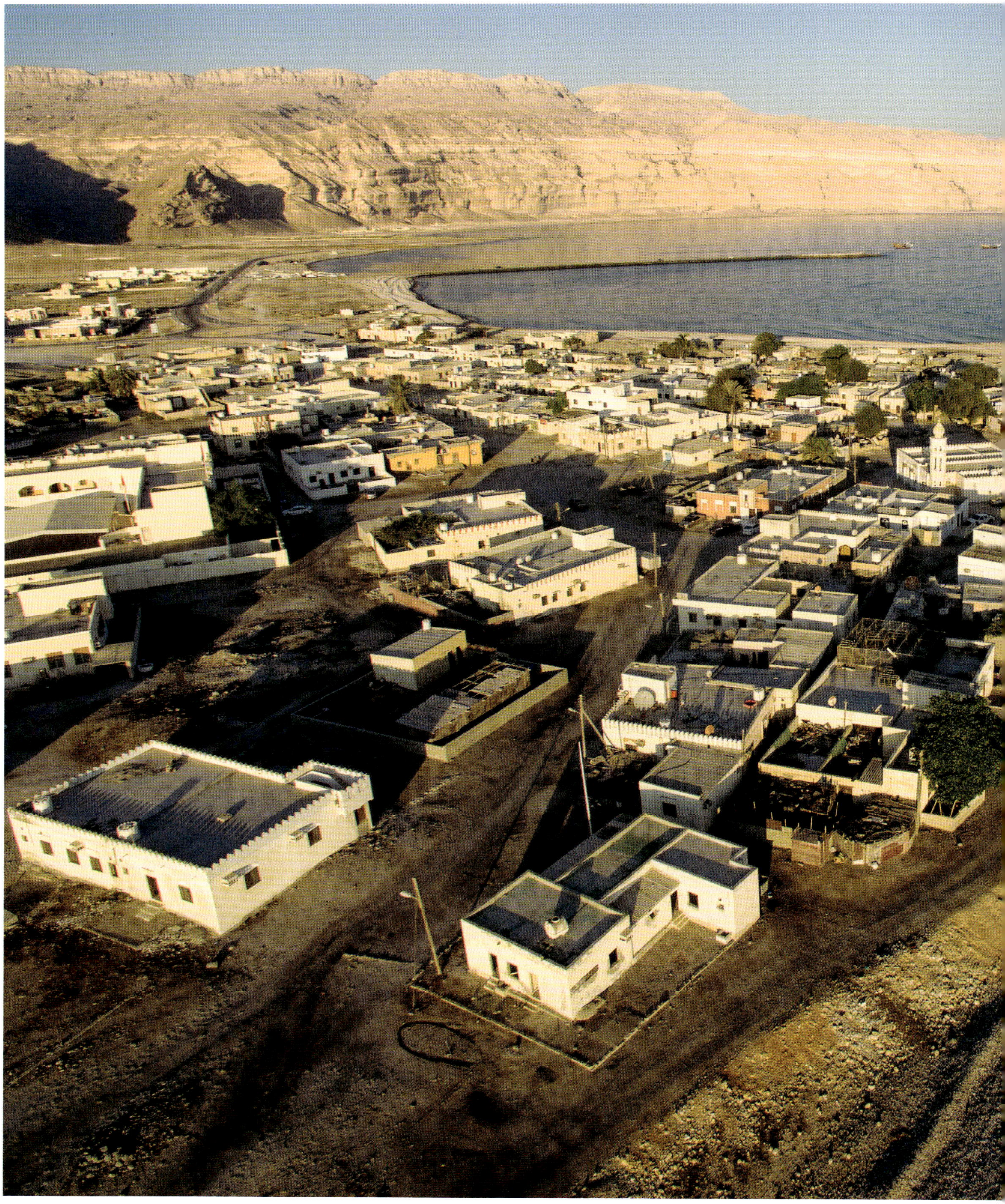

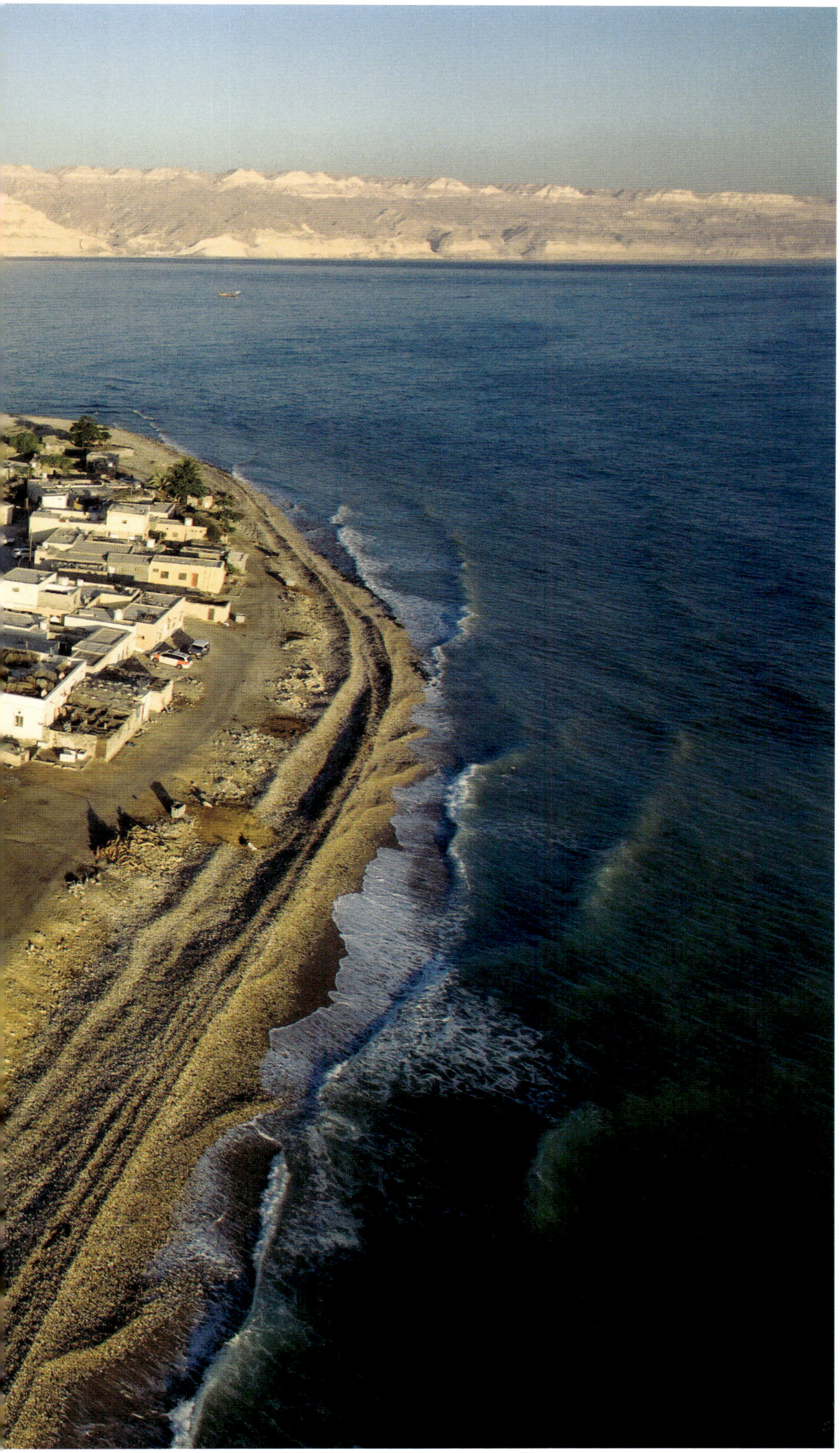

Hasik to Sharbthat

On the narrow coastal plain north of Hasik are the dominant, 300-metre-high limestone cliffs of Natif, famous for their springs that, during heavy rain, become waterfalls. Water trickling and tumbling off the limestone cliffs carries dissolved calcium carbonate, which precipitates out to form highly sculptured travertine structures.

Heading north, the coastal plain soon disappears and the pale cream cliffs of Jabal Samhan, towering above a turquoise sea, sweep north-east. Interrupted only by the occasional eastward-flowing wadi and the impressive Khawr Sinaq, they seem to go on forever. However, eventually the northern extent of Jabal Samhan is reached and the cliffs are replaced by flat coastal hills and a sandy beach that stretches in a gentle arc for more than 30 kilometres. Here is found the village of Ash Shuwaymiyyah, which sits on a raised terrace at the mouth of the great Wadi Ash Shuwaymiyyah, which drains the north-eastern reaches of Jabal Samhan.

At the northern end of the Ash Shuwaymiyyah bay, the sandy beach and plain are replaced by dark cliffs that

(Left) Until the early 2000s the small town of Hasik was a remote settlement reachable only on foot and by boat. Today it is reached by a highway that hugs the shoreline from Hadbin in the south before climbing the steep coastal cliffs of Jabal Samhan to reach Ash Shuwaymiyyah in the north.

mark the south-western extent of the Jiddat Arkad, a largely flat and dry sedimentary plain. The coastal rock, also sedimentary, is darker and older than the inland formations. Though only 150-200 metres high, the cliffs are sheer and the coastline, largely devoid of vegetation, feels harsh and remote. Broken only by the occasional small wadi and associated *khawr*, the coastline is uniform until the ancient ruined settlement of Manji. From here to Sharbthat there is a low-lying but broad coastal plain with occasional poorly vegetated *khawrs* and areas of *sabkha*. At the northern end is the large settlement of Sharbthat, dominated by modern buildings spread largely across a raised central plateau. Beyond the village is a *khawr* and beyond that Ras Sharbthat, which marks the northern limit of the Dhofar coast.

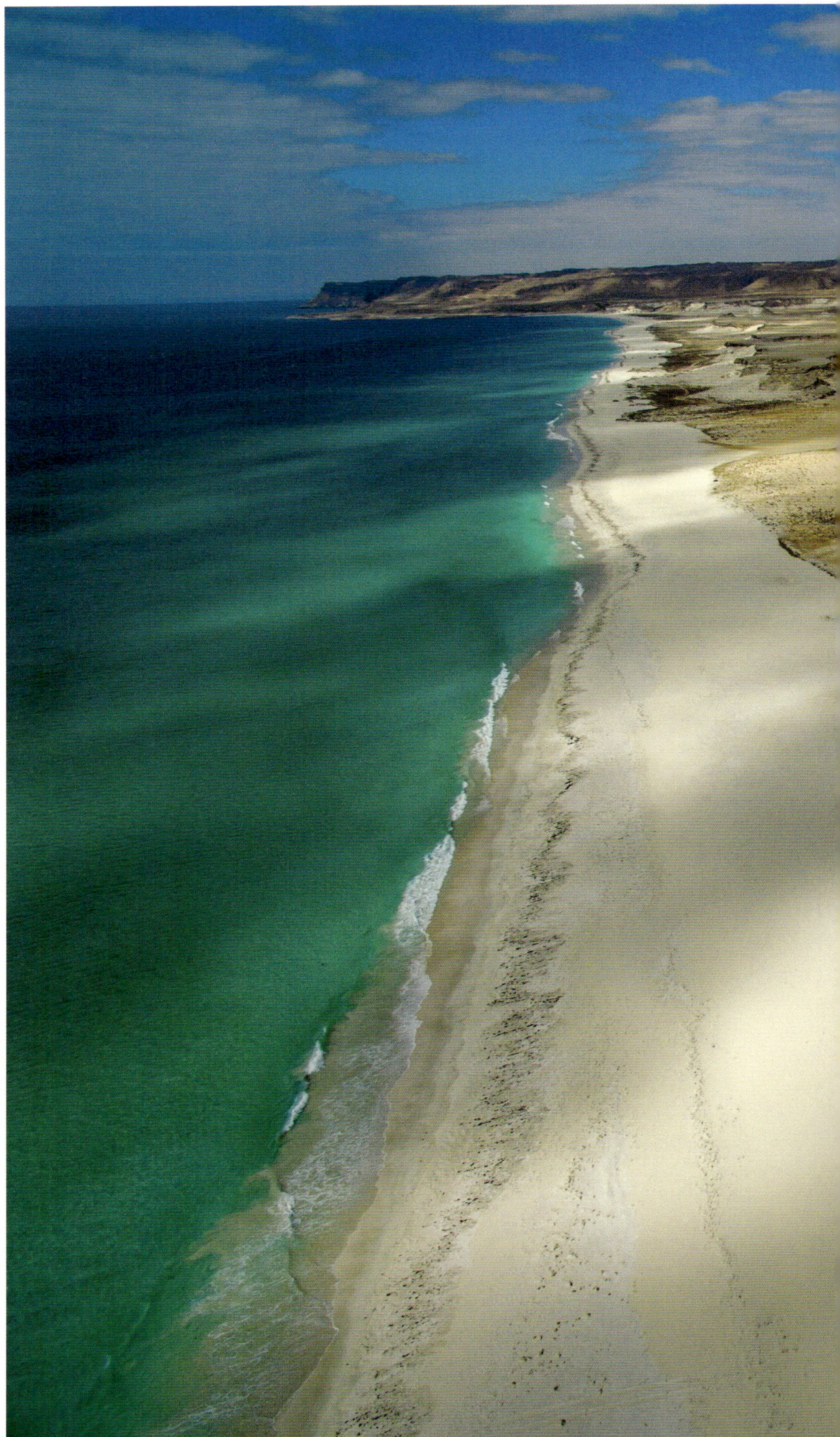

(Right) The coastline north of Ash Shuwaymiyyah and south of Sharbthat remains quite remote and is characterised by shallow coves, sandy beaches and coastal lagoons.

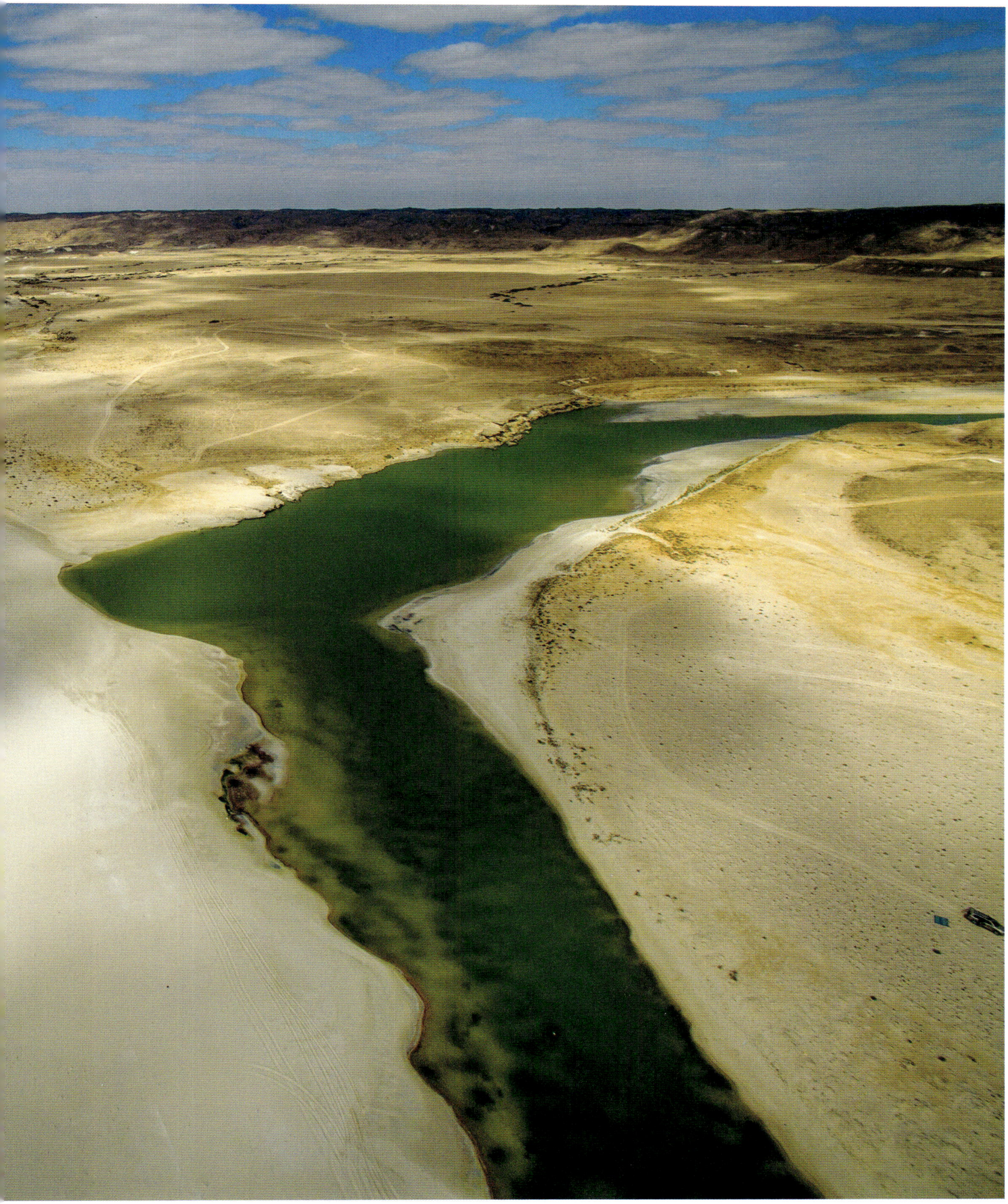

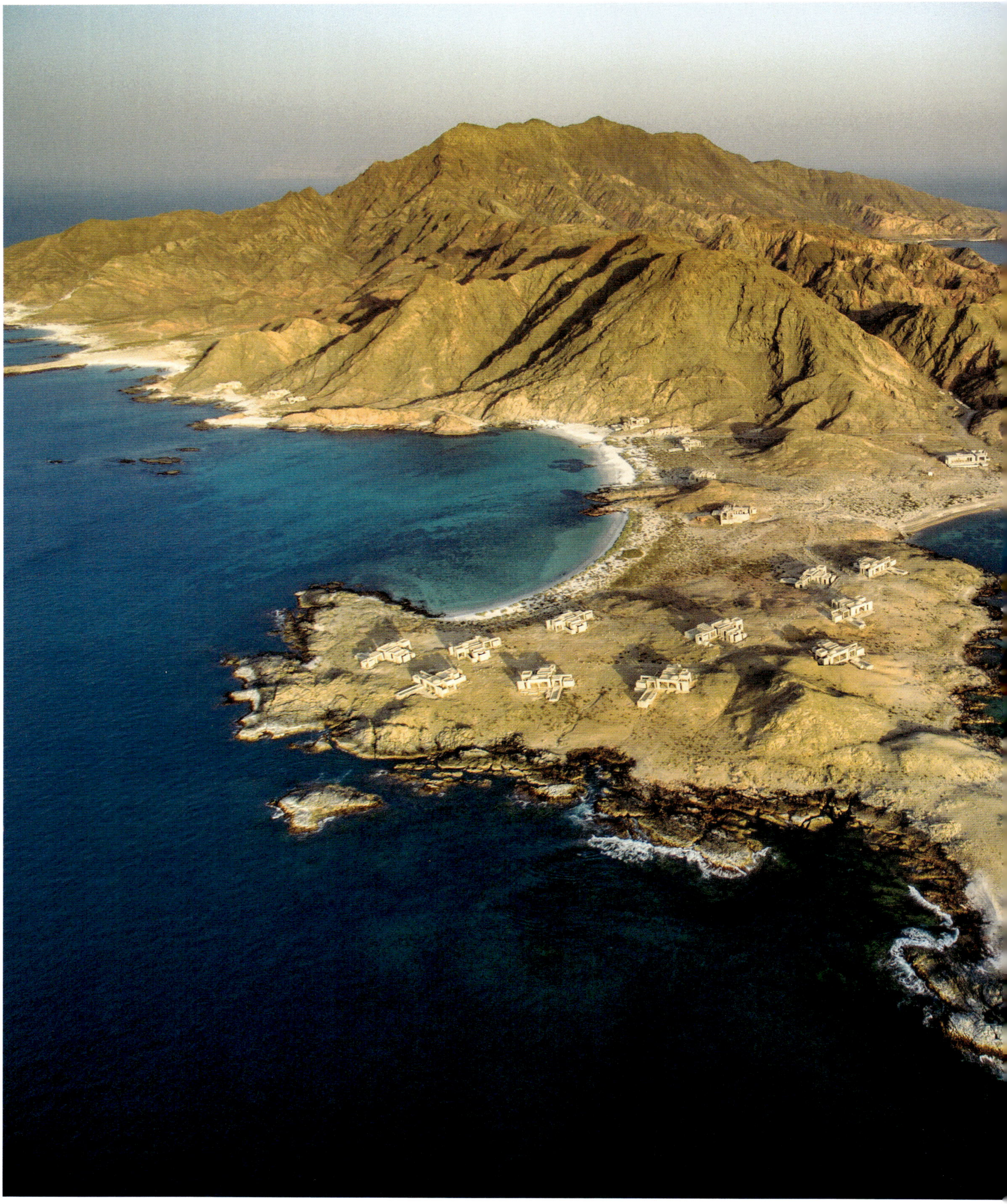

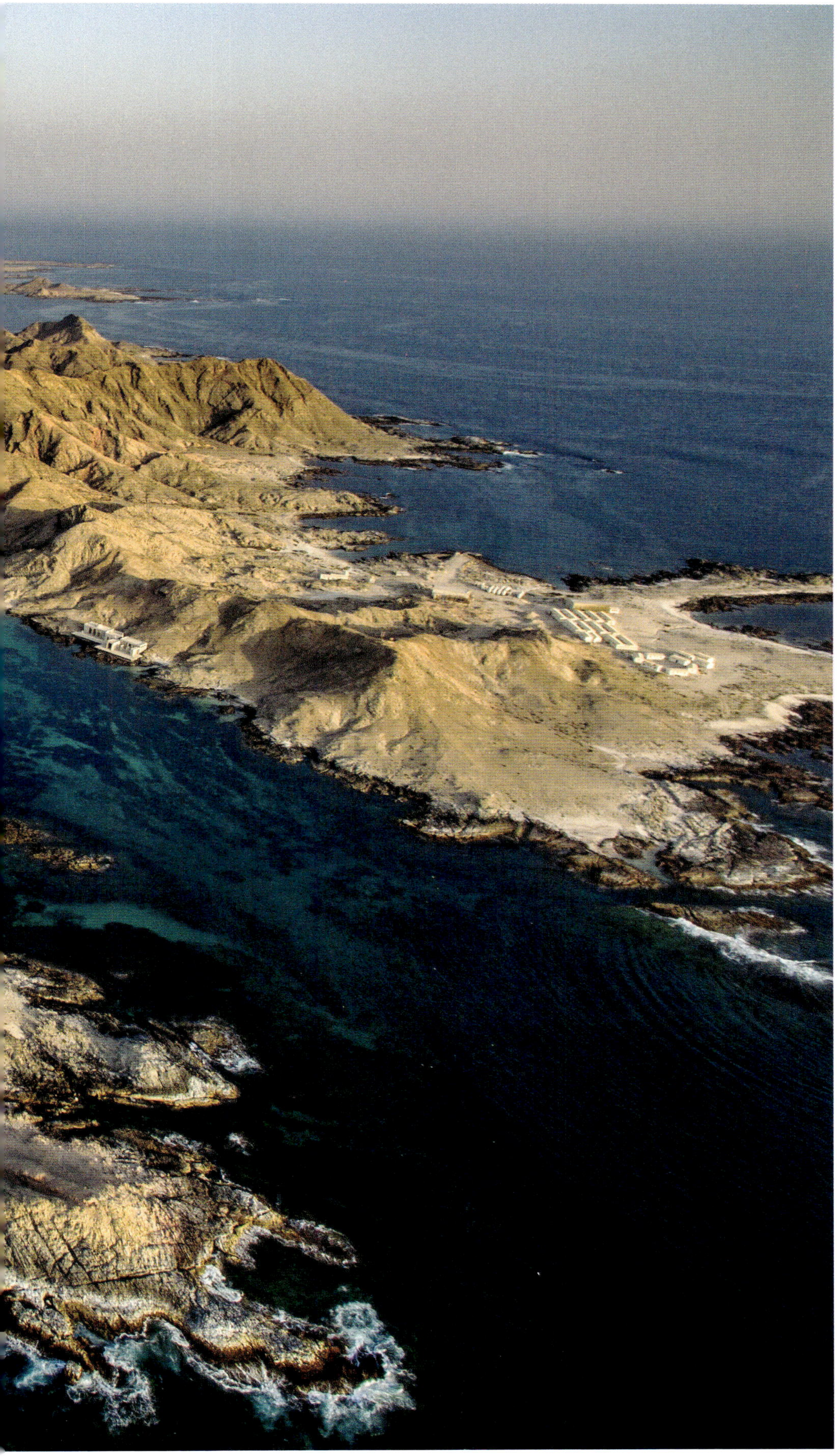

The Al Hallaniyyat Islands

The five islands of the Al Hallaniyyat archipelago lie approximately 40 kilometres off Dhofar's north-eastern coast, equidistant from Ash Shuwaymiyyah and Sharbthat, from where on a clear day they are easily seen. The islands are: Al Hasikiyyah; As Sawdah, the second largest; Al Hallaniyyah, the largest and the only one with permanent human habitation; Al Qibliyyah, in the east; and finally the tiny outcrop of Shinays.

There is a strong sense of remoteness to the islands that is not only a question of distance but also remoteness from the everyday world. Isolated by the stormy seas and mists for most of the summer monsoon, there is little respite before the winter *shamal* whips up the sea again, cutting off the islands from the mainland. This sense of remoteness is reinforced by the barren and waterless landscape that is dominated by hard, craggy, volcanic and metamorphic basement rocks, found only elsewhere in Dhofar on the Salawt Plain east of Mirbat.

The main island of Al Hallaniyyah, measuring approximately 15 kilometres east to west and seven kilometres north to south, rises to

As Sawdah ***(left)*** is the second largest of the Al Hallaniyyat Islands.

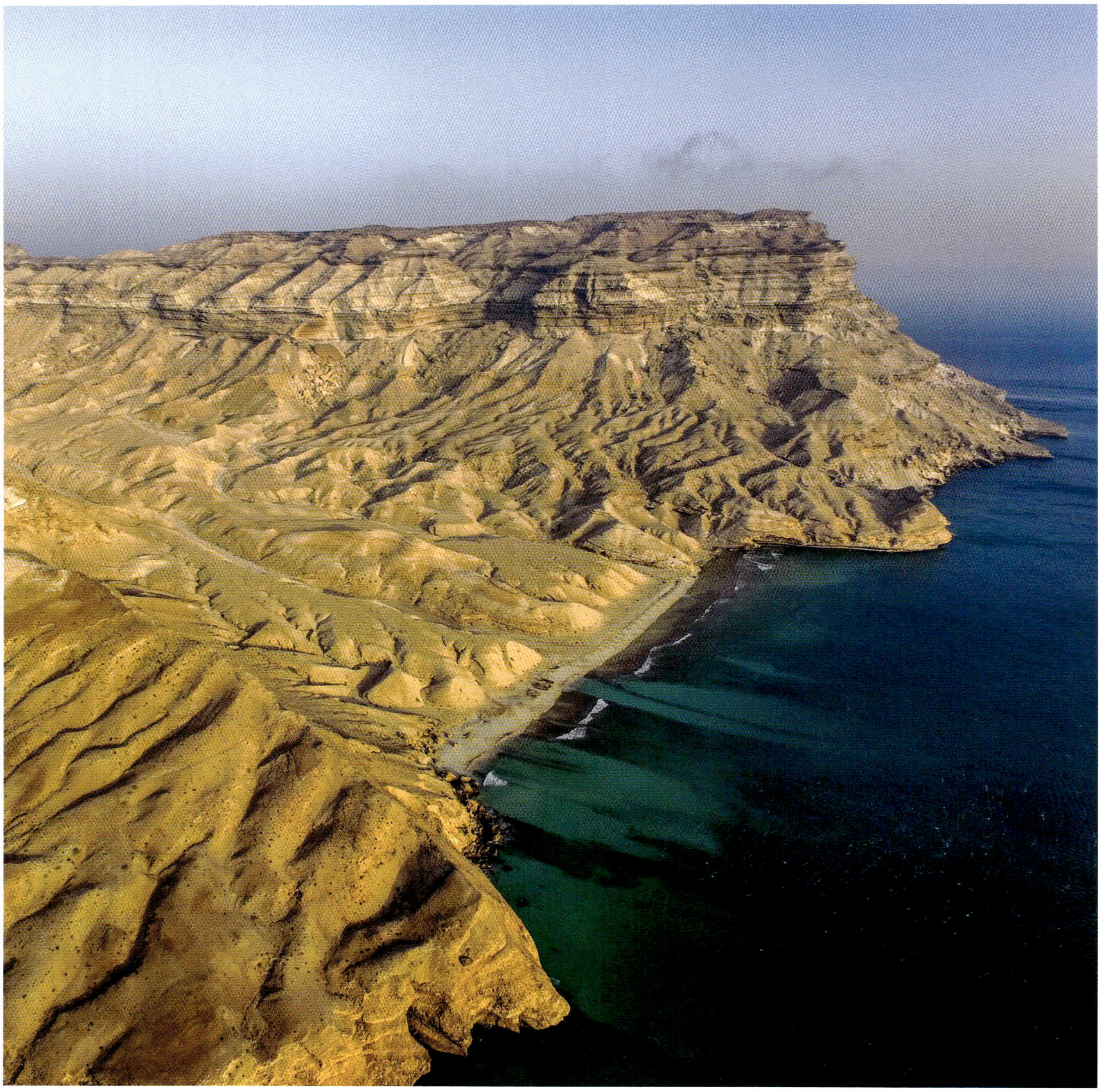

460 metres. Much of the island comprises caramel, pink and rusty-red ancient basement rocks (gneisses and granites) cut by numerous igneous dykes (basalts) that form prominent dark ridges. In the north is Ras Al Hallaniyyah, an impressive headland formed from the familiar pale limestone and sandstone that make up most of Dhofar's mountains. There are no major wadis but small gorges drain the mountains, some with brackish water springs and some ending in a coastal *khawr*. The small, wind-blown settlement of Al Hallaniyyah sits on a coastal platform at the western end of the island and from it runs the islands' only road. About two kilometres east is a modern fishing harbour.

As Sawdah is the second largest island, approximately six kilometres from west to east, and is formed entirely from metamorphic and igneous basement rocks. The north-south dykes and ridges are particularly striking. It is believed that the island was inhabited until the mid 19th century.[21] At the eastern end of the island is a coastal platform on which sits a partially-built tourist

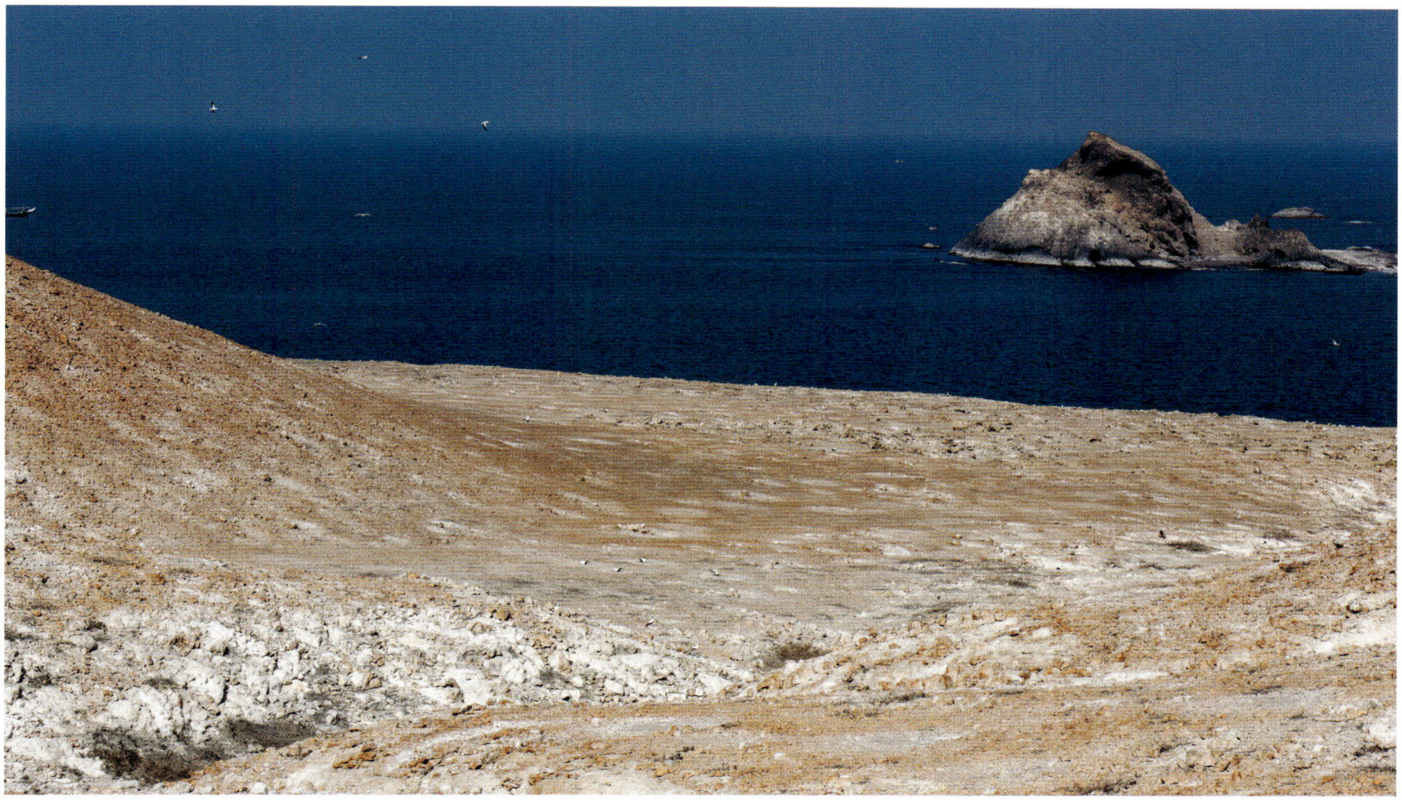

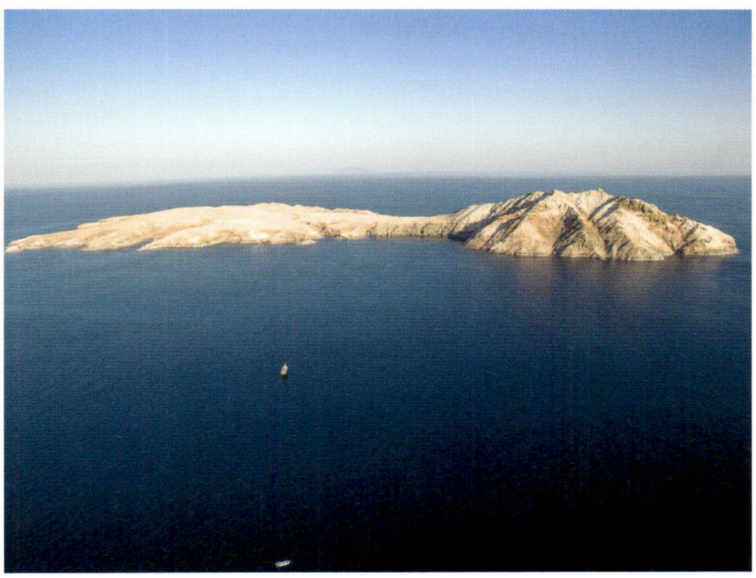

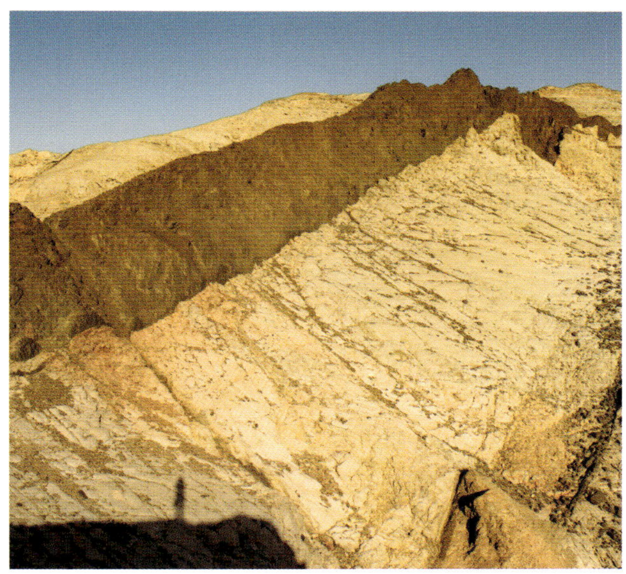

resort complete with infinity swimming pools but seemingly abandoned some years ago.

Al Qibliyyah and Al Hasikiyyah are much smaller islands, both about 2.5 kilometres at their broadest. Shinays is significantly smaller again, being no more than 600 metres long. All are made of volcanic rock and marked by the dried guano of large colonies of nesting seabirds. Al Qibliyyah is the highest, with a peak of 190 metres, and is the most accessible. On Al Hasikiyyah and Al Qibliyyah are found signs of former habitation. None of these small islands has potable water.

The limestone massif of Ras Al Hallaniyyah reaches 460 metres ***(far left)*** and dominates the main island of Hallaniyyah. In places, veins of anc ent volcanic rock contrast with the pale limestone ***(above right)***; the shadow of the photographer, (bottom left of the picture), shows the scale of the formation. The white colour of the islands of Al Qibliyyah ***(top)*** and Al Hasikiyyah (Island) ***(above left)*** comes from the guano of the colonies of thousands of nesting seabirds.

The Jabal

The Dhofar Mountain Chain forms a crescent-shaped arc that is tilted north and consists of Jabal Samhan, Jabal Al Qara and Jabal Al Qamar. Locally the three mountains are known simply as the Jabal from the Arabic word for mountain but there are numerous other names, some very old, that are still widely used. For example, in the languages of the mountain people the mountains of Jabal Al Qara and Jabal Al Qamar, which receive the monsoon rains, are known as śḥɛr.

The three mountains are contiguous and there are no formal boundaries between them. In the west, Jabal Al Qamar rises from the sea to face head-on the Southwest Monsoon that cloaks it in fog and low cloud from June to September, supporting lush forests and grasslands. This runs east to an area of dry lands, close to Wadi Ashawq, that marks the transition to Jabal Al Qara, which is the central block and overlooks Salalah and the coastal plain or Jarbib.

Jabal Al Qara also faces the monsoon, and like Jabal Al Qamar its south facing slopes and plateaus are transformed each summer by the seasonal rainfall. As the mountain sweeps east there is a point east of Tawi Aatayr and above the town of Mirbat where it begins to rise and its south-facing escarpment veers north-east. Now angled more east than south, and several hundred metres higher, the Jabal is no longer in the direct path of the monsoon, is hyper-arid and is commonly referred to as Jabal Samhan. This towering mountain is the highest and driest of the three mountains and extends east to the coastal village of Hasik.

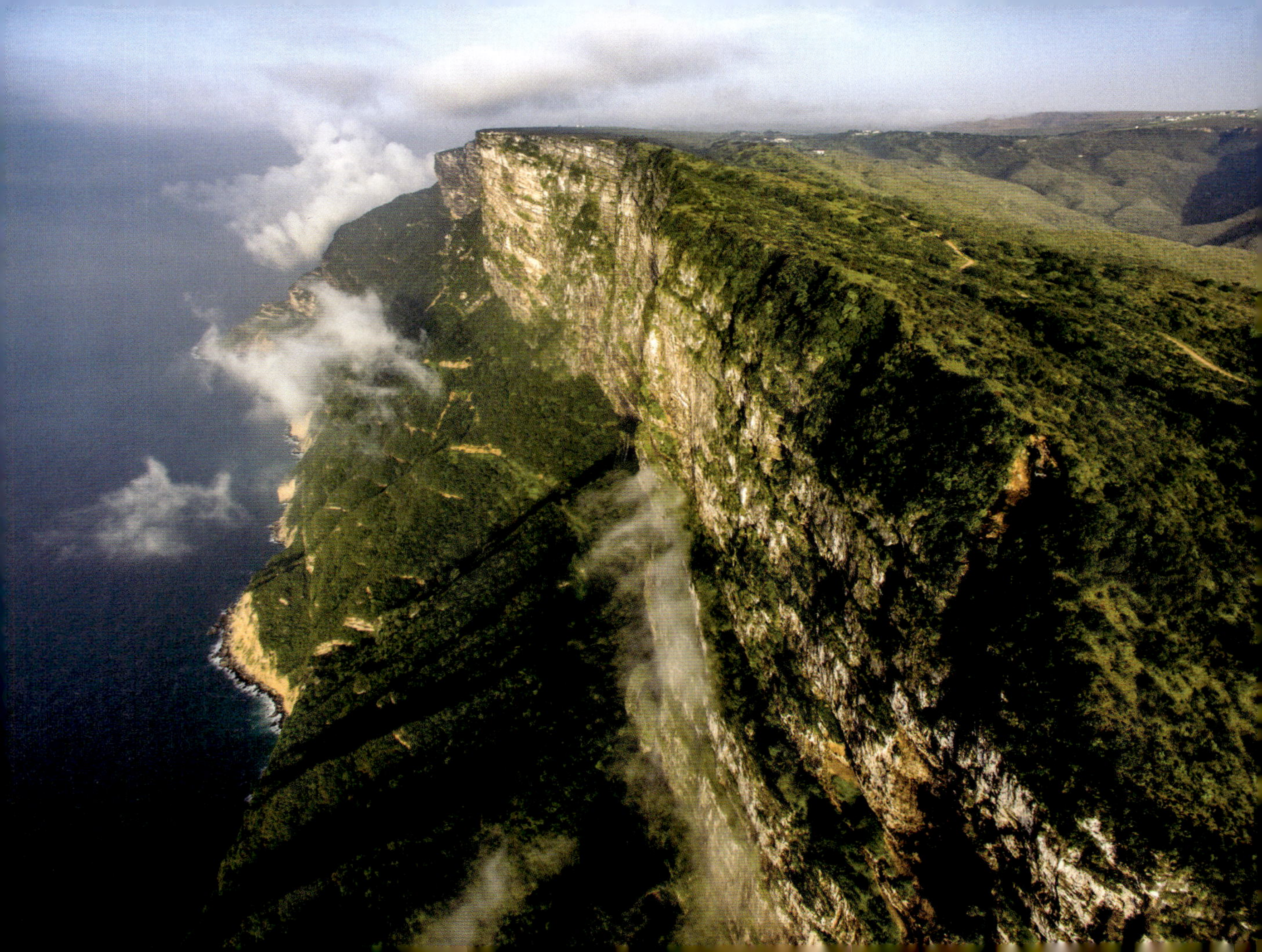

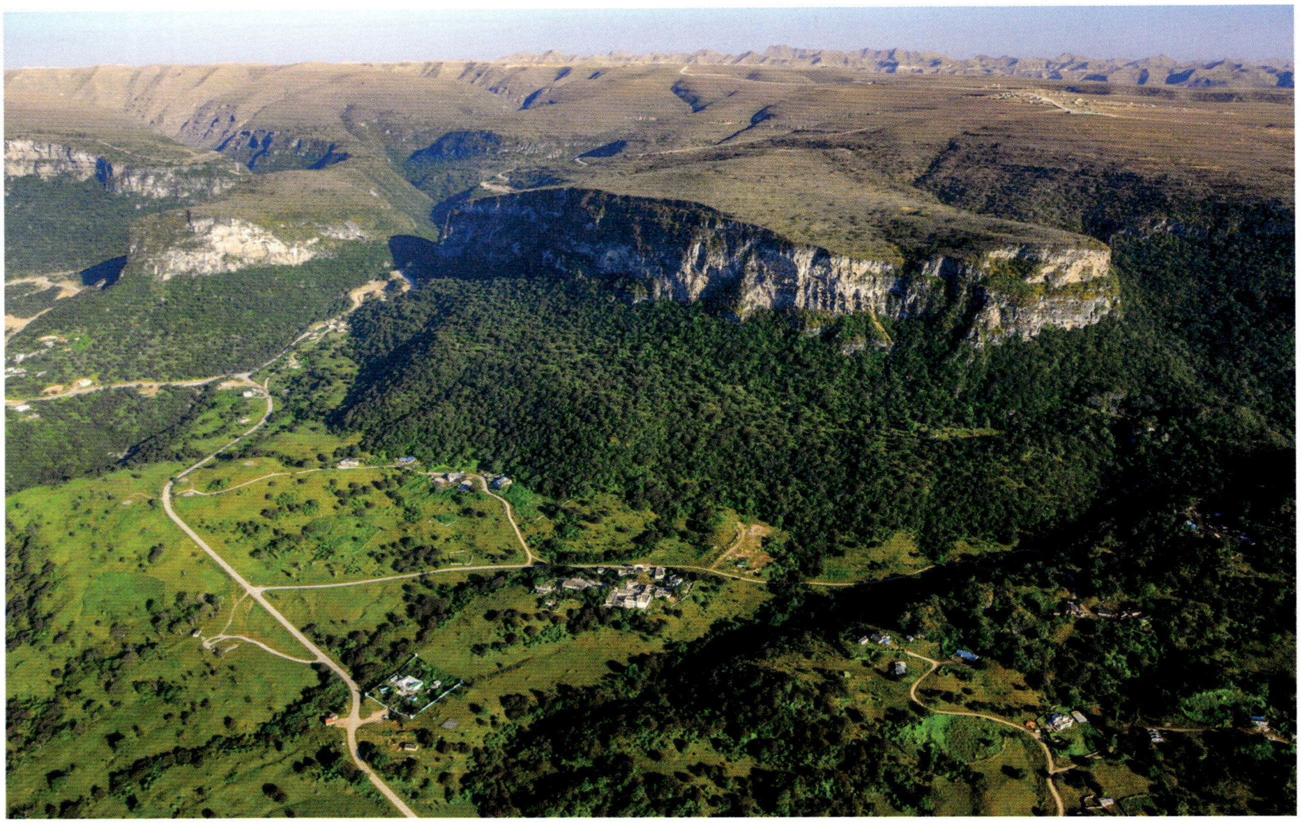

Jabal Al Qamar

Jabal Al Qamar is the westernmost range of Jabal Dhofar and runs approximately 60 kilometres east to west. It is a long narrow range and, unlike the other Dhofar mountains, it is not separated from the coast by an extensive plain. It is formed from the usual limestone found in Dhofar although there is a band of older limestone at mid-elevation on the southern slopes. At its highest point, just north of the border town of Sarfayt, the mountain reaches a height of 1,403 metres above sea level. It is bordered in the east by Jabal Al Qara, in the south by the Arabian Sea, in the north by the Najd and to the west by Al Mahrah Governorate of the Republic of Yemen.

It lies in the path of the Southwest Monsoon and consequently its southern slopes and escarpments are heavily vegetated while the northern aspects remain largely dry and devoid of vegetation. The plateau, which is in places touched by the monsoon, is deeply incised by a series of wadis that mostly drain north from the watershed to the Najd or south to the sea.

The largest of the wadis, and appearing to split the Jabal in two, is the mighty Wadi Sayq. It rises in very arid country close to the Yemeni border but as it flows east to south-east it falls under the influence of the monsoon and is transformed from a harsh, waterless gorge to a lush, wooded valley rich in flora and fauna. The wadi reaches the sea at Khawr Kharfut, a brackish lagoon that lies equidistant from the village of Rakhyut and the small town of Dalkut, the principal settlement of Jabal Al Qamar.

West of Wadi Sayq and towering over Dalkut is a high inland escarpment that runs west to the border with Yemen. Below the escarpment are forested slopes and a raised coastal platform that face the full force of the monsoon. Above the escarpment are plateau grasslands that extend no more than a kilometre inland before they vanish where the desert heat draws the moisture from the monsoon winds.

East of Wadi Sayq the landscape is less regular and in places the presence of an inland escarpment, steep wadis, ridges above and coastal cliffs makes for a stepped topography. Here, above Wadi Rakhyut and east as far as Al Hawtah are found the most extensive woodlands and grasslands of Jabal Al Qamar. At the foot of the escarpment are occasional freshwater springs while above it the landscape is dominated by dense shrubland, often strewn with rocks, that extends up the gentle slopes

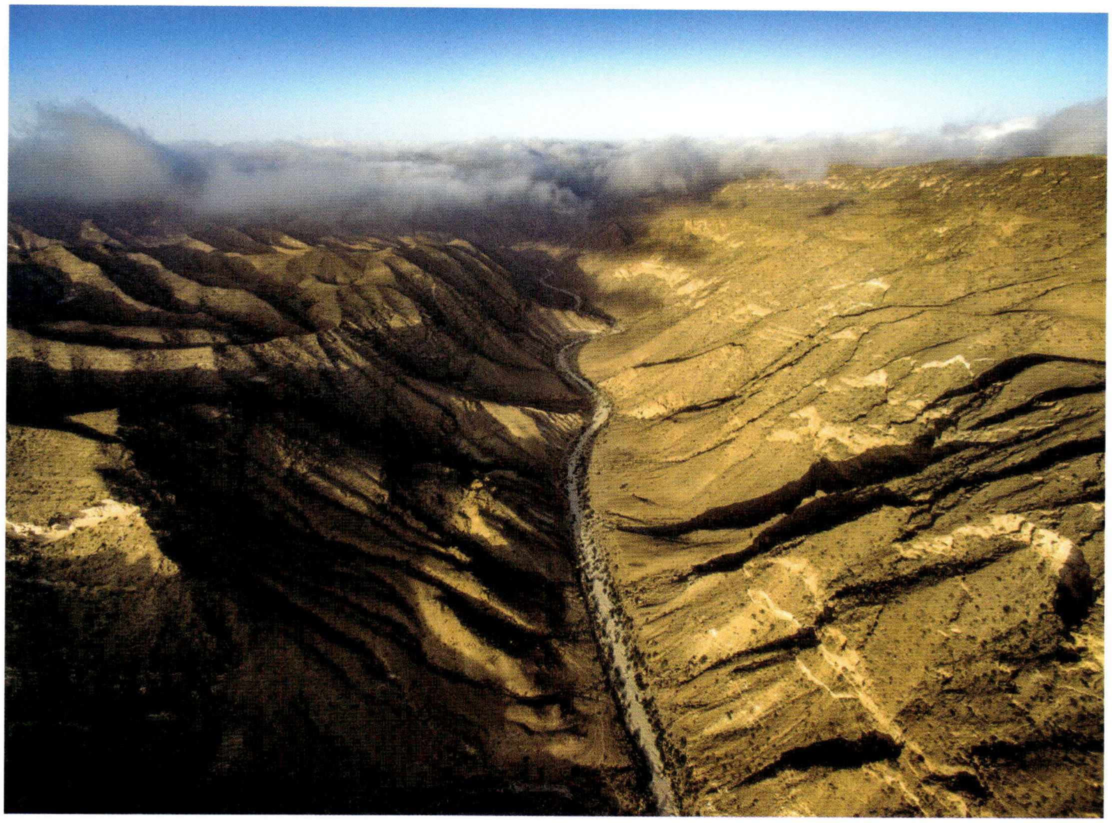

towards the almost barren summit plateau. Beyond the summit the Jabal drains north into the dry Najd.

From Al Hawtah eastwards, Jabal Al Qamar seems to rise directly from the sea and almost vertical cliffs tower as high as 800 metres above a narrow coastal terrace. Perhaps most spectacular are the cliffs at Shaat from where, outside the monsoon, there is a clear vista west and to the seashore far below. During the monsoon the clifftops become a place of swirling mists and silence, bar for the sound of crashing waves far below. Nearby is Shaat sinkhole, the opening to an extensive cave system.

East of Shaat is Ras Sajir beyond which the coast turns north-eastward and the influence of the monsoon weakens. The wooded areas are limited to a very narrow strip on the lower slopes of the seaward-facing escarpments that dwindles to nothing east of Al Fazayih. The plateau reaches over 1,000 metres in height and overlooks a number of spectacular south-eastward-flowing wadis that drain the heavily faulted arid zone where Jabal Al Qamar merges with Jabal Al Qara. The most important of these are Wadi Aful, Wadi Ashawq and Wadi Al Mughsayl.

The majority of human settlements on Jabal Al Qamar are on the plateau, close to the watershed and at the northern edge of the area under the direct influence of the monsoon. These are linked by the main arterial road from Salalah that ascends the mountain from Wadi Aful before following the watershed for about 60 kilometres, where it descends into Wadi Sayq before again climbing up the mountain towards Sarfayt, close to Oman's border with Yemen. Settlements include (from east to west) Arift, Shahb Asaayb, Thatniti, Ardit and Shirshatti. Branch roads enable access to coastal settlements including Dalkut, Rakhyut, Al Hawtah and Al Fazayih and to villages in the Najd including Aydam.

The monsoon rainfall supports rich grasslands and woodlands, such as those at Khadrafi ***(top left)*** but beyond the reach of the monsoon the plateaux and wadis, including Wadi Aful ***(top right)***, are dry and sparsely vegetated.

Jabal Al Qara, which overlooks the coastal plain, or Jarbib, is dry and brown for most of the year but from June to September its south-facing slopes and plateaux ***(right top)*** are transfigured by the clouds of the annual monsoon ***(bottom right)***. The most famous geographical feature of Jabal Al Qara are the mighty travertine falls of Wadi Darbat ***(below)***.

Jabal Al Qara

The mountain is crescent-shaped, runs approximately 120 kilometres east to west and is the largest of the three mountains. However, it is lower than both Jabal Al Qamar and Jabal Samhan, reaching an elevation of 1,232 metres above sea level at its highest point, just west of Qaftawt. To the north the mountain is bordered by the Najd and to the south it dominates the Salalah coastal plain, the Jarbib, which separates it from the Arabian Sea.

There is no particular location where Jabal Al Qamar stops and Jabal Al Qara starts but usually the range east of Wadi Ashawq and Wadi Al Mughsayl is referred to as Jabal Al Qara. Here the dry and barren Jabal runs north-east, following a fault line, but as it gradually entraps increasing amounts of summer monsoon precipitation it is transformed to a land of thickly forested slopes and tall grass plateaux.

In the west the striking southern escarpment, which overlooks Adawnab and Raysut, is not a continuous cliff face but a deeply dissected landscape of rounded buttresses, vertical cliffs and gullies that are the

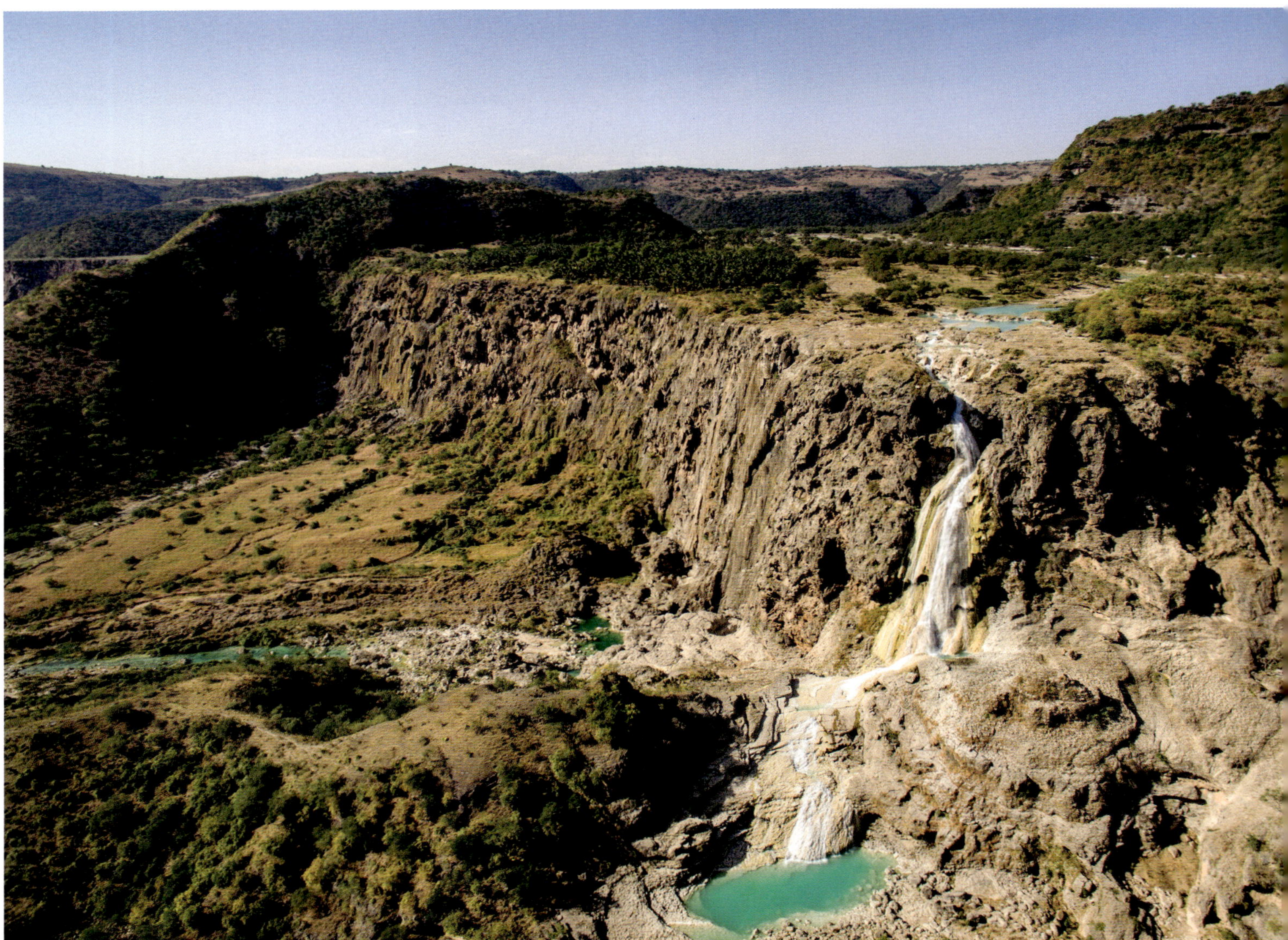

upper reaches of wadis that flow south to the sea. These include Wadi Ishat, Wadi Suqah, Wadi Saarit and Wadi Shaykh. All have freshwater springs and some, like Ayn Ishat, have a surface stream that nurtures diverse flora and fauna throughout the year. Above the escarpment the plateau areas extend no more than seven kilometers north before the watershed is reached and the landscape turns arid, being beyond the reach of the *khareef* rainfall.

Immediately behind Salalah city the escarpment is more broken still, with extensive foothills, pocked with termite mounds, marking the edge of the Jarbib. Here the Jabal is dominated by three major south-flowing wadis, Wadi Jarziz, Wadi Nahiz and Wadi Razat, that are formed by multiple tributaries rising many kilometers to the north. Each of the wadis is heavily forested, with trees being replaced by grassland on ridges, and headlands that overlook the Jarbib. There are numerous caves. Suhur Cave in Wadi Nahiz is the finest known example and comprises two chambers, the inner of which is occupied by colonies of bats. To the north, above the wadis, the Jabal extends about 17 kilometres and is dominated by extensive grasslands that in years of a heavy monsoon reach beyond the watershed to the edge of the northern escarpments and wadis that mark the beginning of the Najd. Scattered over the grasslands are small woodlands, copses and individual trees.

East of Wadi Razat the Jarbib narrows as the mountain orientation shifts south-easterly towards the sea. Here the escarpment is rarely more than 500 metres above sea level and is dominated by Wadi Darbat, the best-known and the most beautiful of Dhofar's wadis. Described by travellers at the turn of the 19th century as 'a real paradise in the wilderness',[3] Wadi Darbat has extensive freshwater lakes set amongst lush meadows where fish hide in bank-side pools and cattle graze in the dappled sunlight under proud fig trees. Above the lakes the wadi sides are honeycombed with caves and fissures. At the end of the wadi is a 150-metre high dry travertine waterfall that some believe gave rise to the famous name 'Abyssapolis', used by the Greek Claudius Ptolemy who lived nearly two thousand years ago, and thought to refer to the ancient incense port of Mirbat that lies close by.[25] At times of heavy rainfall this towering waterfall is brought back to life as water flows over and crashes onto the rocks below before flowing into the coastal lagoon of Khawr Rawri. There are numerous caves in the wadi and just to the west is Shihait sinkhole.

On the Jabal highlands above Wadi Darbat are found the most extensive grasslands of Dhofar – in fact, in all of Oman. Between Madinat Al Haq in the west, Jibjat in the north and Tawi Aatayr in the east are open landscapes of

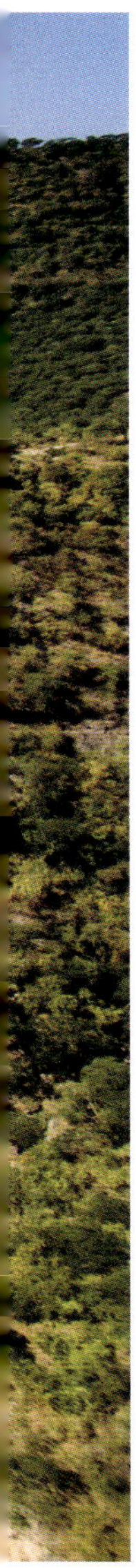

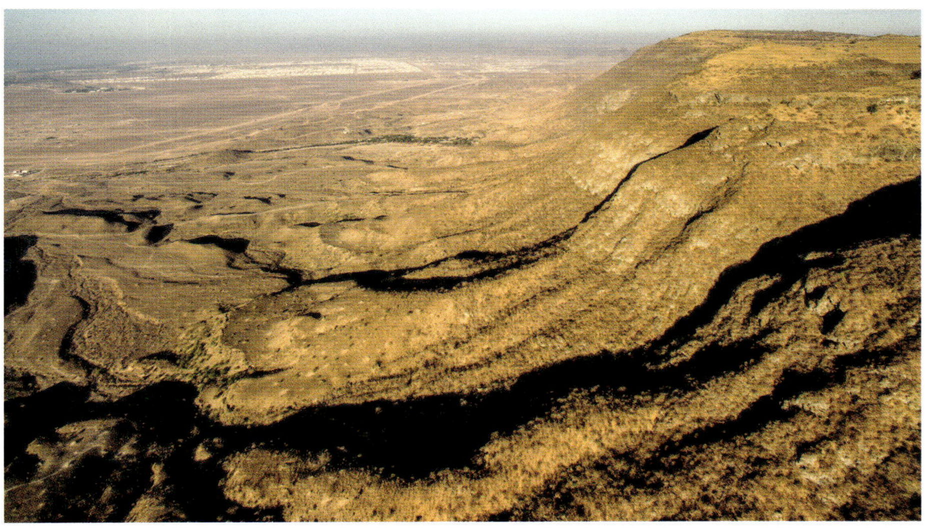

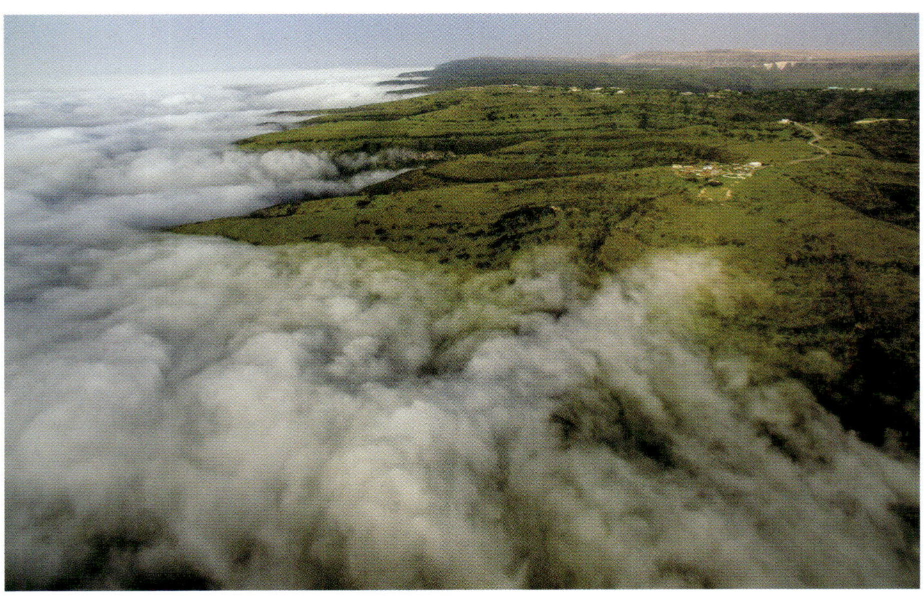

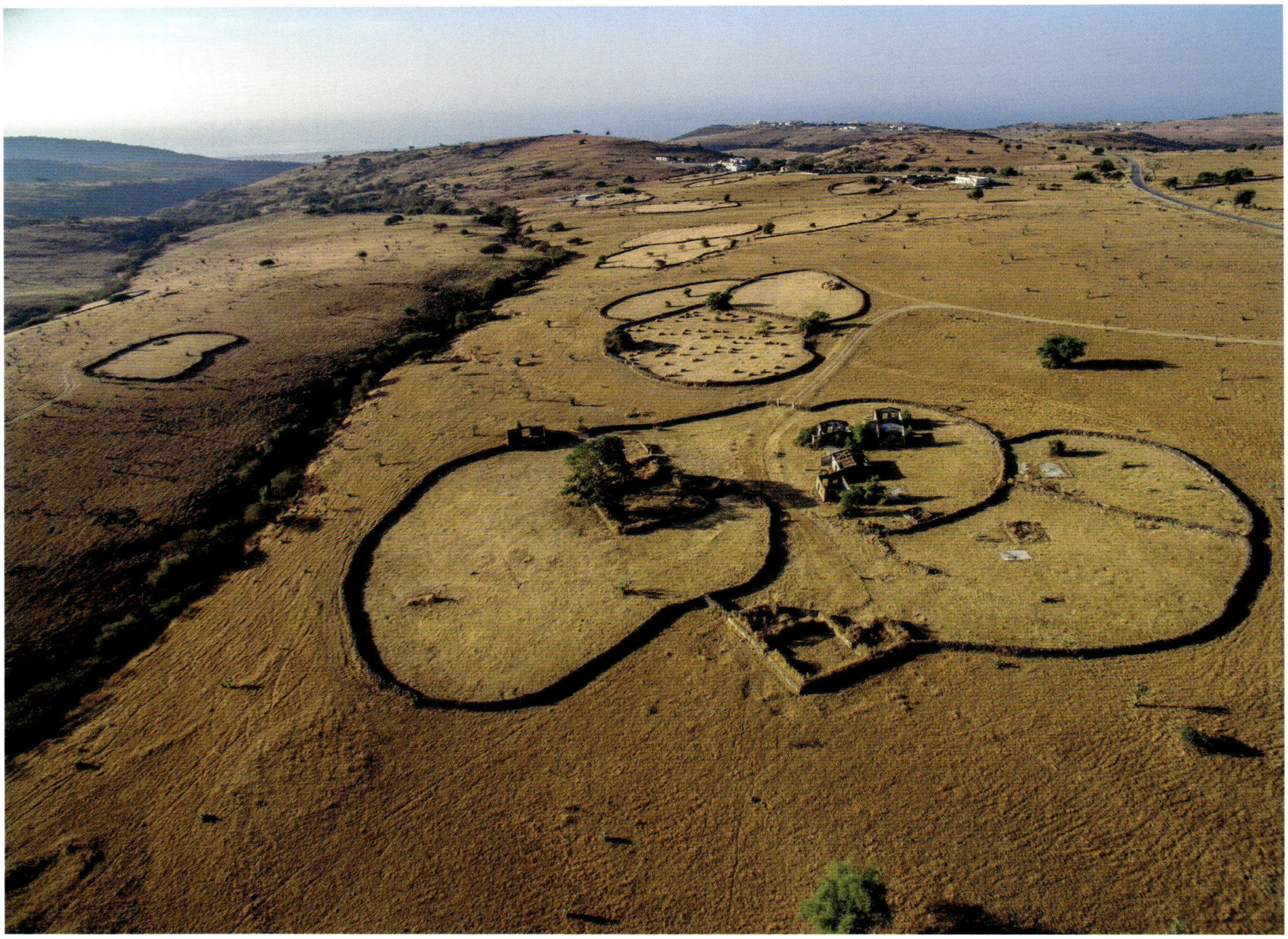

gentle slopes and rolling hills that seem to be never-ending, broken only by small settlements, copses and occasional trees. After the monsoon, herds of cattle, and increasingly camels, move lazily across these verdant pastures, stopping only to seek the shade of giant fig trees during the heat of the day. Within just a few weeks the sun turns the green grass golden brown.

The eastern region is karst country, typical of much of Dhofar's mountains, formed from the crumbling of soluble limestone, dolomite and gypsum. The grasslands, especially in the east, are strewn with rocks and the mountains are littered with caves and sinkholes, many yet to be discovered. The best-known sinkhole is Tawi Aatayr 'Well of the Birds' just outside the town of the same name. It is 130-150 metres in diameter and 211 metres deep-taller than the greatest pyramid in Egypt.[26] However, the nearby Tayq sinkhole is significantly bigger, being 800 metres long, 600 metres wide and 200 metres deep. An extensive underground cave is reached via a water pool at the bottom of the sinkhole.

In the far east, beyond Tawi Aatayr, there are extensive open woodlands over grasslands, and in the distance the high ground of Jabal Samhan. To the south, in the vicinity of Wadi Hinna, the *Jarbib* is gone and the southern escarpment overlooks the sea. Here the alignment of the Jabal shifts north-east and a rapid rise in elevation to over 1,000 metres above sea level marks the beginning of Jabal Samhan, Dhofar's highest mountain.

Jabal Al Qara is the least rugged of Dhofar's mountains and has the most extensive pasturelands; this, combined with its proximity to Salalah city, has meant that it is the most populated. There are numerous villages and small settlements that are connected by a network of asphalt roads. Though a few traditional Dhofari roundhouses remain, most have been replaced by concrete-block houses that are occupied year-round. Many villages have schools, government offices, shops and other services.

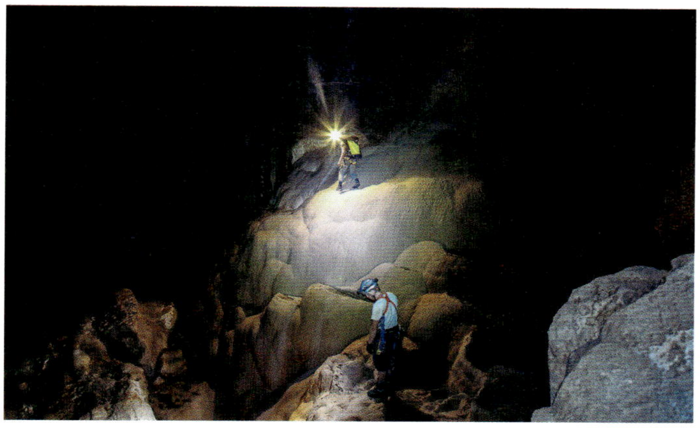

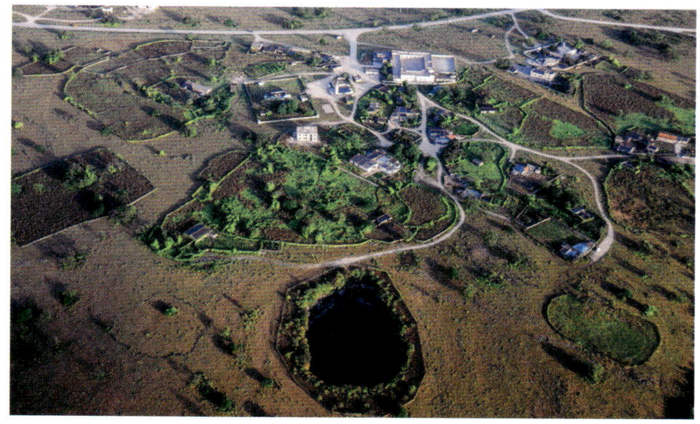

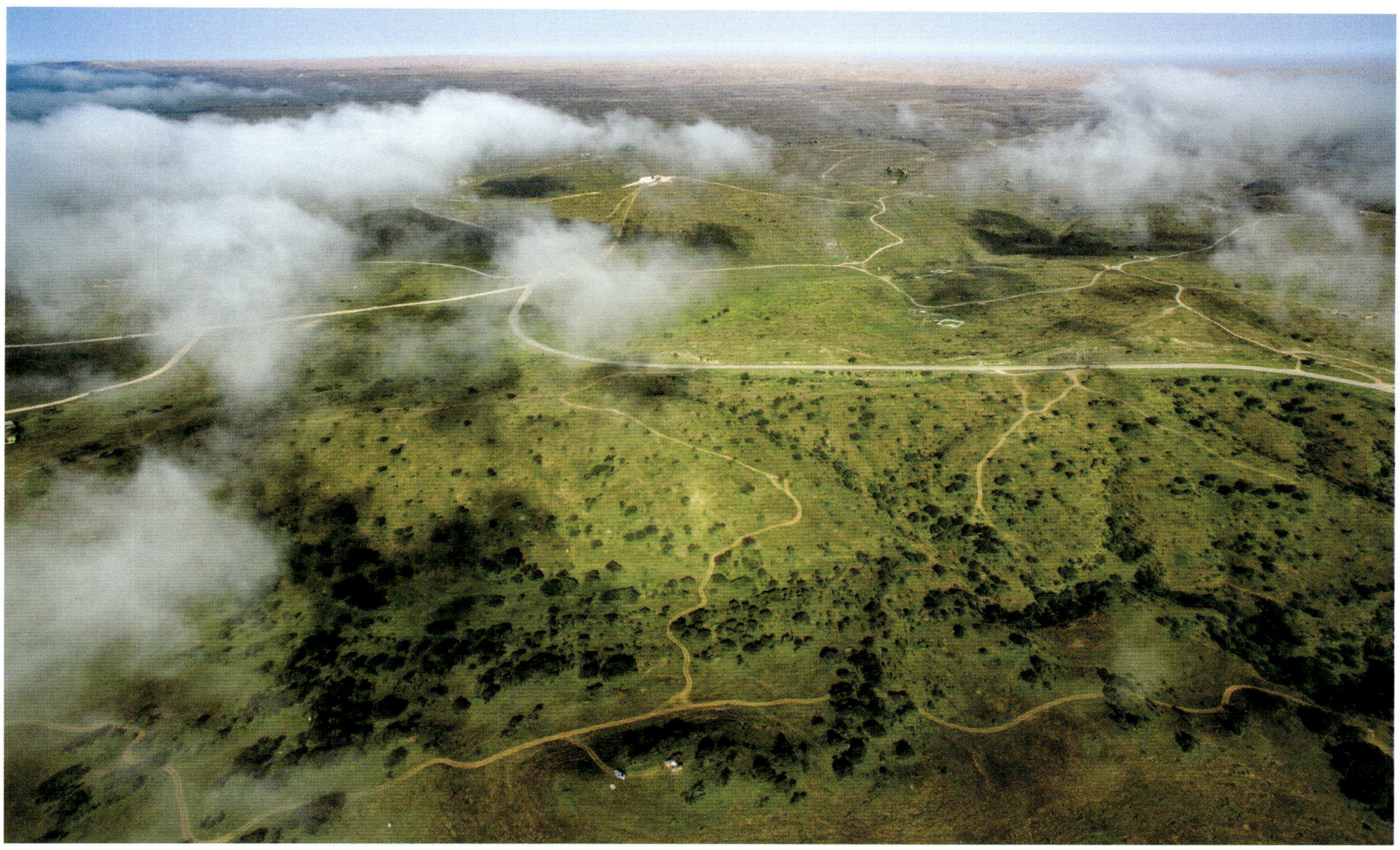

In the west the principal settlements include Itin, which is connected north to Uyun and west to Qaftawt, where there are extensive limestone quarries. These in turn are connected to Salalah by several roads that have been cut into the southern escarpment, leaving deep scars visible from across the Jarbib. Further east, on the Muscat-Salalah highway, is the village of Qayrun Hayrti, from where a road runs east along the watershed to Jibjat, which sits above Wadi Saalafan, overlooking the seemingly endless expanse of the Najd. From there roads lead south to a number of smaller settlements and to the towns of Tawi Aatayr and Madinat Al Haq, which are amongst the largest settlements of Jabal Al Qara. Roads connect Tawi Aatayr with Madinat Al Haq, Wadi Hinna on the southern escarpment, and with the high plateau of Jabal Samhan.

The monsoon clouds define the boundary between the green pastures of the Jabal and the hyper-arid desert of the southern Najd ***(above lower)***.

Once the monsoon ends, the pastures turn a golden-brown colour, and in ancient stone-walled fields grass is cut and arranged in stooks ***(opposite)***.

Caves such as Tawi Aatayr ***(top left)*** attract cavers from around the world, while the bottom of Shihait sinkhole ***(top right)*** has a small forest rich in wildlife.

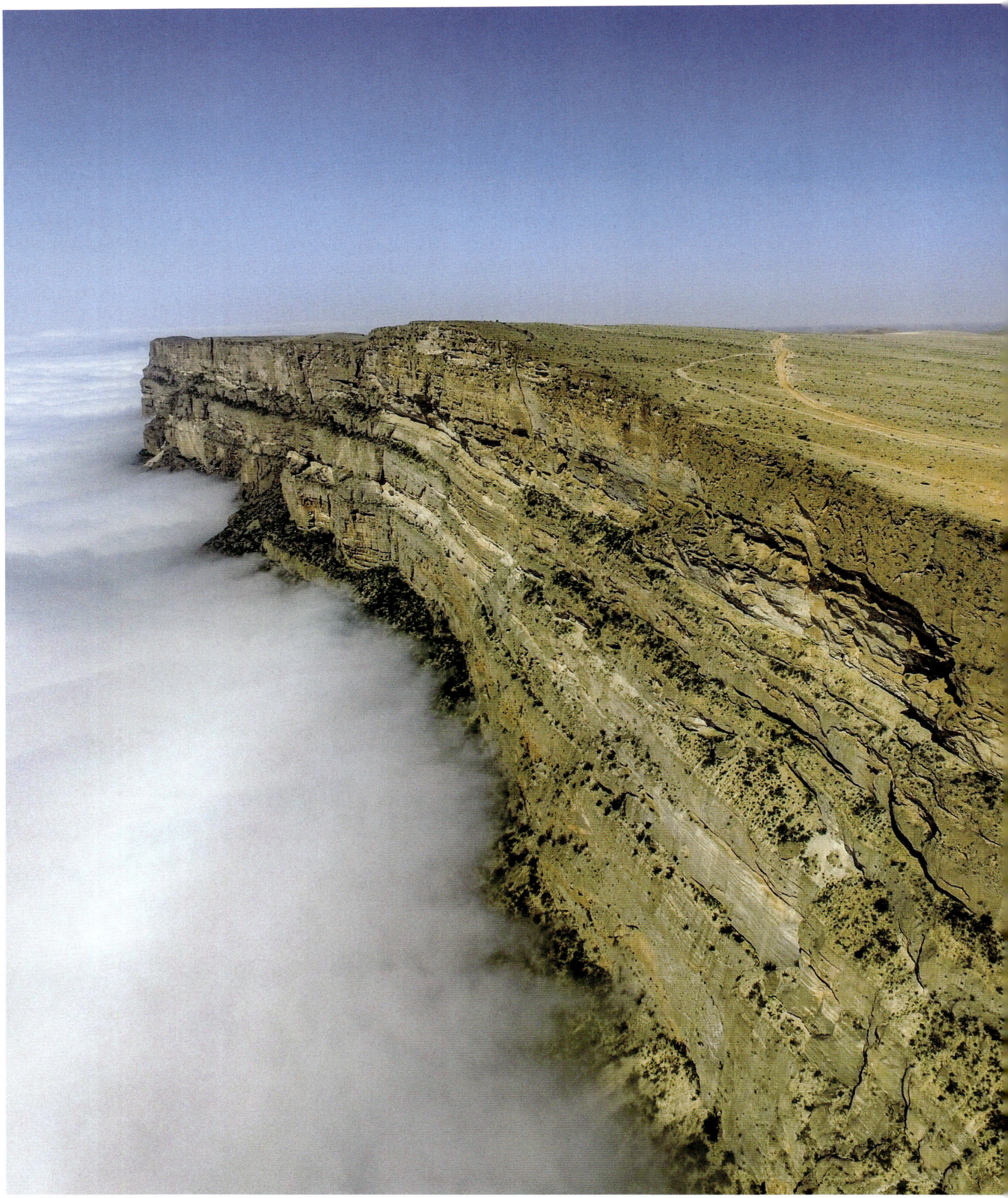

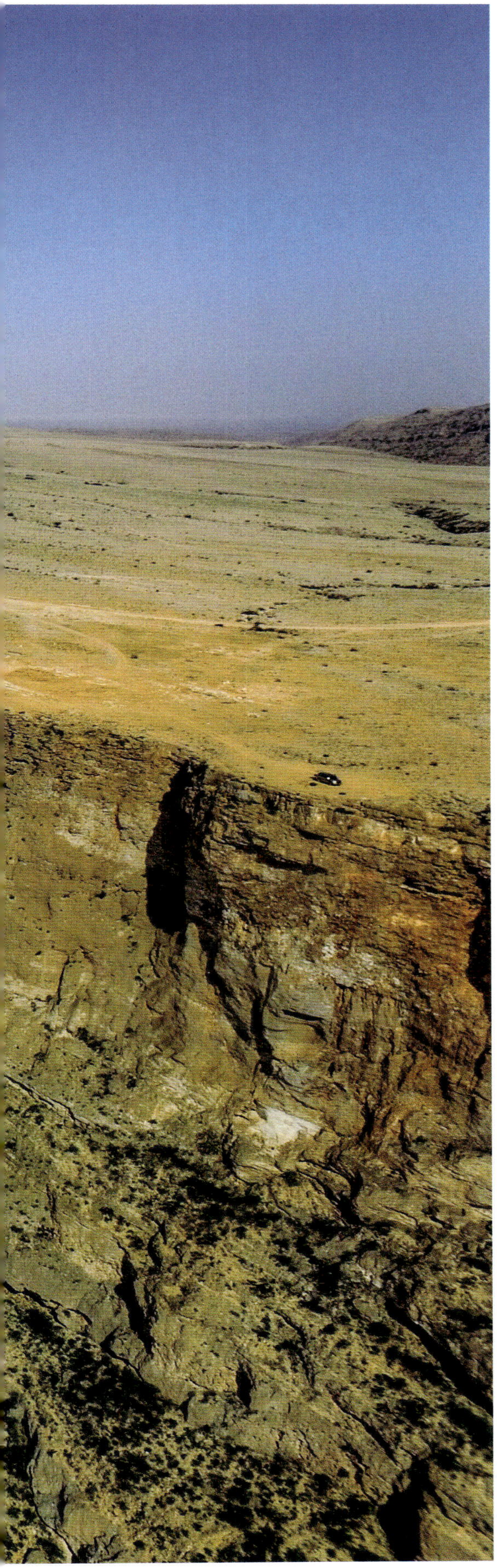

Jabal Samhan

There is no clear point where Jabal Al Qara ends and Jabal Samhan starts but above the town of Mirbat the towering cliff turns north-east, shedding most signs of the summer monsoon, the greens, browns and greys being replaced by the pale yellows and whites of arid landscapes. This is Jabal Samhan, a massive limestone mountain lying on top of the ancient basement rocks that are seen to the south on the Salawt Plain.

Jabal Samhan, a nature reserve and proposed as a National GeoPark, dips north and is deeply dissected by wadis that rise almost at the edge of the southern escarpment. Consequently, the plateau is rarely flat and the escarpment clifftop rises and falls where it has been cut by the upper reaches of the northward-flowing wadis. It is at its highest (1,760 metres) in the vicinity of Kharish, about 20 kilometres east of the ever-visible communications tower that sits at its western extremity. It extends east-northeast for about 70 kilometres and is bordered to the west by Jabal Al Qara, to the south by the Salawt Plain, to the north by the Najd and to the east by the Arabian Sea.

Wadi Saalafan and Wadi Halit drain the western end of Jabal Samhan but it is Wadi Andhur and Wadi Arah that dominate the northward-flowing wadis. Each wadi system is formed from a myriad of small gulleys, that drain the high plateau and come together to carve out gorges a few metres wide and 200-300 meters deep. In places these meandering gorges are choked by great boulders and dry waterfalls while elsewhere there are deep freshwater pools and lush vegetation. These gorges wind their way almost 30 kilometres north before coming together to form broad wadis, up to 500 meters across, that meander gently north through the Najd before disappearing under the sands and gravels of the Empty Quarter.

The eastern part of the Jabal Samhan massif, beyond the waterhole at Ayn Shayrukh, drains not north to the desert but east to the sea. Here distinctive surface channels resembling herringbones, best observed from an aircraft, drain water from the plateau into the upper reaches of several eastward-flowing wadis. The greatest of these is Wadi Rabkut, which seems to follow a fault line east to the coastal village of Hasik. Water pools and sculptured travertine are amongst the highlights of this impressive wadi. Other wadis, all with permanent water, include Wadi Samhal to the south and Wadi Hadbaram, Wadi Dahnat and Wadi Sinaq to the north.

However, it is the southern aspect of Jabal Samhan that is best known and is the most visible landscape feature. The towering southern escarpment rises approximately 1,000 metres above the Mirbat plain and runs east-northeast towards Hasik and the sea. The top 200-400

The vehicle at the right of the photograph ***(left)*** provides a sense of the great height of Jabal Samhan's southern escarpment.

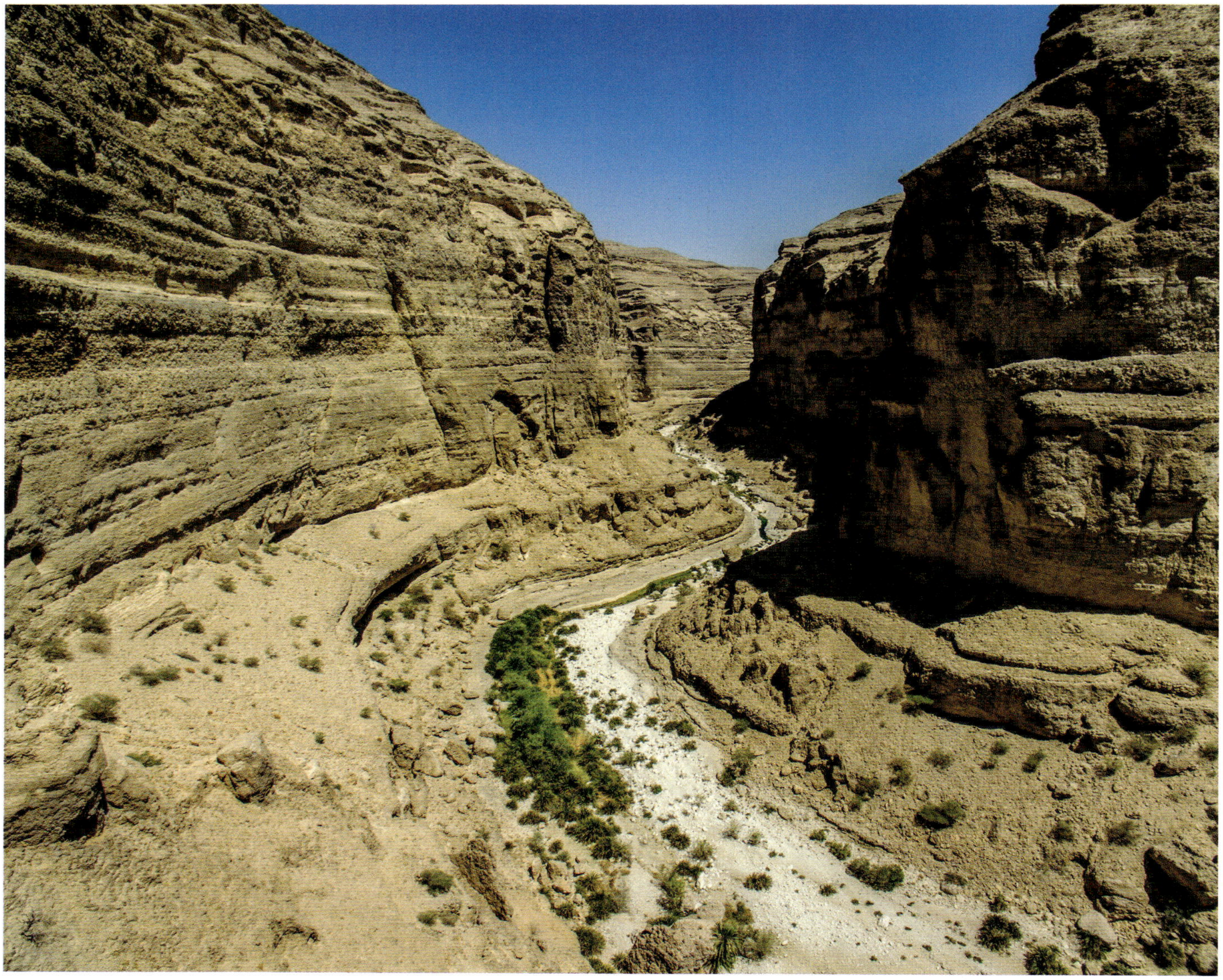

metres comprise an almost vertical cliff while the boulder-strewn lower slopes have been shaped by thousands of years of water erosion as gullies come together to form a series of wadis that cross the Salawt Plain. These include Wadi Ayn, Wadi Fushi, Wadi Shaat and Wadi Shilyun.

Beyond Ayn Laja Shilyun, the main Jabal is dissected by the eastward-flowing wadis and the plateau is reduced to a narrow ridge, sometimes less than one kilometre wide and reaching an elevation of more than 1,400m. This towers over Wadi Rabkut to the north and Wadi Samhal to the south before petering out just south of Hasik. A little to the south and above Hadbin is the isolated Jabal Jashim (894 metres above sea level), which is considered to be the most south-eastern extremity of Jabal Samhan.

North of Hasik, the main massif of Jabal Samhan abuts the sea forming milky-white-coloured sea cliffs, particularly striking in the dawn light, that sweep north-east in an arc towards the distant Ras Qanawt, which marks the most easterly point of this extraordinary mountain. Wadi Kawbawt drains north but here the landscape is dominated by the upper reaches of the great Wadi Ash Shuwaymiyyah, which flows into the Najd for more than 60 kilometres, first north, then east and finally south to the sea, by which time it has formed a great sculptured canyon 300 metres deep and more than two kilometres wide. It has been deemed to be worthy of designation as a National GeoPark.[24]

By virtue of the harsh, arid climate, poor accessibility and its status as a protected area, there is no significant permanent settlement on Jabal Samhan. In the west, above Tawi Aatayr, there are a number of small settlements, recently established,

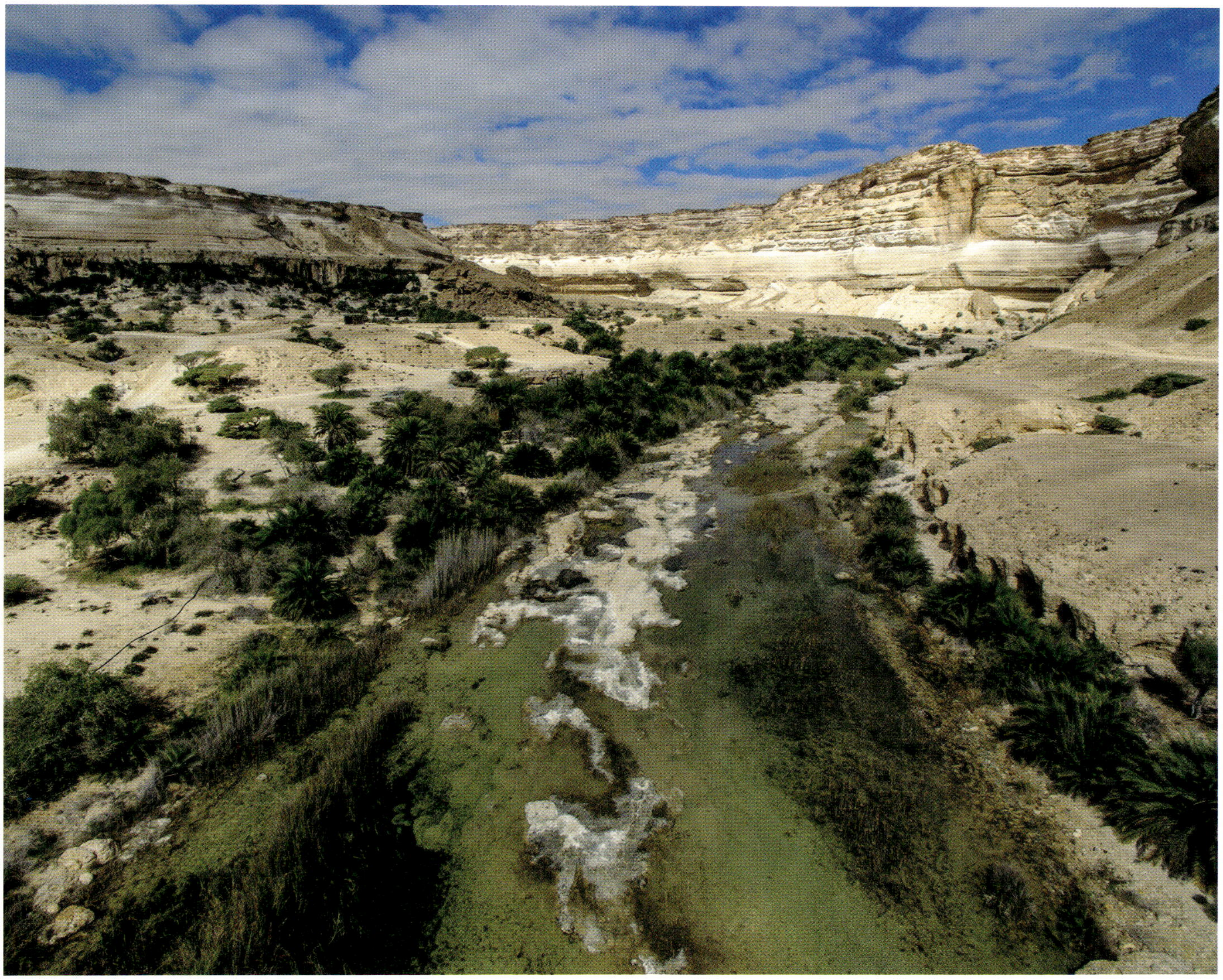

from where a graded track extends 12 kilometres east, but otherwise there are no formal roads and few vehicular tracks on the plateau. However, there are a number of trails, mostly associated with the harvesting of frankincense, that traverse the plateau from west to east while others descend into the upper reaches of the northward flowing wadis. Below the plateau there are small settlements in the southern foothills from where roads have been driven up the escarpment to access freshwater springs, such as Ayn Laja Shilyun and Ayn Shayrukh. Otherwise, dense thorn-scrub makes access difficult, although in a few places walking trails used by local people and their livestock ascend the southern escarpment to reach the plateau above.

In the east the spectacular coastal highway follows the seashore from Hadbin to Hasik, and from Hasik to Wadi Sinaq. Thereafter it cuts inland by up to 10 kilometres, skirting frankincense groves, before rejoining the coast at the southern end of Ash Shuwaymiyyah bay. From the highway a number of unpaved roads provide limited access to the eastern *wadis* including Wadi Kawbawt.

Wadi Arah ***(left)*** and Wadi Ash Shuwaymiyyah ***(right)*** are the most spectacular of Jabal Samhan's numerous wadis.

The Najd

At the height of summer a person may stand on the high watershed of Jabal Al Qara or Jabal Al Qamar, looking north; under their feet is lush grassland, against their back is swirling mist, but in front of them is a vast landscape of emptiness and desolation. Here the heat of the Arabian desert sucks the moisture from the air and reclaims the land as its own. This is the great Najd of central Dhofar, and though sometimes it is considered a middle ground between 'here' and 'there', people have survived here for longer than anywhere else in Dhofar.

The Najd occupies the interior heart of Dhofar, and though there are no formal boundaries, early maps of Oman show it occupying the area north of the Jabal, south of the Empty Quarter and south-west of the Jiddat Al Harasis. It comprises nearly 70% of the land mass of Dhofar, is full of wild and wide-open spaces and is hugely important for its natural resources, including hydrocarbon reserves and fossil water.

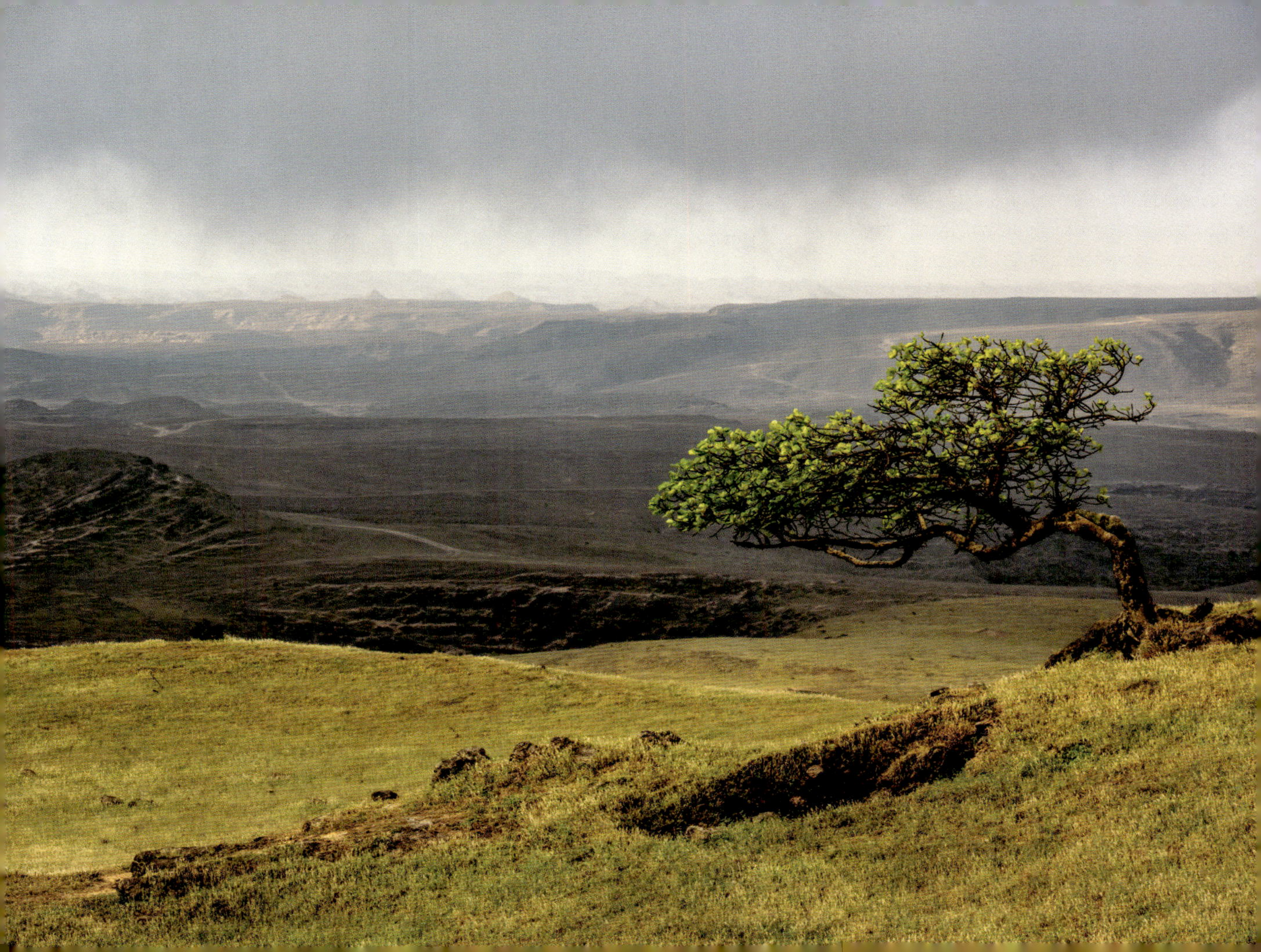

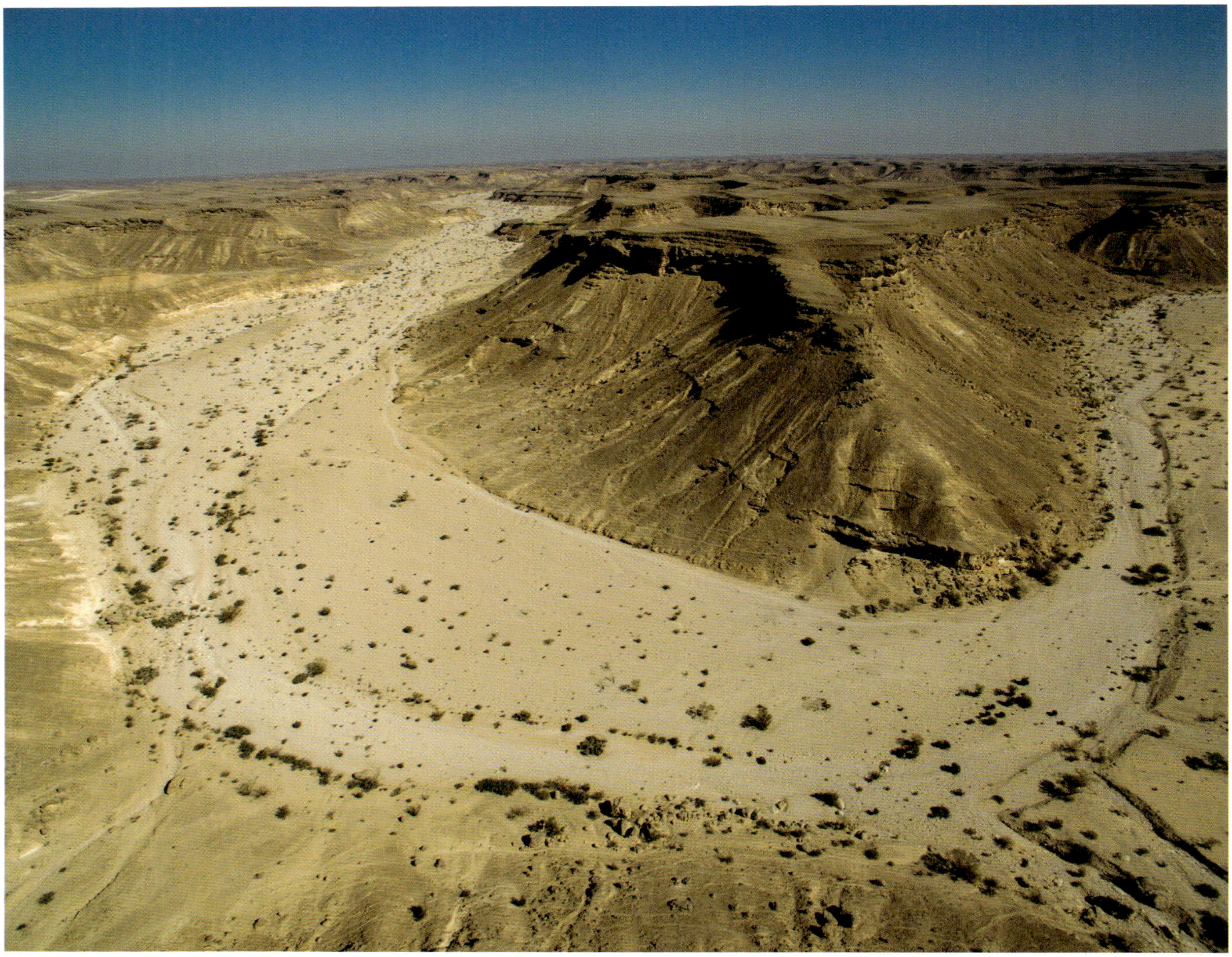

The great wadis, such as Wadi Aydam ***(above)***, meander north across the southern Najd and enter a Martian landscape characterised by rocky outcrops ***(opposite, top and bottom)*** and occasional settlements such as the town of Muday ***(opposite centre)***.

The Southern Najd

North of the watersheds of Jabal Samhan, Jabal Al Qara and Jabal Al Qamar the monsoon influence is soon left far behind except for the occasional relief from cool winds. Here the usually dry wadis begin as an intricate series of small channels but soon come together to form steep-sided gorges that twist and turn before converging and meandering gently north. In the east are Wadi Kawbawt, Wadi Arah, Wadi Andhur, Wadi Halit and Wadi Saalafan, which drain Jabal Samhan, while in the centre and draining Jabal Al Qara are Wadi Dhahbun, Wadi Dawkah, Wadi Uyun, Wadi Amat, Wadi Gharah and in the west, flowing north from Jabal Al Qamar, are the many tributaries of the mighty Wadi Aydam. In the upper reaches of these complex wadi systems, and touched by the cool winds of the distant monsoon, is found the iconic frankincense tree that seems to thrive in the dry landscape and yields Dhofar's finest *hojari* and *najdi* resin. A number of the deep gorges, including Wadi Arah, Wadi Uyun and Wadi Aydam, have clear spring-fed water pools that are usually fringed by reeds and are havens for wildlife.

Further north the *wadis* slow

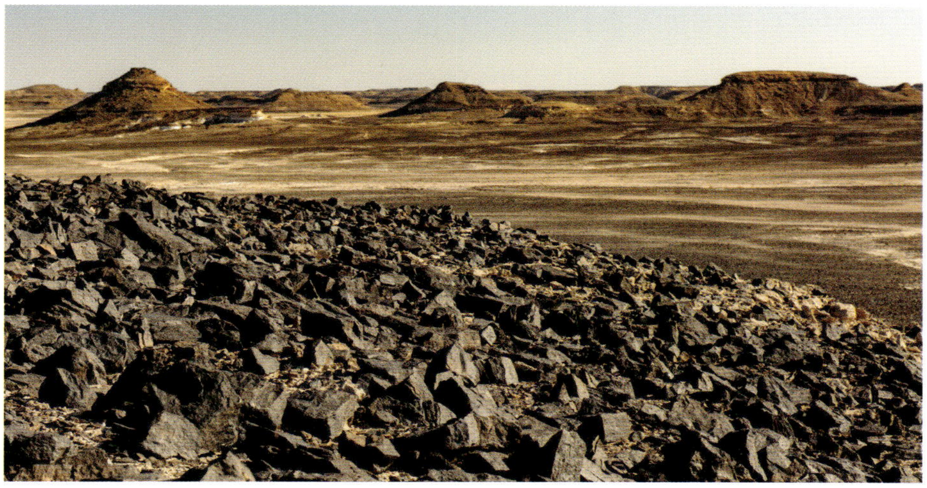

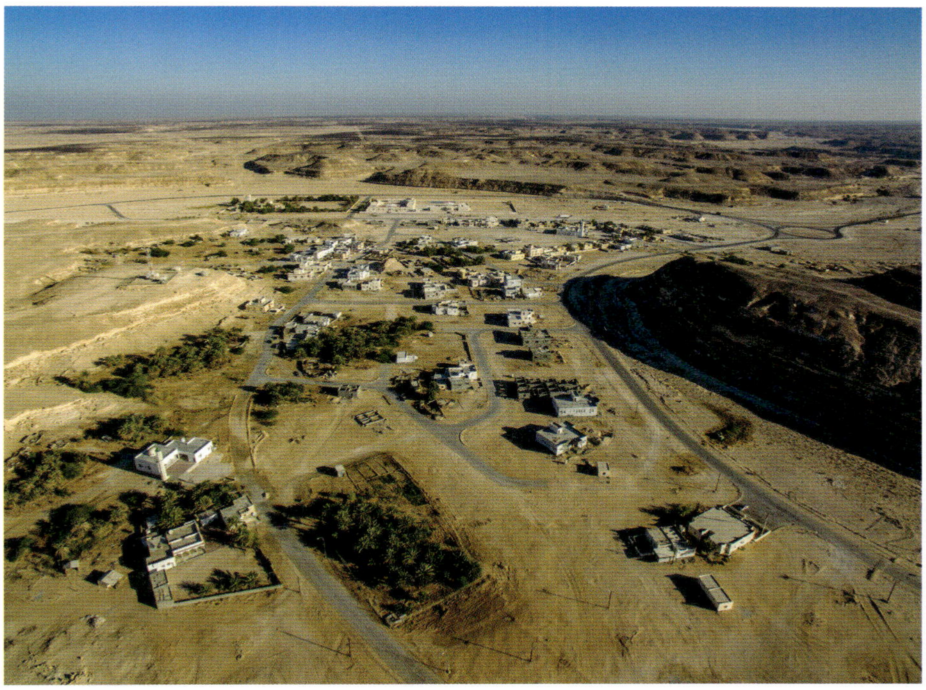

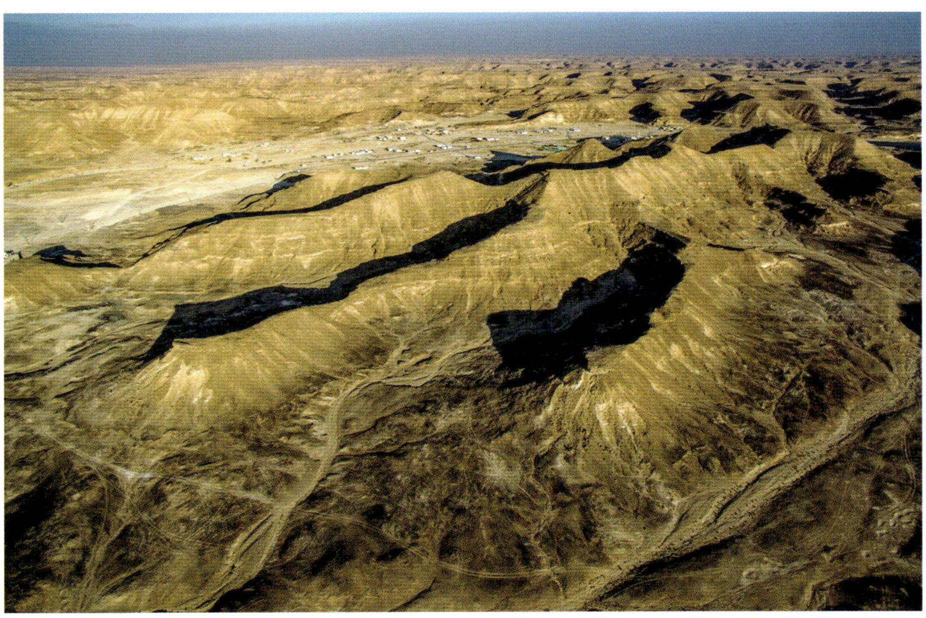

to form broad open landscapes with a pebble or gravel-filled watercourse and elevated terraces and platforms sparsely vegetated with occasional acacia and tamarisk trees and dense clumps of dwarf palm. Also on these terraces are signs of former human occupation including graves of the current Islamic period, triliths from the Iron Age and even stone tools from the Stone Age. Some of these ancient sites, such as Hanun and Muday, are close to springs that in more recent times were pivotal to the survival of nomadic herdsmen during the long harsh summer. They also provided travellers and their camels a last opportunity to drink before heading north to cross the vast gravel plains and the sand-seas of the Empty Quarter.

As the wadis start to leave the Jabal far behind, they flatten out and, in the central area in particular, are replaced by what has been described as a Martian landscape that is harsh and flat but dotted with isolated hills known as *inselbergs* (from the German words for island and mountain) that rise above the desert plains. These are formed from the tertiary limestones that make up much of the southern Najd and are about 40 million years old. This landscape is particularly striking east and west of the town of Thumrayt.

The oldest settlements of the southern Najd include Habrut, Uyun and Muday, which are associated with waterholes and thus with old camel caravan routes. However, the largest is Thumrayt, while numerous smaller settlements have sprung up, from Aybut in the west to Barbazum, Dhahbun, Dimit and Kawbawt in the east.

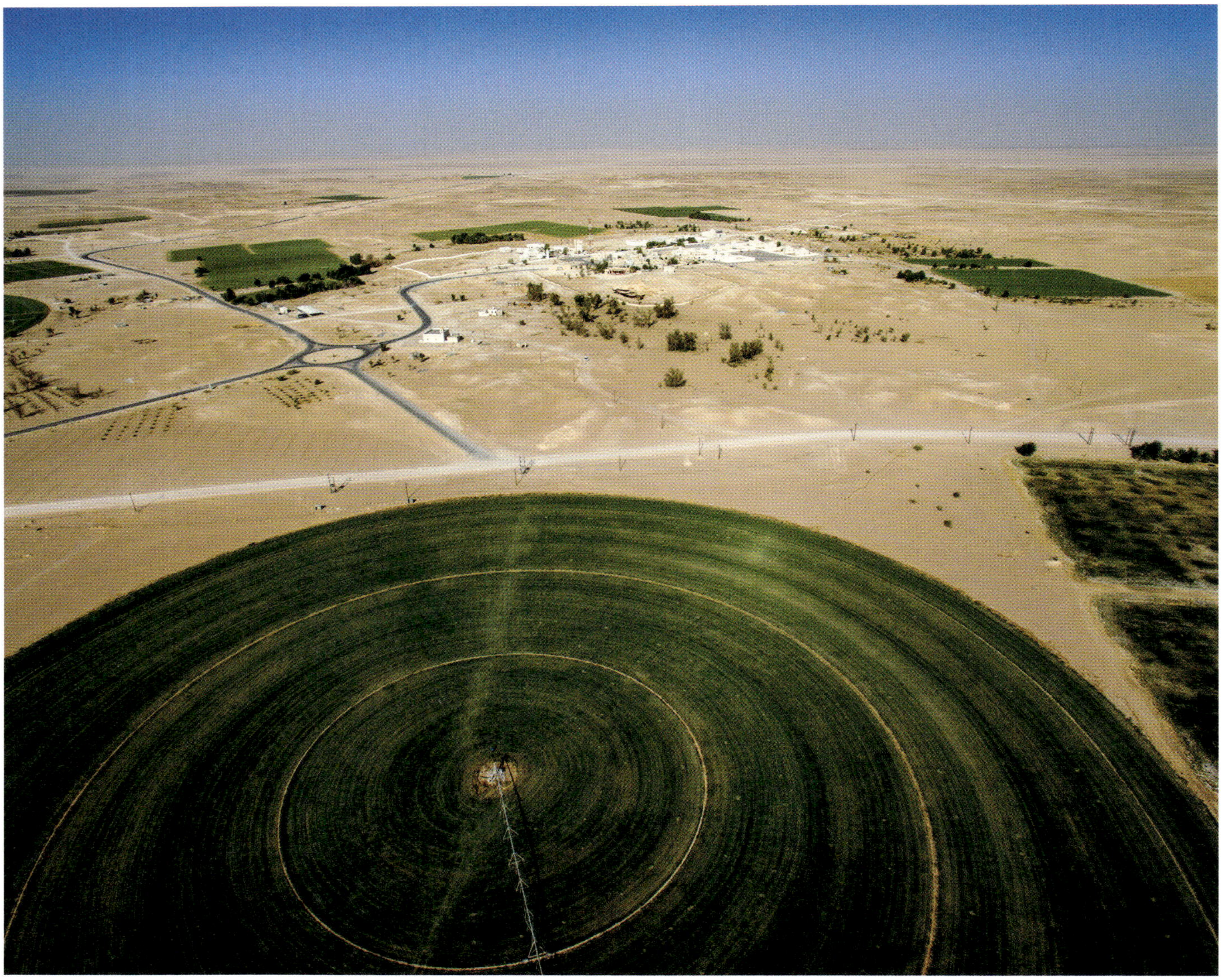

Northern Najd

The northern Najd is generally considered to be the area north of the Marmul-Thumrayt-Muday road and south and east of the sands of the Empty Quarter. Most of the area is hyper-arid, too far north to benefit from the *khareef* and too distant from coastal fogs or the rainfall associated with Oman's northern mountains. Even the tropical storms and cyclones that occasionally reach Dhofar rarely bring rainfall to this region, and lacking the beauty of the equally arid Empty Quarter, the northern Najd is the most desolate of Dhofar's landscapes.

In the central area, north of Thumrayt and each side of the Salalah-to-Muscat highway, the flat plains appear to roll to an unbroken horizon without tone or shadow. The landscape is made up of the sands and gravels of ancient lakes and deltas that the desert swallowed up long ago. However, in recent times the ancient water stored underground has been accessed to transform some areas of desert into farmland. Ash Shisr, for example, once a tiny spring in a sea of aridity, is now surrounded by vast fields of green fodder irrigated by an army of roving sprinklers.

There is less farming to the west and to the east, where the broad, northward-flowing wadis continue to provide some relief. In the west these include the great Wadi Ghadun, Wadi Aydam and Wadi Mitan, which eventually disappear into the dune fields of the Empty Quarter. In the east, wadis such as Arah wend their way north and in places a seemingly monotonous landscape is interrupted by forests of ghaf (*Prosopis cineraria*), the principal tree of the desert. The largest such forest is found at Muqshin in the far north of Dhofar and close to the dunes of the Empty Quarter.

In the far east is the Jiddat Arkad, a stony, windswept plateau

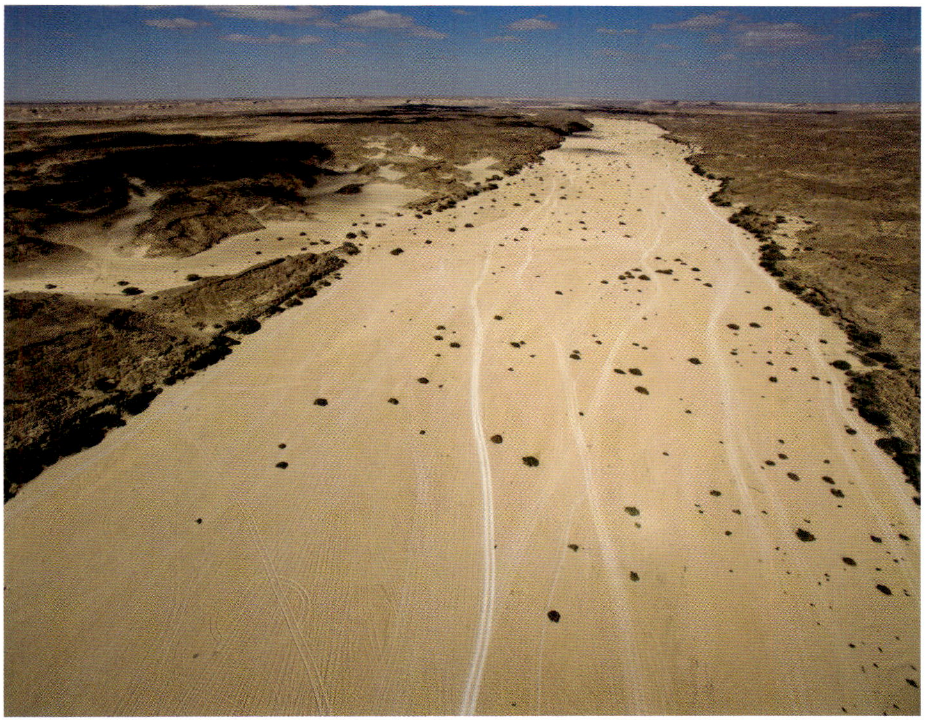

Broad open wadis such as Wadi Aynaynah *(top)* dominate a generally flat and barren Northern Najd. In the east, much of the landscape is dominated by the oil and gas industry *(bottom right)* and includes the constructed Nimr Wetlands *(bottom left)* that treat produced water and are a haven for wildlife. In the west the ancient fossil water is used to irrigate the desert; Ash Shisr was once a remote spring in the harshest of landscapes but is today surrounded by green cultivated fields *(far left)*.

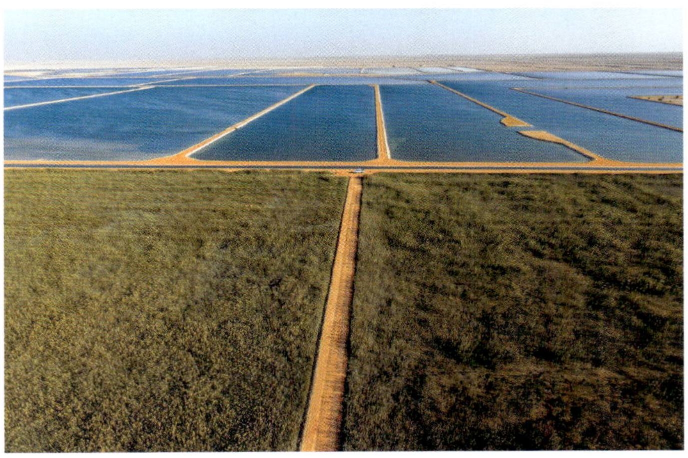

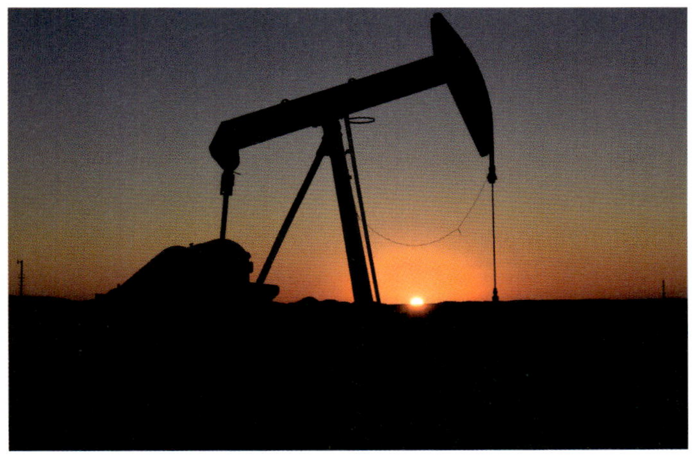

that separates the coastal plains of Ash Shuwaymiyyah, to the south, and Al Jazir, to the north. It is drained by eastward-flowing wadis including the giant Wadi Aynaynah. Benefiting from seasonal coastal fogs, the Jiddat Arkad is home to plants and animals that are unique to this area of the northern Najd.

Though lacking natural features, the skyline of the eastern Najd is dominated by the hydrocarbon industry and includes, amongst others, Marmul, Amal and Nimr oil and gas fields. Hundreds of pumps, known as 'nodding donkeys', silently draw oil from deep underground while rigs search for more, and all are connected by a maze of pipelines, power lines and roads. Seen from the air the land is crisscrossed by seismic lines and it seems that hardly a stone has been left unturned. In the far north, and visible from space, is the Nimr Wetland, which forms a green island in the barren desert. Reed beds and settlement pools– for the treatment of 'produced water' (the water by-product brought to the surface with oil and gas) –cover an area the size of 640 football pitches.

Historically there were few permanent settlements in the northern Najd as the lack of water meant that it was almost uninhabitable during the summer months. Exceptions were Mughsin and Ash Shisr, where there were freshwater springs that for centuries served as waterholes for camel-mounted travellers. However, today there are many small towns and villages where traditionally nomadic peoples have settled, including Al Mazyunah in the west, Dawkah and Qatbit in the central area and Shalim, Marmul and Nimr in the east.

The Empty Quarter (Ar Rub Al Khali)

In the north-west of Dhofar is the iconic sand-sea of the Empty Quarter-or Ar Rub Al Khali - that to many people of Dhofar is simply known as the 'Sands'. Considered to be the biggest continuous body of sand anywhere in the world, its natural beauty is striking, with its orange-reddish dunes, sculptured by the wind, extending as far as the eye can see. The explorer Wilfred Thesiger first saw the Sands from afar, at sunset, as a 'shimmering rose-coloured wall, seemingly as intangible as a mirage'.[27]

The Empty Quarter makes up about 22% of the land mass of Dhofar, stretching from Al Wusta Governorate in the north-east along the more than 300 kilometres length of the border with the Kingdom of Saudi Arabia to the Yemen border in the south-west. At the heart of the dune fields is a continuous series of *seif* dunes (from the Arabic for 'sword') that are aligned almost north—south and parallel to one another and the direction of the prevailing wind. They rise to more than 100 metres high and are up to 1.5 kilometres wide, with inter-dune corridors up to three kilometres wide.

In places the *seif* dunes are topped by so-called 'star' dunes that dominate the sand-seas further east and north. Typically the star dunes are pyramidal sand mounds with three or more arms that radiate from the high centre of the mound-reflecting more varied wind conditions and probably formed as a result

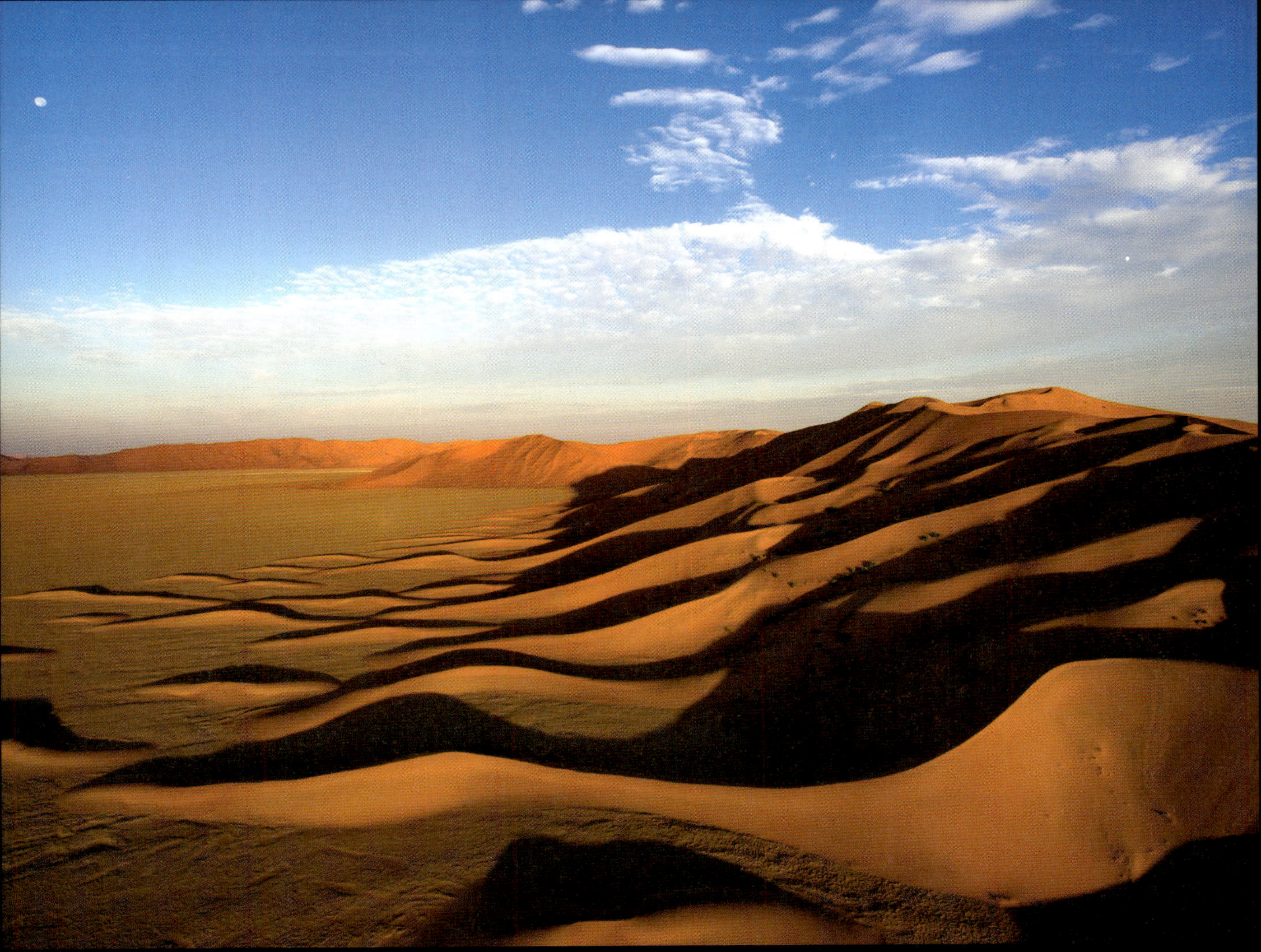

In 1930 the explorer Bertram Thomas, accompanied by Sheikh Saleh Bin Kalut Al Kathiri, sighted the sands for the first time. Thomas later recalled, 'Scarcely had we been on the move an hour when my companions started shouting excitedly, *'ar raml! ar raml!'* sweeping their canes as they did so along our right front, where in the far distance a sunlit yellow ribbon now edged the skyline; and I gazed eagerly towards this southern bulwark of the

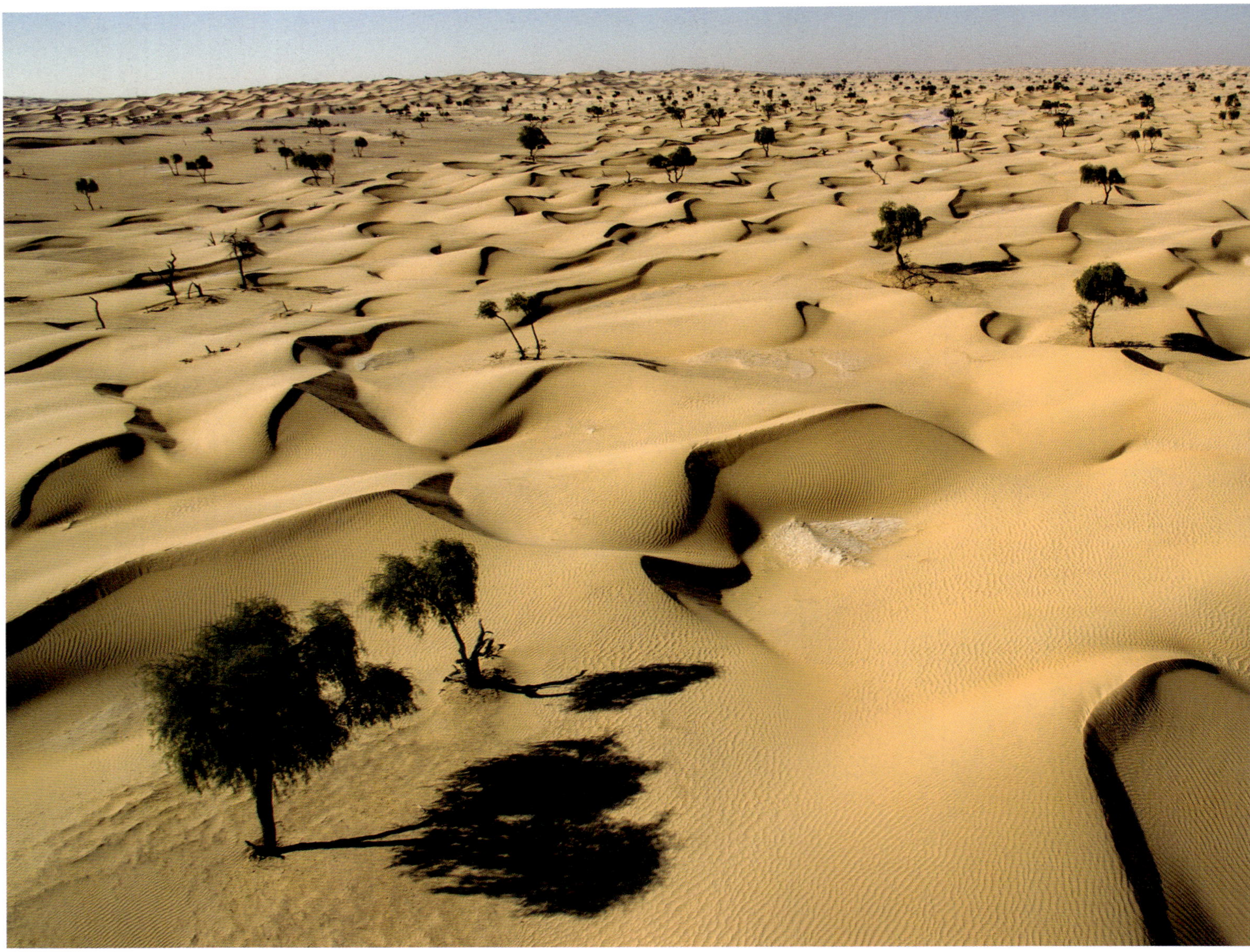

of the opposing winds of the Southwest Monsoon (*khareef*) and the Northeast Monsoon (*shamal*).[28] The star dunes include Ramlat Jadaylah, just north of Mitan, which was identified in 2017 as the world's highest dune.[29] At a height of 455 metres above sea level, it rises about 120 metres over the surrounding *sabkha* plain. Elsewhere, particularly in the north east, are found Barchan dunes that face south-east.

Though the height of the dunes is impressive, it is their colour that provides the strongest contrast with the grey-coloured gravel plains. The sand is composed mainly of quartz and some feldspar but it is an iron oxide coating of the sand grains that give the dunes their strong orange-reddish colour. Generally, the plains and dune valleys are unremarkable though in some areas, particularly close to Al Hashman, the plains are strewn with geodes – spherical rocks, varying in size from a table tennis ball to a football, that contain hollow cavities lined with crystals. The dunes and dune valleys of Al Hashman and Mitan are considered to be worthy of designation as National Geo-Parks.[24]

Most of the dunes of the Empty Quarter are not thought to be particularly old and formed only 6,000 years ago, at the beginning of the current period of hyper-arid climate.[30] Before that the area was much wetter, with freshwater lakes and grasslands frequented by grazing herbivores[6] and by cattle herding stone aged man who moved between the Empty Quarter and the Najd.[8] However, the wet times passed, animals died and humans retreated south leaving only fossilised animal teeth and chipped-stone

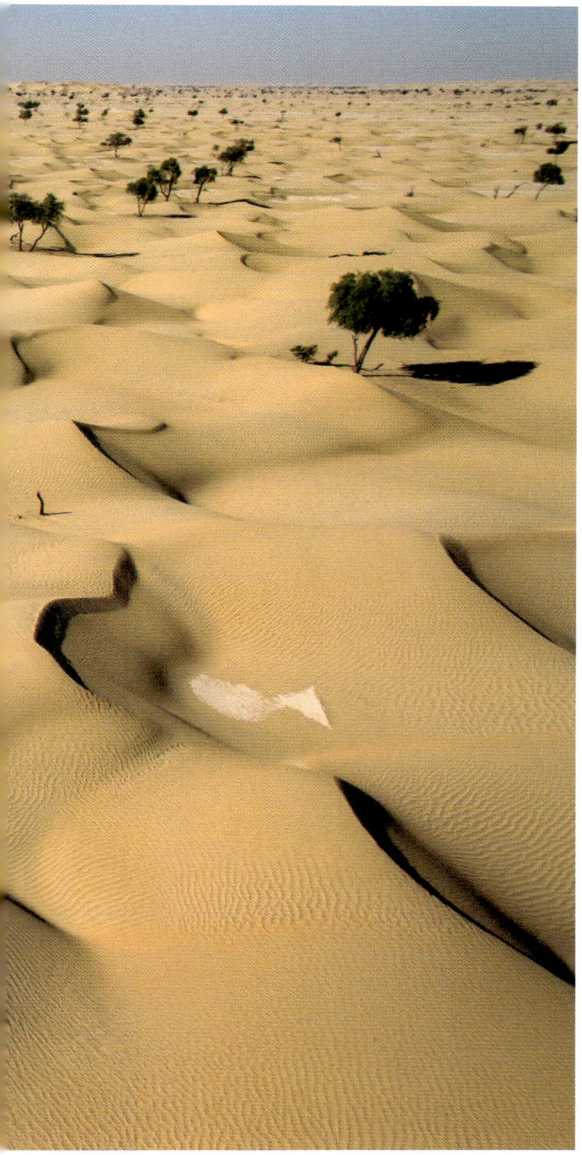

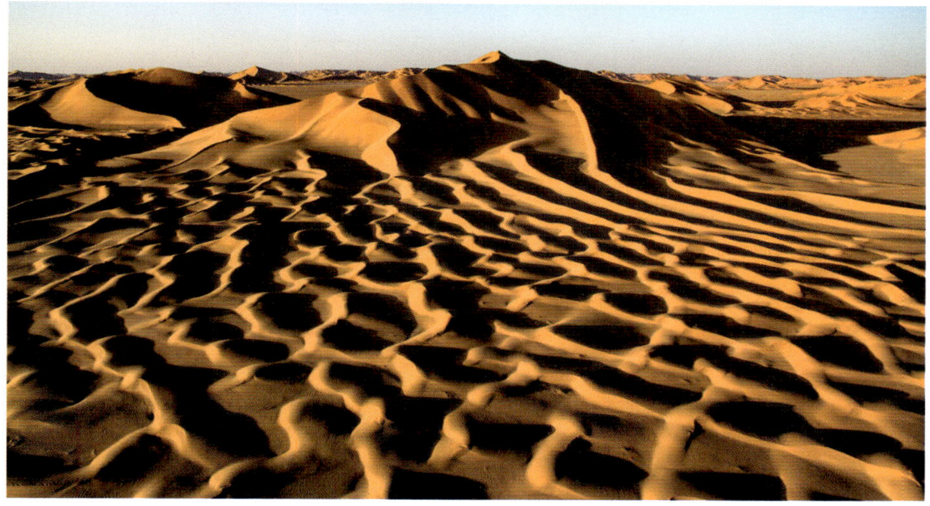

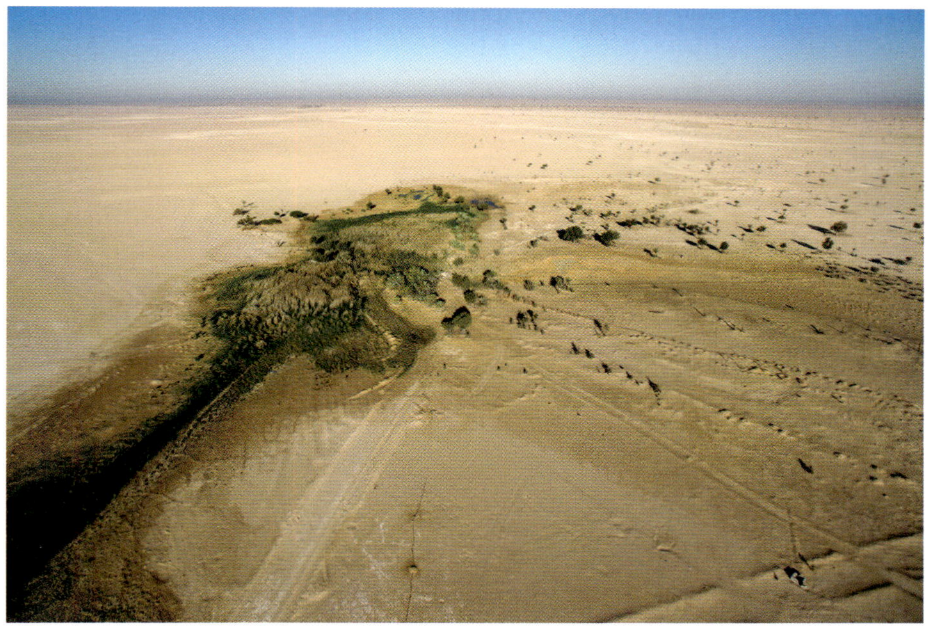

tools to tell the story of times long past.

Since that time the Empty Quarter was long judged too unforgiving for all but the most resourceful humans and those who did venture there only did so in the relative cool of winter. However, today where once the camels of desert nomads passed the dunes are traversed by a number of vehicle tracks while graded roads connect modern settlements that have grown up at the margins of the dunes. These include Mitan and Al Hashman in the south and Dawkah, Mawsaddid and Muqshin in the east. Elsewhere often-sulphurous wells, such as at Muntasar, support small islands of vegetation in an otherwise seemingly lifeless, though bewitching, landscape.

The star dunes of Mitan ***(top right)*** are the highest of the Empty Quarter while in the north-east ghaf trees (*Prosopis cineraria*) provide the only shade in an endless landscape of marching Barchan dunes close to Mawsaddid ***(top left)***. At the edge of the dune fields the sulphurous well of Muntasar ***(bottom right)*** is a local hotspot for wildlife in an otherwise barren landscape.

3 Climate

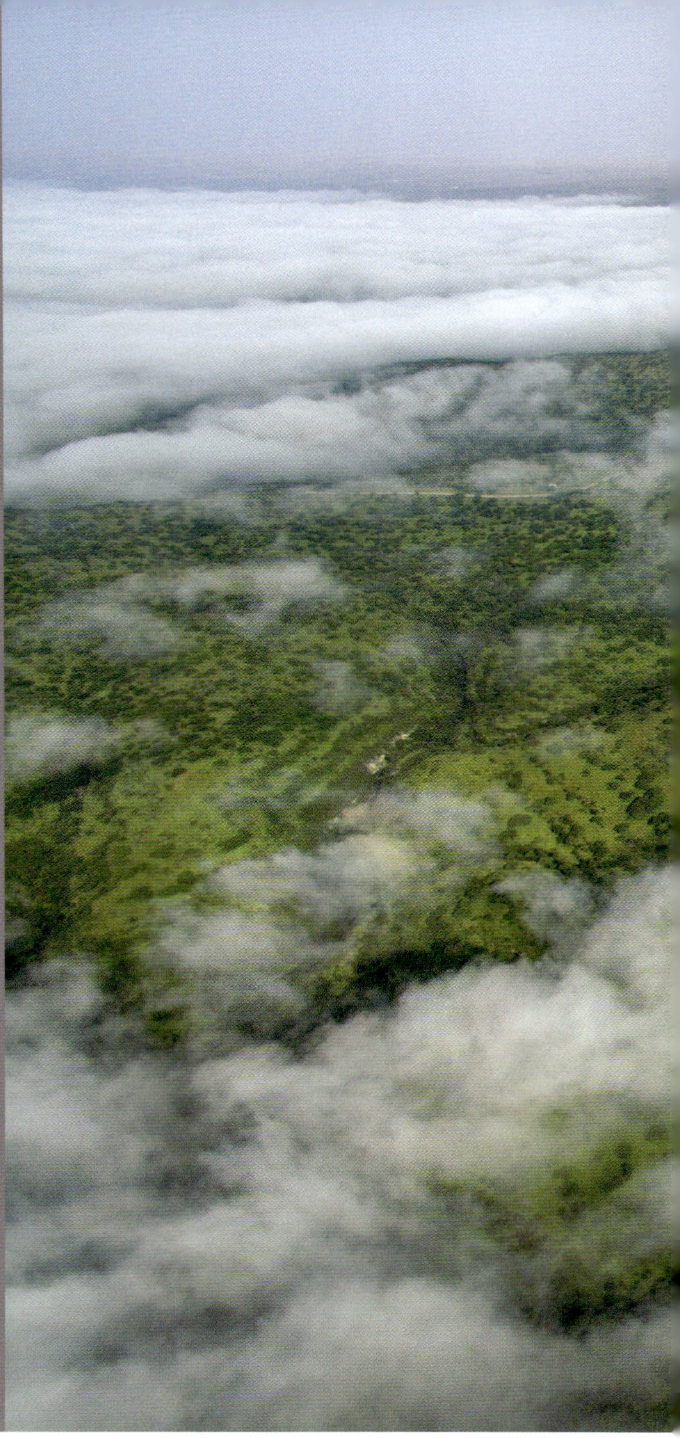

Introduction

The climate of Dhofar is dominated by the Southwest Monsoon and is unlike that found anywhere else in Oman. Broadly, it is subtropical and ranges from hyper-arid in the Najd and the Empty Quarter to semi-arid on the Jabal, where each year, from June to September, the Southwest Monsoon, or *khareef,* sweeps in from the Arabian Sea. Much of the Jabal disappears under a blanket of fog and the constant drizzle transforms the landscape. Consequently, while the rest of Oman faces the intense heat of an Arabian summer, much of Dhofar enjoys light rainfall, cool breezes and temperatures that rarely exceed 25°C.

The temperate summer conditions are not found throughout the Jabal, but are confined to the south-facing and south-west-facing slopes and plateaux of Jabal Al Qara and Jabal Al Qamar, extending into Al Mahrah Governorate of Yemen. Other parts of Dhofar, including Jabal Samhan and the southern Najd, are hyper-arid but they do not

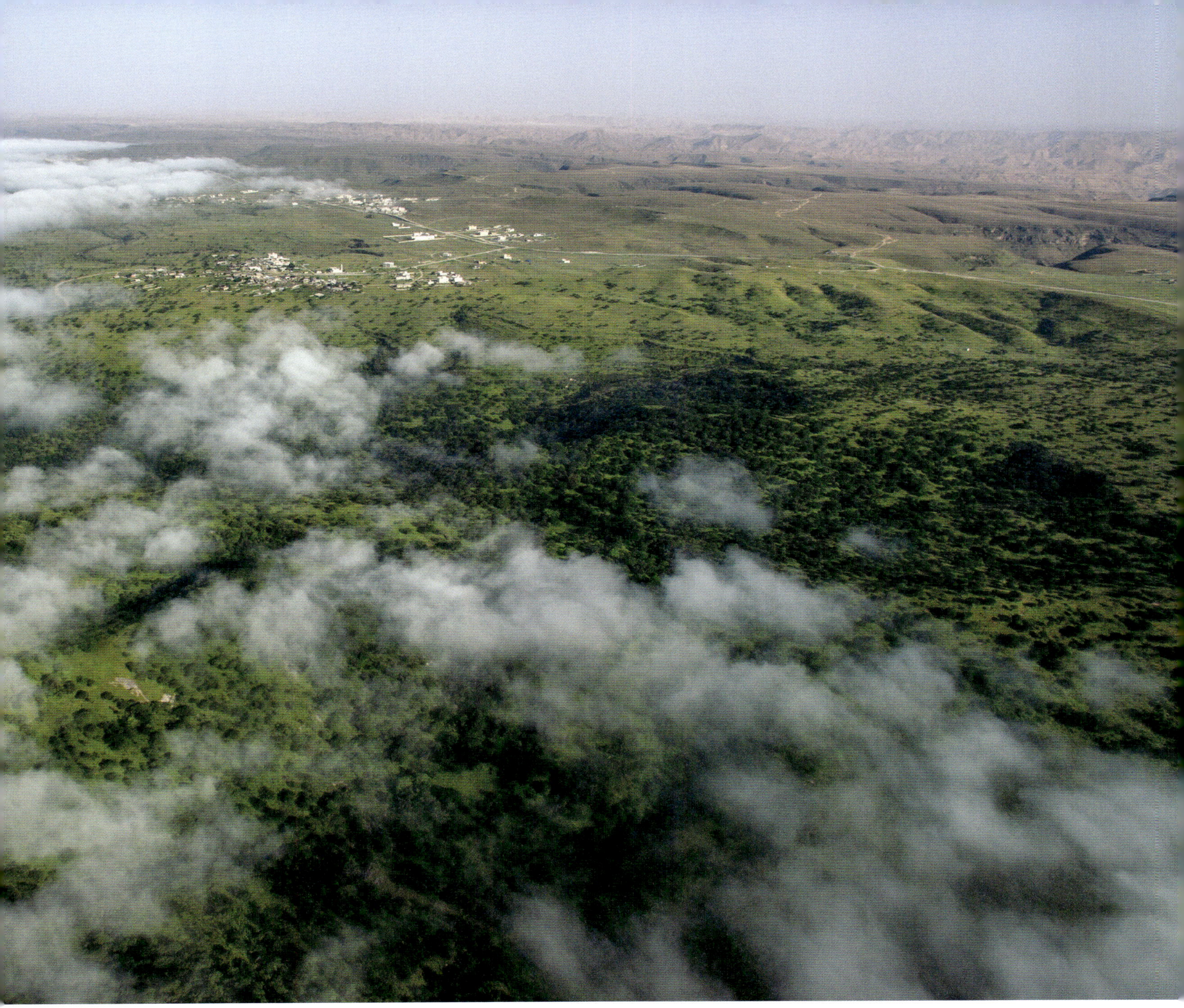

completely escape the influence of the monsoon, which brings small amounts of moisture and cooling winds to these areas at the height of summer. Further north, the northern Najd and Empty Quarter are beyond the reach of the monsoon and temperatures can rise as high as 50°C during the summer months.

Outside the summer monsoon the climate of Dhofar is characterised by dry winters with cold, northerly winds; temperatures may fall close to 0°C in the true desert of the Empty Quarter and rainfall is very low and erratic. The seasons between the *khareef* and winter are times of change as tropical storms and cyclones form in the south-east of the Arabian Sea. These sweep north and most make landfall in Pakistan and India, but on occasion they veer west and – like the powerful cyclone Mekunu, in May 2018 – make landfall in Dhofar.

(Above) Dhofar is known across the region for its seasonal weather and particularly for the summer *khareef*, when the mountains are cloaked in clouds. Yet these clouds stretch no more than 30 kilometres inland before the desert heat removes their life-giving water, the hyper-arid desert replacing lush grasslands.

General Conditions

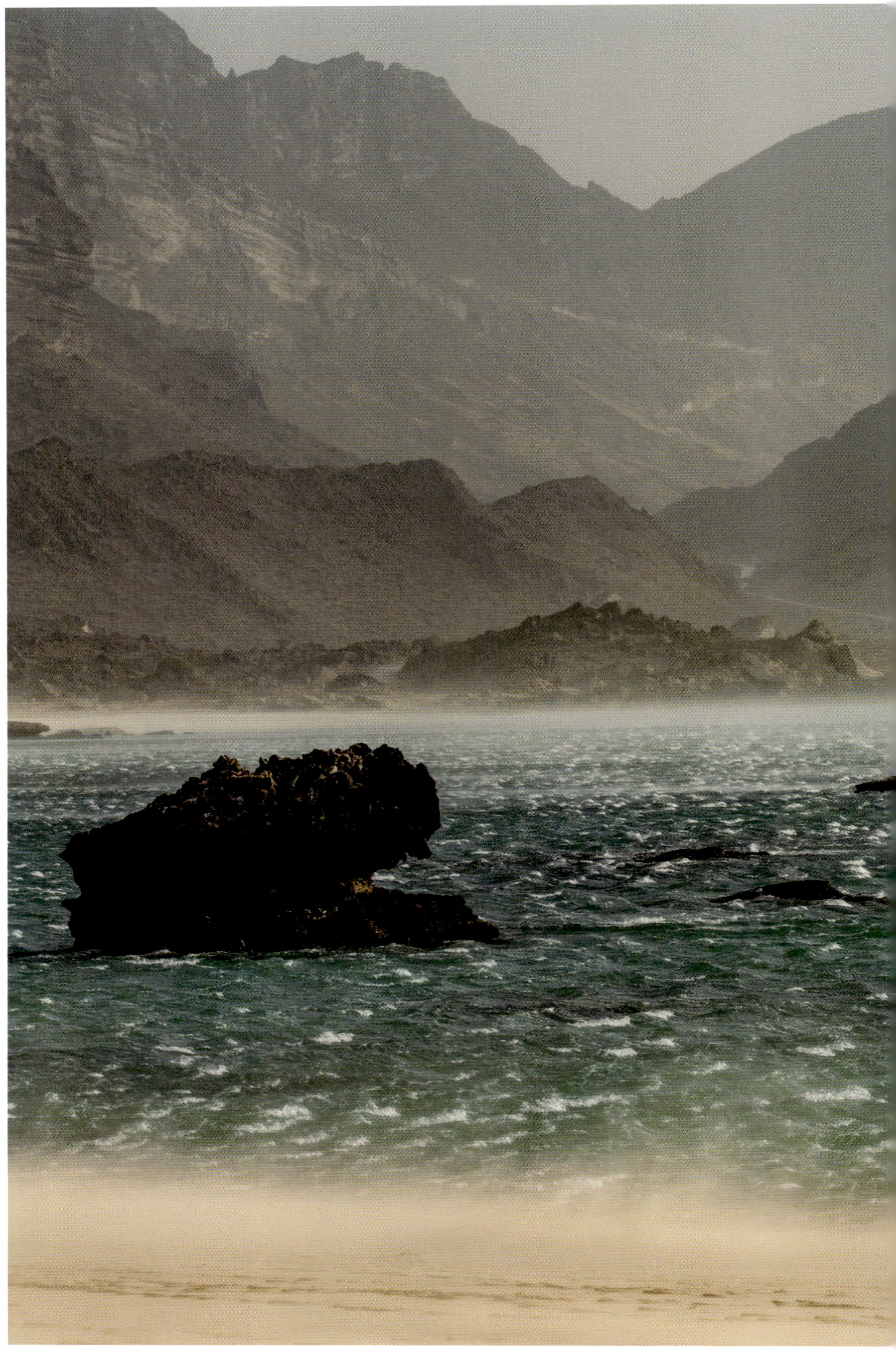

In the winter months the subtropical climate of Dhofar and most of the region is dominated by polar continental air masses carried into the region by the Siberian high-pressure system. These bring cool and dry conditions with clear skies, and the prevailing north-easterly winds, often referred to as trade winds, flow outward from the Siberian high-pressure area to a belt of low pressure near the equator known as the Intertropical Convergence Zone (ITCZ). These are the winds of the Arabian winter that were once used by traders to sail south to the coast of Africa.

However, these normal winter conditions may be interrupted by moisture-bearing low-pressure frontal systems that build up in the Mediterranean and move south-east.[31] Usually these bring patchy cloud and a wind shift, with strong northerly winds, known by the Arabic name *shamal*, that can lead to dust storms that typically blow for three days. Visibility falls, as does temperature. These are more common in northern Oman but will on occasion reach Dhofar. On other occasions the frontal systems may bring rain to the Gulf and northern Oman but again only rarely does this reach Dhofar.

The spring or pre-*khareef* period of March to June is a time of transition. As the summer approaches the sun is seen higher in the sky, days are longer, and sunset and sunrise make their way north. The ITCZ also moves north and there is an increasingly strong contrast in temperature between the cool seawaters and the hot desert interior.[32] This is an important time for rainfall in Dhofar, when tropical storms and cyclones might occur. Along the coast there is often a southerly onshore breeze, locally called the *kos*, that can bring heavy dewfall and morning fogs to areas north of Jabal Samhan, particularly the Jiddat Arkad and coastal areas.

The summer, or *khareef*, season, late June to September, is the season of the monsoon, when cool and wet conditions are found over the Jarbib, Jabal Al Qara and Jabal

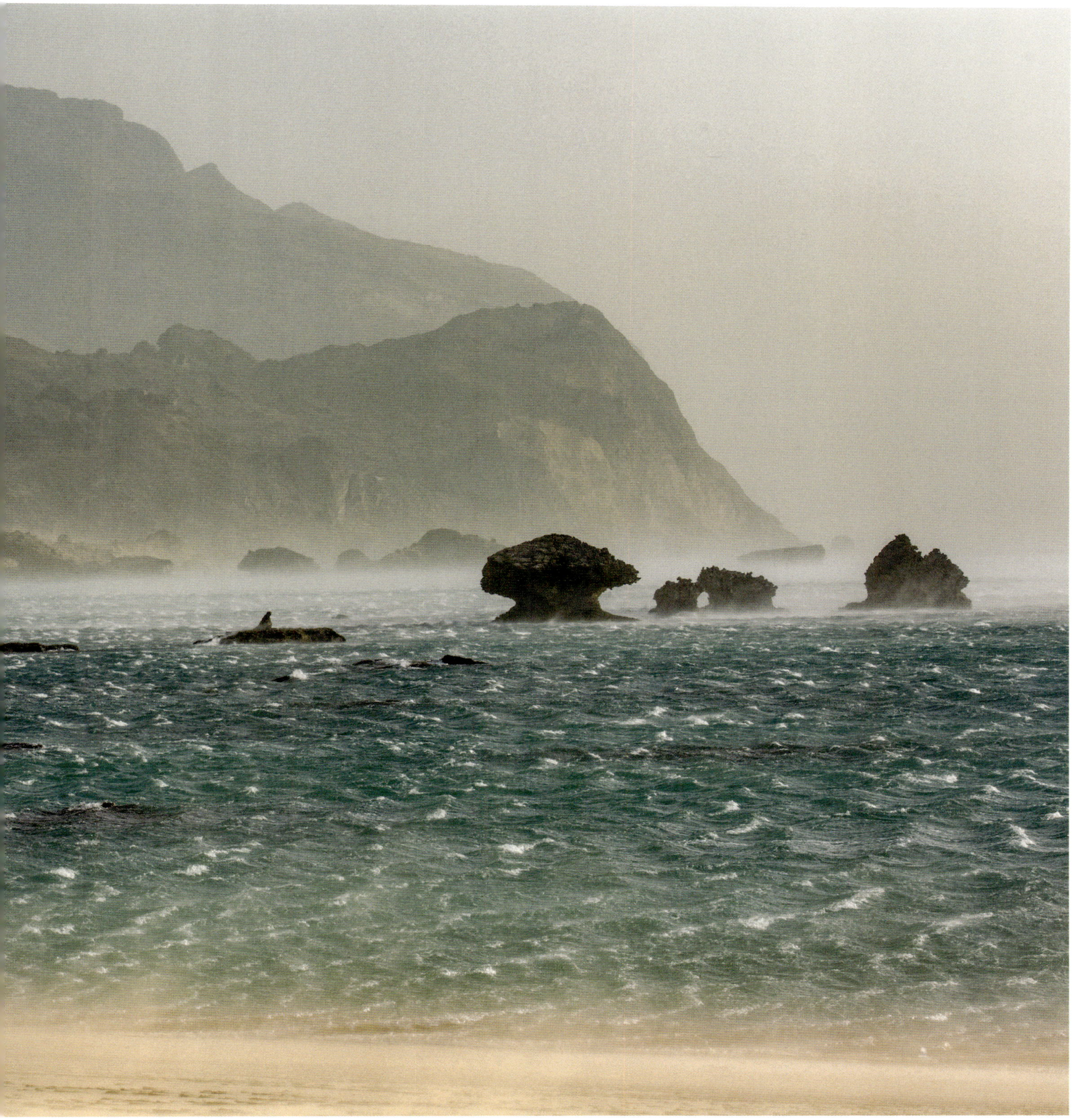

Al Qamar, while most of the rest of Dhofar experiences the very harsh weather that is characteristic of the Arabian Peninsula at this time. By the summer solstice of June 21st the low-pressure ITCZ zone has reached its northernmost extent, close to the Gulf, and the north-easterly winds are replaced by south-westerly trade

(Above) Strong winter *shamal* winds churn up the sea at Al Fazayih, Jabal Al Qamar.

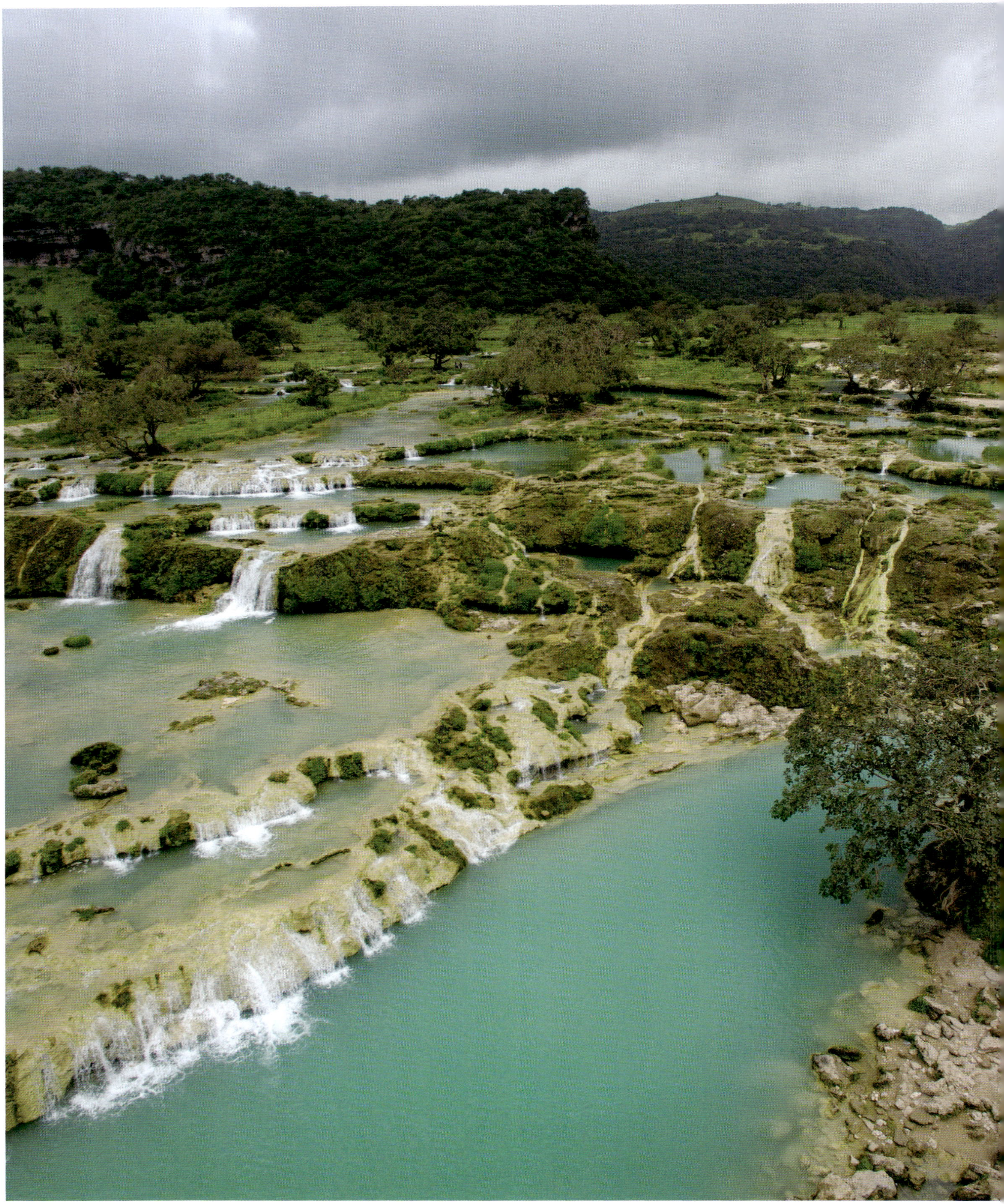

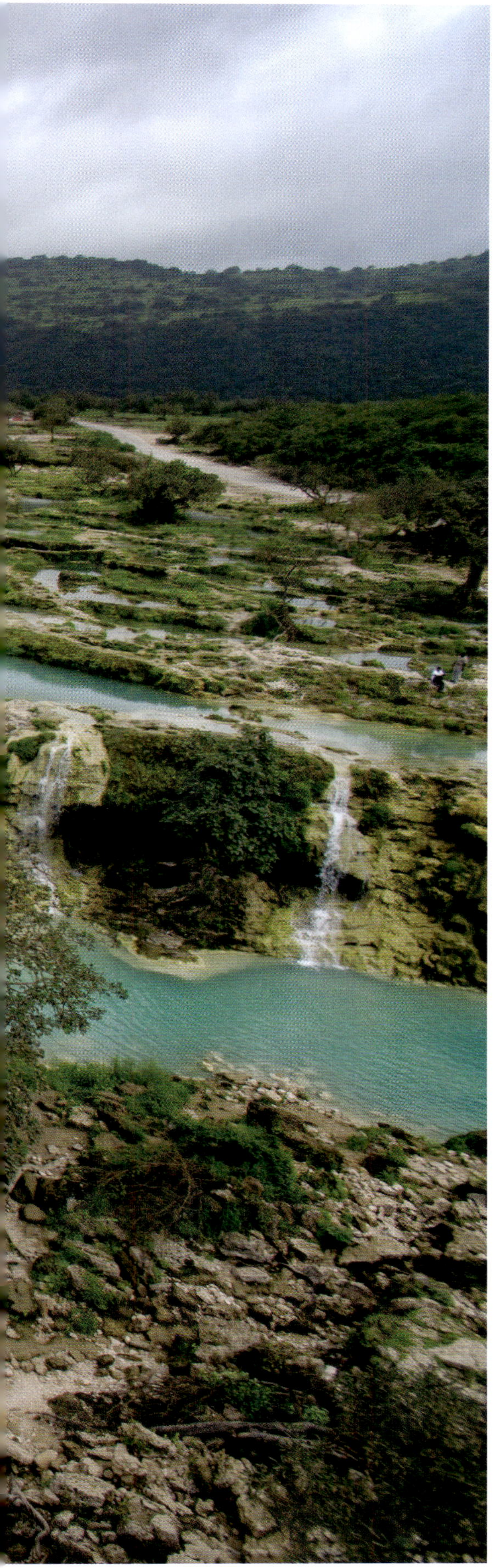

winds that blow from the high-pressure areas over the equator to the low-pressure ITCZ. As these winds travel north over the Indian Ocean they pick up huge amounts of moisture-resulting in heavy rainfall over the subcontinent. The winds and associated rainfall are known as the Indian or Southwest Monsoon, a word that comes from the Arabic word *mausim* meaning season. It was at this time that Arab traders would find favourable winds to return from the coast of East Africa. It is the Southwest Monsoon that brings the *khareef* to Dhofar.

The autumn transitional period of October to December is generally a quiet time except for the threat of tropical storms and cyclones. The sea is often calm and coastal areas north of Jabal Samhan, especially the Jiddat Arkad, may experience heavy dewfall and morning fogs.

In most years the monsoon is often the only source of rainfall but in some years tropical storms and cyclones result in torrential downpours and widespread flooding, as occurred in Wadi Darbat ***(left)*** and throughout Dhofar following Cyclone Mekunu in 2018.

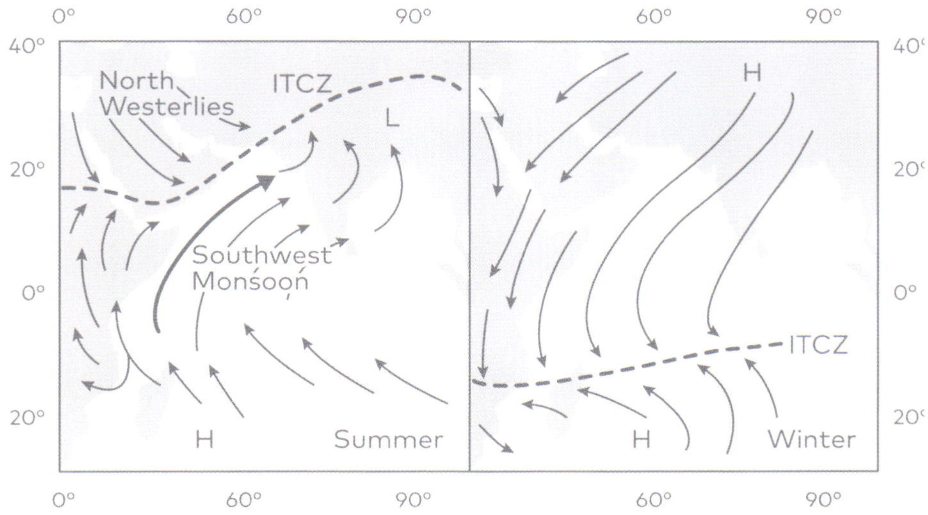

Fig. 3 The climate of Dhofar is largely driven by the ITCZ.

(Below) In the swirling mists of the *khareef* season, visitors to Dhofar can enjoy temperatures that rarely exceed 25°C in the mountains – a respite from the Arabian summer heat where temperatures can reach 50°C.

Temperature and Humidity Patterns

Typically, subtropical deserts are the hottest deserts in the world, being very hot and dry in the summer and cooler, although still dry, in the winter. This is certainly the case for much of the Najd and especially the Empty Quarter, where summer temperatures regularly exceed 45°C in June, July and August and have been recorded at 49°C at Marmul and Muqshin. In the winter, temperatures are often below 10°C in January and February, and have been recorded to fall as low as 4°C and 2°C in Al Mazyunah and Muqshin respectively. Unsurprisingly, the northern Najd and Empty Quarter are the driest places in Dhofar and humidity remains

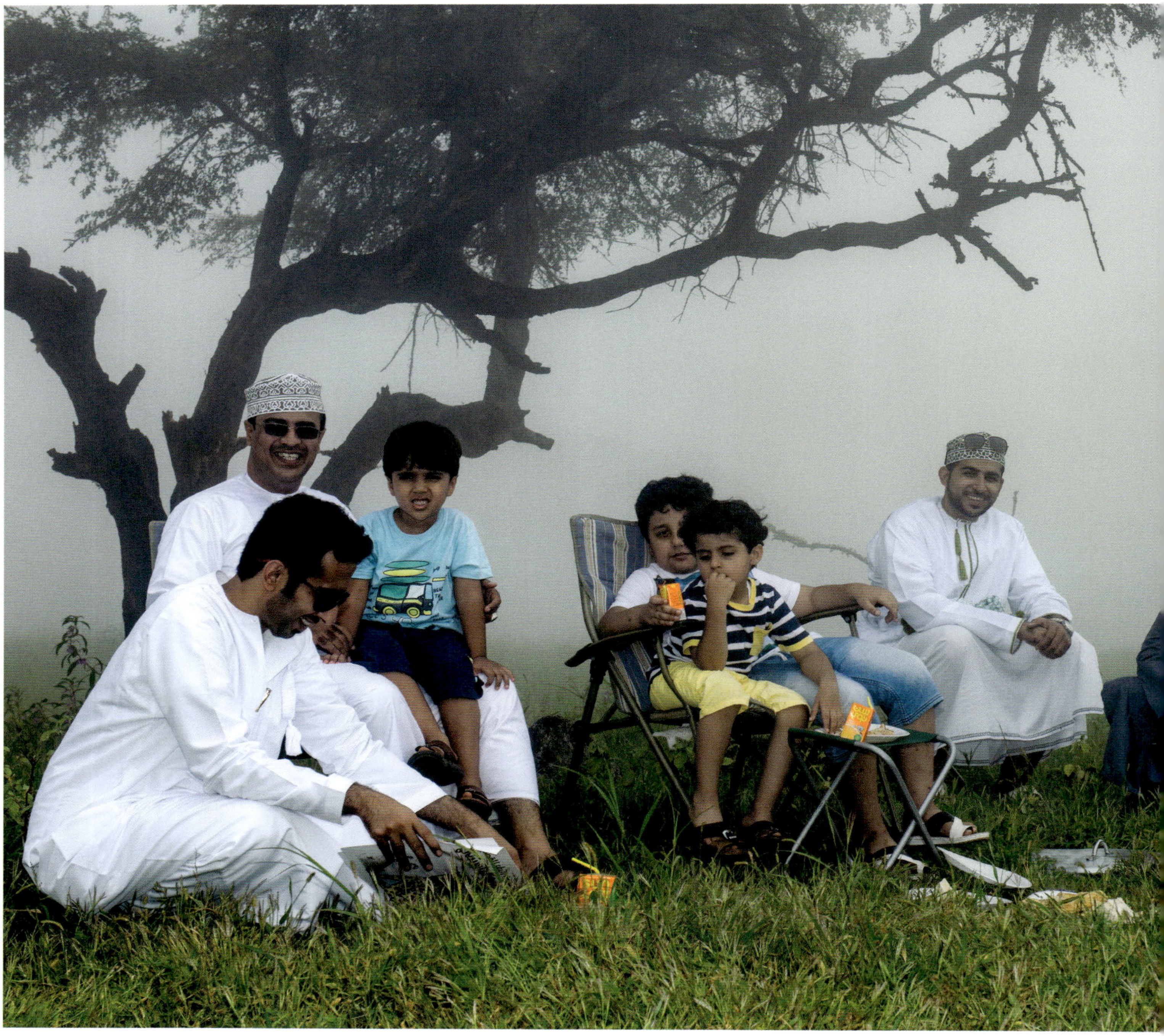

low year-round, rarely exceeding 30% at Al Mazyunah and 50% at Muqshin.

All other areas of Dhofar, including the Jarbib, the Jabal, the southern Najd, the coast and the Al Hallaniyyat Islands, have patterns of temperature and humidity that are not at all typical of subtropical deserts. This of course is because the *khareef* ameliorates the hot summer conditions, arriving just as the rest of the region is entering high summer. In late June the first of the cool moist winds rush in from the sea and for up to three months much of Dhofar enjoys temperatures of 20-30°C and humidity of 80-100%. The dip in temperature in most regions of Dhofar during the *khareef* is clear on the graph below (Fig. 4), while in the northern Najd temperatures remain high.

Although the *khareef* winds make landfall over the Jarbib, the coolest and most humid conditions are to be found on the Jabal and in particular at mid-elevation, where temperatures are 20-22°C and the air is saturated, forming a heavy fog. As can be seen from Fig. 4, the lower temperatures of the Jabal compared to the Jarbib are not only a feature of the *khareef* but remain throughout the year.

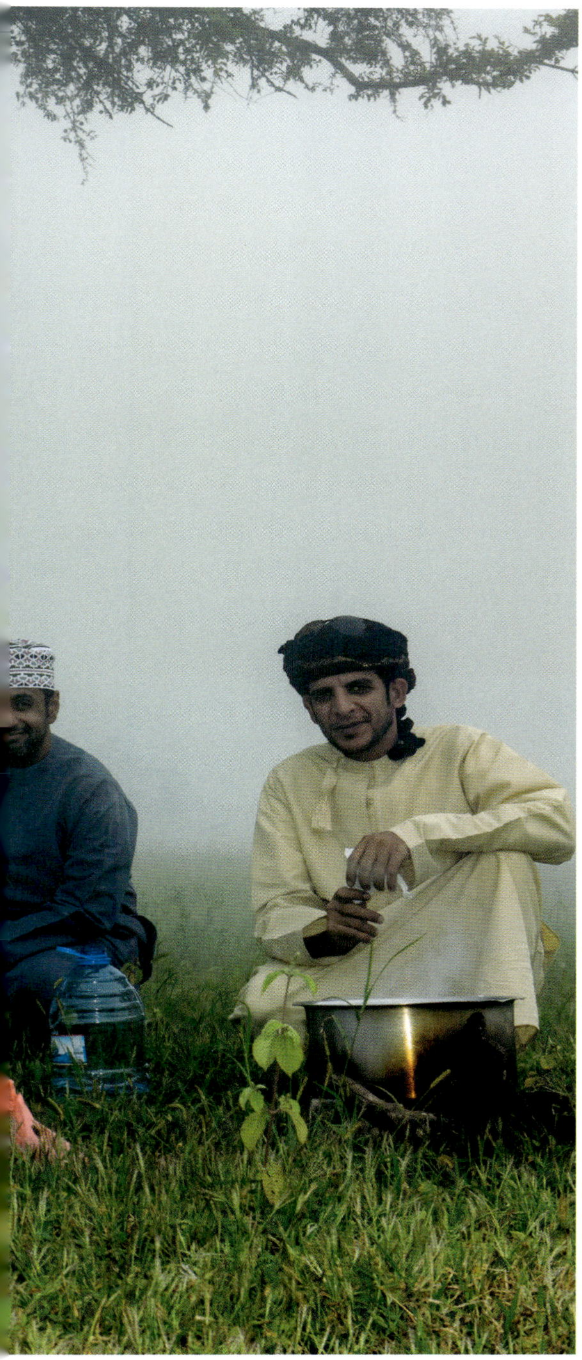

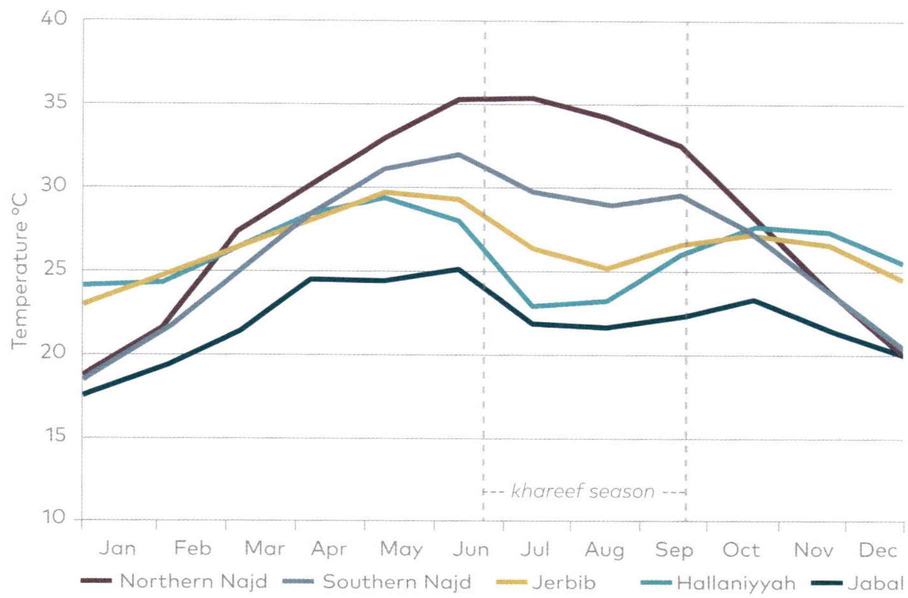

Fig. 4 Average monthly temperatures for different regions of Dhofar.[33]

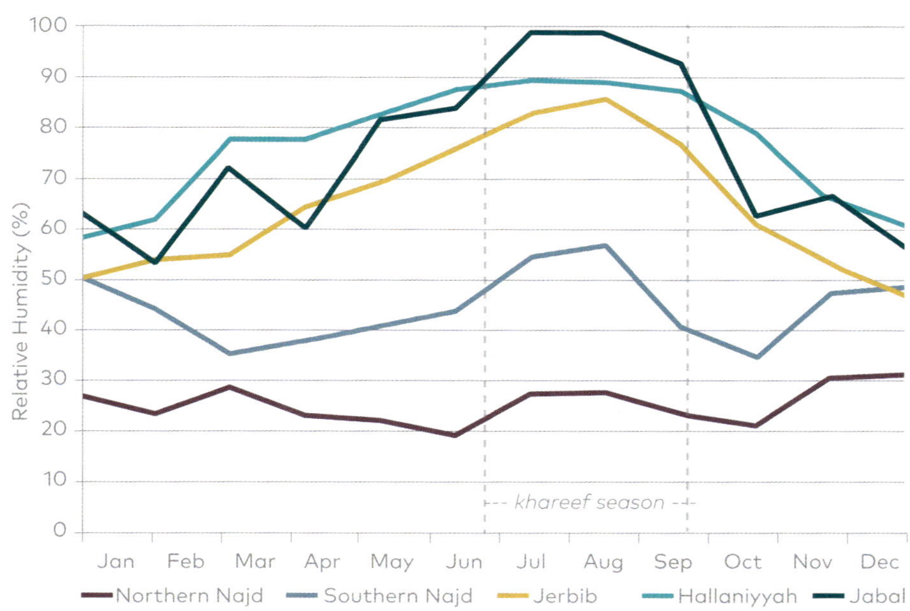

Fig. 5 Average monthly relative humidity for different regions of Dhofar.[33]

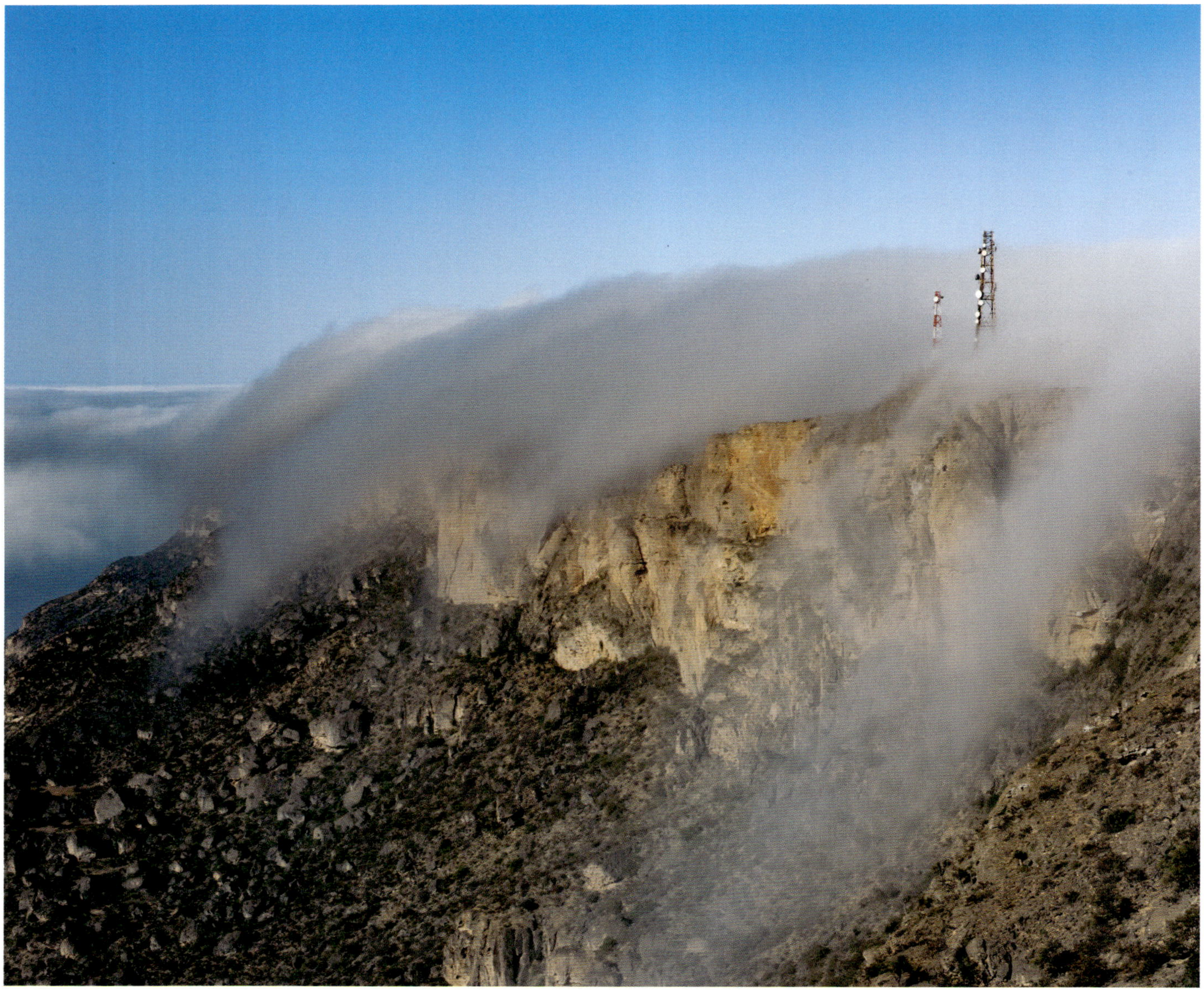

(Above) Monsoon clouds reach the western slopes of Jabal Samhan and cascade over the southern escarpment.

For example, at Qayrun Hayrti on a typical April day average temperatures are 23°C while close to Salalah temperatures are more typically 28°C. This is largely due to the greater elevation of the Jabal and exposure to cooling winds.

After the Jabal the lowest temperatures and highest humidity during the *khareef* are found on the Al Hallaniyyat Islands. There the hottest month is May, before the first of the *khareef* winds, after which time temperatures fall and humidity continues to rise. However, unlike on the Jarbib, there is almost no rainfall and the very strong winds are not conducive to the formation of fog. Once the *khareef* has passed temperatures rise, and typically October is the second-hottest month on the islands.

Although the southern Najd is very arid, it is reached by the cool, moist *khareef* winds. For example, at Thumrayt, 40 kilometres north of the main *khareef* zone, the cooling effect of the *khareef* is only felt once it is in full swing in July. Temperatures can reach 45°C, especially when there is a summer *shamal*, but overall temperatures are about 5°C lower than the northern Najd and Empty Quarter to the north.

The *Khareef*

The Southern Monsoon, or *khareef*, is at the heart of the climate of Dhofar and it is not surprising that the people of the Jabal and the Najd recognise four seasons that are different from the conventional four seasons of a temperate climate; after all the *khareef* was central to their subsistence pastoral lives. Each season is further divided into seven sub-seasons that reflect small changes in climatic parameters such as the subtle changes in precipitation during the *khareef*.

In early summer, usually late June, strong south-westerly winds are the first sign of the imminent arrival of the summer Southwest Monsoon, or *khareef*. These monsoon winds, which blow north-east and parallel to the coast of Oman, are of such strength that, combined with the rotation of the Earth, they cause an eastward movement of the relatively warm coastal surface waters of the Arabian Sea. As these waters shift out to sea they are replaced by cold, nutrient-rich waters, that rise up from the deep ocean in a process called upwelling. The upwelled water is 4-8°C cooler than the moist air flowing over it and consequently the water in the moist air condenses to form fog and low cloud which is then driven onshore by the south-westerly winds.[32]

Once onshore the fog and low clouds face the vertical barrier of the Jabal as well as a horizontal barrier created by a strong temperature inversion layer, at about 1,200 metres above sea level, where the hot air of the desert lies above the cool maritime air (Fig. 6). In the case of Jabal Al Qamar and Jabal Al Qara this is about the

Seasons of the Dhofar Mountain Chain			
Period	English	Arabic	Jibbāli
21 December – 20 March	*Winter*	*Shitā*	Śete
21 March – 20 June	*Pre-khareef*	*Ḳayḏ*	Ḳayḏ
21 June – 20 September	*khareef*	*khareef*	Khorf
21 September – 20 December	*Post-khareef*	*Sarb*	Serb

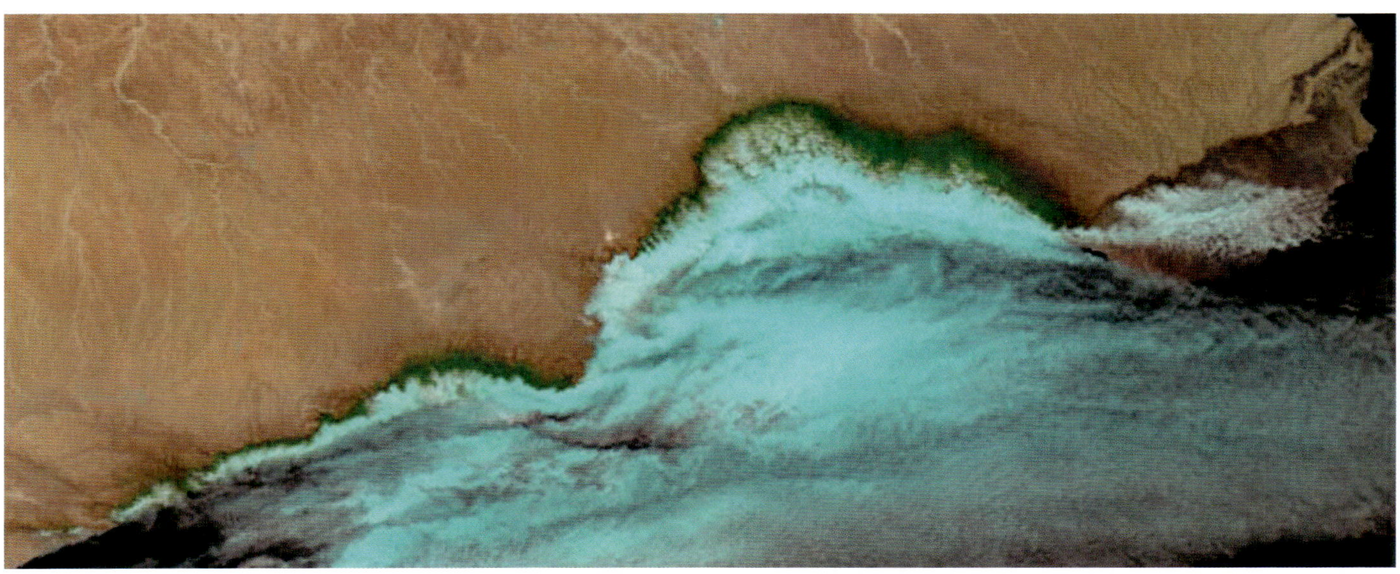

(Below) Seen from space, the extent of the monsoon influence is very clear; this image taken in mid-September shows the cloud cover (mint green) and vegetation (deep green) of Jabal Al Qara and Jabal Al Qamar while Jabal Samhan is barely touched by the monsoon (https://reverb.echo.nasa.gov/).

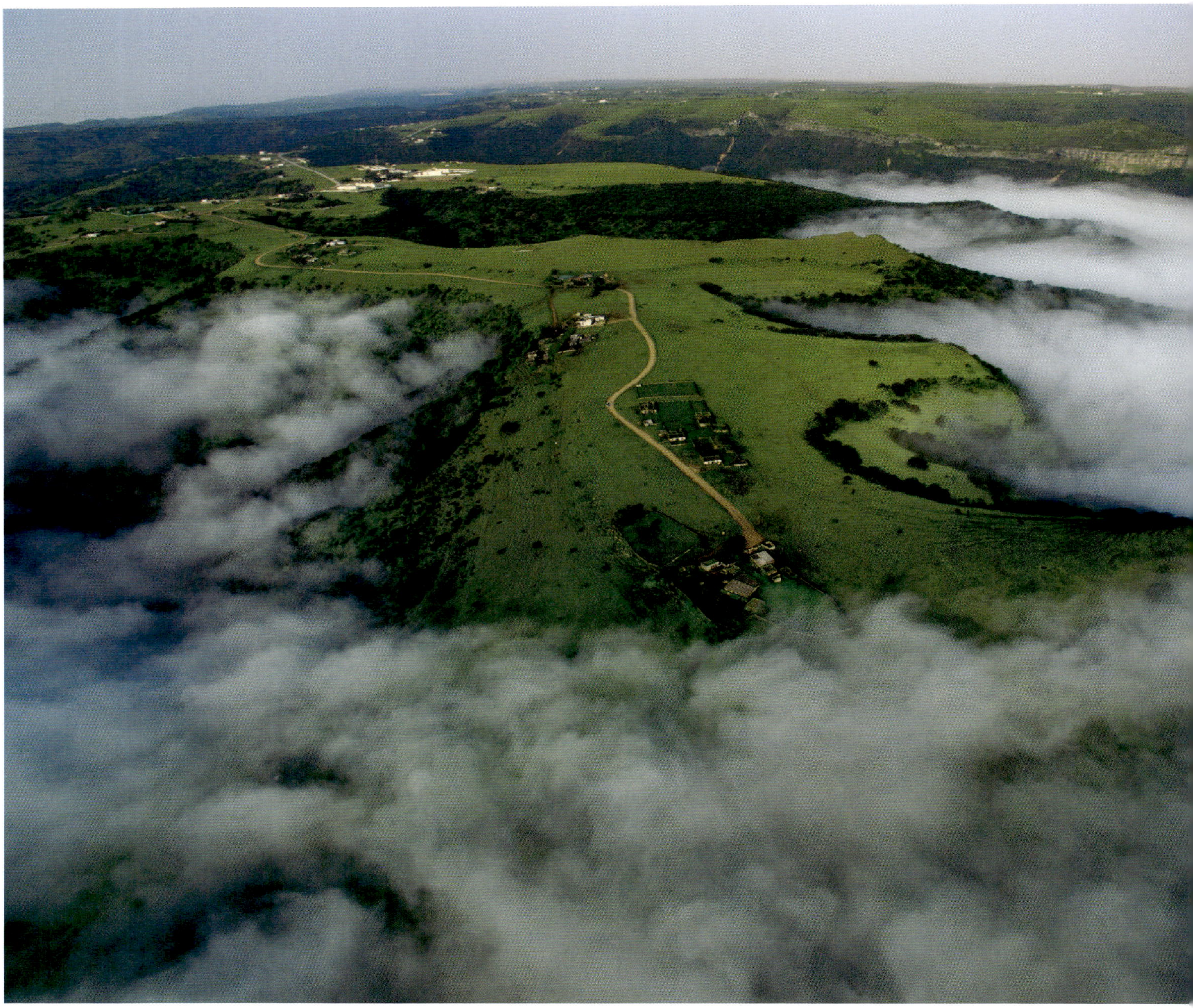

During the monsoon, hot air is blown south from the Empty Quarter and sits above the cool moist air blown in from the ocean, creating an invisible ceiling just above the mountains. Jabal Al Qara and Jabal Al Qamar remain below the ceiling and are transformed by the monsoon drizzle ***(above left)*** while the summit of Jabal Samhan is above the ceiling and remains dry ***(above right)***.

level of the mountaintop, though it is considerably below the summit of Jabal Samhan. Together the mountains and the inversion layer trap the fog and cloud, and much of the moisture falls as light rain or drizzle or is captured and condensed by vegetation on the south-facing slopes and plateaux of Jabal Al Qamar and Jabal Al Qara. Jabal Samhan, however, remains largely dry, presumably in part because the inversion layer prevents precipitation from reaching the summit and the mountain's southern escarpment faces south-east and not south-west into the prevailing *khareef* winds.

On Jabal Al Qamar precipitation extends about 10 kilometres inland and quickly tapers off close to the watershed at about 1,000 metres elevation. On the lower-lying Jabal Al Qara, precipitation extends about 20 kilometres but there is little beyond the watershed at about 800 metres

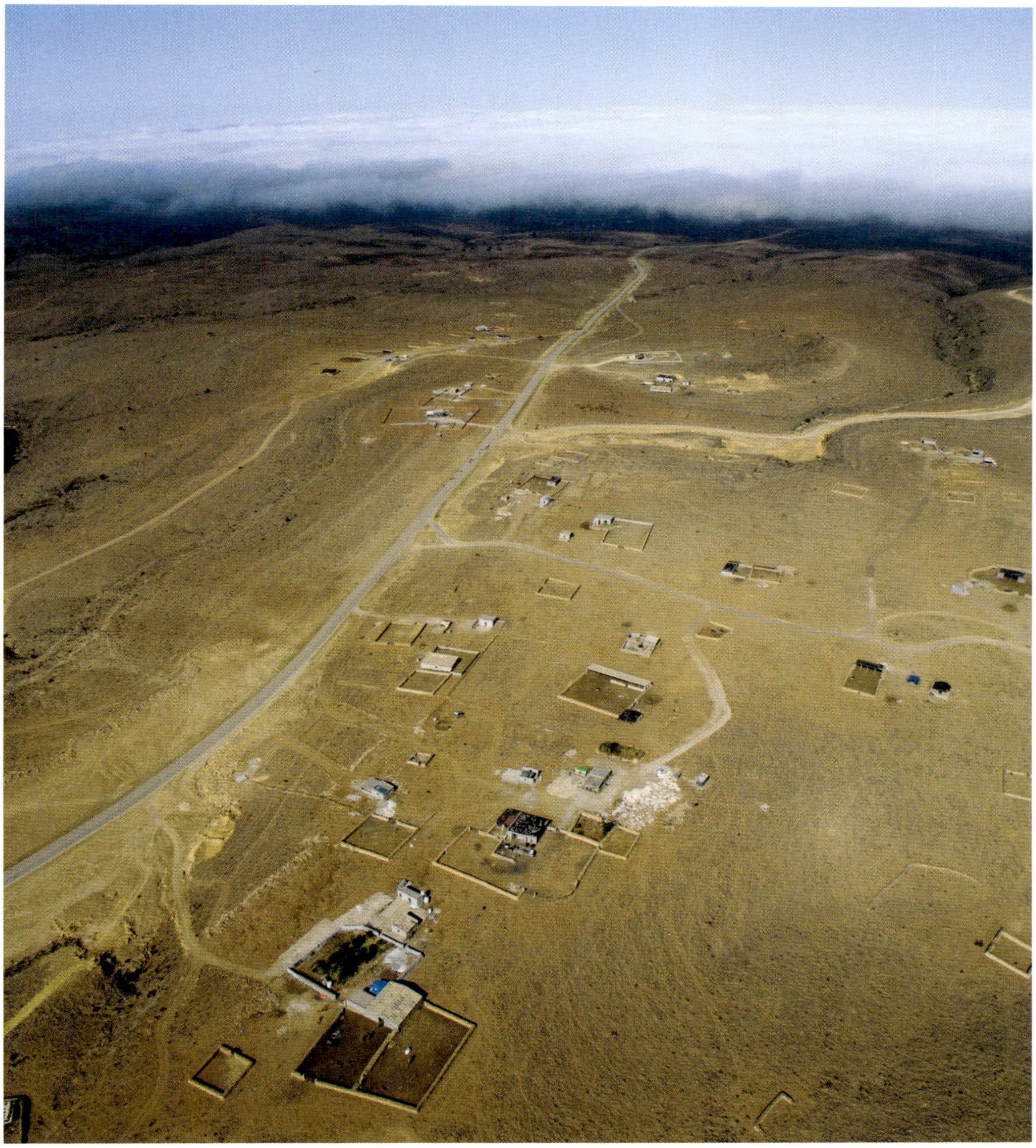

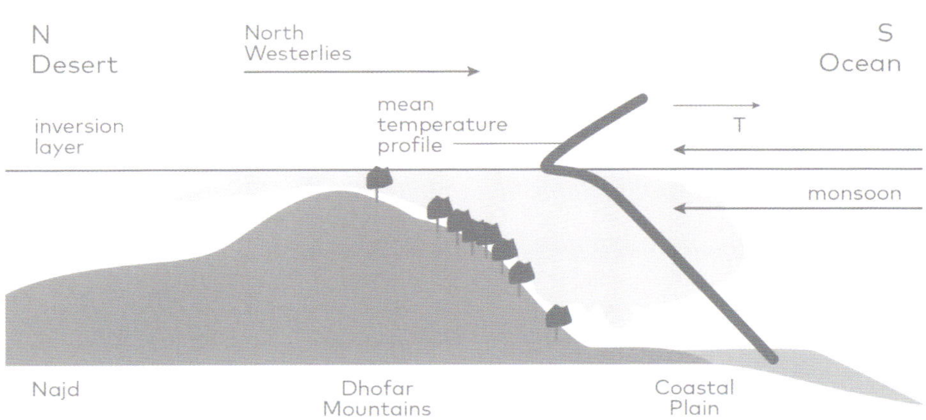

Fig. 6 *khareef* clouds trapped between the Jabal and the temperature inversion layer above.

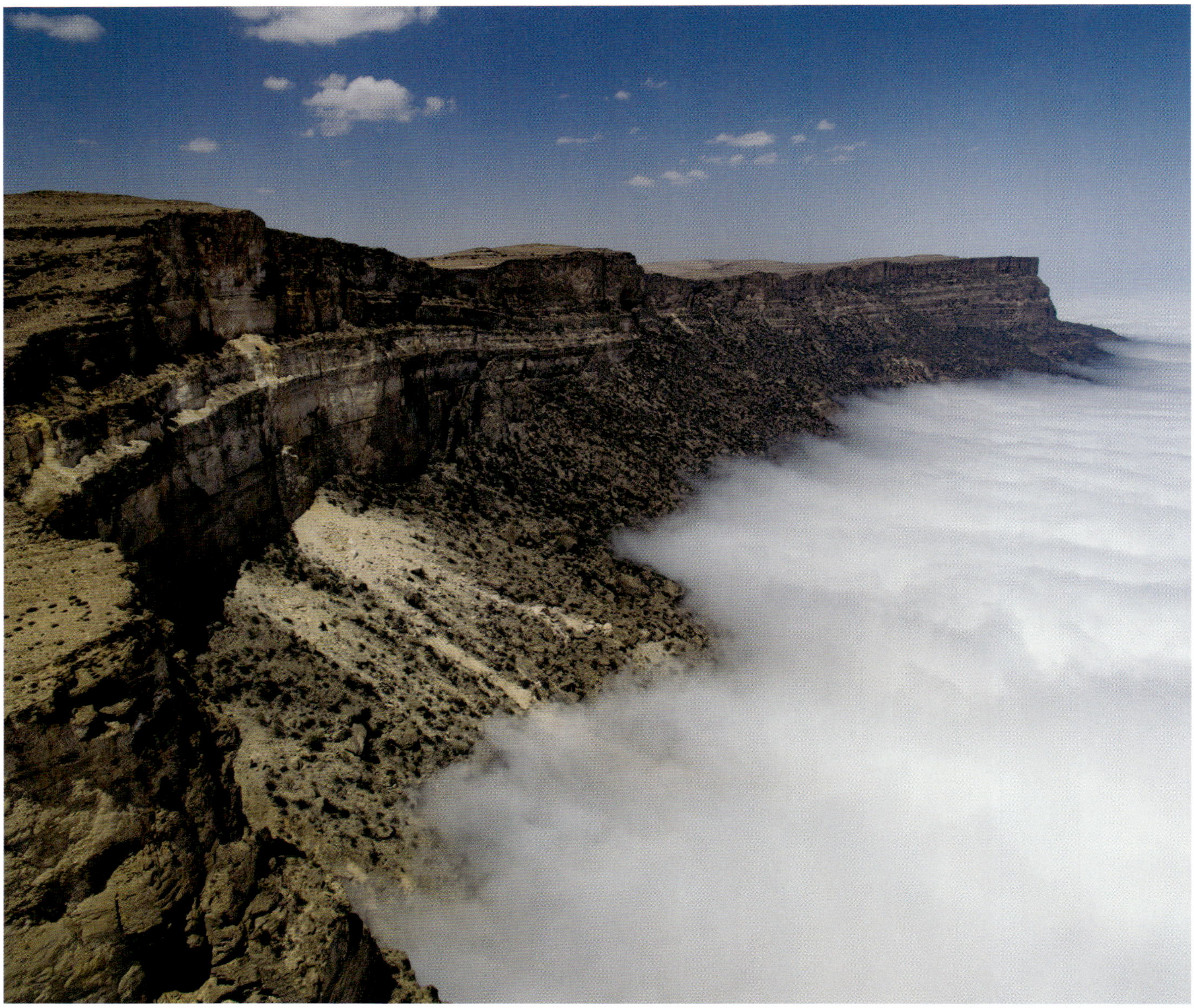

(Above) Jabal Samhan receives little monsoon precipitation, largely by virtue of its higher elevation but also because of its more south-easterly alignment.

elevation. Maximum precipitation on both mountains is not on the mountaintops but at about 700-800 metres above sea level, an area known as the *khatm* by the rural communities.

The timing of the *khareef* is usually June to September but there is considerable yearly variation in its onset and its end. For example, in 2014, when the *khareef* was considered to be weak, the first record of rainfall was July 1st and the last record was September 12th. In 2016 the *khareef* was reported as exceptional and for the first time in many years the *Jarbib* saw a good growth of short grasses. That year the first record of rainfall was on 11th June and the last of the season on 30th September. Across 23 rainfall stations the *Jabal* enjoyed an average of 32 days of precipitation in the *khareef* of 2014 compared with 60 days in 2016. During that time the average rainfall at the stations was 64 millimetres in 2014 and 144 millimetres in 2016. Thus between these two years there is almost a doubling in the days of rainfall and more than a doubling in the volume of rainfall collected.

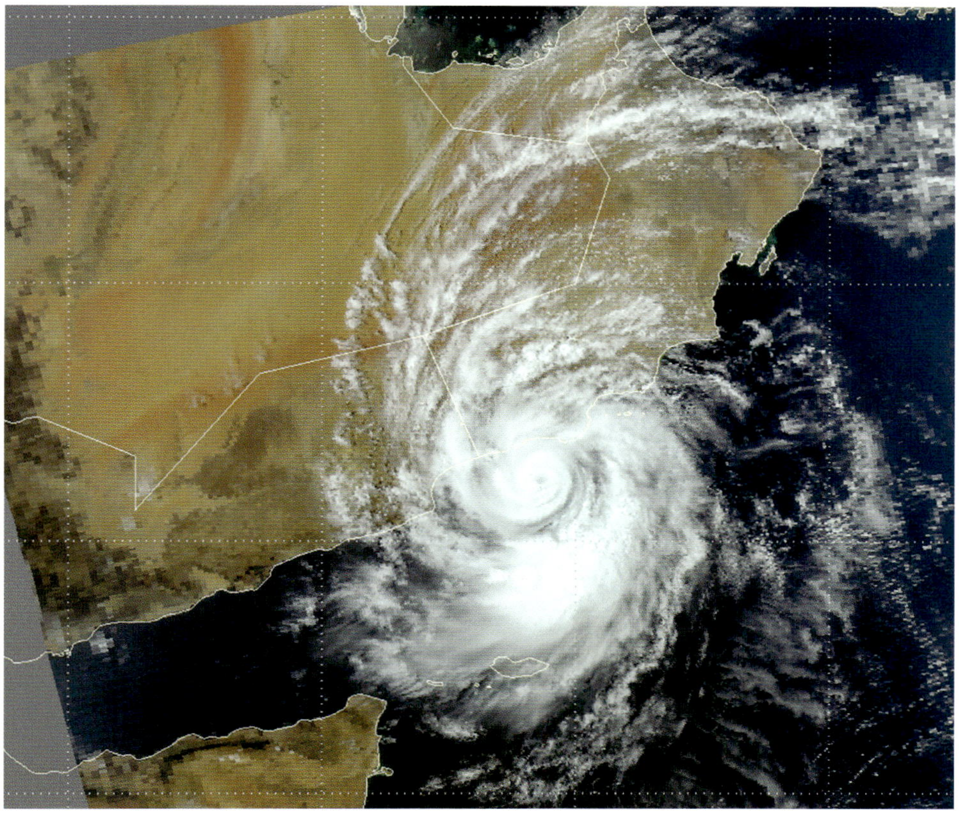

The cyclonic storm Mekunu *(left)*, classified as Extremely Severe, was the most intense tropical cyclone to make landfall in the Arabian Peninsula since records began. It battered Dhofar during the last days of May 2018 with wind speeds reaching 175 kilometres per hour (image courtesy of Directorate General of Meteorology, Public Authority for Civil Aviation, Oman).

Tropical Storms and Cyclones

Storms and cyclones usually form over the warm waters of the south-east Arabian Sea, often close to the Laccadive Islands, when areas of low-pressure air are heated, causing thunderstorms. When several thunderstorms come together a tropical depression is formed and, as it grows, it becomes increasingly severe, with rising wind speeds. Above wind speeds of 34 knots the depression becomes a tropical storm that in turn is upgraded to a cyclone when wind speeds exceed 63 knots.[34]

Once formed, tropical storms and cyclones usually move north-westerly towards the Arabian Peninsula though most eventually curve eastwards towards Pakistan and India. However, about once every three years they cross the coast of Oman. Fortunately some of the most severe cyclones, including Gonu in 2007, which brought widespread destruction to northern Oman, have missed Dhofar.

In Dhofar tropical storms and cyclones are almost entirely associated with the transitional periods before and after the summer *khareef*. Of the 15 tropical storms and cyclones that have impacted Dhofar since records began more than 100 years ago, nine have taken place in May-June, four in October-November, one in December and one in August.

One of the earliest cyclones for which there are detailed records occurred in late May 1959.[35] It crossed Raysut, then a village, with wind gusts reaching 90 knots and left a trail of devastation. Eighty-two millimetres of rain was recorded at Salalah airport and the Salalah-to-Raysut road was swept away by a raging torrent from the mountains. Offshore, a passenger *dhow* en route from Zanzibar to Sur sank close to the Al Hallaniyyat Islands with the loss of all 141 people on board.

Prior to Gonu the most powerful cyclone to strike Oman was the Masirah Island cyclone of June 1977, when winds gusted to 110 knots, causing widespread damage and leaving 100 people dead and 2,000 families homeless. The cyclone brought heavy rain and flooding to much of Dhofar, with the heaviest recorded rainfall at Madinat Al Haq on Jabal Al Qara, where 482 millimetres was recorded over five days – more than three times the average annual rainfall.[35] In May 2002 a cyclonic storm hit the coast close to Salalah port, with heavy rainfall across the Jabal and a maximum of 251 millimetres at Qayrun Hayrti. Nine people lost their lives and there was widespread loss of livestock and damage to homes and infrastructure.[33]

In November 2011 Cyclone Keila made landfall close to Salalah. It had relatively low wind speeds but heavy rainfall that caused the deaths of 12 people in northern Oman. In Dhofar maximum rainfall was at Ras Naws, near Hadbin, where 700 millimetres fell over seven days, at least 10 times more than might be expected in a normal year. Floods from wadis flowing from the Jabal to Salalah caused damage estimated at 32 million Omani Rials. In response to the damage flash-flood protection dams were constructed, the largest being Salalah and Sahalnawt dams, built to protect the city of Salalah.

The most powerful tropical cyclone to make landfall over Oman was Mekunu, a Category

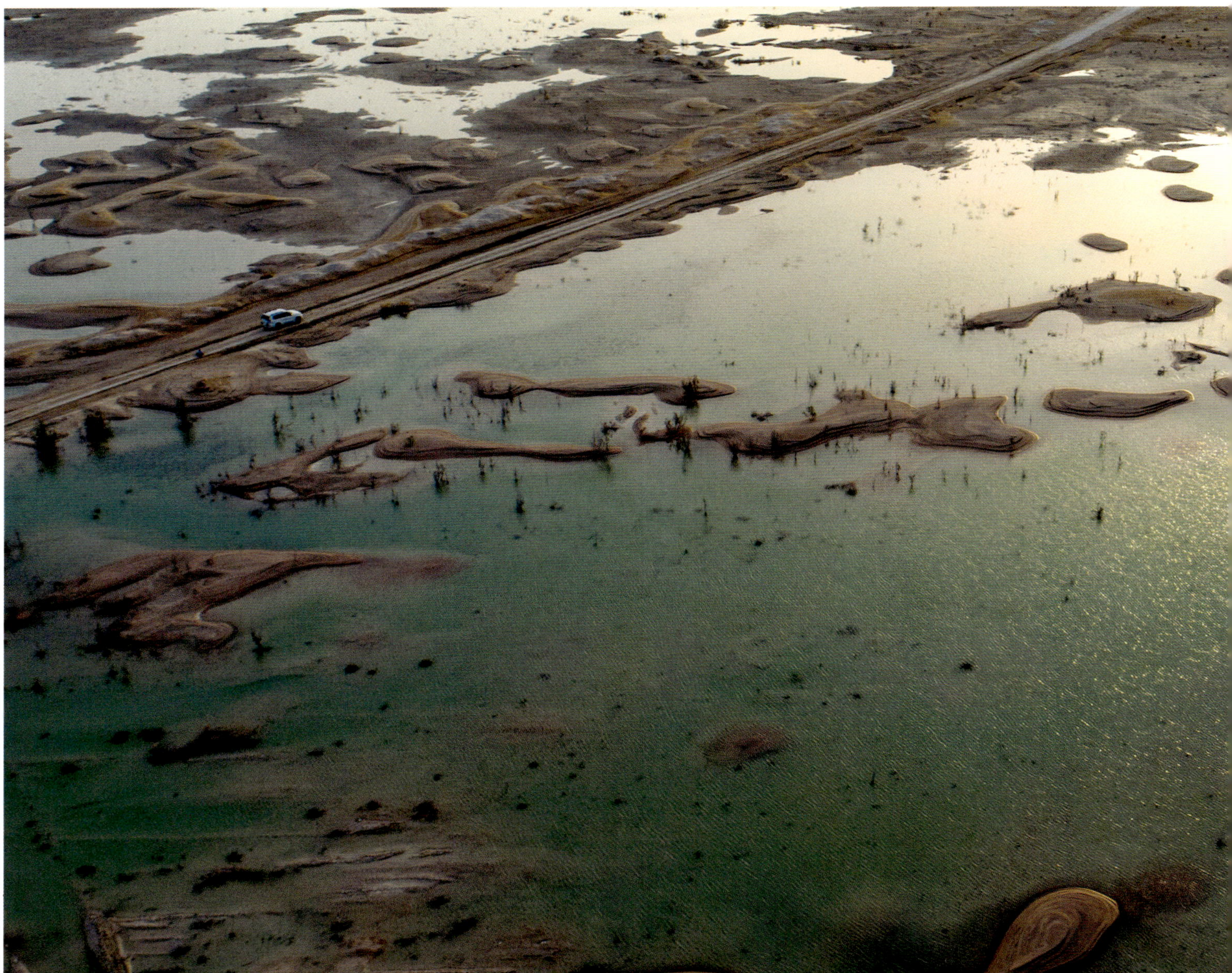

Two cyclone that hit Dhofar on May 26th, 2018. Making landfall close to Al Mughsayl, just west of Salalah, Mekunu battered Dhofar from 24th to 28th May as wind speeds gusted to 100 knots and rainfall reached almost 700 millimetres on the Jabal. In spite of the intensity of the cyclone, damage was limited, with just four casualties, largely as a consequence of the flash-flood protection dams and early warning systems that allowed the necessary evacuation and other precautions.[33]

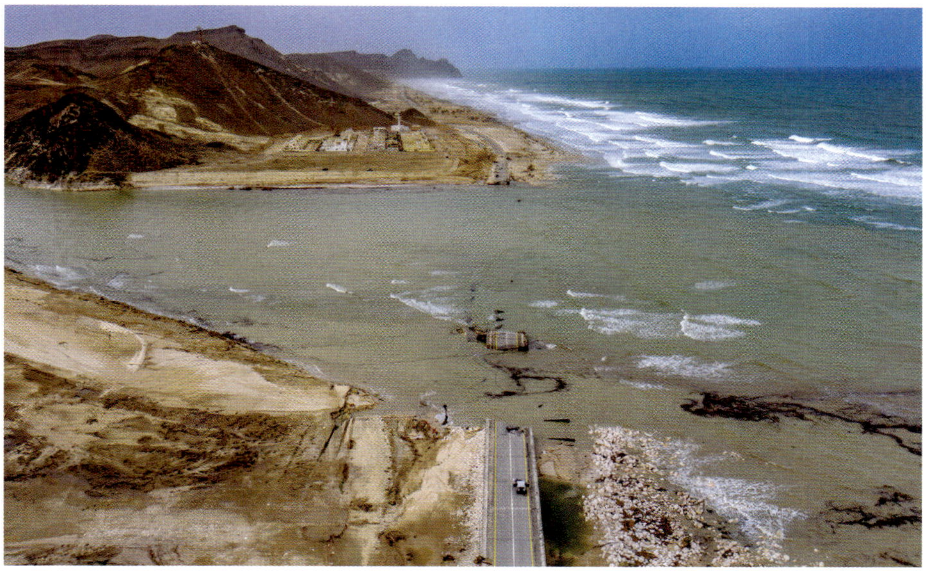

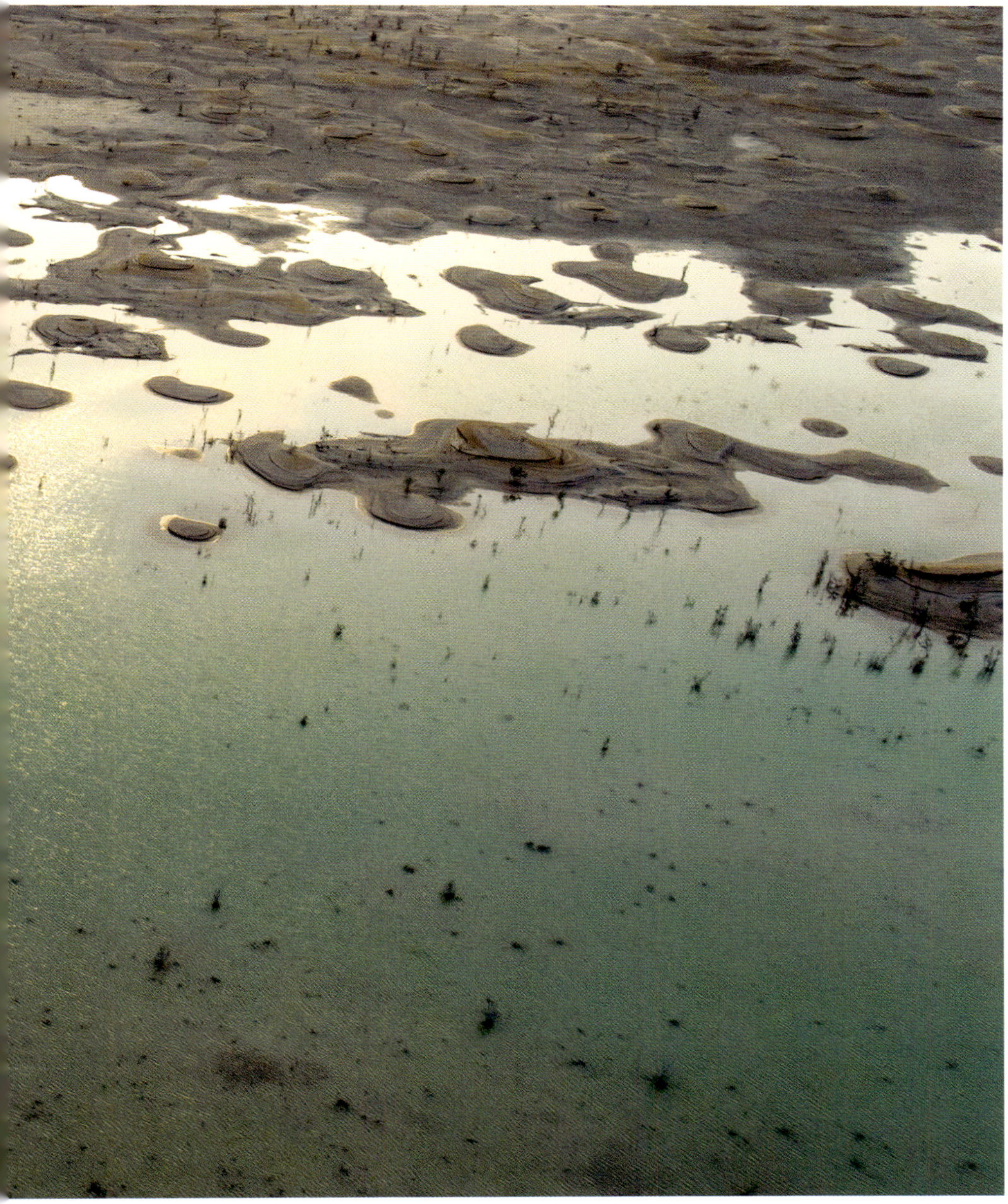

(This page) Flash-floods as rainfall turns dry wadis into thundering rivers is the major threat from cyclonic storms. In 2018 Cyclone Mekunu made landfall close to Al Mughsayl and floods washed away Khawr Al Mughsayl and the coastal road *(above)*. To the north of the mountains the great wadis carried water more than 250 kilometres north to the sand-seas of the Empty Quarter *(left)*.

Rainfall

The average annual rainfall in Oman is approximately 117 millimetres, while that of Dhofar ranges from 460 millimetres (Kanzir on Jabal Al Qara) to seven millimetres (Muqshin at the edge of the Empty Quarter). The bulk of the annual rainfall comes from the *khareef* but its influence is largely limited to Jabal Al Qamar and Jabal Al Qara. Other rainfall, such as from cyclonic storms, is very variable both in terms of when it may fall and where it may fall.

When does the rain fall?

The summer *khareef* means that the rainfall pattern is strongly seasonal; in an average year, 80% of annual rainfall occurs in the months of June to September (Fig. 7). However, in 2011, when Cyclone Keila made landfall in November, the *khareef* rains amounted to less than 50% of rainfall for most of Dhofar while in the following dry years of 2012, 2013 and 2014 the *khareef* rainfall was the only rainfall across most of the governorate.

The first of the *khareef* rains fall in late June but the bulk of the rainfall is in July and August, with little difference between the two months in terms of the volume of rainfall. The *khareef* peters out in September and only in exceptional years, like 2016, is there significant rainfall during this month.

Outside the *khareef,* rain has

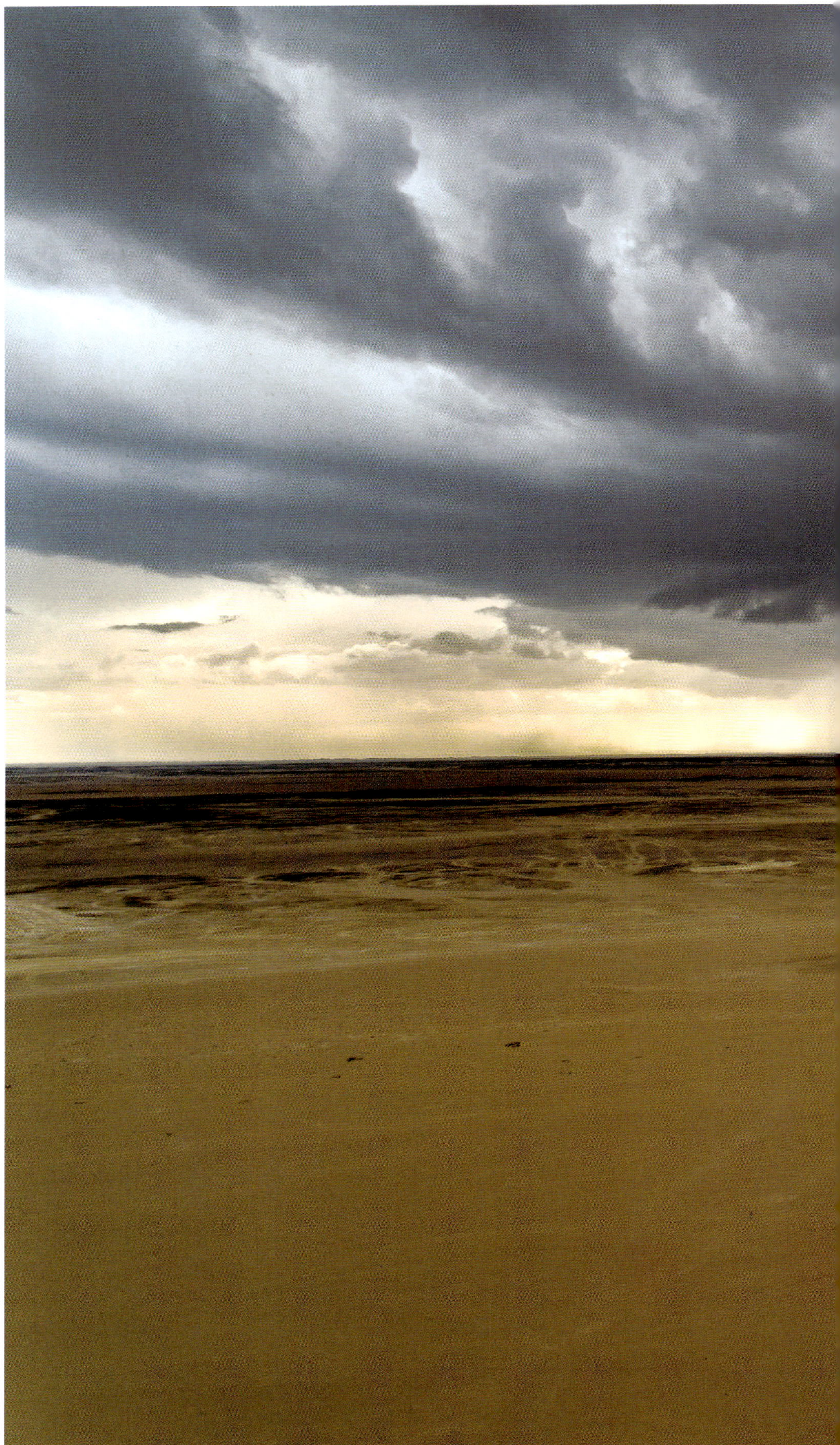

(Right) Cyclonic rainfall is usually in the months just before and after the *khareef*, and where and when it may fall is largely impossible to predict.

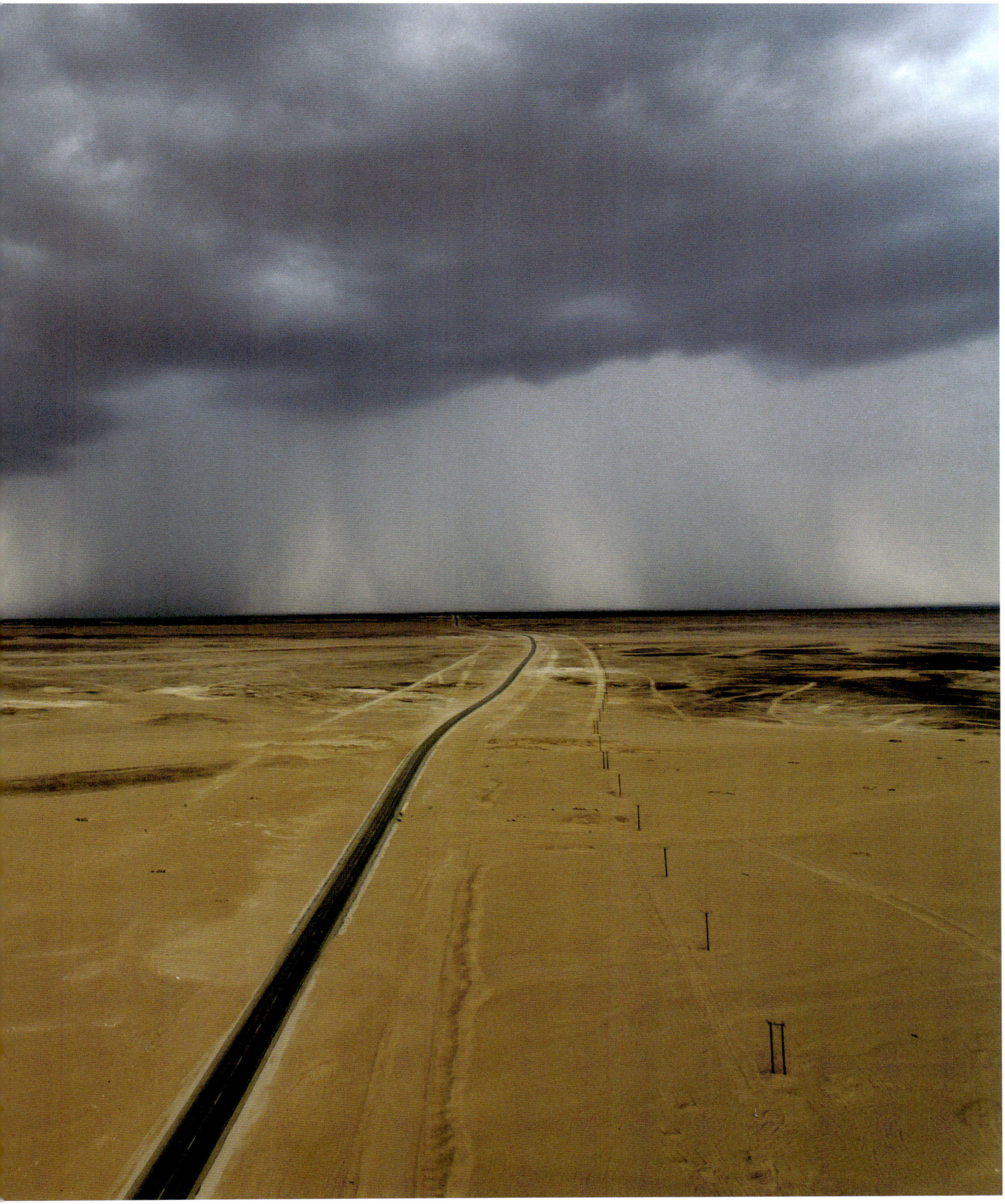

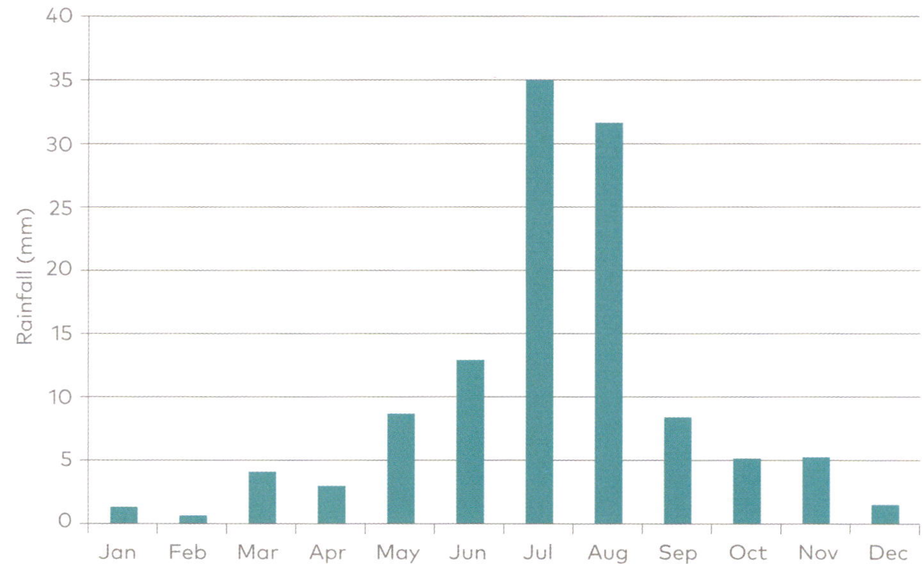

Fig. 7 Average monthly rainfall for Dhofar (data from 43 rainfall stations, 1992-2016)[36]

been recorded in each month but most is associated with the two periods of change, or transition, between the winter weather and the summer *khareef*– March to May and October to November. It is at this time when cyclonic storms are most likely; for example, Cyclone Mekunu of May 2018 brought 700 millimetres of rainfall to Shahb Asaayb on Jabal Al Qamar and 688 millimetres to Titam on Jabal Al Qara, many times the annual rainfall from the *khareef*. Elsewhere these storms are the only rainfall and the figure of 651 millimetres recorded in Hasik in May 2002 was greater than all the rainfall at Hasik over the preceding 10 years.

Where does the rain fall?

The *khareef* rainfall is mainly on the Jarbib, Jabal Al Qara and Jabal Al Qamar but it is not evenly distributed. The herdsmen have names for the different zones of the Jabal that reflect the quantity of available pasture and these in turn are the result of different amounts of *khareef* rainfall. The *khatm* is the southward escarpment up to about 800 metres, while most of the upper slopes and plateaux are collectively known as the *qatn*.

As the *khareef* clouds are blown across the Jarbib they yield a heavy drizzle, with much falling at the base of the *khatm*, where the plain meets the foothills. In good years, such as 2016, the *khareef* rainfall may reach 100 millimetres on the Jarbib, transforming it into a carpet of green. But in years of a weak *khareef*, like 2014, there may be just a few millimetres of rainfall and the Jarbib remains a dusty brown.

However, it is higher up the *khatm* where rainfall is highest. As the wind continues to push the clouds against the Jabal there is little escape as they are almost trapped between the Jabal and the temperature inversion overhead. Maximum rainfall is from 450 metres to 800 metres above sea level. Amongst the wettest places are Ambruf on Jabal Al Qamar and Arkabit, Tawi Aatayr and Kanzir on Jabal Al Qara– all 500-600 metres above sea level. Kanzir, on a ridge just west of Wadi Jarziz, enjoys an average annual rainfall of 427 millimetres, nearly 200 millimetres greater than any other location, making it the wettest place in Dhofar.

At elevations exceeding 800 metres– in the *qatn*– there is a noticeable, indeed more than 50%, decrease in rainfall to approximately 70 millimetres. These areas, reaching just over 1100 metres, straddle the watershed and in years of a weak *khareef* receive little rainfall. Jibjat (78 millimetres) in eastern Jabal Al Qara and Hijayf (74 millimetres) in central Jabal Al Qara are typical of the *qatn*, a combination of elevation, aspect and distance from the coast leaving them at the edge of the best of the *khareef* rainfall. Argut on Jabal Al Qamar lies at the edge of the *qatn* and the Najd, with an annual rainfall of just 29 millimetres.

Beyond the watershed is the arid southern Najd, where the *khareef* seems to have no discernible effect on the barren landscape. Here the clouds slip between the Jabal summit and

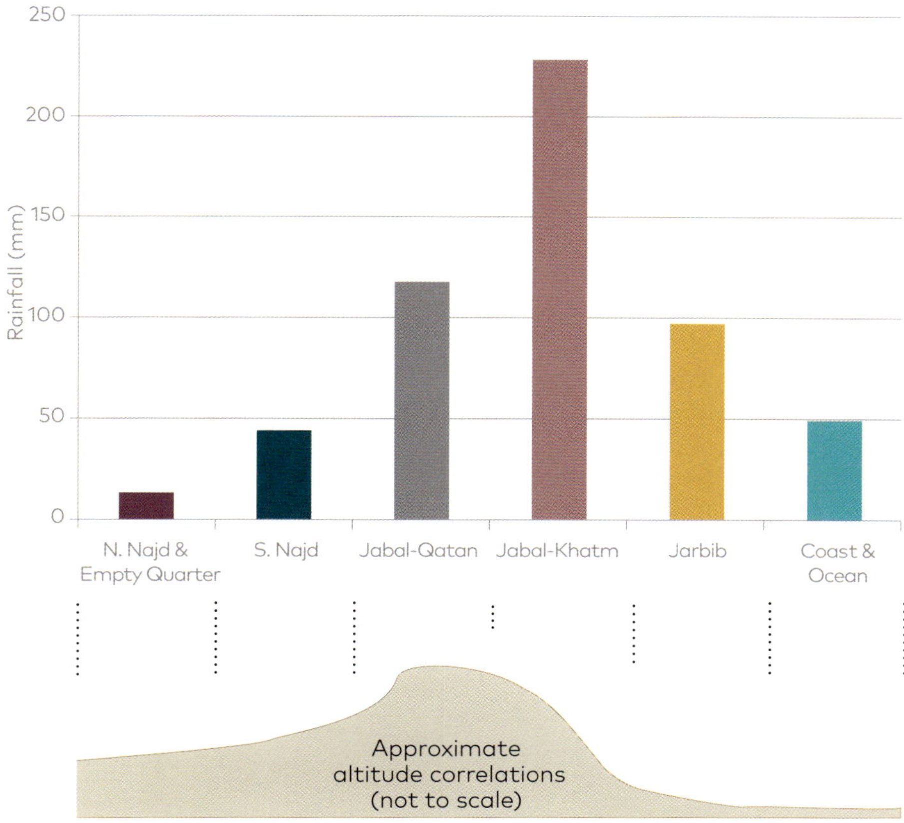

Fig. 8 Cross section of Dhofar showing annual rainfall for the different regions (data from 43 rainfall stations, 1992-2016).[36]

the inversion layer overhead and are blown north to evaporate over the hyper-arid desert. However, in doing so there is some rainfall. For example, both Uyun in Jabal Al Qara and Aydam in Jabal Al Qamar lie about 16 kilometres north of the discernible influence of the *khareef* but have rainfall of 11 millimetres and 24 millimetres respectively for the *khareef* months of June to September. Similarly, in the far east there is also a low level of precipitation at the west end of the largely arid Jabal Samhan although most of the southeast-facing mountain is unaffected by the *khareef*.

In addition to the *khareef* there are rain events, usually cyclonic, that can– as in the cyclones of 1996, 2007, 2011 and, especially, Mekunu in 2018–bring rainfall to most of the governorate, but on other occasions can be extremely localized, falling over just a few square kilometres. Although there is no clear pattern to where the non-*khareef* rainfall occurs, storms often arrive from the Arabian Sea, resulting in rainfall on the coast, the Al Hallaniyyat Islands and the Jabal. Rain rarely reaches the hyper-arid areas north of the Jabal and consequently the northern Najd and Empty Quarter are the driest zones of Dhofar. Here there are often many years without any rain and annual rainfall remains less than 30 millimetres for most areas, with Al Hashman, Ash Shisr and Muqshin having annual rainfall of 13, 12 and seven millimetres respectively, making them amongst the harshest places in Dhofar.

In May 2018 Cyclone Mekunu hit the coast near Al Mughsayl and tracked north and north-west. It brought up to 700 millimetres of rainfall to the Jabal (Shahb Asaayb), 172 millimetres to the southern Najd (Muday), 80 millimetres to the northern Najd (Mazunah) and 145 millimetres to Al Hashman in the Empty Quarter.

(Right) Mud cracks give the feeling of a parched desert landscape yet the flooding that followed Cyclone Mekunu in 2018 brought the first rainfall in many years to vast areas of the Najd and the Empty Quarter.

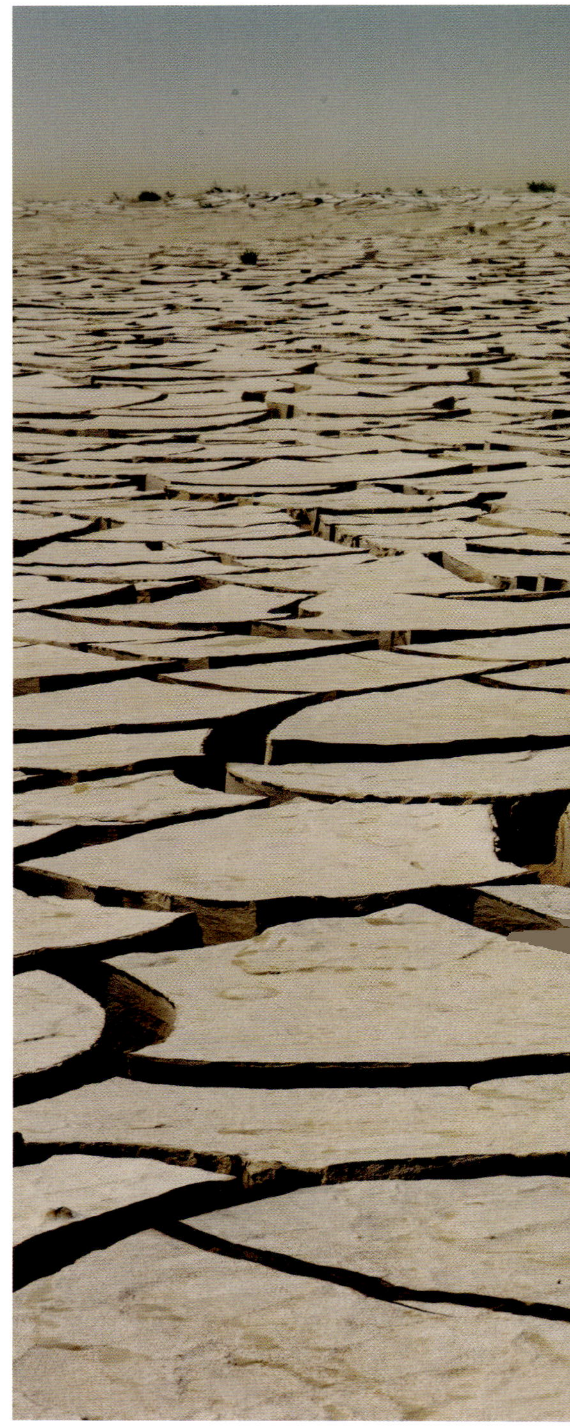

Climate Change

It has been forecasted that by 2100 the temperature will have risen across the globe by 1.4-1.5C since 1990.[37] In the Middle East and North Africa maximum temperatures are expected to increase from around 43°C to 50°C by the end of the century.[38] A study of temperature and rainfall data from Salalah from 1943-2008 recorded a significant increase in temperature over that time but not of yearly rainfall.[39] However, the same study concluded that *khareef* rainfall had declined by 3.72 millimetres every 10 years while another study of rainfall records from 1977 to 2003 found no significant trends of increase or decrease.[40]

Not surprisingly the situation with respect to climate change is not clear. There is some evidence of warming and of a reduction in *khareef* rainfall but this is not conclusive. Interestingly some local herdsmen do feel that the *khareef* is weakening each year and consider that this explains the deteriorating condition of the *khareef* woodlands and grasslands.

Fig. 9 shows *khareef* rainfall on the *khatm*, the wettest area of the Jabal, and there is some suggestion of a decline since the 1990s. However, the chart also suggests a slight increase during recent years. Clearly there is great variability and a

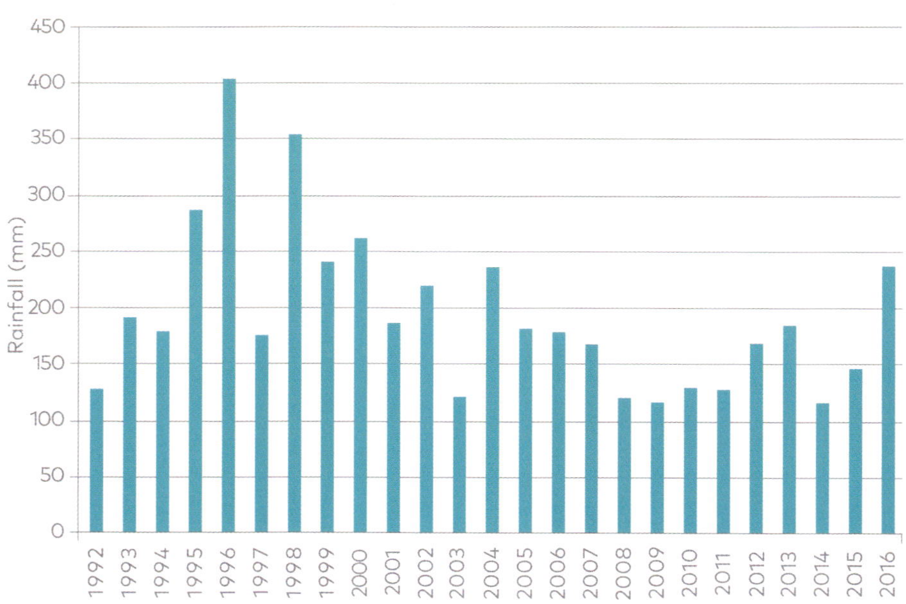

Fig. 9 Average annual *khareef* rainfall for the *khatm* zone of the Jabal (data from 43 rainfall stations, June-September, 1992-2016).[36]

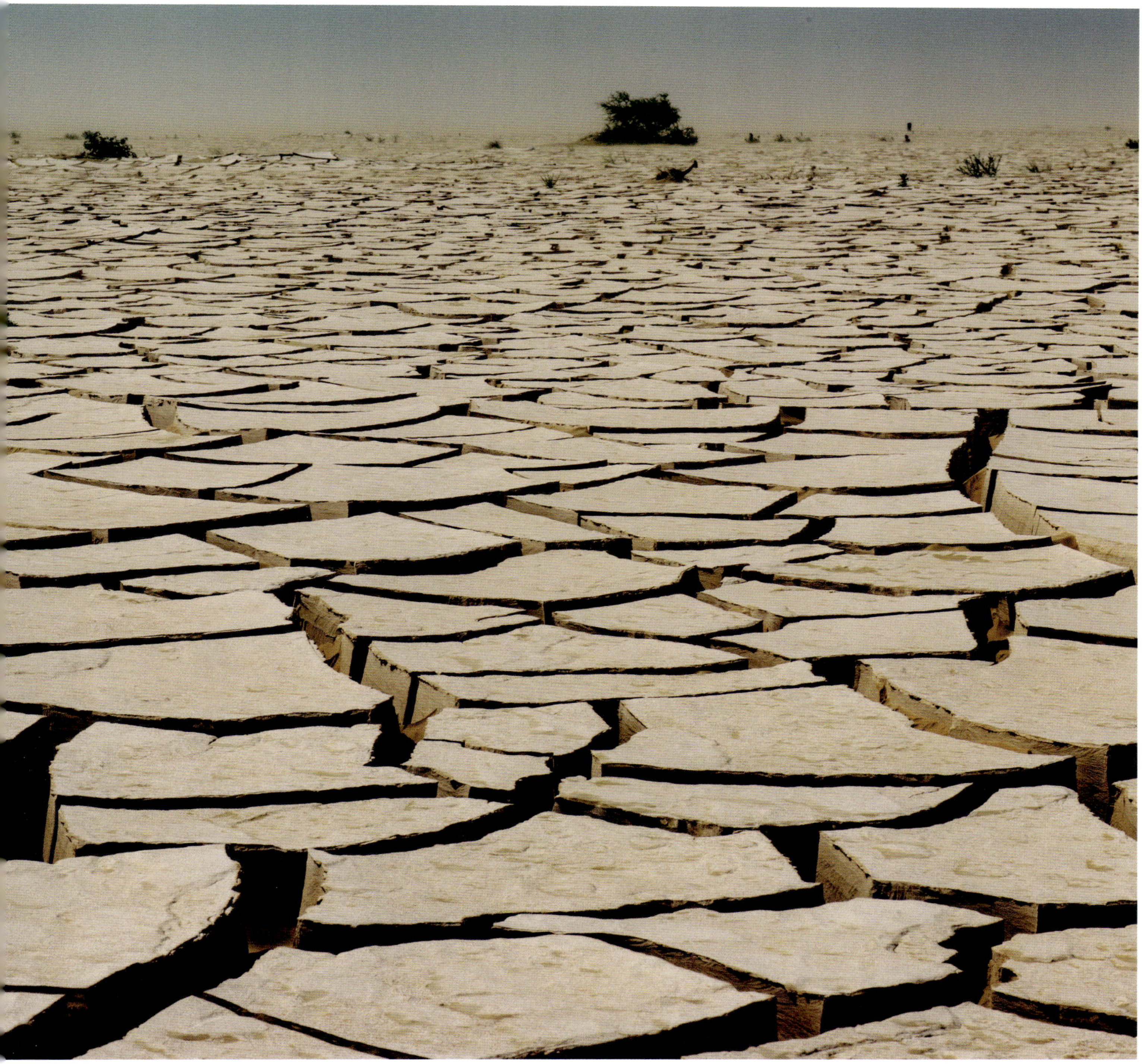

very recent study of Dhofar's *khareef* cloud cover, using satellite imagery, for 17 years (2000-2016) concluded that the annual variability in *khareef* cloud cover masked any long-term trend.[41] In other words, there were years of strong *khareef* and years of weak *khareef* but no evidence of any overall increase or decrease in cloud cover and thus, by implication, also rainfall. Interestingly, climate models for the Indian or Southwest Monsoon do not predict a future decrease but rather an increase of 5-10% in rainfall.[42] Indeed, the strengthening of the Southwest Monsoon has recently been linked to the increased occurrence of harmful algal blooms in the Arabian Sea, including off the coast of Dhofar.[43] The Dhofar *khareef* might in fact not be weakening but strengthening, which could be good news for the Jabal though the downside is that more extreme climate events, including cyclones, are likely.

4 Water

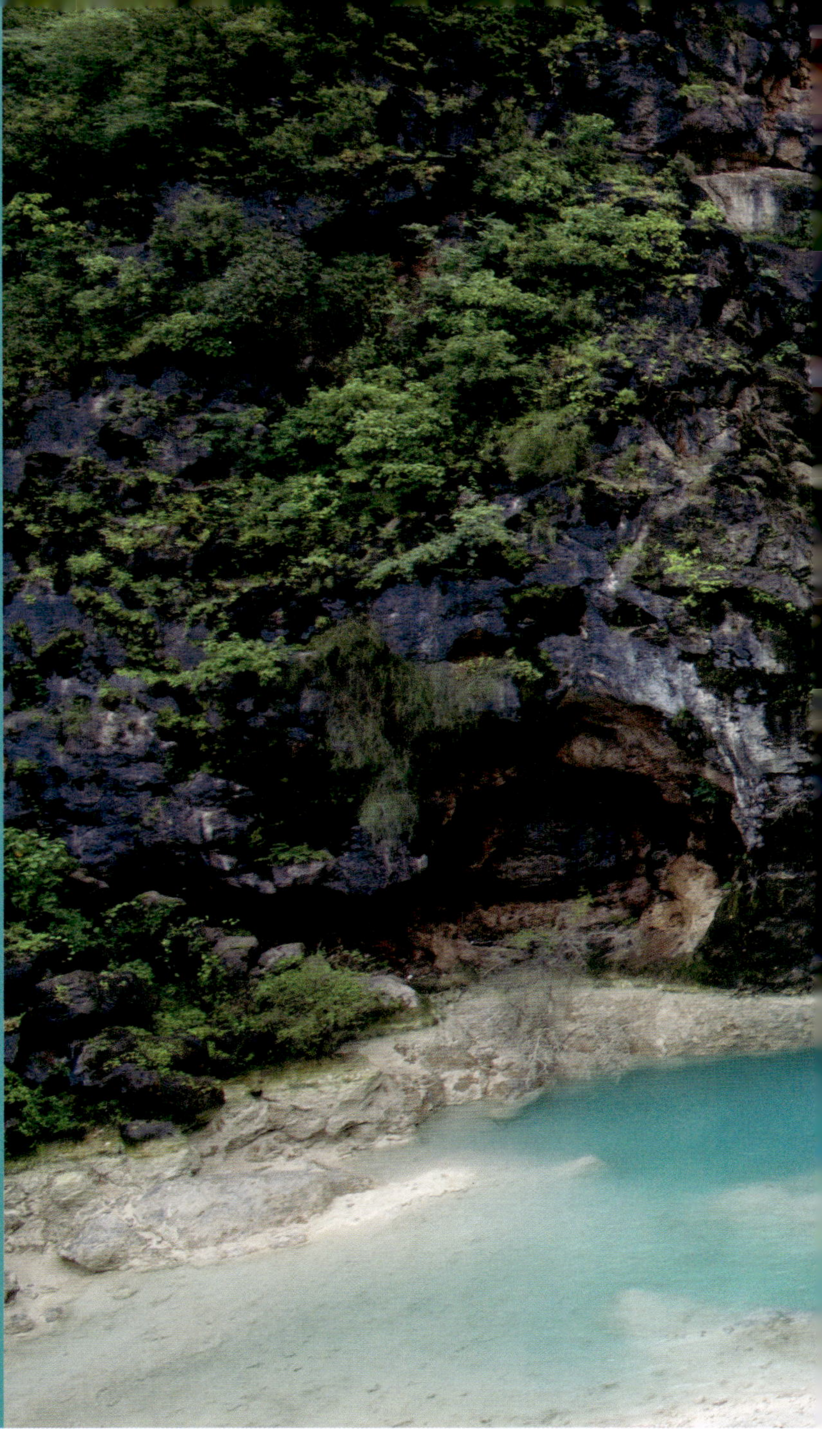

Introduction

Most of Dhofar is true desert yet the region has broad freshwater lakes, pools, numerous springs and coastal lagoons. Some are short-lived but many are permanent. Underground there is an enormous reservoir of ancient water. Without water there would be no life, and as the people of the desert know, water must be cherished.

There is no single source of water in Dhofar; there are many and they are connected. First and foremost is the annual *khareef* or Southwest Monsoon that brings water to the Jabal and the *Jarbib*. Second is rainfall that falls outside of monsoon (often in the form of tropical storms and cyclones), which can bring huge volumes of water and

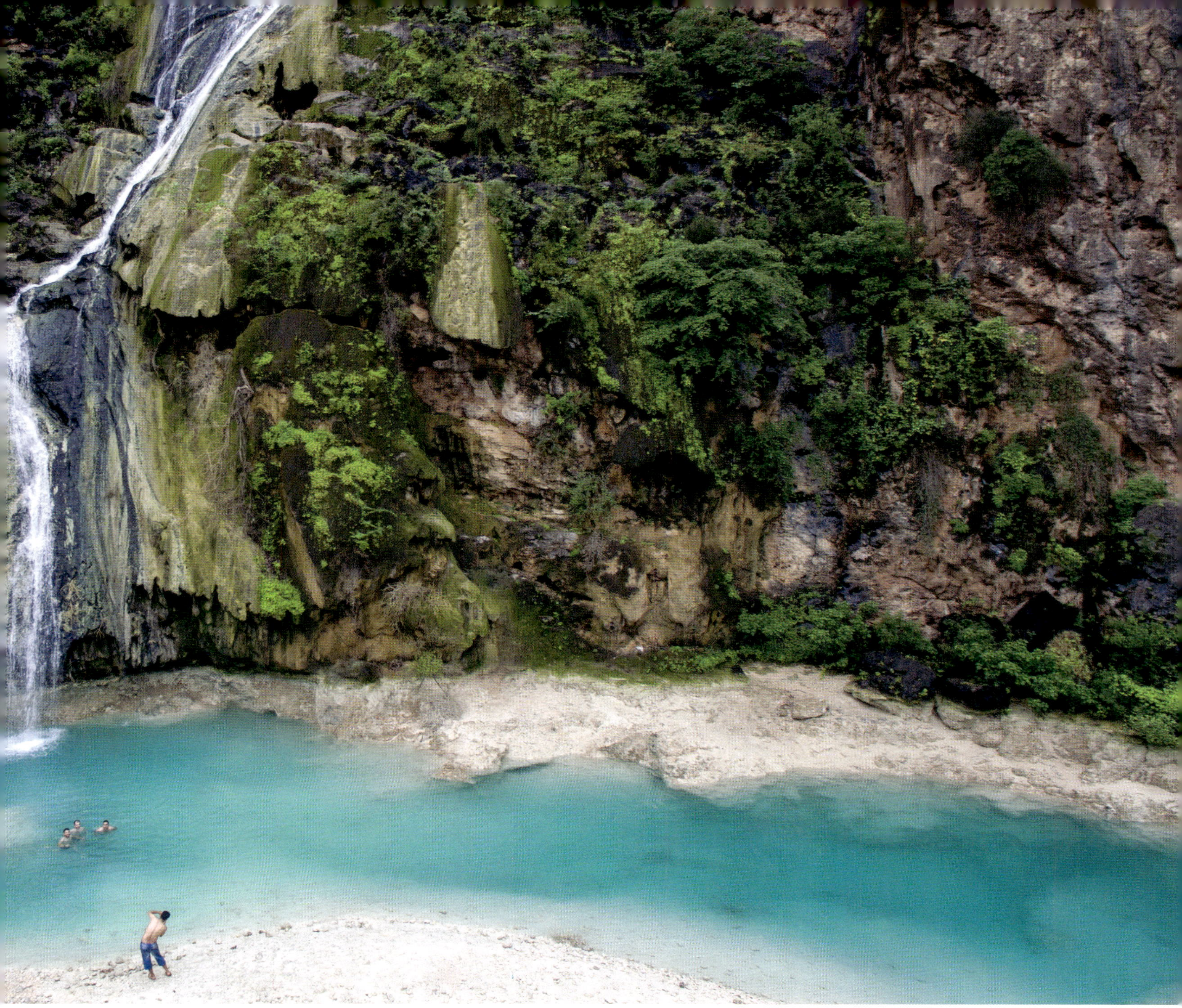

can reach areas of the Najd and Empty Quarter that have been dry for years. Third is groundwater, some ancient, from which water seeps to replenish Dhofar's springs and lakes and in modern times is pumped to the surface for man's use. Then there are the fogs and dews, especially in coastal areas, that are a small but important source of water. Finally there is seawater that is turned into fresh water.

(Above) Water is Dhofar's single most valuable resource and, during the monsoon, water that is captured by the mountains, especially by the trees and shrubs, helps recharge aquifers and replenish surface pools. In years of a strong monsoon, overflowing springs, such as Ayn Kur, attract large numbers of visitors.

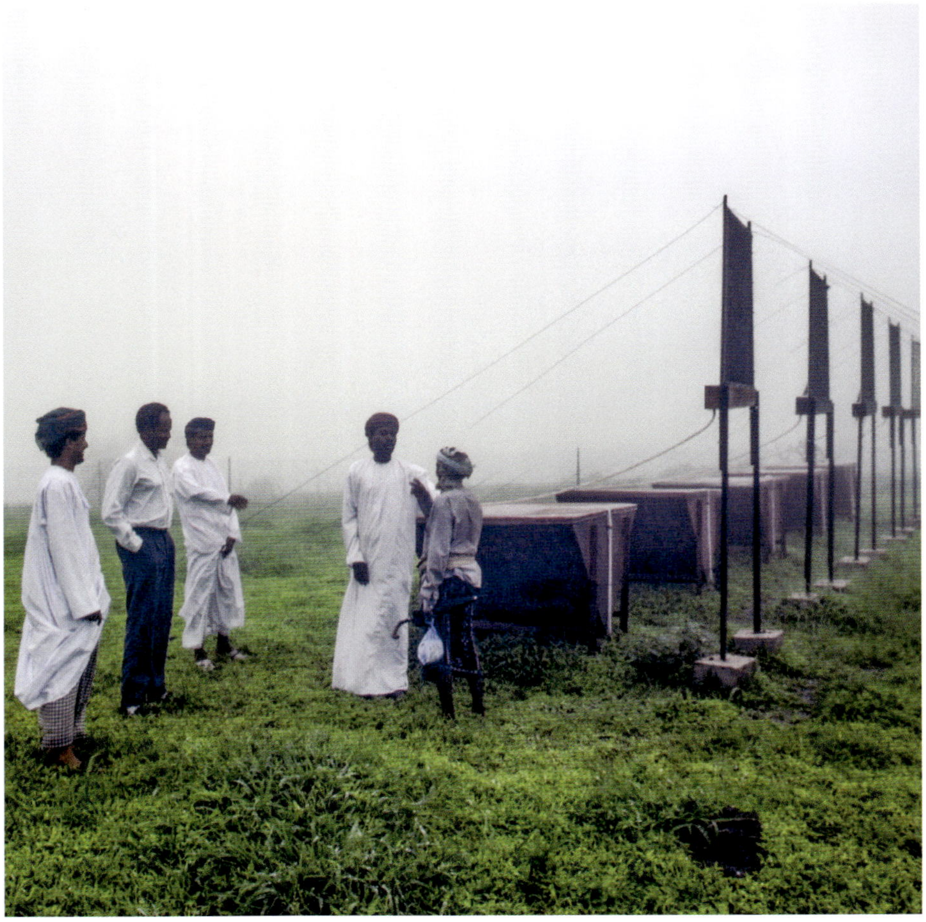

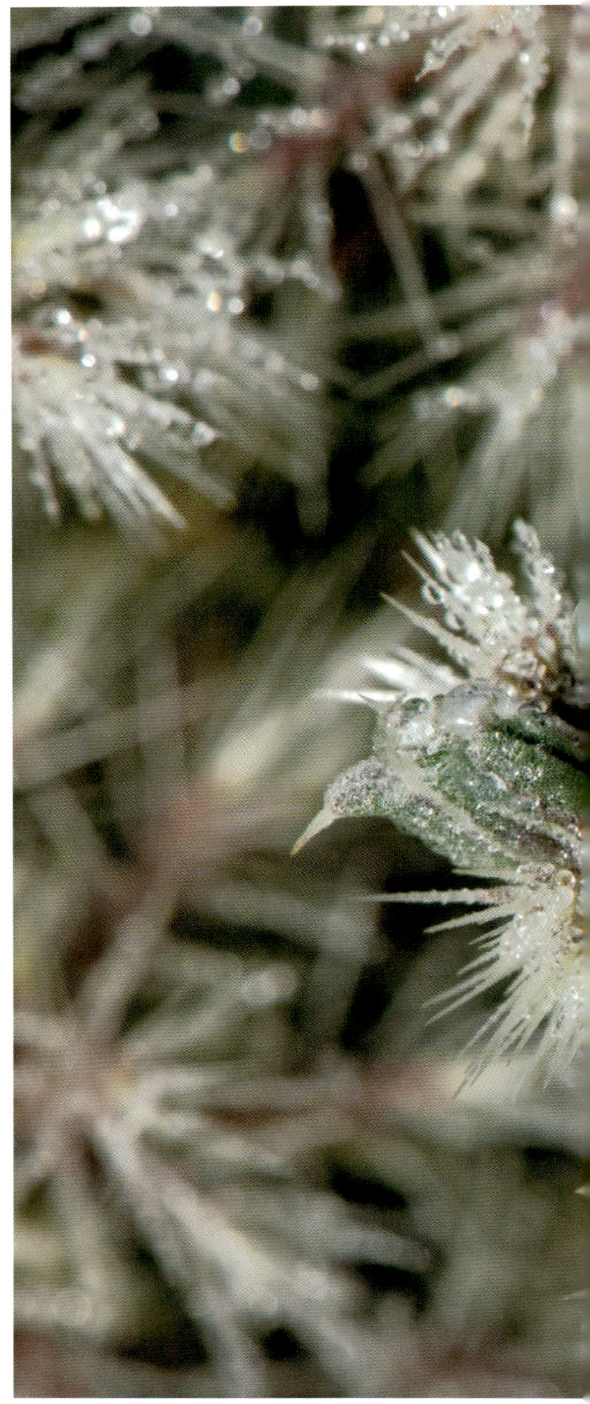

Monsoon Rainfall

In late June the clouds gather over the Jabal and light rainfall and drizzle fall on the parched earth. The cracked clay soils absorb large amounts of water but when they are saturated the water begins to fill surface pockets and trickles underground to replenish aquifers in the limestone below. In years of a strong *khareef*, such as 2016, the prolonged drizzle leads to surface-water flow, with small streams forming amongst the forests on the south side of the Jabal. Permanent springs flood and give rise to waterfalls that in turn fill deep plunge pools that may have been dry for years. Ayn Kur on Jabal Al Qara is a good example and in 2016 the waterfall flowed continuously from late July to mid-September.

The rainfall and drizzle that is enjoyed by summer visitors to Dhofar is not the only source of monsoon water. The low-lying cloud that blankets the Jabal is essentially fog and is made up of countless tiny water droplets that are blown north. Unless they are blown onto a surface or intercepted by trees, the droplets are pushed to the top of the Jabal where they meet the blistering heat of the Najd; the water evaporates and is lost. However, lots of these droplets do get intercepted by trees, and this condensation is a major source of water in Dhofar. In a study of this phenomenon, 60,000 litres of water was collected under a single dripping fig tree during the monsoon season at Masroob on Jabal Al Qara.[44] At Jawjab, also on Jabal Al Qara, it was estimated that total precipitation under the canopy of *Anogeissus dhofarica* trees was three times as high as rainfall, indicating that the trees capture significant quantities of fog water as it is blown through the canopy.[45] It is believed that in turn this captured water contributes significantly to recharging the

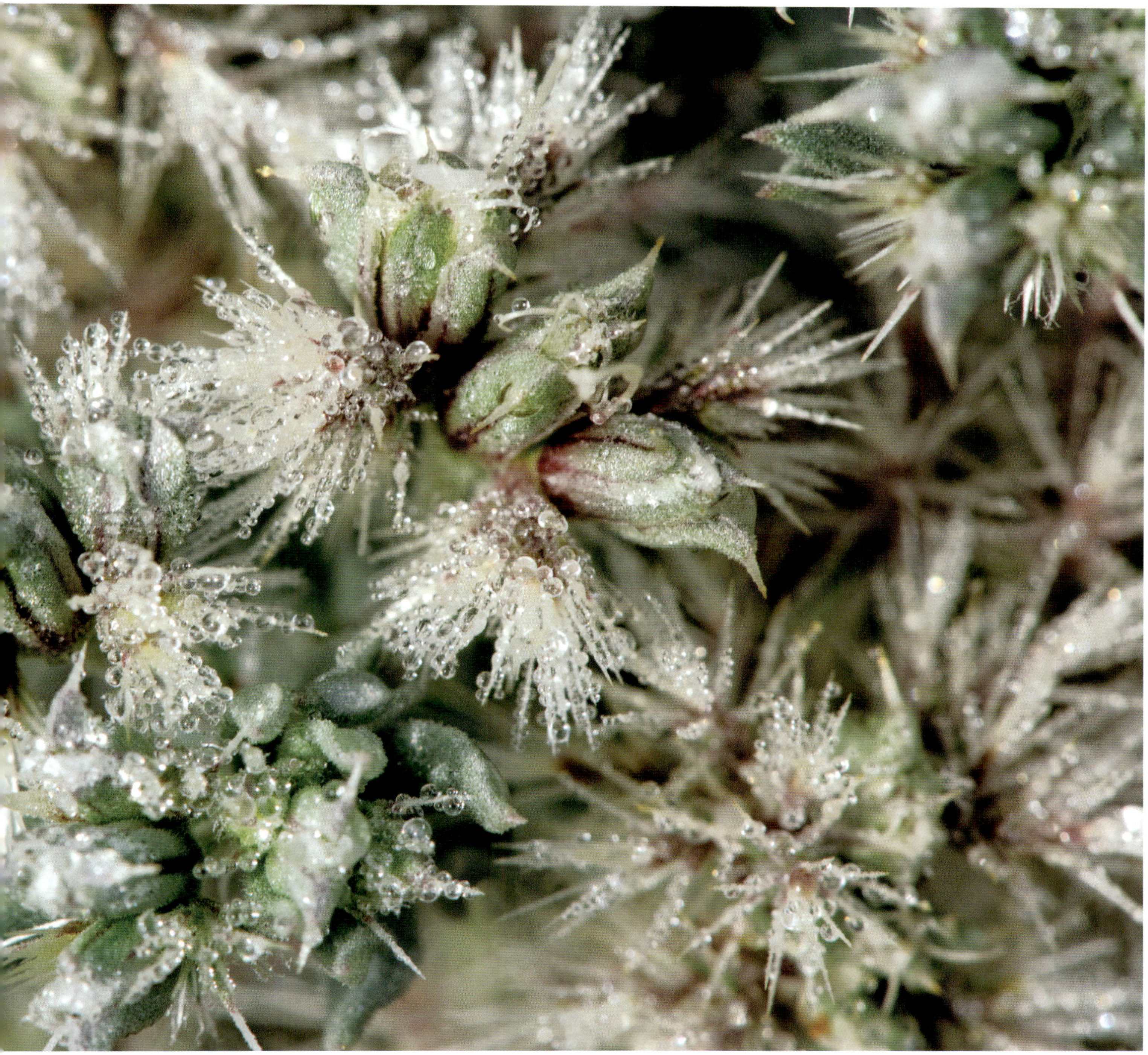

Salalah plain aquifer.[46]

The potential of Dhofar's monsoon fog as a source of water was recognised in the 1980s and mesh screens, erected at different locations on the Jabal, yielded average collection rates of 30 litres of water per square metre per day during the monsoon season.[44] In the early 2000s further experiments were carried out and mesh mist-collectors erected just south of Qayrun Hayrti produced an average of 60 litres of water per square metre of mesh per day during July and August.[47] Daily collection rates are amongst the highest in the world and the water is considered to be potable.[48]

Studies of the collection and use of fog water began in the early 1980s ***(above left)***. Even the tiniest plants, such as *Blepharis dhufarensis*, Ji. 'Ayźob ***(above right)*** collect fog water. Where vegetation is absent, fog water is blown north over the Jabal, where it evaporates and is lost to the system.

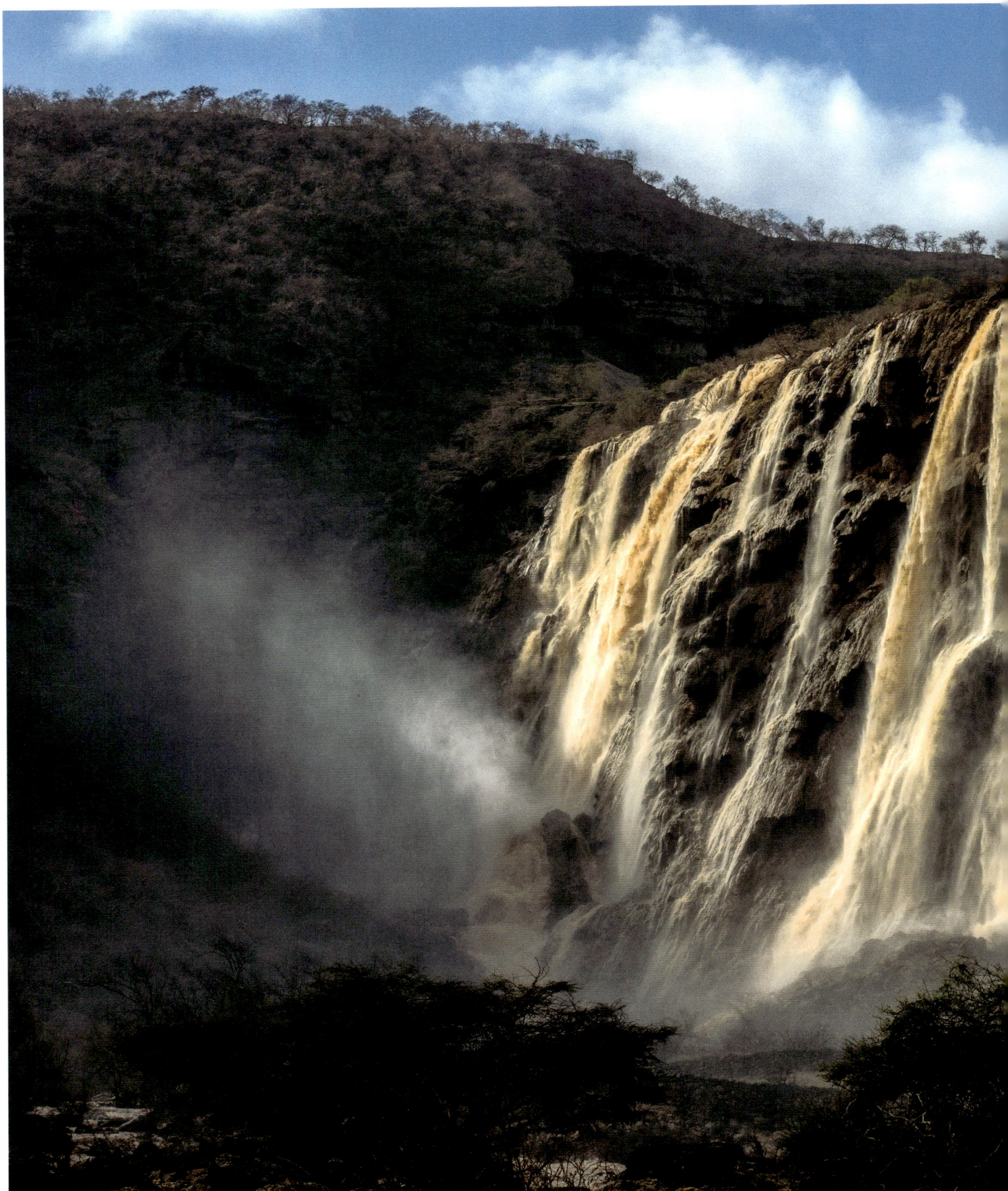

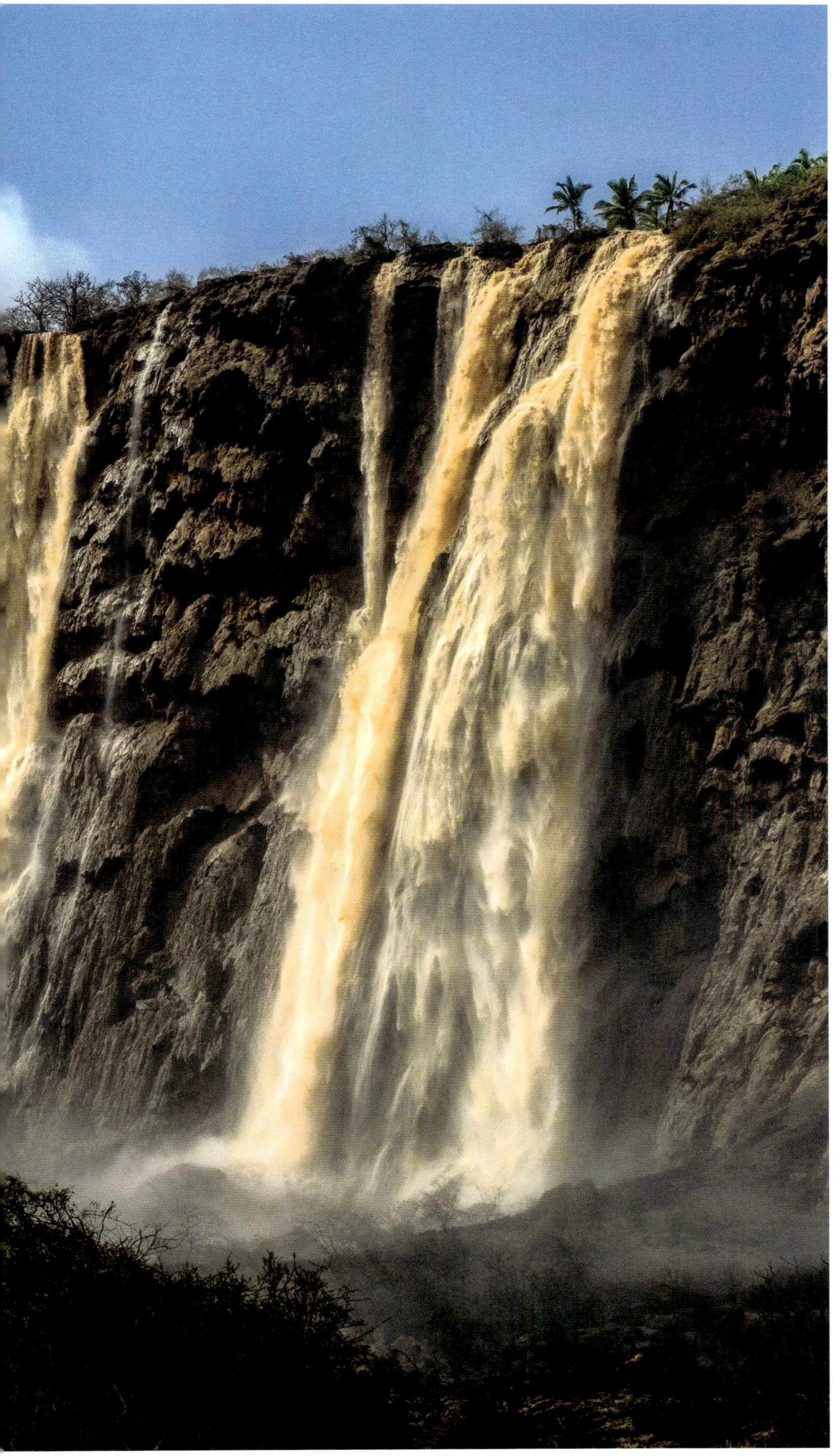

Rainfall

Across the world, rainfall is the primary source of fresh water, whether collected in surface catchments or accumulated in underground aquifers. In Dhofar rainfall is rare but every few years frontal rainfall, tropical storms and cyclones result in heavy downfalls. Sometimes they can be very localised, perhaps falling over just a few square kilometres, while at other times there is rainfall throughout the governorate. When rainfall is particularly intense it may result in flash floods, especially in the Jabal, where floods typically last a few hours and usually come with little warning. The usually dry wadis are transformed into raging torrents, and waterfalls such as the towering Darbat Falls, which may have been dormant for years, come alive.

In May 2018 Dhofar was struck by Mekunu, a Category Two tropical cyclone that made landfall just west of Salalah. Up to 700 millimetres of rain fell, wadis and waterfalls across Dhofar flooded, and record flow-rates were recorded. On the north side of Jabal Al Qara, in the southern Najd, peak flow rates reached 2,411 cubic metres per second while in Wadi Darbat a maximum rate of 4,043 cubic metres per second was recorded– more than double

(Left) Only after heavy rainfall, in this case Cyclone Mekunu in 2018, does water plunge over the 150-metre-high travertine falls of Wadi Darbat.

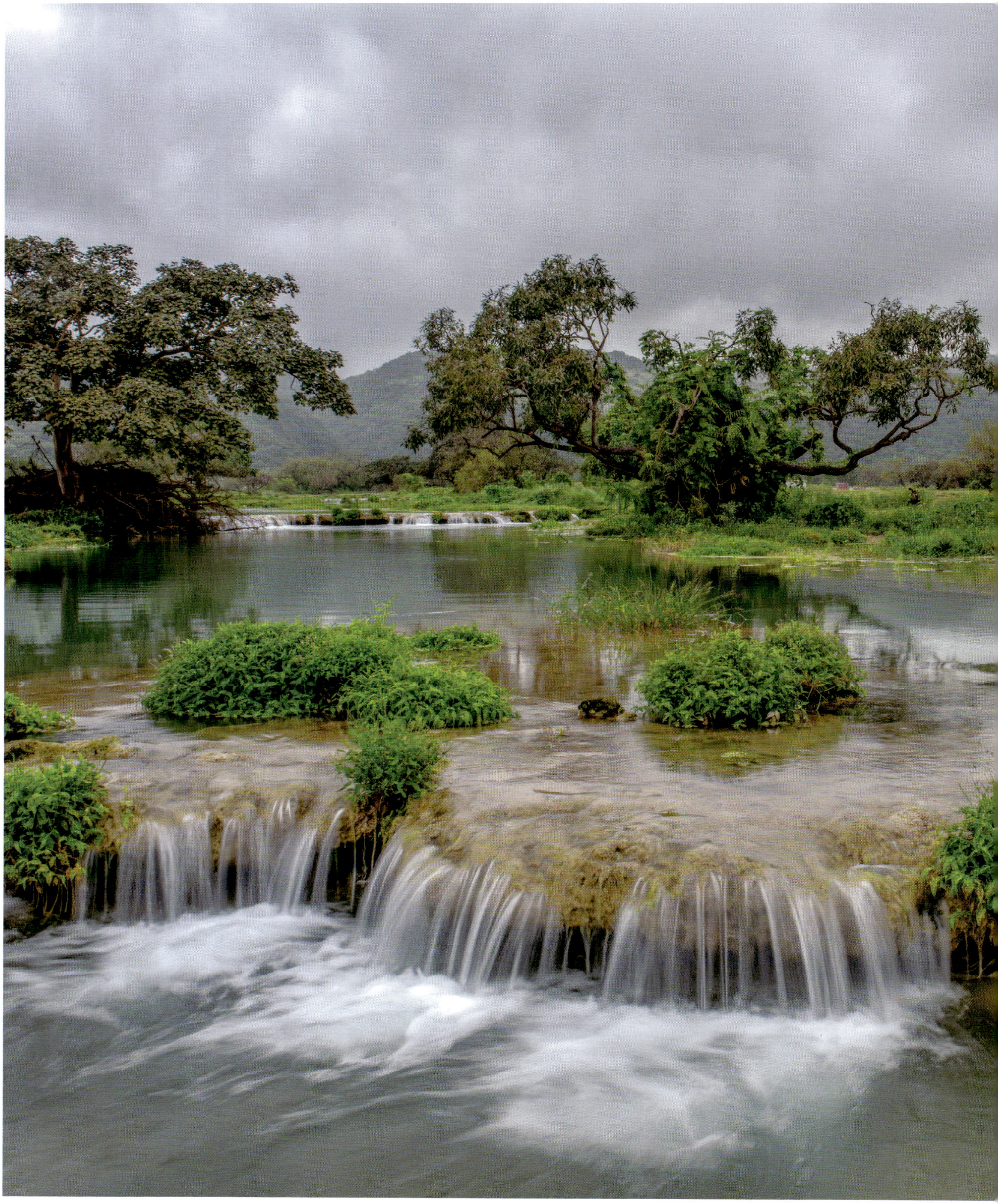

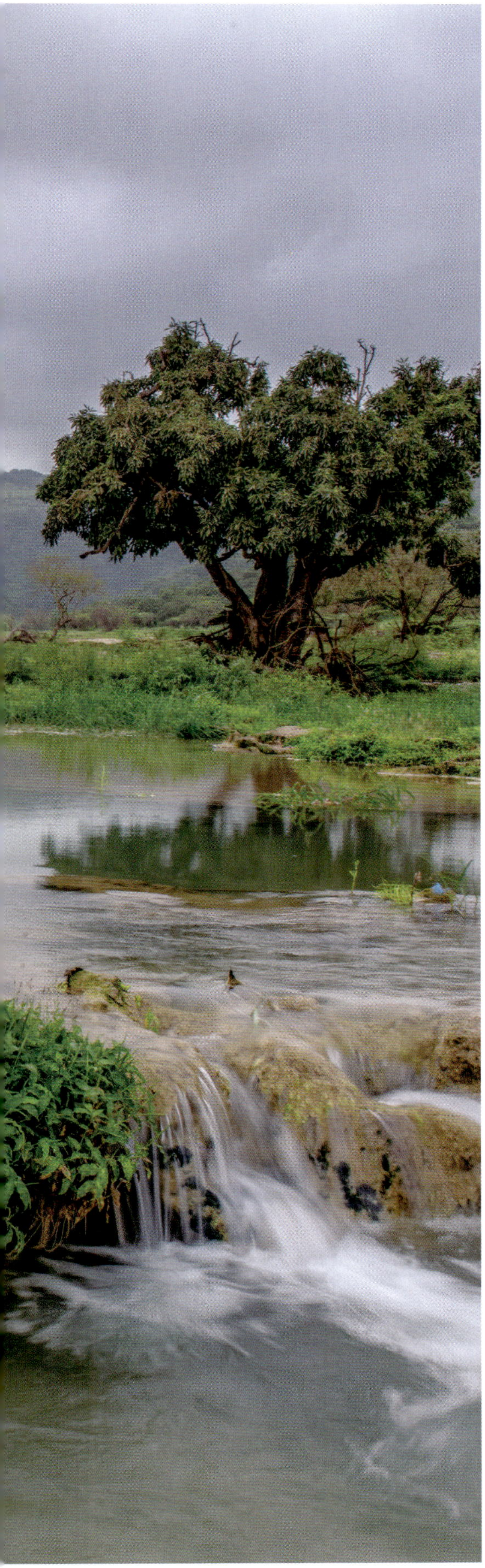

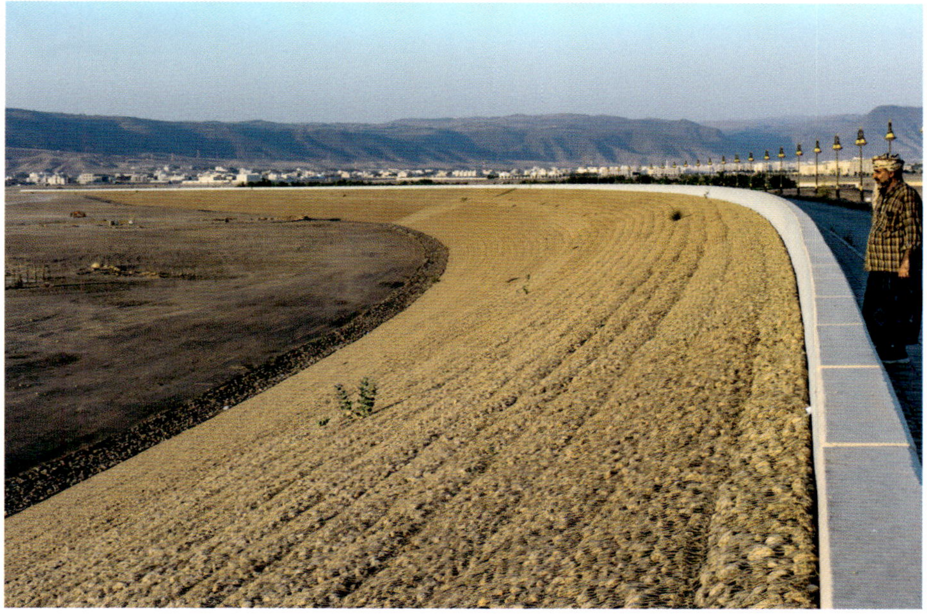

the existing record of 1,700 cubic metres per second for a cyclone, in 1977.[36]

Although most water from heavy rainfall finds its way deep underground or reaches the sea, floods also replenish existing spring-fed pools and form new pools that may remain for several months. In the Jabal and the Najd these pools are typically found on the dry wadi bed where flooding over thousands of years has scoured out potholes and other shallow structures capable of holding water. Further north in the open and largely flat desert, heavy rain and flooding may leave expansive open pools in shallow surface depressions, particularly in the broad courses of northward flowing wadis. Following Cyclone Mekunu, flooding wadis flowed north, where they formed huge lakes close to Muqshin in the northern Najd, more than 250 kilometres north of where most rain had fallen.

These ephemeral pools, whether in the Jabal or the open desert, quickly become havens for wildlife and in the past were life-giving for rural people and their livestock. Many waterless areas were largely inaccessible to people and rainfall not only provided them with a supply of drinking water but also meant that fresh grazing could be found for their goats and camels.

Since 1970 dams have been built to prevent flooding, for surface-water storage and to allow recharge of the aquifers. The largest of these dams is the 6.1-kilometre-long and 20-metre-high crescent-shaped guard dam built to protect the city of Salalah. Also close to Salalah is the Sahalnawt recharge dam, while there are a number of small storage dams built across the Jabal, including one on the plateau of Jabal Samhan. The dams, particularly Sahalnawt dam, protected Salalah City during cyclone Mekunu.

Winter rainfall as well as tropical storms and cyclones help replenish groundwater, often leading to increased flows of springs, as occurred in Wadi Darbat ***(left)*** and across Dhofar following Cyclone Mekunu in 2018.

Salalah dam ***(above)***, built following Cyclone Keila in 2011, proved very effective in preventing flood damage from Cyclone Mekunu.

Groundwater

In the limestone rocks that underlie most of Dhofar there are vast aquifers where water is stored in saturated rock, fractures and caverns. The water can only be brought to the surface by natural springs or by pumping from boreholes. In the hyper-arid Najd and the Empty Quarter, where rainfall is extremely rare, this is usually the only available water.

North of the Jabal is the Umm Er Radhuma aquifer system, known as the UER, which underlies much of southern Arabia and in Oman extends over a large area from the Dhofar Jabal in the south to the edge of the Al Hajar mountains in the north. The width of the UER is 200-600 metres and the general flow of water is north- and north-eastward. The bulk of the water is very old and has long been considered to be between 20,000 and 35,000 years old, but recent studies suggest this may as much as 550,000 years.[49] The UER is recharged very slowly by water from the annual monsoon but more quickly by rare cyclonic rainfall.

South of the Jabal the limestone rock and the covering of alluvium that underlies the Jarbib close to Salalah City form the distinct Adawnab aquifer that is connected to the UER. The maximum width of the aquifer is about 120 metres, close to Al Husaylah, and this is where the best-quality water is found. However, it is generally 60-70 metres wide and thins to the east and west where the water becomes increasingly brackish.[50] This water is recharged by water flowing from the mountains following rainfall and during the monsoon.[46]

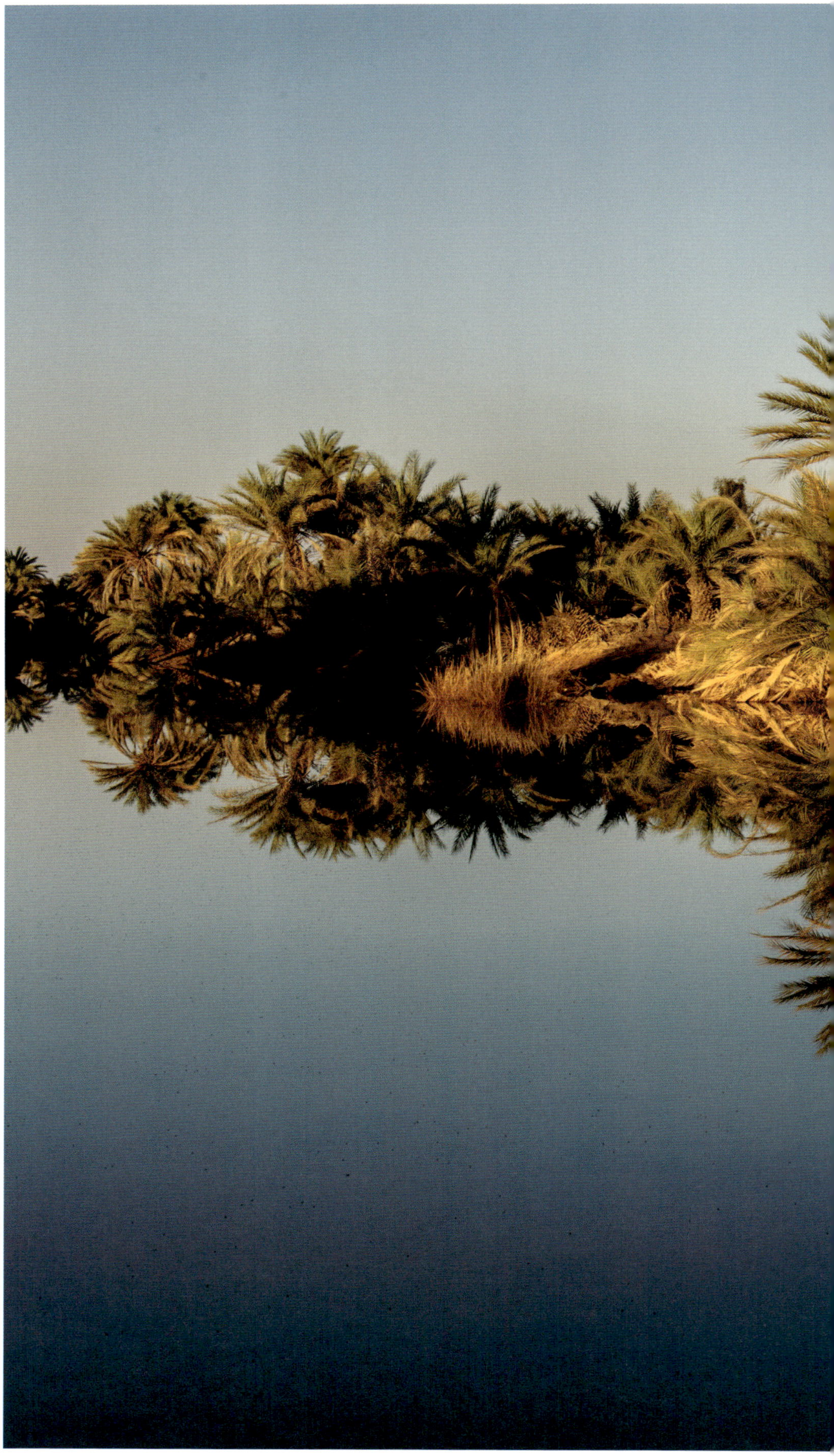

There are just a handful of natural springs in the northern Najd. Wadi Muqshin ***(right)*** is by far the largest.

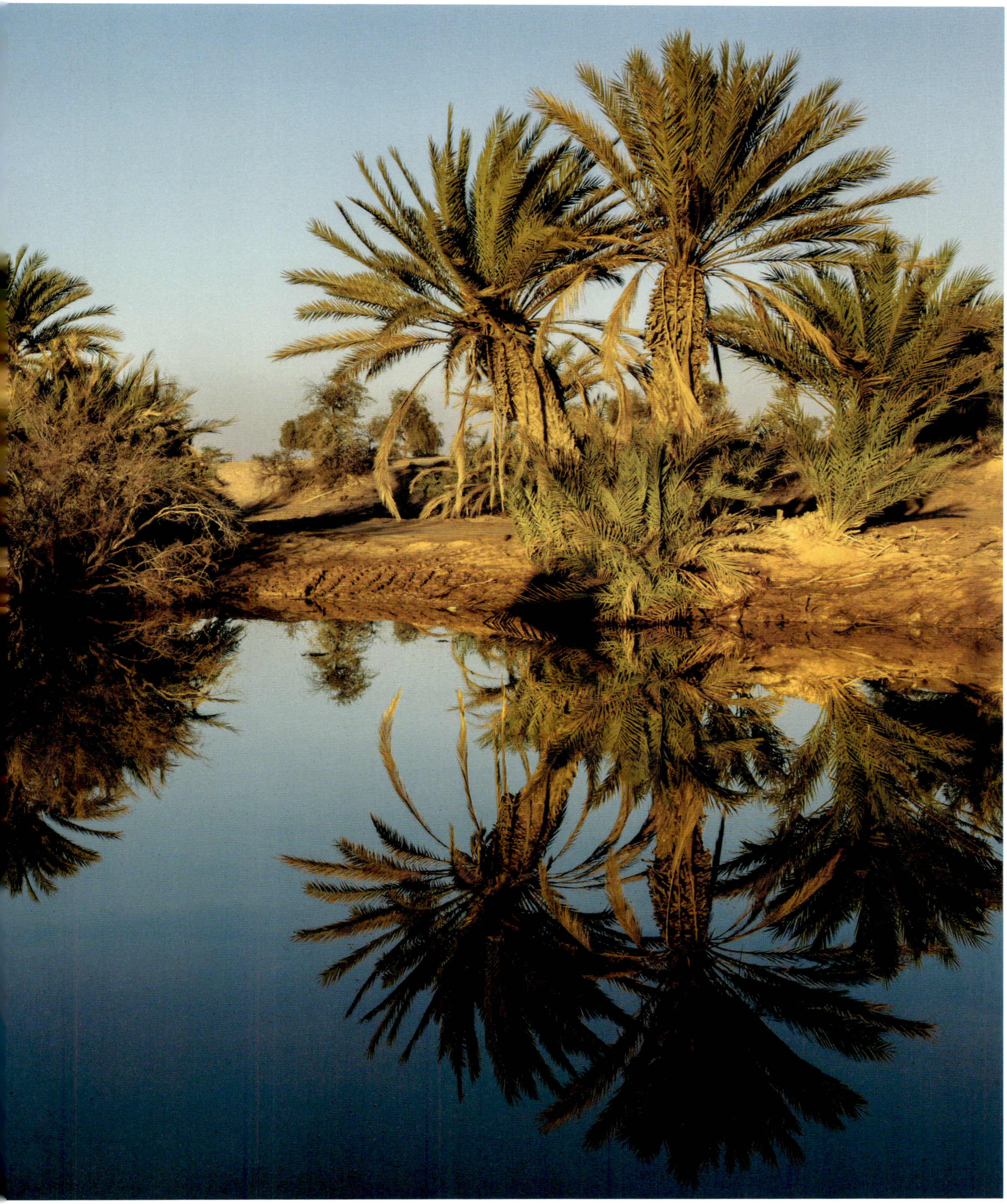

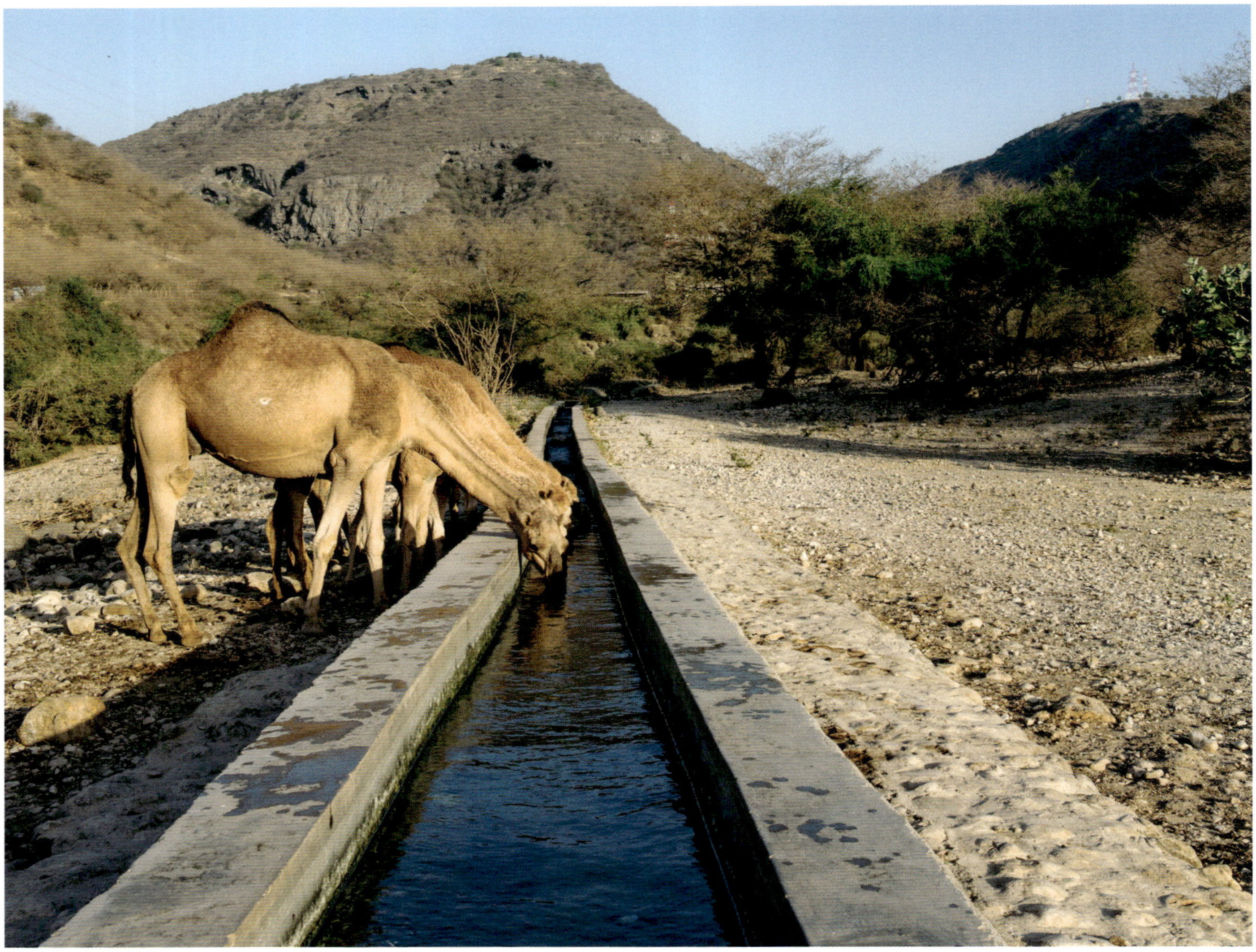

Springs and Seepages

A spring, know as *ayn* in both Arabic and Jibbāli, is any natural situation where underground water reaches the Earth's surface. Springs range from tiny seeps, characterised by low flow-rate and little volume, such as those seen on the Al Hallaniyyat Islands, to the gushing springs of the southern foothills of Jabal Al Qara.

Historically springs were the most important source of water in all regions of Dhofar. They determined where people lived and, most importantly for the predominantly rural community, where they grazed their livestock. For the largely cattle-owning people of the Jabal, water was often a greater constraint than the availability of grazing. The location of springs and access to them, especially during the driest months just prior to the monsoon, were the main factors determining the location of permanent and temporary encampments. Cattle could not be grazed where areas were waterless or where traditional agreements prevented access to springs. Similarly, in the Najd the camel-and goat-herders, especially at times of drought, had to remain close to permanent springs.

The routes of travellers were also largely defined by the availability of water. Bertram Thomas and Sheikh Saleh Bin Kalut Al Kathiri,

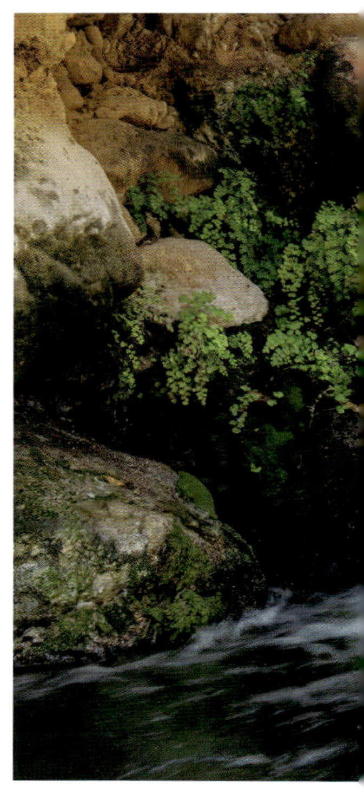

who crossed the Empty Quarter in 1930-31, took water from Hanun, south of Thumrayt, before heading north to Ash Shisr, where on arrival Thomas noted, 'for it is the first water-hole we meet for five days, and after leaving it there will be none for a further seven or eight.'[23] While Thomas went west from Ash Shisr, in 1946-47 Wilfred Thesiger, went north from Ash Shisr, taking nine days to reach water at Wadi Muqshin.[27]

Springs of the Jabal

Most of Dhofar's springs are in the southern foothills of Jabal Al Qara and Jabal Al Qamar and while some are permanent many flow only after the monsoon rains and are dry by the following summer. The major springs, most of which are permanent, arise from the base of the southern escarpments close to the 100-metre contour and include Ayn Jarziz, Ayn Sahalnawt, Ayn Razat, Ayn Hamran and Ayn Tabruq in Jabal Al Qara. Of these, Ayn Razat has the highest rate of discharge, with an average annual flow-rate of 188 litres per second.[50] Rates of discharge fall slowly with time after the monsoon to reach their lowest levels in May, indicating the important role that the annual monsoon plays in recharging the aquifer. It has been estimated that these five principal springs contribute an estimated 30% of the total recharge to the Salalah plain and in most cases the water-quality is good.[51] In the 1930s, on the instruction of Sultan Said Bin Taimur, three water channels (*aflaj*) were constructed to carry water from the springs of Jarziz, Sahalnawt and Razat more than 10 kilometres across the coastal plain to farms close to Salalah.[52] In Jabal Al Qamar the major springs include Ayn Sarfait, Ayn Khadrafi, Ayn Al Mughsayl (Wadi Sayq), Ayn Adi, Ayn Hiak and Ayn Habreyat.

Springs are also found along the coast and many of the coastal *khawrs* have an inflow of fresh water either from springs upstream of the *khawr* or that

Small springs in the foothills of Jabal Al Qara flow throughout the year ***(centre)***, and close to Salalah city water is carried across the plain by channels ***(e.g. Falaj Jarziz, left)*** for drinking and agriculture. Several springs are popular tourist sites ***(e.g. Ayn Razat, below)***.

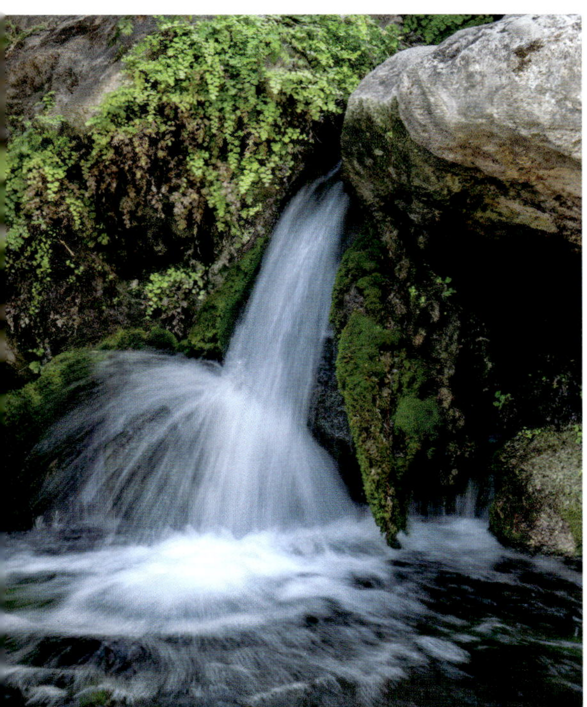

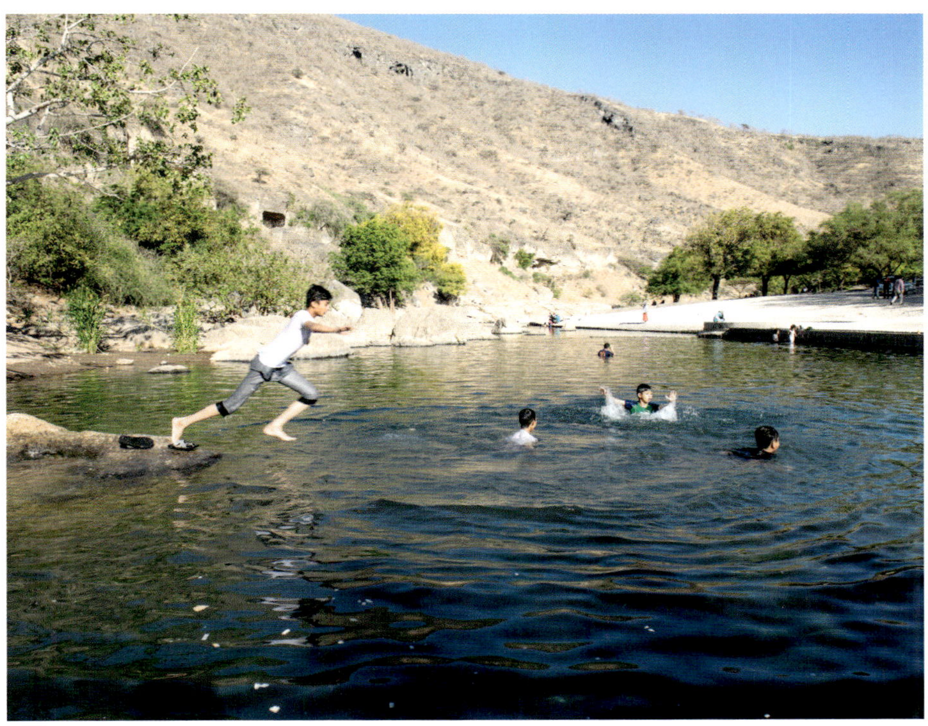

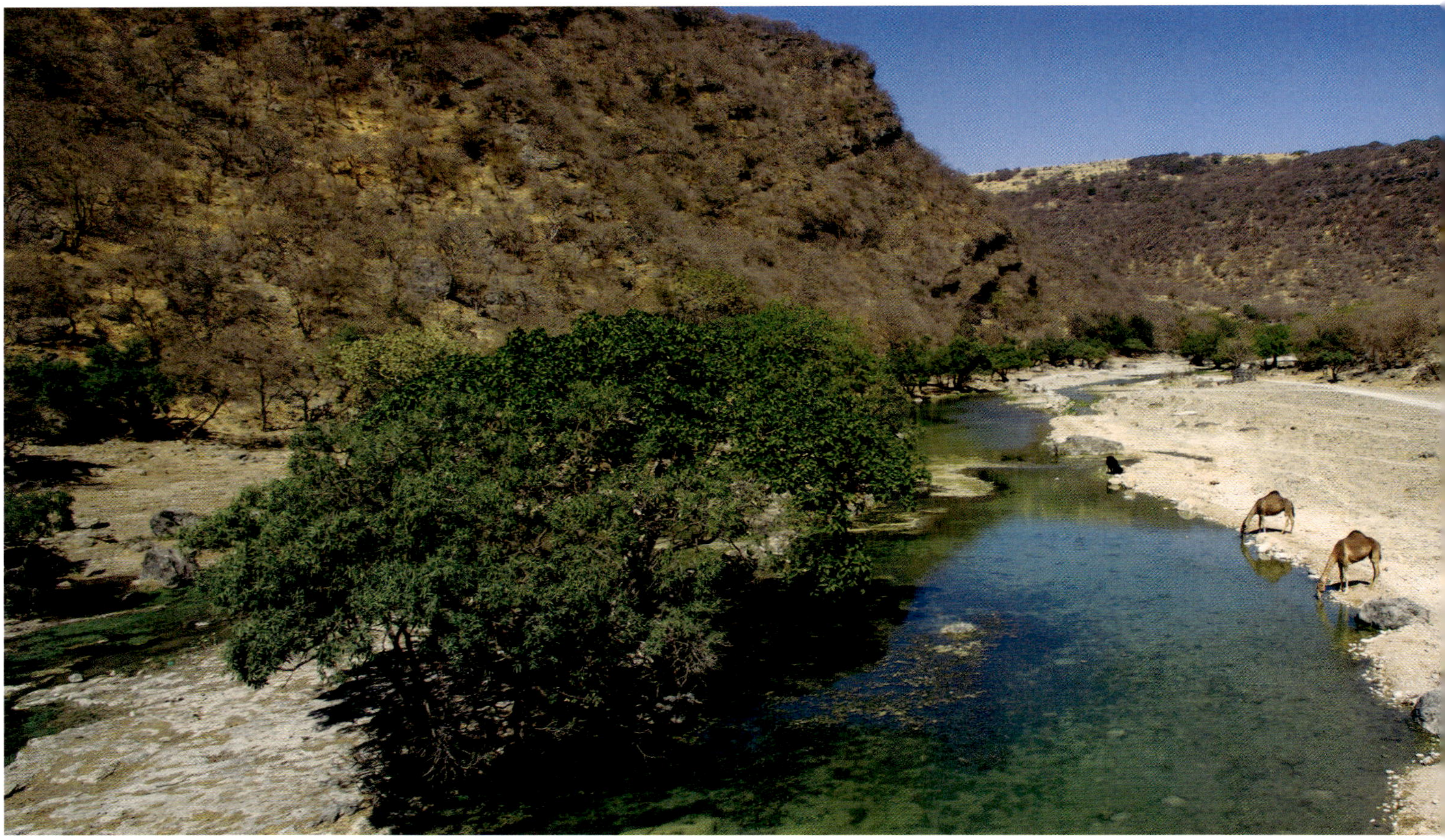

rise under the *khawr*. *Khawrs* with significant volumes of fresh water include Taqah, Rawri, Al Mughsayl, Awqad, Sawli, Al Balid, Ad Dahariz and Salalah.[53]

The lakes of Wadi Darbat are undoubtedly the largest and best-known freshwater bodies of Dhofar. Stretching over nearly four kilometres, the lakes are connected by shallow surface streams, and with a rich ground flora and majestic overhanging fig trees the wadi resembles a temperate river valley. With a catchment area of approximately 300 square kilometres that extends nearly 20 kilometres north, Wadi Darbat collects significant volumes of water. This replenishes the springs that form the Wadi Darbat lakes and some water finds its way underground to Khawr Rawri. The Wadi Darbat springs are an important source of water for the towns of Taqah and Mirbat.

In the east there are a small number of springs on the southern escarpment of Jabal Samhan. Ayn Ghaefat, north-east of Mirbat, is unusual as it shows little seasonal fluctuation, but perhaps the most important is Ayn Laja Shilyun, which supplies piped water to Sadah and other smaller settlements on the Salawt Plain. Closeby is Ayn Shayrukh, which lies on an important trail up the escarpment. In the eastern-flowing wadis of Jabal Samhan, including Wadi Samhal, Wadi Rabkut, Wadi Hadbaram and Wadi Sinaq, there are numerous small seeps and extensive spring-fed pools. Some of the seeps, such as that on the cliffs just north of Hasik, have significant travertine formations, including well-developed stalactites. These springs attract wildlife, and the remains of ancient settlements and graves are testimony to their importance to humans in the distant and recent past.

Not surprisingly there are very few springs on the high Jabal. Where they do occur they are found at the top of small tributaries that flow south to the Jarbib or to the coast. For example, there is a small cluster of springs just a few kilometres south-east of Qayrun Hayrti. There are also springs in many sinkholes and caves including Tawi Aatayr, Tayq Cave, Shaat sinkhole and Shihait sinkhole. In the inner chamber of Suhur Cave (Wadi Nahiz) is a natural basin that collects water from a seep above and in former times was used by herdsmen.

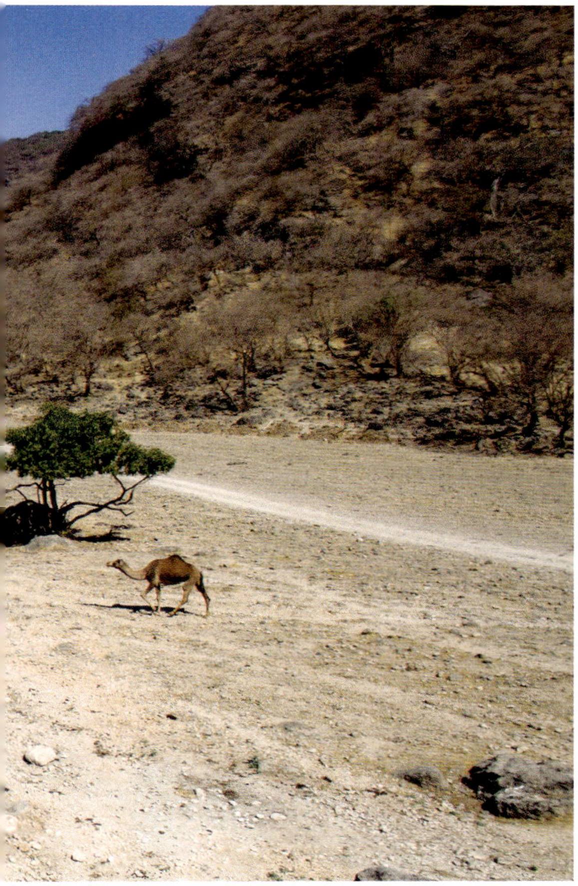

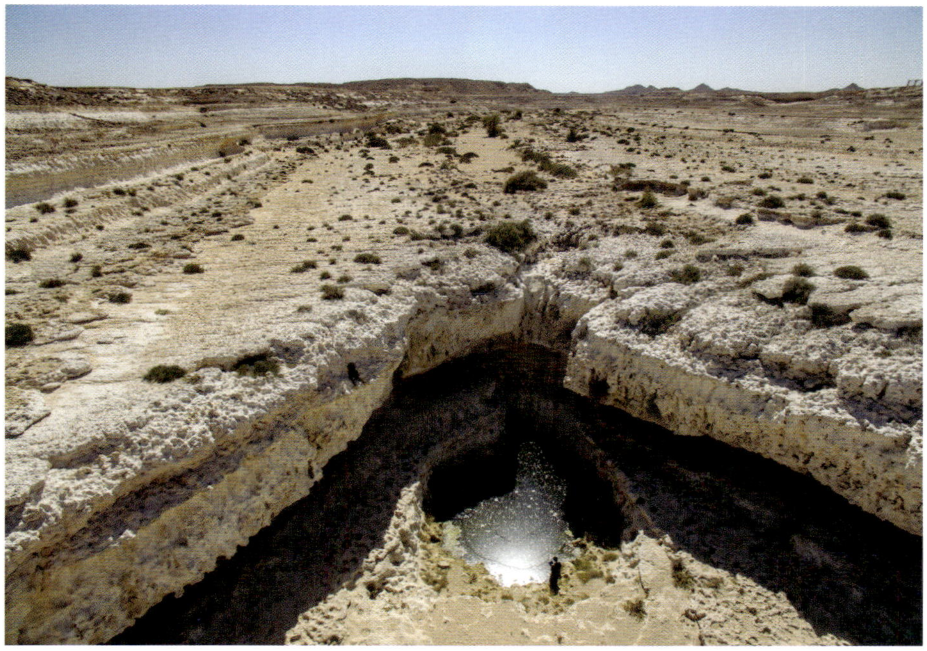

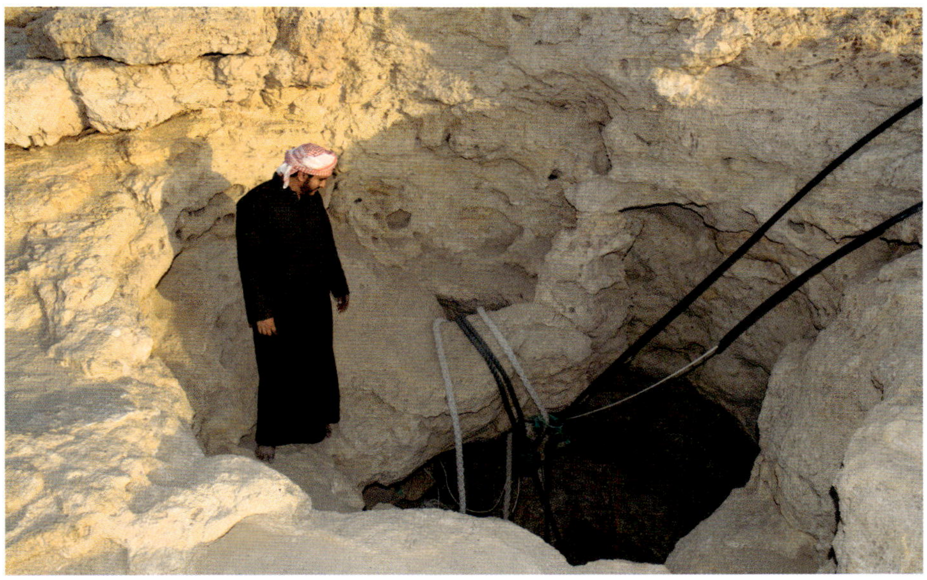

Springs of the Najd

In the southern Najd a number of springs are found in some of the northward-draining wadis. Most notable are those of Jabal Samhan, including Wadi Arah and Wadi Andhur, while further west are the pools of Wadi Uyun and the spring at Hanun that has watered travellers since the height of the frankincense trade more than 2,000 years ago. Deeper into the Najd there are key springs at Muday, Habrut and Ma'shadid; all were important watering points for travellers crossing the desert and of course for pastoralists and their livestock. Many of the springs were difficult to access and Ma'shadid – where the water can be reached only by descending a narrow limestone sinkhole with the aid of a rope – is a fine example. The name Ma'shadid comes from the Arabic words for 'water' and 'strength' and reflects the difficulty of access.

Much of the northern Najd and the Empty Quarter is waterless, but important and ancient seeps exist, including Manji in the north-east, Ash Shisr in the west and Muqshin in the far north. The traveller Wilfred Thesiger,[27] who crossed the Empty Quarter in 1946-47, drank at Ma'shadid before going on to Ash Shisr, which he describes in detail:

Up in the mountains most springs are very small but in a small number of cases, such as Wadi Darbat and Ayn Ghaydah ***(above left)***, they give rise to extensive lakes. In the northern foothills the springs of Ayn Hanun ***(top)*** and Ayn Mas'shadid ***(bottom)***, though difficult to access, were vital waterholes for travellers and their camels before heading north to cross the Najd and Empty Quarter.

> *'At the bottom of the large cave [sinkhole] which undercuts the mound there was a trickle of water in a deep fissure. This water could only be reached with difficulty down a narrow passage, between the rock wall and a bank of sand, thirty feet in height, which half filled the cave. When we arrived at the well the water was buried under drifted sand and had to be dug out.'*

This contrasts with Muqshin, where there are extensive pools, stretching over several kilometres, set amongst date palms and against the backdrop of Dhofar's largest forest of ghaf trees (*Prosopis cineraria*). In 1930 Bertram Thomas[23] journeyed north by camel from Salalah described Wadi Muqshin as *'surely the Prince of Wadis in all South-east Arabia'.*

Although tankered, piped and bottled water meets most water demands today, Dhofar's springs remain important water sources and are still utilised by many communities. Livestock continues to be watered at some springs but more often spring water is piped, often great distances, to local settlements for livestock, agriculture and some household use. Some springs, like the famous Hanun, seem to be no longer in use while others, especially Wadi Darbat, are very popular tourist attractions.

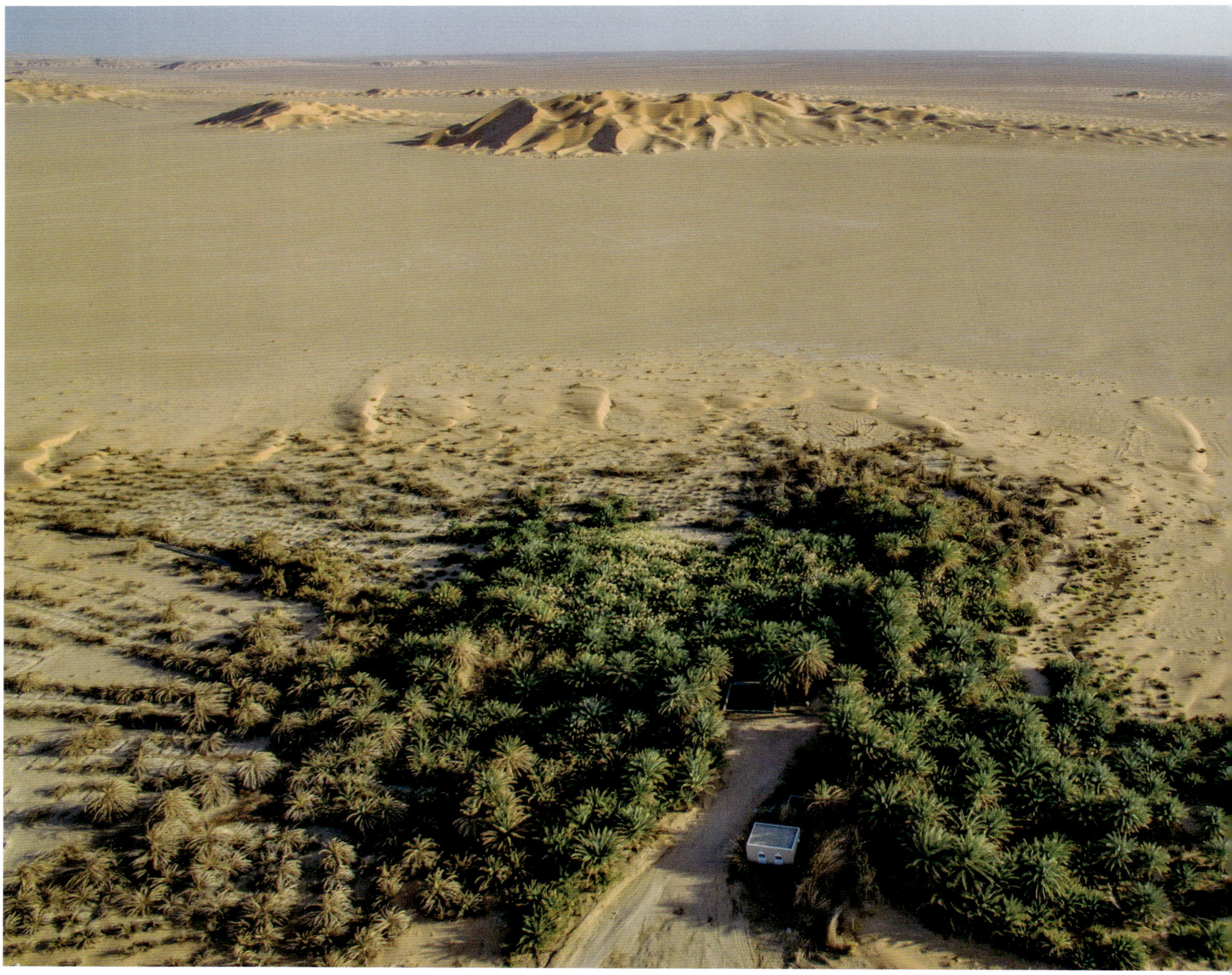

Until the late 20th century the main source of water in the open desert of the northern Najd and Empty Quarter was shallow hand-dug wells ***(below right)***. Drilling by oil prospectors opened up new deeper artesian wells, though the sulphurous water from many, such as Al Hashman ***(below left)***, was barely potable.

Wells

Shallow hand-dug wells have been a feature of the farms of Salalah and Taqah for centuries. They were not deep and water was drawn in buckets by hand or using livestock, particularly camels. The area of agriculture was small and the volumes of water drawn were not large. But wells were not common elsewhere in Dhofar and people relied on natural springs and seeps to access the groundwater.

This changed with the arrival in the 1950s of oil prospectors whose efforts to drill for oil often resulted in the discovery of water. Most of the activity was in the Najd, where companies also drilled water wells for their own use and for local communities. At a number of locations wells were drilled into confined aquifers, where the water is under great pressure, causing the water to gush out. Some of these artesian wells were capped but others were left to discharge freely for many years, forming lakes in the desert with a richly vegetated fringe. Muntasar, just south-west of Muqshin, and Al Hashman, both at the edge of the sand, seas of the Empty Quarter are two examples. The former is used occasionally by livestock herders while the latter is used both for livestock and for the growing of crops tolerant of the warm and very sulphurous water that is typical of the artesian wells. Shijaj, deep inside the Empty Quarter, was drilled in about 1973 and was gushing about 4,000 gallons of water per hour at that time, while further east water from an artesian well was used to establish Rahab experimental farm at Marmul in 1985.

Though most of the early drilling was confined to the Najd this changed after 1970 when programmes for the drilling of water wells commenced on the Jabal and elsewhere in Dhofar. The government set out to provide water supply-points within 5-6 kilometres of every village on the Jabal and by 1994 this was largely achieved, with 113 boreholes, 103 reservoirs and 346 kilometres of pipeline on Jabal

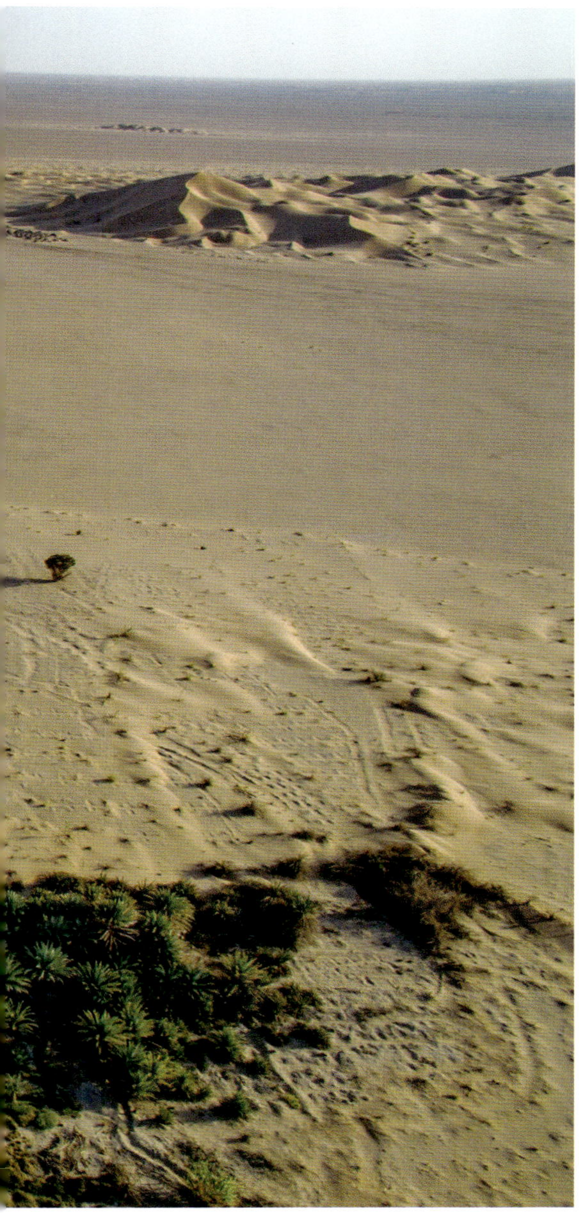

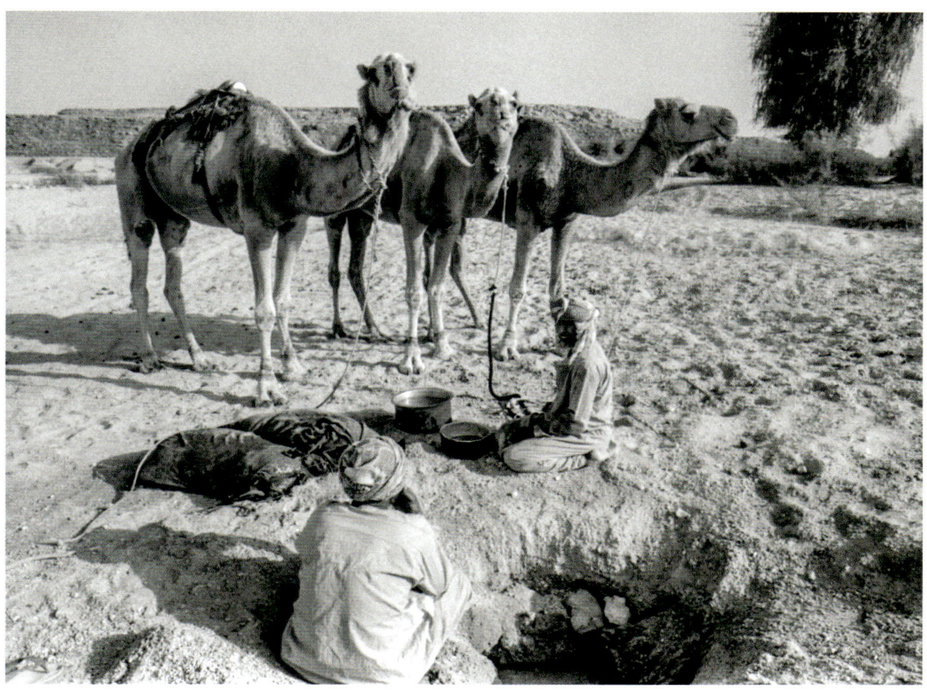

Al Qamar and Jabal Al Qara.[51] Meanwhile, in the Najd small farms had grown up around the artesian wells including at Dawkah and Marmul; but, except for Rahab experimental farm at Marmul, farming was on a small scale and thus water use was therefore very limited.

However, in northern Oman there was growing evidence that the rapid increase in wells and the overuse of groundwater for the growing of fodder on farms of the Al Batinah coastal plain was leading to salt water intrusion and the loss of date groves and other agricultural land. All eyes turned to the vast water reserves of the Umm Er Radhuma aquifer and a decision was taken in the early 1990s to move fodder farms from the Al Batinah to the northern Najd. This marked the beginning of the large-scale use of the aquifer, with Wadi Dawkah, Ash Shisr, Hanfit and Qitbit identified as the most suitable for agricultural development and in particular for the growing of livestock fodder. By 2013 there were 17,810 hectares of agricultural holdings in the *wilayats* of Thumrayt and Muqshin reliant on borehole water production, growing 4,328 hectares of crops of which 61% was forage for livestock.[54]

On the Salalah plain the expansion of agricultural areas, drilling of new wells and introduction of pumps led to a significant increase in demand for water by the 1990s. Since that time the area of agriculture has stabilised at about 2,700 hectares but the human population has increased considerably. Water demand tripled between 1985 and 2010.[50]

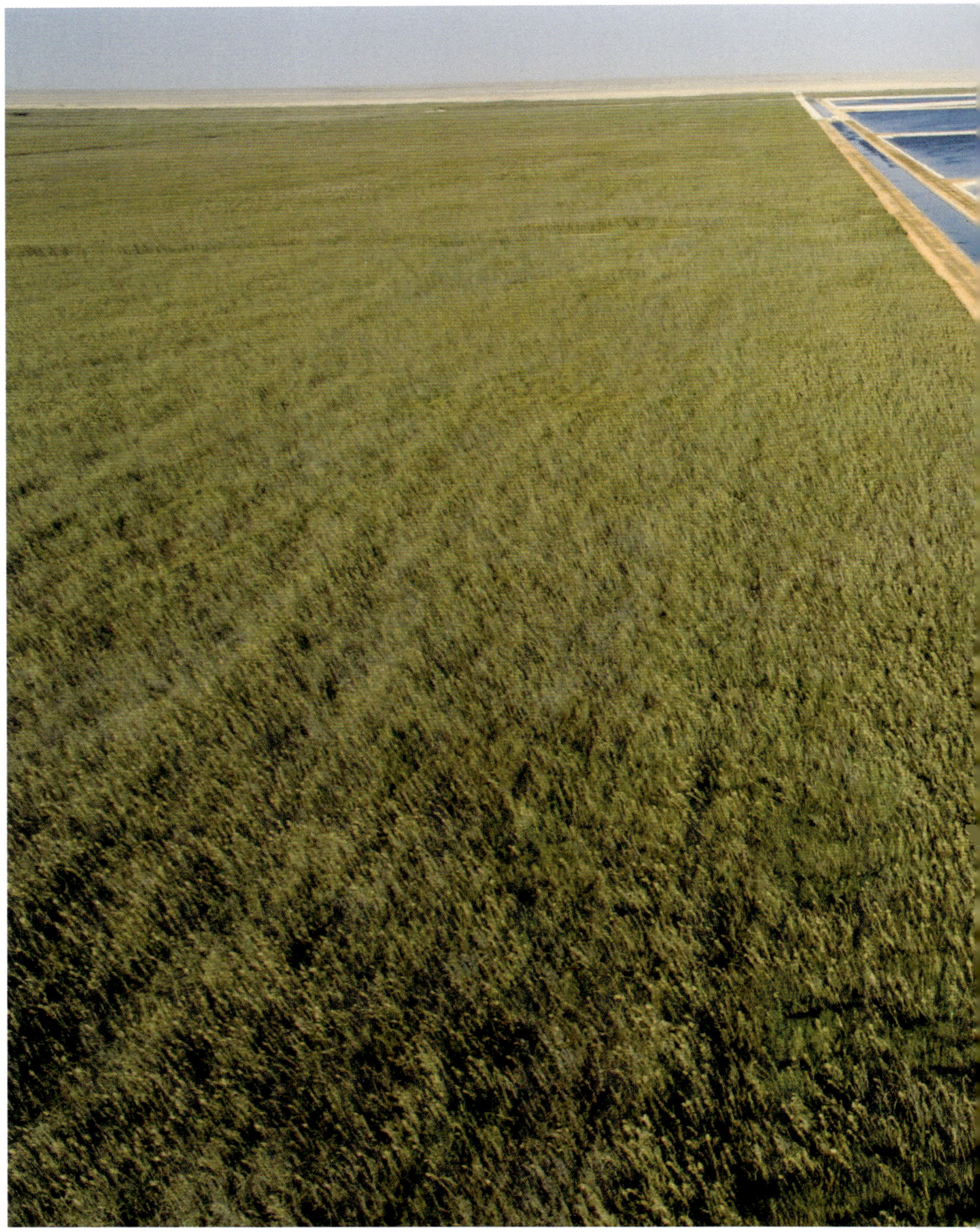

Produced Water

Produced water is the single largest associated waste product of the oil industry. Over the lifetime of an oil field water production is expected to be more than ten times that of oil.[55] As this water is contaminated by oil it is not fit for human use and the usual solution is to remove the oil and pump the treated water into very deep aquifers. This is expensive and carries the risk that freshwater aquifers become contaminated.[56]

At the Nimr Reed Beds Project in the northern Najd an exciting solution has been found. Since 2011 a vast plantation of reeds and evaporation ponds, the size of 640 football pitches, has been used to treat produced water. The produced water first passes into a settlement tank, where residual oil is removed, before entering a series of reed

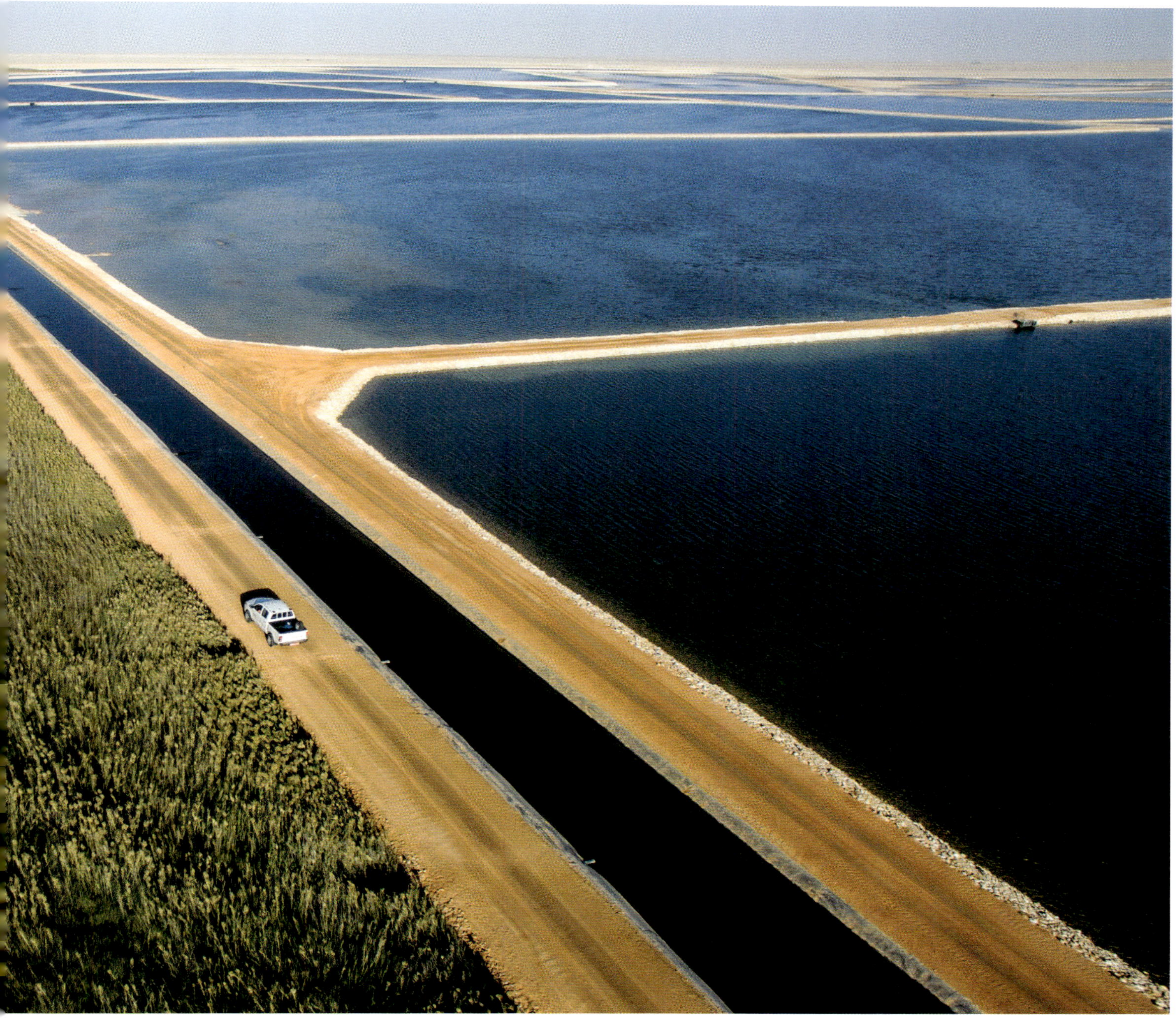

beds where it is 'cleaned' by microorganisms that live among the roots of the reeds. By 2017 the site was treating 110,000 cubic metres of produced water a day. Furthermore, more than 370,000 barrels of residual oil have been recovered from the water since operations began in 2010 and energy savings have reduced carbon dioxide emissions by 300,000 tons every year.[57]

The planted reed beds not only treat the produced water but have formed an important wetland and local biodiversity hotspot. More than 100 species of bird have been recorded, many of which are migrants that stop over while making the long and exhausting journey between Africa and Asia. Natural wetlands are in decline and thus artificial wetlands will take on an increasing importance for biodiversity conservation.

(Above) At Nimr, produced water is cleaned by the reeds before passing into huge evaporation ponds. The reeds have become a haven for wildlife.

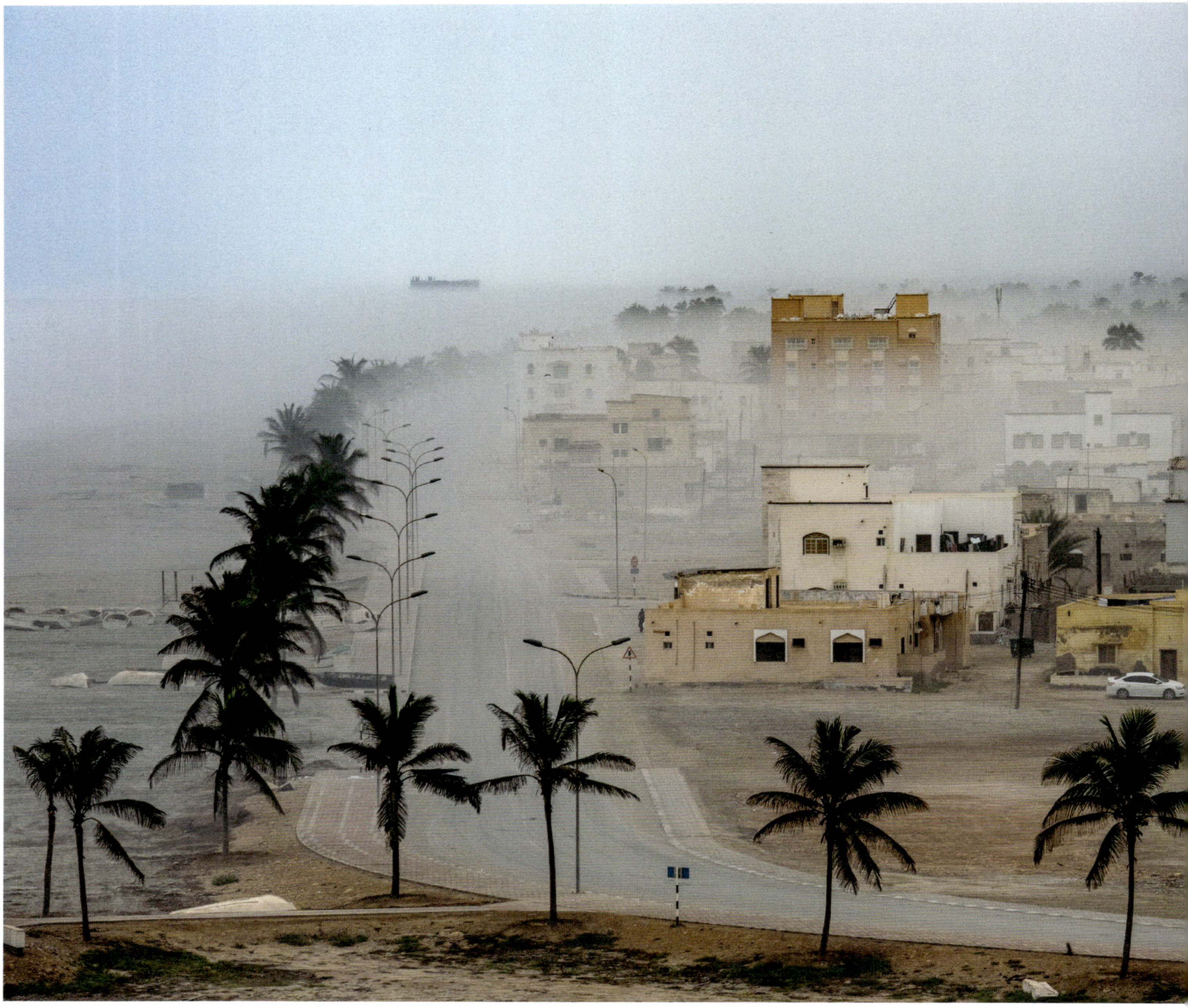

(Above) The town of Taqah stands here shrouded in fog.

Fogs and Dews

In Dhofar fog is normally associated with the swirling mists and low cloud of the annual *khareef* monsoon. But elsewhere, especially at the eastern coast, dew and fog can occur throughout the year and are an important source of water for the flora and fauna of these areas. This is particularly the case in the north-east, where the Jiddat Arkad and Wadi Aynaynah are often enveloped in fog, especially during the autumn and spring. There is no information as to how much water the fogs yield but in the Jiddat Al Harasis of central Oman 1-square-metre mesh screens produced up to five litres of water in a single night. In the past, nomads recognised the importance of fog water and harvested it from the saturated canopies of *Acacia tortilis* trees.

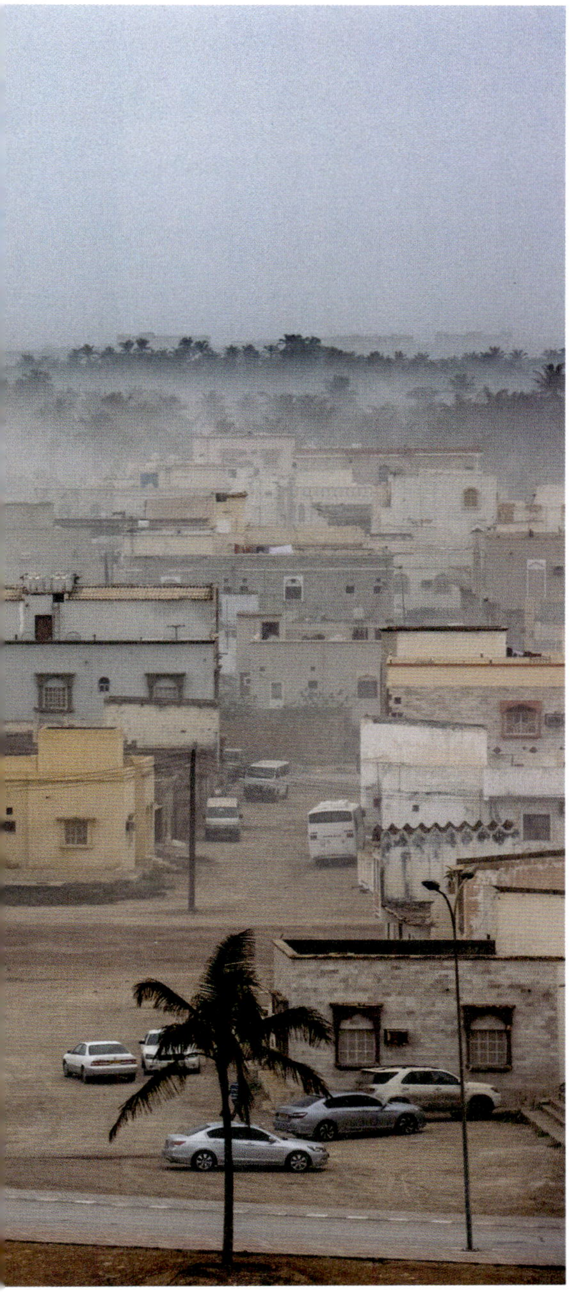

Desalination

Desalination of groundwater has been practised since the 1970s and small reverse osmosis plants are found throughout Dhofar's interior. Some communities, such as those of the Al Hallaniyyat Islands, are entirely dependent on treated groundwater.

In southern Dhofar (namely Salalah, Taqah, Mirbat) all potable water was obtained from underground aquifers until the 1990s, when concern at falling water tables and increasing demand led to plans to introduce desalination of seawater. A huge plant built between Taqah and Mirbat came on-stream in 2012 and when working at full capacity it met local needs. However, demand continued to rise rapidly and by 2017 demand was already exceeding supply by more than 50% and the shortfall was being obtained from groundwater. A new desalination plant, announced in 2018, will almost triple capacity to approximately 180 cubic metres per day. However, rising demand means that within a few years there will be a further shortfall in supply, especially as other areas of the Jabal and Jarbib become connected to the water distribution network. This shortfall will be met from groundwater or additional desalination plants.[58]

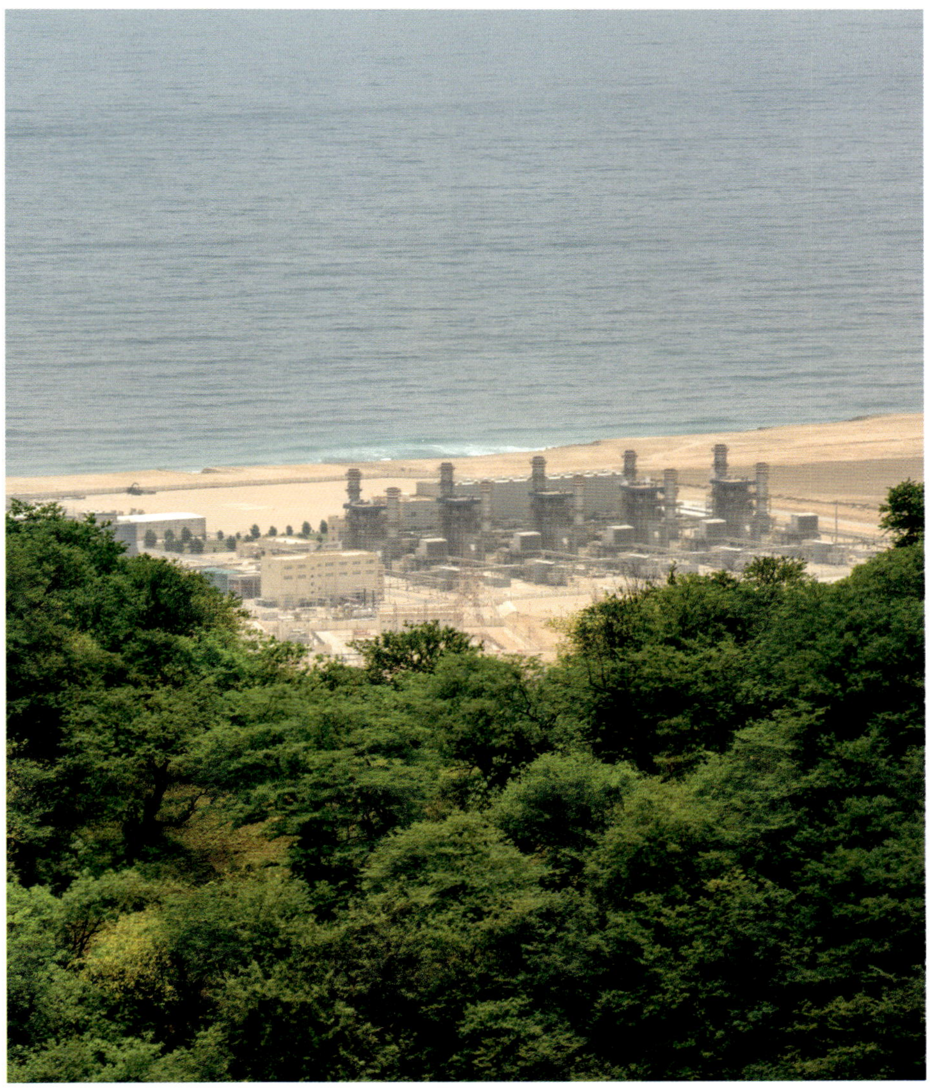

(Right) The desalinisation plant just west of Mirbat will continue to meet much of Dhofar's growing demand for fresh water.

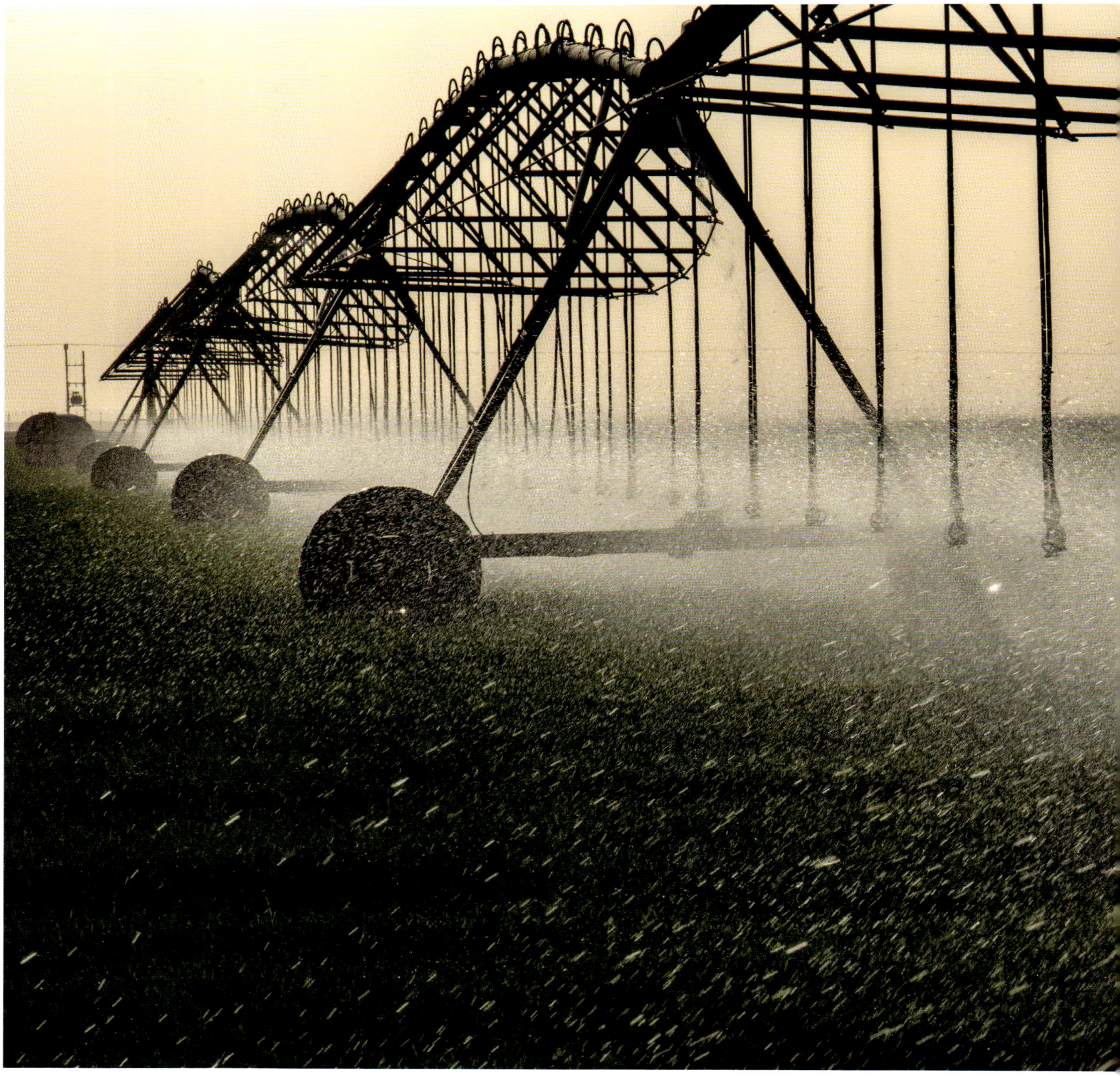

(Above) Modern irrigation systems have allowed the fossil water of the Najd to be used for growing vast acreages of vegetable and fodder crops. However, care needs to be taken to ensure that this finite water resource is not over-exploited.

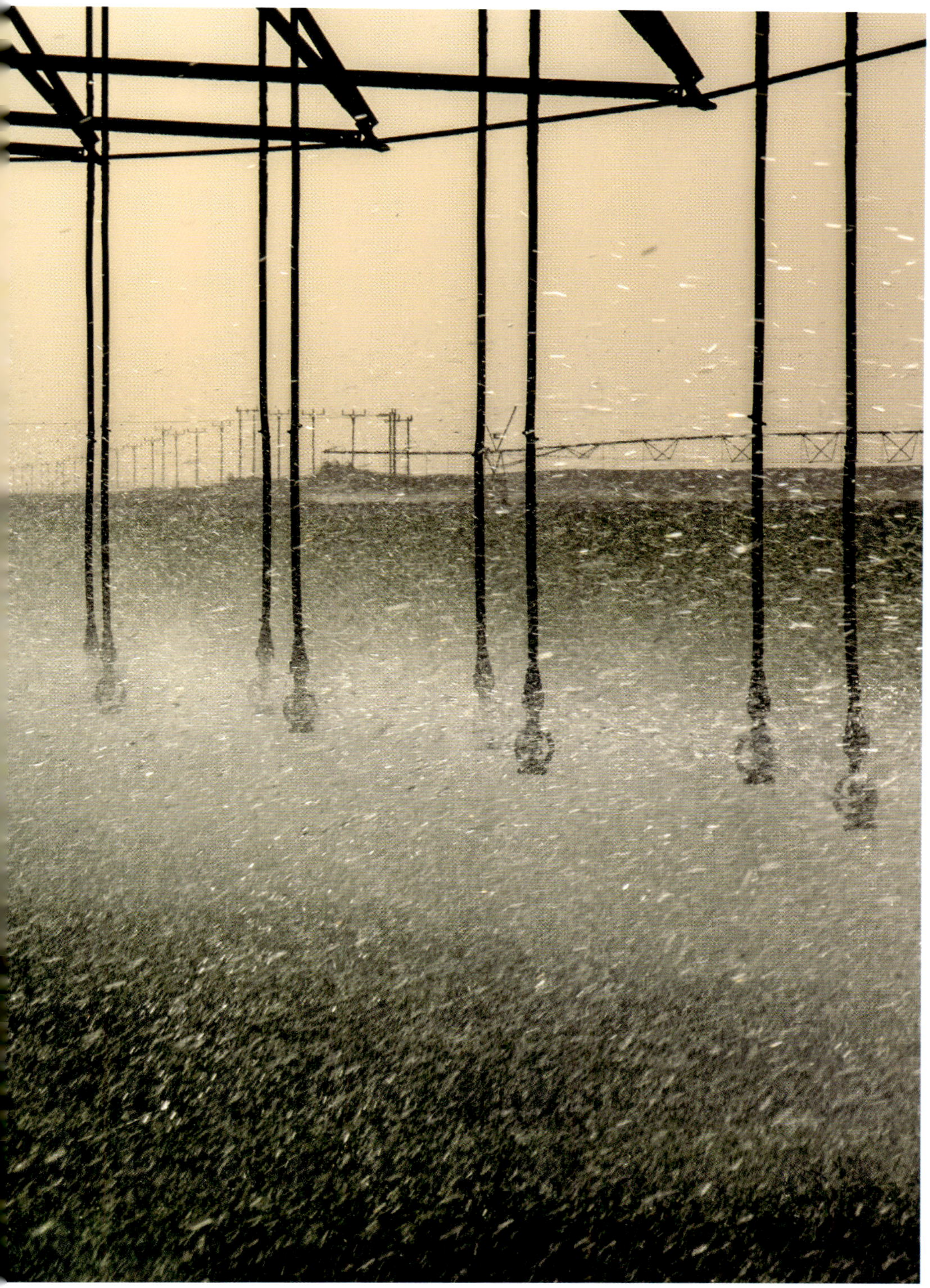

Sustainability

Since 1970 Dhofar's scarce water resources have been successfully managed to supply water to the cities, towns and villages of Dhofar, for drinking, domestic use, industry and agriculture. Existing springs have been harnessed, dams have been built, ancient fossil water has been tapped, hundreds of new boreholes have been drilled and seawater is being desalinated.

There have been challenges, however. On the Salalah plain groundwater levels have fallen,[59] which has led to increased salinity as fresh water was replaced by seawater and, in turn, crop yields have declined while in some cases farms have been abandoned.[60] However, this decline seems to have been reversed by the adoption of a suite of different approaches including the construction of dams, the shifting of forage agriculture to the northern Najd, the construction of a new desalination plant and the injecting of waste water into the aquifer to displace seawater.[61]

In the Najd significant challenges remain. The fossil water reserve of the Umm Er Radhuma aquifer is vast but it is not unlimited and there are worrying indications that the aquifer is being depleted by agricultural projects in the northern Najd. Water is being pumped out faster than rainfall can recharge it. A study of the UER aquifer showed that groundwater levels decreased slowly over the period 2002-2010 but significantly more rapidly from 2010-2014,[62] when the water table fell by up to two metres per year. Although rainfall from storms and cyclones, such as Cyclone Mekunu in May 2018, will help to recharge the UER aquifer, the current over-pumping of water is not sustainable in the long-term. The principal crop of the farms is Rhodes grass, which is used to feed livestock, whose numbers have risen rapidly across Dhofar, but especially on the Jabal. In order to halt or reverse the falling water levels in the Najd it will almost certainly be necessary to find new ways to manage the region's livestock.

Elsewhere desalination is likely to continue to be a major component of water management. However it is a costly process and not without negative environmental consequences for Dhofar's biodiverse coastline. Other elements of an ongoing integrated approach to water management might include the expansion of existing schemes using recycled waste water for irrigation in Salalah while in the oilfields of the northern Najd the enormous volumes of produced water should be considered an opportunity for conservation and reuse. Improved water conservation on farms might include metering of water use, the wider use of modern irrigation systems, particularly to replace flood irrigation, and in the Najd the expansion of existing schemes that use hydroponics. At the community level, better use of fog water might be considered, with schemes to use the water for small-scale agriculture or local reforestation. Across all sectors the raising of awareness of the need for wise water use together with new pricing policies would discourage wasteful water use.[50]

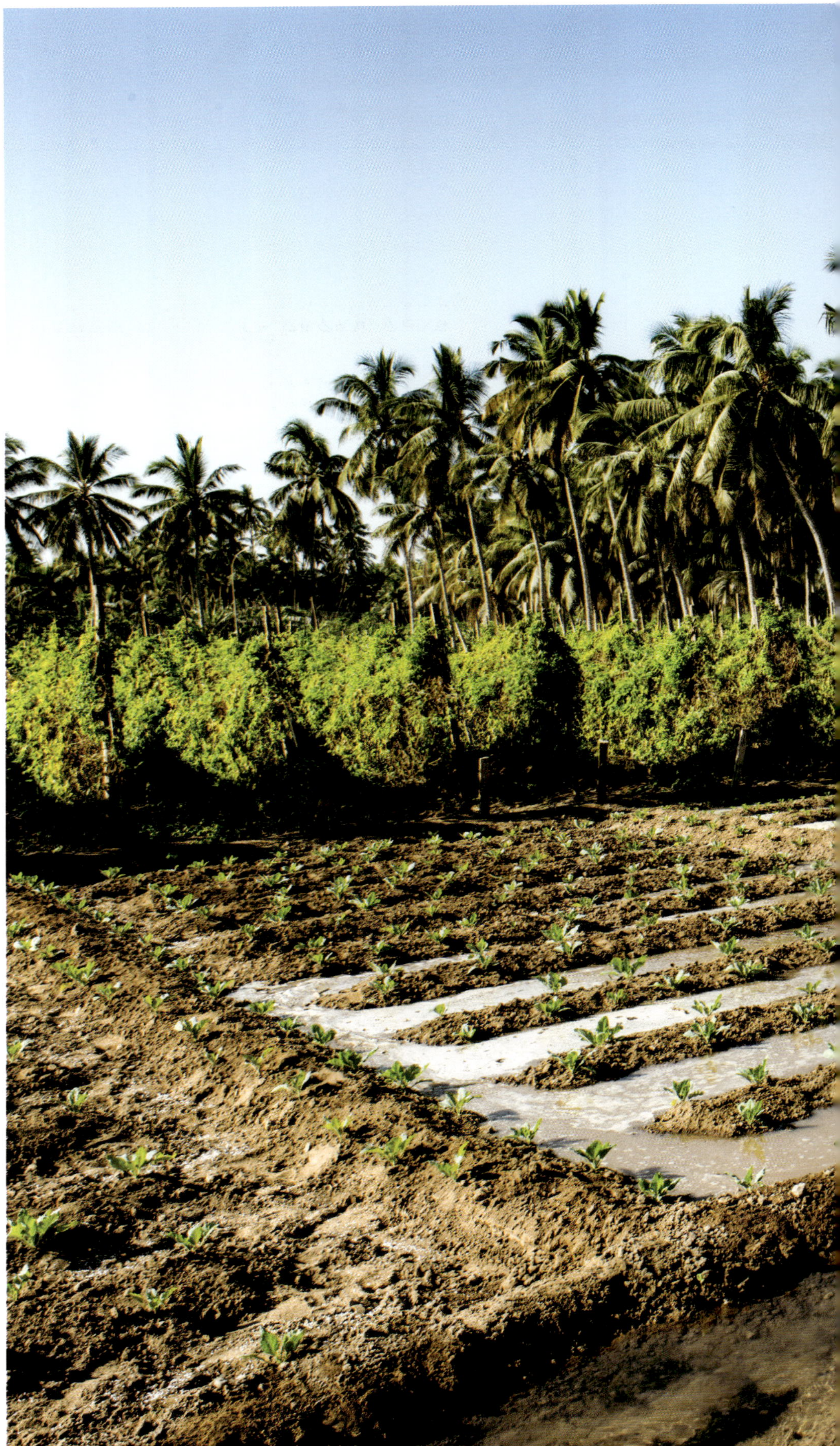

(Right) Flood irrigation, seen here in Salalah, is effective, but modern irrigation systems are more efficient and help to conserve valuable water resources.

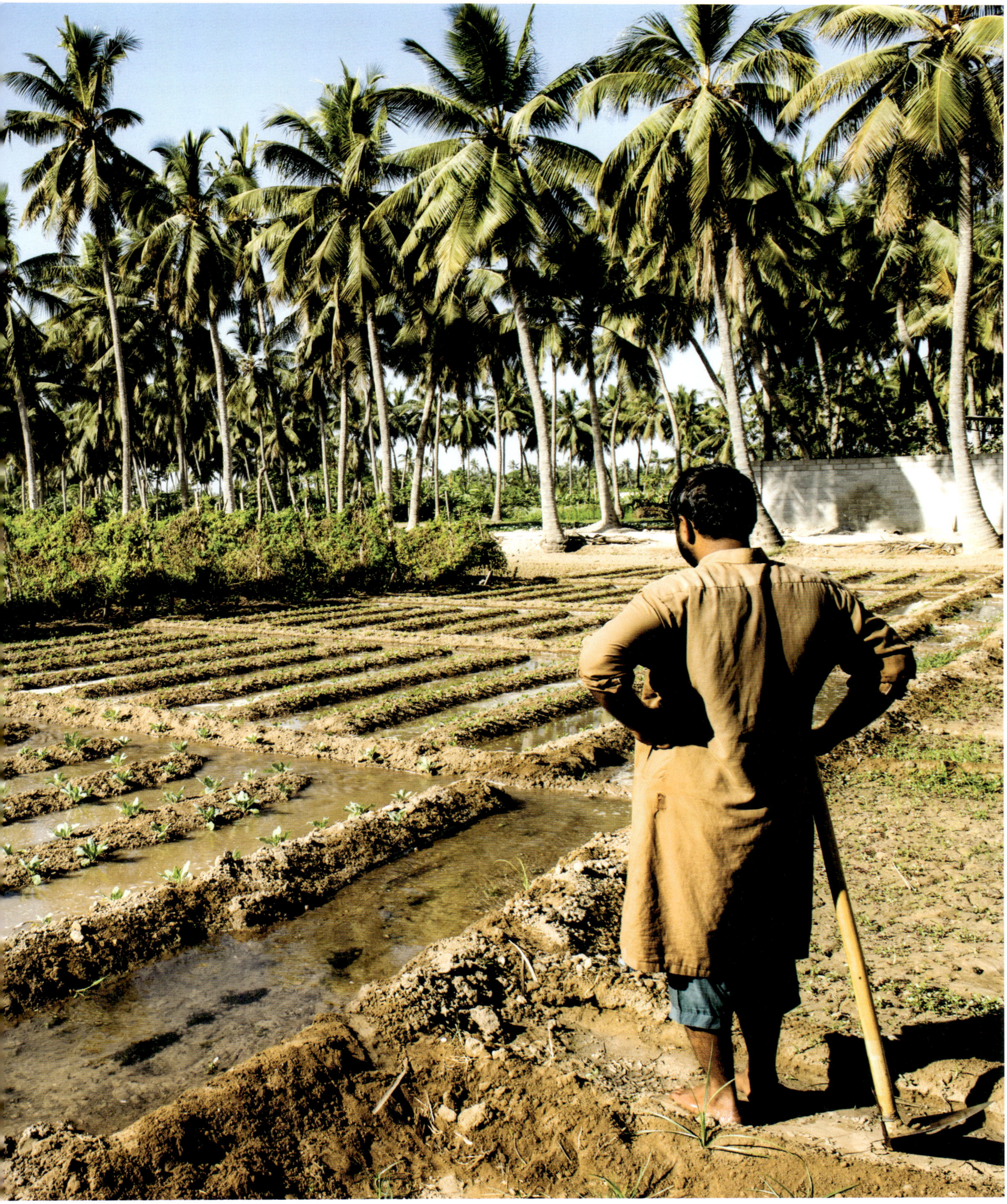

5 Flora

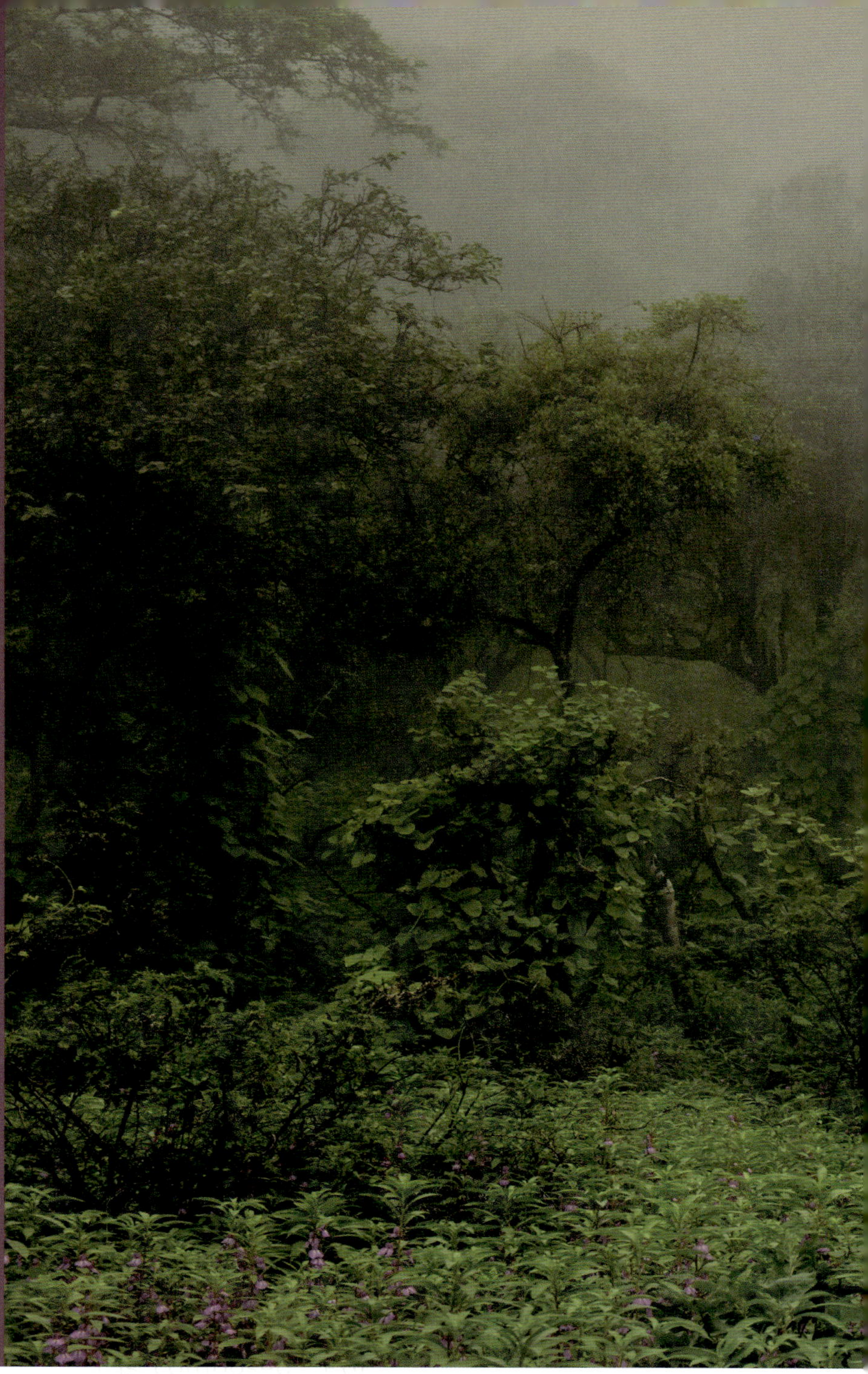

Introduction

The Southwest Monsoon supports dense subtropical forests ***(above)*** unique to southern Arabia. They are dominated by *Anogeissus dhofarica* and are home to many species that are not found elsewhere.

The geographical position of Dhofar, being only 600 kilometres from the Horn of Africa, combined with the climatic influence of the *khareef,* or Southwest Monsoon, has resulted in a unique flora that is amongst the most diverse of the Arabian Peninsula. Of Oman's 1,407 plant species, 867 are found in Dhofar.[63]

To the north of the Jabal are found species that are typical of the Arabian deserts (known as the Nubo-Sindian zone) while species occurring to the south and directly impacted by the Southwest Monsoon more closely resemble the flora of north-east Africa (the Somali-Masai zone).

The seasonal monsoon brings precipitation and cool temperatures to Dhofar at the height of the Arabian summer. This has allowed the evolution and establishment of plants that would not survive in the Arabian deserts. Furthermore, the influence of the monsoon is

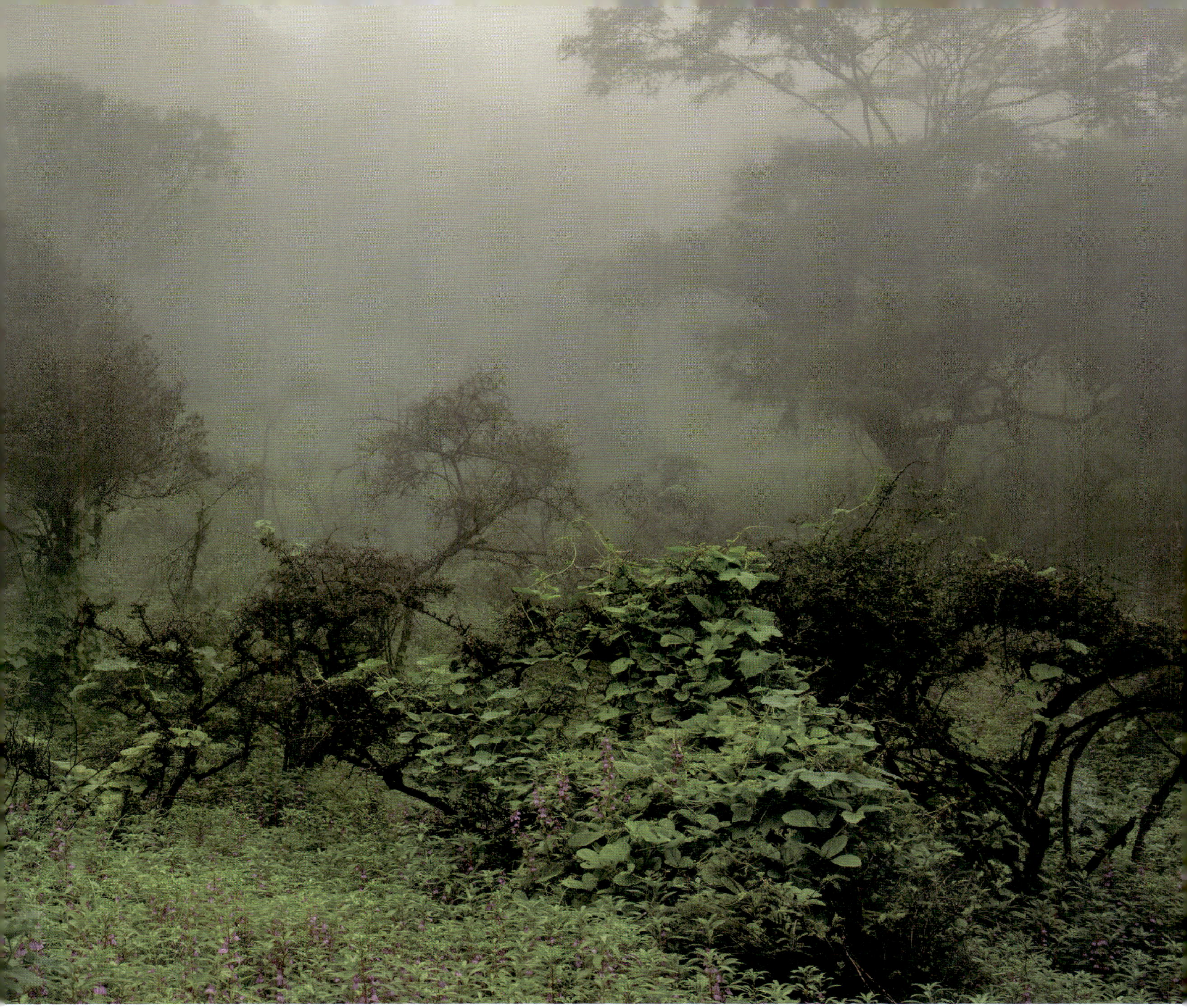

not uniform across Dhofar, with often very subtle differences in precipitation and rainfall associated with differences in elevation, orientation and distance from the coast. For example, during the monsoon the wettest areas are neither by the coast nor high on the Jabal; they are at mid-altitude, and it is here where the thick forest of *Anogeissus dhofarica* (Ji. Ṣġót) is found. Similarly, the Jiddat Arkad seems to be typical of the arid interior of Dhofar but the very slight influence of the summer monsoon and coastal fogs has resulted in a unique flora that is found nowhere further inland.

Thus the proximity to both the Arabian desert and Africa, combined with a rich diversity of micro-climates associated with the summer monsoon, has allowed the evolution of an enormously diverse plant community that includes 41 species that are not found anywhere outside Dhofar.[64]

NB where possible the common plant name is used followed, when the species is first mentioned, by the scientific name and if known the local Jibbāli (Ji) or Arabic (Ar) name.

Vegetation Zones

Beaches and Khawrs

Coastal habitats include the productive environment of the coastal *khawrs* and the less rich though interesting environment of the beaches and sand dunes.

The flora of Dhofar's *khawrs* varies with the salinity of the water. Just nine of the more saline lagoons contain mangrove communities; all are on the Jarbib coastal plain and typically are fringed with a band of grey mangrove (*Avicennia marina*), a species that is particularly tolerant of arid and hyper-saline conditions, grows to six metres and forms a dense canopy. The two *khawrs* known as Khawr Qurm (Al Kabir and As Saghir) on the road from Salalah to Raysut provide the best examples of mangrove woodland. Many of the *khawrs* also support stands of common reed (*Phragmites australis*) and hard sea rush (*Juncus rigidus*), and away from the water's edge salt-tolerant grasses can be found including *Sporobolus virginicus* and *Aeluropus lagopoides*.[65] The two *khawrs* of the Al Hallaniyyat Islands are without mangroves or reeds but are fringed by relatively extensive and woody stands of tamarisk (*Tamarix senegalensis,* Ji. Terfal).

The coastal beaches, sand dunes and *sabkhas* are relatively species-poor, with *Atriplex farinosa* (Ar. *afar*), *Limonium axillare*, (Ji. Sizyit), *Cyperus conglomeratus*, *Sporobolus virginicus* and the saltbush *Tetraena qatarensis*. Species of note include the desert hyacinth (*Cistanche phelypaea*) and the Omani endemic shrubby seablight, (*Suaeda moschata*).

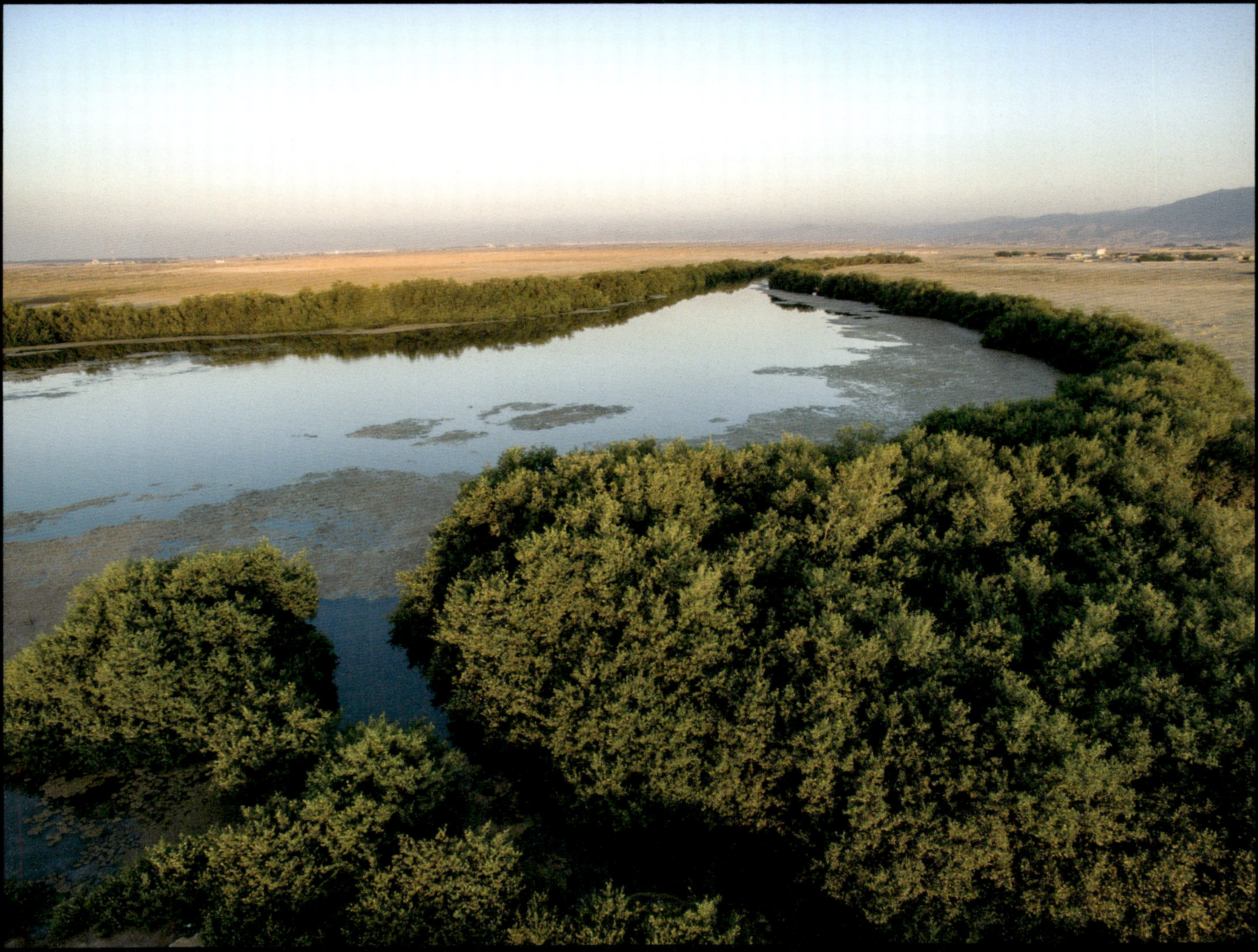

The natural drainage of the mountains has produced more than 50 *khawrs*, where the wadis reach the sea. These harbour important plant communities but are also important for fauna, particularly birds, and also function as nursery grounds for marine fish while in some cases they are sources of fresh water. Many, like Khawr Jnawf ***(above)***, just east of Salalah, are fringed by mangroves.

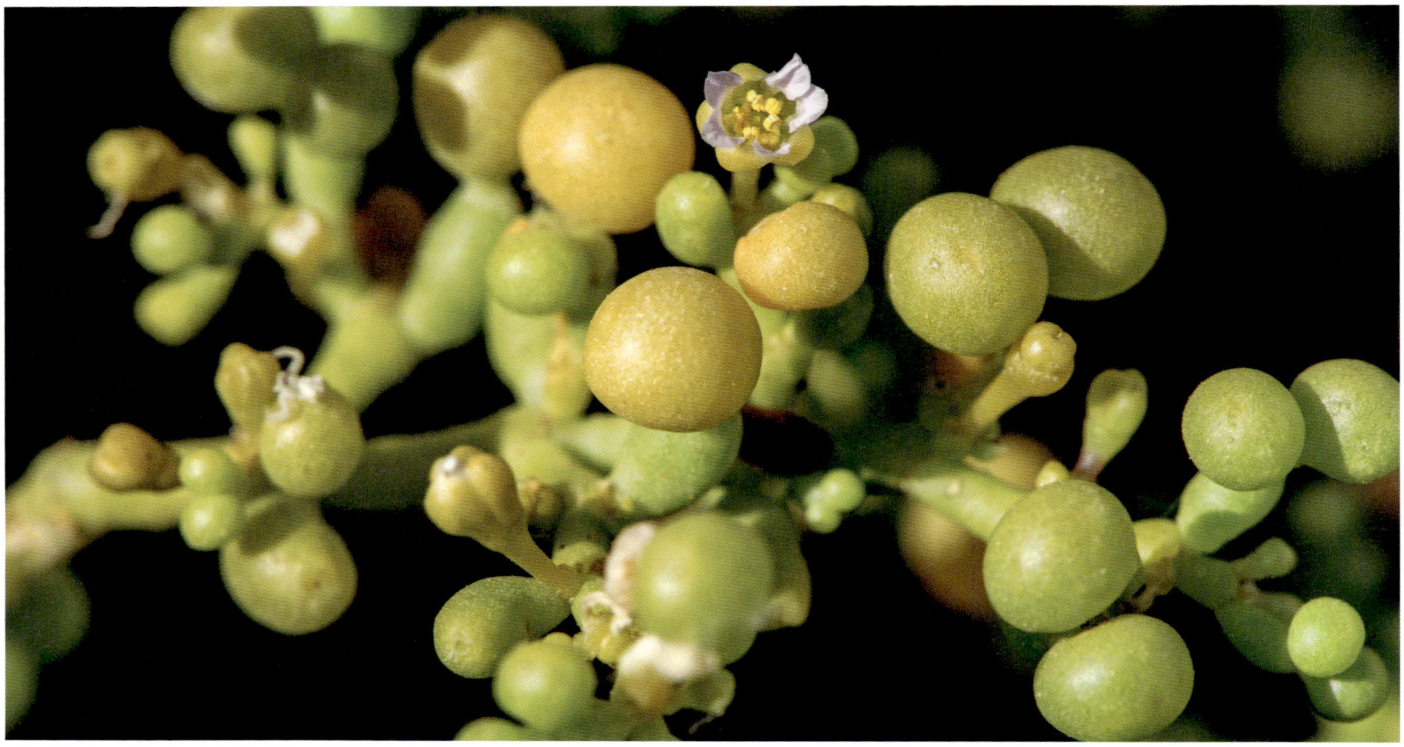

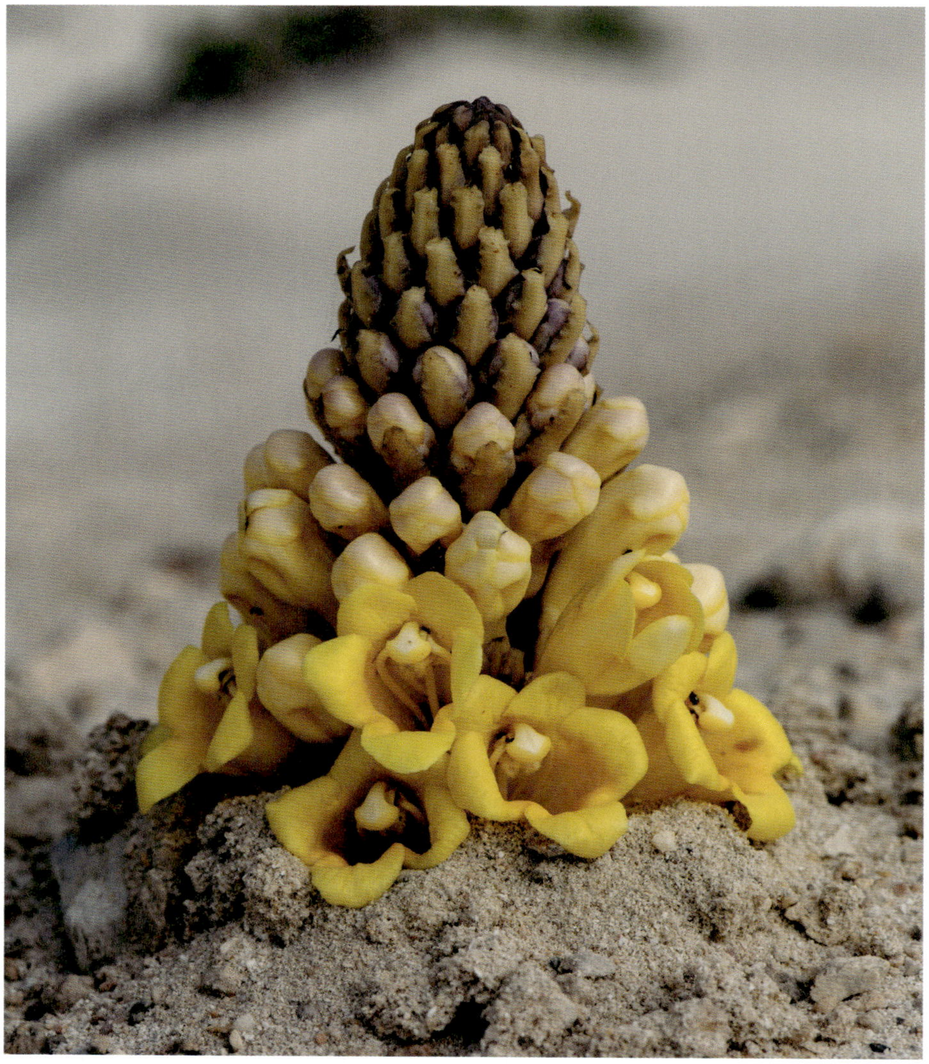

The tough environment of the coastal beaches and sand dunes gives rise to specialist plants. *Tetraena qatarensis* ***(above)*** is salt-tolerant while desert hyacinth ***(right)*** has no chlorophyll and obtains its nutrients and water from the host plants whose roots it parasitises.

Coastal Plains, the Jarbib and the Salawt Plain

The coastal plain is reduced to a very narrow shelf for most of Jabal Al Qamar but in the vicinity of the coastal bays of Al Fazayih, Al Hawtah, Rakhyut, Khawr Kharfut, and Dalkut the landscape is more level. In these more open habitats species of acacia are found, as are trees and shrubs of Arabian balsam tree (*Commiphora gileadensis*, Ji. Škóf) and ground flora including the grass *Dichanthium micranthum*. Late in the monsoon, species such as the bright-yellow-flowered *Ipomoea obscura* and *Crotalaria retusa* add striking colour to the otherwise green landscape.

East of Al Mughsayl are the low hills and shallow southward-flowing wadis of Adawnab. This area receives only very light monsoon precipitation and is sparsely vegetated with scattered trees that include *Acacia senegal* (Ji. Tur), *Acacia hamulosa*, wild drumstick tree (*Moringa peregrina*, Ji. Yen) and Arabian balsam tree. Stands of frankincense trees (*Boswellia sacra*, Ji. Meġerót) occur in the upper reaches of wadis such as Wadi Ishat. The coastal headland of Ras Hamar receives more rainfall than much of the Adawnab area and in years of a strong monsoon is blanketed in green. Nevertheless it is very overgrazed and the presence nearby of a coastal stack that is inaccessible to livestock but covered with dense *Commiphora* shrub serves as a stark reminder of how the entire coastal hills must once have been.

The Jarbib – sometimes meaning the Salalah plain and at other times considered to mean the entire area from Wadi Hinna in the east to Al Mughsayl in the west – dominates the coastal plains of Dhofar. Although today it is heavily developed, severely overgrazed and populated by the invasive mesquite (*Prosopis juliflora*, Ar. *Ghaf Al Bahri*), it once supported a rich flora under open woodlands.[66] These are largely gone but after exceptional monsoon rains, such as those of 2016, the entire Jarbib turns green with a covering of ephemeral grasses and herbs dominated by the near-endemic grass *Dichanthium micranthum*, a species restricted to Dhofar and Yemen. In the wadis that cross the plain the flora is more intact and includes *Acacia tortilis* (Ji. Ṭulḥ) trees, shrubs of *Cadaba farinosa* (Ji. Simar) and *Dyerophytum indicum* (Ji. Melheloh).

East of Mirbat and beyond the reach of the monsoon the Salawt Plain supports a sparse, scattered shrub land dominated by *Acacia tortilis*, *Cadaba farinosa*, tamarisk and occasional Christ's thorn (*Ziziphus spina-christi*, Ji. Zed) trees. Closer to Sadah are frankincense groves, and although the resin is not considered to be the best quality the trees continue to be cut and harvested.

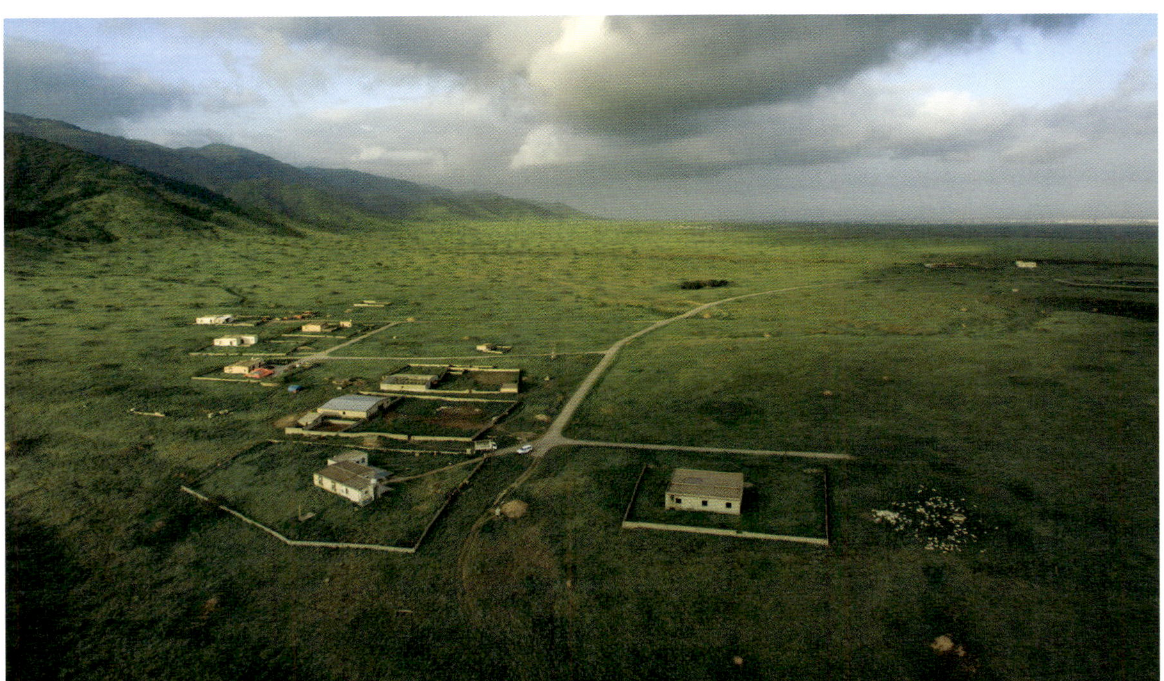

In years of a strong monsoon, such as in 2016, or following cyclonic rainfall such as that of Cyclone Mekunu in 2018, the Jarbib is transformed, with a carpet of herbs and short-lived grasses ***(left)***.

The salt-tolerant *Tamarix senegalensis* occurs in small stands on Dhofar's islands ***(bottom)*** while short-lived perennials such as *Aizoon canariense* ***(below)*** are more sparsely distributed.

Islands

The hyper-arid conditions of the Al Hallaniyyat Islands support a surprisingly high diversity of plants and to date surveys have recorded 67 species, all of which are also found on the mainland.[67] The only tree species is *Acacia tortilis*, which is present in small numbers, while tamarisk is found around coastal lagoons and small brackish water inland springs. Dominant coastal plants include *Atriplex farinosa* and *Suaeda moschata* while ephemeral species include the woody-stemmed, purslane-leaved *aizun* (*Aizoon canariense*, Ar. *Shuheymat ard*) and the grass *Stipagrostis dhofariensis*, which is endemic to Oman. The people of the islands still have local names for many plants, suggesting that many were used in the past for food and medicine, which is not surprising given that life before 1970 was a grim struggle for survival.[68] The soft-spined fruit of *Glossonema varians* (Ji. Tekelum) is considered a delicacy and is still harvested.

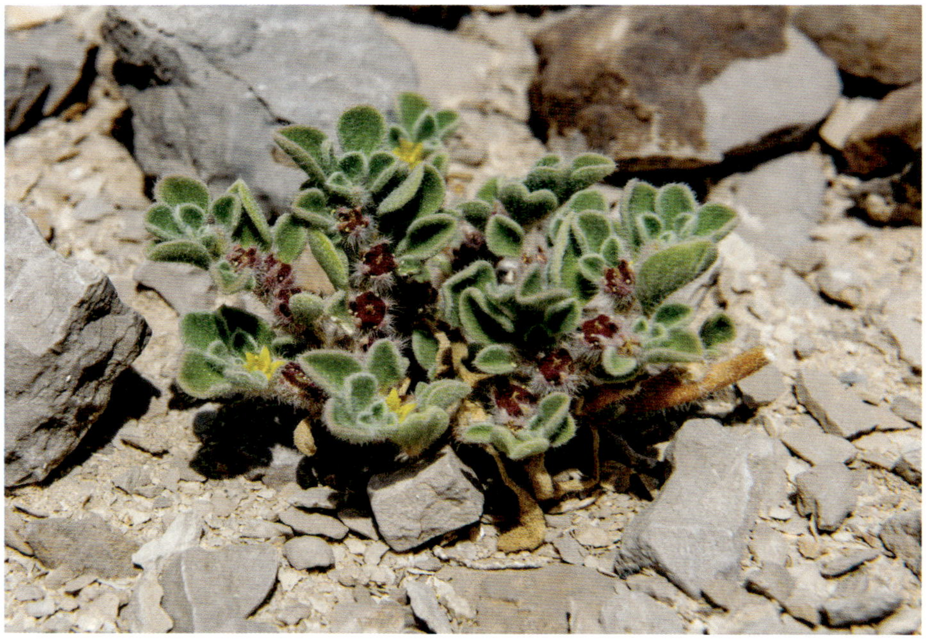

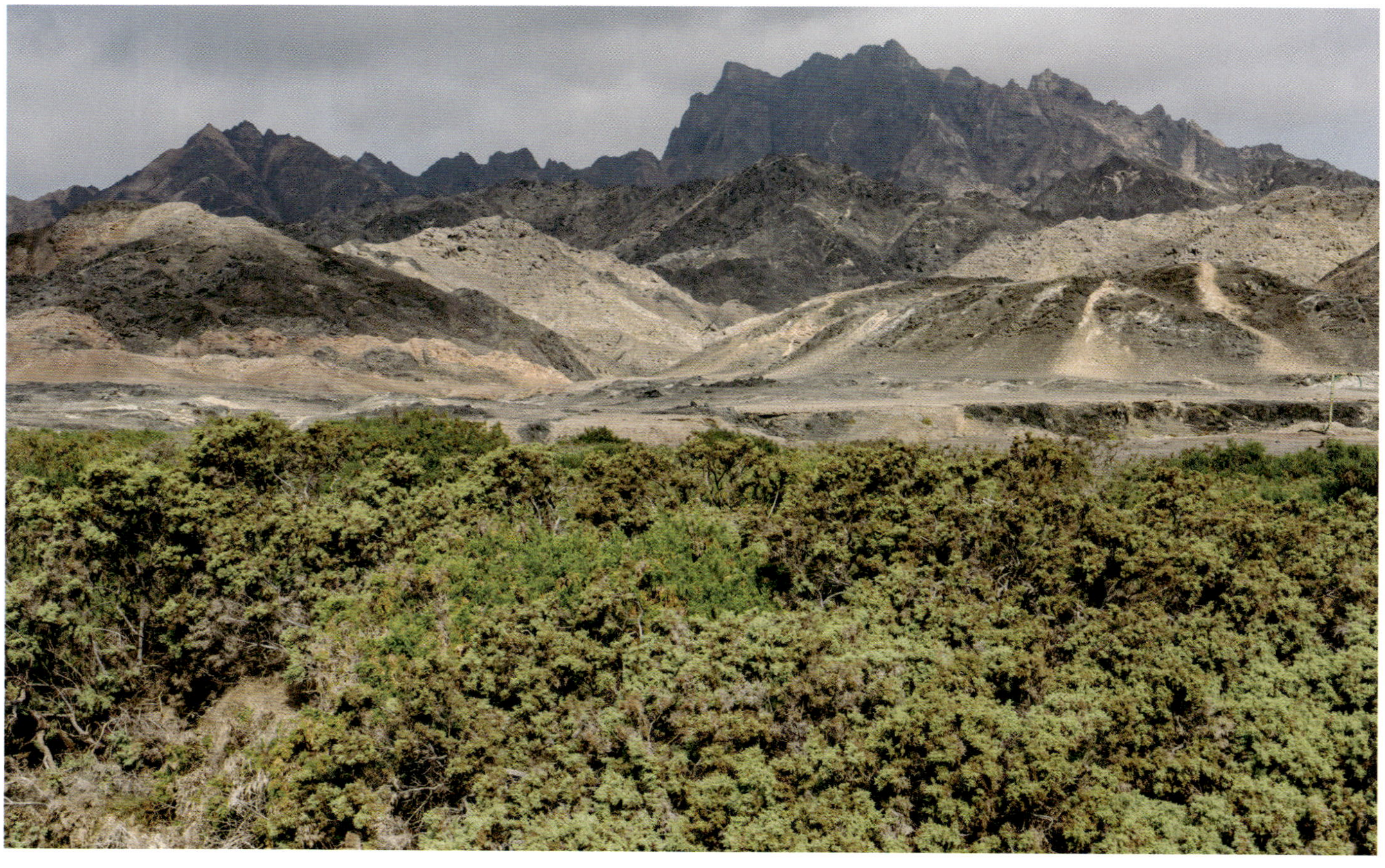

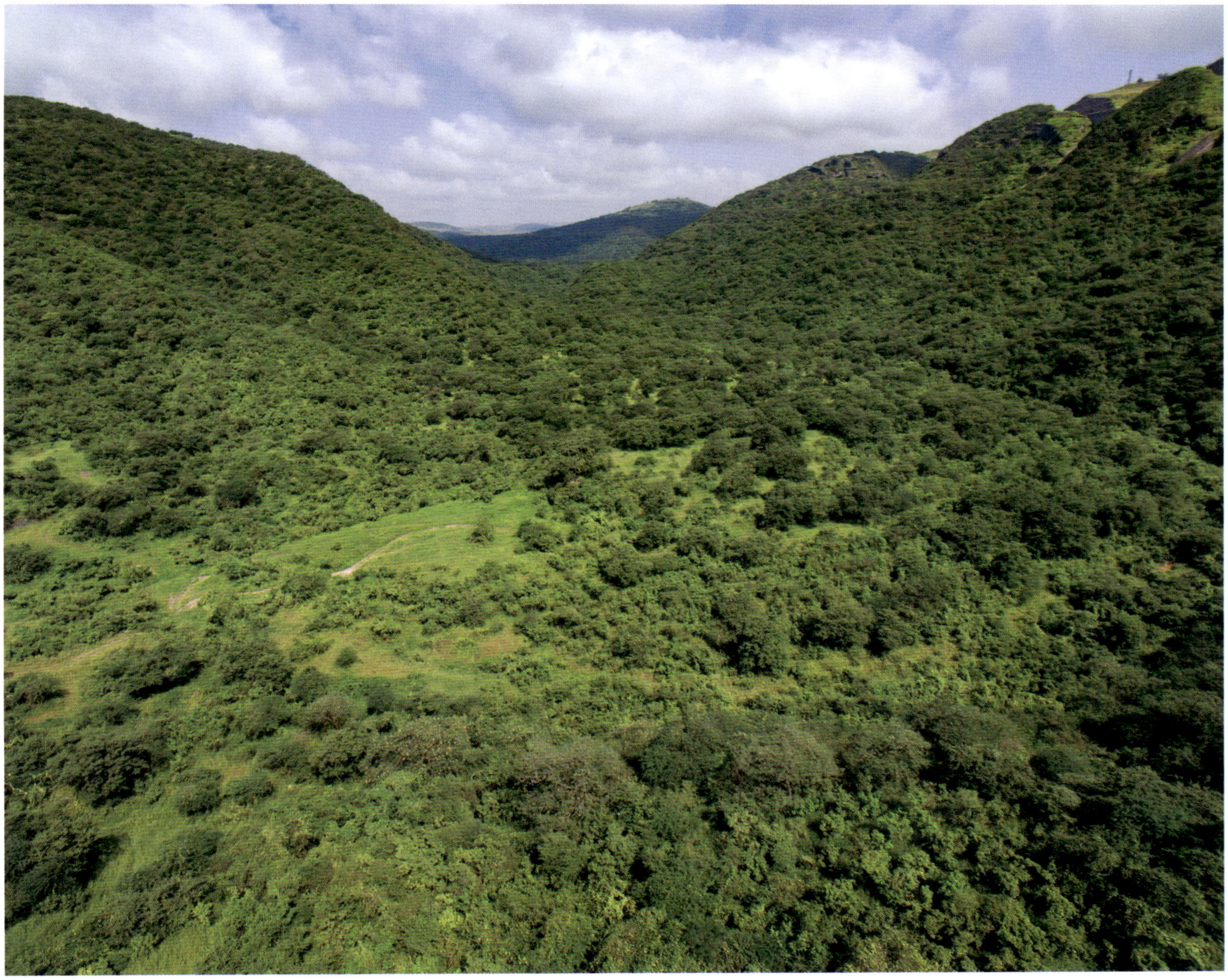

Jabal: South-Facing Escarpments

The south-facing escarpments are the seaward-facing slopes of Jabal Al Qamar, Jabal Al Qara and Jabal Samhan, including foothills, steep cliff faces and the valleys of southward-flowing wadis.

Jabal Al Qamar and Jabal Al Qara

In Jabal Al Qamar and Jabal Al Qara this zone is made up of monsoon woodlands and tall grasslands and is known locally as the *khatm*. It runs from the border with Yemen in the west to Wadi Hinna in the east but does not include the rain-shadow region of the arid wadis and slopes of Wadi Aful, Wadi Al Mughsayl and Wadi Ashawq that separate Jabal Al Qamar from Jabal Al Qara.

The broad foothills of Jabal Al Qara are dominated by termite mounds, most of which are inactive, and above which is a narrow belt of open woodland comprising the evergreen *Boscia arabica* (Ji. Sĩr), a tree that is also present on the lower slopes of Jabal Al Qamar. Above this, and also common to the lower and drier slopes of Jabal Al Qamar, is a community dominated by *Commiphora* species, the resin

The thickly-wooded Wadi Nahiz ***(above)*** is typical of the south-facing wadis that come under the influence of the monsoon.

The splendid flower of *Delonix elata* ***(right)***, one of the most common trees on the lower slopes or southern foothills of the mountains. In previous times the wood of the tree was used for making lime in the lime kilns of the Jarbib.

The endemic *Aloe praetermissa* ***(far right)***, only known from Dhofar, is widespread including on the south-facing escarpment of Jabal Al Qamar.

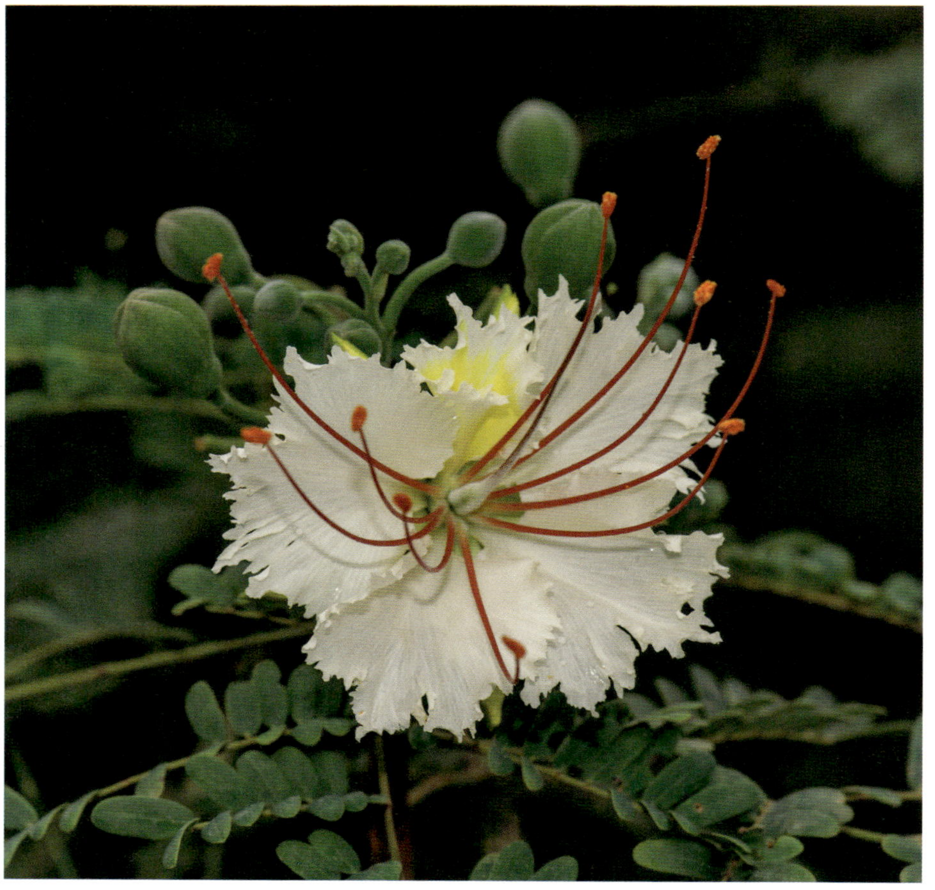

of one, *C. kua* (Ji. ʻÓḳor), being known as myrrh. It is one of four species of *Commiphora* that were used to produce myrrh in Oman and Yemen and was immensely important in local medicine as well as being one of the staple medicaments, along with antimony, aloe juice and indigo, which the mother of the family would keep in her private medicine bag.[66]

Above the gentle foothills is the true cloud forest dominated by *Anogeissus dhofarica*, usually referred to by its local name, Sġót, a regional endemic only occurring in Dhofar and across the Oman–Yemen border, where the monsoon forest extends west for about 50 kilometres. Sġót is a deciduous tree and comes into leaf in June, at the beginning of the monsoon, transforming the grey-brown mountainsides and wadis. Leaf-fall is usually by November but in years of a very heavy monsoon, as happened in 2016, many trees come back into leaf and flower in March of the following year.

Other trees growing alongside Sġót include *Delonix elata* (Ji. Érír) as well as two south Arabian endemics, *Euphorbia smithii* (Ji. Hiok) and *Gymnosporia dhofarensis* (Ji. Sérbit). Under the canopy, thriving in dappled shade, is a carpet of shrubs including *Croton confertus* (Ji. Ḥōr), creepers such as wild cucumber (*Cucumis sativus,* Ji. Aḥsebe), bulbs such as *Gladiolus candidus* (Ji. Bedah) and grasses including *Arundinella pumila*. The epiphytic herb *Remusatia vivipara* (Ji. Fóḍe), which has huge leaves up to 40 centimetres long and whose tubers are gathered and eaten, is very characteristic of the wet undergrowth. In places *Impatiens balsamina* (Ji. Sefer) forms a broad carpet while on shaded banks and damp rocks are delicate ferns including the maidenhair fern (*Adiantum capillus-veneris*).

The Sġót forests coincide with the areas of heaviest monsoon precipitation and remain under thick cloud for most of July and August. On top of the water that falls as drizzle the Sġót captures significant amounts of water that is blown as fog through the forest canopy. Known as 'horizontal precipitation', this contributes significantly to the water economy of the mountain vegetation.[69]

At mid-elevations (500-800 metres), on plateaux between the wadis, the Sġót forests are replaced by open tall grasslands dominated by *Themeda quadrivalvis* (Ji. Ēlí), which can grow to 2.5 metres if cattle do not graze on them. These grasslands are rich in species; on Jabal Al Qamar 112 species have been recorded

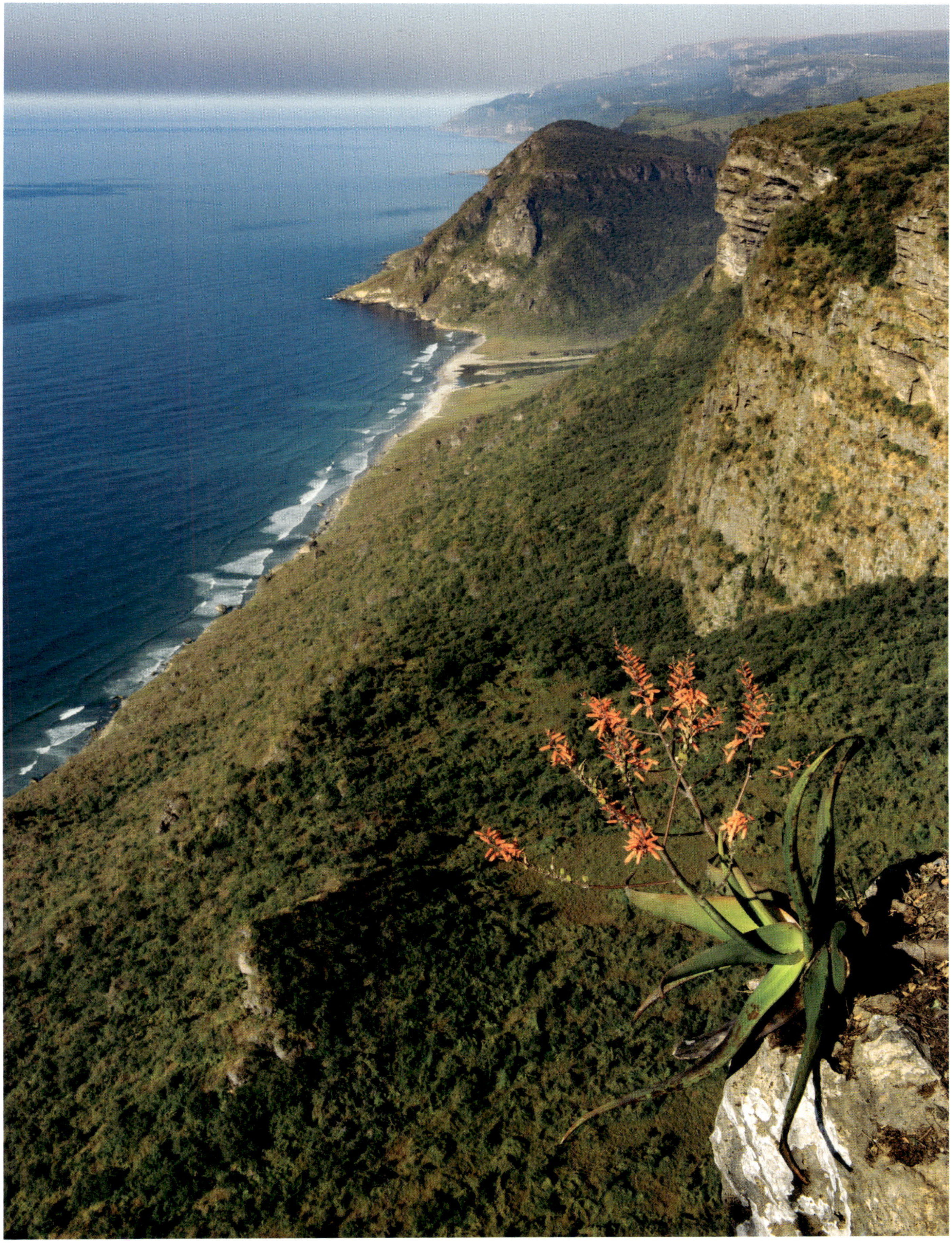

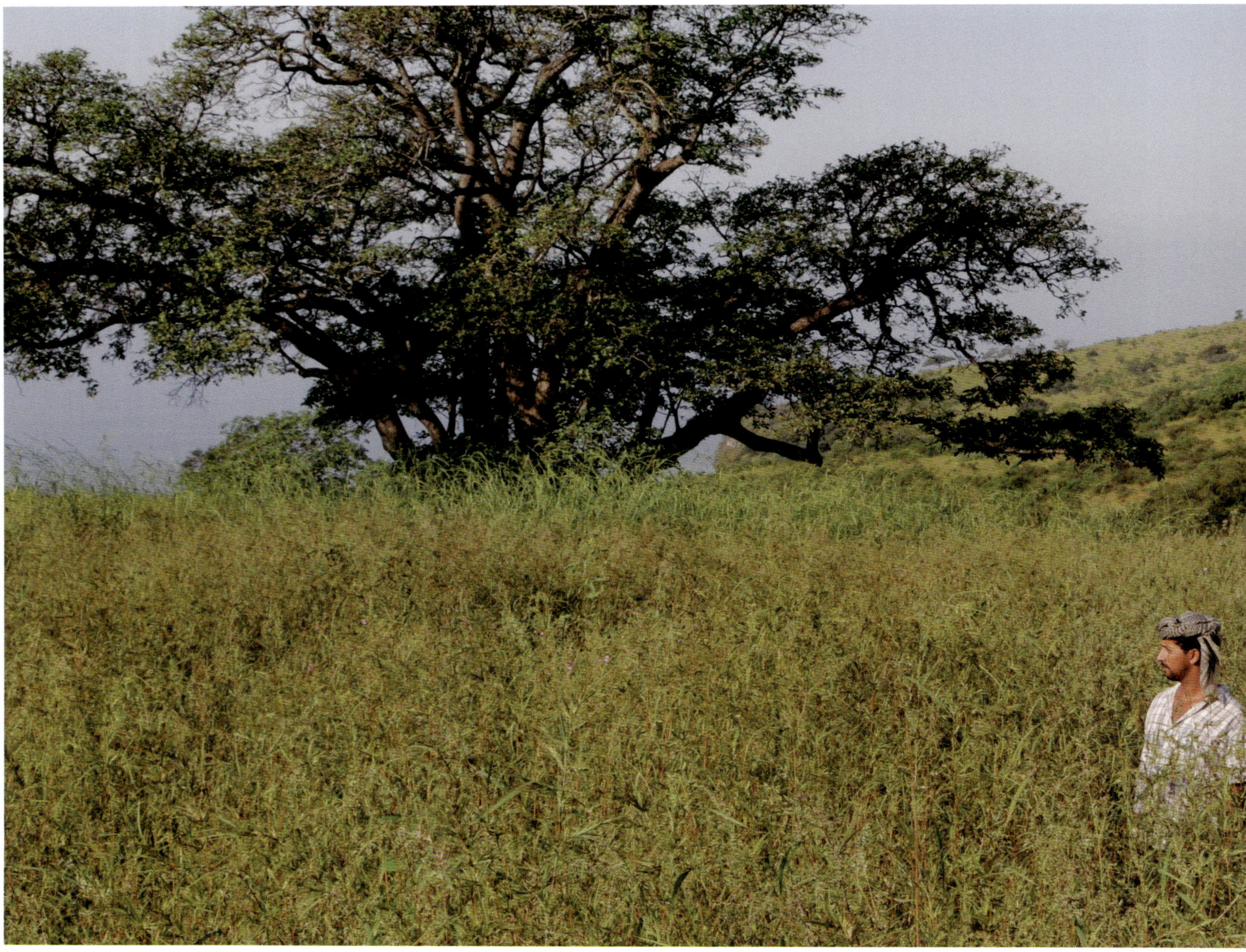

and, of these, 11% are unique to the region and five occur only in Dhofar.[70] Growing amongst the grasslands are scattered trees and, in many locations, particularly on Jabal Al Qamar, extensive stands of the very conspicuous and unpalatable evergreen *Dodonaea viscosa* (Ji. Sires). In contrast, the Sġót is a very important browsing food for camels, with the result that it is often cut to feed livestock. Another important fodder species is *Plectranthus barbatus* (Ji. Źefúbreḳ), which grows on rocky outcrops and is also used as a deodorant.

The grasslands are most extensive on Jabal Al Qara and in many places, particularly north of Madinat Al Haq, they stretch over the rolling hills to a horizon that is only rarely broken by occasional specimens of Sġót and scattered ancient fig trees (*Ficus vasta*, Ji. Ṭiḳ). On Jabal Al Qamar these grasslands are less developed although extensive pastures are found, particularly on the plateau west of Wadi Sayq. These are Dhofar's best rangelands.

On Jabal Al Qamar the Sġót again dominates a second, higher escarpment above the grasslands. On Jabal Al Qara there is little Sġót at higher elevations but in places it forms open woodland while elsewhere it occurs as isolated clumps amongst a landscape dominated by fig trees, Christ's thorn, *Gymnosporia dhofarensis* and *Commiphora spp.*

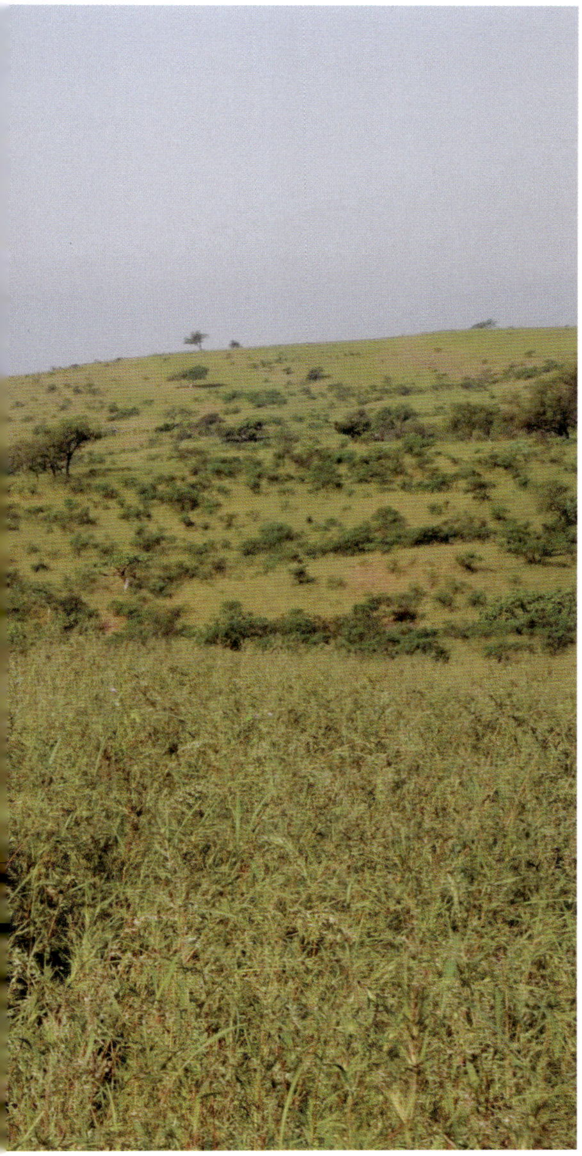

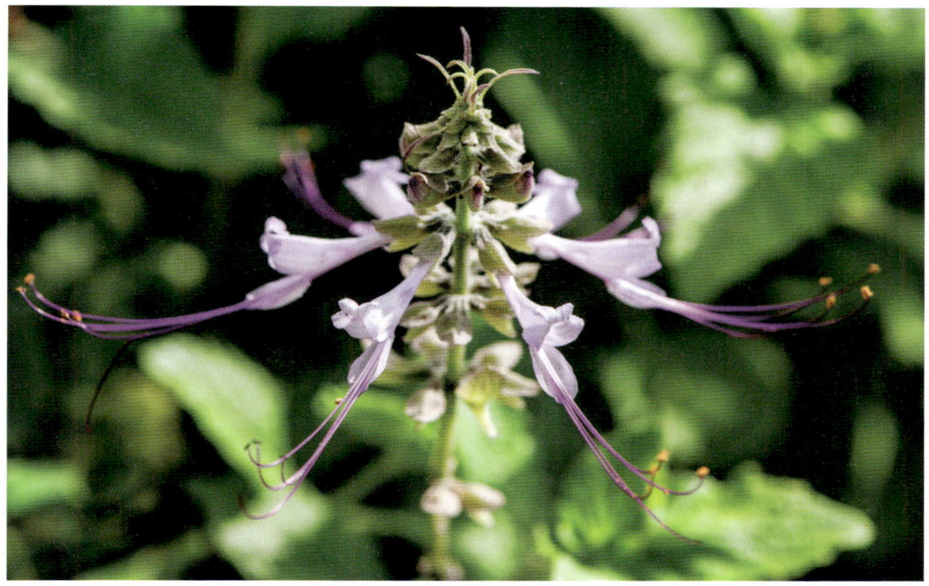

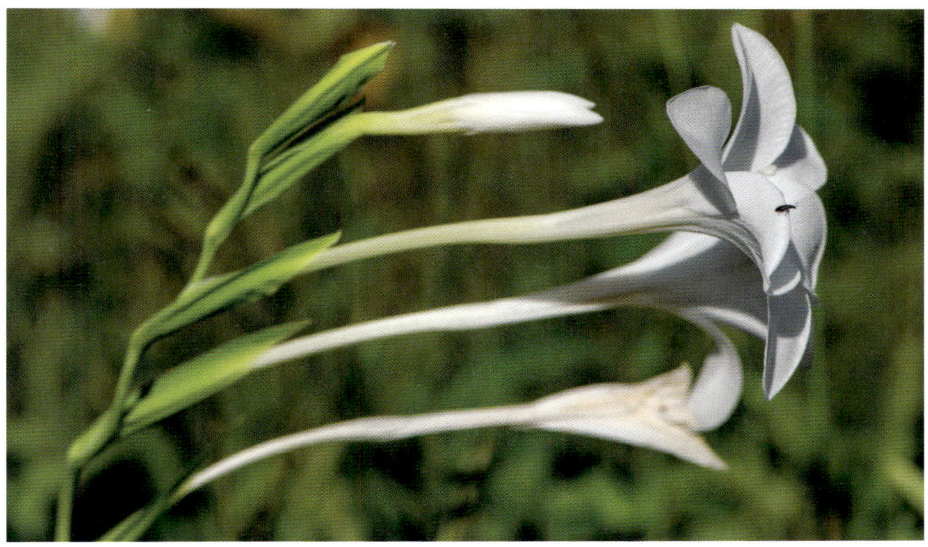

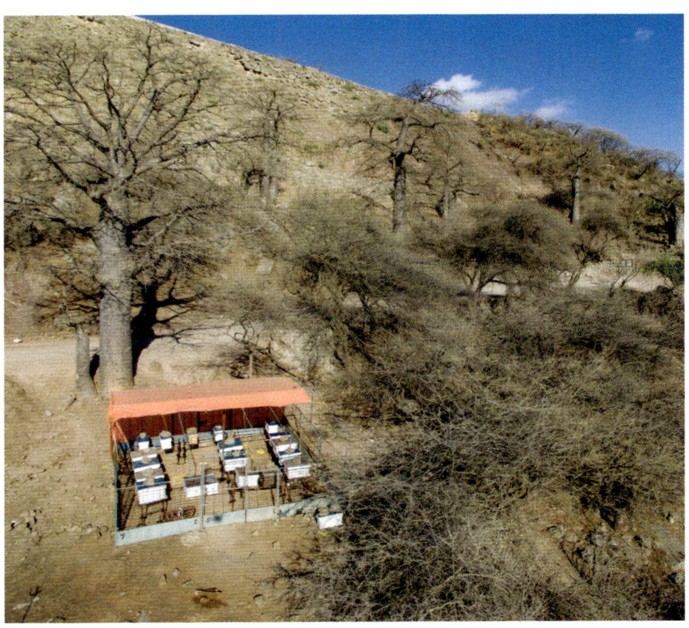

Local people recall when the tall *Themeda quadrivalvis* grasses were at least as tall as a man. Today, outside of exclosures ***(above left)***, the grasslands are heavily grazed by livestock.

Species common to the south-facing slopes include the almost endemic *Ocimum dhofarense* (Ji. Ho *dem*) ***(top)*** and *Gladiolus candidus* ***(above)***.

A lone baobab *Adansonia digitata*, (Ji. enkize) grows near Dalkut while about 30 trees are found in Wadi Hinna ***(left)***.

Wadi Aful, Wadi Al Mughsayl and Wadi Ashawq Drylands

East of Shaat on Jabal Al Qamar the alignment of the coast and the Jabal shifts more north than east, the elevation rises to over 1,000 metres and the landscape is shaped by three southward-flowing wadis, beyond which Jabal Al Qara rises. Here is a dry belt where the influence of the *khareef* is much reduced and the area has an arid feel, reminiscent of the Najd.

The escarpments, wadis and cliffs are dominated by arid-land species. Above Wadi Aful the slopes and horizons are dotted with the endangered Arabian dragon tree (*Dracaena serrulata*, Ji. ʿÁyrób), a close relative of the famous dragon's blood tree of Socotra. It is endemic to Oman, Yemen and Saudi Arabia and occurs here at high densities not seen elsewhere in Dhofar. Another widespread species in close association with the Arabian dragon tree is *Euphorbia momccoyae* (Ji. Zuger), which in spite of its cactus-like appearance, with angular stems and spines, is not a cactus. *Commiphora kua* is common and frankincense is found high on the cliffs and on the wadi floors. Resin from these trees is known as *shazari*. Also found at exceptionally high densities is *Aloe dhufarensis* (Ji. Tuf), endemic to the mountains of Dhofar and Hawf (in Yemen), and one of the most important medicinal plants. At lower elevations, in association with *Aloe dhufarensis*, are the succulents *Monolluma quadrangula* (Ji. Zoja) and *Sansevieria ehrenbergii* (Ji. Śēbṯeh).

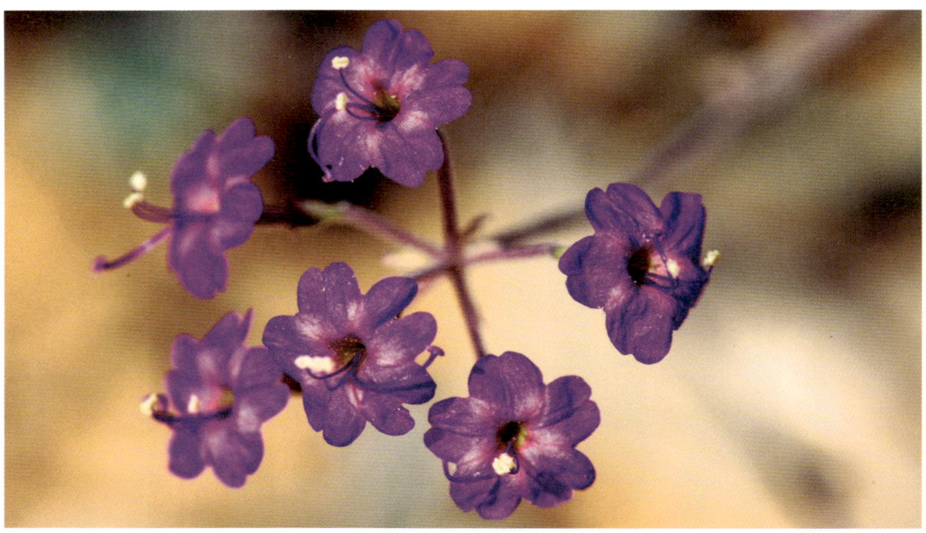

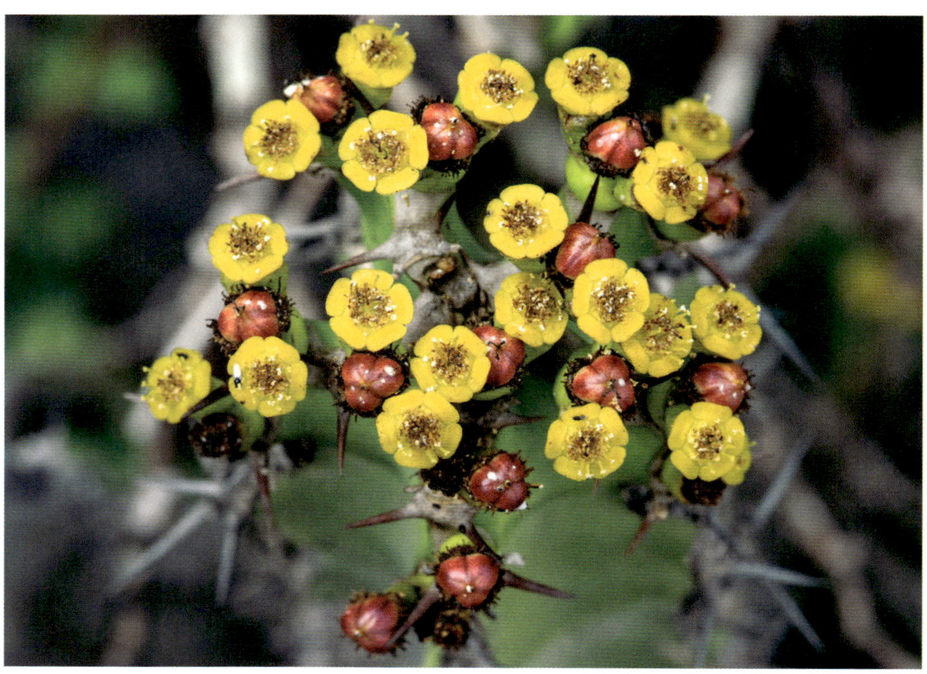

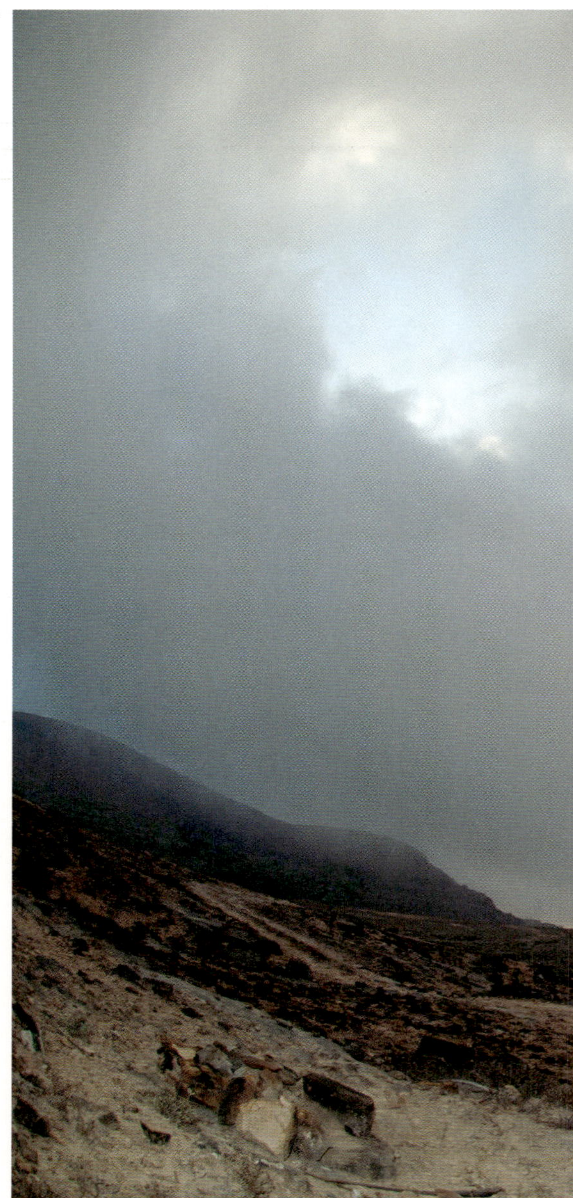

Jabal Samhan

Although clouds are often seen along the Samhan escarpment there is very little precipitation and thus the vegetation is very different to that of the adjacent Jabal Al Qara. Sġót is almost absent, except in the far west, and is replaced by an open woodland community dominated by species of acacia and *commiphora*. At least three species of acacia are found, including *Acacia asak,* which has not been recorded anywhere else in Oman, and two species of myrrh. Frankincense is widespread in a small number of wadis, particularly Wadi Akaloo, just north of Mirbat.

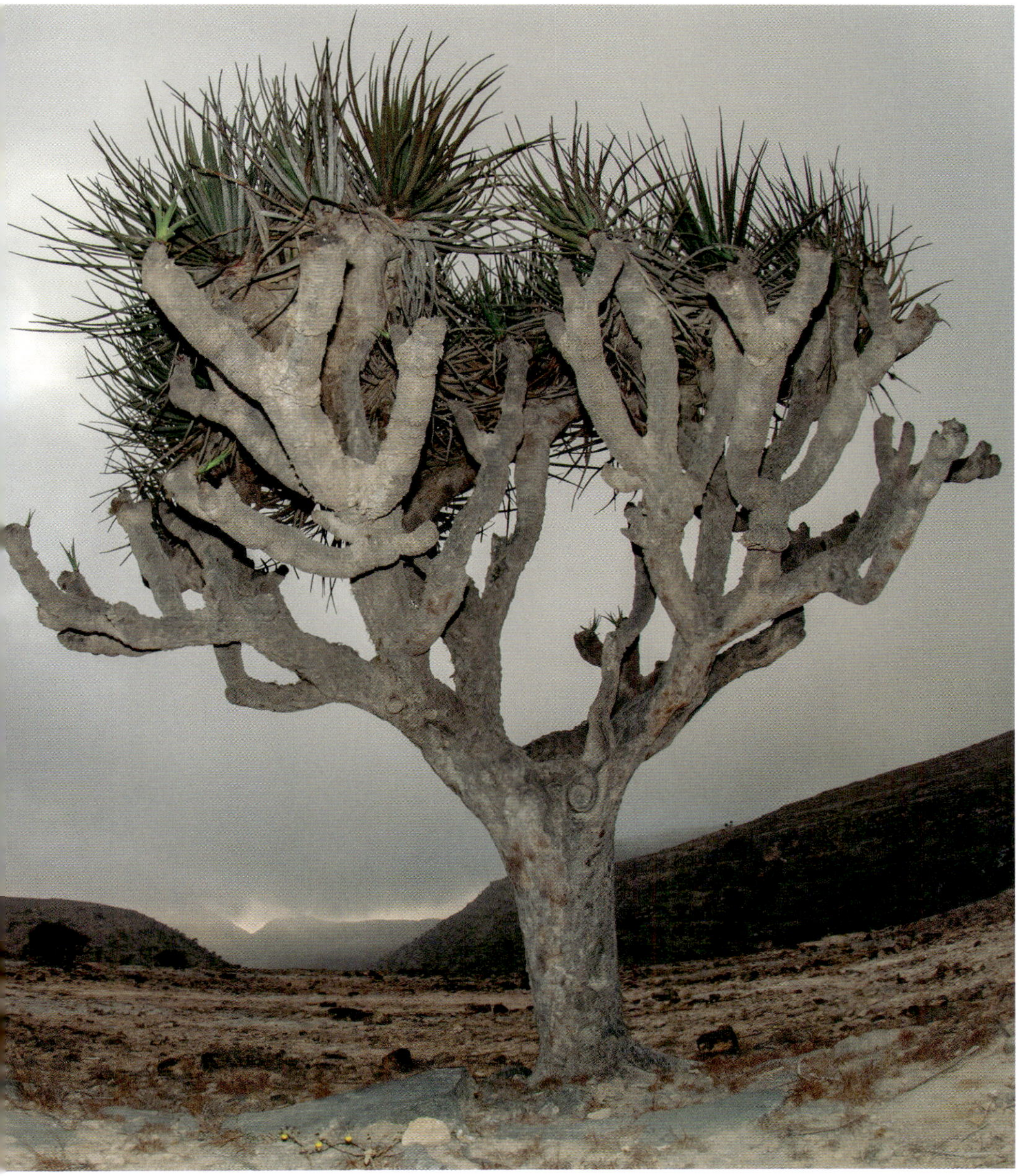

Though the monsoon clouds reach Wadi Aful, Wadi Al Mughsayl and Wadi Ashawq, they leave little or no precipitation. Hence this area, marking the eastern end of Jabal Al Qamar, remains dry and the landscape is dominated by dryland species, particularly the Arabian dragon tree ***(left)***. Other species include the cactus-like *Euphorbia momccoyae* ***(far left, bottom)*** and *Boerhavia boissieri* (Ji. *Aytif*) ***(far left top).***

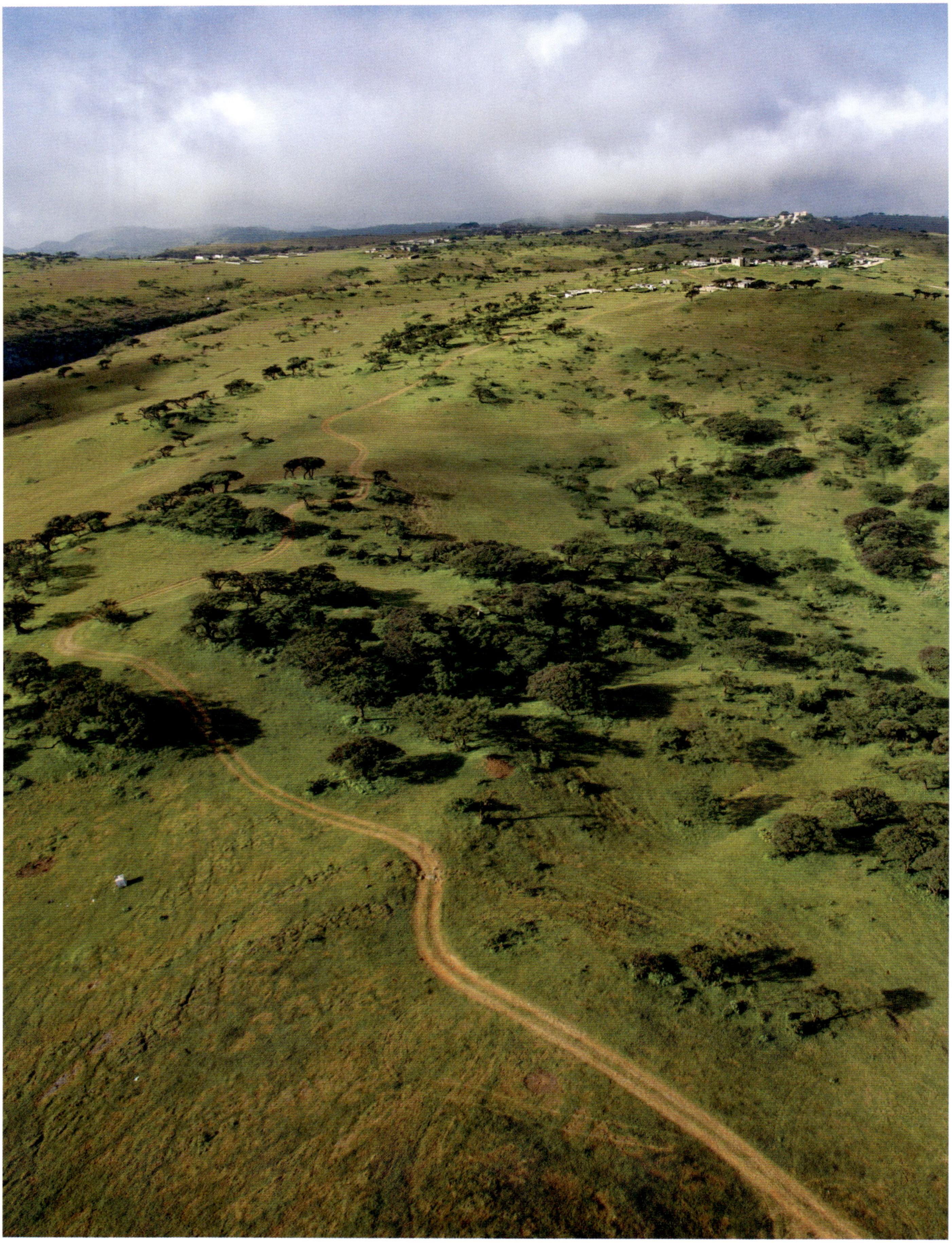

Jabal: Summit Plateaus

Jabals Al Qamar and Al Qara

Above the escarpments and wadis, approaching the watershed, the influence of the monsoon weakens and there is an abrupt change in the vegetation. This zone is known locally as the *qatn* and is considered by the herdsmen to be inferior to the *khatm*. On Jabal Al Qamar the *qatn*, south of the Salalah to Sarfayt highway, comprises a very distinctive scrubland dominated by *Commiphora species*, the Arabian balsam tree, *Cissus quadrangularis* (Ji. ʿAteré) and desert rose (*Adenium obesum*, Ji. Esféd). It is in this zone that many of the permanent settlements are found and thus there are very large numbers of livestock. North of the highway the increasingly arid plateau is much more sparsely vegetated, with *Aloe dhufarensis*, *Euphorbia momccoyae* and the Arabian balsam tree the most visible species.

On Jabal Al Qara the summit plateau, or *qatn*, is dominated by short grasses, with the characteristic shrub *Commiphora gileadensis* and, beyond the watershed, the Arabian balsam

On the summit plateaux of Jabal Al Qara are open woodlands dominated by wild olive. Particularly fine examples are found close to Titam ***(left)***. On Jabal Al Qamar the vegetation of the south-facing aspects of the plateaux comprises a low and heavily grazed scrubland with species such as *Commiphora* and desert rose ***(below)***.

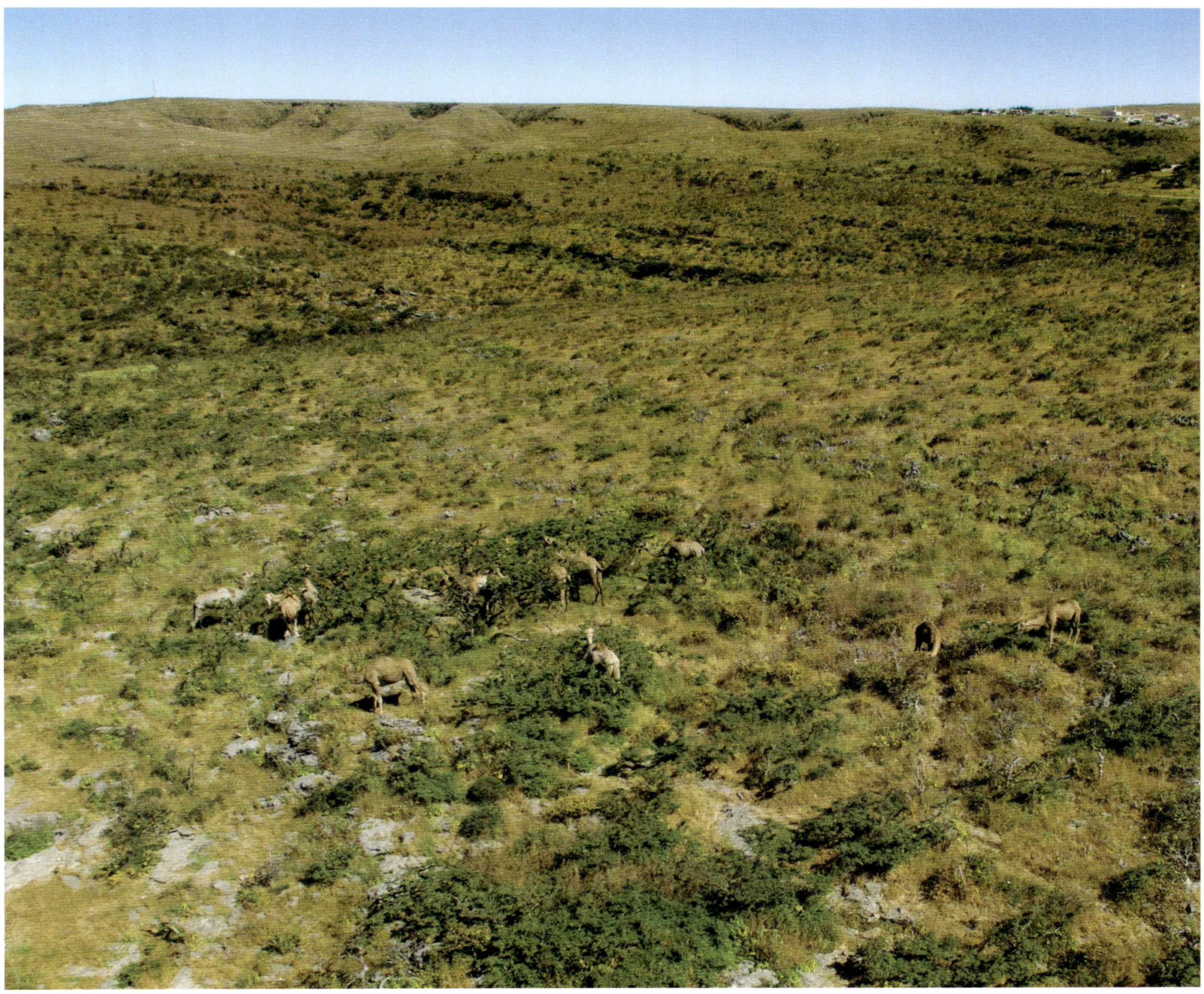

Magnificent fig trees dominate the skyline **(below)** in many areas, particularly the rock-strewn plateaux of eastern Jabal Al Qara. In places the woodlands have a rich ground flora **(right)** that includes species such as *Gladiolus candidus*, whose roots were once one of the most important wild food sources in Dhofar. In years of a strong monsoon the upper slopes of the north-facing escarpments on Jabal Al Qara boast a surprisingly rich flora with species such as *Kleinia saginata* (Ji. hubberaldi) **(opposite bottom left)** and *Teucrium nummularifolium* **(opposite bottom right)**.

tree quite common. There are open woodlands in this zone, including stands of ancient wild olive (*Olea europaea*, Ji. Mótin) in the west, in particular close to Titam. At the height of the monsoon the olive woodlands are shrouded in mist that supports a rich ground flora dominated by the grass *Arundinella pumila* and includes colourful species such as *Gladiolus candidus*, *Impatiens balsamina* and *Ipomoea nil* (Ji. *Kemerot*).

Beyond Tawi Aatayr where the Jabal rises east to Jabal Samhan, there are significant woodlands of *Acacia etbaica* (Ji. Ṣá'b), with undergrowth dominated by *Commiphora* species and the almost ubiquitous creeper *Cissus quadrangularis*. At slightly higher elevations the acacia is replaced by a dense population of *Adenium obesum* together with the Arabian balsam tree. Further north, close to Jibjat, are open woodlands of *Acacia etbaica* in an otherwise heavily overgrazed barren landscape. The northern limit of the *qatn* is the escarpment that overlooks the harsh Najd landscape.

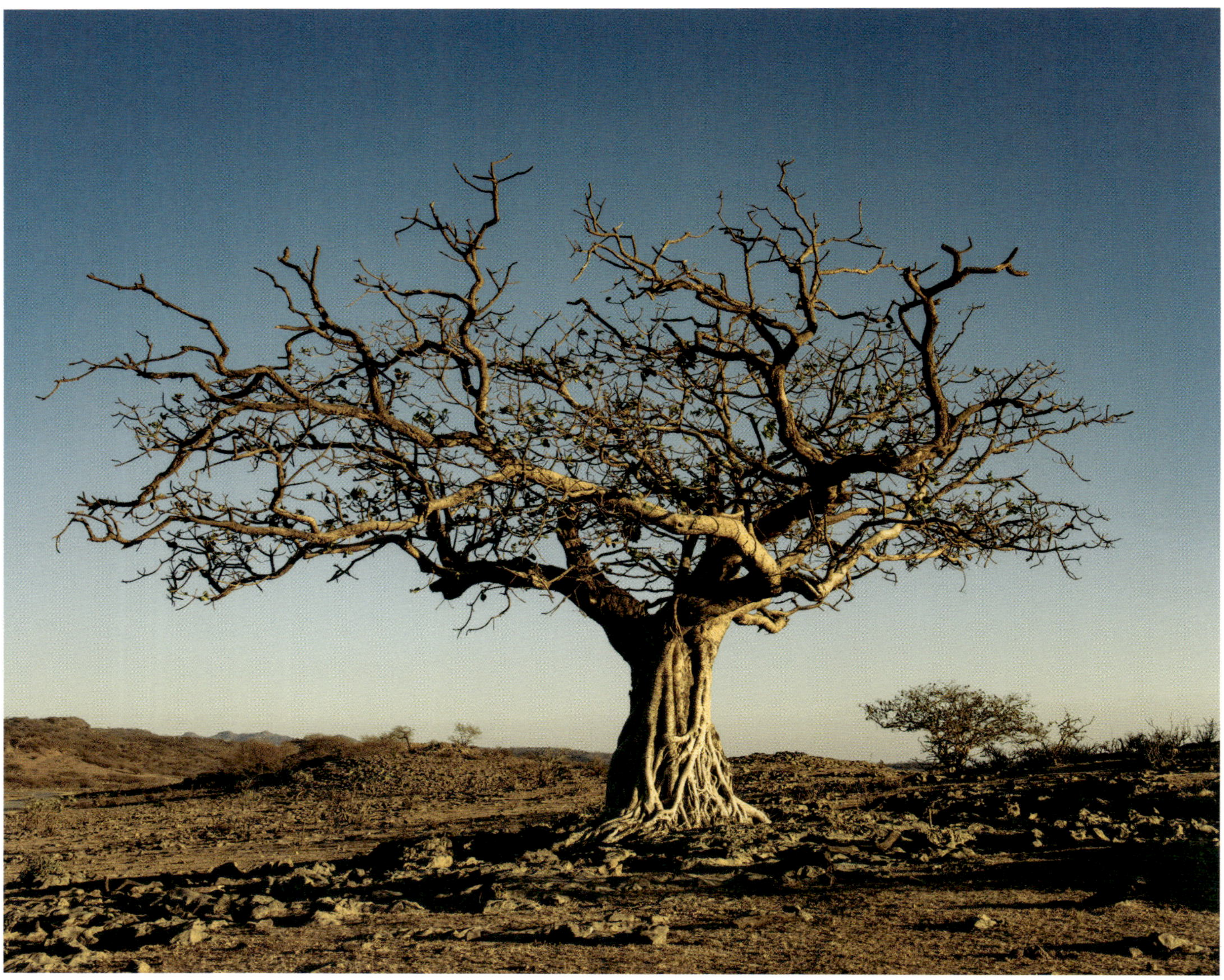

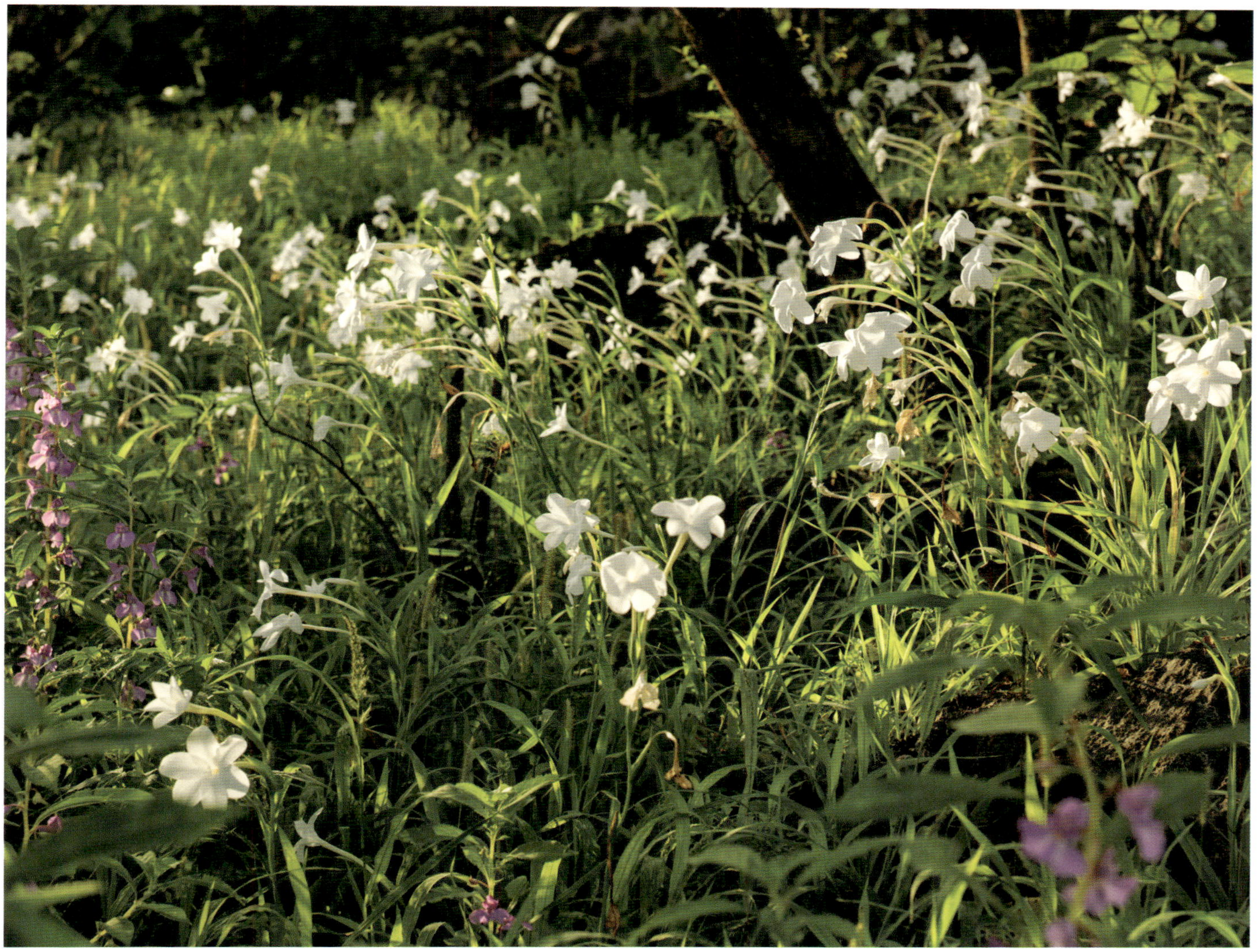

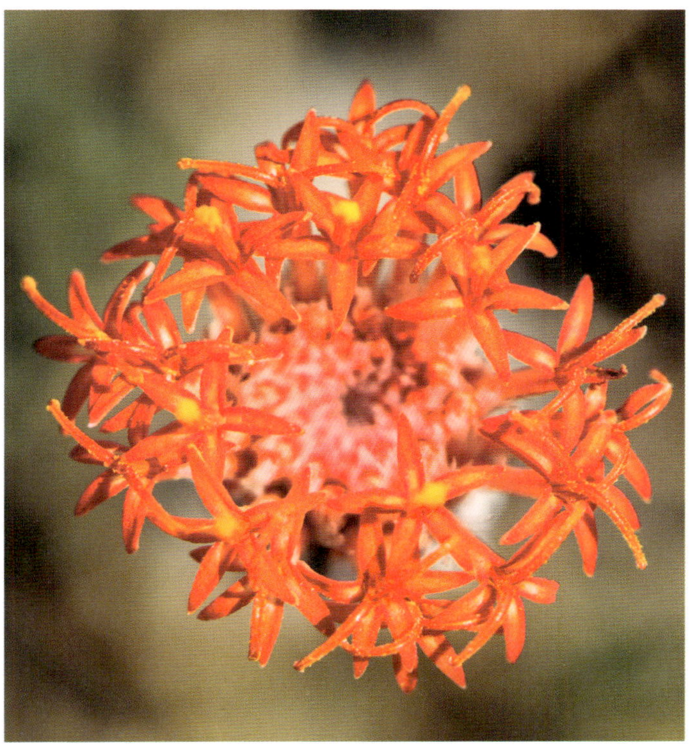

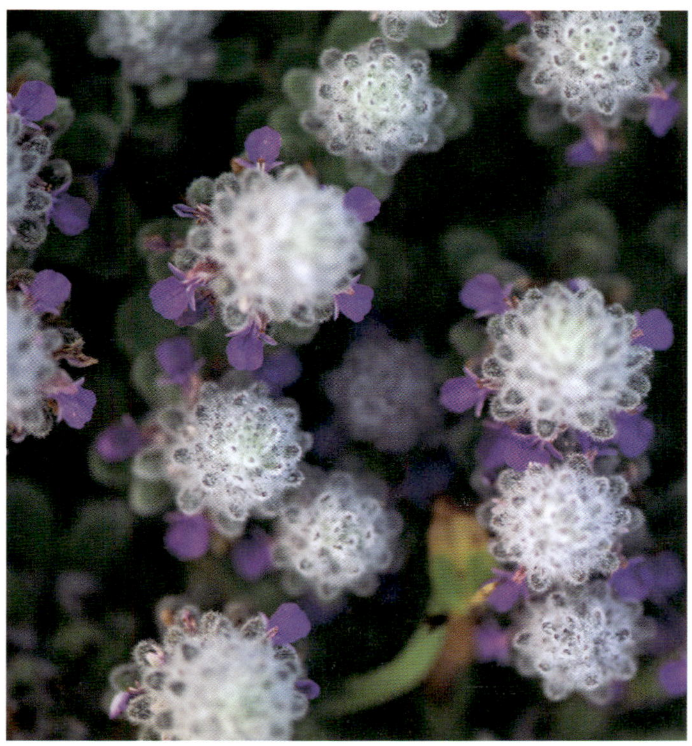

Jabal Samhan

The summit of Jabal Samhan is arid and after the richness of the adjacent Jabal Al Qara first impressions are that there is little vegetation. However, it seems that the plants benefit from the clouds that sit over the escarpment during the monsoon as there is a sparse but very interesting flora and the area is one of only five local centres of endemism in Oman.[71] Most conspicuous, though present only in small numbers, is the Arabian dragon tree, which is also found in the drier, high-altitude areas of Jabal Al Qamar. As a high-altitude species it is considered to be particularly susceptible to the rising temperatures associated with global climate change. The only other conspicuous plant is the leafless spurge (*Euphorbia schimperi*) but amongst the much smaller flora there are four species that are endemic to Jabal Samhan – *Salvia hillcoatiae*, *Barleria samhanensis*, *Pulicaria samhanensis*, and *Lavandula hasikensis* – and thus the mountain holds 100% of the global population of these species.[71]

While the *khareef* provides some relief in the form of cool moist winds, the plateaux may go several years without rainfall. Some plants remain dormant but spring to life after rain with a profusion of flowers. One example is the herb *Diplotaxis harra* (Ji. Ġaśór), whose bright yellow blooms give the impression that the plateau is carpeted yellow. After very exceptional rains the desert truffle (*Tirmania nivea*, Ji. Bahath) may erupt and is quickly gathered by local people; the truffles command a very good price in international markets, especially in other Gulf states.

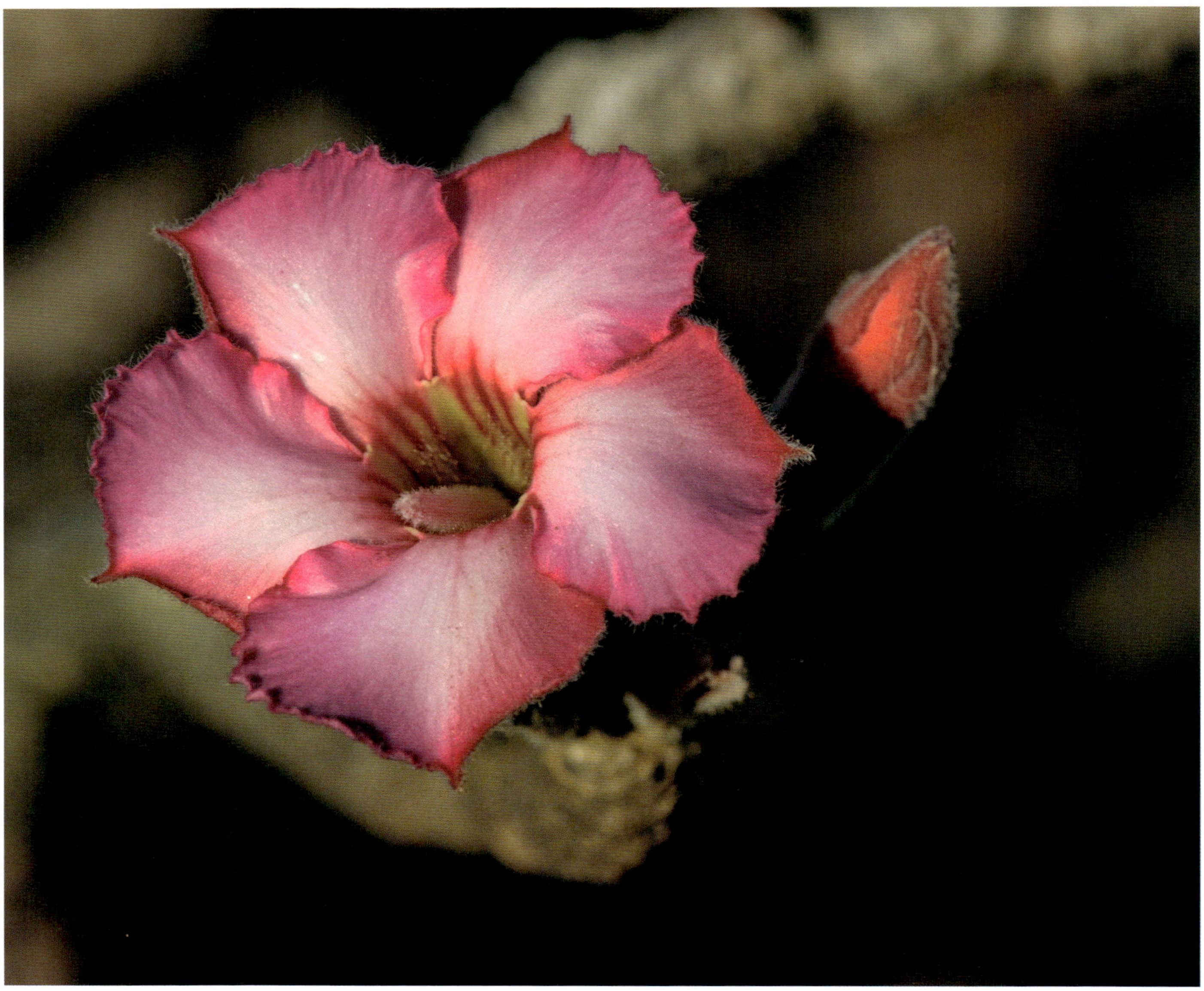

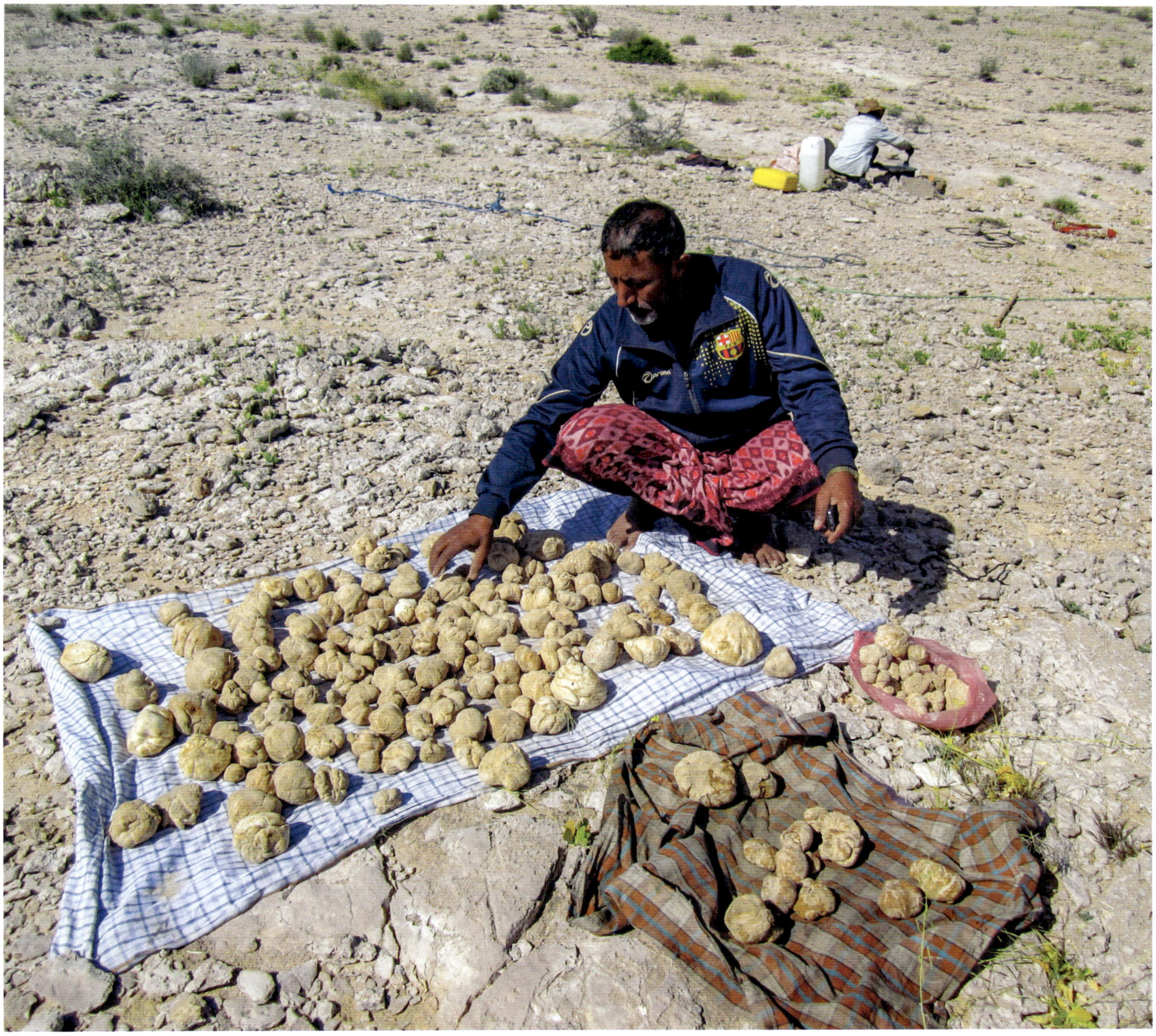

Jabal: Springs and Lakes

The south-facing escarpments and wadis include numerous springs that on Jabal Al Qara form significant water bodies, particularly in Wadi Darbat. The open lakes are dominated by the pondweed *Potamogeton nodosus* and *Najas graminea* but it is the smaller springs where the most interesting species may be found. For example, the eastern marsh helleborine orchid (*Epipactis veratrifolia*) is found in small springs, seeps, and in rock cavities while the regionally endemic Arabian violet *Exacum* aff. *affine* occurs in a few locations at springs on the southern foothills of Jabal Samhan. The aquatic fern known as water lettuce (*Ceratopteris cornuta*) has been recorded at limestone springs while the attractive Indian red water lily found at Ayn Razat was introduced and is now considered naturalised.

One of the most conspicuous plants of the western slopes of Jabal Samhan is the desert rose ***(left)***. Unlike many plants, it has few traditional uses and was often avoided for it was believed that snakes obtain their poison from it. Conversely the very rare desert truffle ***(above)*** is highly sought-after as it fetches extraordinarily high prices.

In the upper reaches of northward-flowing wadis are groves of frankincense *(below right)* while further north the flora is dominated by a small number of species including *Maerua crassifolia, acacia* species and extensive stands of dwarf palm *(below)*.

The Southern Najd

The Najd commences at the upper limits of the northward- flowing wadis and continues north into the open desert. It largely lies beyond the influence of the monsoon and consequently vegetation cover is typically sparse, with hotspots close to desert springs and on wadi beds.

The upper wadis of the Najd, from Jabal Al Qamar east to Jabal Samhan, are sometimes referred to as 'the frankincense zone' as this is often the only tree in this area. It prefers the north-facing slopes of the plateaux and the floor and valley sides of the steep tributaries, but is largely absent from lower elevations, where the great wadis become broad open riverbeds gently meandering north. On Jabal Samhan the major areas of frankincense are in the headlands of Wadi Arah and Wadi Andhur as well as further east in the wadis north of Hasik. North of Jabal Al Qara the important wadis include Wadi Amat, Wadi Uyun, Wadi Hirayt, Wadi Dhahbun and Wadi Dawkah. In the Najd regions of Jabal Al Qamar frankincense occurs in a number of wadis including Wadi Aydam that flows north to the desert and Wadi Sayq that flows south to the sea.

Amongst other plants in this zone *Tetraena decumbens*, *Heliotropium bacciferum*, *Launaea castanosperma* and *Ochradenus giffrii* have been recorded on Jabal Al Qamar[72] while those of Jabal Al Qara include *Convolvulus hystrix*, *Heliotropium bacciferum*, *Cleome brachycarpa* (Ji. Źaʿāf), *Tetraena decumbens*, *Salsola rubescens* and the endemic *Fagonia mahrana*.[73] In the east, on Jabal Samhan, species on the wadi edges

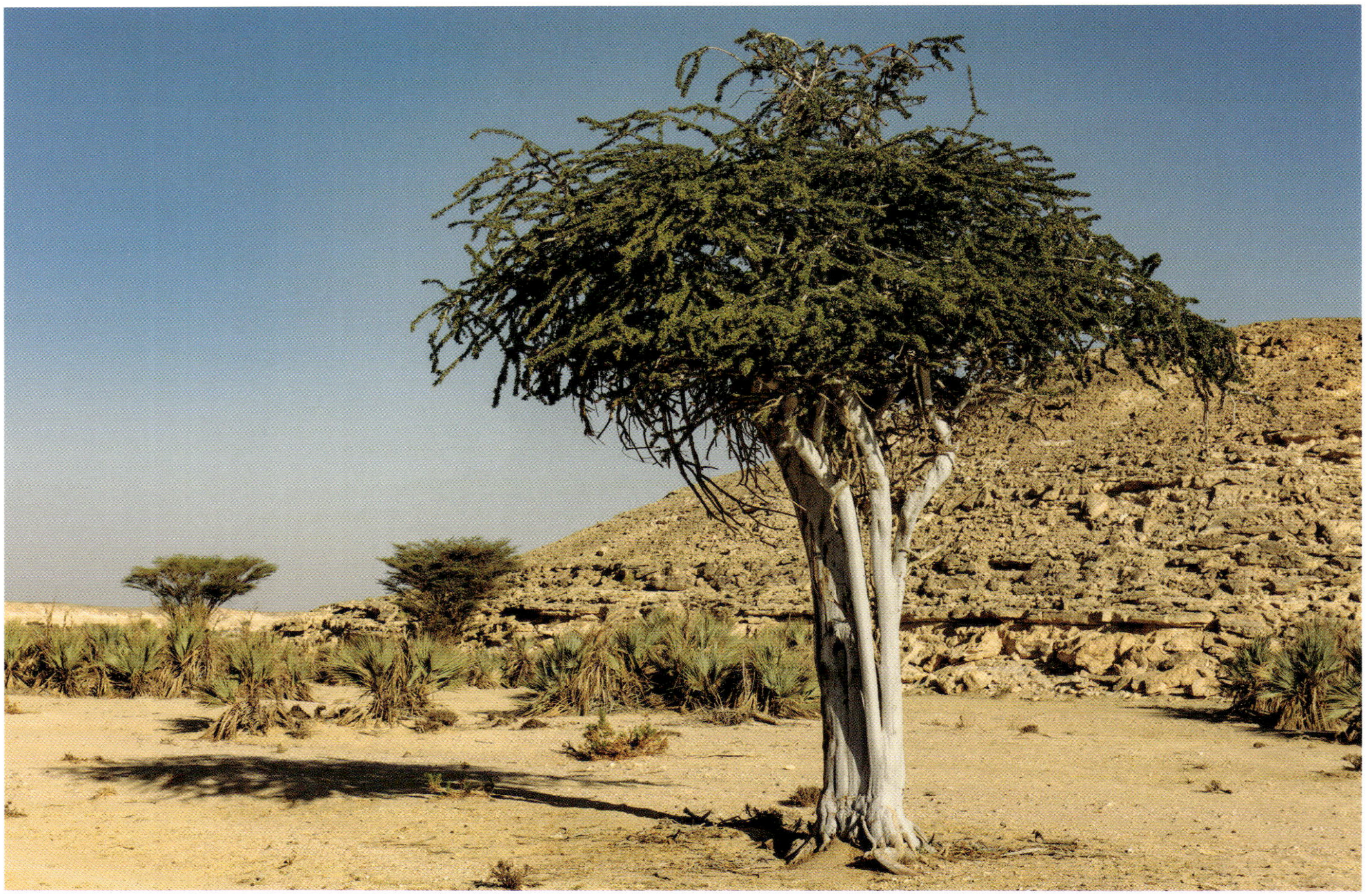

and slopes include the yellow-flowered *Kelleronia revoillii*, the endemic *Dhofaria macleishii* and the near-endemic *Gymnosporia dhofarensis*.[74]

As the wadis flow north the landscape becomes more open and frankincense no longer occurs; other trees, including *Acacia gerrardii*, *Acacia tortilis*, *Maerua crassifolia* (Ji. Sir śeherét), *Moringa peregrina* and tamarisk are found. The timber of both *Moringa peregrina* and tamarisk is highly resistant to termites and thus both species were historically highly sought-after for making the traditional Dhofari roundhouse as well as other household items. However, the most conspicuous species is the dwarf palm *(Nannorrhops ritchiana, Ji. 'Arf, Ar. Ghaẓf)*, which occurs in large clumps in the open wadis of the Najd. This was one of the most important plants for the pastoralists of the Jabal and the Najd and was used to make numerous household items, from rope to camel-milking bowls. Along the wadi margins meanwhile is found the so-called toothbrush tree (*Salvadora persica*, Ji. Eherik).

The larger pools of the Najd, such as those of Wadi Uyun, Wadi Andhur and Wadi Arah, are typically fringed by southern cattail (*Typha domingensis*), *Phragmites australis* and sea rush (*Juncus rigidus*). The date palm (*Phoenix dactylifera*, Ji. Xus) also occurs at many of these pools, both as tall mature trees and clumps of immature plants. They rarely bear edible fruit but traditionally the leaves and branches were used to make household items including bird traps to catch desert species, particularly the Arabian partridge (*Alectoris melanocephala*).[66]

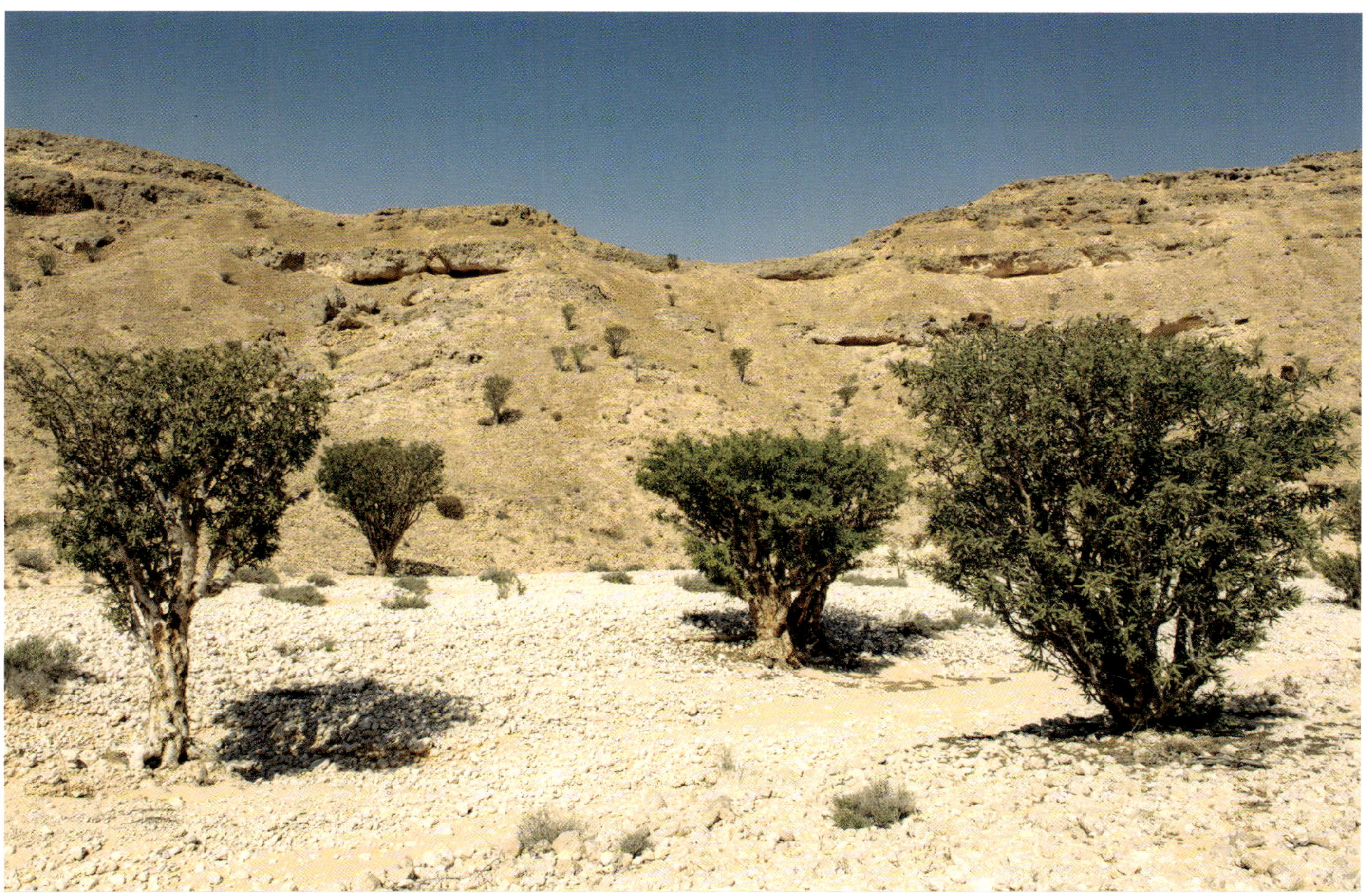

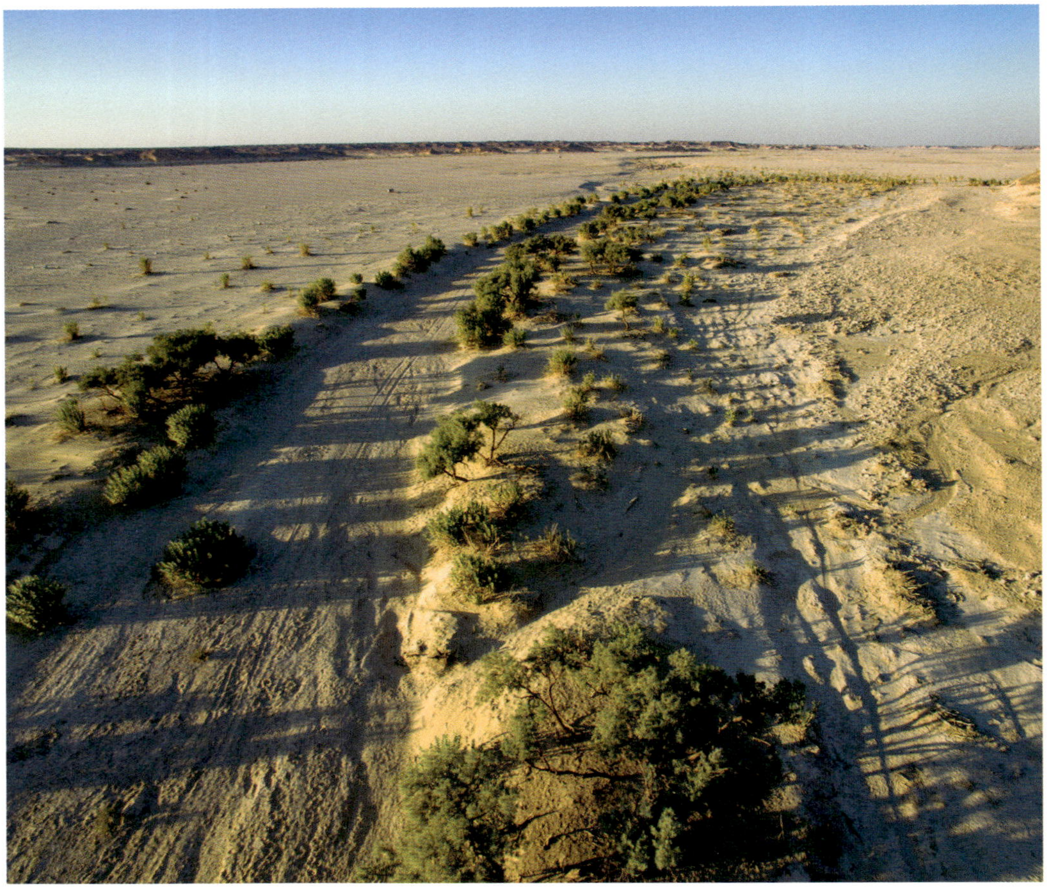

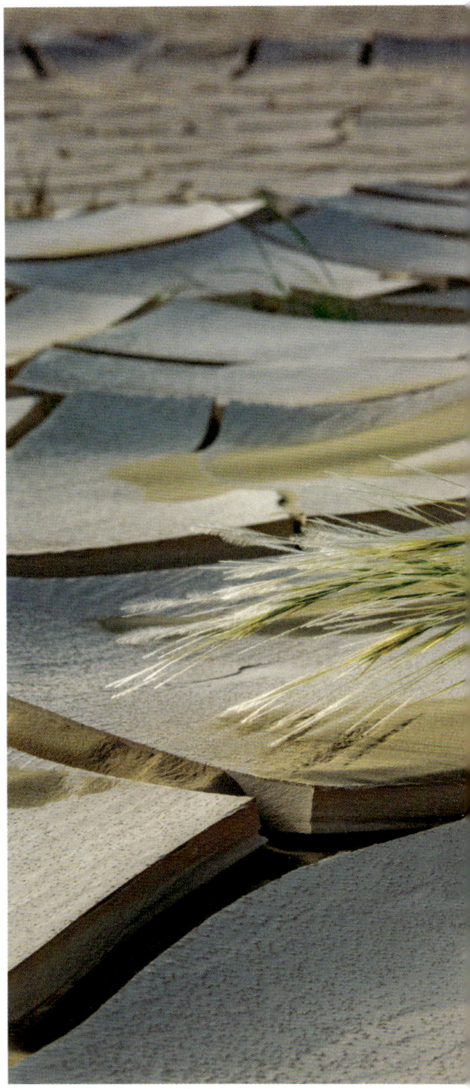

The Northern Najd

The northern Najd is hyper-arid and consequently large areas are barren and without vegetation. At the northern extent of many of the major wadis there are stands of trees that in the west – for example at Wadi Ghadun – are dominated by *Tamarix aphylla* and also Sodom's apple (*Calotropis procera*, Ji. Úṭeb), an indicator of overgrazing. In the east, including the lower Wadi Arah, there are extensive woodlands of Ghaf (*Prosopis cineraria*, Ar. *ghaf*). On the gravel plains the dominant tree is Simr (*Acacia tortilis*), which occurs in different forms. Typically it resembles an umbrella but in the north-east, it has the appearance of a ground-hugging shrub, mostly likely a response to the strong winds of the summer monsoon and coastal winds. During seasonal fogs the small, fine leaflets of the Simr trap water that drips to the floor and is taken up by the tree's shallow root system.

The sparse ground flora includes *Rhazya stricta* (Ji. Adfir), which is considered the chief medicinal plant of the central desert while also used to fend off the *jinn* and 'evil eye'. Other shrubs include *Heliotropium bacciferum* (Ar. *hahhfa*), *Crotalaria aegyptiaca*, *Limonium stocksii* and species of *Tetraena*. Grasses flourishing after rain include species of *Stipagrostis*.

In the north-east the vegetation is very different. At first glance the Jiddat Arkad and plateau above Ash Shuwaymiyyah seem bleak, with only the stunted Simr trees visible on the gravel horizons. However, on the stony plateaux, shallow wadis and coastal escarpments there are a remarkable number of small endemic species including at least five known only in central Oman.[71] One such species is *Hyoscyamus gallagheri*, one of several species named after the first curator of Oman's Natural History Museum, and first described in 1988. Others include *Ochradenus harsusiticus* and *Pulicaria pulvinata*. This region differs from that of the rest of the northern Najd as a consequence of its proximity to the coast and thus its exposure to seasonal fogs as well as summer cooling associated with the monsoon. These conditions have allowed the development of a specialist plant community that extends north as far as the Jiddat Al Harasis and is recognised as one of Arabia's most important centres of plant endemism.

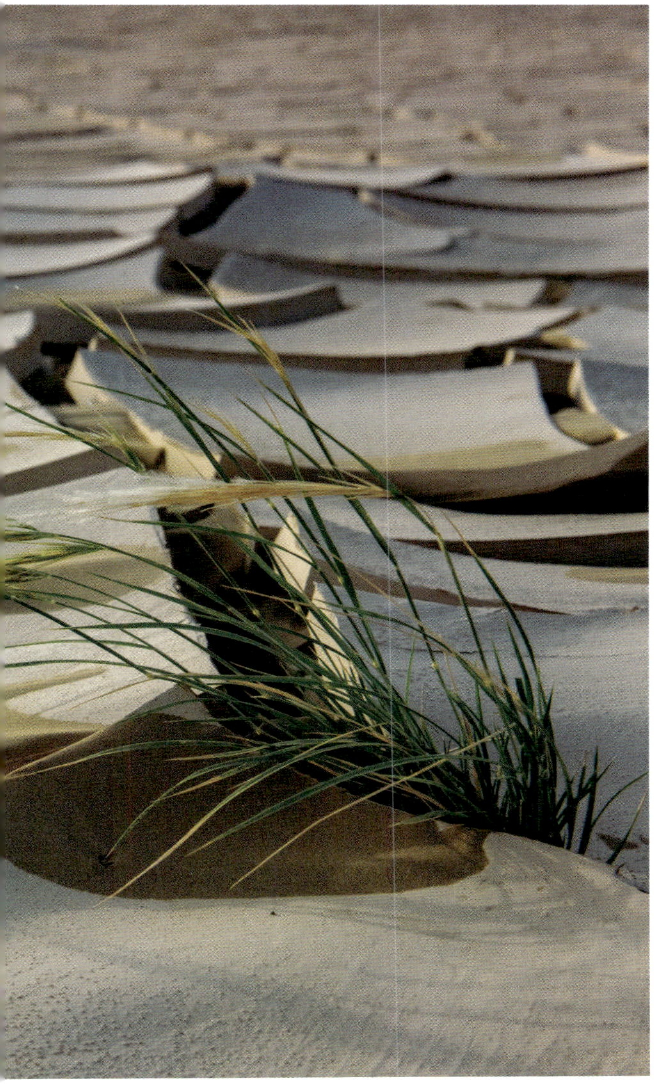

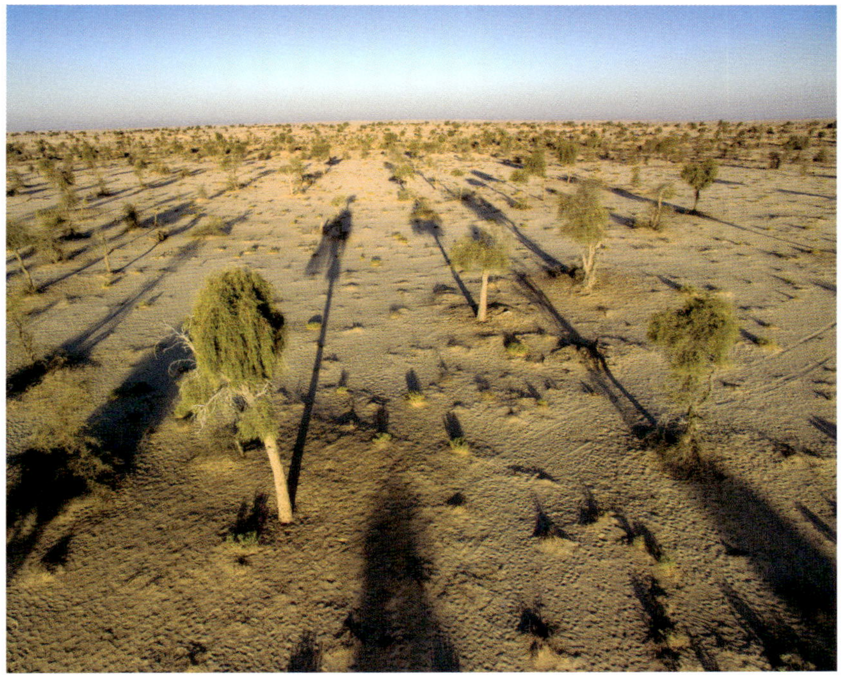

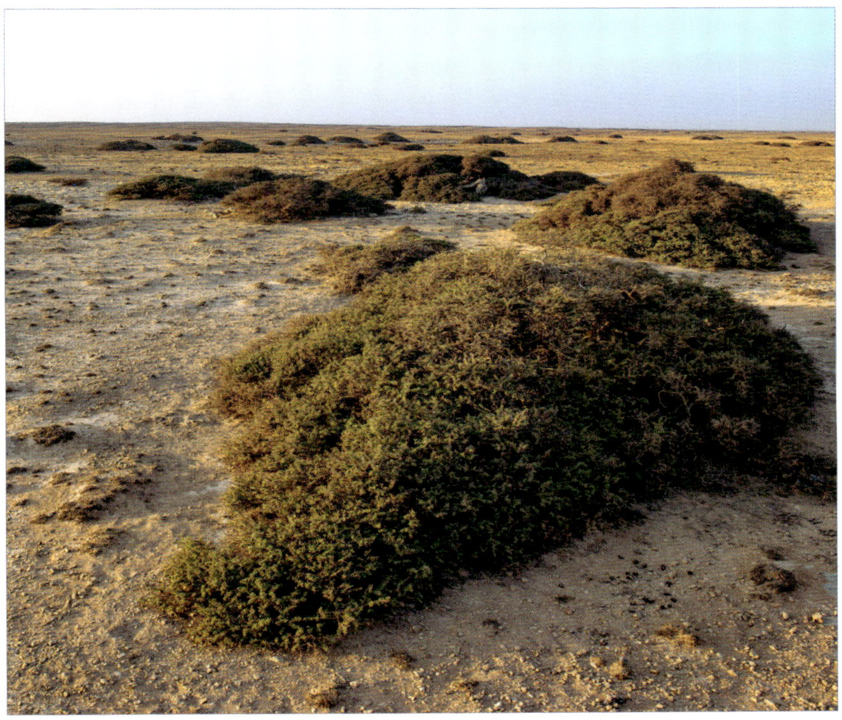

In the north-west the gravel plains merge with the *sabkhas* and sands of the Empty Quarter. Here there are open woodlands of Ghaf, of which the largest by far is at the oasis of Wadi Muqshin. The woodland stretches out over several square kilometres of the wadi, with over 1,000 trees. On the east side of the woodland and on the fringes of the shallow lakes are large numbers of date palms.

The northern Najd is sparsely vegetated, though wadis include stands of tamarisk ***(far left)*** and, particularly in the north and east, extensive Ghaf woodlands ***(above top)*** while in the wind blown north-east a stunted form of *Acacia tortilis* ***(above bottom)*** is common. After rainfall ephemeral grasses such as species of *Stipagrostis* are common ***(centre)*** and readily eaten by livestock.

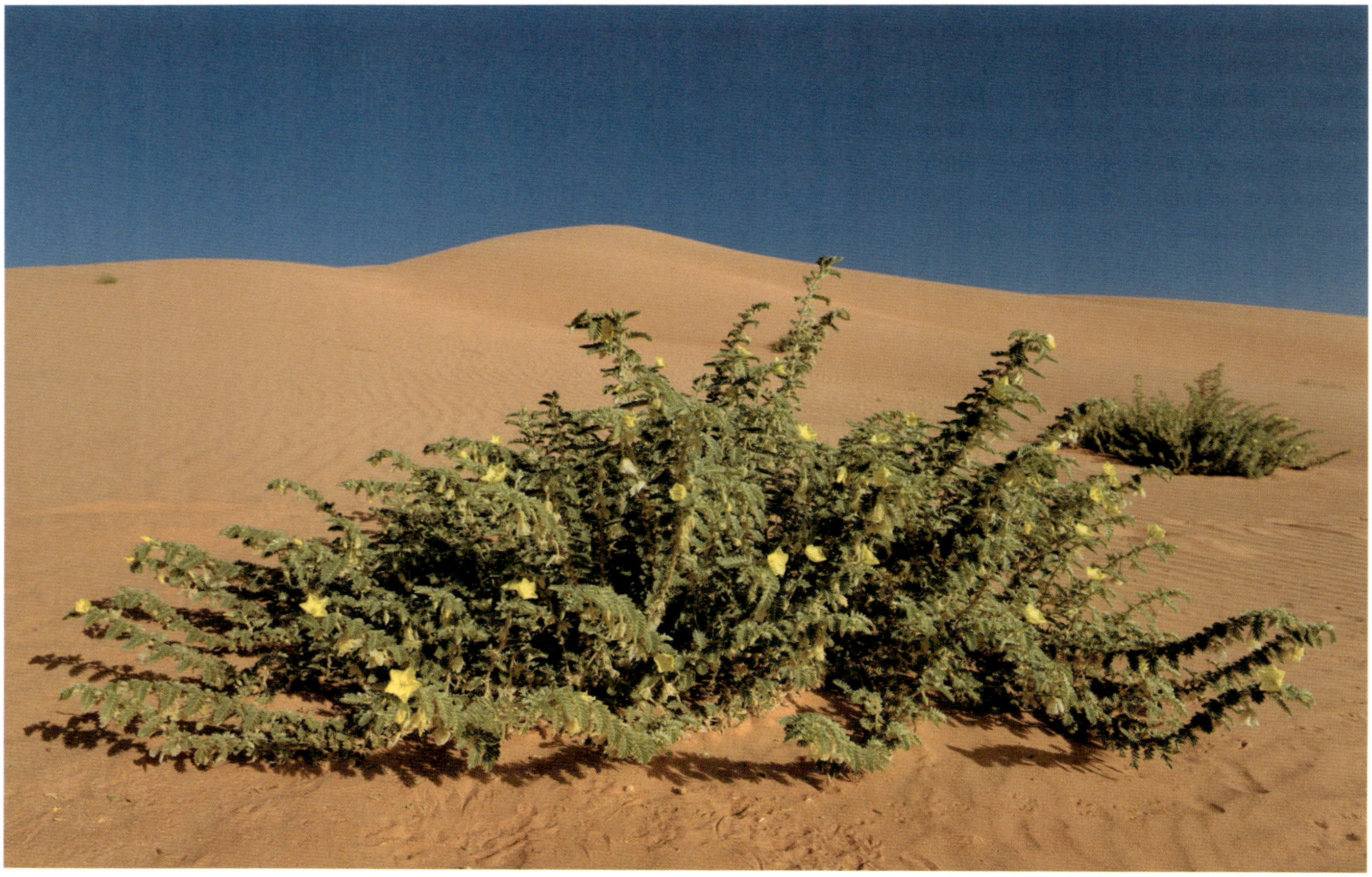

The Empty Quarter

The sands are characterised by very low species diversity. Trees are absent from many areas but the iconic Ghaf tree is found around the outer margins and in drainage lines and pans between dunes. Ghaf trees are dependent on groundwater and a study in the Ramlat Al Wihibah (Sands) of eastern Oman found that the tree's tap roots were able to reach water aquifers 60 metres below the surface. The same study also revealed that the trees are able to absorb moisture from dew and mist.[75] The Ghaf is highly prized by the nomadic herdsmen of the desert; it often provides the only shade for many kilometres, as well as firewood and vital grazing for camels. It is also a haven for wildlife, providing nest sites for brown-necked ravens (*Corvus ruficollis*) and, increasingly rarely, for the golden eagle (*Aquila chrysaetos*). Today many trees are overgrazed and branches are lopped when no other green fodder is available. Most seriously there is virtually no natural regeneration as seedlings are grazed before they can become established.

Other species include the woody *Calligonum crinitum and Tetraena qatarensis,* which often are the only plants present on dune slopes, while in dune valleys *Dipterygium glaucum* and *Heliotropium bacciferum are found*. After rainfall the sedge *Cyperus conglomeratus* and the beautiful yellow-flowered *Tribulus omanense* become more common. Both species are highly valued as fodder for camels, and as the traveller Wilfred Thesiger wrote, nomads will not burn *Tribulus* 'for it is venerated as the best of all food for their camels.'[27]

Sand dunes are extremely poor habitat for plant growth as they contain little organic matter and few nutrients, while rainfall tends to be almost absent. Yet when rain does fall the dunes spring to life. Following cyclone Mekunu in 2018 the striking *Tribulus omanense* ***(above)*** could be found on the slopes of even the highest dunes.

Many areas of Dhofar, especially the Jabal and including the forests of *Anogeissus dhofarica* ***(right)***, are criss-crossed by the tracks of thousands of cattle, camels and goats.

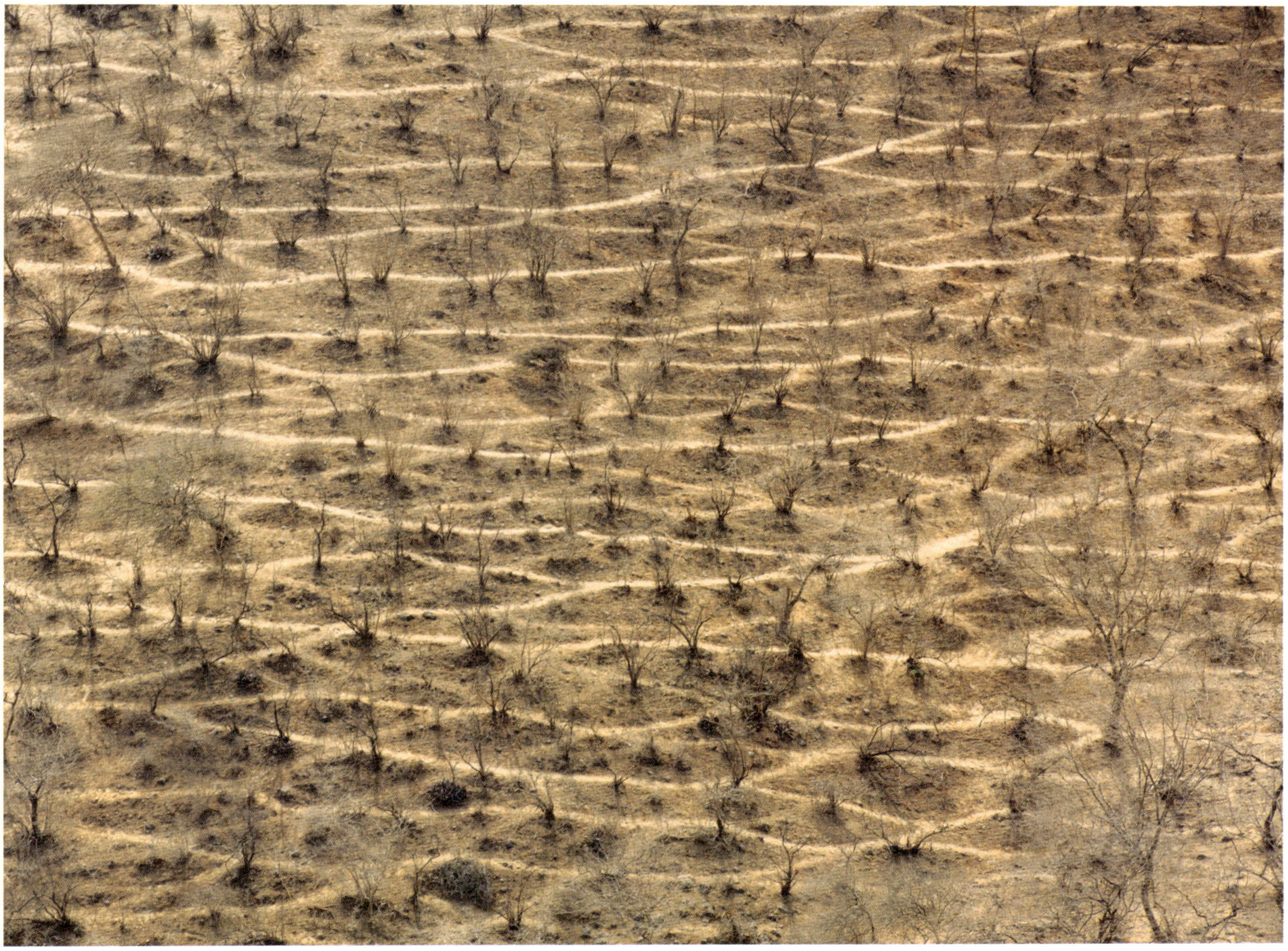

Conservation

Endemism and Extinction Threat

Endemism is the ecological state of a species being unique to a defined geographic location. Dhofar has high rates of endemism, with some 43 plant species that are found only in Dhofar and across the border in Yemen and a further 41 species that occur in Dhofar alone. These species tend to be found in unique areas of habitat known as local centres of endemism. There are five such centres in Oman, of which three are in Dhofar: the monsoon-affected mountains of Jabal Al Qara and Jabal Al Qamar, the high plateaux and wadi systems of Jabcl Samhan, and the limestone plateaux and escarpment of the Jiddat Arkad, part of which is within Al Wusta Governorate.[71]

An example of a uniquely Dhofari species is *Aloe praetermissa*, one of four *Aloe* species that occur in Dhofar. Found in the drier parts of the mountains, *Aloe* was widely used as a medicinal treatment, the juice from the leaves considered a cure for many conditions, from breathing difficulties to eye ailments.

In addition to having a high level of endemism, many of the plants of Dhofar are at risk of extinction. The *Oman Plant Red Data Book* lists 110 species in the Sultanate that meet the three highest categories of threat and, of these, 82 occur in Dhofar and are listed as Vulnerable (56), Endangered (10) or Critically Endangered (16).[64] Many of these species are endangered because their populations are naturally small, but others face threats caused by man.

At least six species of the succulent *Caralluma* are considered to be Critically Endangered, the highest category of threat, and wild populations are at risk of extinction. They are often collected by local people for food but are also at risk of being illegally collected as part of a growing international trade in succulents. Succulent plants are traded in large volumes for the global horticultural market and the majority of these are then artificially propagated for sale.

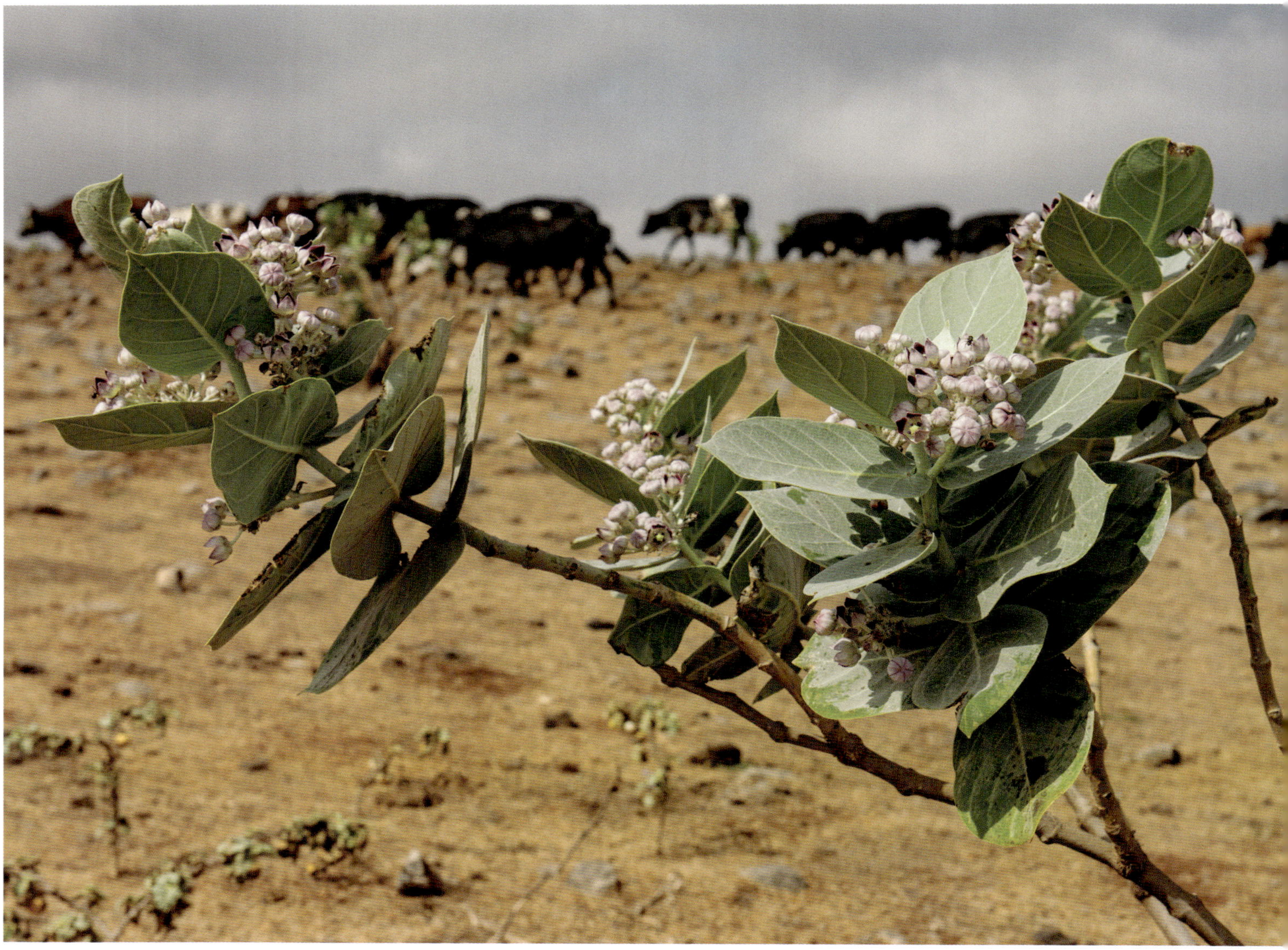

Overgrazing

For generations the monsoon forests, woodlands and grasslands supported rural livelihoods based on the herding of cattle, goats and camels. Natural checks and balances along with a subsistence economy meant that livestock numbers did not exceed the carrying capacity of the Jabal and thus the plant habitats remained healthy. However, following the change from a subsistence-to cash-economy in 1970, the number of livestock has increased exponentially, with very significant consequences for the plant communities both of the Jabal and elsewhere in Dhofar.

The signs of overgrazing are there for all to see and many are provided by the plants themselves. For example, large parts of the Jabal grasslands, particularly in the eastern part of Jabal Al Qara, are today dominated by Sodom's apple, a plant unpalatable to livestock that is indicative of overgrazing the world over. Elsewhere dense stands of the bright-green *Dodonaea viscosa* suggest to the visitor that the woodlands are healthy, yet this species and others like it, unpalatable to livestock, are spreading at the expense of plants eaten down by the animals. Where trees remain their canopy is neatly cropped at about three metres above the ground, marking the limit of the camels' reach. Other trees are stripped of their bark.

Local people commonly recall earlier times when *Themeda quadrivalvis* grasslands grew taller than a man. However, even after the exceptionally good monsoon of 2016 it was very unusual to see this grass standing more than one metre tall. In most areas the monsoon pastures hardly have time to mature and seed before they

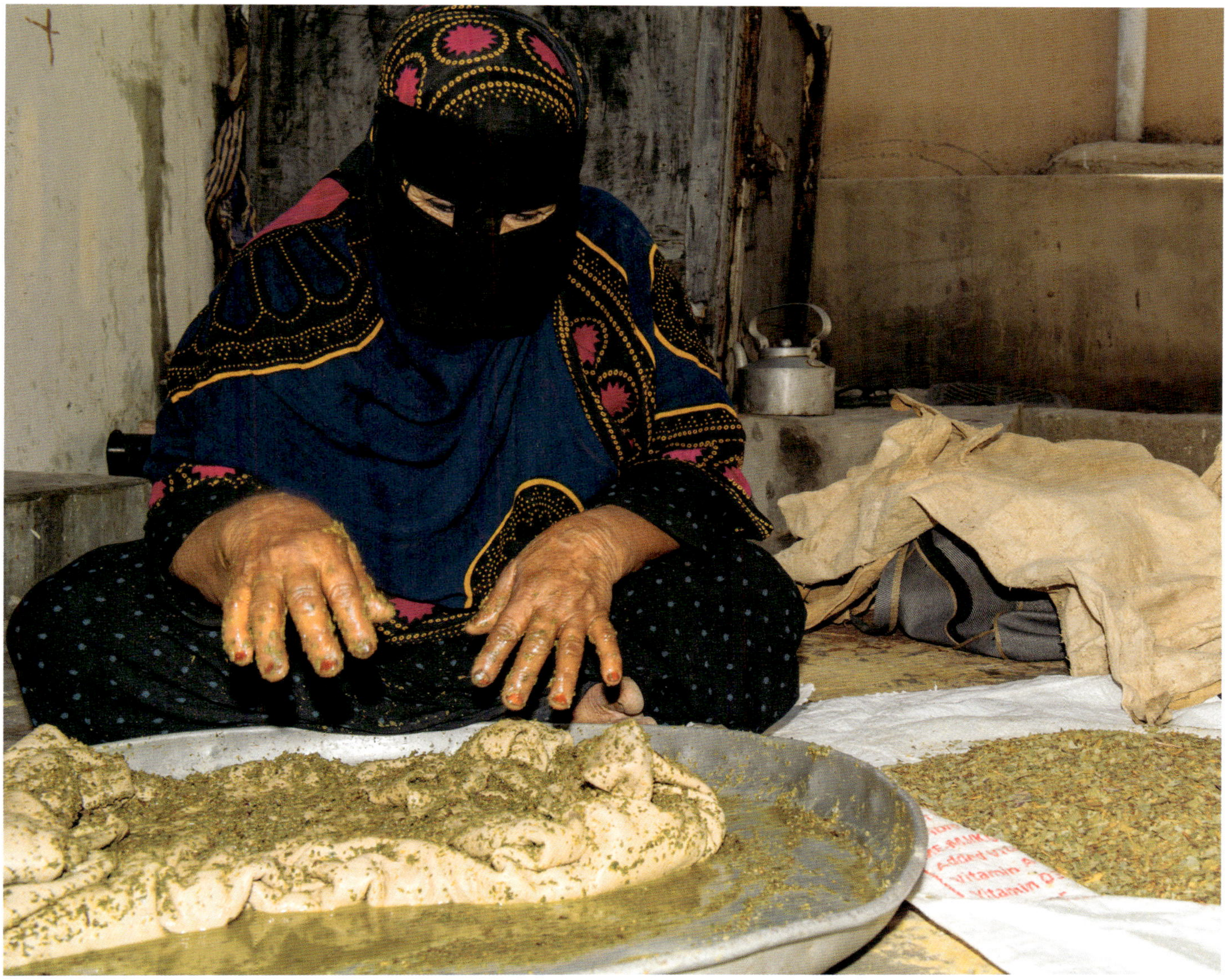

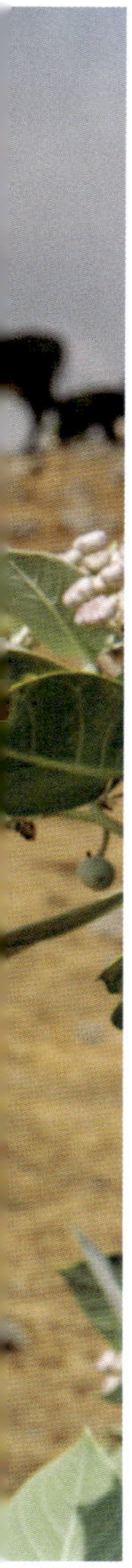

are eaten to the ground. Fenced enclosures, mostly established in the 1980s, demonstrate not only that grassland species, when left ungrazed, can still grow to the height of a man but also that many grassland areas of the Jabal had a diverse flora that included trees and shrubs. The thickly vegetated coastal stack at Ras Hamar is also evidence of former times.

The rich woodland communities of the Jabal, especially the Sġót forest, are not free of overgrazing and in spite of the almost vertical slopes, grazing livestock, especially camels, reach even the least accessible areas. In many places there is little undergrowth, and increasingly trees are being stripped of bark as livestock are unable to find green fodder. Trees die, the ground is compacted, and as elsewhere on the Jabal, there is little or no sign of regeneration. The loss of trees impacts the entire ecosystem for they play a vital role in the capture of water from the monsoon clouds, and in their absence most of the moisture is blown north towards the desert, where it is then lost.[69]

In past times the people of Dhofar utilised many plants for food, clothing, medicine and other aspects of day-to-day life. Today most such uses have been replaced by modern materials and medicines. However, some plants are still used; for example, *Aloe dhufarensis* continues to be used for the tanning of raw animal hides ***(above right)***.

Sodom's apple thrives when pastures are heavily grazed ***(above left)***.

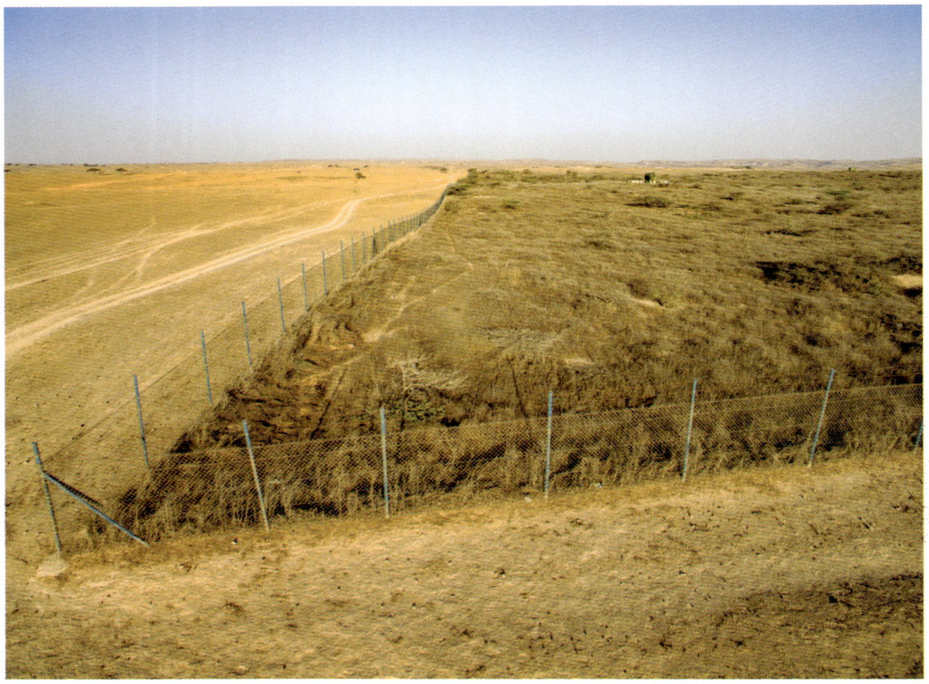

In the 1980s animal exclosures were established to monitor long-term vegetation change in relation to livestock grazing ***(left)***.

Lantana camara is an invasive species, not eaten by livestock, that has very recently become established over large areas of the Jabal including areas close to the town of Tawi Aatayr on Jabal Al Qara, where it forms a dense carpet crowding out native species and reducing biodiversity ***(opposite)***. Other invasive species that are rapidly spreading through grassland areas include *Parthenium hysterophorus* and *Nicandra physalodes*.

Invasion

Prosopis juliflora, otherwise known as mesquite, or *Ghaf Al Bahri* in Arabic, is a native tree species of Central and South America that was introduced to northern Oman in the 1960s or 1970s and to Dhofar somewhat later. It is fast-growing and drought-resistant and grows well in desert conditions. It flowers throughout the year and its seeds are spread by grazing livestock, particularly goats. Once the seeds germinate the roots develop rapidly and can reach 40 centimetres in eight weeks.

In some parts of the world this species is regarded as a useful resource for rural communities, providing fuel-wood, timber and fodder for livestock.[76] Experiments conducted in Oman concluded that sheep and goats could be fed up to 20% with mesquite seed pods without adverse effects.[77] However, generally *Prosopis juliflora* is considered to be of no fodder value, a threat to limited water resources, poisonous to livestock, of limited value as fuel-wood and a threat to native flora.[76]

In Dhofar the largest and most dense populations of mesquite are on the Jarbib between Salalah and Taqah. Here the trees resemble sprawling woodlands stretching over many hectares with little sign of other plant species or animal life. The tree is also found on coastal areas of Jabal Al Qamar, north of the Jiddat Al Arkad and even on the Al Hallaniyyat Islands. A few specimens have been found in the lower reaches of the south-flowing wadis of Jabal Al Qamar and Jabal Al Qara but thus far the species has not established itself on the upland areas of the Jabal.

Mechanical cutting and removal of *Prosopis juliflora* has been ongoing on the Jarbib for many years. This remains a reasonably effective way to control the spread of the species, though it needs to be frequently repeated. The removal of plants from areas closer to the Jabal and in remote areas where they are still only present in small numbers, such as the Al Hallaniyyat Islands, would seem prudent.

Protected Areas

The Global Strategy for Plant Conservation of the Convention on Biological Diversity states that at least 60% of threatened plant species should be within protected areas. The declaration of Jabal Samhan and ten coastal *khawrs* as nature reserves is helping Oman to reach this target, although none of these reserves was established specifically to conserve the flora. The establishment of the reserves has helped safeguard plant communities but threats remain. In Jabal Samhan light grazing by livestock is not incompatible with conservation objectives but the ever-increasing number of goats, camels and feral donkeys, especially in the west, is impacting the flora of the plateaux. Frankincense harvesting should also be part of the sustainable management of the reserve but the current practice of overcutting and overharvesting is killing some trees and resulting in declining yields.[78]

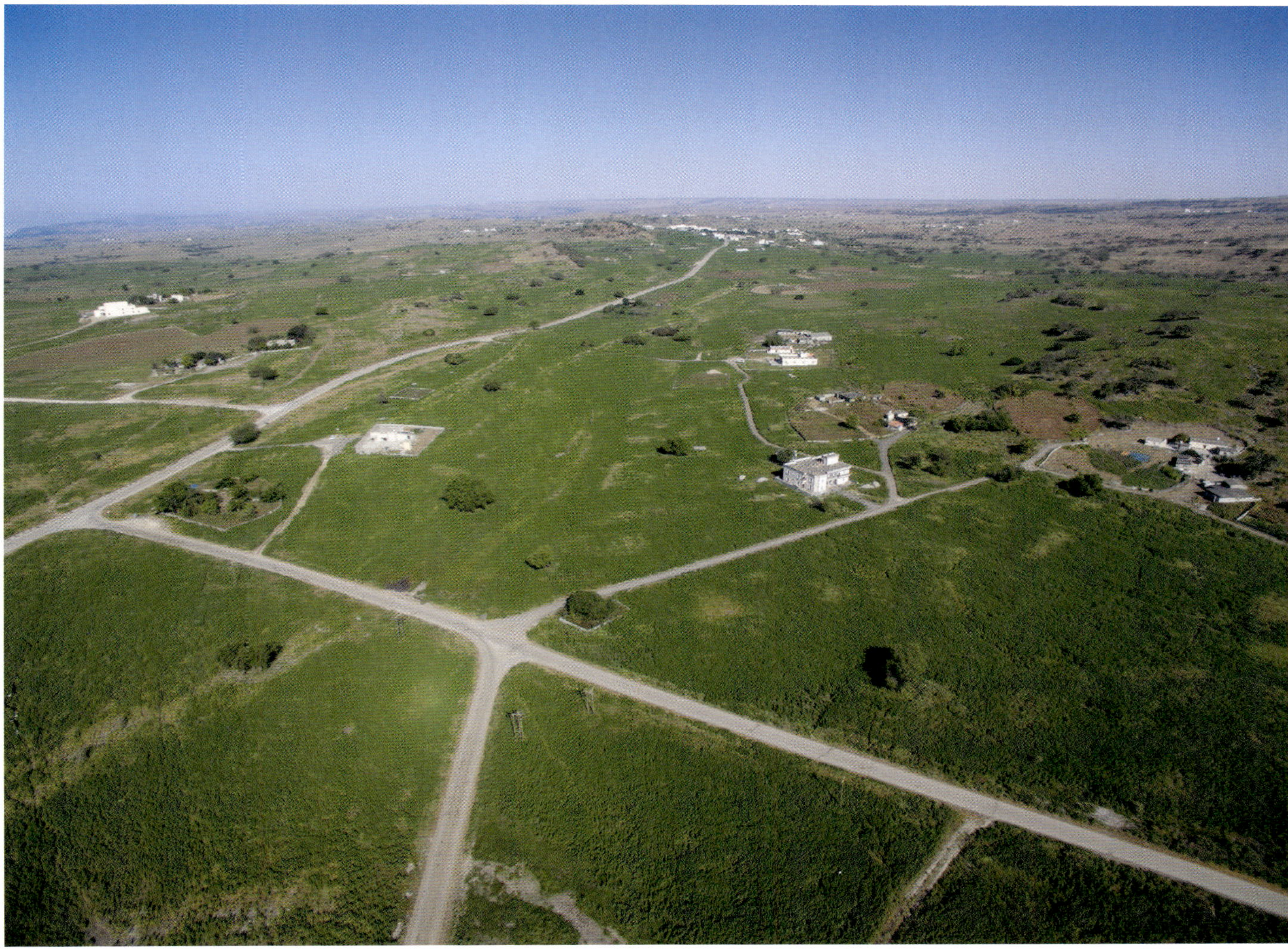

Currently there is no protected area in the monsoon habitats of Jabal Al Qamar and Jabal Al Qara, yet this is one of Oman's five centres of plant endemism. Wadi Sayq on Jabal Al Qamar – with its largely intact forests of Sġót, coastal lagoon and uplands areas of the Najd – might be considered a strong candidate for Dhofar's first monsoon forest reserve. The Jiddat Arkad, another centre of plant endemism, is also worthy of protection.

'Ex situ' Conservation

A further target of the Global Strategy for Plant Conservation is for 75% of threatened species to be conserved in *ex situ* collections. Oman is currently creating the Oman Botanic Garden at Al Khawd (in Muscat), which will be a world-class facility preserving Omani flora ex-situ while supporting in-situ conservation. The garden will feature different habitats of Oman including those of the monsoon mountains of Dhofar, which will be housed in a large climate-controlled biome open to the public. The garden intends to hold plant material, whether plants or seeds, from all threatened species. Currently the garden nursery and seed bank already hold 153 taxa of Oman's threatened species and thus Oman is well on track to meeting the target for *ex situ* conservation.

6 Fauna

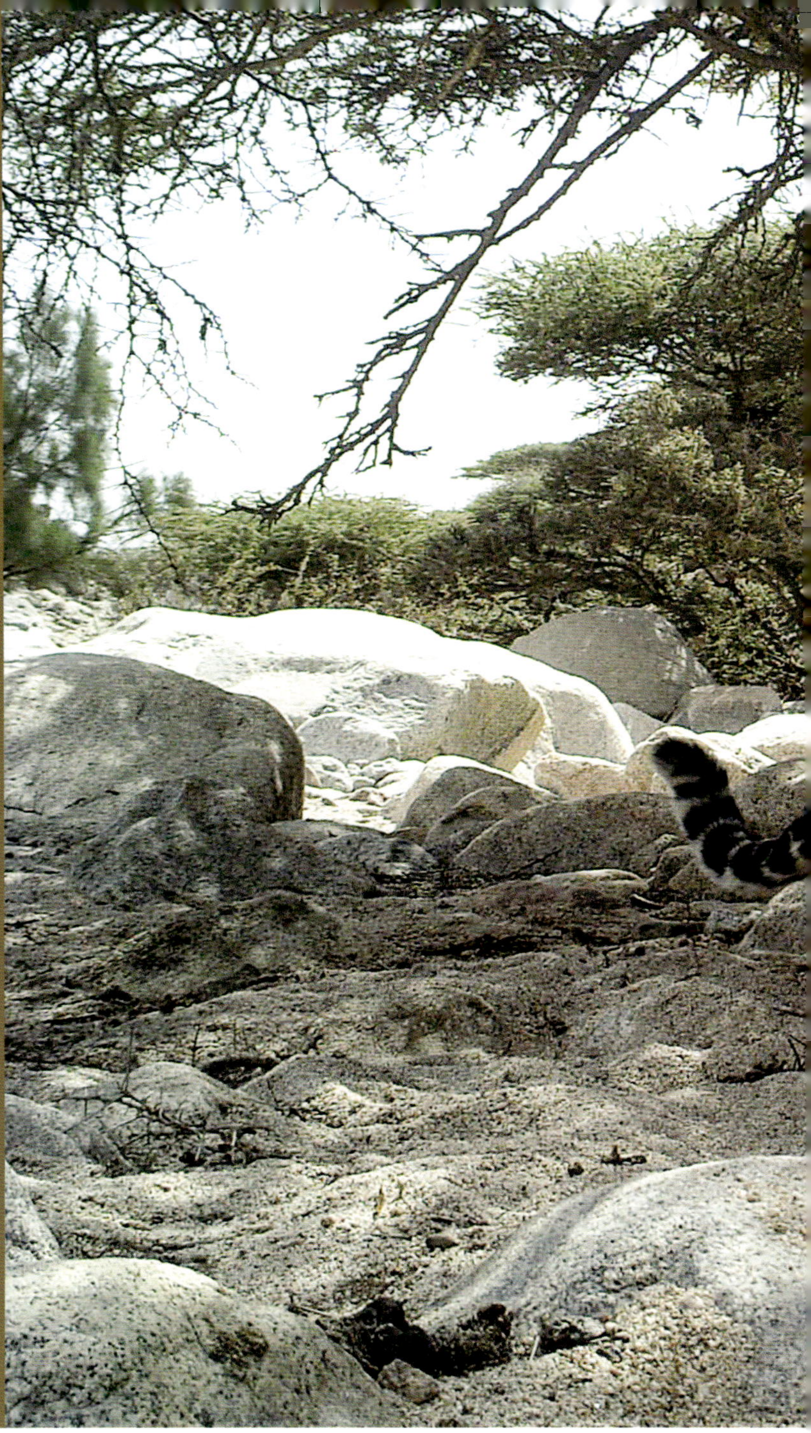

Introduction

Dhofar's wonderfully diverse landscapes include true desert, saturated cloud forests, lakes, rocky shores, remote islands and deep upwelling seas, all of which are habitats for a rich assemblage of fauna that reflects this variety of landscapes.

The presence of certain species of fauna, such as the Indian crested porcupine (*Hystrix indica*), is evidence of strong links with Asia. However, much of Dhofar's fauna reflects ancient links with Africa. For example, the humble snails of Dhofar's forests share a common ancestry

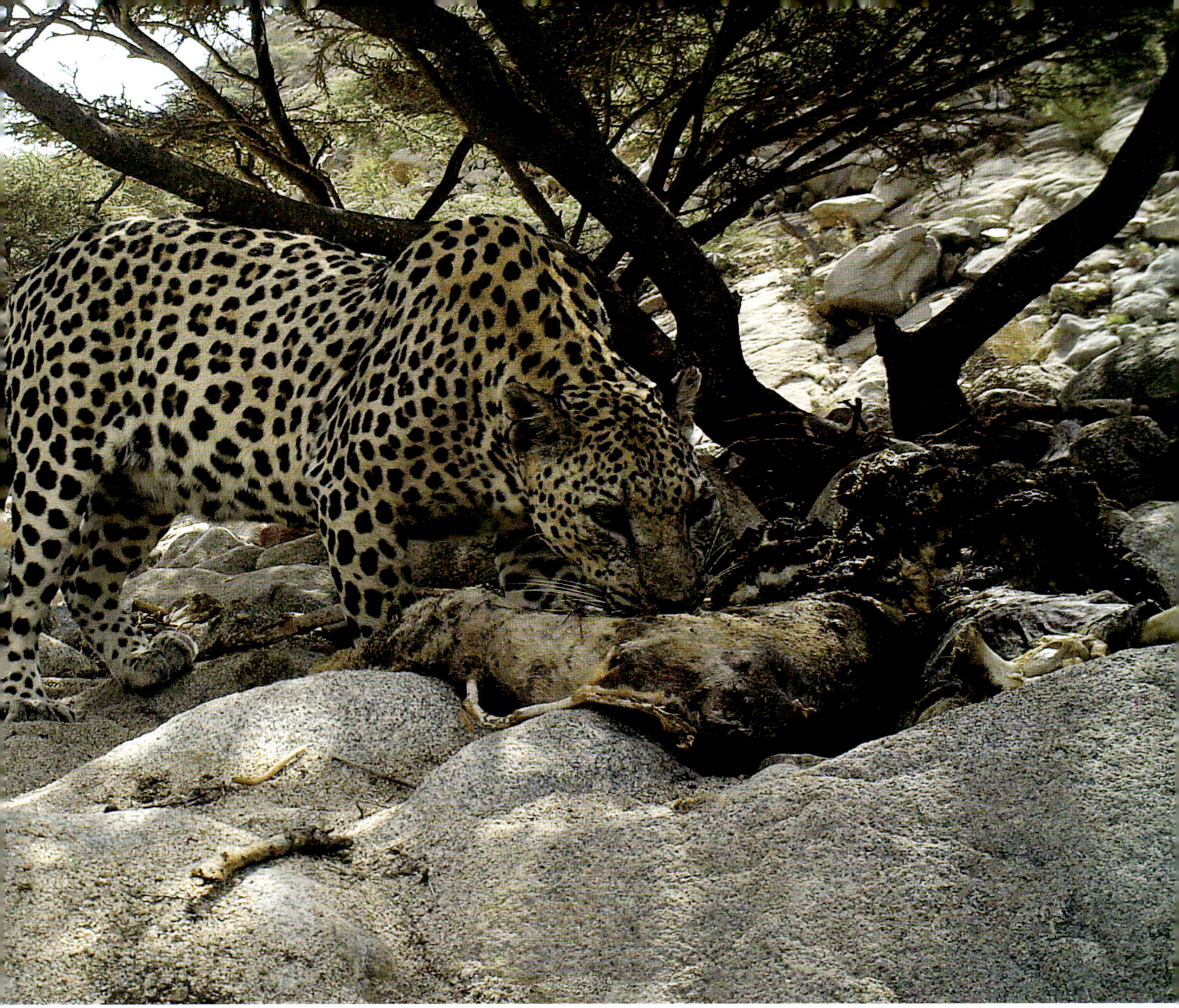

with continental Africa while those of northern Oman are closer to the snails of Europe and Asia. Similarly, species such as the Verreaux's eagle (*Aquila verreauxii*) and their favourite prey the rock hyrax (*Procavia capensis*) have a largely African distribution, evidence of previous eras, as much as 100,000 years ago, when the strait of Bab Al Mandab formed a land bridge between Africa and Asia.[79]

(Above) The iconic Arabian leopard (Ji. ḳe'źer' Ar. *'An Nimr Al 'Arabi*), here feeding on a Nubian ibex, is perhaps the best-known of Dhofar's animals. However, it is just one of hundreds of species of animal, from mammals to molluscs, that inhabit the land and the sea of the region. Almost certainly there are still new animal species to be discovered.

Terrestrial Mammals

Carnivores

At the top of the food chain are the carnivores, and of these the Arabian leopard (*Panthera pardus nimr*), striped hyena (*Hyaena hyaena*) and Arabian wolf (*Canis lupus arabs*) are the largest. A fourth large carnivore, the Asiatic cheetah (*Acinonyx jubatus venaticus*), once roamed throughout the Najd and north as far as the Empty Quarter but became extinct in 1977 when the last specimen on the Arabian Peninsula was shot north of Jibjat.

The most iconic of the carnivores is the elusive Arabian leopard, which once roamed throughout the mountains of Oman but is today only found in Dhofar. It is the smallest of the world's leopards, half the size of its African cousin, with males and females in the wild weighing up to 34 kilograms and 20 kilograms respectively. They are generally most active between sunset and sunrise though have been sighted throughout the day, especially during the monsoon. Their natural prey in Dhofar ranges from the tiny Arabian spiny mouse, weighing just 50 grams, to large Nubian ibex (*Capra nubiana*), which can weigh as much as 65 kilograms. Leopards once lived in the Jabal and coastal wadis, from Sarfayt in the west to Wadi Aynaynah in the north-east, but today they are largely confined to the south-facing wadis and scarps of the Jabal, with a small number of animals in the wadis of the central southern Najd. Dhofar represents the last stronghold for

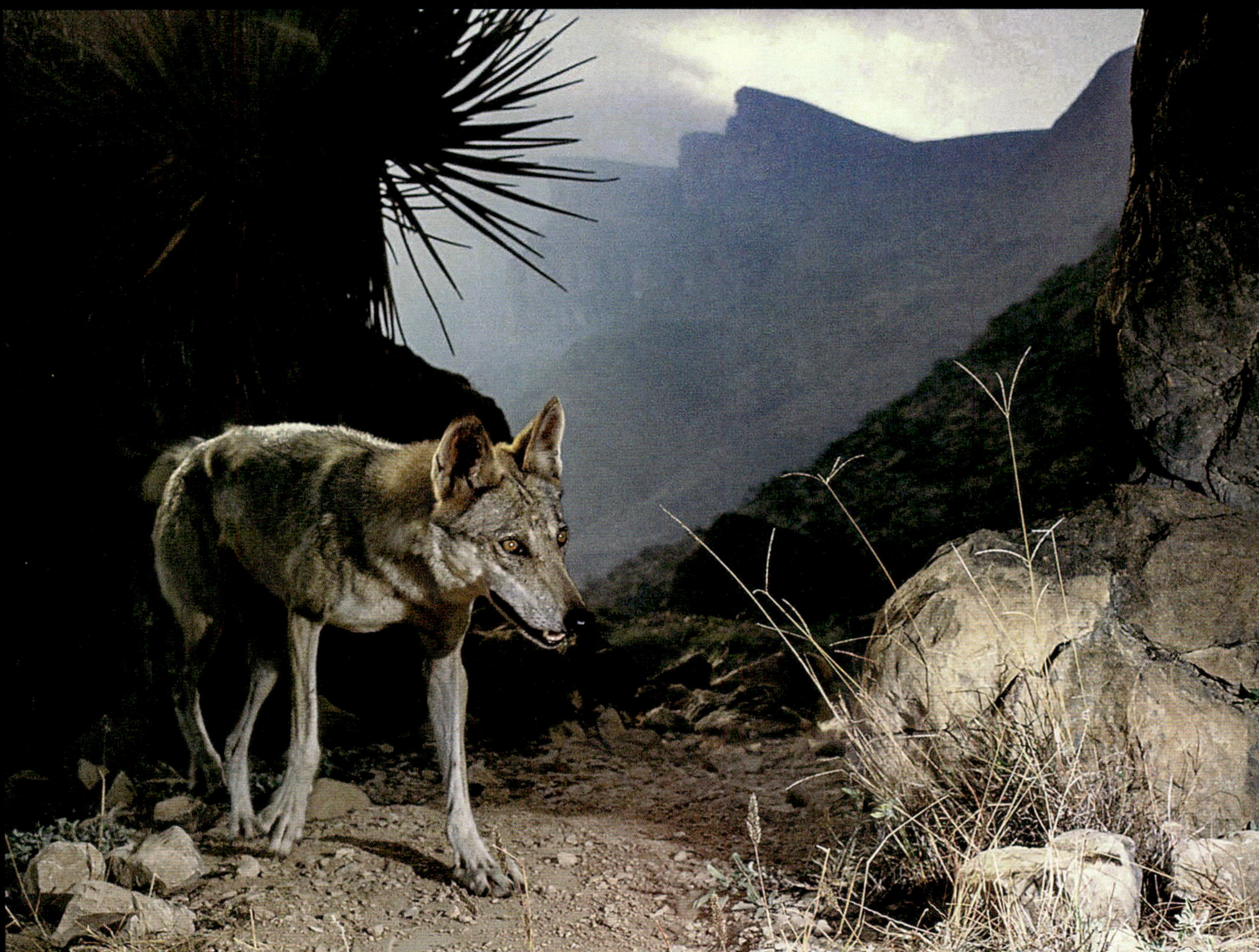

(*Above*) The Arabian wolf, here on the southern escarpment of Jabal Samhan, is one of 53 species of terrestrial mammal found in Dhofar. As well as bats (18 species) and rodents (13 species) there are 12 carnivores, five herbivores and five insectivores (see appendix).

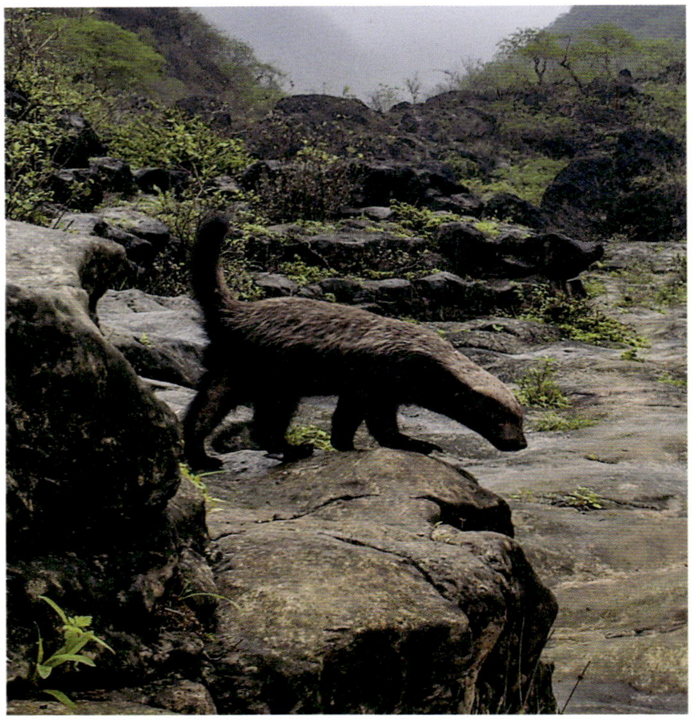

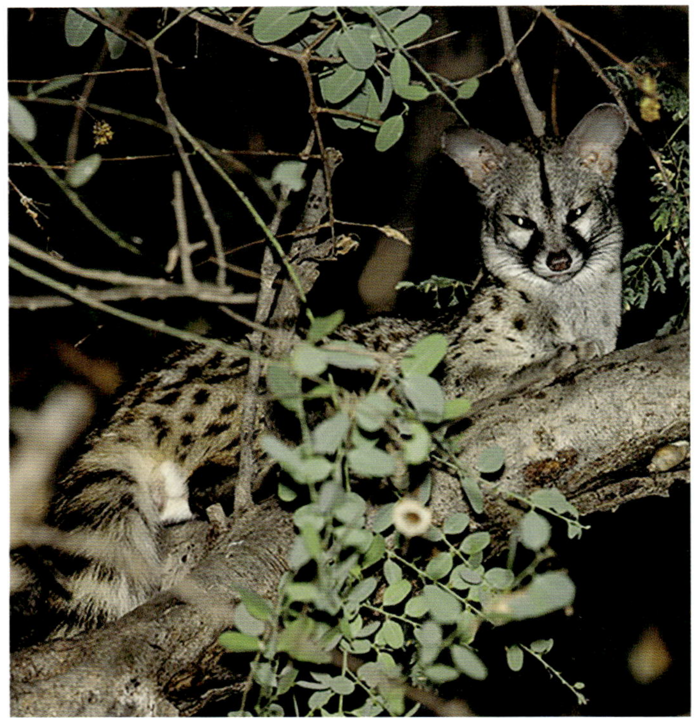

the Arabian leopard in the wild.[80]

Striped hyena are the largest of Dhofar's carnivores and like the Arabian wolf they largely live in the Jabal and the Najd, where there is more prey and they are safer from human persecution. However, both species have been known to leave the protection of the Jabal and range over the Jarbib in the south, while in the north tracks have been recorded at Ash Shisr in the north-west and Sharbthat in the north-east. Hyenas, often solitary, are scavengers and will forage near settlements, including municipal rubbish dumps. Both the hyena and the wolf benefit from the large numbers of livestock on the Jabal and may be seen at night or in the early morning feeding on carcasses, particularly of cattle, killed on roads. Coinciding with the abundance of prey during the monsoon, wolves are known to form large packs, numbering at least 12 individuals, on Jabal Al Qara and can be heard calling, particularly on the grasslands above Wadi Darbat.

Of the medium-sized carnivores, caracal (*Caracal caracal*) are the largest and a large male might almost reach the size of a small Arabian leopard. Like the leopard, the majority of the caracal's diet comprises small species of lizard, birds and mammals but they are also known to prey on the young of ibex and on adult Arabian gazelle (*Gazella arabica*). Unlike the leopard, caracal are found throughout the Najd and, as elsewhere in Oman, this species seems to be increasing in distribution, occupying the empty niche or vacated habitat of the leopard.

There are three fox species in Dhofar. The shy Blanford's fox (*Vulpes cana*) with their characteristic big ears and black-tipped bushy tail are found only in the mountainous Jabal, where they feed on a diet of small rodents, reptiles and birds. Rüppell's sand fox (*Vulpes rueppellii*), as the name indicates, are found in the Empty Quarter but have also been reported in the gravel plains of the Najd. Overlapping the ranges of both species and becoming increasingly ubiquitous are red foxes (*Vulpes vulpes*), whose global geographical range is greater than any other carnivore. Though native to Dhofar, their range has extended hand-in-hand with the increase in human settlements. There is some indication that this seemingly more aggressive species is driving out the smaller Blanford's and Rüppell's foxes.

Dhofar is also home to two small cats: the African wildcat (*Felis lybica lybica*) and the sand cat (*Felis margarita*). Wildcats are found in most areas though they have not reached the Al Hallaniyyat Islands. Sand cats are the only felid found primarily in true desert of the Empty Quarter, where they seem to prefer the vegetated wadis and dune valleys, which support good populations of rodents, including gerbils. Though sand cats were recorded further north, at the edge of the sand dunes in

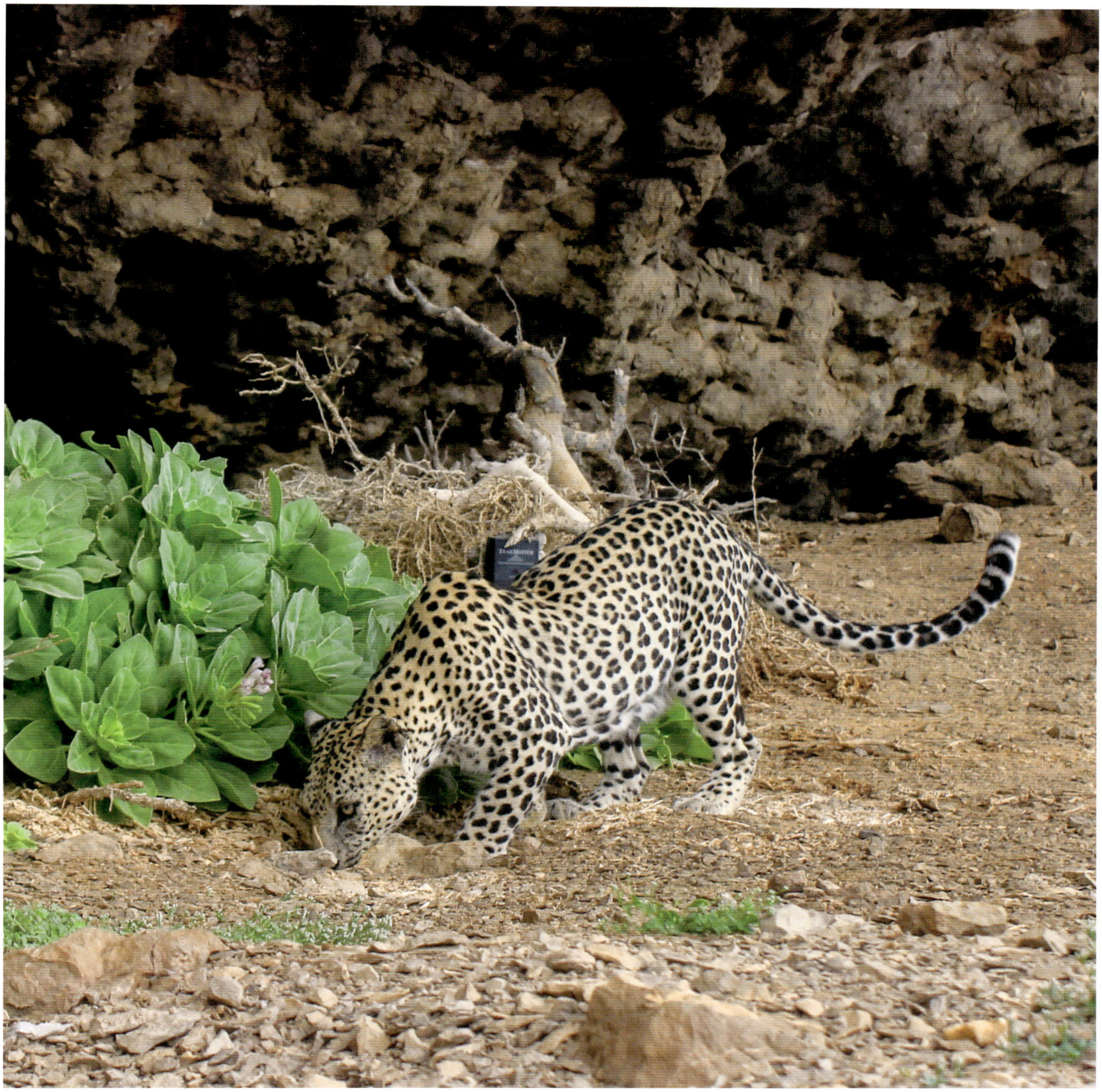

Ad Dhahirah Governorate, as recently as 2007, they have not been recorded in Dhofar for more than 20 years.

Common genet (*Genetta genetta*) is another species that occurs only in Dhcfar and was first recorded only in 1977. However, genets are widespread and are found in both the monsoon and dry areas of the Jabal.

Two species of mammal known to raid Dhofari homes and gardens are the ferocious honey badger (*Mellivora capensis*) or ratel and the white-tailed mongoose (*Ichneumia albicauda*); the former seems to seek out dates and sugar while the latter is in search of insects, fruit and occasionally chickens.

The sweet-toothed honey badger or ratel ***(far left)*** and the shy common genet ***(centre left)*** occur both in the monsoon and dry areas of the Jabal. The Arabian leopard ***(above)*** is one of the most endangered large cats on earth.

Herbivores

Until relatively recently Dhofar was home to four species of ungulate: the Arabian oryx (*Oryx leucoryx*), Nubian ibex, Arabian gazelle and Arabian sand gazelle (*Gazella marica*). The sleek, horned Arabian oryx became extinct in the wild in 1972, killed by hunters. Fortunately, however, some animals had been captured in the Yemen–Oman border area in 1962 in order to establish a captive breeding group and it was the descendants of these and other captive animals that were successfully reintroduced to Jiddat Al Harasis in 1982.[81] By 1995 this wild population numbered nearly 500 and roamed free over an area of more than 20,000 square kilometres. However, in the late 1990s and early 2000s illegal capture for live trade decimated the reintroduced population and once again no oryx roamed free in the wild in Oman. However, in 2020 oryx were again reintroduced and now roam free inside the partially fenced Al Wusta Wildlife Reserve in the Jiddat Al Harasis. The last record of oryx in Dhofar was in 1970 when four animals were sighted in Wadi Mitan, western Dhofar, just 50 kilometres from where the animals were captured in 1962.

The oryx shared much of their desert range with two species of gazelle. The very pale *reem* or Arabian sand gazelle is, unlike the oryx, a species of the true desert. Largely confined to the sand-seas of the Empty Quarter, they would occasionally, move east to the gravel plains usually following rainfall. Today few remain in the wild, although a small herd was seen by local people near Ramlat Al Hashman in 2018. Arabian gazelle are a species of the gravel plains, open *wadis* and foothills and were once found through much of Dhofar. They live in small female-dominated herds while males establish and defend territories. Though they prefer to graze on grasses and shrubs, they can often be seen standing on their hind legs to browse the leaves of acacia trees. Some animals remain in the north-west and north-east but the healthiest populations are found in the northward-flowing *wadis* of the central southern Najd and in the southern foothills of Jabal Samhan and the nearby Salawt Plain, east of Mirbat.[82]

Majestic Nubian ibex are often depicted in the ancient rock art and petroglyphs of Dhofar. The species is a true mountain ungulate that was once found throughout the arid mountainous areas of the Jabal, coastal *wadis* and the cliffs from the Yemen border north to the mighty Wadi Aynaynah of the northern Najd. They are usually found in small, mainly female, groups and the males are usually solitary. However

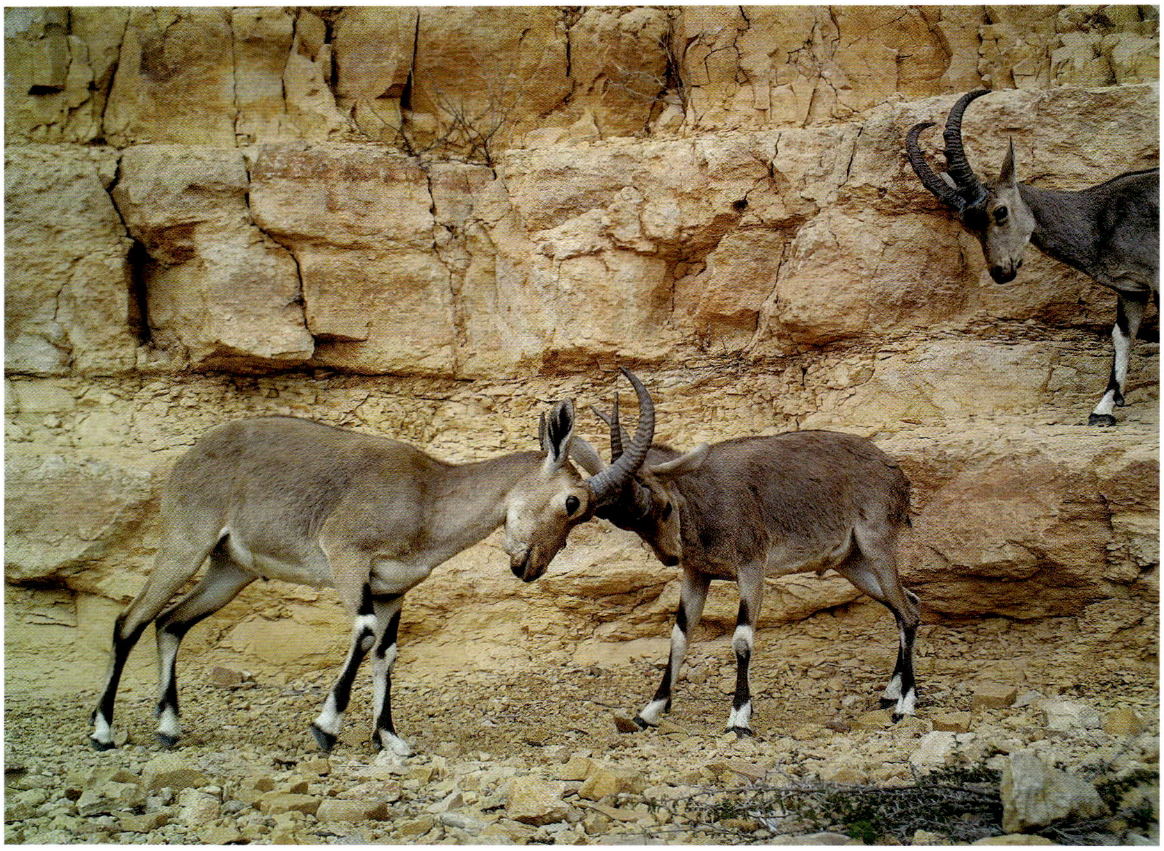

(Right) Young Nubian ibex spar on the southern escarpment of Jabal Samhan. As a dryland species, the ibex avoids the monsoon rangelands of Jabal Al Qamar and Jabal Al Qara.

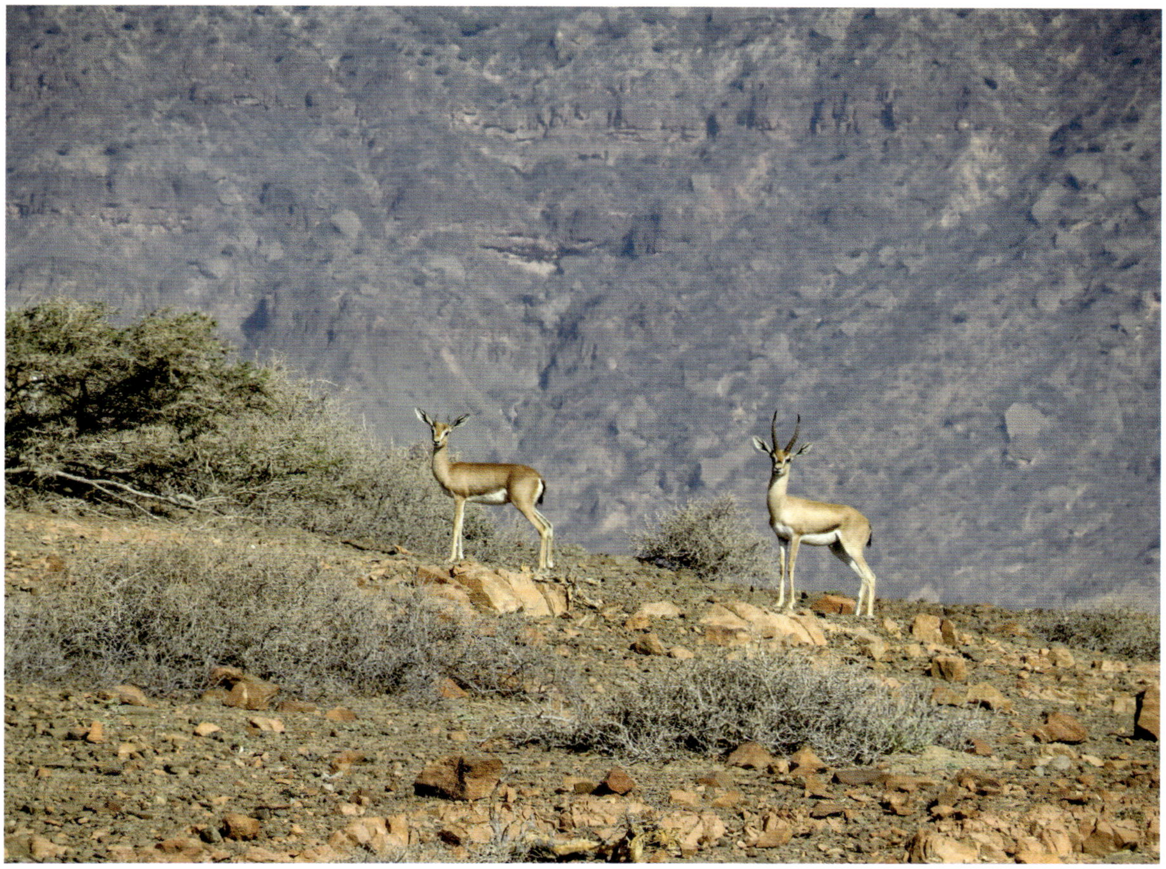

(Left) male and female Arabian gazelles in the southern foothills of Jabal Samhan, one of last strongholds for the species in Dhofar.

large groups form when animals come together for the annual rut that begins late in the monsoon period and extends into the autumn. At this time large males do battle, with much clashing of horns. Today ibex may be seen on the dry plateaux and north-facing slopes of Jabal Al Qamar and Jabal Al Qara and throughout Jabal Samhan, including the southern escarpment. However, they no longer occur east of Jabal Samhan and are therefore isolated from the populations of Ad Duqm and the Al Wusta Wildlife Reserve, more than 300 kilometres to the north.

Surprisingly, none of Dhofar's wild ungulates inhabit the monsoon woodlands and grasslands of Jabal Al Qamar and Jabal Al Qara. The lush rangelands would seem suited to wild herbivores and though Nubian ibex are found in the southward-flowing wadis of Wadi Ashawq and Wadi Aful, at the fringes of the true monsoon areas, they remain outside. Perhaps the grasslands were once grazed by the auroch, the ancestor of domestic cattle, which roamed the Empty Quarter as recently as 10,000 years ago, when the region was significantly wetter.[6]

One herbivore that is found in both the monsoon and arid areas is the rock hyrax (*Procavia capensis*). These gregarious creatures have an interesting evolutionary history, being related to both the elephant and the dugong. In Dhofar today they are the principal wild herbivore of the monsoon areas and consequently are important prey for larger carnivores, though they are also popular with hunters. They can be found on the south-facing slopes, plateaux and upper reaches of northward-flowing *wadis* of Jabal Al Qamar, Jabal Al Qara and Jabal Samhan. Records from Wadi Aynaynah suggest that in past times they were also found in the coastal *wadis* of the northern Najd.

The Cape or desert hare (*Lepus capensis*) is a most adaptable animal, being found in a variety of habitats, from the sands of the Empty Quarter south to the Jarbib coastal plain. The hares seem to survive where there is a minimum of vegetation and are important prey for the desert carnivores. Like other desert mammals they do not occur in the monsoon woodlands or grasslands.

Insectivores are amongst the most elusive of Dhofar's mammals. Sightings of Brandt's hedgehog ***(below right)*** and the desert hedgehog ***(below left)*** are rare but the tiny shrews are almost never seen; there have been just five sightings of the three shrew species since records began.

Insectivores

Dhofar has five mammals that feed almost entirely on insects: two species of hedgehog and three species of diminutive shrew. Desert hedgehogs (*Paraechinus aethiopicus*) are quite common in the Najd, particularly where there is some vegetation. They seem to prefer lowland areas and avoid the higher elevations of the Jabal, where their cousin the Brandt's hedgehog (*Paraechinus hypomelas*) is found. This species is darker than its desert cousin and has a more upright posture. It was first recorded in Dhofar only in the late 1990s and is found on the plateaux areas of both Jabal Samhan and Jabal Al Qamar. However, neither species of hedgehog has been recorded in the rich monsoon grasslands and woodlands.

Shrews are Dhofar's smallest mammals and though they resemble mice they are not rodents and are closer to moles. The white-toothed pygmy shrew *(Suncus etruscus)*, the world's smallest mammal, is only known in Oman from a single animal found in Salalah in 1977. Arabian shrews (*Crocidura arabica*) were found first at Khadrafi in Jabal Al Qamar in 1977 and later at Tawi Aatayr in Jabal Al Qara. Dhofarian shrew (*Crocidura dhofarensis*) were also first recorded in Khadrafi though until recently there was some doubt whether the species existed at all. However, in 2006 they were found in the province of Hawf in Yemen[83] and in 2017 a single animal was live-trapped at As San on Jabal Al Qara.

Rodents

By far the largest of Dhofar's rodents is the Indian crested porcupine, which is principally a species of south-west Asia but

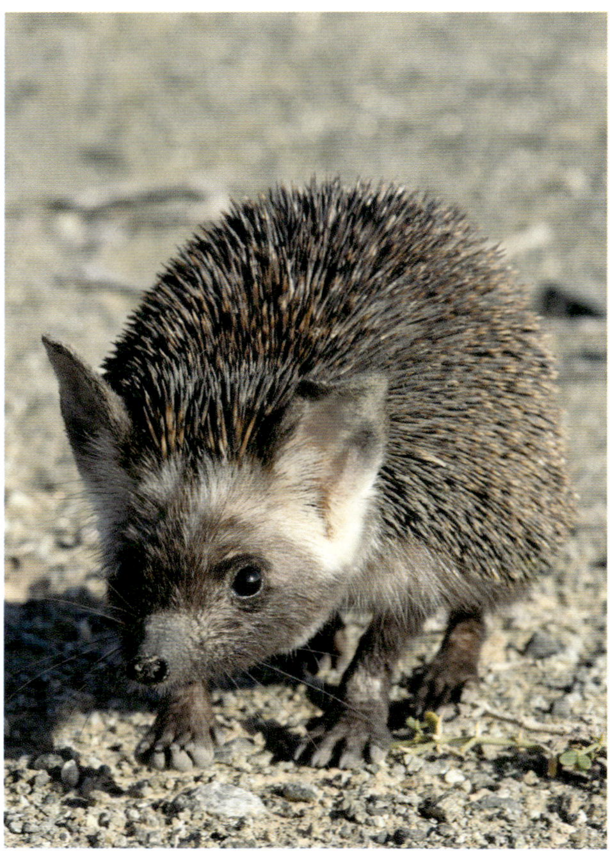

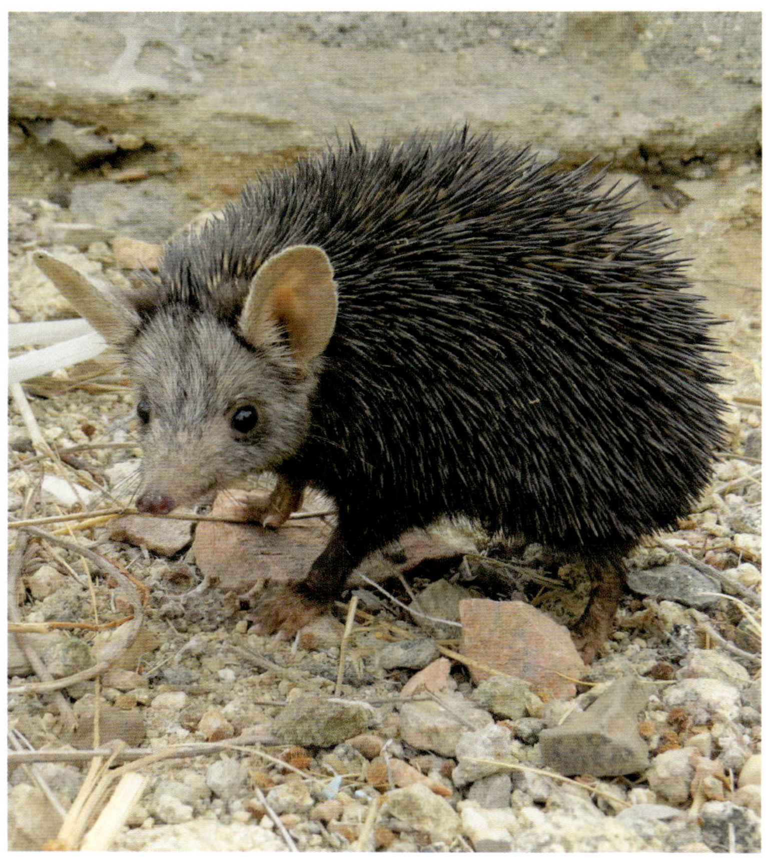

occurs at a small number of localities in south and west Arabia. Porcupines are not present in northern Oman but are found in the Jabal and Najd areas of Dhofar. They are mostly nocturnal and often spend daylight hours in underground dens. Though porcupines themselves are rarely encountered, broken quills can be found on animal trails and close to dens.

There are at least 12 species of rat, mice, gerbil, jird and jerboa in Dhofar and there may be more to be discovered. Most are nocturnal and therefore difficult to see, and when threatened they move quickly to their dens which may be in rocky crevices, termite mounds or the soft sand of the dune deserts. The most common is the Arabian spiny mouse (*Acomys dimidiatus*), which occurs throughout the Jabal and as far north as Wadi Aynaynah in the northern Najd. It shares part of its range with the golden spiny mouse (*Acomys russatus*); one species comes out at night and the other in the daytime. Towns and villages are home to the house mouse (*Mus musculus*) and black rat (*Rattus rattus*).

In the Najd the occurrence and distribution of rodents remains poorly understood. In some areas it is difficult to find rodents while in other areas several species live close together. For example, in Wadi Kawbawt in the eastern southern Najd there are at least three species in the lower reaches of the wadi: dawrf gerbil (*Gerbillus nanus*), Sundevall's jird (*Meriones crassus*) and the bushy-tailed jird (*Sekeetamys calurus*), which was first recorded in Dhofar in 2015.[84] The principal rodent of the Empty Quarter is the Cheesman's gerbil (*Gerbillus cheesmani*), which burrows into the sand to avoid the desiccating heat.

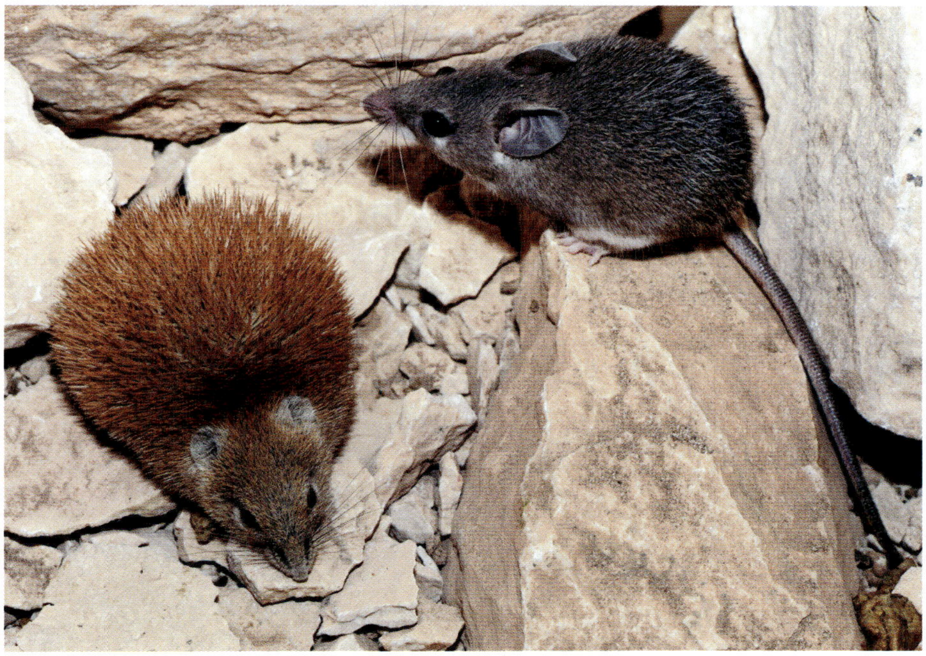

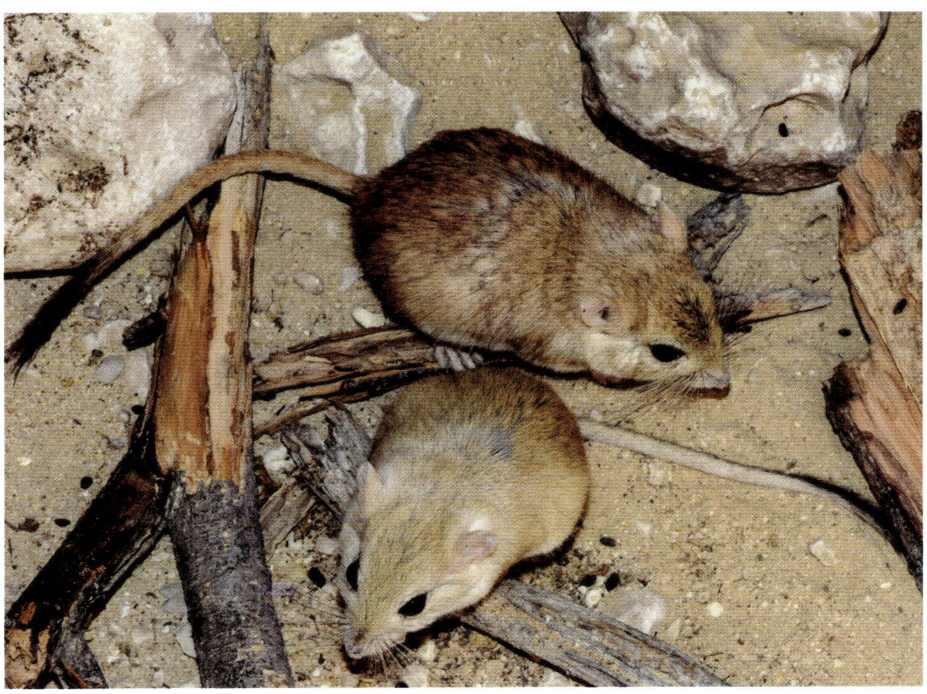

Much remains to be understood about the distribution of rodents in Dhofar. Of the two species of spiny mouse ***(left above)***, the darker Arabian spiny mouse has the widest distribution, being found in the Jabal and the Najd. Sundevall's jird ***(left below)*** seems to prefer the drylands.

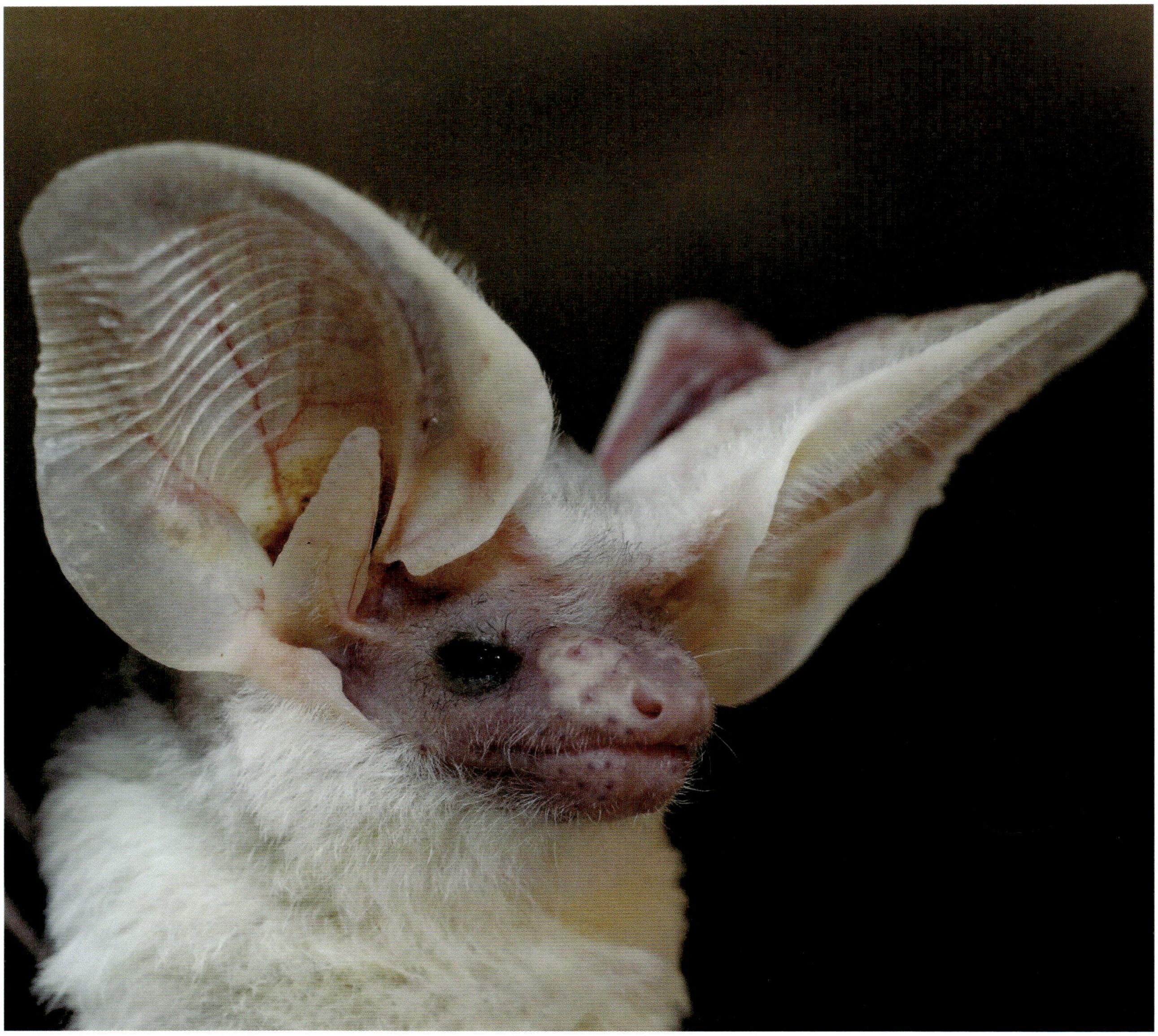

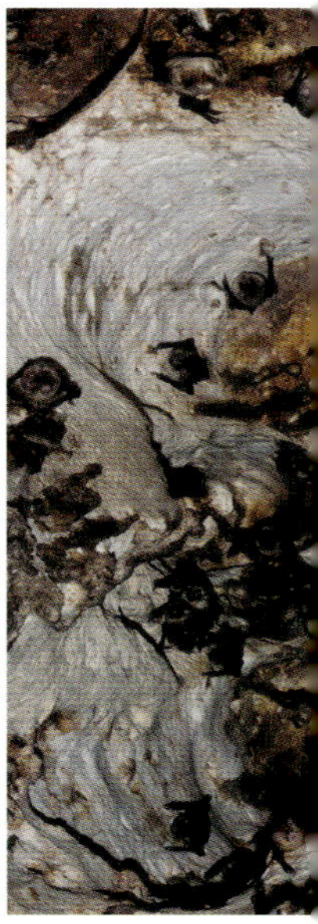

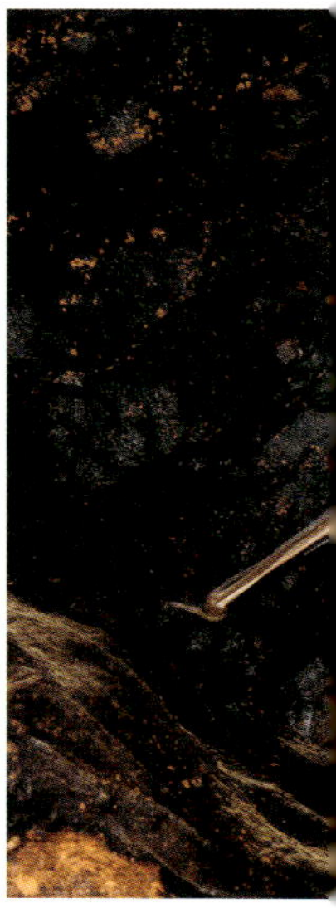

Bats

A visit to most of Dhofar's many caves will be rewarded with the sight of bat roosts. There are at least 18 species of bat in Dhofar; all but two are insect-eating and most are found on the Jabal. Largest and most easily seen are Egyptian fruit bats (*Rousettus aegyptiacus*), with a body-length of about 15 centimetres and wingspan of approximately 60 centimetres. They emerge from their daytime roosts, such as caves and old buildings, just after sunset, and with a very sophisticated sense of smell go in search of fruit. This may be wild fruits such as figs or the abundant fruits of the farms close to Salalah, including mangoes, papayas and coconuts. The fruit bat may be the largest of the bats but are extremely gentle when handled correctly.

Amongst the smallest of Dhofar's bats are the pipistrelles, which weigh about five grams and are the size of a human thumb. The recently-discovered Dhofarian pipistrelle (*Pipistrellus dhofarensis*) is unique to Dhofar and the adjacent monsoon mountain of Hawf in Yemen.[85] They are widely distributed but do not venture into the arid wadis of the southern Najd, which is the domain of a desert specialist, the ghost bat (*Otonycteris hemprichii jin*). These very striking, slightly frightening-looking bats have huge ears that help them to listen for the movement of ground-living animals such as scorpions, known to be amongst their favourite food.[86]

Most bats are not blind but have poor eyesight and use echolocation, similar to sonar, to fly and to hunt for insects in the dark. As they fly they make calls and can tell how far away something is by how long it

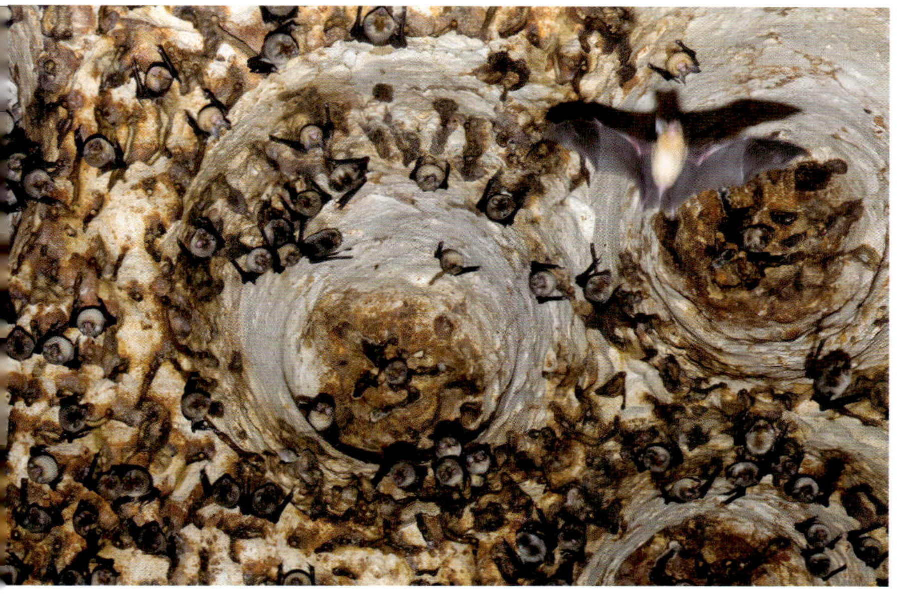

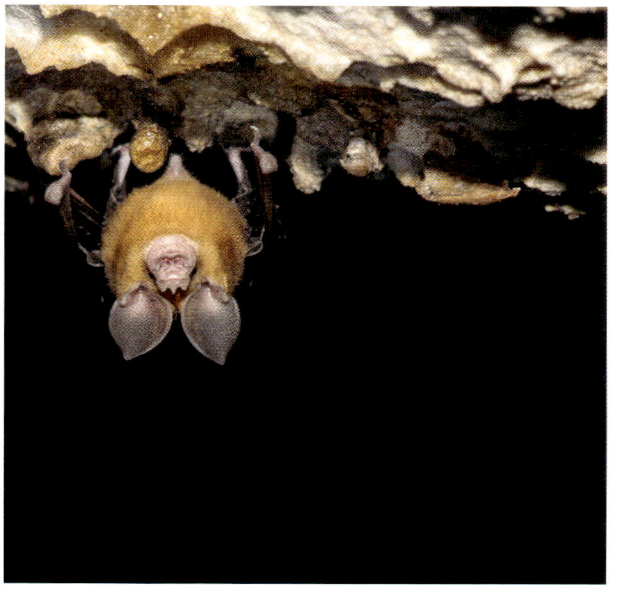

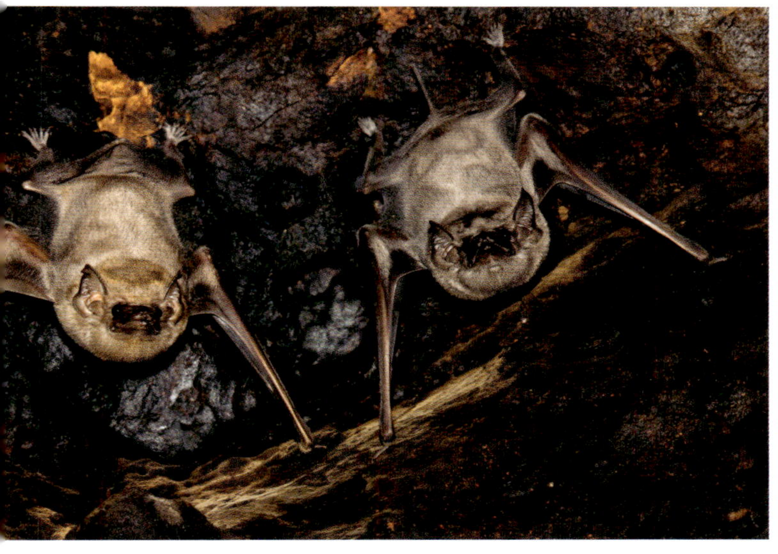

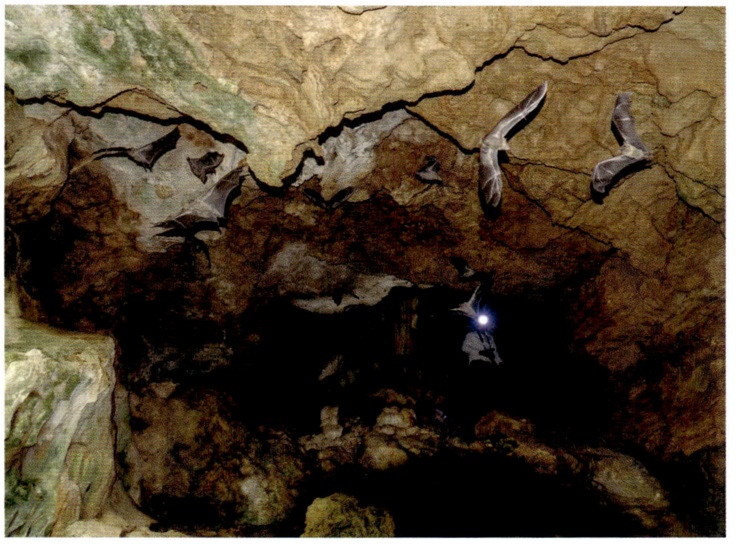

takes for the echo of the call to return to them. Just as radio stations broadcast at different frequencies, bat species call at different frequencies and these can be listened to with a bat detector to determine which species is calling.

Bats are wonderfully beneficial creatures but are amongst the most misunderstood of animals, often feared as sinister and unclean creatures of the night. Many plants, wild and agricultural, rely on bats to pollinate their flowers, others to spread their seeds. They are also pest controllers and eat insects that are harmful to agricultural crops and to man. Ultimately bats are a good indicator of the health of natural habitats.

The ghost or long-eared bat ***(far left)*** is a desert dweller and has only been recorded in the Najd while the Arabian trident bat *(Asellia arabica)* prefers the monsoon forests and grasslands. Many hundreds of Arabian trident bats roost in Suhur Cave of Wadi Nahiz ***(top centre and top right)*** and emerge each day at sunset to forage in the wadis and elsewhere for insect prey. Egyptian fruit bats have a wide distribution and are most easily seen flying over the gardens and farms of Salalah City. Some roost in abandoned buildings while others prefer caves in the Jabal ***(bottom right)***. The tomb bat *(Taphozous perforatus)* is more elusive but has been recorded at several locations including Wadi Rakhyut in Jabal Al Qamar ***(bottom centre)***.

Marine Mammals

The rich coastal waters of Dhofar are a favourite place for a wonderful array of whales and dolphins. In total nine species of whale and nine species of dolphin have been sighted in the sea off Dhofar; those most likely to be encountered in coastal waters are the Indian Ocean humpback dolphin (*Sousa plumbea*), Indo-Pacific bottlenose dolphin (*Tursiops aduncus*), Arabian Sea humpback whale (*Megaptera novaeangliae*) and Indo-Pacific common dolphin *(Delphinus delphis tropicalis)*.

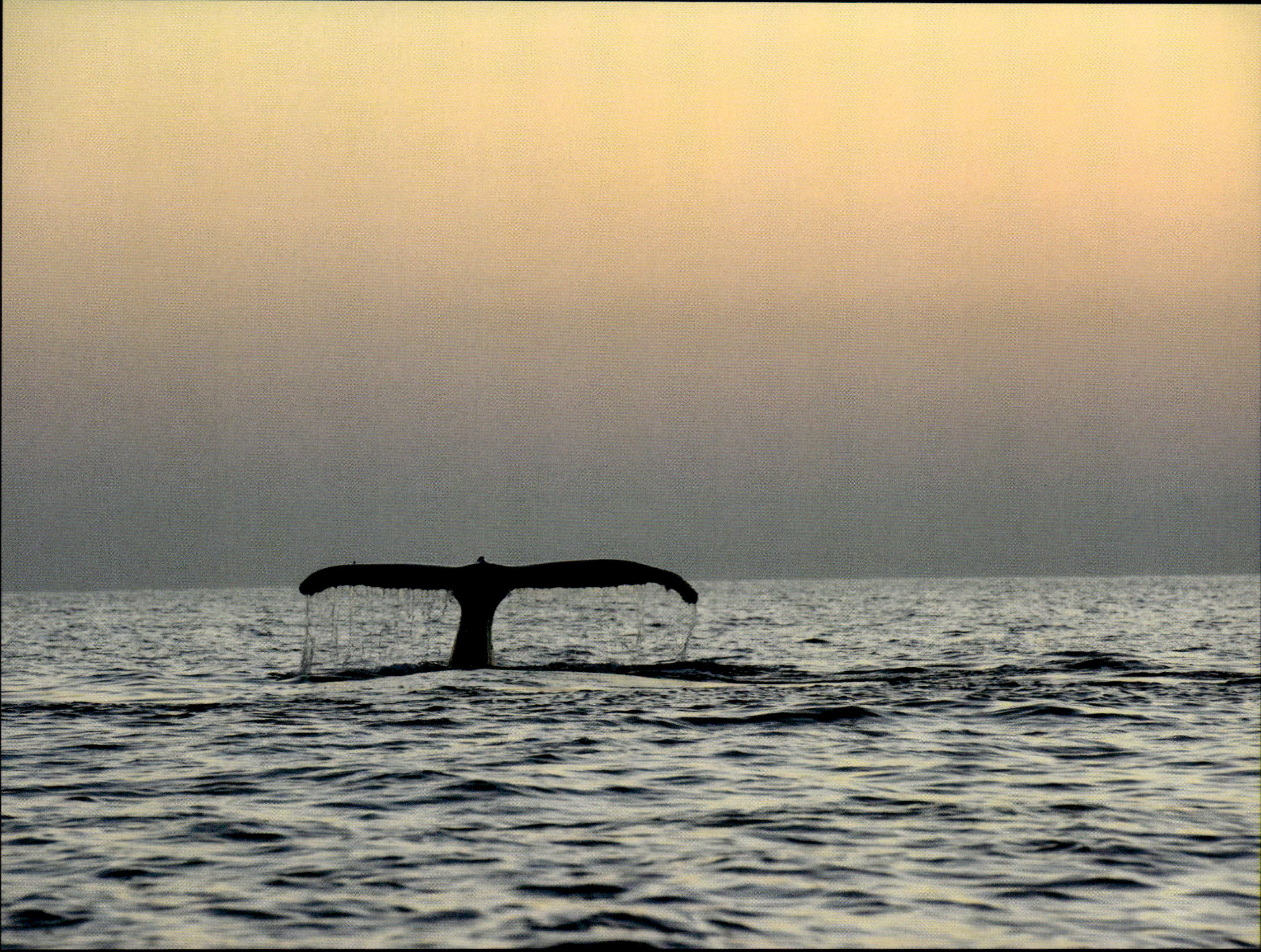

(Above) The humpback whale is one of the world's most popular mammals and Oman has its own unique subpopulation known as the Arabian Sea humpback whale. Here a humpback dives in the rich

Whales

Arabian Sea humpback whales are magnificent mammals that grow up to 15 metres[87] long and weigh up to 36,000 kilograms.[88] They are baleen whales, having no teeth, and are most commonly found in coastal waters, stretching from Masirah Island in the north, south to Dhofar and further south to the coast of Yemen's Al Mahrah Governorate, although they have also been observed further north, in the Sea of Oman and the Arabian Gulf.[89] Although some of the animals have left the area, even travelling as far as the coast of India, Al Hallaniyyat Bay is one of the two 'hotspots' off the coast of Oman for this species.[90]

Humpback whale populations throughout the world are known to be migratory, the animals travelling to the cold and rich polar waters to feed in the summer before returning to the warm waters of the tropics to breed in the winter. But, the Arabian Sea humpbacks are effectively land-locked to the north and thus unable to move to Northern Hemisphere polar waters in the summer. However, the upwelling of deep, nutrient-rich cold water off the coast of Oman during the *khareef* supports a plentiful supply of crustaceans and schooling fishes, including sardines, upon which humpback whales can feed in the summer. Thus the Arabian Sea humpbacks remain in the same area all year round, where they both feed and breed, making them the world's only non-migratory population.[90]

In the 1960s Soviet whaling fleets operating illegally in the Arabian Sea killed 242 humpback whales off the coast of Oman, India and Pakistan.[87] Today humpback whales are beginning to attract the attention of whale-watchers, who come to see the whales perform spectacular acrobatics. Often just a few hundred metres from the coast, they can be seen jumping out of the water and then slapping the water as they come back down, a behaviour known as 'breaching.' As well as being spectacular to watch, male humpbacks sing complex songs, a behaviour that is associated with breeding. Researchers have recorded humpback whale song around the Al Hallaniyyat Islands, often 24 hours a day, between November and May, confirming the importance of this area for breeding.[91]

Other whale species encountered in Dhofar's coastal waters include the Bryde's whale (*Balaenoptera edeni*) which, like the humpback whale, is a baleen whale that filters krill, small fish and plankton through specialised feeding plates in its mouth. The deep-diving sperm whale (*Physeter macrocephalus*) can be found further offshore; even larger than the humpback whale, sperm whales are toothed whales and can dive to depths reaching 1,500 metres in search of food such as squid.[92]

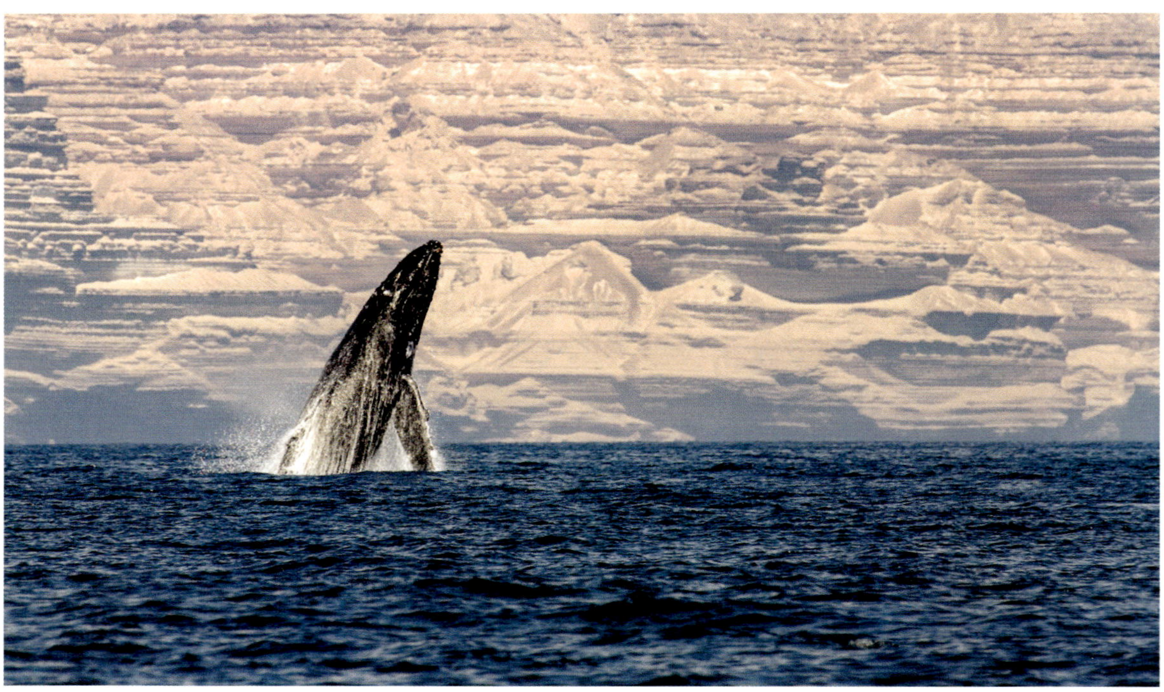

(Right) The sea cliffs of Jabal Samhan provide a backdrop to a breaching Arabian Sea humpback whale.

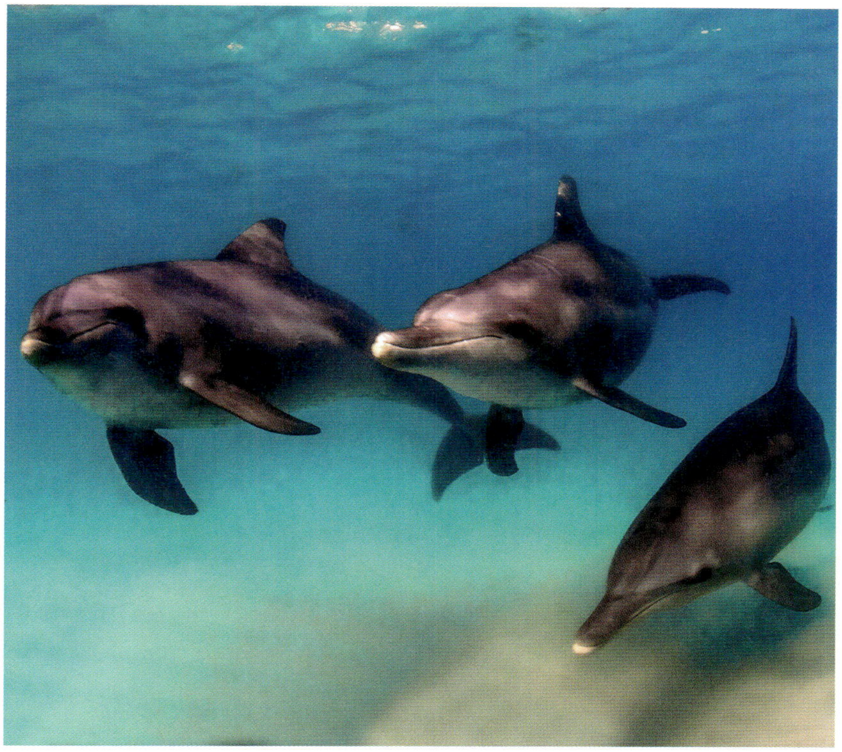

The most commonly encountered dolphins are the Indo-Pacific bottlenose dolphin ***(left)***, Indian Ocean humpback dolphin ***(below)*** and Indo-Pacific common dolphin ***(bottom)***.

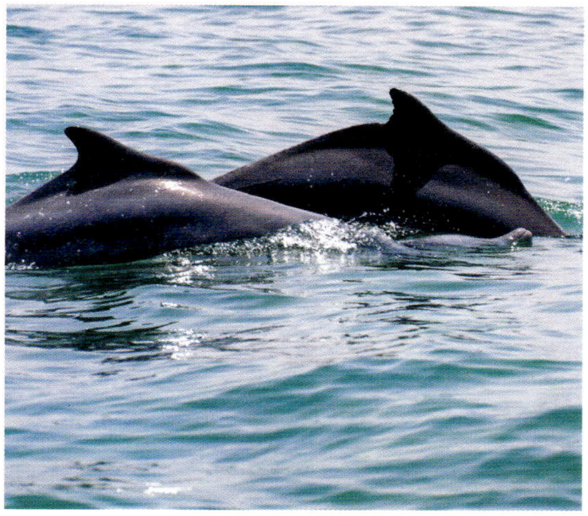

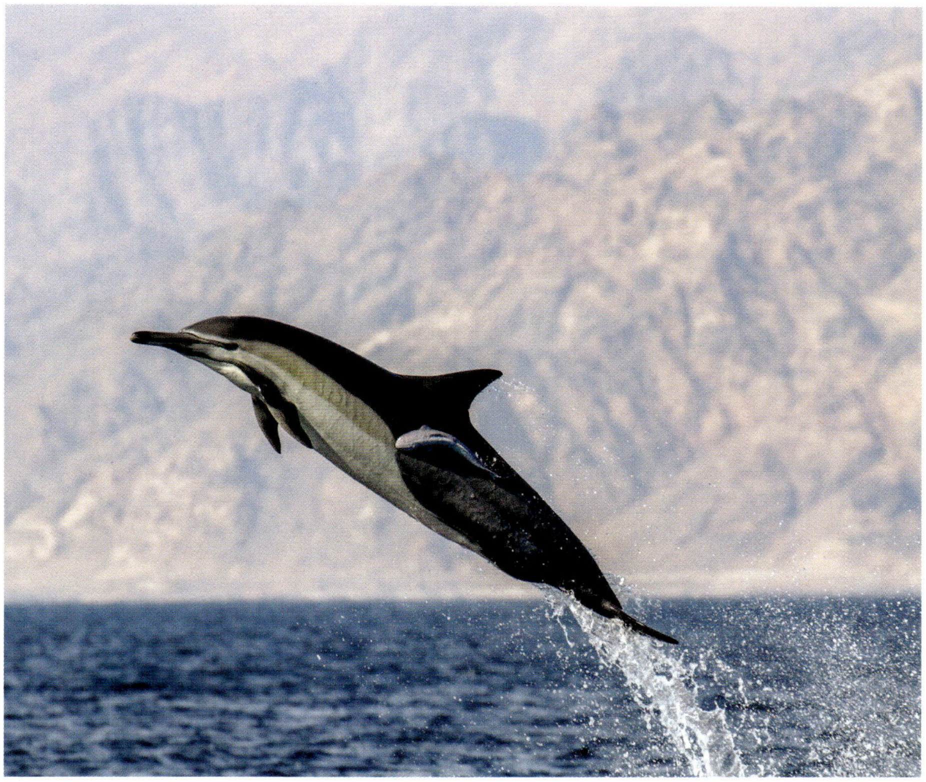

Dolphins

Unlike baleen whales that filter small fish and shrimp-like prey from the water, dolphins have teeth which they use to grasp fish or squid when they feed. They use echolocation, a form of sonar, to navigate and to hunt fish and other prey. They do not sing, as the humpback whale does, but communicate through clicks and whistles. The marine mammal most commonly observed by boat or from shore in the coastal waters of Dhofar is the bottlenose dolphin. Though the larger common bottlenose dolphin (*Tursiops truncatus*) has been observed in the region, the more petite Indo-Pacific bottlenose dolphin is more likely to be observed in Dhofar's coastal bays.[93] These live in close-knit family groups and are found near to shore, particularly between Hadbin and Hasik and on the Al Hallaniyyat Islands, where they can be seen feeding in the breaking waves.

Indian Ocean humpback dolphins can also be observed close to shore in Dhofar's coastal waters, especially off the coast at Hasik and Salalah. This species is easily recognised by the fleshy hump its dorsal fin sits on. These dolphins seem to prefer shallow water and thus do not venture far offshore while feeding on fish, squid and crustaceans.[94]

Birds

As a consequence of the summer monsoon and the resultant richness of habitats, Dhofar is a haven for birdlife. Some birds are breeding residents, others come to breed during the monsoon, many come as winter visitors and others are passage migrants.[95] However, there can be considerable variability; for example Bonelli's eagle (*Aquila fasciata*) is a common passage migrant, a winter visitor and also a breeding resident.

In terms of numbers, the vast majority of birds seen in Dhofar are migrants. Twice a year millions of birds migrate vast distances across the globe from breeding grounds, usually in the colder polar and temperate regions, to wintering grounds in the temperate and tropical areas. To do this they follow one of eight different established routes known as flyways. Dhofar lies on the East Asia–East Africa flyway linking northern and north-eastern Asia with eastern and southern Africa.

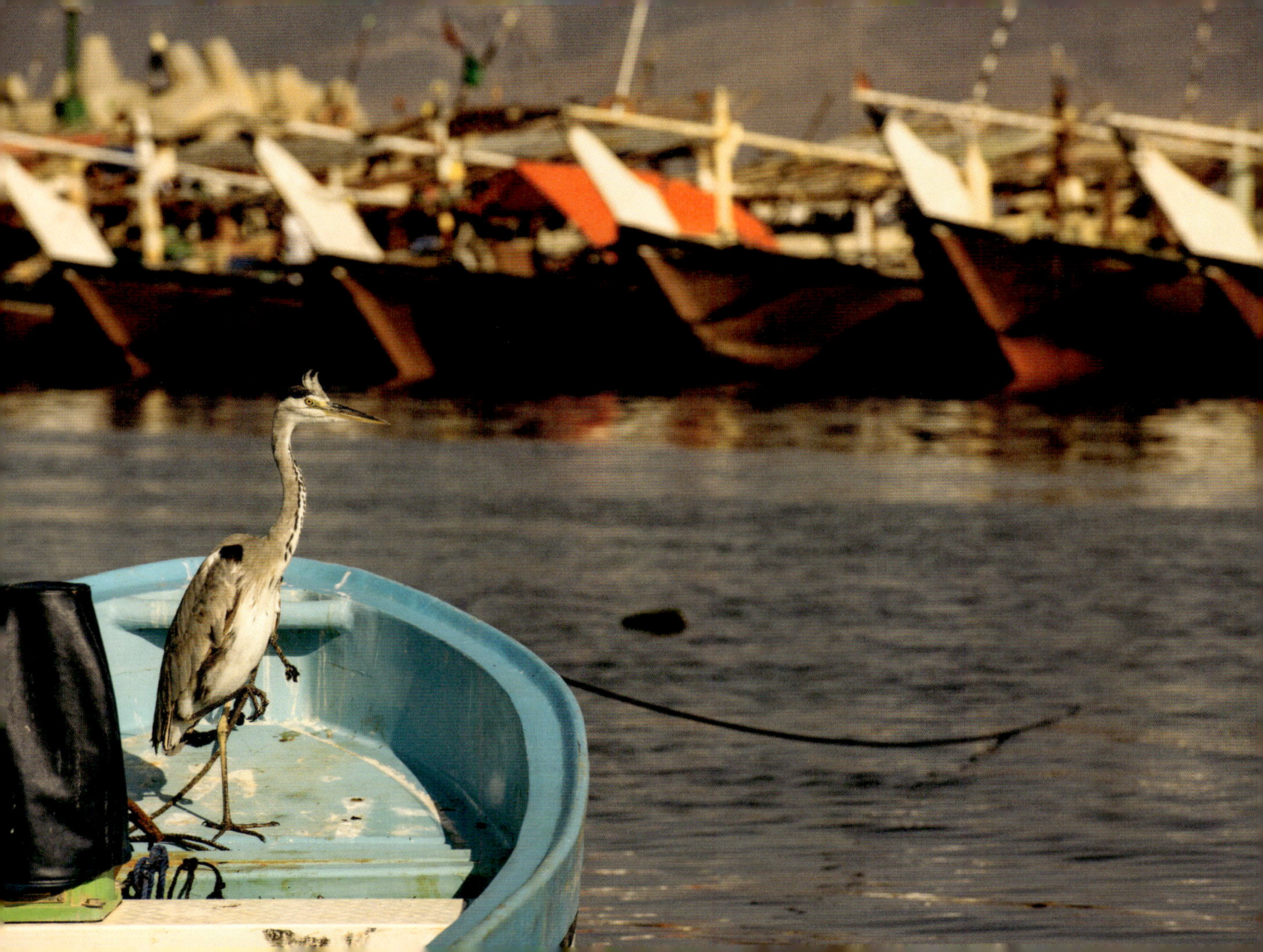

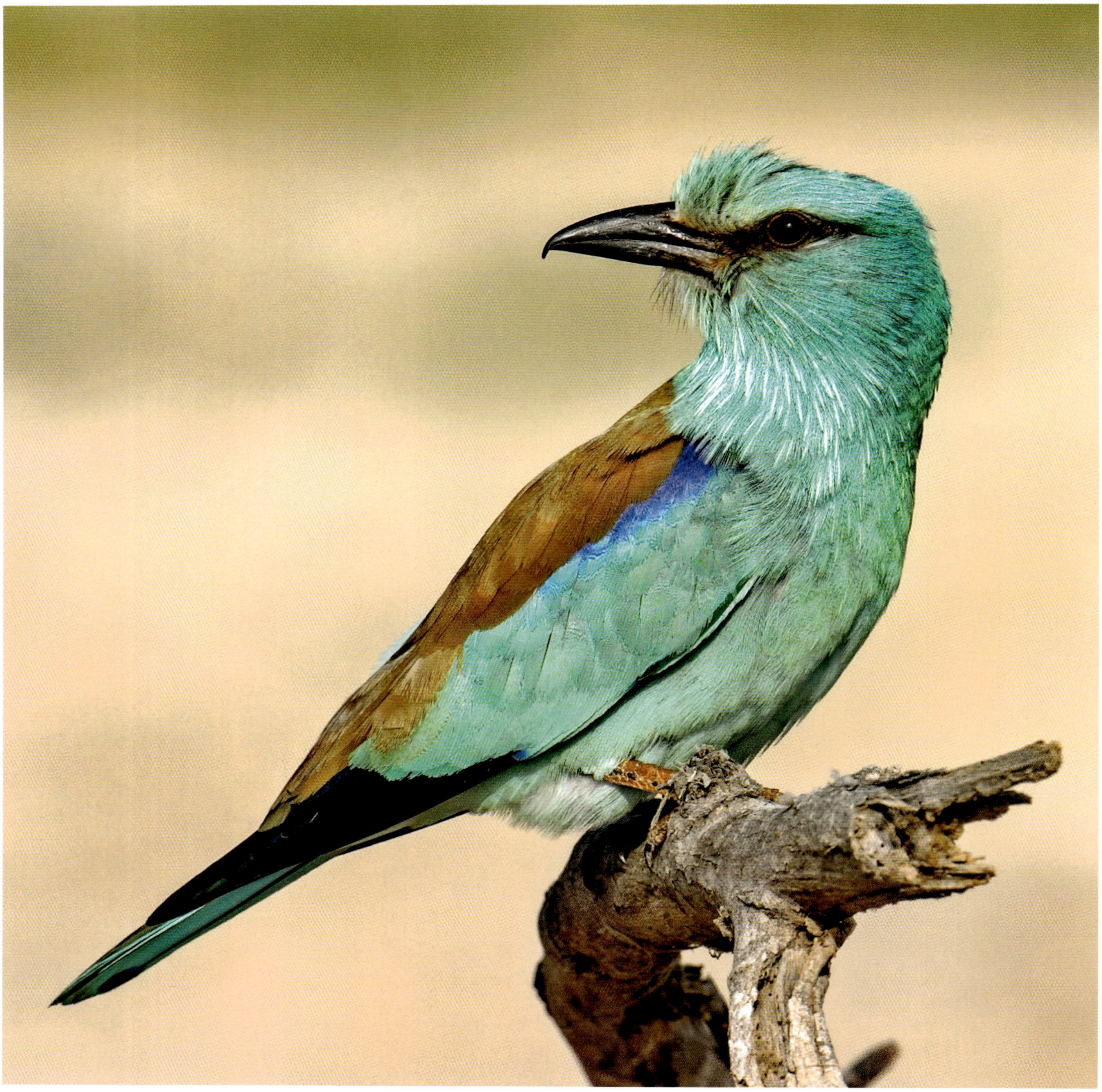

The European roller *(above)* breeds in Iraq and Iran during the summer months before migrating to sub-Saharan Africa for the winter. On their migration the birds often stop in Dhofar to refuel for the onward journey.

Passage Migrants

The first migrants leave Asia in the autumn and for many Dhofar is an important stopover to rest and feed before continuing south to Africa. All over Dhofar migrants appear wherever there is a chance of food, whether at a desert spring such as Muntasar, on farm land in the Najd or on one of the many *khawrs*. Highly visible species include the white stork (*Ciconia ciconia*) that can be seen strutting over grasslands looking for insects or the European roller (*Coracias garrulus*) perching on overhead wires also watching for insects. Species such as nightjars, are less visible, and are active by night flying close to the ground in search of insects.

Winter Visitors

While some species continue south many settle for the winter. These winter visitors include numerous warblers, chats, flycatchers and shrikes as well as coastal waders, gulls and terns.

Distinctive visitors include the Eurasian hoopoe (*Upupa epops*), which has a striking long pinkish-brown crest that they raise when excited. Hoopoes appear in the Quran, where they are known by the name *hudhud*. On the coast, especially in the shallow waters and amongst the mangroves of the *khawrs*, large wading birds are found, including the greater flamingo (*Phoenicopterus roseus*), egrets, herons, spoonbills and ibises.

Away from the coast the most visible of the winter visitors are the birds of prey, also known as raptors, that come south from colder climes. Common kestrels (*Falco tinnunculus*) may be seen hovering while seeking out a small rodent and small groups of eagles may gather around a cow carcass, but it is at the municipal rubbish dumps where there is a real spectacle. On one occasion 825 steppe eagles (*Aquila nipalensis*) together with 20 eastern imperial eagles (*Aquila heliaca*) and 20 greater spotted eagles (*Clanga clanga*) were counted at one of Dhofar's rubbish dumps.[96]

Some birds visit throughout the year. The masked booby (*Sula dactylatra*), for example, is a large seabird that breeds throughout

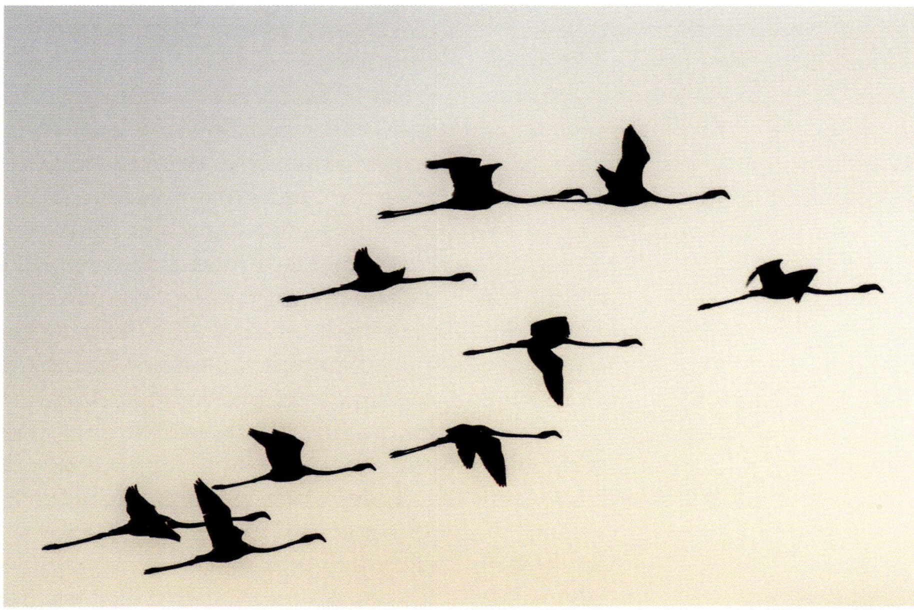

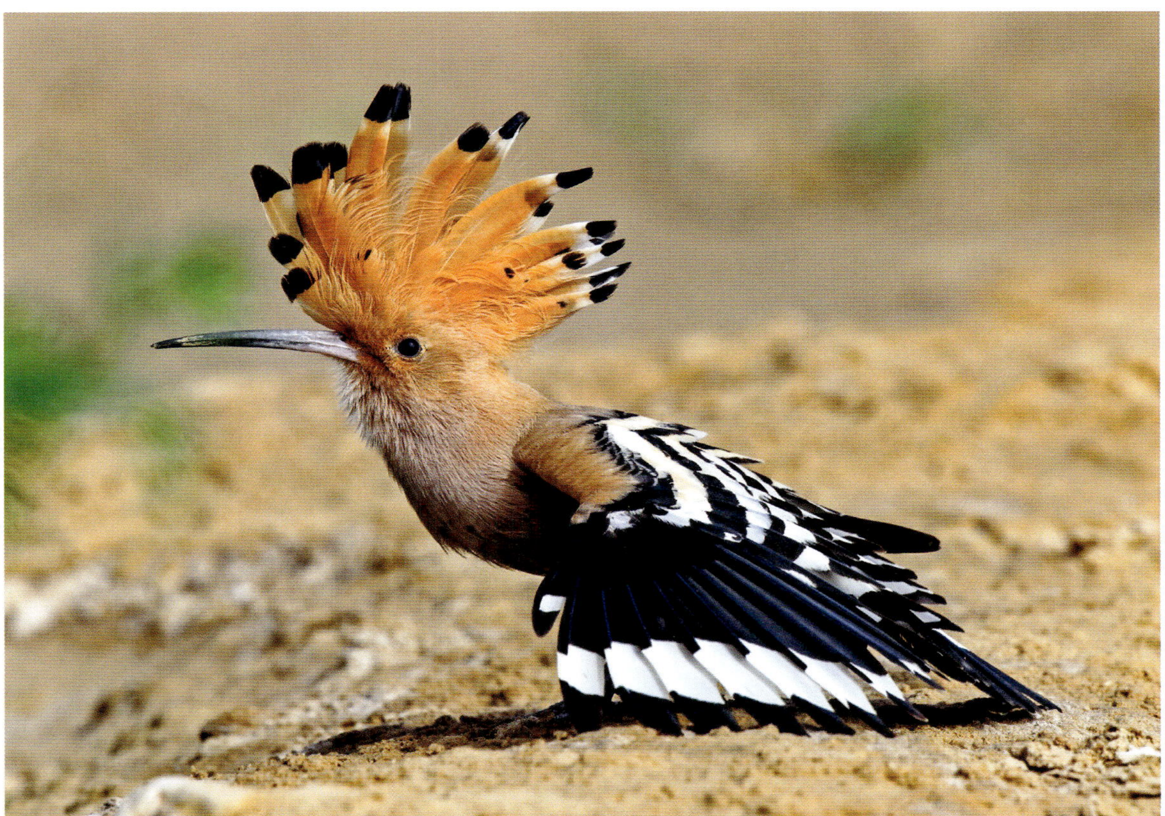

Visitors that may choose to spend the winter in Dhofar include the hoopoe ***(left)*** and greater flamingo ***(above)***.

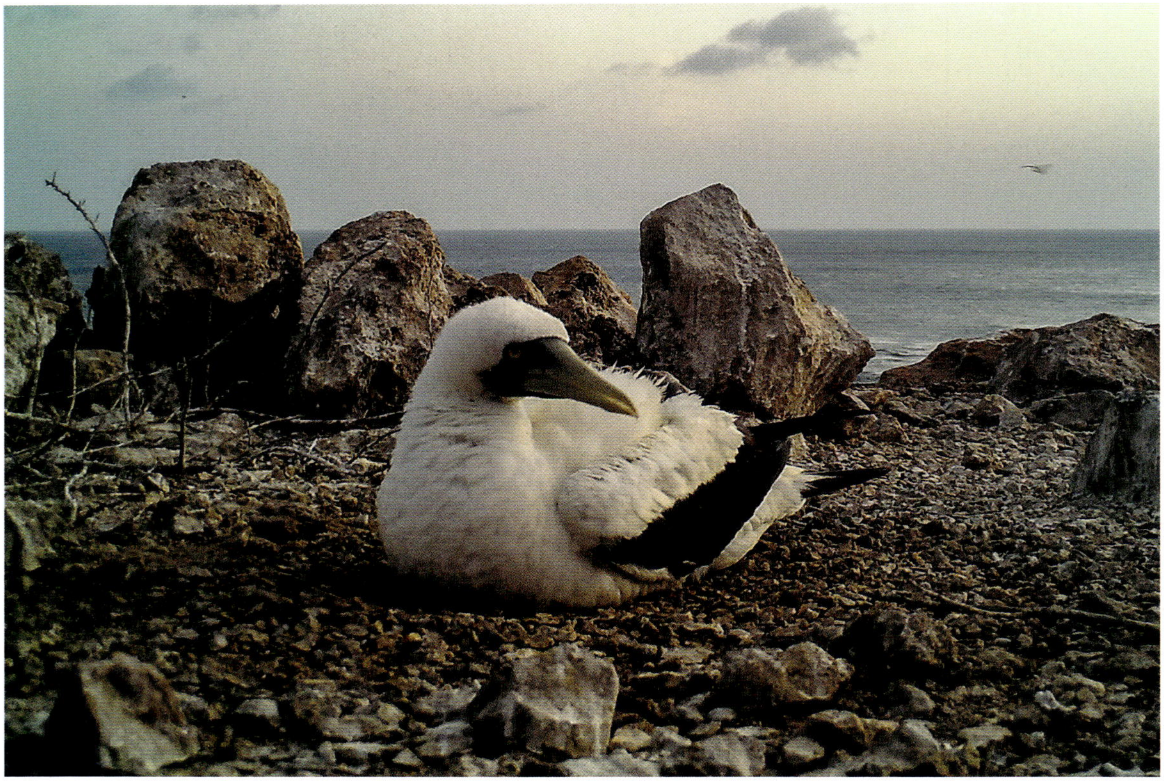

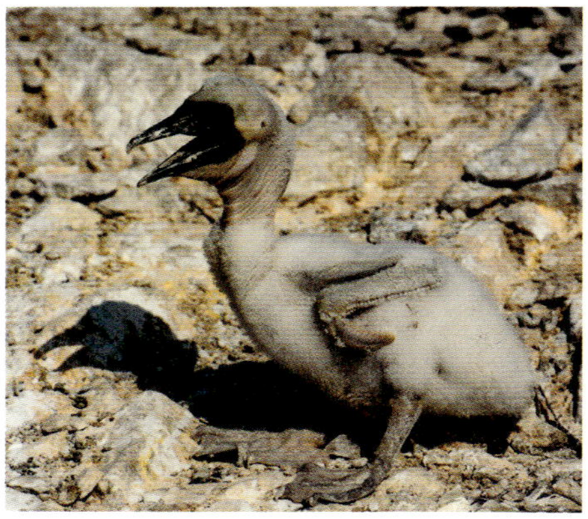

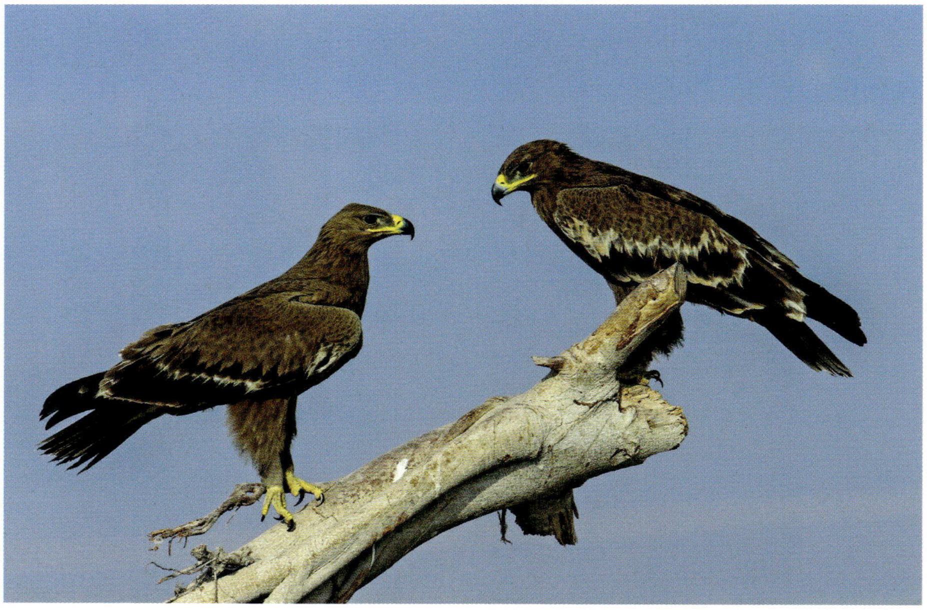

Camera-traps left on masked booby nests on Al Qibliyyah island showed that while birds laid two eggs only one hatched ***(top & above left)***. While steppe eagles ***(right)*** visit Dhofar in huge numbers, their global population is declining and they are endangered.

the year on the three smaller, and uninhabited, islands of the Al Hallaniyyat Islands – Al Qibliyyah, Al Hasikiyyah and Shinays. Up to 15,000 of the birds nest in colonies, generally away from the beach, on the gentle slopes of the islands.[97] Nests usually contain two eggs but the adults may abandon the second egg or, if it hatches, the first chick will kill its smaller sibling. Boobies are not considered a resident of Dhofar as they spend most of their life on the wing, returning to land only to court a mate and to breed.

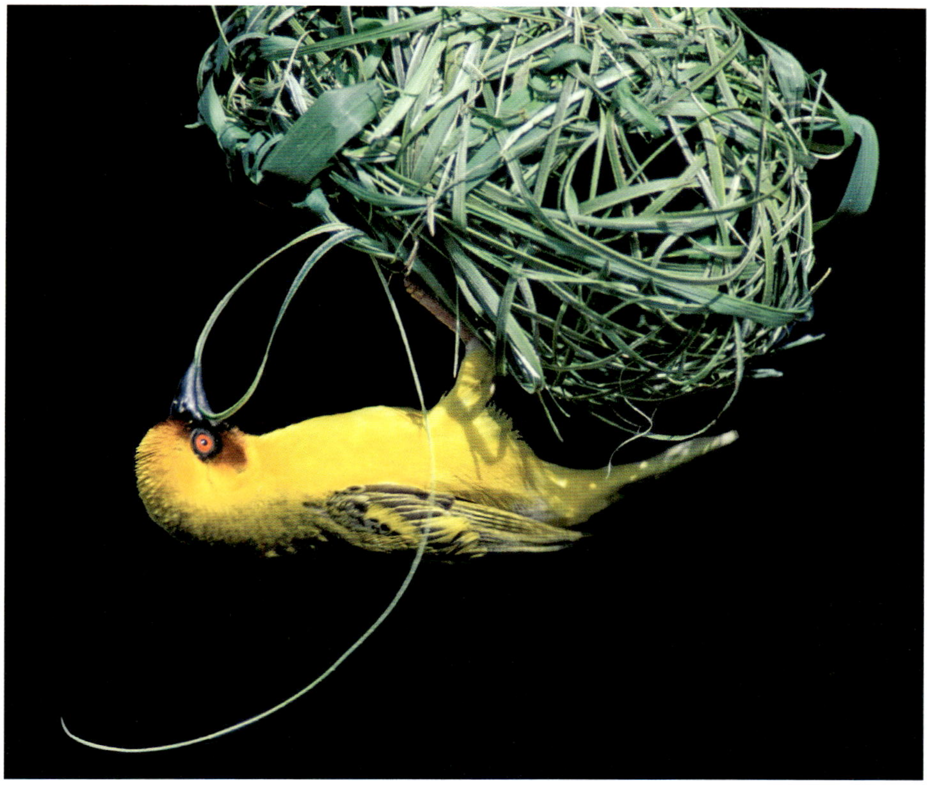

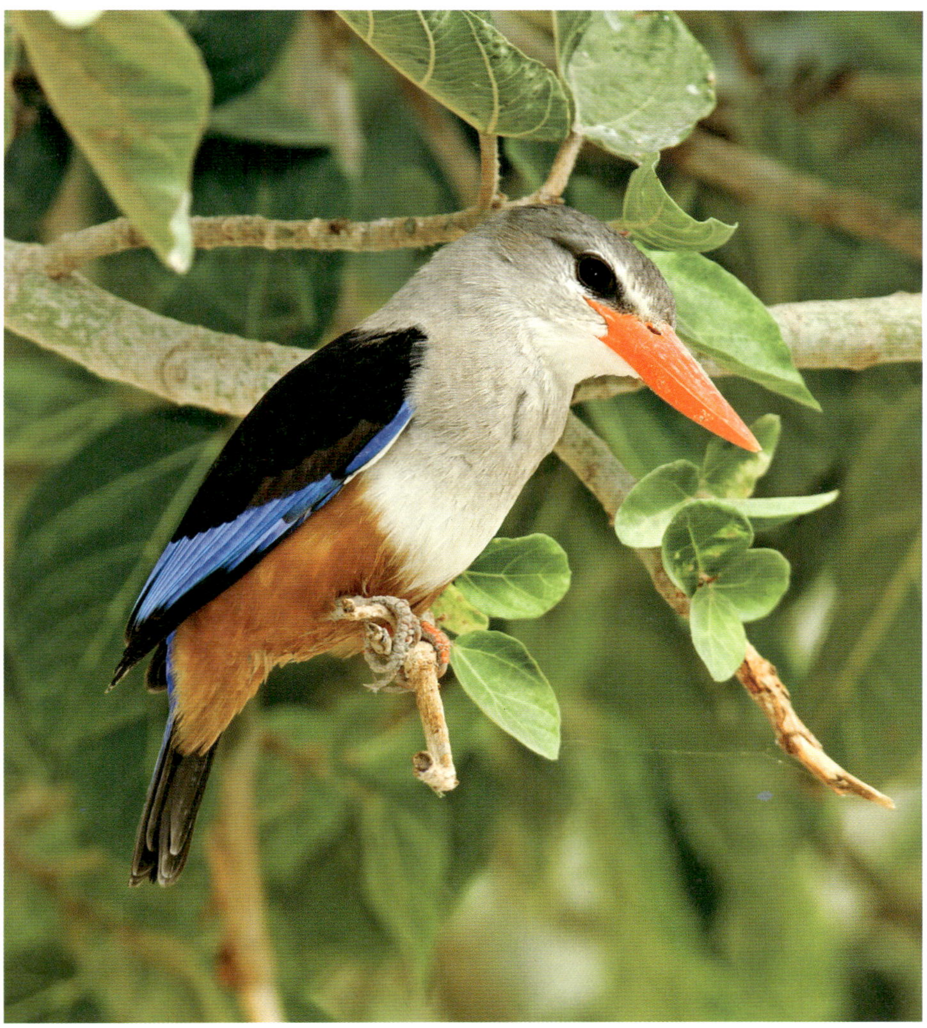

Summer Visitors

Shortly after the winter visitors head north the first of the summer visitors arrive, mainly coming north from Africa. They appear when the monsoon woodlands and grasslands of the Jabal are at their driest but after a period of nest-building and egg-laying they hatch young at the beginning of the monsoon, at a time when there is abundant food. Birds of particular interest include the noisy and colourful grey-headed kingfisher (*Halcyon leucocephala*), which can be found in the woodlands of Jabal Al Qara and Jabal Al Qamar, where insects are their principal prey. One infamous visitor is the Diederik cuckoo (*Chrysococcyx caprius*), which lays a single egg in the nest of resident Rüppell's weaver (*Ploceus galbula*). When the young cuckoo hatches it pushes out the eggs of the weaver bird, leaving the unwitting host to raise the single cuckoo as its own offspring. Not surprisingly, few visitors come to other parts of Dhofar during the summer. One exception is the European turtle dove (*Streptopelia turtur*), which has been recorded breeding in the Ghaf woodlands of Wadi Muqshin, at the edge of the Empty Quarter, at the height of the Arabian summer.[95]

Summer visitors to Dhofar include the Rüppell's weaver ***(above)*** and grey-headed kingfisher ***(below)***.

Breeding Residents

While the winter visitors are mainly from the north and are therefore Palaearctic species (from northern Asia, Europe and northern Africa), the breeding residents, unlike those of northern Oman, are generally Afrotropical, coming from central and southern Africa. For example, majestic Verreaux's eagles (*Aquila verreauxii*) are mainly found in the Great Rift Valley region of Africa but breed in isolated pockets of southern Arabia. In Dhofar they can be seen hunting along the southern escarpments of Jabal Al Qara and Jabal Samhan, where their preferred prey, as it is in Africa, is the hyrax. In Jabal Samhan Nature Reserve they are known to nest on the steep rock faces of the southern escarpment between November and February.

Rüppell's weavers are a bird of the Ethiopian and Yemen highlands but their range extends to the monsoon areas of the Dhofar Jabal. In spring the male, in his bright yellow and black plumage, builds several hanging nests under the canopy of forest trees. The female selects a nest and eggs are laid so that hatching takes place close to the arrival of the monsoon.

A number of resident species, not found in northern Oman, are restricted to the Arabian Peninsula and fringes of the Red Sea. Desert owls (*Strix hadorami*), closely related to the Omani owls (*S. butleri*) of the Al Hajar Mountains, are found in the wadis of the Jabal, where they are largely nocturnal. Yemeni serin (*Crithagra menachensis*) are a species of finch that are found at the sink hole at Tawi Aatayr.

The Najd is home to far fewer birds than the monsoon woodlands and grasslands of the Jabal. There is less food here and water is scare, and the birds tend to have wide distributions. Although the brown-necked raven (*Corvus ruficollis*) is not found on the Jabal or Jarbib, where their niche is occupied by the fan-tailed raven (*Corvus rhipidurus*), they appear throughout the rest of Dhofar, including even the remotest areas of the Empty Quarter. They are a true bird of the desert, with a broad diet ranging from snakes to dates, and seem to thrive around human settlements.

Four species of sandgrouse are found across the Najd, and at many water holes, such as Qatbit and Muntasar, many hundreds, if not thousands, of crowned sandgrouse (*Pterocles coronatus*) and chestnut-bellied sandgrouse (*P. exustus*) come to drink each morning. The spotted sandgrouse (*P. senegallus*) is less numerous while the beautiful Lichtenstein's sandgrouse (*P. lichtensteinii*) drink at sunset and usually in smaller numbers.

Few coastal birds are breeding residents; most are migrants and winter visitors. Of 14 species of gull and 16 species of tern, just the ubiquitous sooty gull (*Ichthyaetus hemprichii*) are

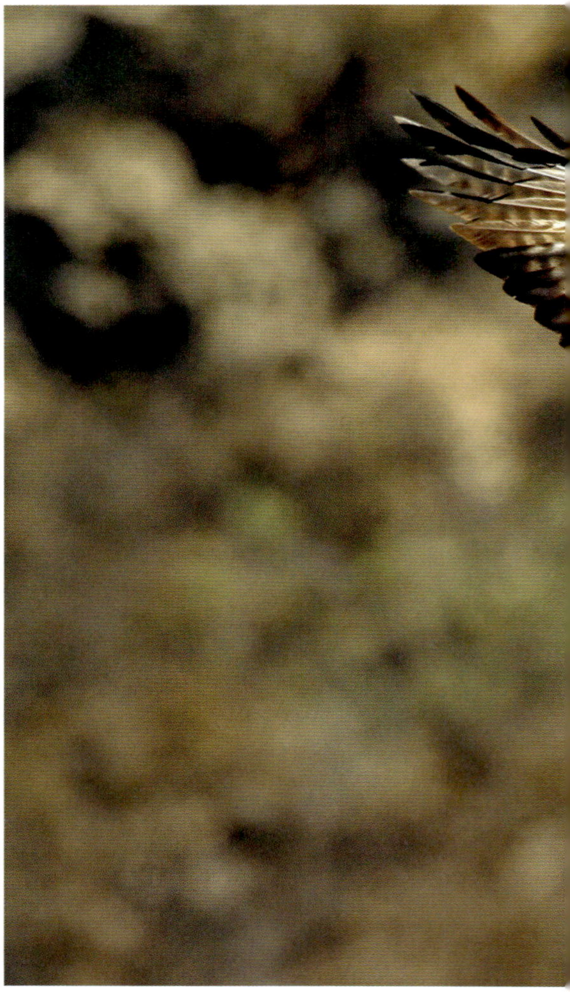

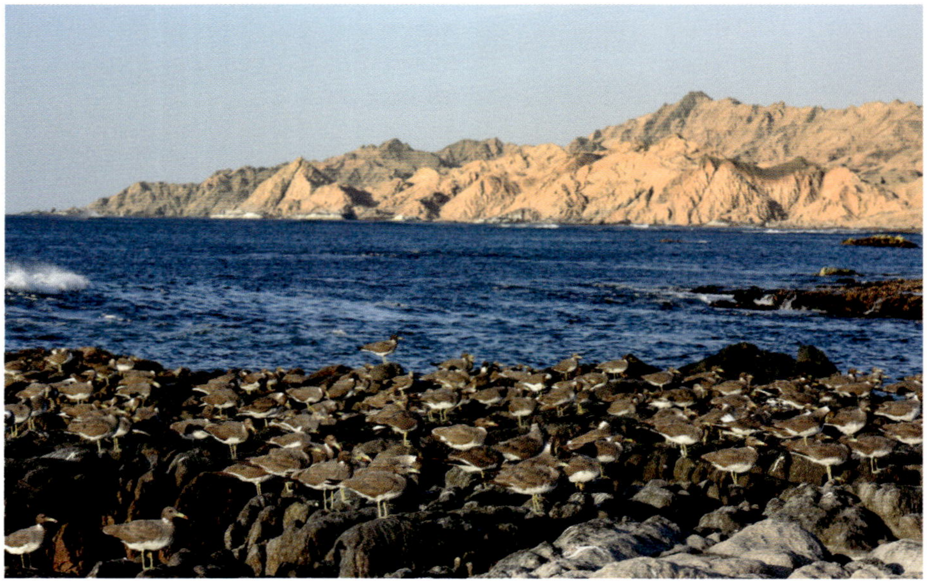

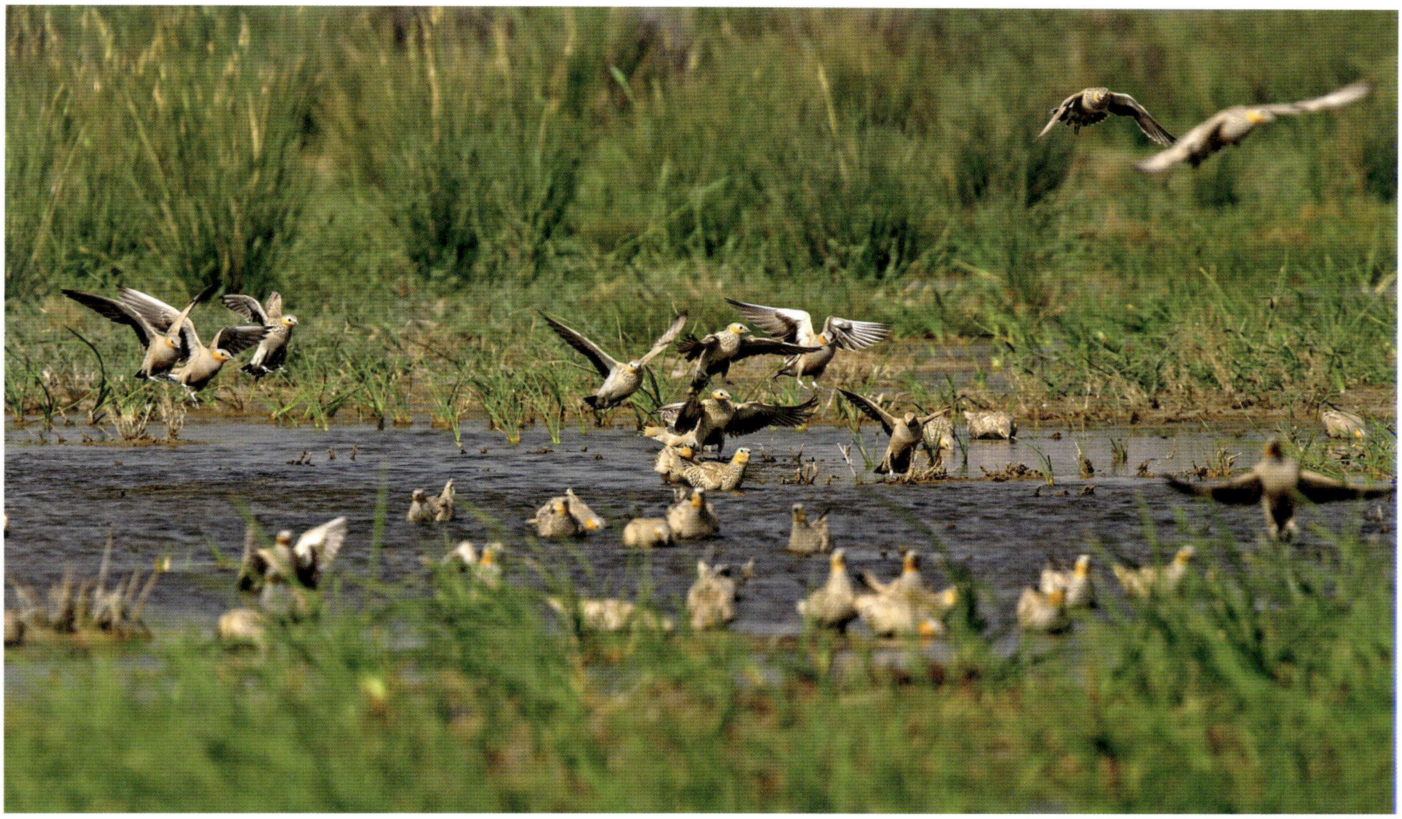

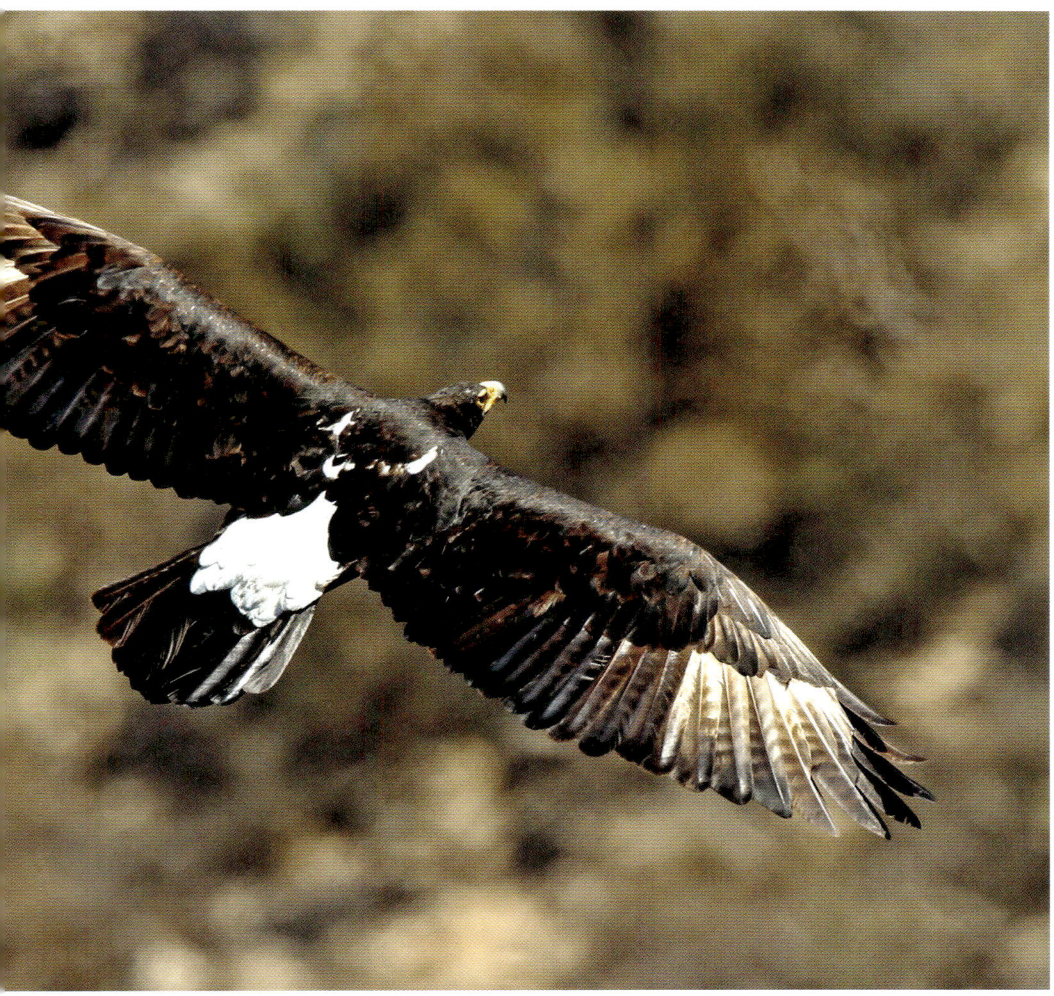

breeding residents. This species is found along the entire coast and breeds on cliff ledges of offshore islands, including the Al Hallaniyyat Islands, during the late summer. Their principal diet is dead fish and offal left by fishermen and thus the greatest concentration of birds can be found close to coastal fishing villages such as Ash Shuwaymiyyah.

(Left) A visit to the escarpment of Jabal Samhan may be rewarded with a sighting of the spectacular Verreaux's eagle ***(left)***. Along the coastline the sooty gull is the most common breeding resident, including on the island of Hallaniyyah ***(far left)***. In the Najd most water pools attract large numbers of sandgrouse; at Muntasar the most common species is the spotted sandgrouse ***(above).***

Amphibians and Reptiles

The first formal surveys of terrestrial amphibians and reptiles in Dhofar, in 1977, recorded 48 species including five new species and many new records both for Oman and Dhofar.[98] Since that time many gaps in our knowledge of the taxonomy, occurrence and distribution of Dhofar's reptiles have been filled and a further 9 species have been identified.[99]

Dhofar has a single species of amphibian but as a consequence of its diversity of climate, habitat and proximity to both Africa and Asia the region has a rich diversity of reptiles including 56 species comprising; geckos, agamas, typical lizards, chameleons, skinks, monitor lizards, thread snakes, typical harmless and rear-fanged snakes, cobras, burrowing asps, and vipers and adders.[100] In addition there are four species of sea turtle that are found in Dhofar.

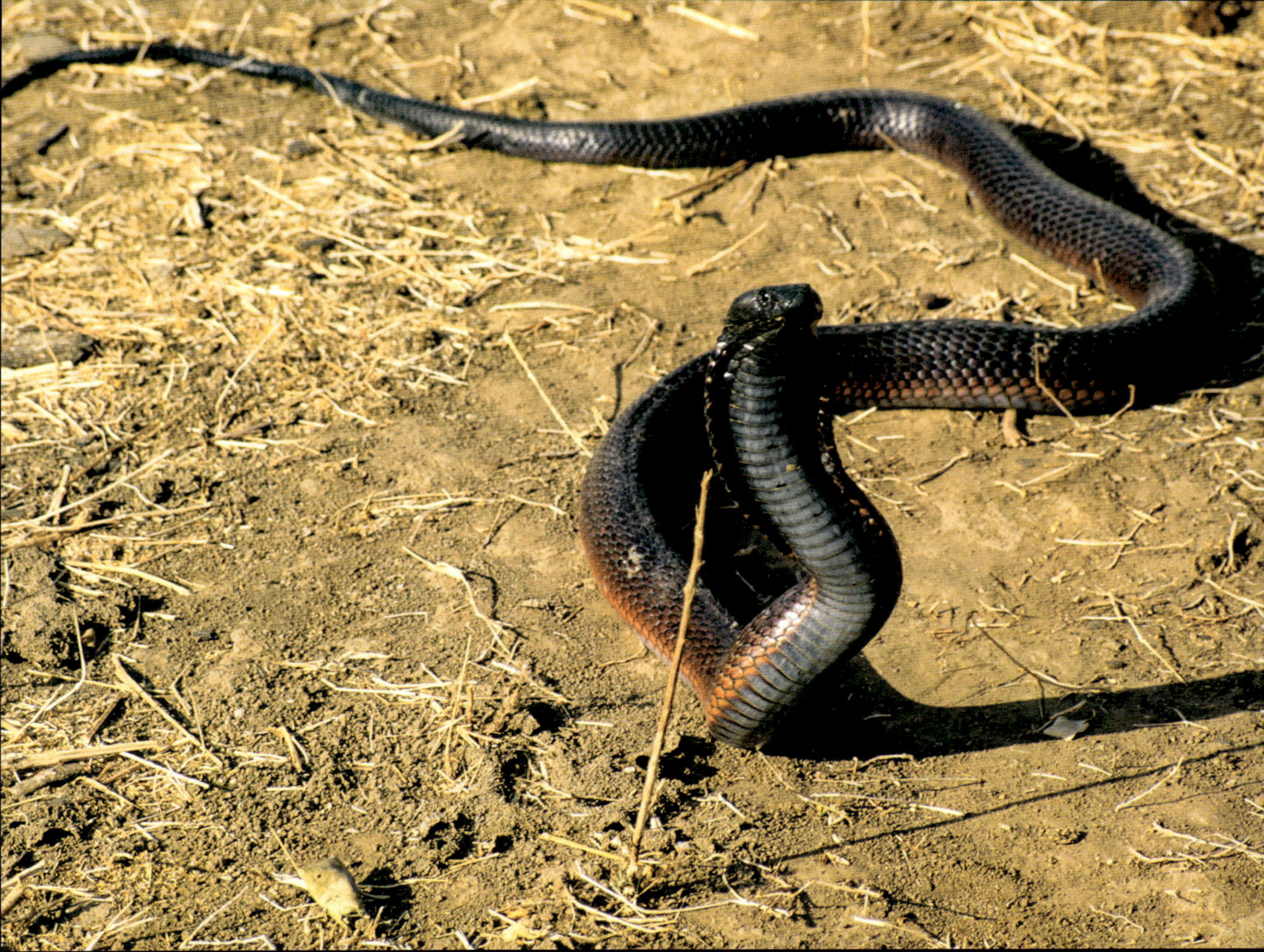

(Above) The Arabian cobra is the largest snake in Oman and is found only in Dhofar. It is potentially dangerous but is shy by nature and only aggressive when provoked

Dhofar's only terrestrial amphibian, the Dhofar toad ***(below)***, can often be heard before it is seen as males have a very distinctive croak. Meanwhile the Arabian chameleon ***(right)*** cannot be heard and its ability to change colour means that it is also very difficult to see.

Amphibians

Oman has two species of toad; the Arabian toad (*Sclerophrys arabica*) and the Dhofar toad (*Duttaphrynus dhufarensis*), though only the latter is found in Dhofar, where it inhabits the monsoon mountains, the Najd and coastal areas. The toads are more or less entirely nocturnal and are most common close to permanent water pools in the Jabal and the Najd as well as other damp environments such as caves. Those toads living close to permanent water breed throughout the year while toads living in dry desert areas will breed only after rainfall. During periods of drought the toads enter a state of dormancy; this is broken by rainfall, after which the toads emerge to breed, a males uttering the distinctive *kra-kra-kra* sound. After breeding, the female lays eggs that develop into tadpoles and these in turn metamorphose into adult toads. Insects form a major component of their diet.

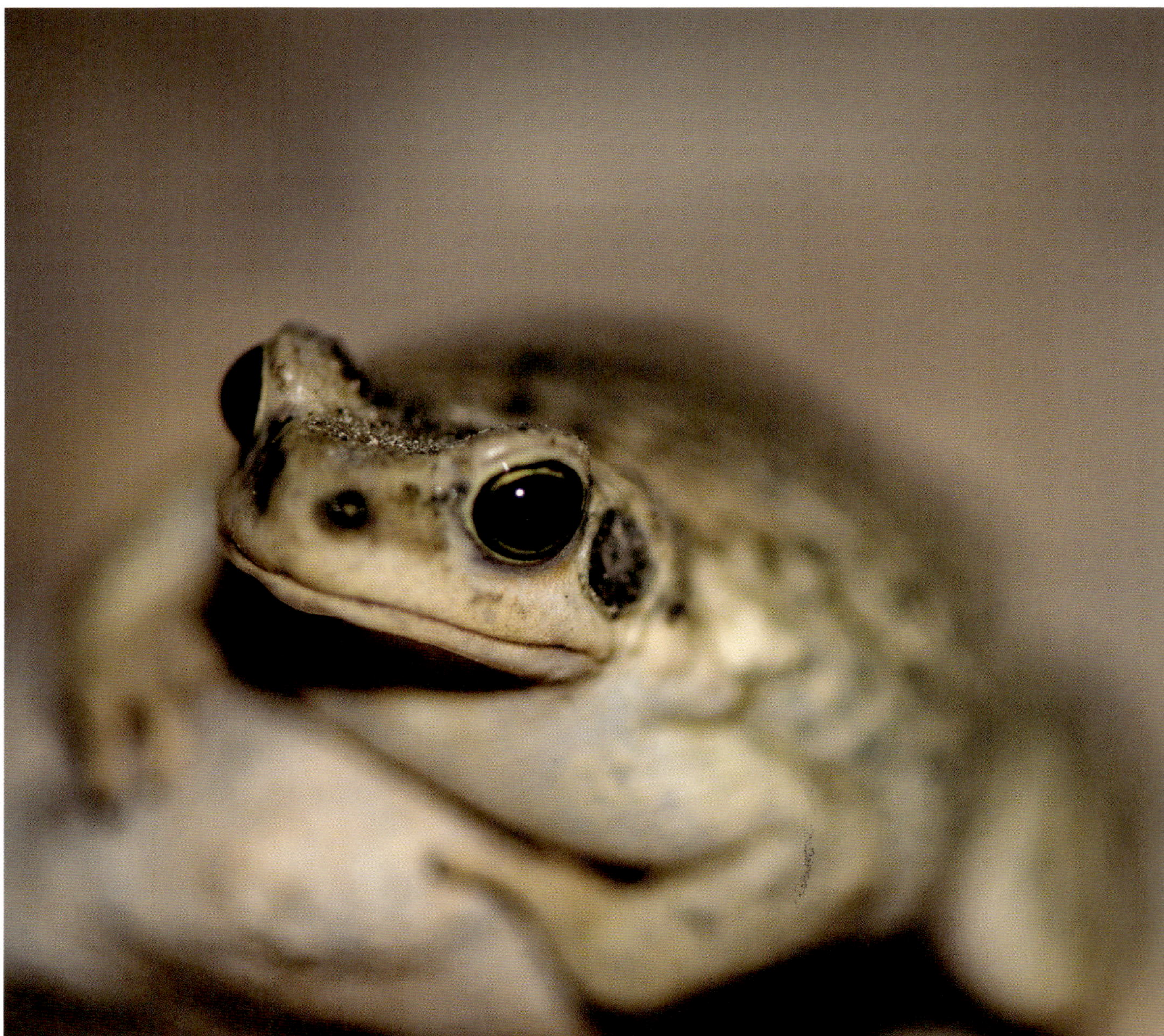

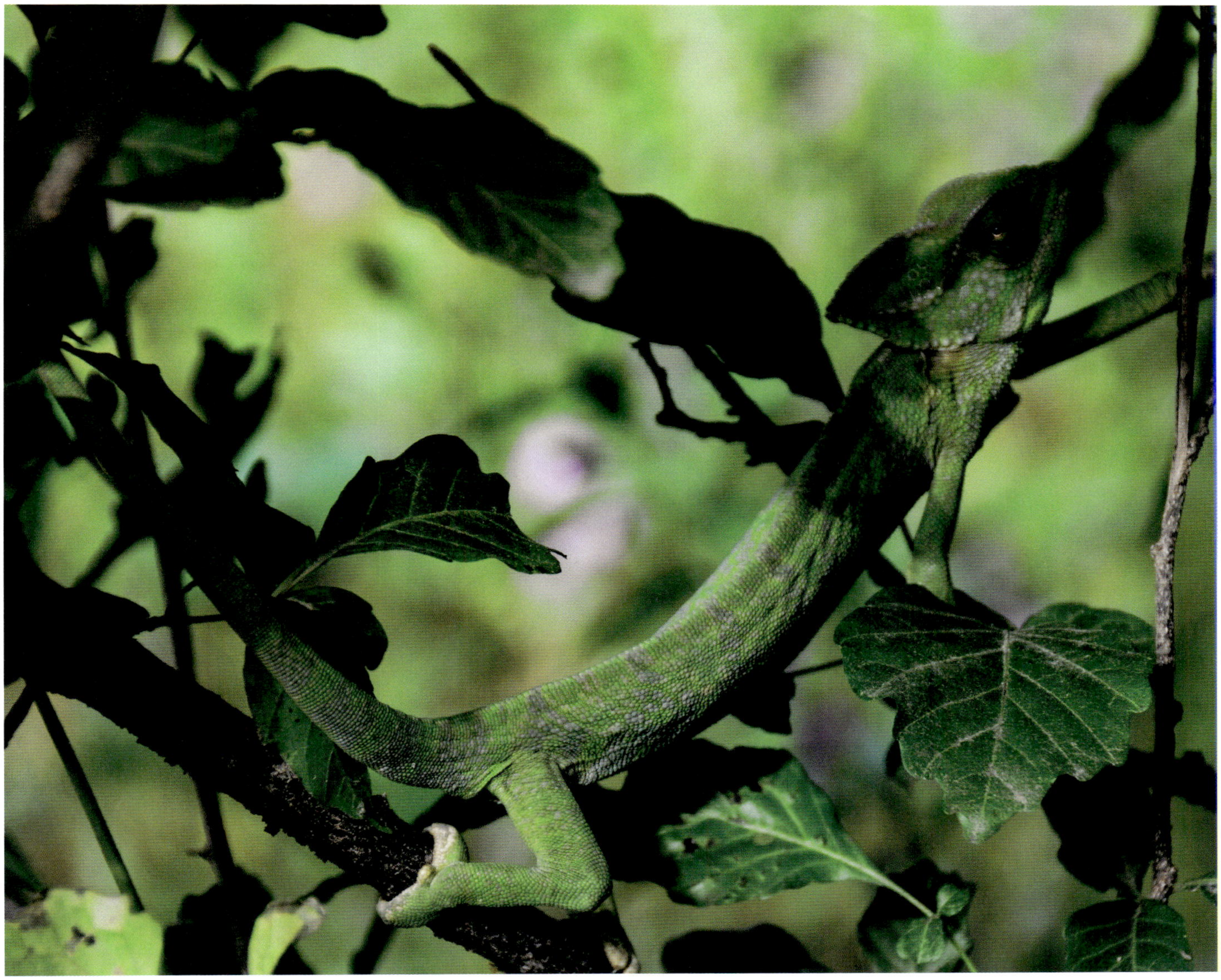

Reptiles

Lizards

The largest family of lizards is the geckos, of which there are 19 species in Dhofar. Geckos are generally nocturnal and, unlike other lizards, have no eyelids; instead they have a transparent membrane that they lick to clean. They prey upon small insects while themselves being prey to larger animals including snakes and foxes. Some geckos can shed their tails when being hunted by predators and it is therefore not unusual to find apparently 'tailless' geckos.

The most widespread of the geckos are the semaphore geckos. These occur on Al Hallaniyyat Islands and on the mainland from the coastal Jarbib through the monsoon forests and grasslands to the dry Najd. However, they are not found in the sands of the Empty Quarter, where they are replaced by the sand geckos that have evolved to survive the harshest of environments. These hunt at night and during the day dig burrows to shelter from the sun.

Not surprisingly, the largest number of gecko species is found on the Jabal, including seven species of leaf-toed geckoes, several of which are endemic to Dhofar and the mountains of neighbouring Yemen. Yellow-bellied house geckoes (*Hemidactylus flaviviridis*) are found only in Salalah, where their diet includes unwelcome house guests such as cockroaches and mosquitoes.

Agama lizards, of which there are 10 species in Dhofar, are known for their beautiful colours. Usually this colour-change is in males and is associated with breeding but yellow-spotted agamas (*Trapelus flavimaculatus*) are able to rapidly change their colour to that of the background to hide from predators. Agamas are found throughout Dhofar and range from the sand-

All lizards found in Dhofar are harmless and most are shy and avoid contact with humans. They include Ali Kiyumi's leaf-toed gecko *(Hemidactylus alkiyumii)* **(top left)**, the Dhofar fan-footed gecko *(Ptyodactylus dhufarensis)* **(centre left)**, Carter's semaphore gecko *(Pristurus carteri)*, **(centre right)**, the east sand gecko *(Stenodactylus leptocosymbotes)* **(bottom left)**, Bent's spiny-tailed lizard *(Uromastyx benti)* **(top right)** and Sinai agama *(Pseudotrapelus sinaitus)* **(bottom right)**.

dwelling Arabian toad-headed agama (*Phrynocephalus arabicus*), usually less than six centimetres in length, to the mighty Egyptian spiny-tailed lizard (*Uromastyx aegyptia microlepis*), often known as the *dhub*, that can reach 70 centimetres in length and favours the gravel deserts of the Najd.

Deserving of special mention are the Omani spiny-tailed lizards (*U. thomasi*) that only occur in the Najd, neighbouring Al Wusta Governorate and on Masirah Island. In Dhofar they have been seen near Thumrayt and Shalim. These lizards have a very distinctive disc-shaped tail that is the origin of their local name, *abu qurush*, or 'Father of the Dollar' – named for the Maria Theresa Thaler, a silver coin once used as currency in the region. These lizards are active by day and are herbivores. In the past they and the *dhub* were eaten by the nomads of the desert as they were often the only available meat.

Typical lizards are generally long and thin, and Dhofar's 9 species are all insectivores and found in a range of habitats across Dhofar, including the Empty Quarter. The only chameleons in Oman are the Arabian chameleons (*Chamaeleo arabicus*), which are found on the Jarbib, the Jabal and the southern Najd. These very striking reptiles are a tree living species that eats mainly insects and has the ability to change colour very rapidly to

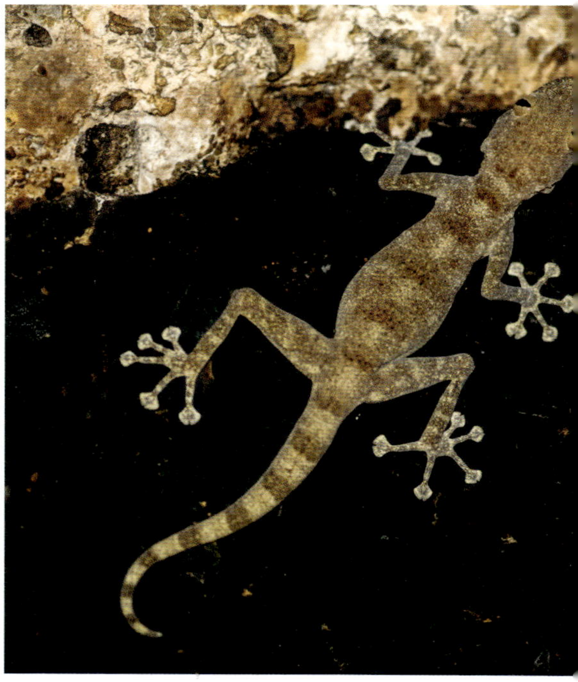

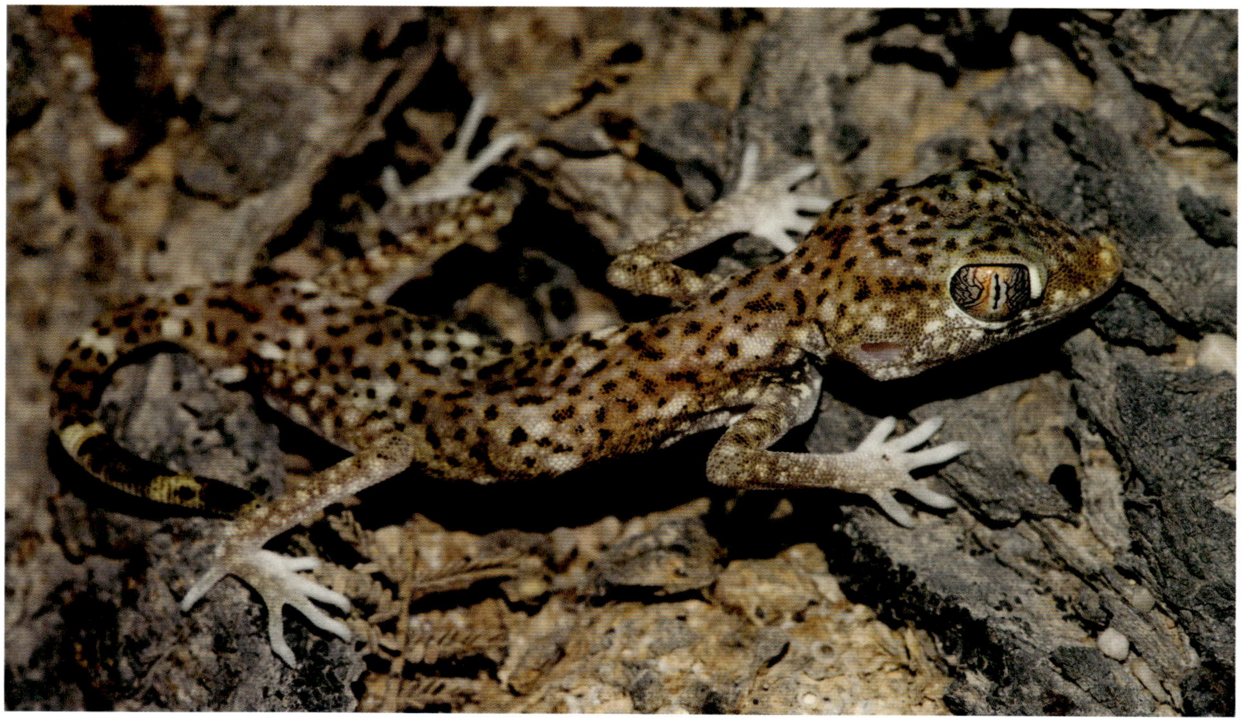

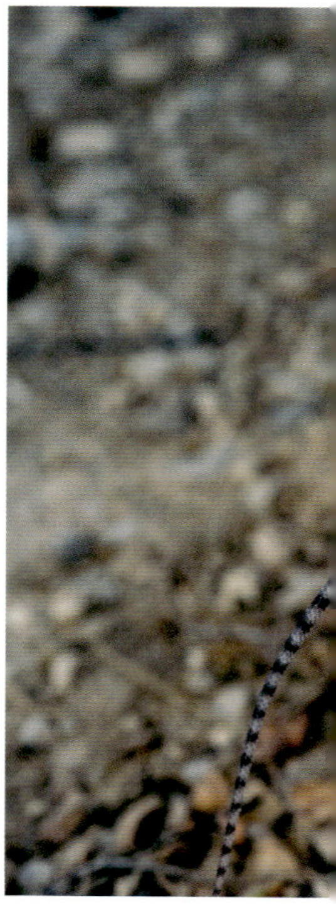

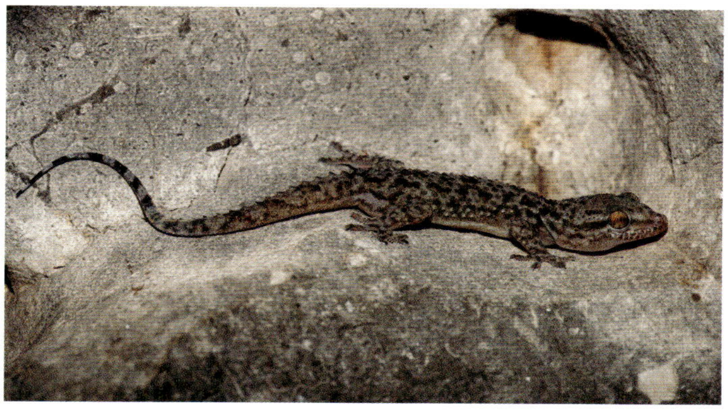

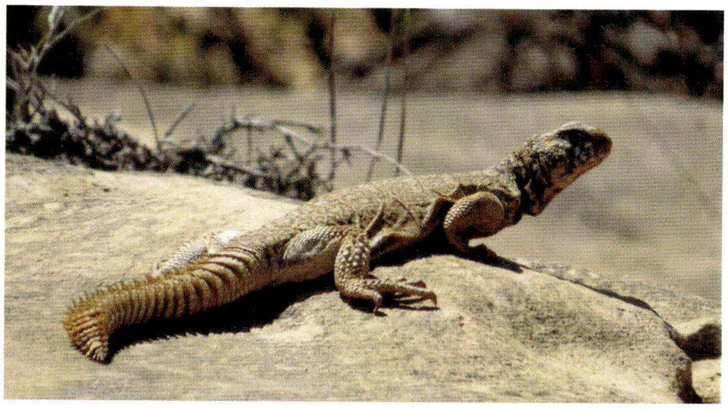

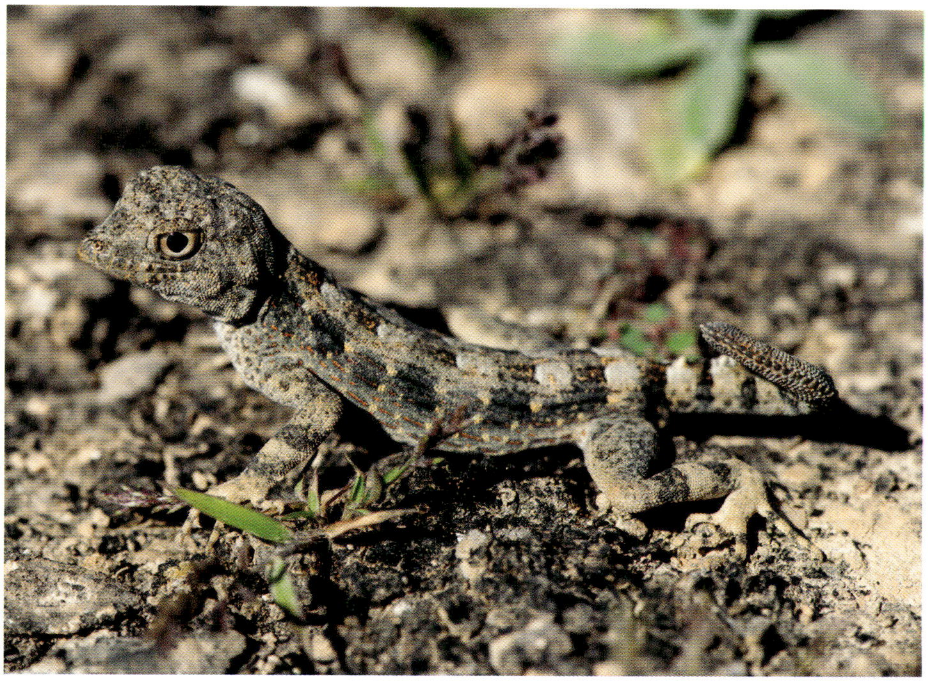

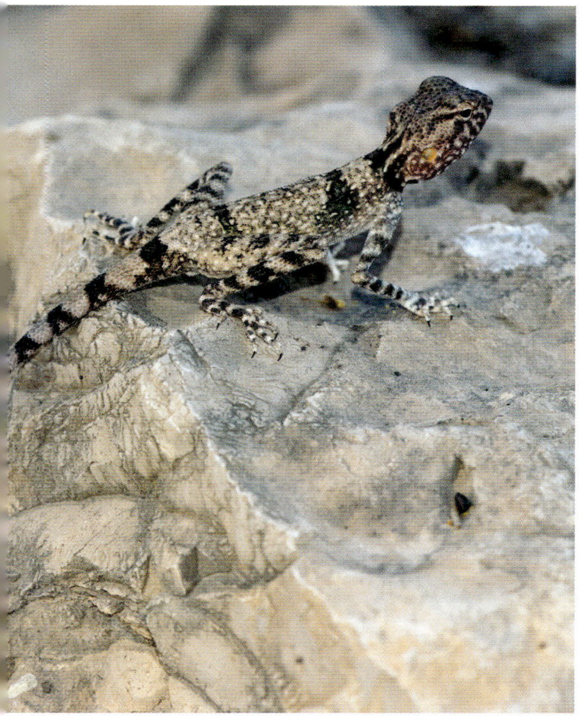

blend in with their habitat.

Of four species of skink, two occur in the monsoon habitats of the Jabal, one in gardens and parks of the Jarbib and Mirbat, while the sandfish occurs in the sandy habitats of the northern Najd and the dunes of the Empty Quarter. Skinks are mainly diurnal, (active during the daytime), but will burrow to avoid the midday heat.

The only monitor lizards are the desert monitors (*Varanus griseus*), which have only been reported from two locations, in the vicinity of Thumrayt and Al Mazyunah. These massive lizards can reach at least 1.2 metres in length and feed mainly on other lizards, snakes and birds.

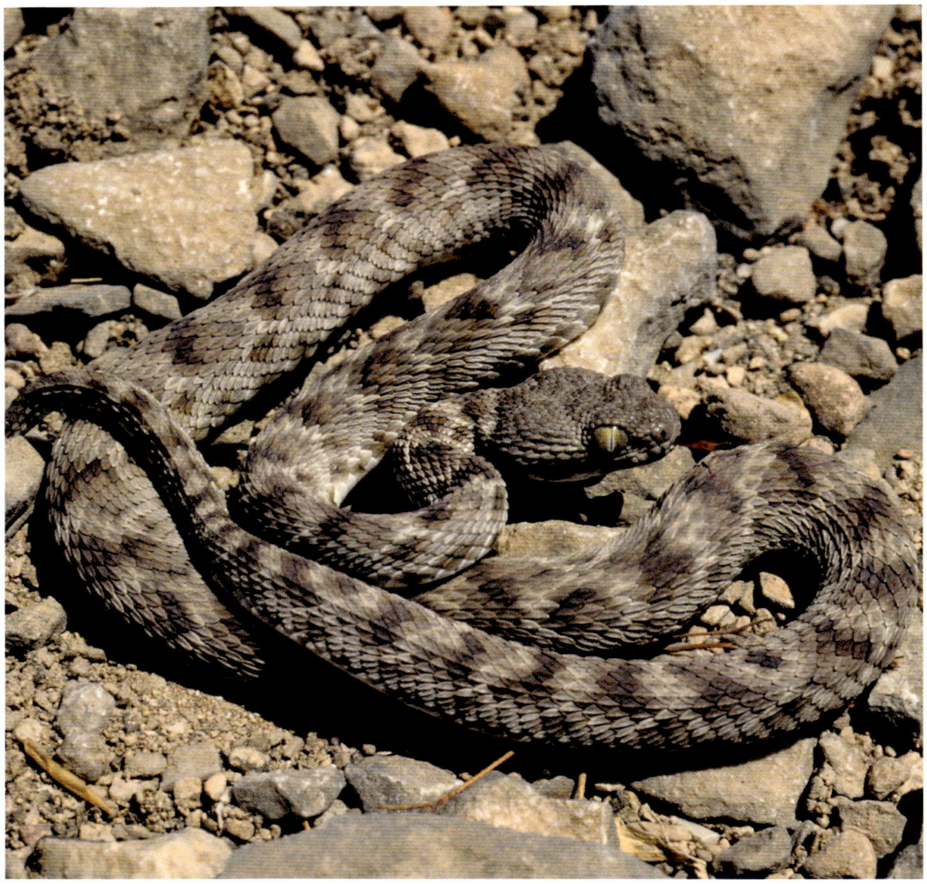

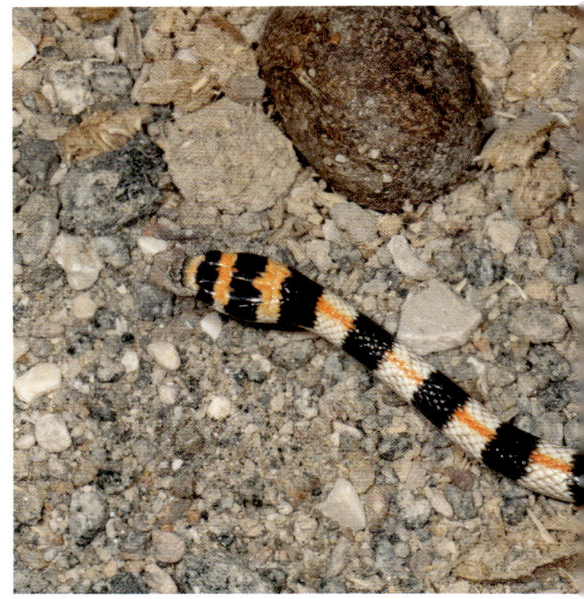

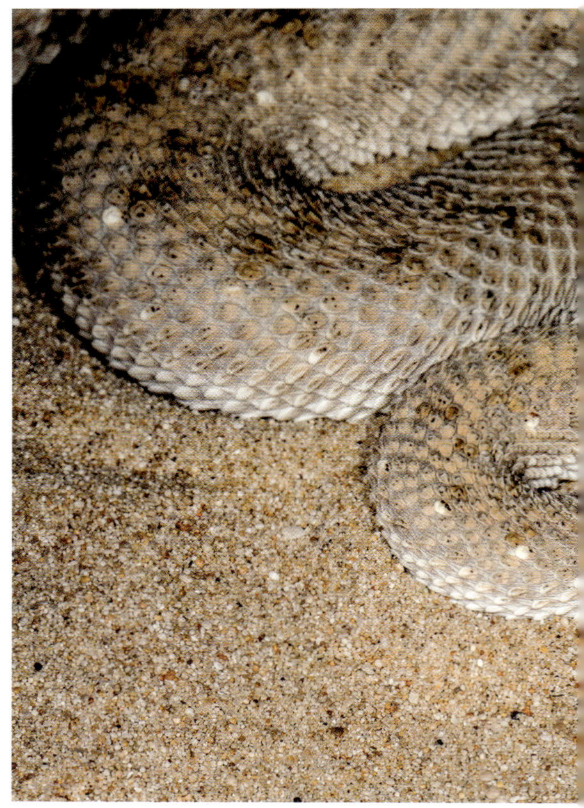

Snakes

Dhofar is home to 17 species of snake, most of which are not considered dangerous.

Thread snakes, recorded from the Najd, are blind and live underground most of their lives, where they eat ants and termites. Similarly the sand boas spend much time underground though they will eat surface prey such as geckos.

Nine species belong to the group of typical harmless and rear-fanged snakes, none of which is considered seriously dangerous to man. This family includes four racers that are confined to the Jabal and the Najd and typically feed on lizards, small mammals, birds and fish. Aden kukri snakes (*Rhynchocalamus arabicus*) have been found at just one location, Wadi Uyun, where they were first recorded in 2013. The hooded malpolon (*Rhagerhis moilensis*), found in the Najd, is a snake of the gravel desert and when disturbed lifts the front third of its body in a threatening posture. This behaviour has not only led people to believe this species to be a cobra but is also the origin of stories amongst the desert nomads that these snakes are able to fly.

Dhofar's only true cobra is the Arabian cobra (*Naja arabica*), which is usually found in well vegetated areas not far from water. Thus most records of this snake are from monsoon areas but Arabian cobras have also been found in arid wadis such as Wadi Rabkut, near Hasik, in dense vegetation close to permanent water pools. They are Oman's largest snake and can reach nearly two metres in length. Though not aggressive, the Arabian cobra will rear up when disturbed and its toxic venom makes them extremely dangerous.

The group known as burrowing asps has only one member, the small-scaled burrowing asp (*Atractaspis andersonii*). These largely live underground and have been recorded just twice on Jabal Al Qara. Though not aggressive,

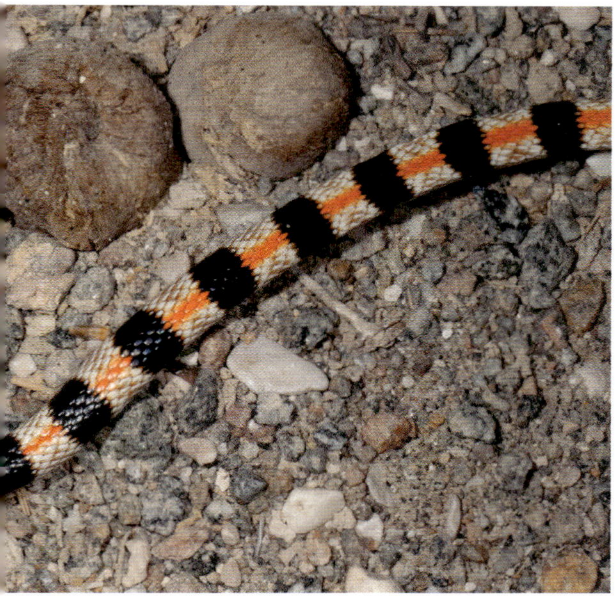

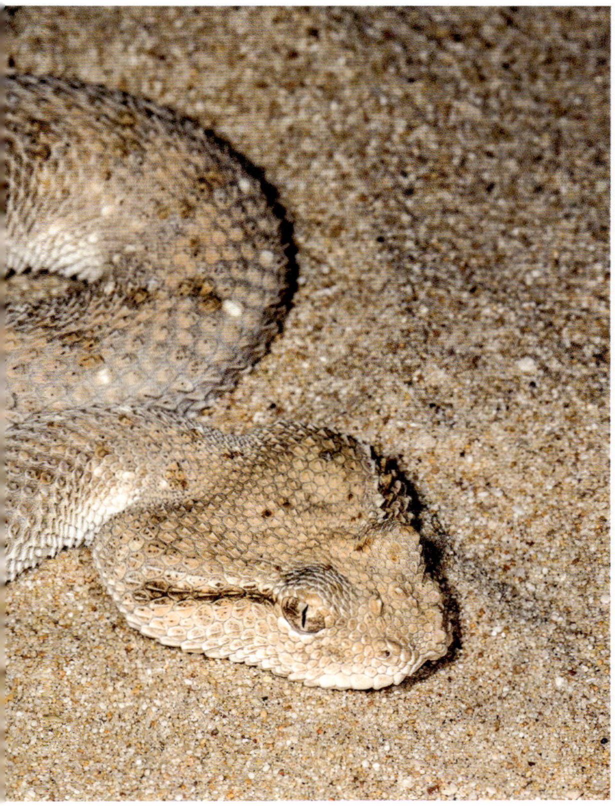

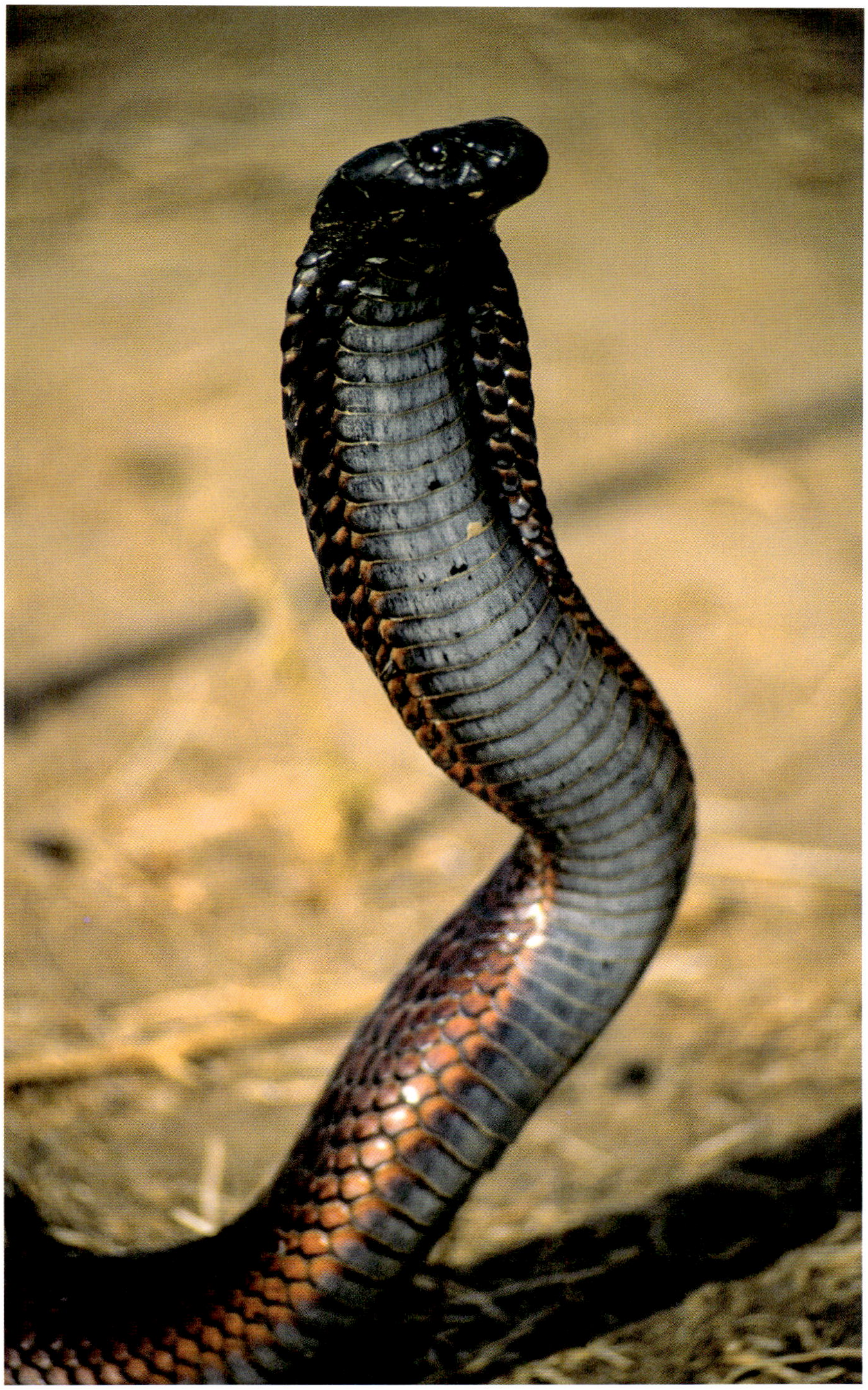

their venom is very toxic.

Of the vipers and adders, the puff adder (*Bitis arietans*) seems to be restricted to the monsoon habitats while the three species of viper have a much broader distribution extending to the northern Najd and, in the case of the Arabian horned viper (*Cerastes gasperettii*), to the Empty Quarter, though this species has been recorded from the Jabal. All four species are primarily nocturnal and feed on lizards, rodents and birds. The venom of the puff adder and the two saw-scaled vipers is highly dangerous while that of the horned viper is less dangerous to humans.

While the brightly coloured Thomas' racer *(Platyceps thomasi)* ***(centre top)*** is harmless, Dhofar's potentially dangerous snakes include Khosatzki's saw-scaled viper *(Echis khosatzkii)* ***(far left)***, Arabian horned viper ***(centre bottom)***, the Arabian cobra ***(above)*** and the puff adder (not pictured).

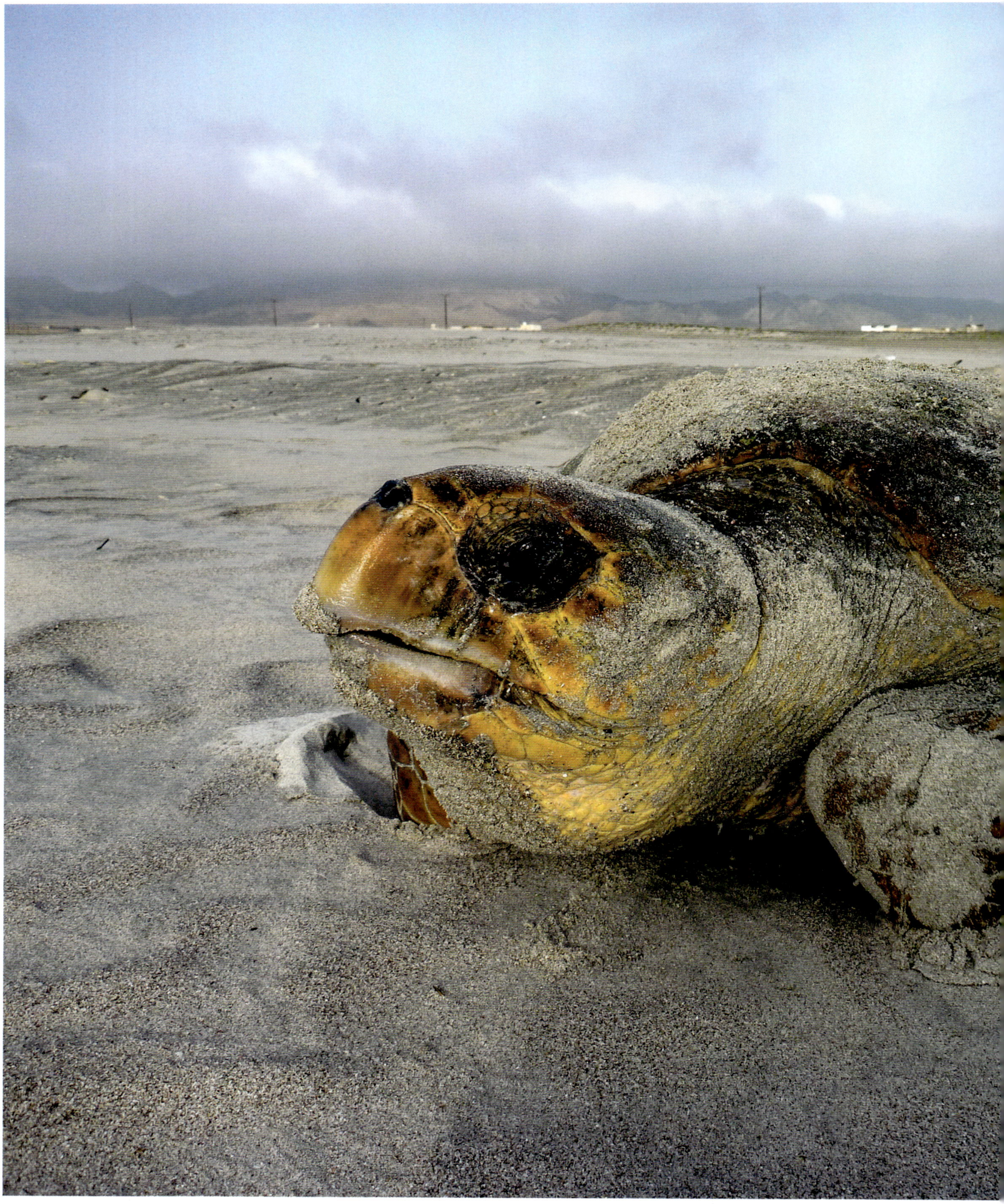

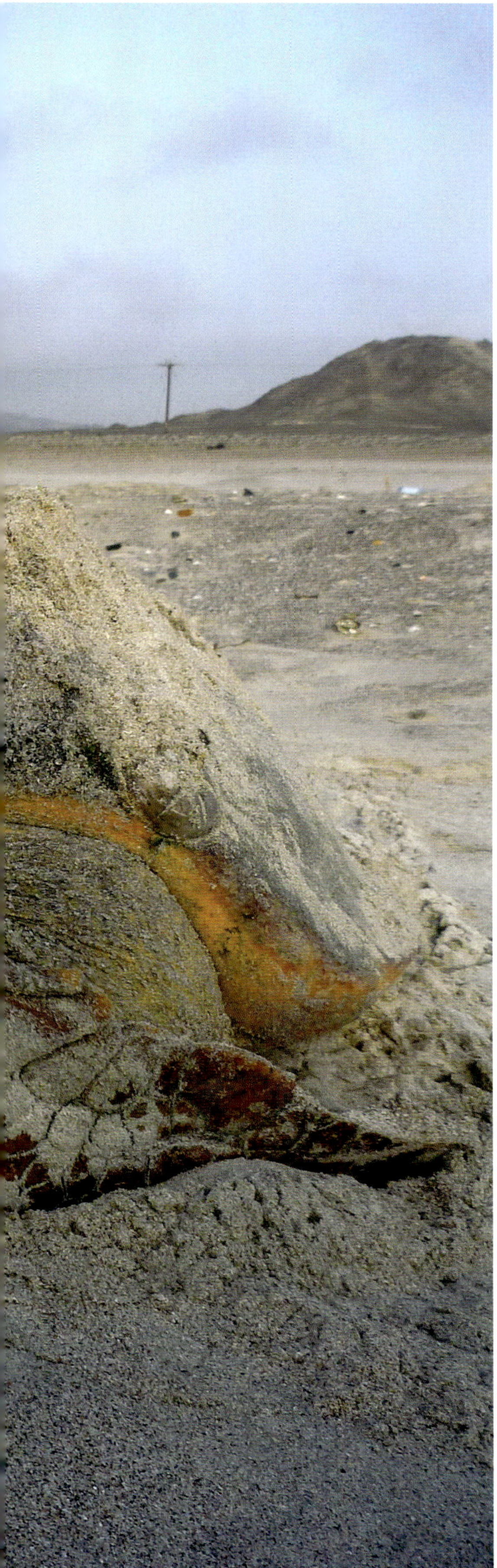

Turtles

Oman is well known for its globally important populations of sea turtles that each year arrive to nest on the sandy beaches of the mainland and offshore islands. In Dhofar four species of the marine reptile nest on about 150 beaches from Sharbthat to Dalkut, including about 50 beaches on the Al Hallaniyyat Islands.[101] In addition many turtles visit Dhofar to feed in the rich coastal waters, especially off the rocky shoreline between Hasik and Mirbat.[102]

Green turtles (*Chelonia mydas*), listed as endangered on the IUCN Red List of Threatened Species, are often encountered in coastal waters, where they regularly feed on the seaweeds that thrive in the cold monsoon waters.[102] They may breed several times in the year but nesting peaks in October. On each occasion they lay as many as 160 eggs; hatching occurs after about 60 days and the young turtles must then run the gauntlet of predatory foxes and gulls to reach the relative safety of the sea. If they survive, it will be another 20-50 years before they are mature and ready to nest on the beach where they themselves were born.

Loggerhead turtles (*Caretta caretta*) nest in the greatest numbers and in 1988 a survey found that of an estimated 4,175 nests in Dhofar 75% were on the islands of Al Hallaniyyah and Al Sawda.[101] The turtles belong to the North West Indian Ocean subpopulation that is considered to be critically endangered, facing a very high risk of extinction in the wild. The tracking of loggerhead turtles that were fitted with satellite transmitters while nesting on Masirah Island showed that they fed mainly in the food-rich waters off Dhofar, Yemen and Socotra.[103]

Hawksbill sea turtles (*Eretmochelys imbricata*) are critically endangered and found in the Sea of Oman but are very rarely seen in Dhofar. Olive Ridley turtles (*Lepidochelys olivacea*) are endangered and also very rare in Dhofar; though many years ago they were found nesting on Hino Island just east of Mirbat.[101]

(Left) A nesting loggerhead turtle. In Dhofar they nest in large numbers on the Al Hallaniyyat Islands and even larger numbers feed in the waters surrounding the islands.

Arthropods

Arthropods comprise the majority of animals in Dhofar but many are small and difficult to comprehend and are thus understudied and the least well known of its fauna. Insects are by far the largest group but others are also of interest and include arachnids (such as spiders and scorpions), myriapods (centipedes and millipedes), crustaceans (e.g. crabs and barnacles) and molluscs.

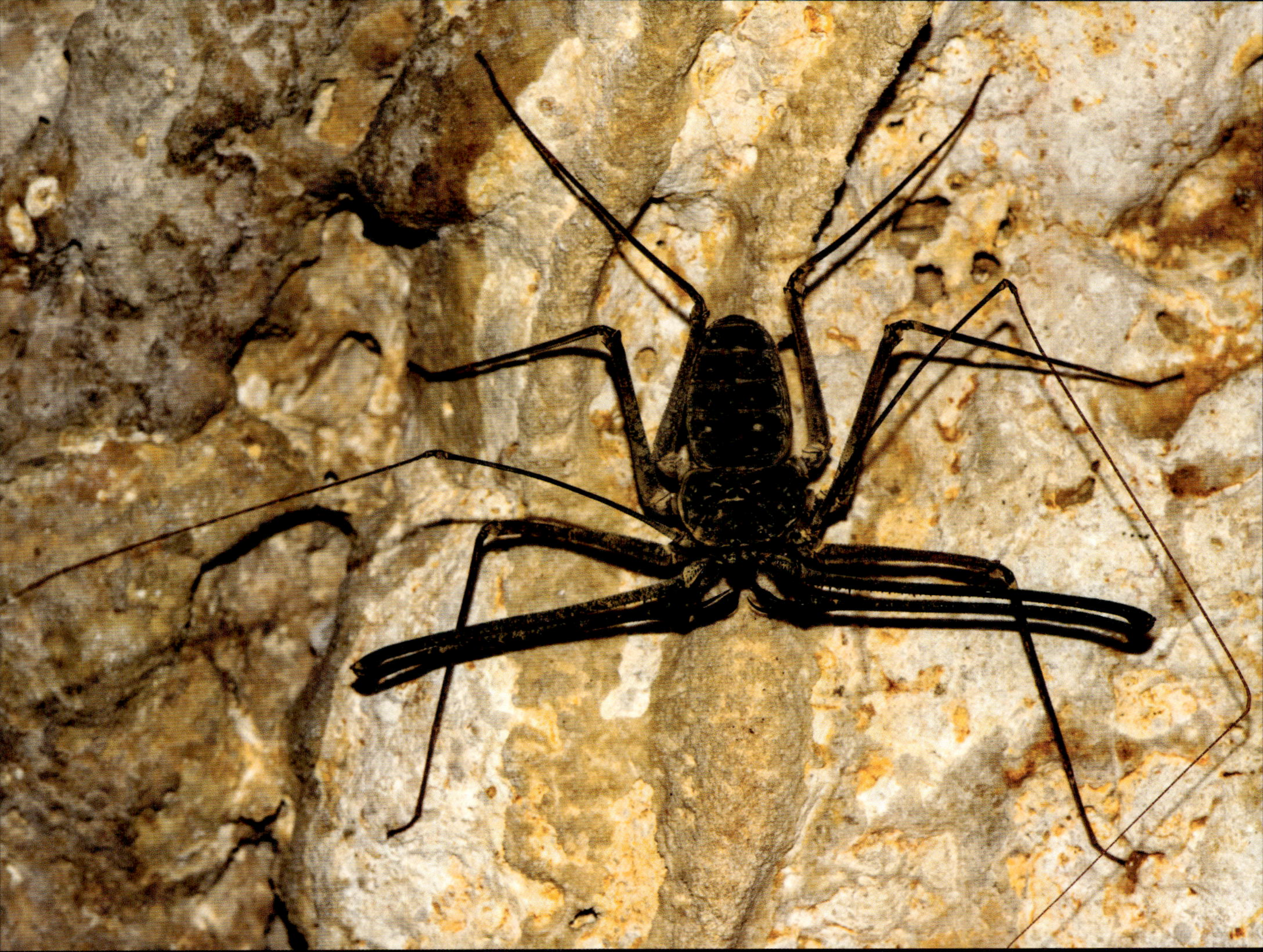

(Above) Arthropods are often misunderstood. The tailless whip scorpion, here in Suhur Cave in Wadi Nahiz, belongs to an ancient order. It is related to spiders and scorpions but it is really neither and is

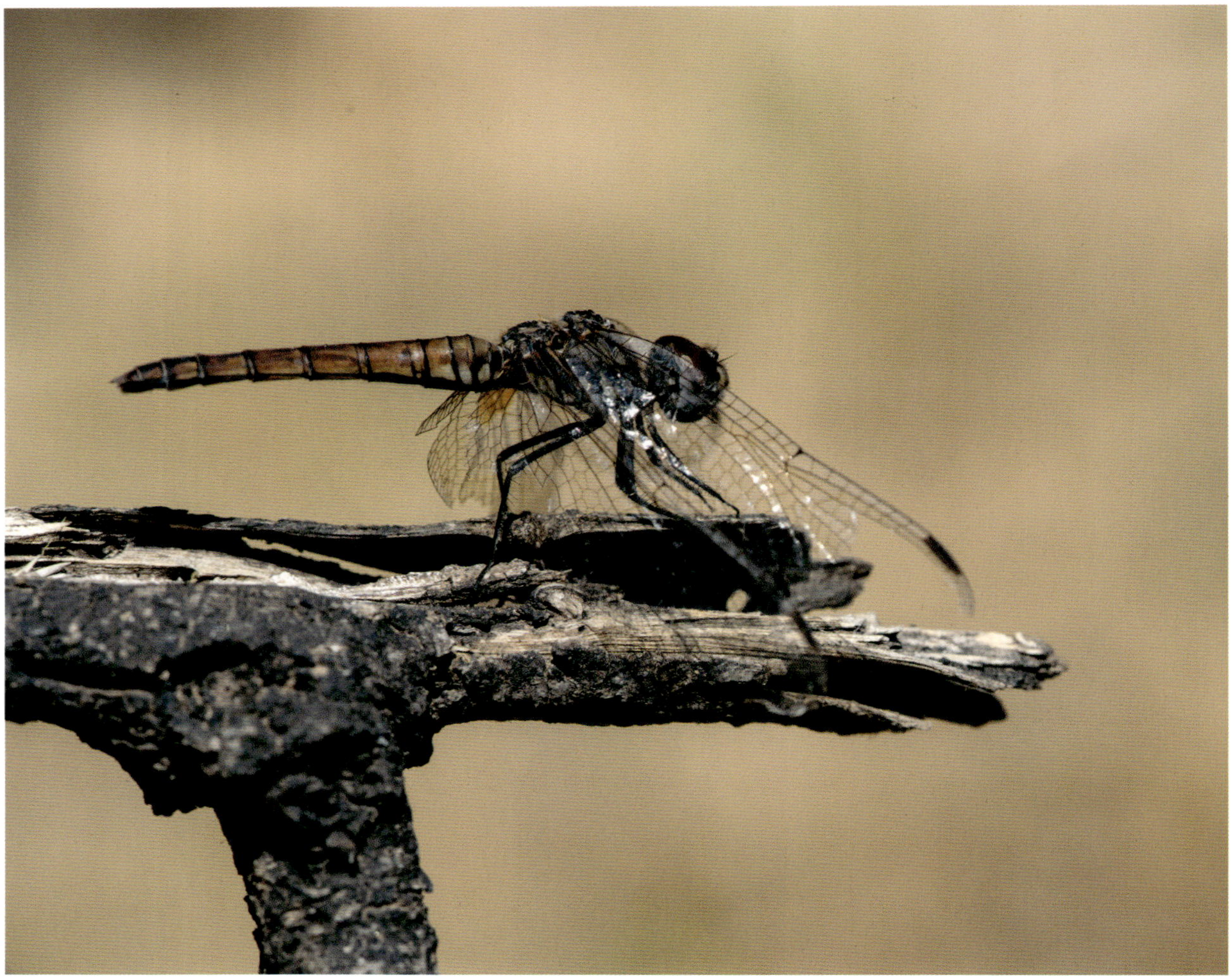

Insects

Globally insects are the largest and most diverse group of animals and include at least thirty different orders including butterflies, dragonflies, moths, beetles, bugs, grasshoppers, termites, antlions, ants, wasps, bees, flies and fleas.

Amongst the most striking of insects are the dragonflies that are found wherever there is water in Dhofar. With two sets of wings they are masters of flight and are able to hover and even move backwards. Forty four species have been identified in Oman[104] and of these 31 have been recorded in Dhofar.[105] Although they are found at springs in the Najd they are most abundant in the monsoon habitats of the Jabal and in the coastal lagoons. The best habitat is provided by the vegetated south flowing wadis that contain permanent water. For example in Wadi Sayq in Jabal Al Qamar, 21 species were recorded with the greatest number of species in the lower wadi, close to Khawr Kharfut.[106] Although some species are migratory, such as the vagrant emperor (*Anax ephippiger*), most are present throughout the year. Dragonflies may be beautiful but they are also brutally effective aerial predators feeding on small insects including mosquitoes.

While dragonflies need to be close to water to breed butterflies require the right food plants and thus are more widely distributed across Dhofar, from the lakes of Wadi Darbat to the true desert of the Empty Quarter. For example the caper white (*Belenois java*) prefers *Maerua crassifolia* trees that are commonly found on the dry mountain slopes and gravel plains of the Najd. The plain tiger butterfly (*Danaus chrysippus*) has a preference for Sodom's apple, a plant that grows on overgrazed rangelands, and thus should thrive under current conditions. Some species of butterfly, including the plain tiger, are poisonous to birds and this is advertised by warning colours. Other species are not poisonous but use mimicry to trick predators. For example the male diadem butterfly (*Hypolimnas misippus*) is quite different to the female but the female looks almost identical to the poisonous female plain tiger. Thus the female diadem is not preyed upon by birds (though it may of course fall prey

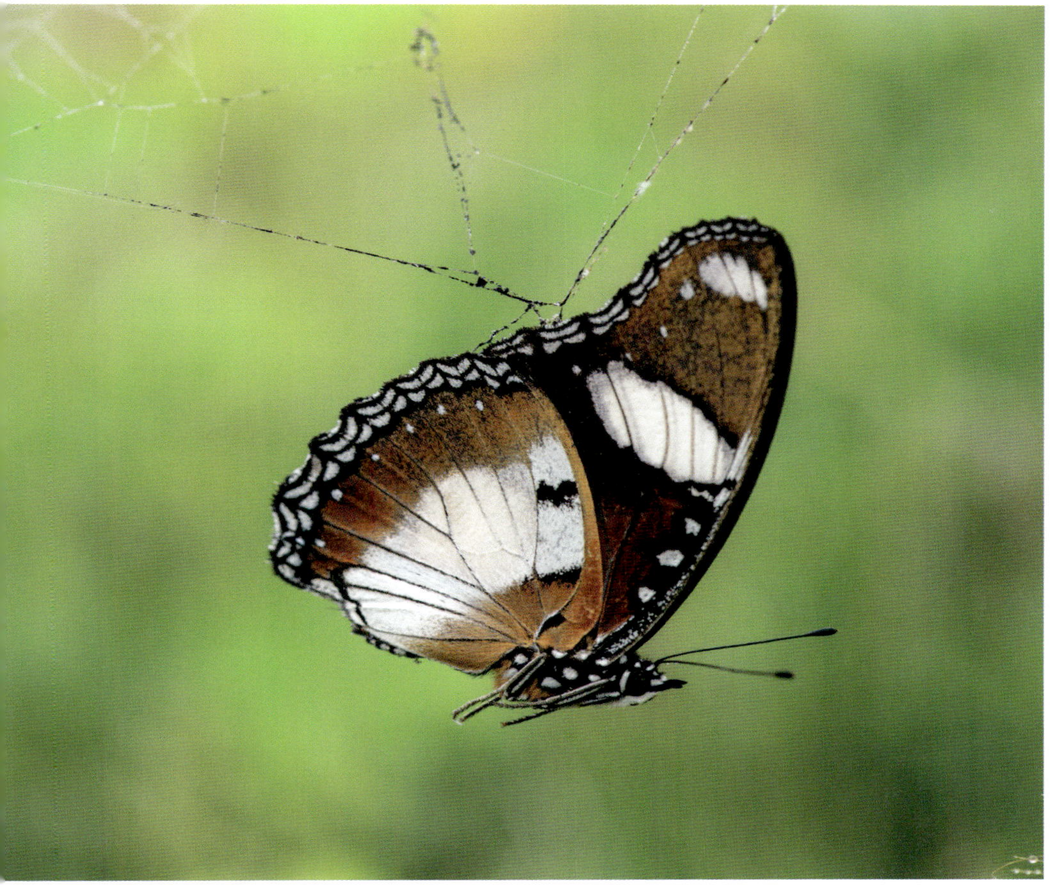

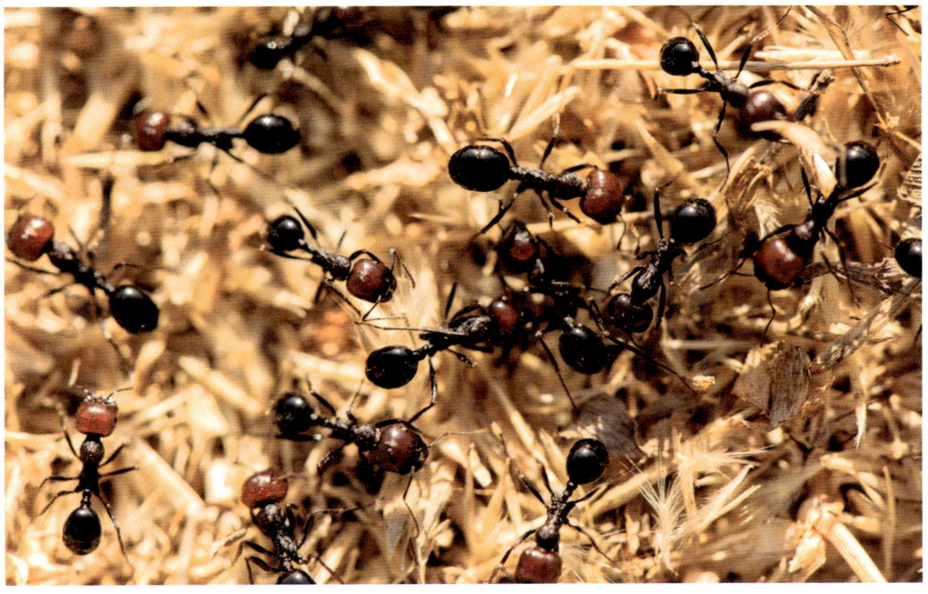

Dragonflies like the violet dropwing *(Trithemis annulata)* ***(above left)*** feed on other insects while the diadem butterfly feeds on plants ***(top)***; here a female diadem has been entrapped in the web of a spider. In the winter and spring harvester ants including *Messor ebeninus* ***(above)*** collect thousands of seeds that are stored in underground nests.

to spiders). There are considered to be 62 species of butterfly in Dhofar found in a range of habitats.[107] Less easily seen and mostly nocturnal are moths of which there are considered to be at least 100 species.[108]

Grasshoppers of Dhofar show a very high degree of endemism; that is many of the species are unique to Dhofar. Of 41 species recorded during the Fauna and Flora Survey of 1977 twelve were new species or sub-species.[109] Most notable was the discovery of a new genus and species *Dhofaria splendens* from near Wadi Uyun in the Najd. This large grasshopper, measuring 50-70 mm, has not been recorded outside Dhofar. Grasshoppers are herbivorous and are found in both the wet and dry zones of Dhofar.

Beetles are by far the largest insect group but are very understudied in most places including Dhofar. The Flora & Fauna Survey of 1977 looked at many insects but not beetles and since that time there have been just a handful of surveys. One such survey was conducted in 2011 when a team visited Jabal Samhan and Jabal Al Qamar where they recorded 16 species of longhorn beetle, including 10 reported for the first time in Oman.[110] Beetles that are known to occur across Dhofar include the scarab or dung beetle that are found in most areas but are most commonly seen on the monsoon rangelands of Jabal Al Qamar and Jabal Al Qara where large numbers of livestock provide ideal habitat. Dung beetles collect dung of livestock and roll it to create a ball that is then buried either for food or for making a brooding ball inside of which the beetles lay eggs. Once the eggs have hatched the larvae feeds on the dung before emerging as an adult.

Termite mounds are very characteristic of Dhofar, particularly along the northern edge of the Jarbib where there is a belt of termite mounds, many up to 3 metres high and 10 metres in diameter. These mounds are made by *Macrotermes subhyalinus*, one of the world's largest termite species and not found elsewhere in Oman. The number of mounds containing living termite nests can be expected to be higher in healthy and productive grasslands. Even in the early 1980s it was considered that only 50% of termite mounds were active and that this was an indication of the poor condition of the Jarbib grasslands.[111] Since that time the number of living termite mounds has fallen, suggesting continued degradation of the rangelands.

A widespread belief is that termites, though certainly not the termites that build the large mounds, are responsible for the loss of woody trees. While it may be true that termites are found on dying trees it is because trees stripped of bark by livestock, are vulnerable to termite attack. Termite nests are considered beneficial and by providing a moist refuge in a dry landscape they allow plants to flourish and keep desertification at bay.

Of the ants, bees and wasps of Dhofar only one family of wasps has been the subject of detailed study. The Flora & Fauna Survey of 1977 recorded 48 species of the so called hunting wasps - species that capture other insects to feed their larvae.[112] Ants can be found in most part of Dhofar and on the Jabal the most visible is the harvester ant (*Messor ebeninus*) which, like most species of ant, live in colonies centred around a queen. In late winter long columns of harvester ants can be seen collecting seeds for their underground stores. Of the bee species the honey bee (*Apis mellifera jemenitica*) and dwarf honey bee (*Apis florea*) are the most conspicuous. Undoubtedly new species of ants, bees and wasps are awaiting discovery.

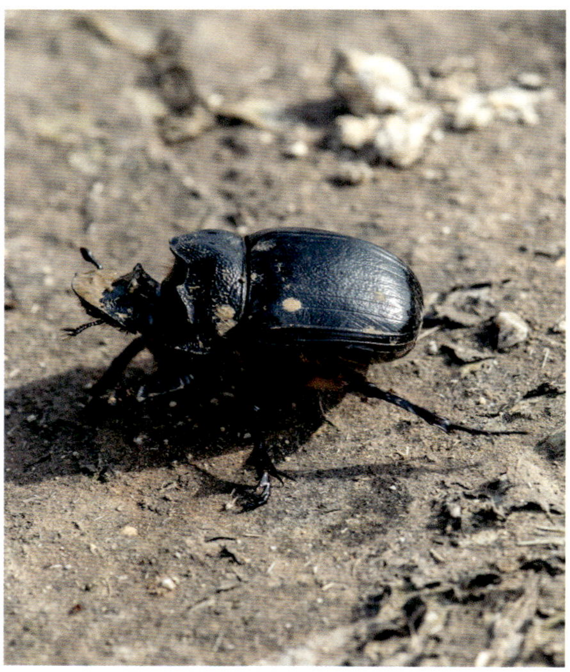

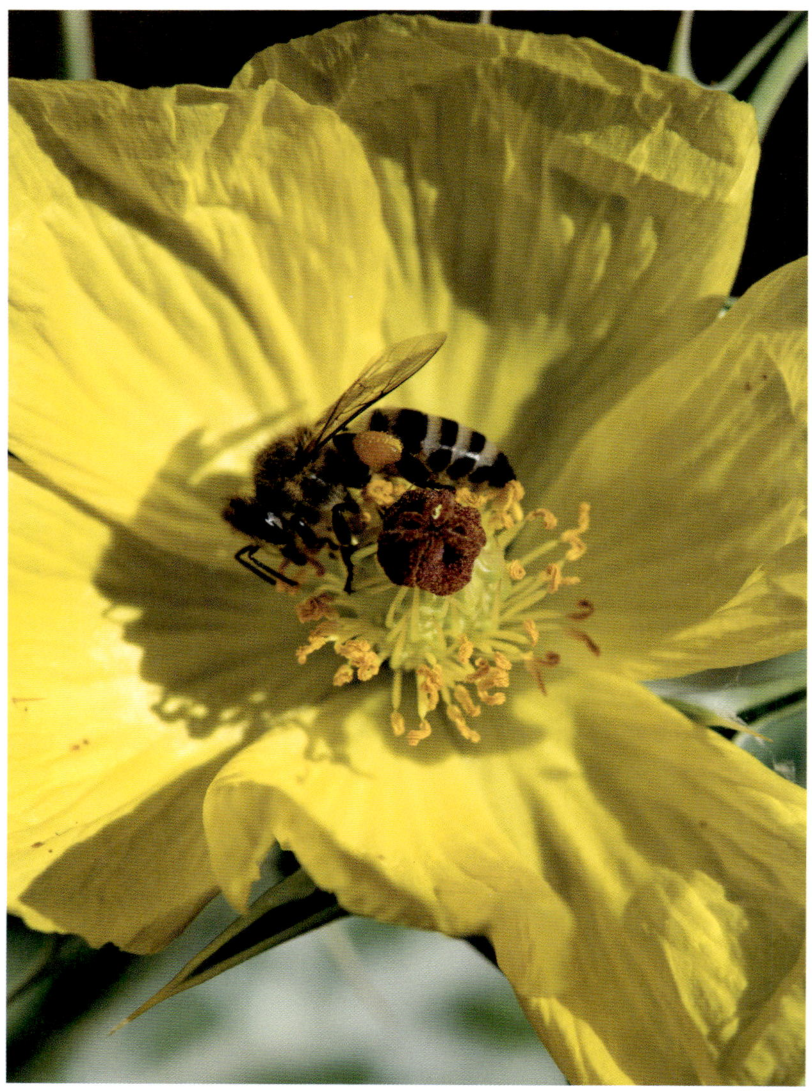

Dung or scarab beetles including species of *Heliocopris* ***(above)*** are particularly active late in the monsoon when camels have returned to the Jabal. Similarly bees, such as the honey bee ***(right)***, are busy as plants come into flower after the monsoon.

The red-legged golden orb-web spider *(Nephila sumptuosa)* ***(below)***, with a cache of prey, is only known from Oman, Yemen and the Horn of Africa while the scorpion *Hottentotta salei* ***(bottom)*** is endemic to Dhofar.

Arachnids

Spiders are not insects but with other groups including scorpions are Arachnids. The spider community of Dhofar seems to be understudied though spiders are frequently encountered, especially in the monsoon when bright water drops hang on the thin silk of their webs. The largest web spinning spiders in Dhofar are the red-legged golden orb-web spiders (*Nephila sumptuosa*) that live on a diet of small insects that have become entrapped in their webs. Once an insect is trapped in the web the spider uses its fangs to inject poisonous venom to kill it.

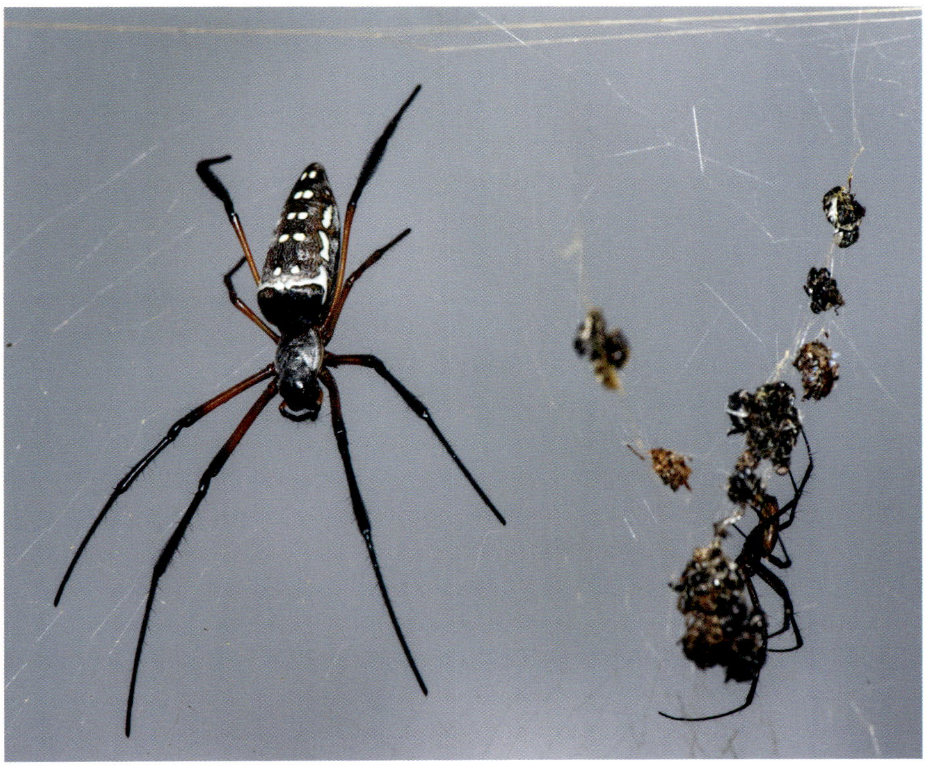

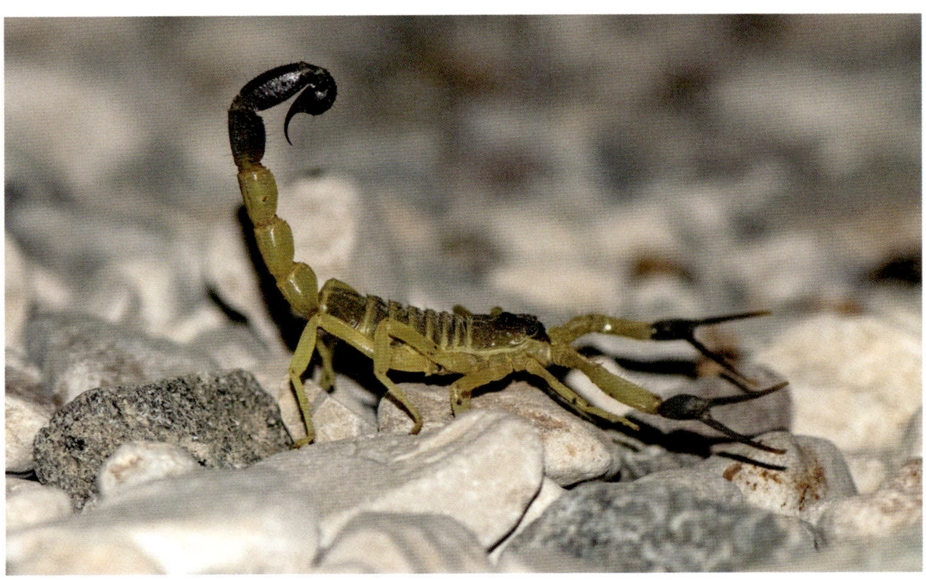

Tailless whip scorpions (*Phrynichus jayakari*) are not scorpions and differ from the other arachnids in that they use only six of their eight limbs to walk; the other two are modified into very long sensory organs. Often found in damp caves they are totally harmless and do not possess venom glands or a sting.

Scorpions are arachnids with eight legs and a large pair of pedipalps used for grasping prey. Most characteristic is the segmented tail that arches forward and ends with a venomous barb. They are not active hunters but wait, often in the entrance of their burrows, for passing prey such as other smaller insects. Though feared by man most scorpions are harmless and their sting will at worst result in local pain and swelling. There are at least twenty species in Dhofar and they are found from the Empty Quarter to the coastal lagoons. There are several endemics including *Hottentotta salei* which occurs on the south side of the Jabal and *Leiurus heberti* that only occurs in Jabal Samhan where it was discovered in 1995.[113]

The camel spider is related to both spiders and scorpions but is neither. They too have eight legs but also a long pair of pedipalps that they keep aloft in front of them. They are aggressive feeders that prey mainly on other invertebrates. Though they often elicit fear they are not venomous although their bite may be painful.

Three common crustaceans of Dhofar beaches are the Red Sea hermit crab *(Coenobita scaevola)* ***(below right)*** and ghost crab ***(below)*** that prefer sandy beaches and the Acorn barnacle found on rocky shores ***(right)***.

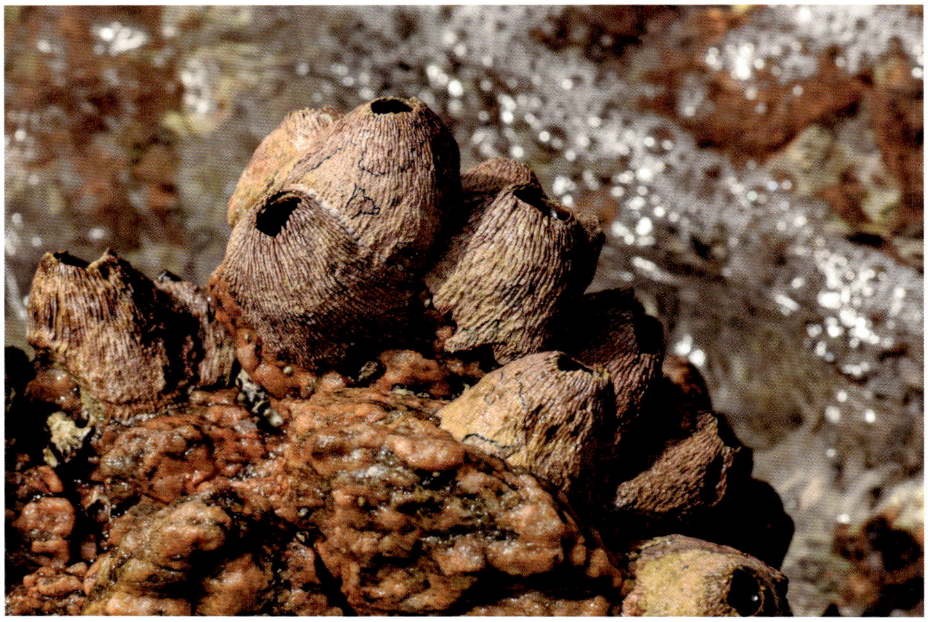

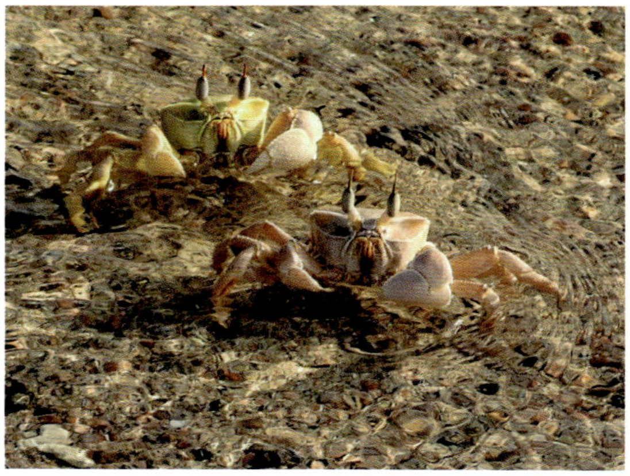

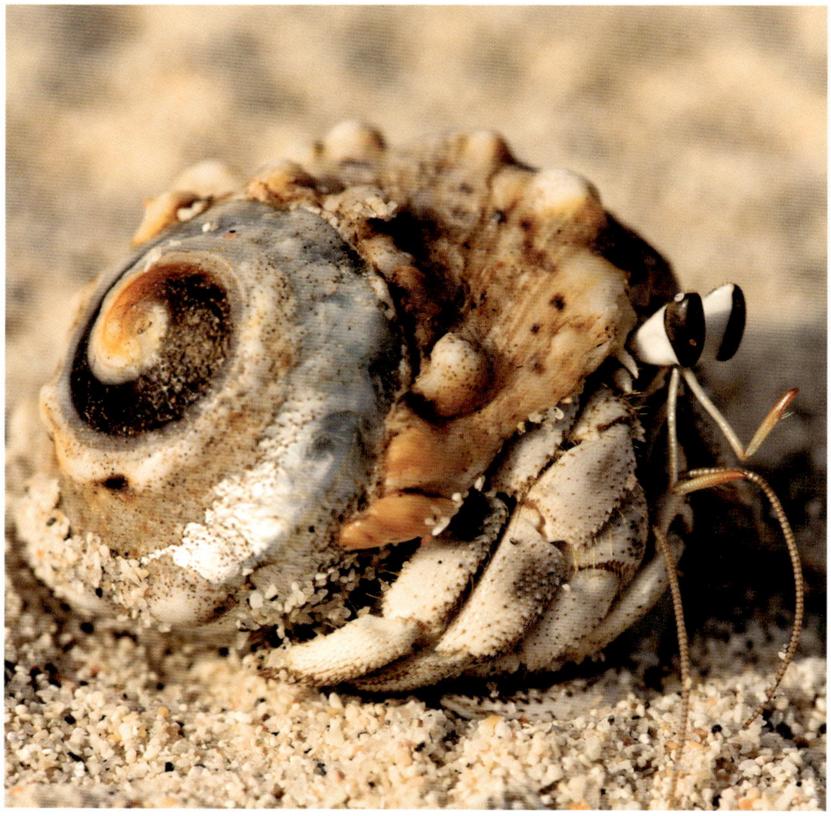

Crustaceans

This is a very diverse group and includes familiar animals such as crab, crayfish, shrimps and barnacles. In Dhofar a few crustaceans inhabit freshwater but most are coastal with diverse communities associated with both the coastal corals and *khawrs*. Perhaps the most frequently encountered are the ghost crabs (*Ocypode saratan*) whose burrows are a major feature of the landscape on beaches close to Salalah. On the beaches of the Al Hallaniyyat Islands, and elsewhere, are large numbers of hermit crabs that scuttle up and down with each breaking wave. Hermit crabs have a soft abdomen that they protect by carrying around a salvaged shell of a sea snail. As they grow they require new shells and these are in limited supply resulting in fierce competition for the best shells. Acorn barnacles *(Tetraclita squamosa rufotincta)* can be found on most rocky shores.

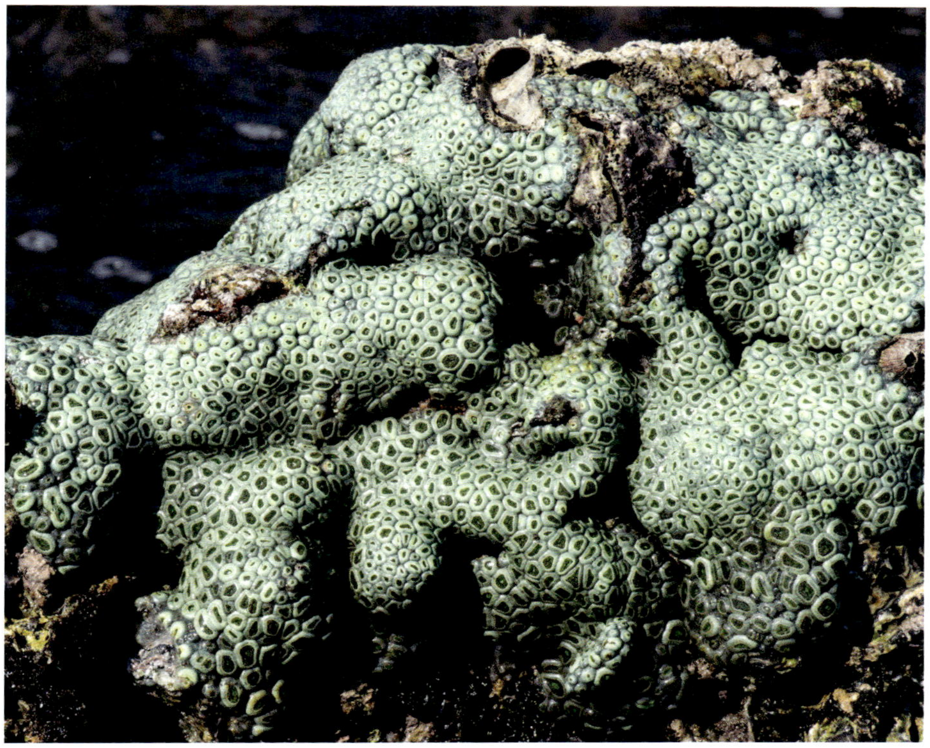

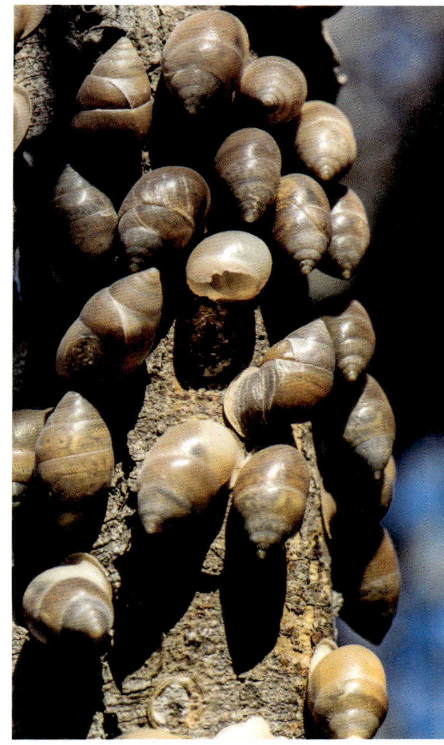

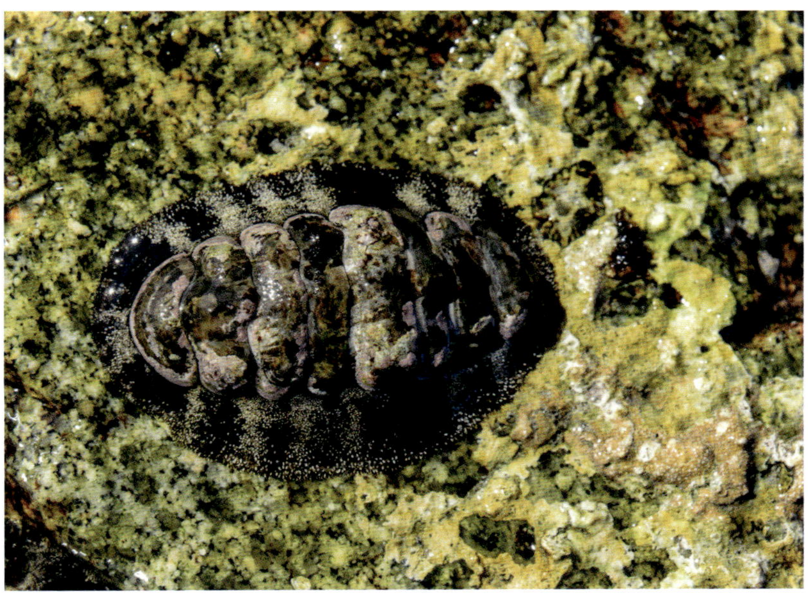

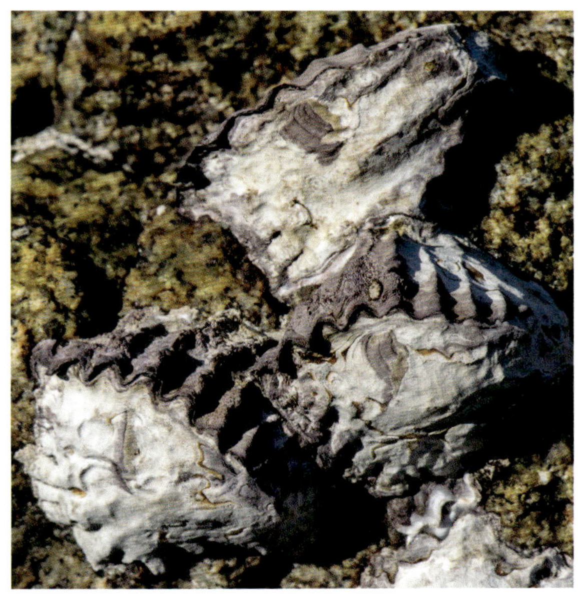

Molluscs

Molluscs include familiar animals such as snails, squid, oysters and chitons. In Dhofar the majority are in the sea where at least 122 species have been recorded but there are at least eight species in the freshwater pools of the Jabal and on the land 10 species of land snail and one slug.[114 & 115] The most easily seen are the sea shells of dead molluscs that litter the beaches while the chiton is common on coastal rocks, just below the low tide level. Land snails (*Euryptyxis latireflexa*) are often found in large numbers on the trunks of trees in the monsoon woodlands. Rock oysters (*Saccostrea cucullata*), locally known as *Zoka*, are one of several species gleaned by local communities.

Rock oysters ***(bottom right)***, Vaillant's chiton *(Acanthopleura vaillantii)* ***(bottom left)*** and the striking green zoanthid ***(top left)*** can be found on rocks in the intertidal zone. Land snails ***(top right)*** are common on the Jabal.

Fishes

Freshwater Fishes

The remote water pools of the Jabal have been isolated since the last wet phase more than 10,000 years ago allowing the evolution of unique animal species, including freshwater fish. In the eastern Jabal Al Qara and Jabal Samhan there are three species of garra, all with very restricted ranges; Tawi Aatayr garra (*Garra dunsirei*) is only found in the sinkhole at Tawi Aatayr, Wadi Hasik garra (*G. smarti*) is restricted to pools in Wadi Hadbaram, near Hasik, and *G. sindhi* is only known from a pool in the lower Wadi Andhur, on the north side of Jabal Samhan.[116] Further undiscovered species may well exist in other pools of Jabal Samhan and the Najd.

The most widespread species is the Arabian toothcarp (*Aphanius dispar*) which is known from the pools on the south side of Jabal Al Qara and eastern Jabal Samhan. However, within the last 10-20 years species of tilapia have been introduced to some of Dhofar's pools and have subsequently colonised others. Water bodies where tilapia are known to occur include Ayn Razat, Ayn Hamran and Wadi Darbat where the

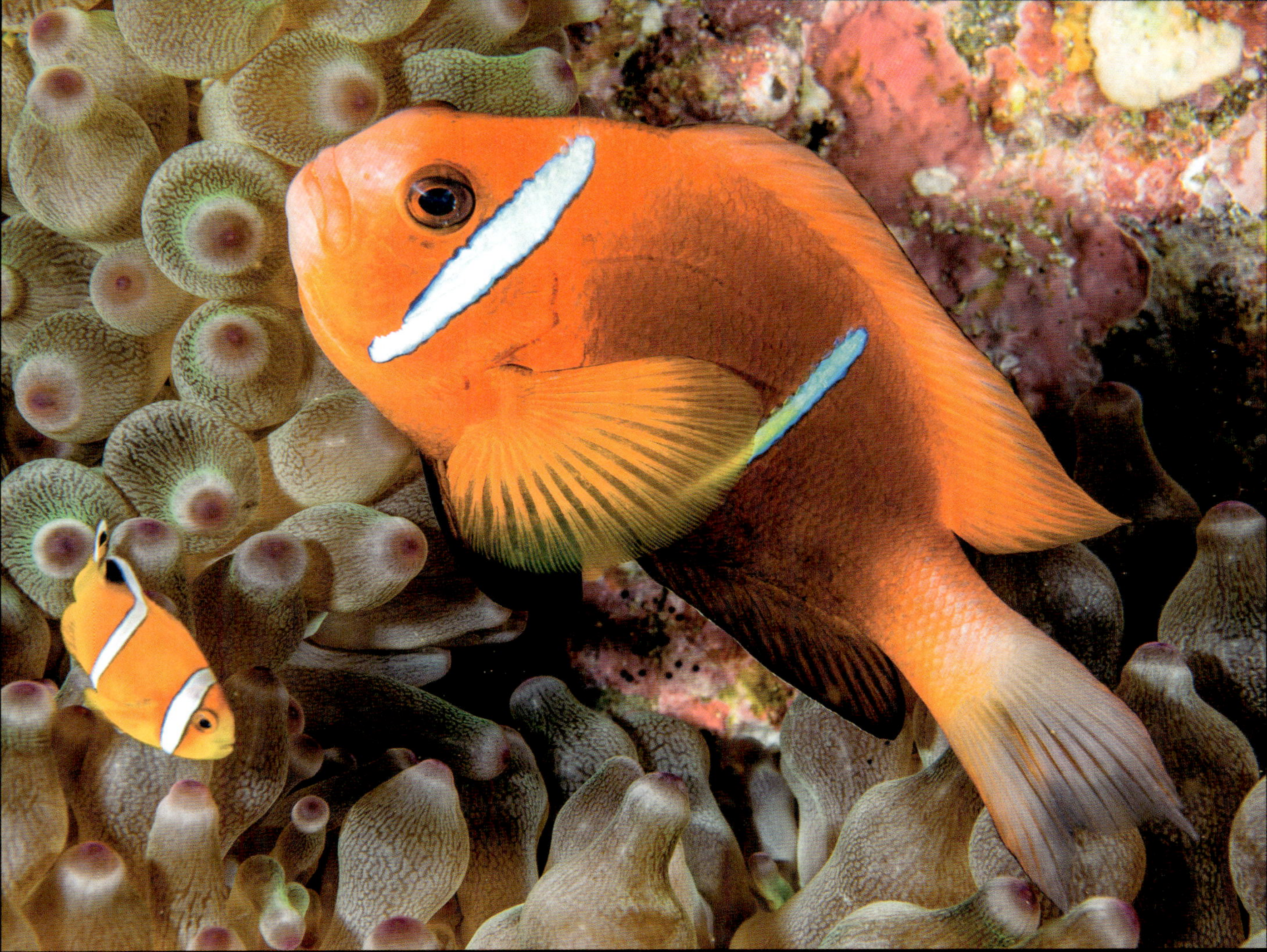

In Oman there are at least 10 species of freshwater fish (five in Dhofar) and 1,179 species of coastal fish; undoubtedly many remain to be discovered. The Oman anemonefish *(Amphiprion omanensis)* ***(above)*** is only known from the Arabian Sea coast of Oman.

Garra sindhi **(below)**, first described in 2016, is one of several freshwater fish species discovered in remote water pools of the Jabal.

tilapia will likely replace the native Arabian toothcarp.

Wadi Hadbaram drains the eastern slopes of Jabal Samhan and its shallow, but permanent pools, have produced interesting records; the pools are approximately 2.5 kilometres from the seashore. In 2002 *Garra smarti* was discovered and in 2015 a survey team found the freshwater goby (*Awaous aeneofuscus*) and Oman's first record of the Indian mottled eel (*Anguilla bengalensis bengalensis*); a freshwater species that breeds in the Indian Ocean. The team also recorded flathead mullet (*Mugil cephalus*) and tiger perch (*Terapon jarbua*); both marine species tolerant of brackish conditions.[117]

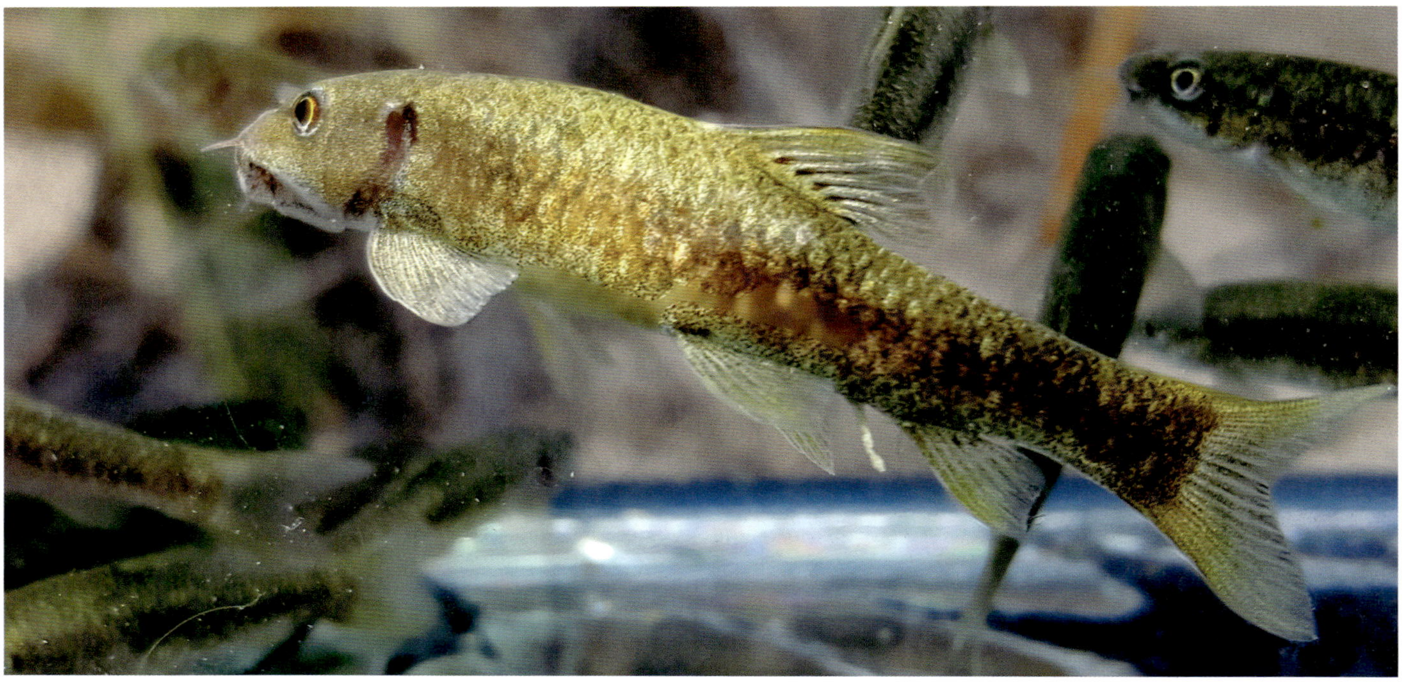

Coastal Fishes

Dhofar's subtropical location in the Arabian Sea and being not so far from either the Arabian Gulf and the Red Sea, combined with seasonal changes in the temperature and productivity of the seas is reflected in the great diversity of coastal fishes. In 1995 a comprehensive survey recorded 930 species of coastal fish for Oman's coastal waters[118] and 15 years later it was considered that there were 1,179 species.[119] Many, if not most, of these species will occur in Dhofar and no doubt the list will continue to grow as the deep and productive waters are better explored and understood. Coastal fishes can be divided into cartilaginous fish (sharks and rays) and bony fish, the latter making up about 98% of all fish on Earth.

Sharks and Rays

There are at least 37 species of shark in Dhofar's coastal waters. Some like the blacktip reef shark (*Carcharhinus melanopterus*) are coastal and range widely across the Indian and Pacific Oceans, others like the oceanic whitetip shark (*C. longimanus*) range across entire oceans while others like the smoothtooth blacktip shark (*C. leiodon*) only occur along the coast of Oman and in the Gulf.[120] Amongst numerous rays and guitar fish both the leopard torpedo electric ray (*Torpedo panthera*) and spotted eagle ray (*Aetobatus ocellatus*) are popular with recreational divers.

Bony fishes

The fish of Dhofar are unusual in that they are representative of several different biogeographic regions and also have high levels of endemism.[121] For example dragon moray eel (*Enchelycore pardalis*) are an Indo-Pacific species, the

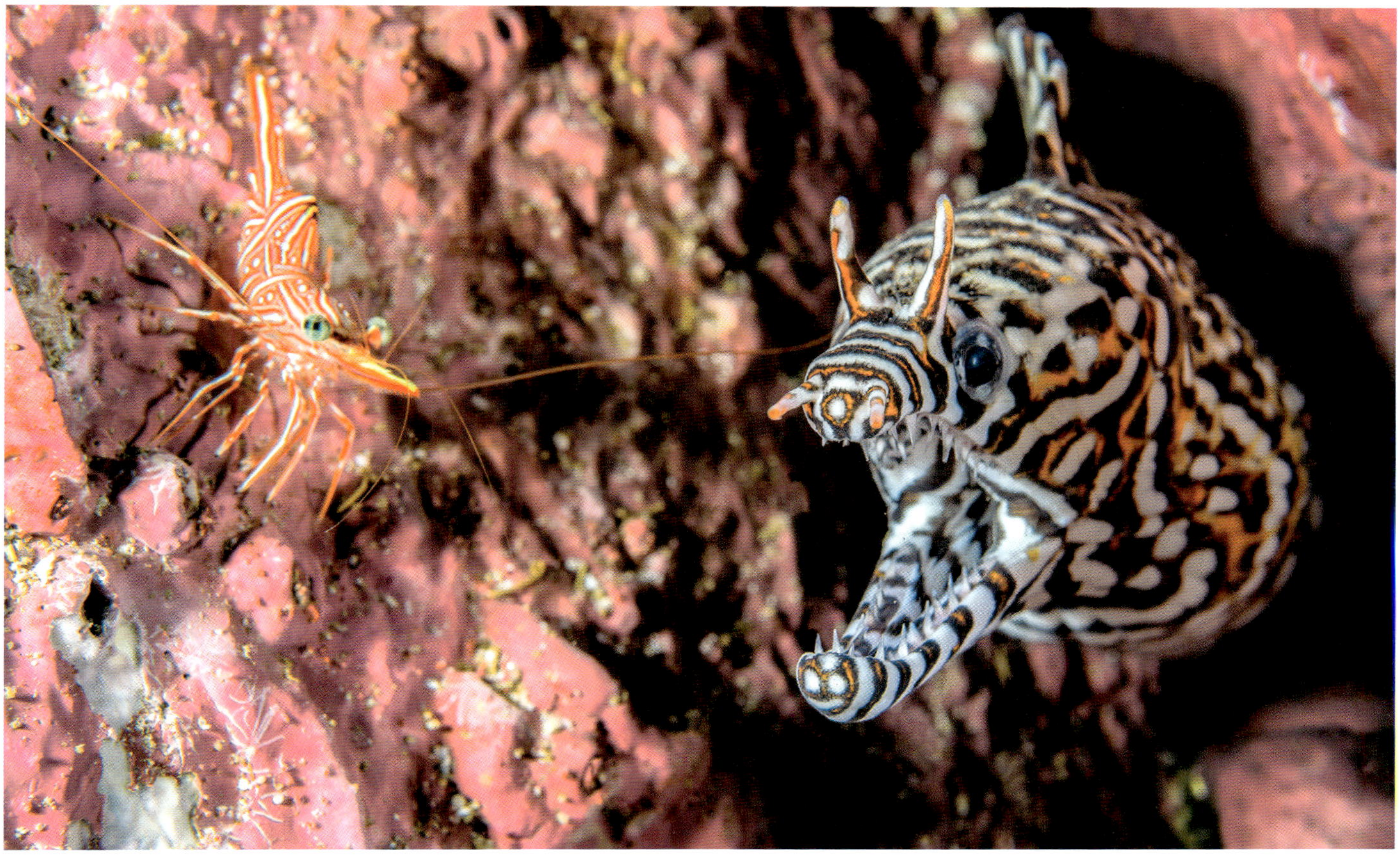

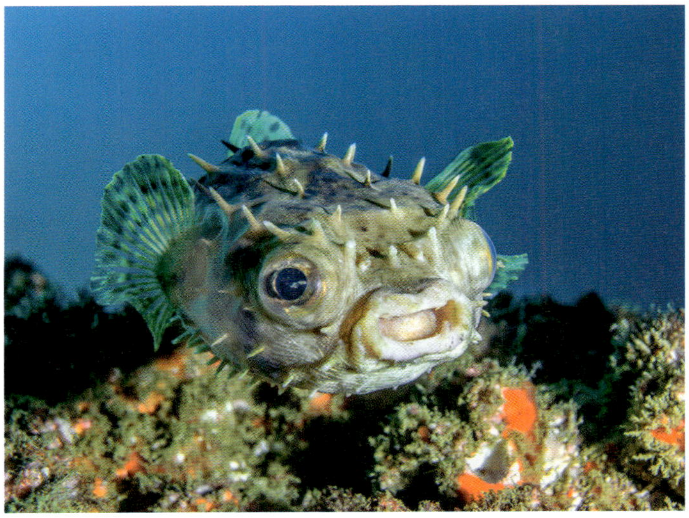

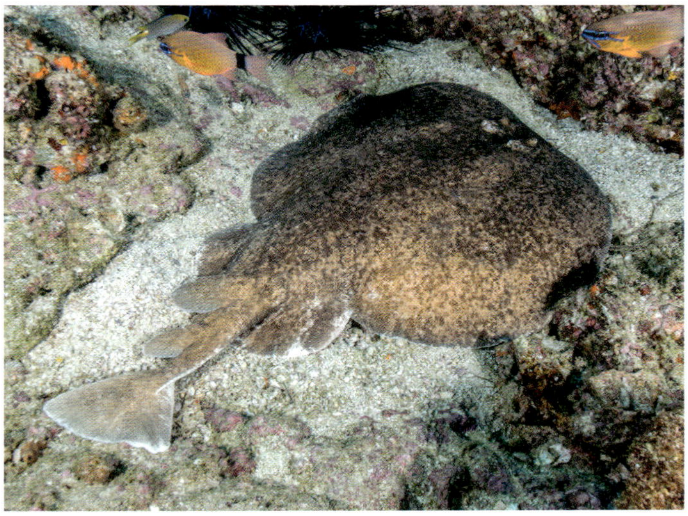

bridled jawfish (*Opistognathus nigromarginatus*) are found in the Red Sea south to South Africa but not the Pacific and orbicular burrfish (*Cyclichthys orbicularis*) are found from the Red Sea to the Gulf. Others like Dhofar cardinalfish (*Apogon dhofar*) only occur in the seas off Al Wusta and Dhofar while Dhofar parrotfish (*Scarus zufar*) are endemic to Dhofar. It seems that many of Dhofar's fish species were more widely distributed before 10,000 years ago, when the region was wetter and cooler. When warming occurred, and the *khareef* weakened, fish retreated to the cool waters of the upwelling off the coast of Dhofar contributing to the high levels of endemism that exist today.[118]

Coastal fish include cartilaginous fishes (sharks & rays) such as the torpedo electric ray ***(above right)*** and bony fish including the dragon moray eel *(Enchelycore pardalis)* ***(top)*** and Orbicular burrfish *(Cyclichthys orbicularis)* ***(above left)***.

Conservation

As a consequence of the summer monsoon that creates a rich variety of mammal habitats and the proximity of the region to three biogeographic regions (Afrotropical, Palaearctic & Indo-Malayan) Dhofar is one of the richest biodiversity hotspots in Arabia. Whether on the land or the sea there are many species of all groups that are regionally endemic (i.e. found only in Arabia) and many amphibians, reptiles, arthropods and fish that occur only in Dhofar and its coastal waters. Furthermore Dhofar is a last stronghold for many species whose populations have drastically declined or disappeared altogether from other countries of the region. The Arabian leopard is perhaps the best-known example.

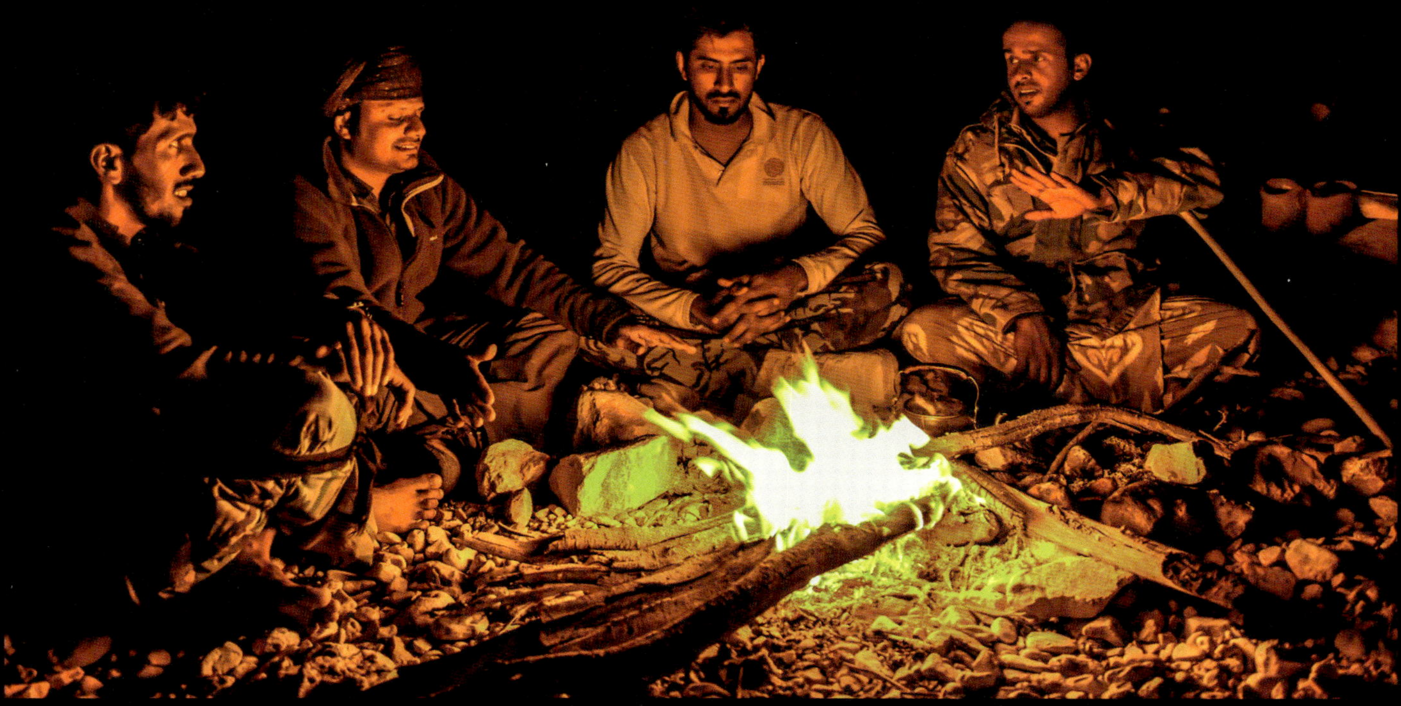

Field biologists and wildlife rangers, recruited from local communities, work at the front line of conservation. Their work involves carrying out surveys of wild animal populations, the use of satellites to track animals and engaging with local communities to resolve human-wildlife conflicts.

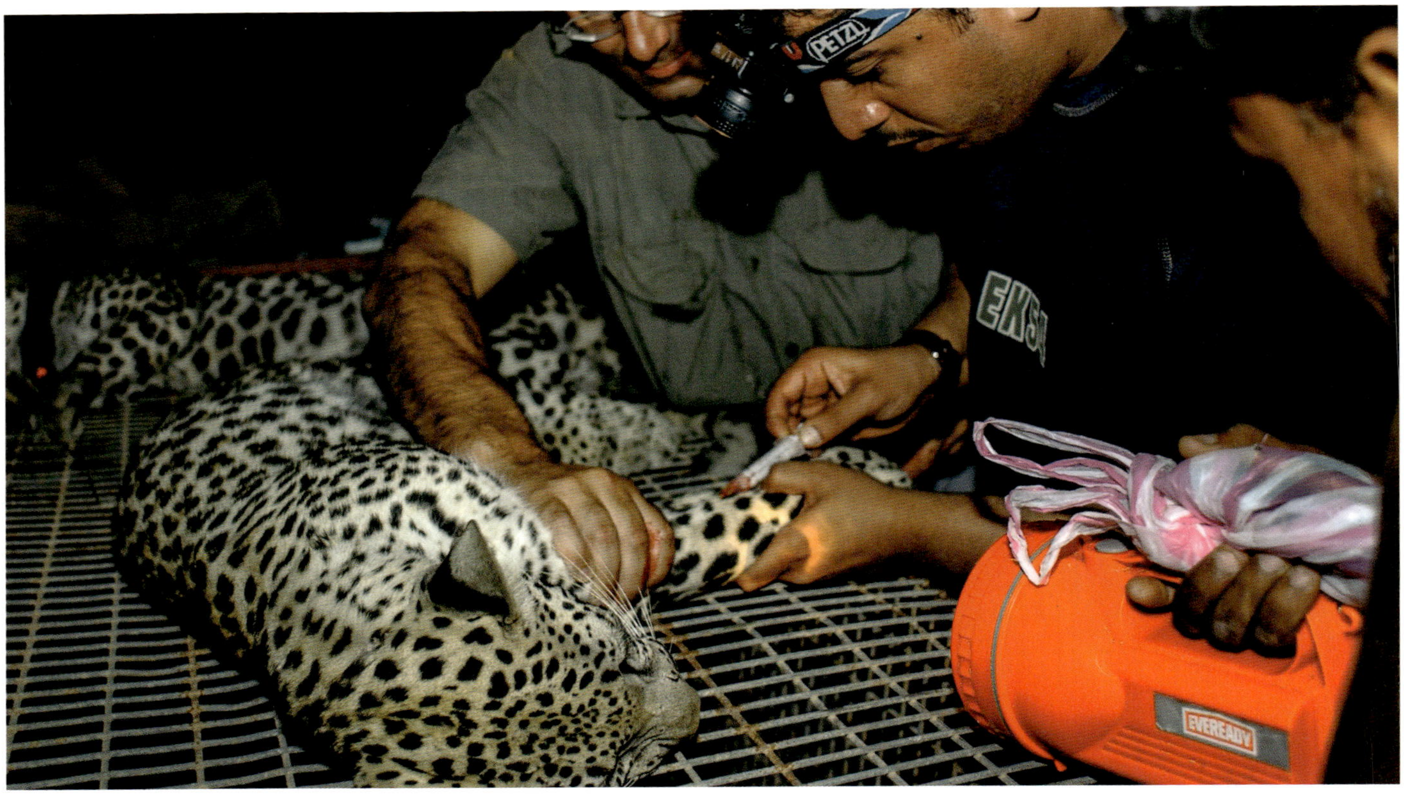

Extinction Threat

As a consequence of the regional, and indeed global, crisis of biodiversity loss some of Dhofar's wild fauna is threatened with extinction. According to the IUCN Red List of Threatened Species, some 65 species that occur in Dhofar, whether as residents or visitors face one of the three highest levels of extinction risk (Fig. 10).

Four species are critically endangered: the Arabian leopard, hawksbill turtle, loggerhead turtle and the sociable lapwing *Vanellus gregarius*. Sociable lapwing are a wading bird that breeds in central Asia and winters in a number of Middle Eastern countries including Oman. This species is threatened by loss of breeding habitat and by hunting along its migration route. Small numbers are reported most years on farms close to Salalah.

Of two whale species listed as endangered one is the blue whale, the world's largest animal. They were very heavily hunted in the 1960s when Soviet whaling fleets took over 1,200 animals from the Arabian Sea.[93] Today they can occasionally be seen off the coast of Dhofar. The Arabian Sea humpback whales have been listed as an endangered subpopulation on the IUCN Red List. Sperm whales are listed as vulnerable and Indian Ocean humpback dolphins are endangered. Like the humpback whales they prefer inshore waters and are thus vulnerable to disturbance from fisheries, tourism and shipping activities, all of which are increasing.

Both Egyptian vulture (*Neophron percnopterus*) and lappet-faced vulture (*Torgos tracheliotos*) visit Dhofar in the winter; both are endangered and are declining through many parts of their global range in the face of threats that include poisoning and loss of habitat. In Oman, populations are considered to be stable though birds occasionally die as a result of electrocution on overhead power lines. Rubbish dumps and carcasses of livestock, particularly on the Jabal, provide important food resources for these birds and for several eagle species, notably the endangered steppe eagle. In some other countries, carcasses are used to establish 'eagle and vulture restaurants' or feeding stations that not only benefit the birds but attract large number of visitors seeking to watch and photograph these spectacular birds. This has been done with great success for the red kite (*Milvus milvus*) in the United Kingdom and setting up something similar in Dhofar could help reverse declining bird numbers.

Arabian sand gazelle, listed as vulnerable, are close to extinction in the wild in Oman. However in 2020 captive bred animals were released into the partially fenced Al Wusta Wildlife Reserve. Arabian gazelle are more widespread but considered vulnerable while the Nubian ibex, also vulnerable, fares

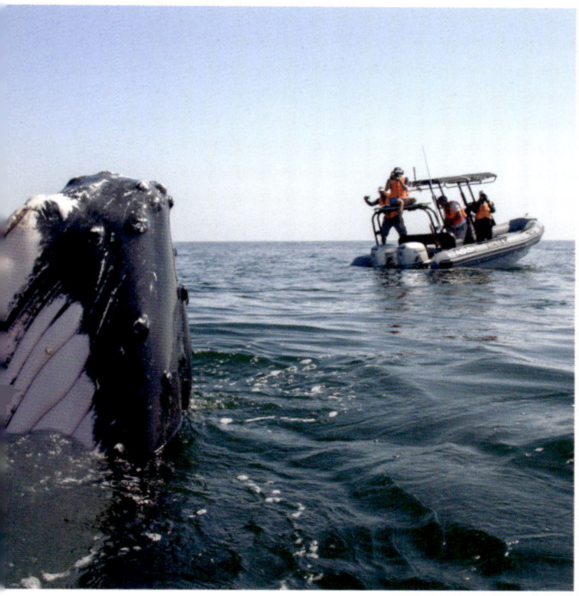

better, largely because hunters are unable to gain vehicular access to their mountainous habitat.

The Asian houbara bustard (*Chlamydotis macqueenii*), categorized as vulnerable, once bred or overwintered in large numbers in the gravel deserts of Dhofar and Al Wusta. However, relentless hunting has pushed the bird close to extinction in the wild and consequently few birds are seen in Dhofar. Ironically one of the birds used by falconers to hunt houbara, the saker falcon (*Falco cherrug*), is also threatened with extinction as a consequence of unsustainable capture of wild birds for the falconry trade.

A number of shark, ray and guitar fish species are threatened as a result of fisheries, particularly for fins, and as bycatch. Sharks include scalloped hammerhead (*Sphyrna lewini*), great hammerhead (*Sphyrna mokarran*) and smoothtooth blacktip shark (*Carcharhinus leiodon*). Corals are particularly endangered with 15 species considered to be vulnerable. In general terms, the major threat to corals is global climate change, in particular, temperature extremes leading to bleaching and increased susceptibility to disease, increased severity of El Niño events and storms, and ocean acidification.[121]

Several animals found in Dhofar are traded for food, traditional medicine, the international pet trade and in the case of the Asian houbara bustard and saker falcon, for falconry. Many are given further protection by the Convention on International Trade in Endangered Species of Wild Fauna and Flora (CITES) that aims to ensure that international trade in specimens does not threaten their survival.

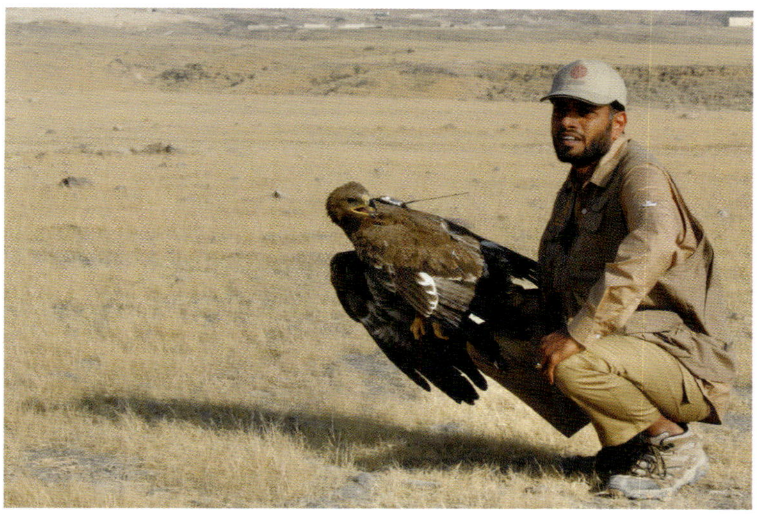

		EXTINCTION RISK			
		Vulnerable	Endangered	Critically Endangered	TOTAL
Mammals	Terrestrial	3		1	4
	Marine	1	3		4
Birds		6	5	1	12
Reptiles	Terrestrial	3			3
	Marine		2	2	4
Fish	Bony fish	10			10
	Sharks & Rays	8	2		10
	Freshwater fish	1			1
Arthropods	Insects	1			1
Corals		15			15
Echinoderm		1			1
TOTAL		**49**	**12**	**4**	**65**

Fig. 10 Dhofar's Threatened Species according to the IUCN Red List.[121]

Research in support of conservation has focused on flagship endangered species including the Arabian leopard ***(opposite)***, Arabian Sea humpback whale ***(centre)*** and steppe eagle ***(above left)***.

Feral and Invasive Species

Dhofar's native fauna is threatened by both feral species and invasive species.

Feral dogs are increasingly encountered on the plains around Salalah and even in the foothills and wadis of Jabal Al Qara. They may spread diseases including rabies that has been recorded in populations of red fox and Arabian wolf and also mange which has been confirmed in Arabian wolves in Dhofar. Furthermore the presence on the Jabal of small pale animals, almost certainly wolf-dog hybrids, poses a serious threat to the survival of the wild wolf population.[122]

Similarly the number of feral cats is increasing and a particular concern is that they are able to mate with the wildcat and produce fertile offspring. Camera-traps have recorded a wide range of coat colours and marking suggesting that domestic-wild hybrids are already widespread. Feral cats are also indiscriminate killers of native wildlife.

Also of concern is the growing population of feral donkeys. Donkeys are still in use by frankincense harvesters in Jabal Samhan and the Najd but over the last 40 or so years many animals have been lost or abandoned. These hardy animals have thrived with the result that there are large numbers of donkeys roaming many areas of the Jabal and the southern Najd. Not only do they contribute to the overgrazing of the rangelands but they contaminate small desert springs and threaten to exhaust the finite water supply.

Three species of non-native bird have become established on the Jarbib in recent years, all most certainly arriving from India. Common myna (*Acridotheres tristis*) are a global pest that aggressively displace local birds and are also a threat to agricultural crops. Rose ringed parakeet (*Psittacula krameri*) are popular in the pet trade but are also very aggressive colonizers of new habitats. They are known to displace other birds and outcompete them for limited food resources. The third and relative newcomer, arriving in about 2010, is the house crow (*Corvus splendens*), considered a pest species and present major problems to native bird species. They are now well established around Salalah and there are numerous anecdotal reports that populations of small native bird species have declined.

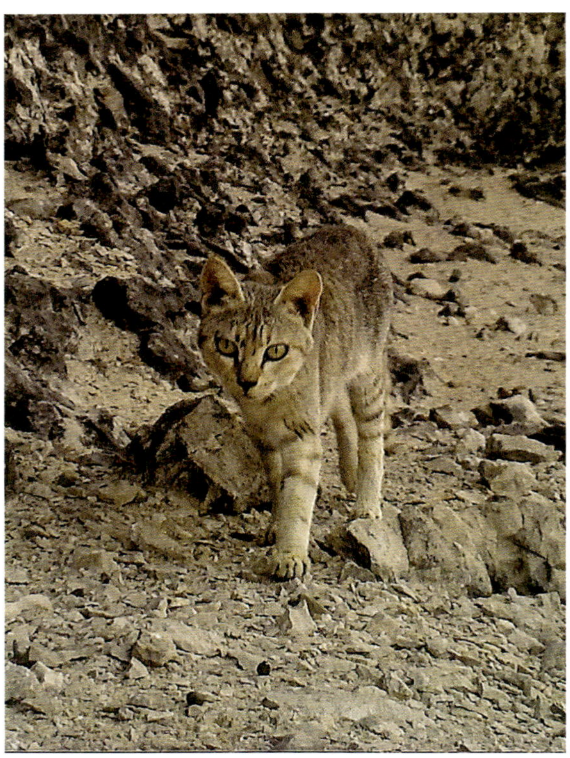

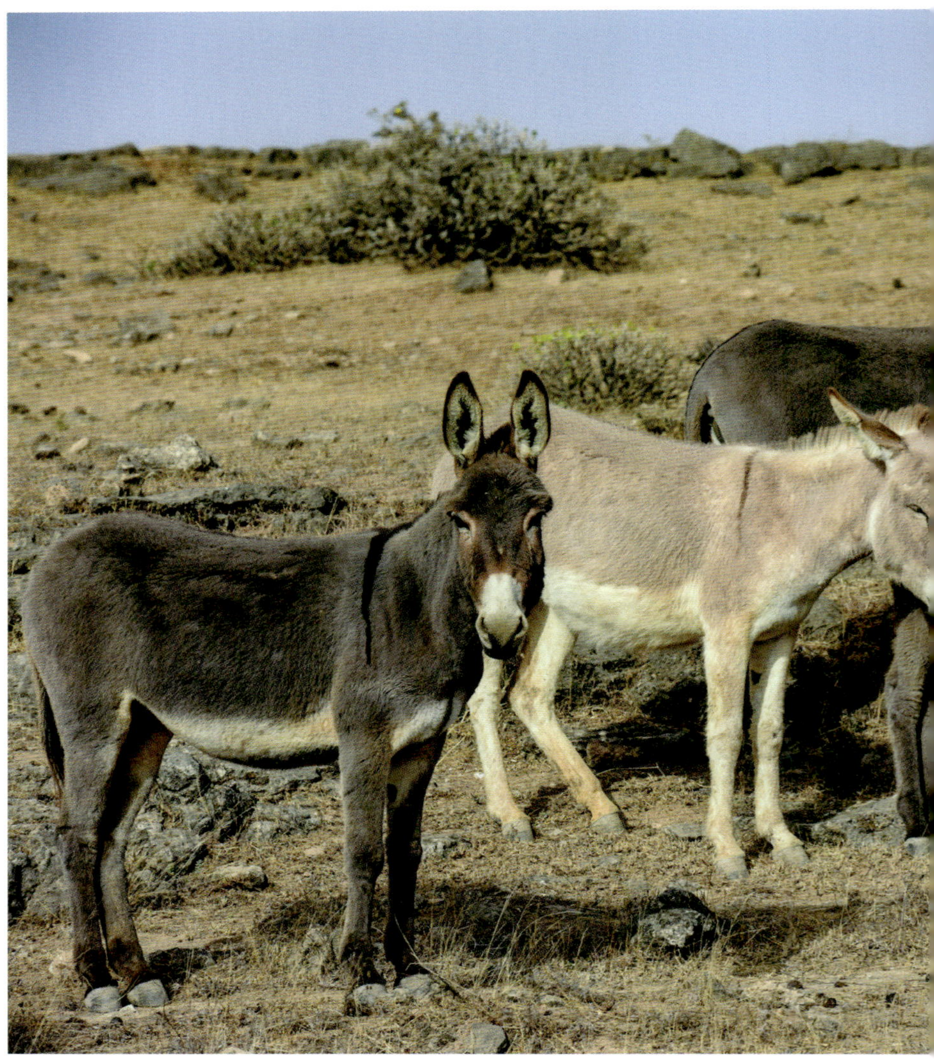

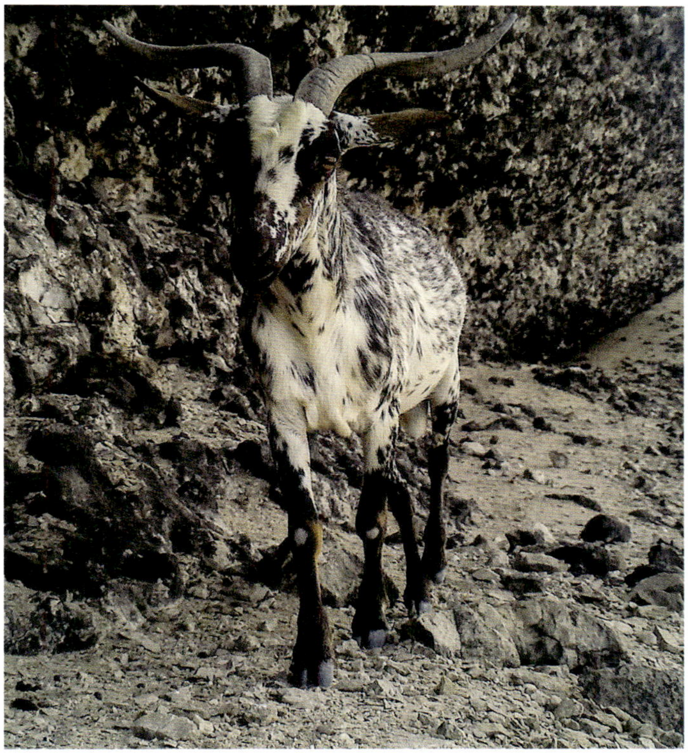

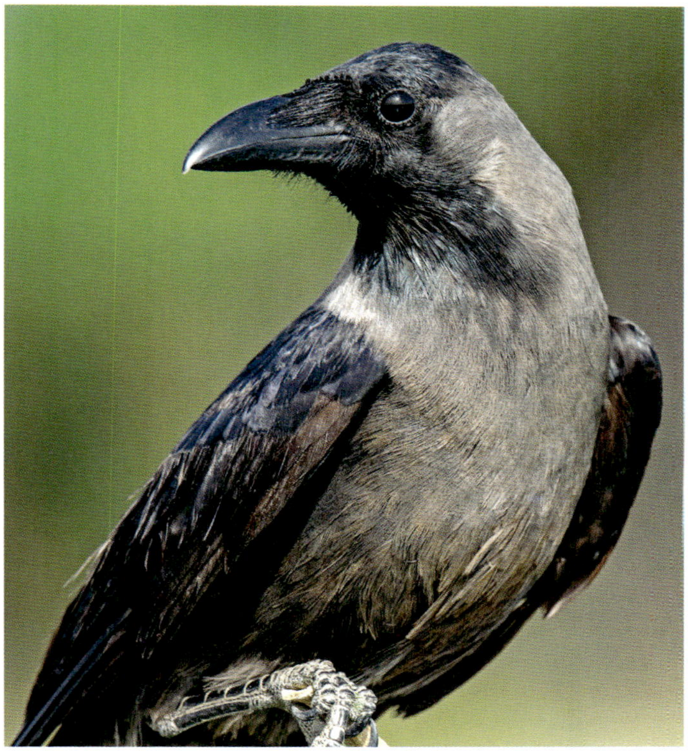

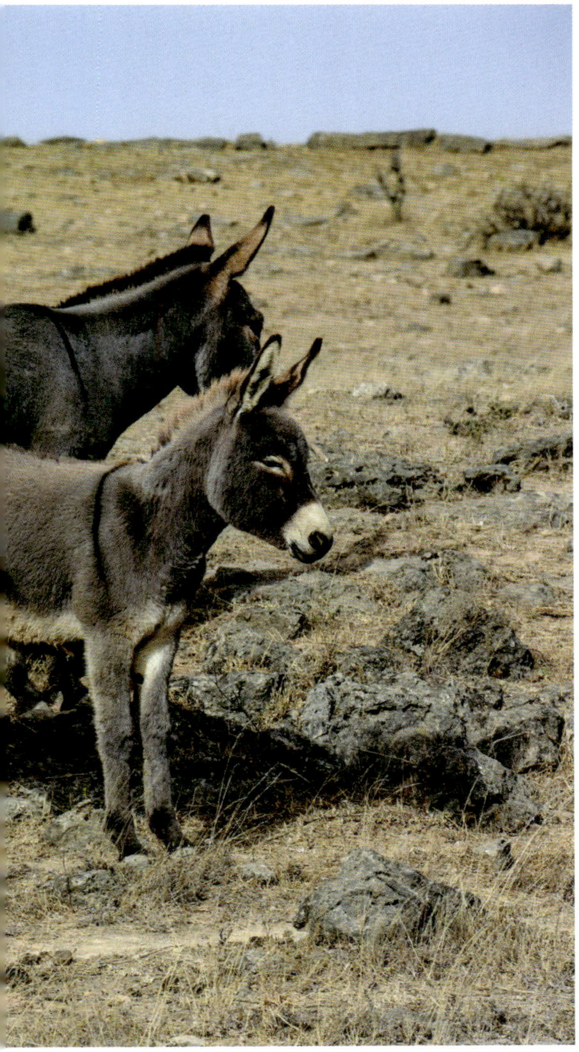

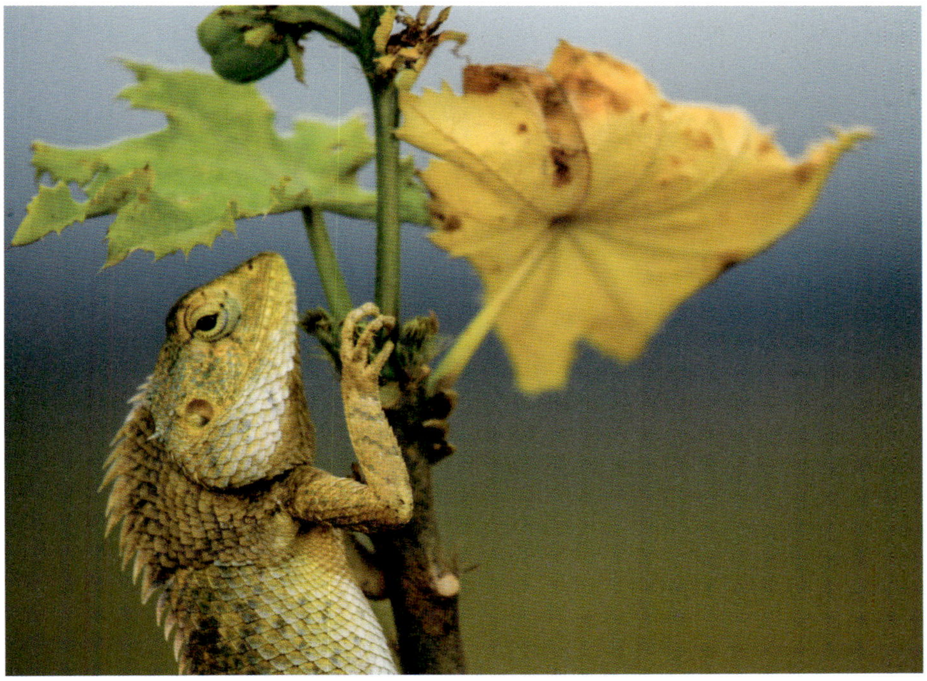

A less familiar invasive species are the bloodsucker agama lizards (*Calotes versicolor versicolor*) that were introduced to Salalah in the early 1980s and are spreading into the foothills of Jabal Al Qara. They are often mistaken for the chameleon.

On the island of Hallaniyyah is Dhofar's only feral goat population ***(upper left)***, which may date back to the early 1800s. Elsewhere populations of feral cats ***(far left)*** and donkeys ***(left)*** together with introduced species including the house crow ***(top right)*** and the bloodsucker agama lizard ***(above)*** threaten the native flora and fauna of Dhofar.

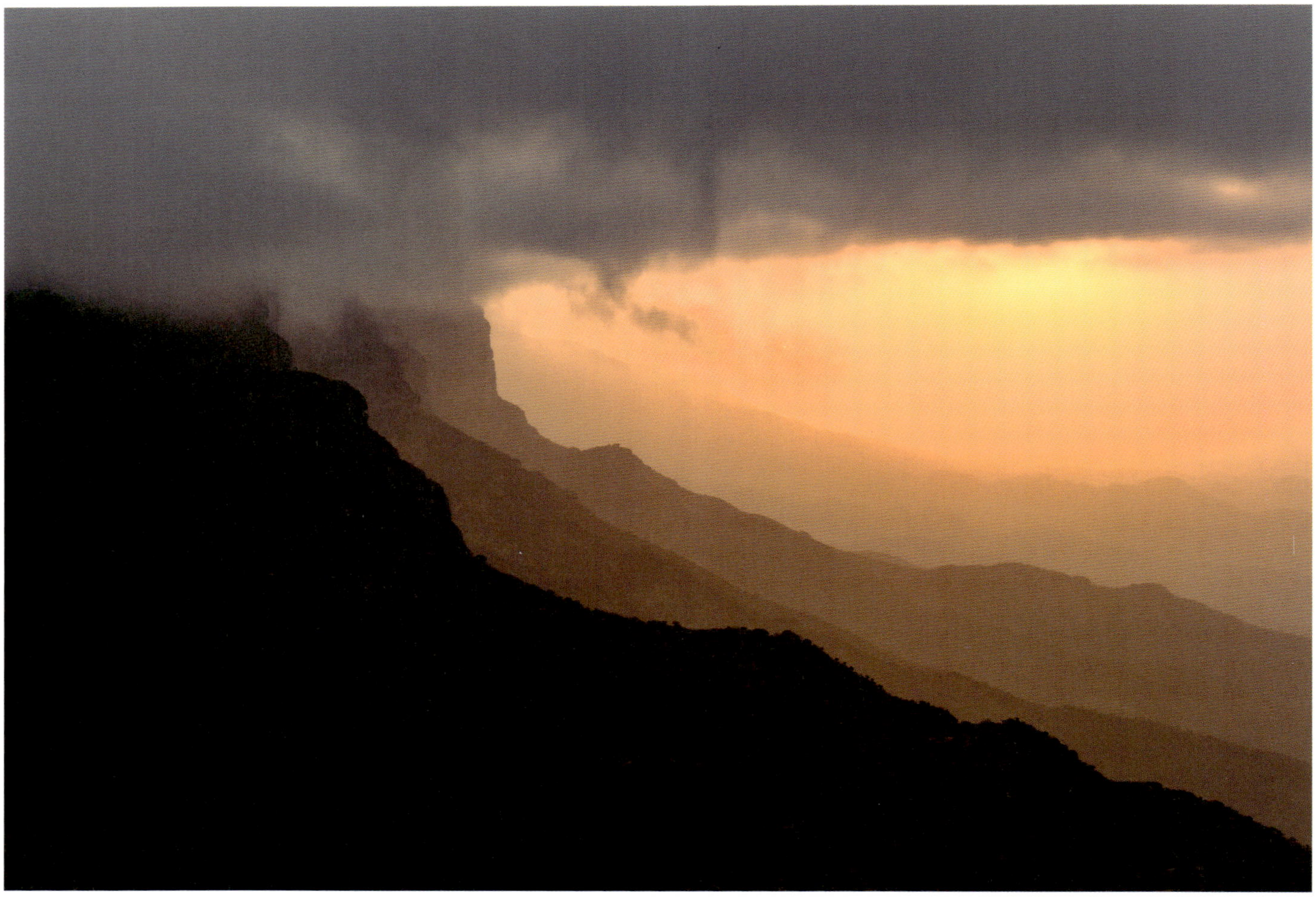

Protected Areas

A number of nature reserves have been established as protected areas for Dhofar's fauna and flora. The best known is Jabal Samhan, established in 1997, and protecting some 4500 square kilometres of dry upland habitat and coastal cliffs between Tawi Aatayr in the west and Hasik in the east. The reserve includes Dhofar's (if not the world's) most important population of Arabian leopard as well as the endangered Nubian ibex and populations of most of Dhofar's arid land mammals. Verreaux's eagle, the desert owl and Bruce's green-pigeon (*Treron waalia*) are among a number of important bird species while reptiles include endemic geckoes and eight species of snake. Permanent water pools are home to freshwater fish such as the vulnerable Wadi Hasik garra.

Ten of Dhofar's coastal *khawrs* are protected areas, nine established in 1997 and Khawr Salalah established in the early 1980s. While of little significance for mammals these are hotspots for birds, reptiles and to some extent arthropods and of course for fish. Khawr Rawri is just over eight square kilometres, the largest of the protected *khawrs*, and on the basis of bird counts was considered the most important for conservation followed by Khawr Ad Dahariz and Khawr Salalah. Species present in Khawr Rawri may typically include several hundred ducks such as ferruginous duck (*Aythya nyroca*) and Eurasian teal (*Anas crecca*) and less common species such as the Arabian warbler (*Sylvia leucomelaena*) in edge vegetation. Waders gather in the shallows.

The *khawrs* are often close to human settlements and several are in Salalah City where they provide important islands of natural habitat on a coastal plain that has been cut up into fragments by roads and development. Most are fenced to prevent over-browsing by camels and some, particularly Khawr Salalah, have hides for bird watching. With the growth of the bird watching industry there are opportunities to further develop visitor facilities hand in hand with local communities who ultimately are the custodians of Dhofar's wild places.

Dhofar's nature reserves help to protect a broad range of species that are representative of the

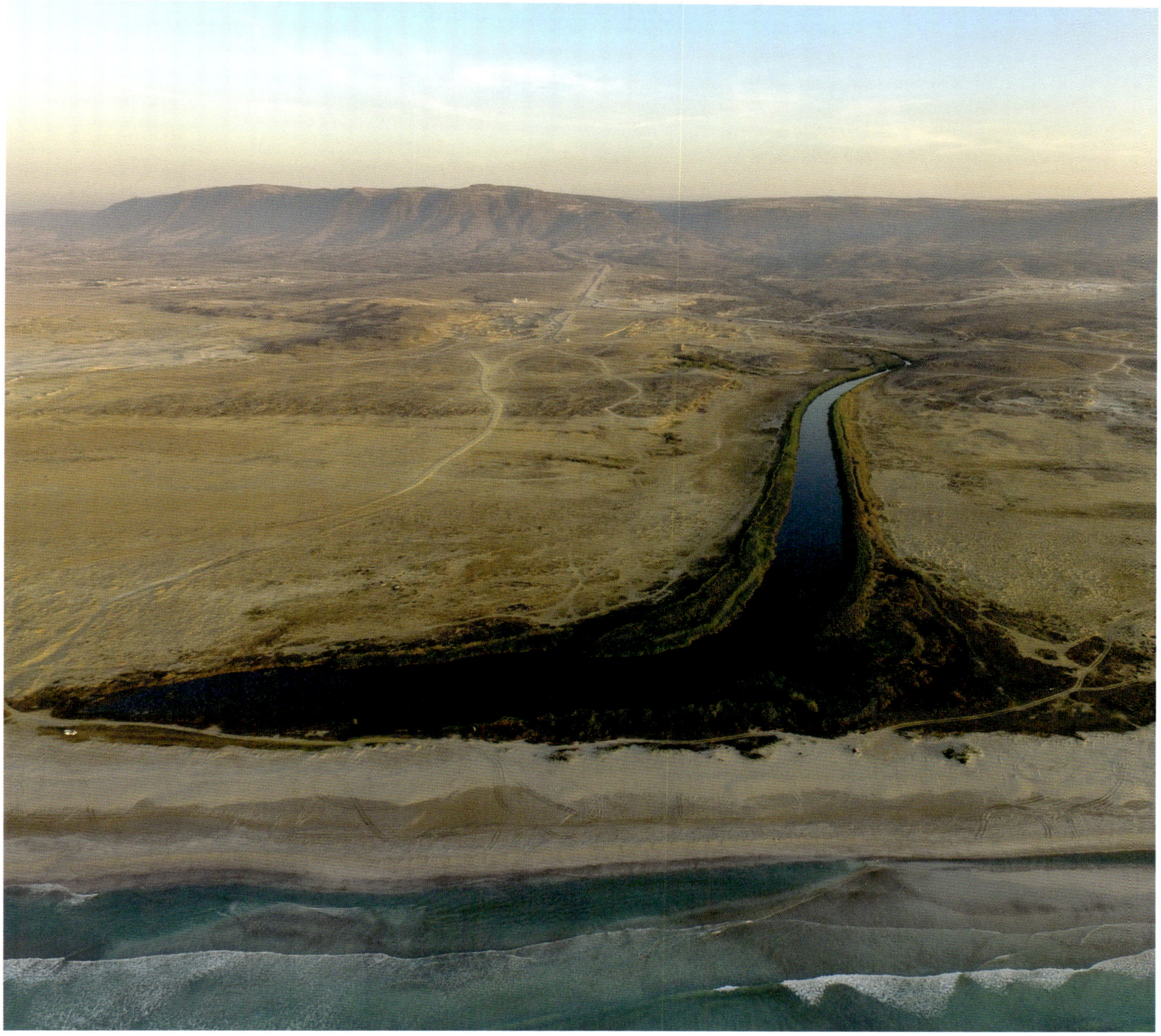

arid land habitats and of coastal lagoons and mangroves. Yet none of the existing reserves is within the biodiversity rich monsoon woodlands and grasslands of Jabal Al Qamar and Jabal Al Qara. A strong candidate for protection is Wadi Sayq, together with Khawr Kharfut, in Jabal Al Qamar where some of the last intact Ṣġót (*Anogeissus dhofarica*) forests are found together with a very diverse fauna including the Arabian leopard.

Similarly there are no marine nature reserves yet the seasonal upwelling of nutrient rich waters gives rise to an extraordinary marine and bird life of international importance. A sanctuary including all or some of the Al Hallaniyyat Islands could provide a perfect opportunity to manage the fisheries sustainably while also providing protection to colonies of breeding birds, to nesting turtles, to reefs and the feeding and breeding grounds of globally important whales and dolphins.

Dhofar's eleven protected areas include Jabal Samhan Nature Reserve ***(left)*** and Khawr Sawli Nature Reserve ***(above)***.

7 Traditional Livelihoods

Introduction

Until the late 20th century, the people of Dhofar were dependent on the land and the sea for their livelihoods and had followed practices and traditions that had remained virtually unchanged over many centuries. The principal activity for most communities, whether on the Jabal or the arid Najd, was the herding of livestock, although some on the Jabal cultivated crops during the period of the monsoon. At the coast, fishing was the main source of sustenance and it was supplemented by coastal gleaning and limited holding of livestock.

On the Jarbib, where water was available, crops were grown throughout the year. Frankincense harvesting was practiced in some areas of the Jabal and the Najd and all communities exploited wild

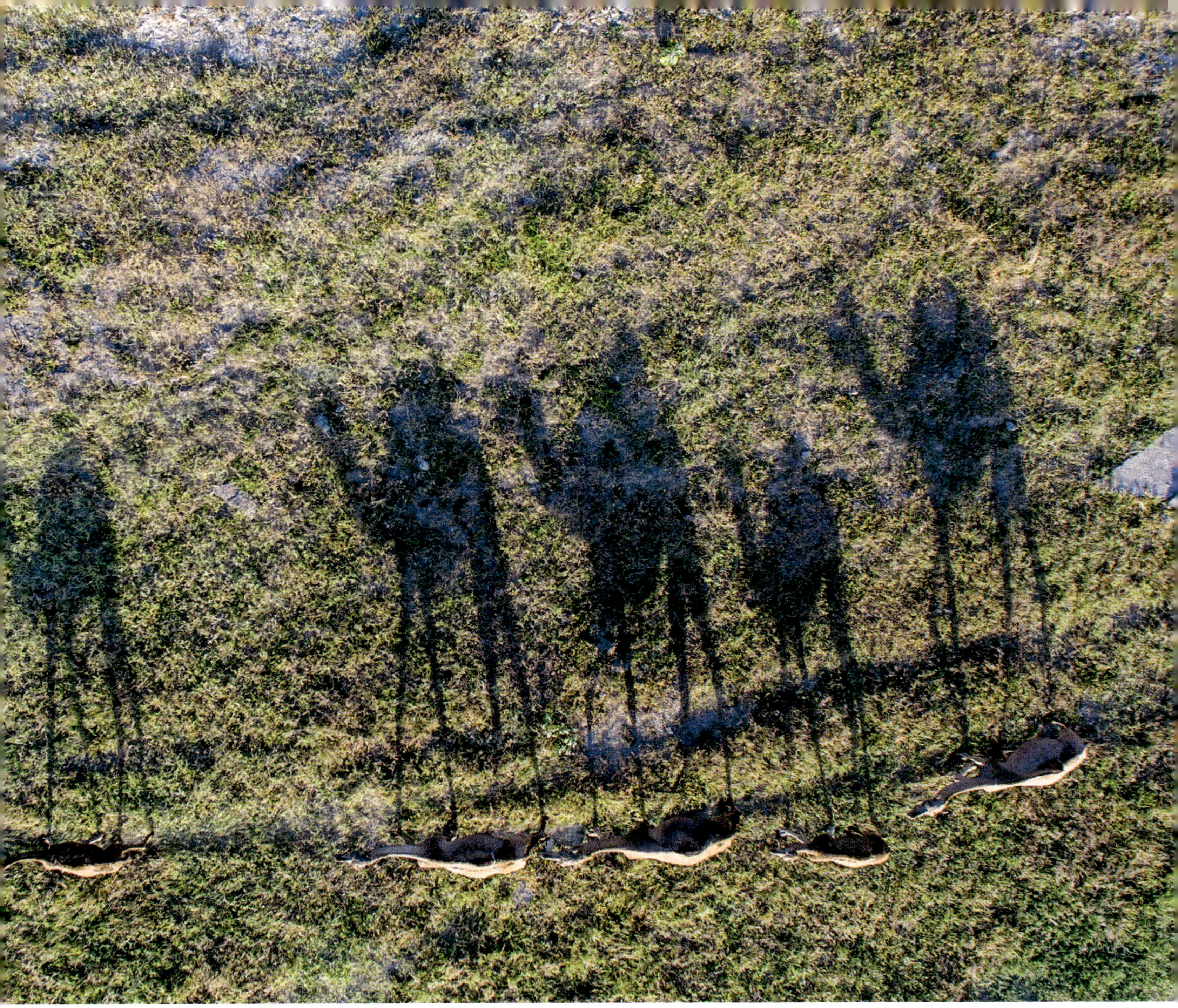

animals and plants for food, medicinal needs and other day to day requirements. Today Dhofar is much changed and a modern developed economy provides diverse opportunities for employment in the government and the private sector. While some traditional livelihood practices have been abandoned and others have been modified, the herding of livestock, fishing and the growing of crops are not only significant to the economy but are also a deeply rooted part of the fabric of society.

(Above) The dromedary, the one-humped camel, was first domesticated in southeast Arabia more than 3,000 years ago.

Pastoralism

Pastoralism is a form of livestock farming whereby herds are constantly kept on the move in search of fresh pasture and water. It is believed that the first pastoral nomads with goats and sheep arrived in southern Arabia approximately 10,000 years ago, with cattle being introduced some 8,000 years ago. Camels were domesticated later and may have been herded for only the last 3,500 years.[123]

Up until Oman's renaissance in 1970, pastoralism in Dhofar was dominated by two groups: on the one hand, the true nomads or Bedouins of the Najd and Empty Quarter, who raised camels and goats, and on the other, the largely cattle-owning mountain people of Jabal Al Qara and Jabal Al Qamar whose seasonal movement between different pastures was determined by the arrival and departure of the summer monsoon or *khareef*. For both groups pastoralism was purely for subsistence but this changed dramatically after 1970 when a new dawn ushered in a modern cash economy.

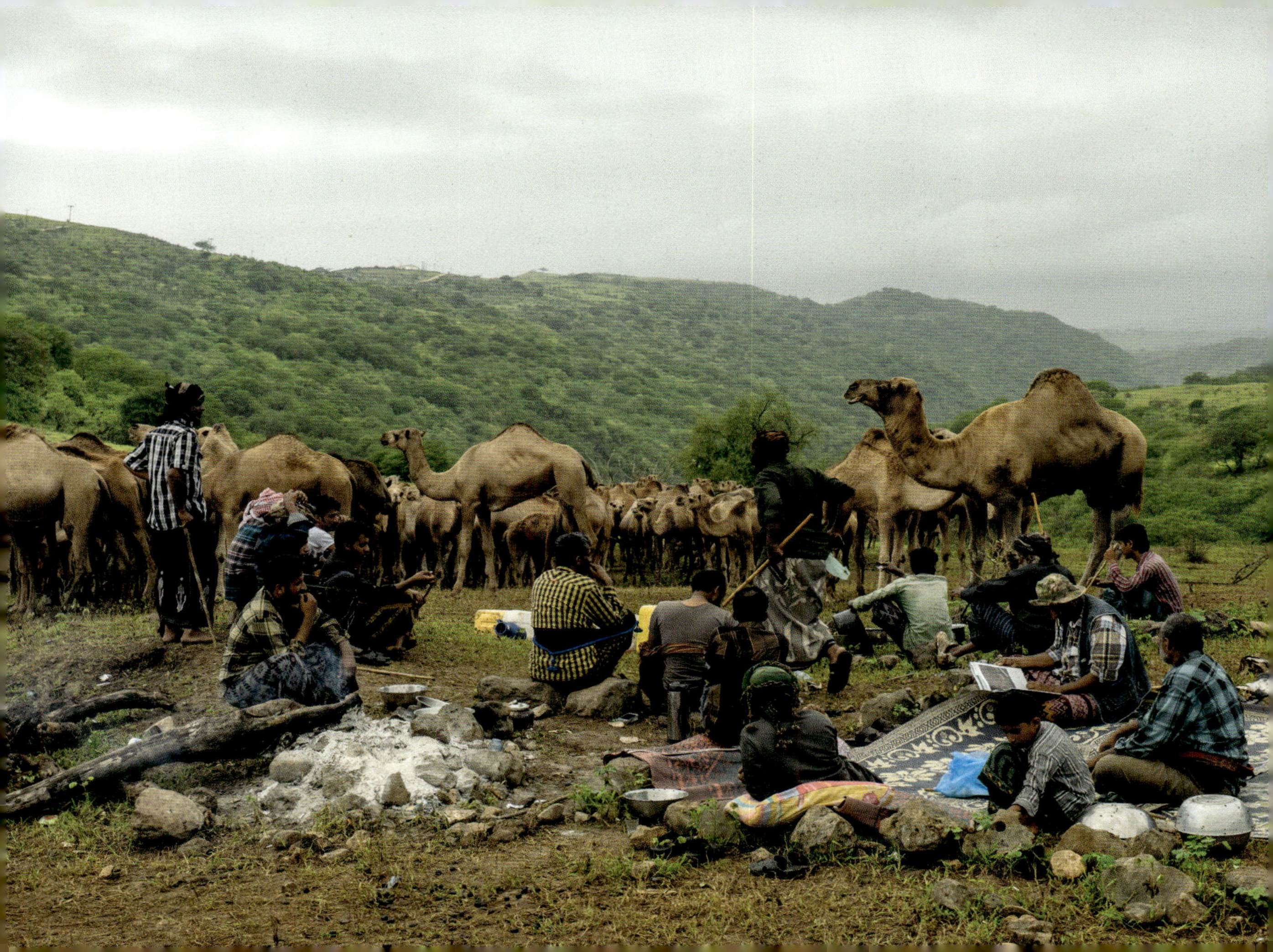

Pastoralism before 1970

The pastoral people use Jibbāli terms to divide Jabal Al Qara and Jabal Al Qamar into a number of grazing zones, largely on the basis of differences in vegetation and elevation.[124]

In the south, the Jarbib comprises the southern foothills of Jabal Al Qara up to about 150 metres and the Salalah plain and then extends east to Wadi Hinna and west to the area of Wadi Al Mughsayl.

The largest zone is the *khatm* of both Jabal Al Qara and Jabal Al Qamar, which is made up of the woodlands of the south-facing slopes and the tall grasslands up to approximately 800 metres. The higher and drier open pasture land of short grasses and scattered low woodland that straddles the watershed is the *qatn*. Beyond this is the Najd (sometimes called the Fejr in Jibbāli) that includes the northern escarpment, the northward flowing wadis and the extensive gravel plains. Further north is the pure desert of the Empty Quarter, sometimes known simply as the 'Sands'.

Nomadic Pastoralists

The nomadic Bedouins occupied the harsh desert lands north of the Dhofar mountains and south of the Al Hajar mountains. Their way of life was based on raising camels and goats for milk. The search for grazing and for water was central to their existence. In some areas seasonal climate events, such as coastal fogs that supported some plant growth and were a source of water, allowed for a seasonal migration. But in most cases the nomads had to rely on largely unpredictable patterns of rainfall: one year widespread flooding would mean good times for the pastoralists while another year drought would bring misery with no rain for many months or even years. These were difficult times for the people and their livestock.

In order to respond to the changing conditions of the desert, the Bedouin had to be highly mobile. They carried few possessions and wasted little. They were constantly on the move, exploiting new pastures and making sure old pastures were not overgrazed.[125] While some Bedouin groups, such as those of the fringes of the Empty Quarter, used goat hair tents for shelter, others had no formal structure and sheltered under *Acacia tortilis* and *Prosopis cineraria* trees or in the shade of rock outcrops and shallow wadis during the hottest times. They were heavily reliant on their livestock. Milk was their staple food and often their only source of water. Although animals were rarely slaughtered they were a source of meat as well as wool for weaving, dung for fuel and skins to make useful objects such as water containers.[126] Where possible, the pastoralists supplemented their diet with game, including Arabian gazelle, Arabian sand gazelle, Arabian oryx, desert hare and large lizards such as the Egyptian spiny-tailed lizard that were dug from their burrows.

Each nomadic group had its own traditional grazing areas, homesteads and watering sites and these were often fiercely guarded, the survival of the clan being paramount.[127] They ranged more widely in the winter months, while in the summer they returned to homesteads to

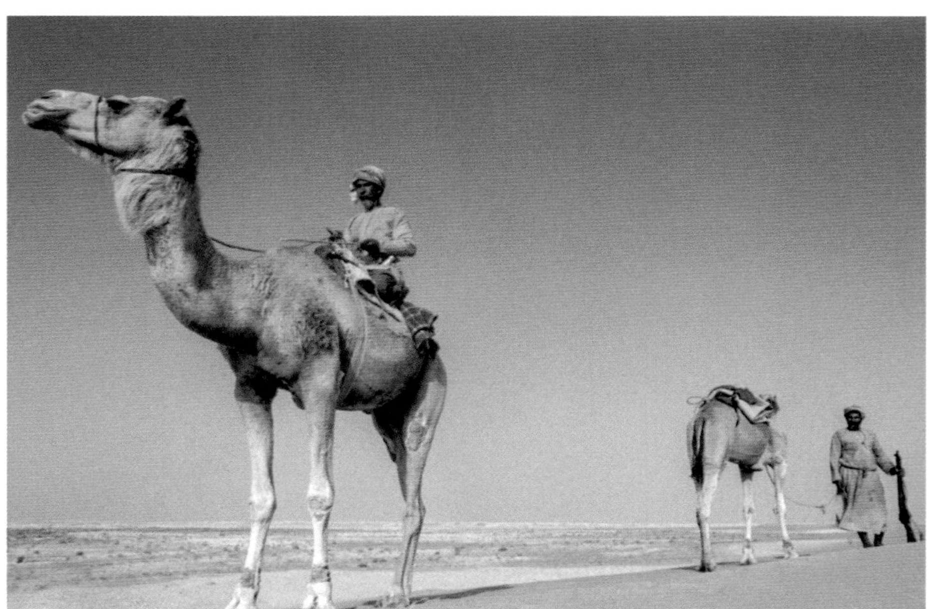

In the Najd and Empty Quarter the nomadic pastoralists ***(right)*** carried only what was necessary for survival.

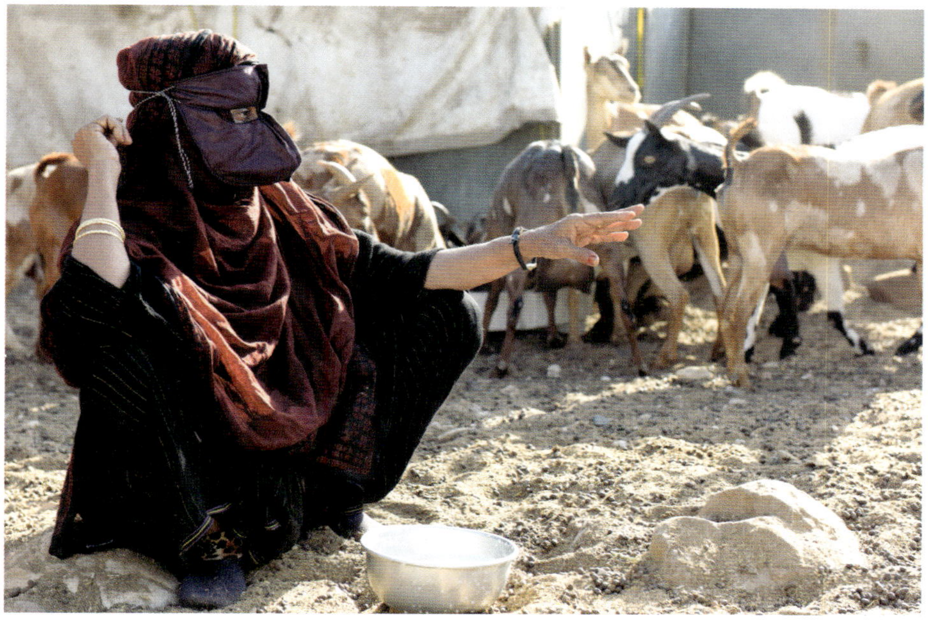

As in past years, goats *(left)* are kept corralled at night but in the daytime, under supervision of a goatherd, roam more abroad in search of forage. Goats are often the responsibility of women while men manage the larger livestock.

escape the extreme heat. For example, groups who roamed the driest areas of the Empty Quarter often spent the summer close to the permanent water pools at Muqshin, Ash Shisr and Habrut where some owned date palms.[125] Others who roamed the plains of the northern Najd retreated to the permanent water pools of the southern Najd such as Uyun, Muday, Hanun, and Wadi Andhur. At the height of the monsoon these groups herded their camels, but not their goats, further south to the *qatn* zone of the Jabal. In the northeast, groups sought the relief of the monsoon winds and the shelter of coastal wadis such as Wadi Aynaynah and Wadi Ash Shuwaymiyyah, where, in the absence of forage, they fed their livestock dried sardines obtained from coastal communities.

Trade was essential to obtain some of the basic necessities of life and each nomadic group had ties with particular settled communities, to the south as far Salalah, to the north the villages of the Al Hajar foothills, and to the east the coastal settlements. Although there were coins in circulation as early as the 18th century, most notably the Maria Theresa Thaler, theirs was basically a subsistence economy, where most products were obtained by barter; goats traded for sardines, dates, sugar and flour, or salt for fish.

To the south of the Dhofar mountains and along the coast there were Bedouin groups that were relatively settled, combining livestock herding with fishing. Only during the monsoon or after good rainfall did they move their livestock inland.[126]

Mountain Pastoralists

The majority of the mountain people were cattle herders who inhabited the most productive rangelands of Dhofar: the monsoon woodlands and grasslands of Jabal Al Qara and Jabal Al Qamar. Here the rich grassland pastures allowed the raising of cattle, a grazing beast, as the principal livestock species. Other herders lived on the lower, usually wooded, slopes of the Jabal and kept camels and goats that, as browsers, are more suited to feed on the trees and shrubs. Further east, the arid terrain of Jabal Samhan was not suited to cattle and there the people herded only camels and goats.

On Jabal Al Qara and Jabal Al Qamar livestock was sometimes kept in association with small-scale crop agriculture, known as *mashādīd*, but the majority of animals were herded as part of a pastoral system. By far the largest group was the cattle-owning herdsmen whose lives revolved around a form of transhumance with permanent settlement areas and seasonal movements to temporary camps, usually within areas defined by clan territories and normally on a north-south orientation.[126]

Permanent settlements were usually within the *khatm* and were inhabited for much of the year, particularly the monsoon and winter seasons. Here cattle were grazed within a few kilometres of home and brought back each night. These settlements usually comprised a dwelling and several cattle byres and each homestead was surrounded by a stone or thorn bush barrier to prevent cattle from straying and for protection against predators. Both dwellings and byres were oval in shape with

On the Jabal domed roundhouses, built with stone walls and timber roofing, were the primary form of dwelling for both people and cattle. In the early 1970s these were reinforced with newly available material such as plastic sheeting and corrugated iron ***(right)***. Since firearms were first introduced to Arabia men have carried rifles to protect themselves and their livestock ***(far right).***

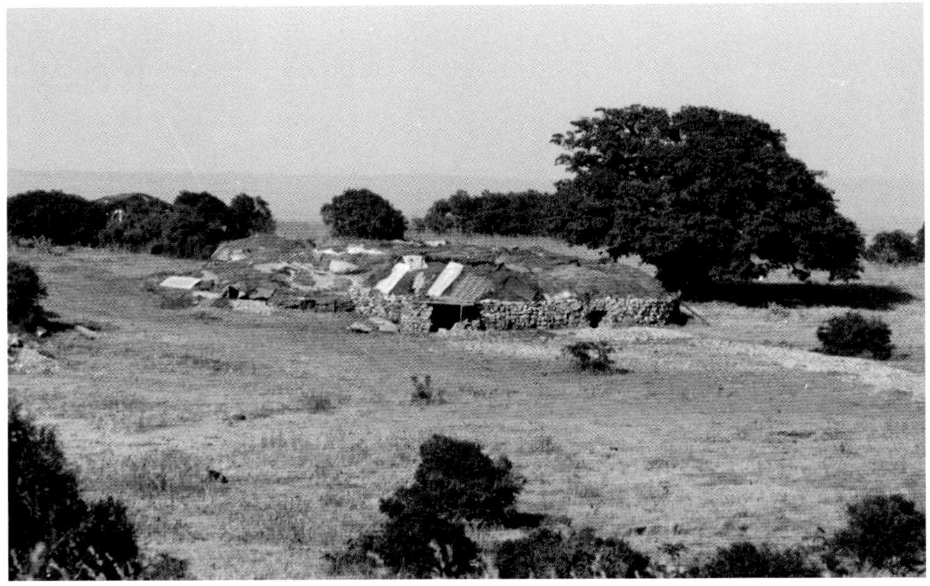

stone walls and timber roofing covered with a mixture of hay and dung.[126] In other cases people and cattle lived in large caves that are found in the southward-flowing wadis of the *khatm*, where ancient rock art is testimony to the long occupation of the area.[128]

For the majority of the mountain people, cattle provided most of the essentials of life, milk being the staple. When animals were slaughtered, meat was eaten or preserved and fat was stored for cooking or used as grease. No part of the carcass went unused: from bone came combs, needles, toys and containers; from hide, storage skins for water, milk and butter, mattresses to sleep on, cradle coverings, wallets, harnesses, amulets and many other household items.[129] The most important product was the milk and the butter (ghee), which was the main commodity to sell or barter for the few goods available from market settlements. On top of this, cattle dung was used for cooking or as manure or was burnt as an insecticide. It was mixed with grass for roofing.

At particular times of the year, in response to shortages of forage, alterations in the weather or the presence of biting flies, the cattle herders moved to temporary settlements. For example, during the monsoon, the cattle on Jabal Al Qara might remain on the *khatm* or be herded up to the drier *qatn* and in both cases they were grazed after sunset to avoid the biting flies. They might then be herded down to the Jarbib after the monsoon. However, in other cases cattle were taken down to the Jarbib for the monsoon before being herded back to the *khatm* for the post-monsoon and winter seasons.[130] On Jabal Al Qamar cattle herders tended to remain in their settlements in the upper *khatm* during both the monsoon and post-monsoon seasons, grazing at night when biting flies were present. They then descended to the lower south-facing slopes of the *khatm* for the winter. Cattle received dried sardines and the straw of sorghum (*Sorghum bicolor*) and millet species during dry season shortages.

In some cases temporary settlements were caves and in others they were simple byres built around a large tree for shade. The timing of these movements varied considerably between herders and was usually a response to access to water - something that was often controlled by traditional land access rights. For example, in the northeast of Jabal Al Qara some cattle herders had no grazing rights in the Jarbib and consequently stayed in their settlements for the monsoon, post-monsoon and winter seasons, leaving only in the pre-monsoon in search of better grazing.[131] Similarly west of Salalah traditional access rights meant that some cattle herders did not have permanent settlements in the Jabal and moved only between the foothills and coastal areas.[132]

Camels and goats, unlike cattle, are not suited to the wet and slippery conditions of the monsoon and therefore must be kept off the *khatm* for the duration of the monsoon and only return once the ground has dried. On Jabal Al Qamar these stock were herded to the drier *qatn* for the monsoon while on Jabal Al Qara they were either moved up to the *qatn* or down to the Jarbib where they lived in large groups made up of many households. This was usually a time of plenty and there was much socialising and people met to resolve issues and to trade

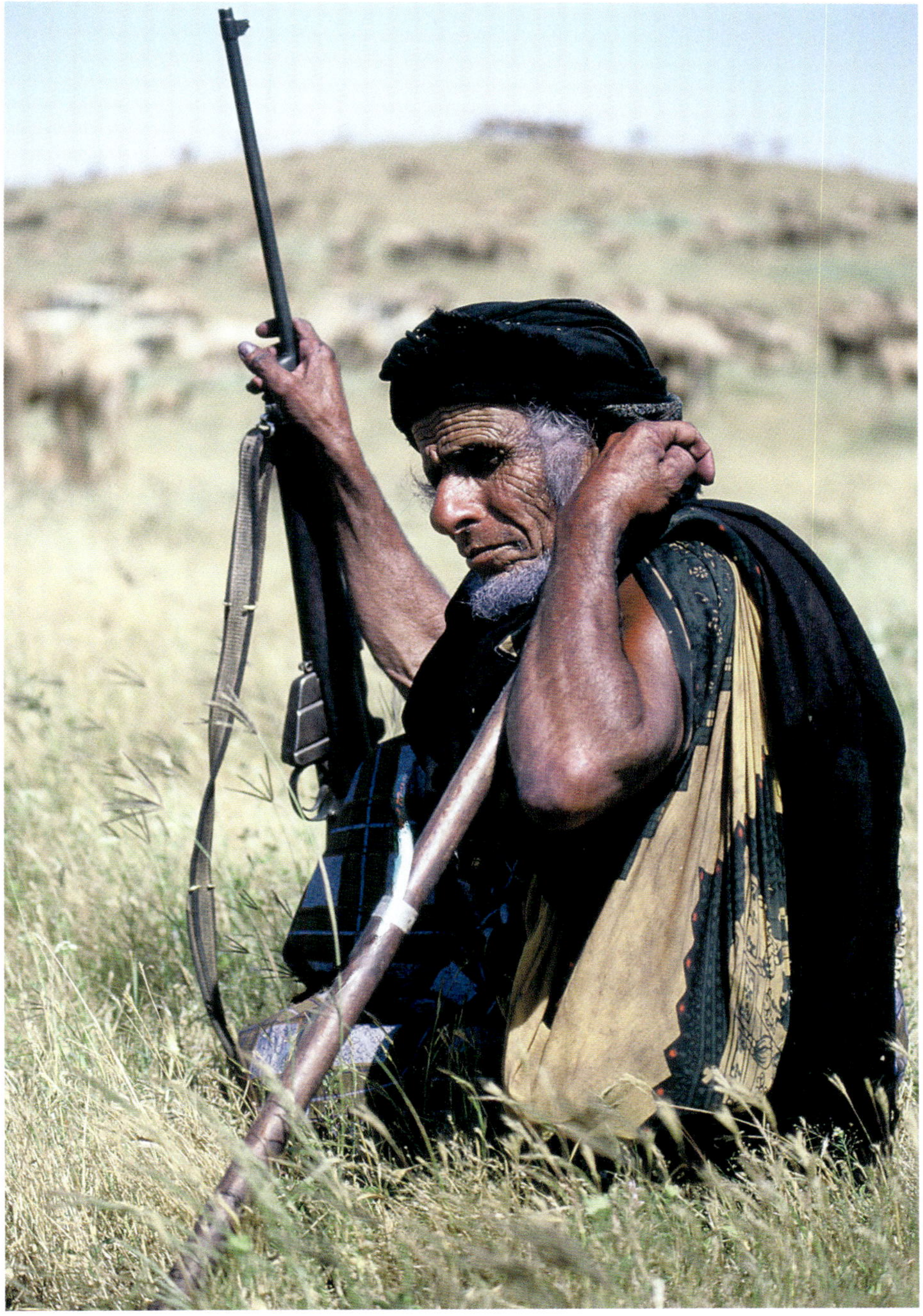

with coastal communities. Once the ground of the Jabal had dried, most herders returned, usually on a date agreed by clan members. In places such as Wadi Nahiz this return was marked by three days of festivities, a tradition that continues today.

In the east the people of Jabal Samhan owned camels and goats, which were best suited to the arid conditions. Typically, these communities had permanent settlements on the southern slopes of Jabal Samhan, often close to springs, where they lived in caves or domed roundhouses, protected by thorn scrub. Most families spent the winter in the foothills or if there had been recent rainfall they herded their stock up the steep trails to the high plateau and into the deep northward-flowing wadis. Here they used caves for shelter from the winter cold. For the pre-monsoon season they preferred to remain on the southern slopes and foothills but for the monsoon many moved to the western slopes of Samhan, east of Tawi Aatayr, or south to the Salawt Plain and coastal *khawrs*. Following the monsoon many herders moved further west to the monsoon grasslands of Jabal Al Qara but remained east of Wadi Darbat.

The mountain folk took full advantage of the richness of the Jabal to ensure their survival. They collected wood for fuel and timber for building and they gathered fruits, tubers, seeds and nuts. They were highly skilled in their use of plants for medicaments, dyes, glues, cosmetics, tobaccos and tanning agents.[66] They hunted wild animals, particularly Nubian ibex, rock hyrax and Arabian gazelle, and nests of wild bees were raided for honey. Those with access to the coast fished, or dived and collected shellfish.

Modern pastoralism after 1970

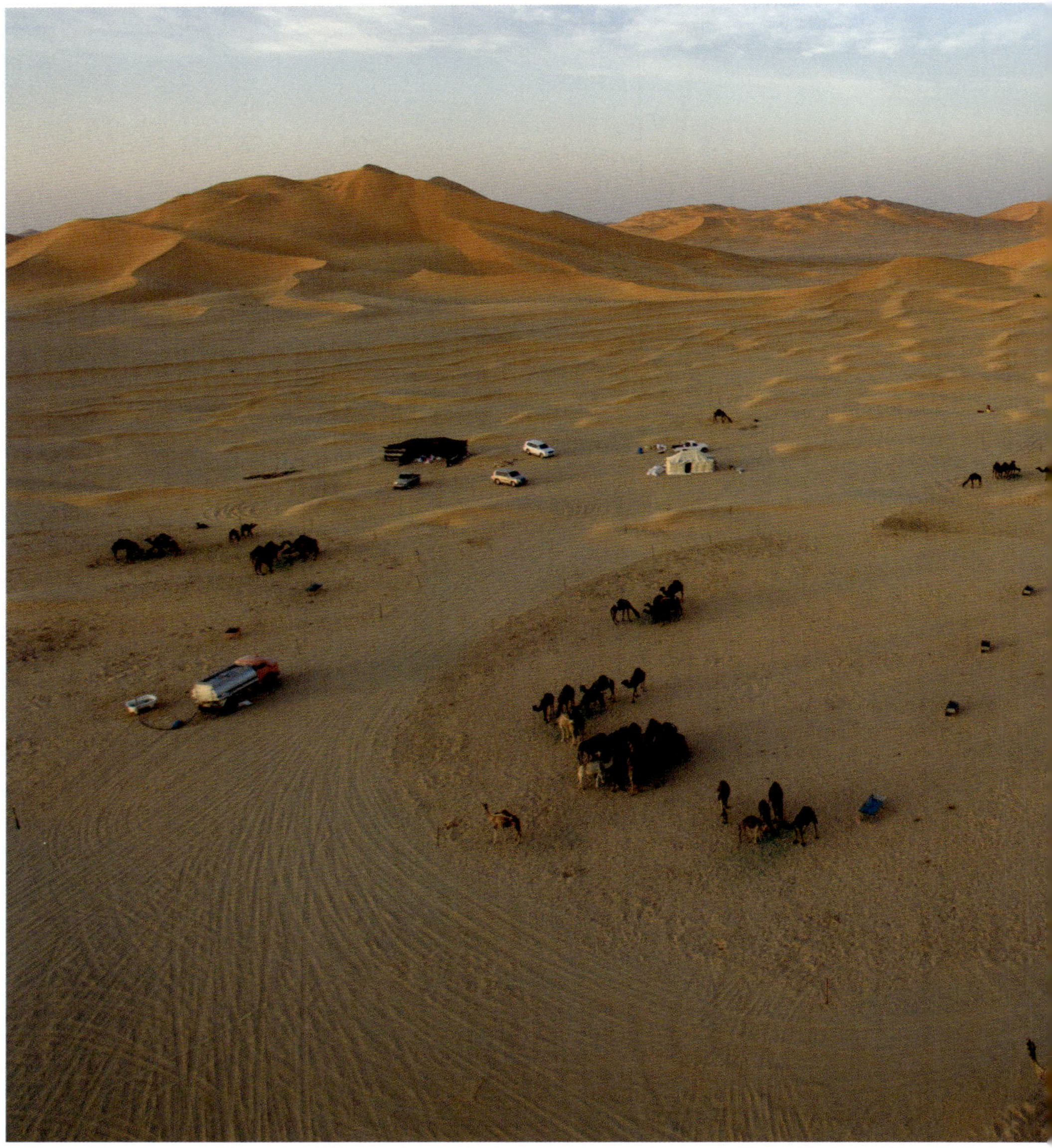

Prior to 1970, livestock farming was for subsistence and the size of herds was limited by a range of factors - primarily availability of forage, availability of supplements (sardines), threat of disease, access to water and traditional land access rights.[130]

However, after 1970 Dhofar experienced rapid political and economic development which changed forever the lives of the pastoralists of the desert and of the Jabal. Seasonal shortages of forage no longer occurred as fodder, especially Rhodes grass and manufactured pelleted feed concentrates, often subsidised, became widely available. Boreholes were drilled where previously there had been no water. Veterinary care and vaccination programmes were introduced and most significantly traditional land access rights were removed.[124]

Roads, government administrative centres and social housing were built and new schools meant formal education where previously there had been virtually none. The introduction of government and commercial salaried jobs introduced cash into what had previously been a largely subsistence economy.

Nomadic Pastoralists

The way of life of the desert people had begun to change in the 1950s with the arrival of oil exploration companies that drilled water wells and provided some opportunities for people to work as camp guards and drivers. But the enormous improvements did not come until the 1970s, when the new cash-based economy brought the many trappings of a modern life style. For the nomads, this meant modern healthcare and education for their families as well as the opportunity to own a vehicle, acquire a house and to find employment or develop a business.

Since camels and goats were no longer essential for day-to-day survival, with even milk available in local shops, a shift away from livestock herding might have been envisioned. However, this was far from the case and suddenly there was an opportunity for the herders, actively supported by government subsidies, to invest in their livestock, which they saw as a capital asset.

The provision of feed supplements, particularly concentrates and Rhodes grass hay, and the availability of tankered water – combined with cash from salaried employment – allowed the pastoralists to increase herd sizes to numbers far greater than they had been in the past. Simultaneously, traditional migration and animal management practices were abandoned as people took jobs, employed labourers and settled in concrete houses close to government centres

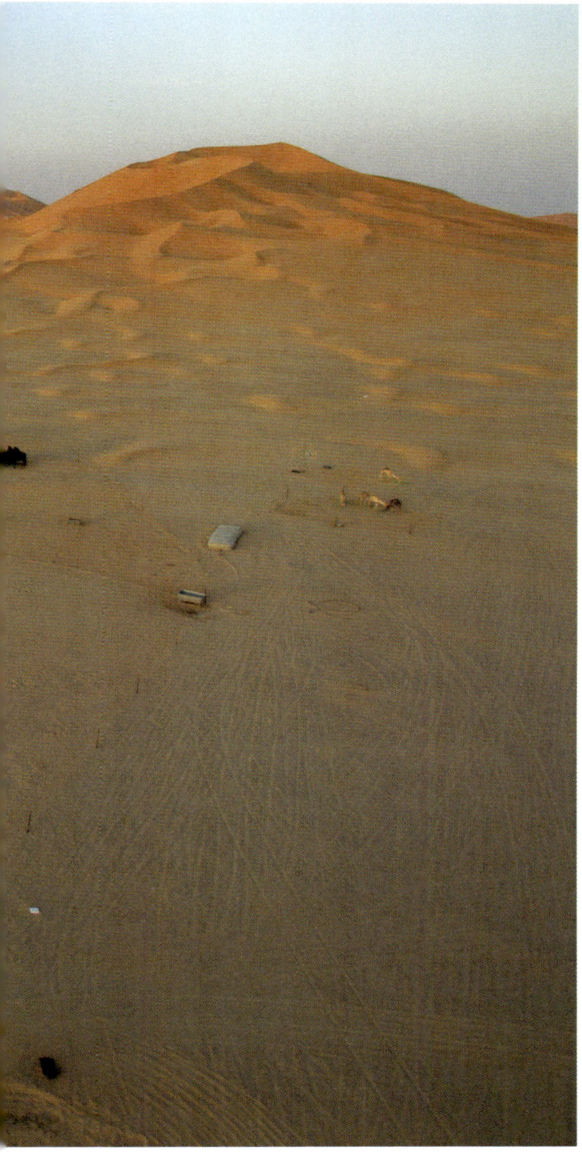

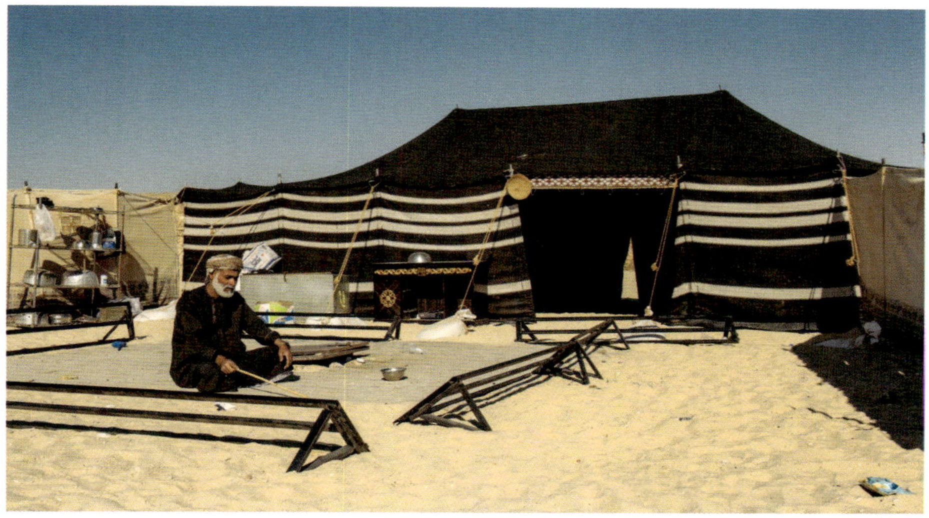

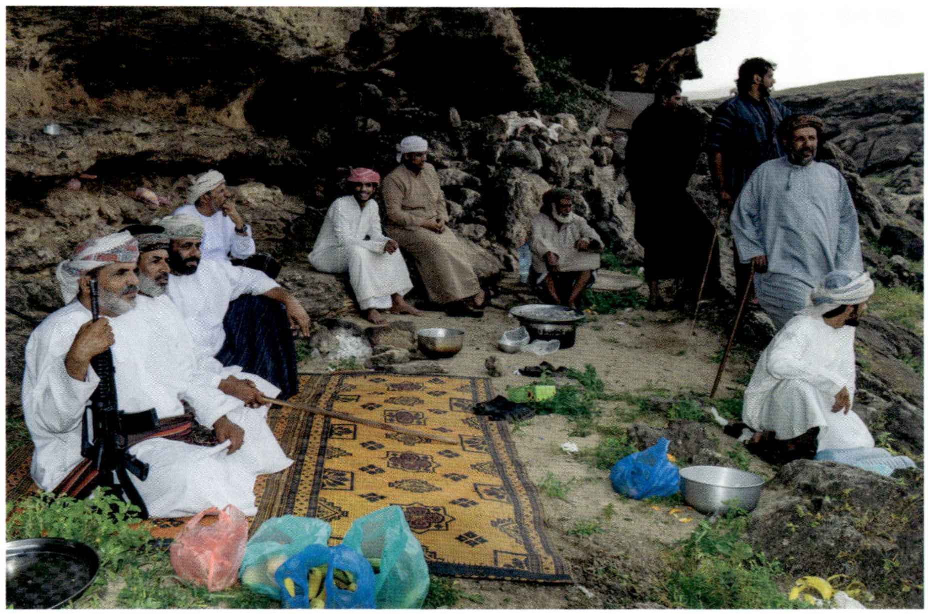

built throughout the Najd and Empty Quarter.

Today camels and goats are still found across the desert but most are concentrated close to permanent settlements. Goats are largely confined to fenced enclosures where they receive water and feed supplements and in some cases, especially following rainfall, are taken out, usually by goatherds, to find natural forage. Some camels are trained for racing, young males are sold to foreign markets and a few animals are slaughtered for special occasions such as the Eids, family weddings or funerals. Camels also spend extended periods close to permanent homesteads and are heavily dependent on supplementary feed. However, male family members and labourers still herd them to desert pastures where they set up temporary camps known as *azba*. In the Najd camel herders continue the tradition of moving their camels onto the *qatn* area of the Jabal after the monsoon but they now remain longer and extend further south than in the past, entering traditional cattle grazing areas.

The people of the Najd and the Empty Quarter are today settled in villages and towns with modern homes, but groups of men establish temporary camel camps, especially after rainfall ***(left)***. Tents are rarely seen but in some areas, especially the Najd, tents are erected at camel camps and visited at week-ends and on holidays ***(above top)***. Similarly, in the southern Najd, caves and rock shelters that once were important dwellings are today places where herders bring their camels and relax with family and friends ***(above)***.

In most areas traditional stone roundhouses have been replaced by cement structures, here used as cattle sheds ***(right)***. Goats are usually kept off the Jabal during the monsoon but are herded up to the luscious green pastures once the ground is dry ***(below)***.

Mountain Pastoralists

The enormous improvements since 1970 have also resulted in a sea change for the mountain people. The once scattered settlements of the cattle and camel herders have become a series of hamlets, villages and small towns. Many have shops, garages and restaurants while the larger settlements include schools, police stations and other government offices. High quality roads, many of which are lit at night, connect most communities. Caves are no longer used, except occasionally to shelter cattle. The domed traditional houses were at first replaced by stone or wood walled structures covered by iron sheet or tarpaulin[133] but today

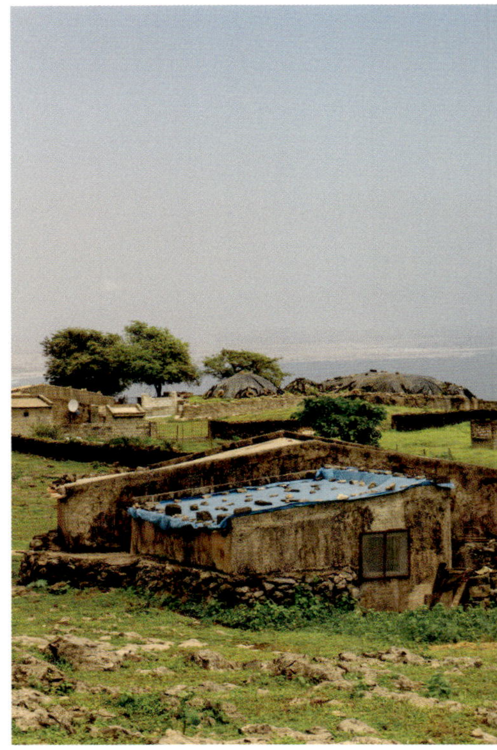

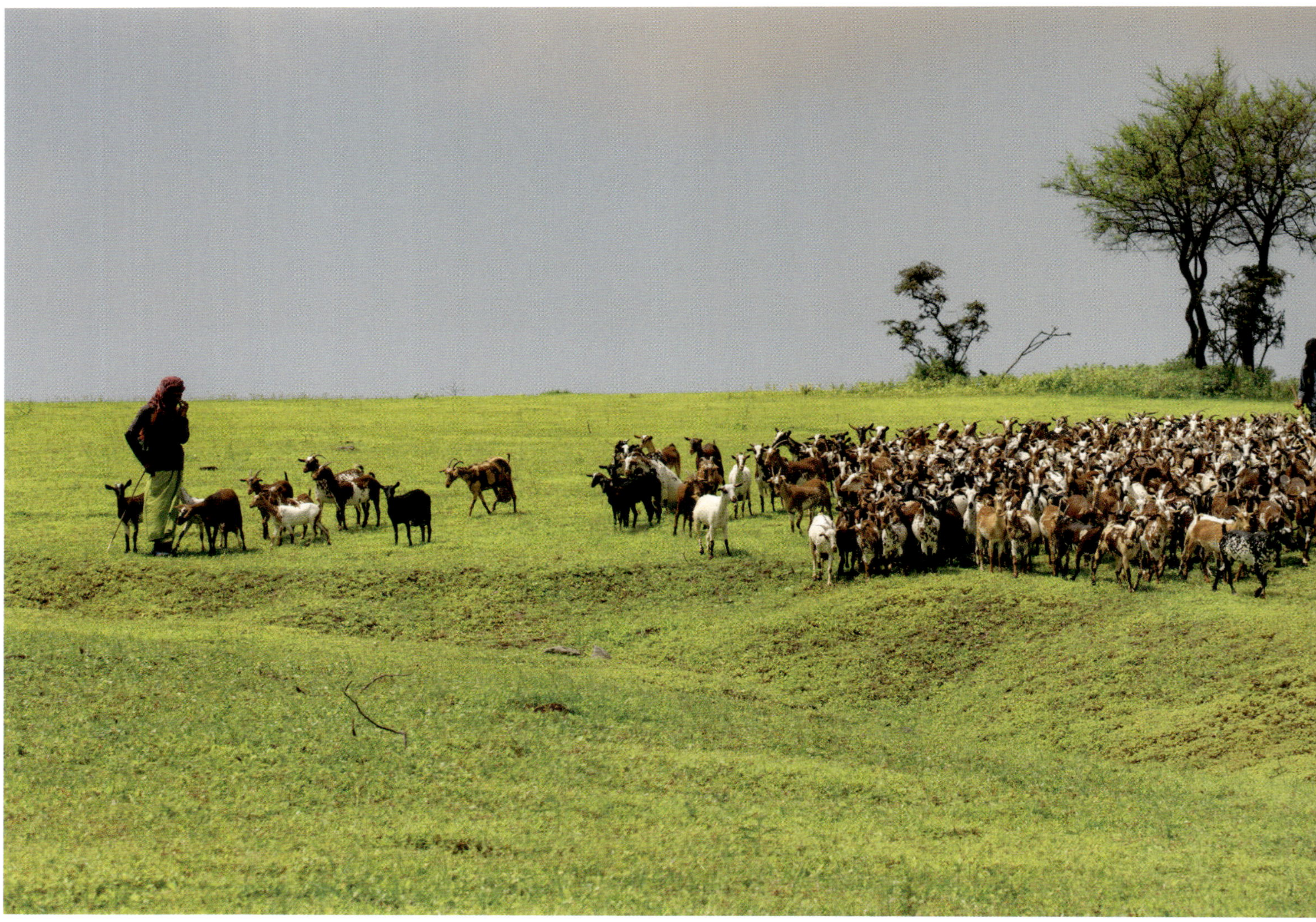

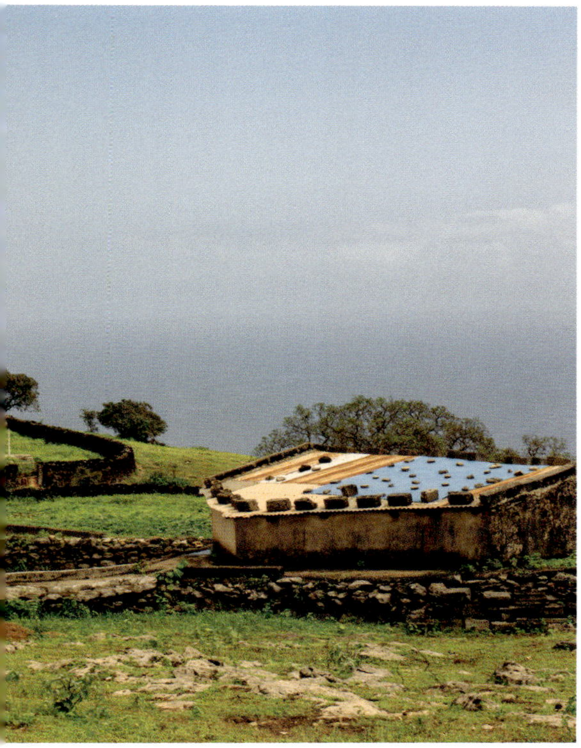

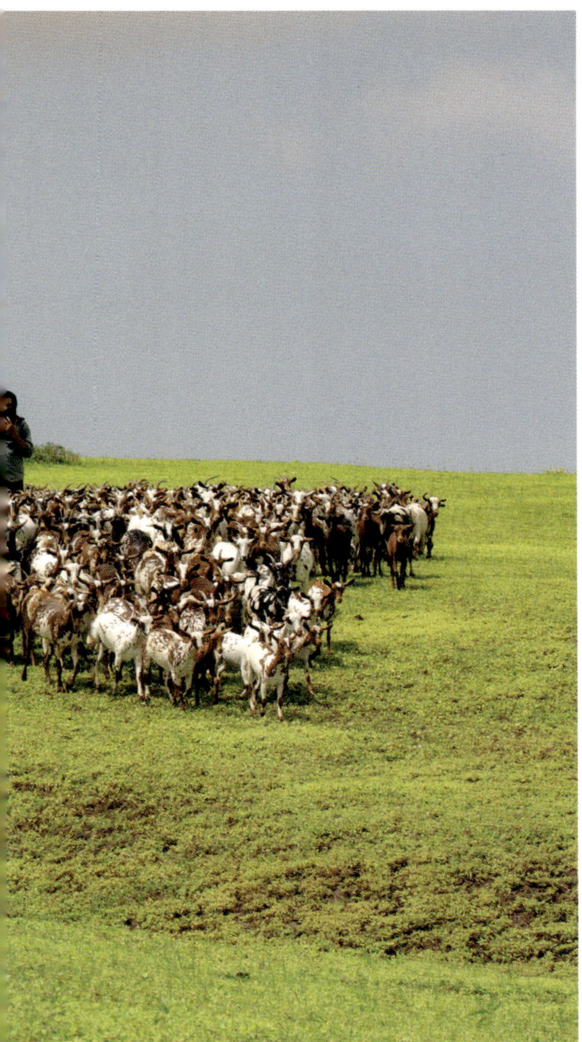

almost all houses are modern reinforced breezeblock with flat concrete roofs and all the usual services such as electricity, piped water and internet access.

The removal of the constraints on increasing herd size, active support for improved production, and a new economy that allowed cash to be spent on livestock farming all led to a rapid increase in numbers of all livestock species. This was at first welcomed, but by the early 1980s concern was expressed at the impact of increasing numbers of cattle on the monsoon rangelands. This led to the introduction in 1984 of a subsidised destocking of cattle that removed 62,000 cattle over five years.[134] Continuing degradation of the Jabal was followed by further subsidised culls of livestock including one of camels in the early 2000s.[135] Though these culls may have temporarily slowed the increase in numbers, census data (Fig. 11) continued to show a rapid growth in all livestock species. Over the 30-year period from 1982 to 2012 the number of cattle, camel and goat in Dhofar had increased by at least 257%, 170% and 96% respectively.

Although numbers of livestock have increased exponentially, herders have derived little economic benefit and spend increasingly large sums on their upkeep. One of the consequences of the rapid increase is that the amount of available forage on the rangelands has greatly declined. Whereas in the past natural grazing was available for approximately nine months, with sardines used as feed in the pre-monsoon season, today livestock are fed pelleted supplements for at least nine months a year and in some cases for 12 months. Indeed many people claim that their entire salary is spent on either commercial fodder or feed concentrates. While the occasional animal is sold for a festive occasion, only the young adult males of camels and cattle are routinely sold.

Today most cattle remain at the settlements on the *khatm* throughout the year where the majority are looked after

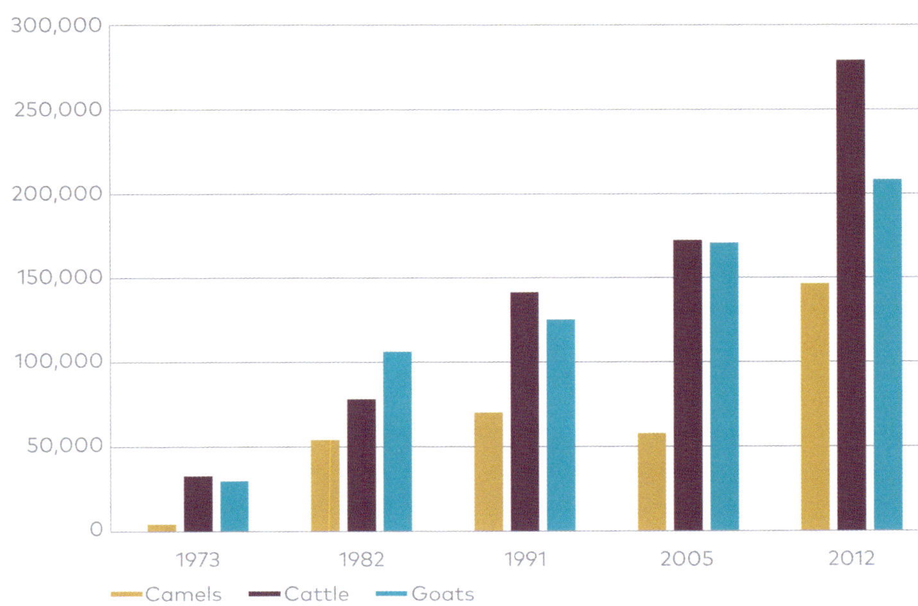

Fig. 11 Livestock numbers, Dhofar.

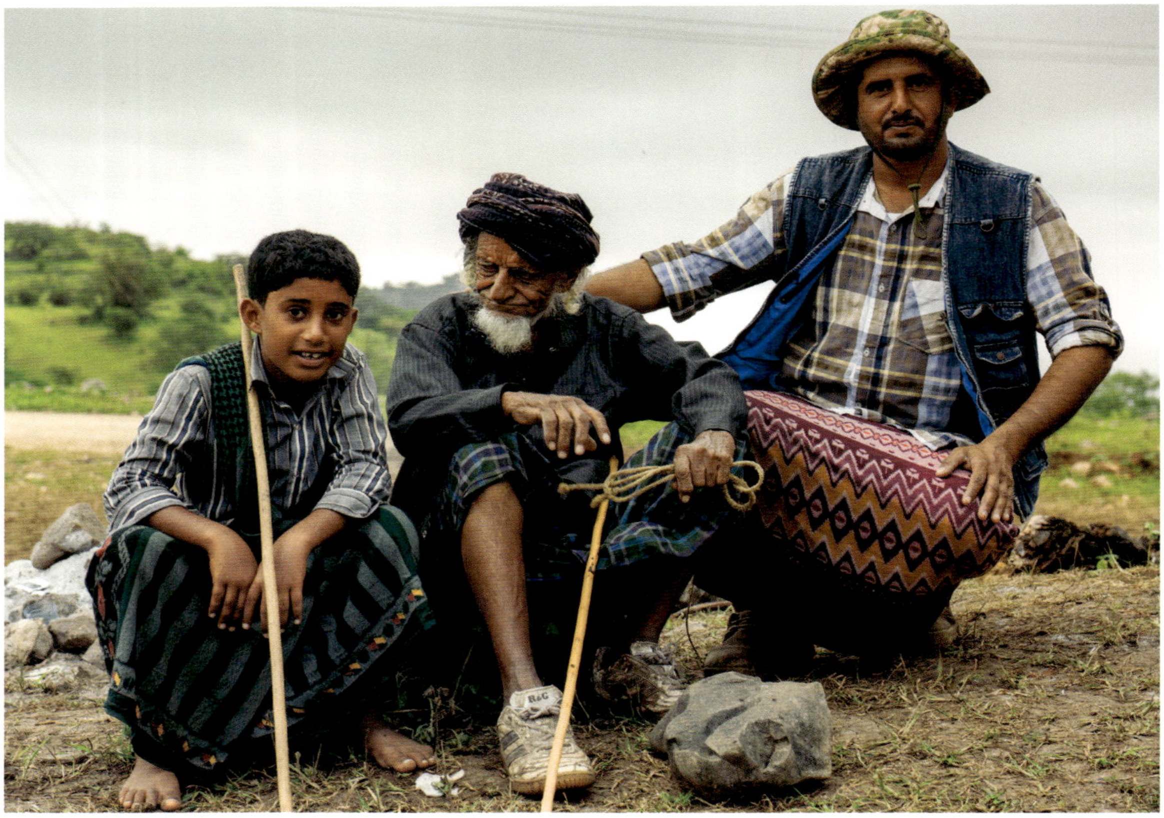

Owning and herding livestock is deeply ingrained into the way of life of the people of the Jabal ***(these pages)***. Many young men share their fathers' and grandfathers' passion for the family livestock, be it cattle or camels.

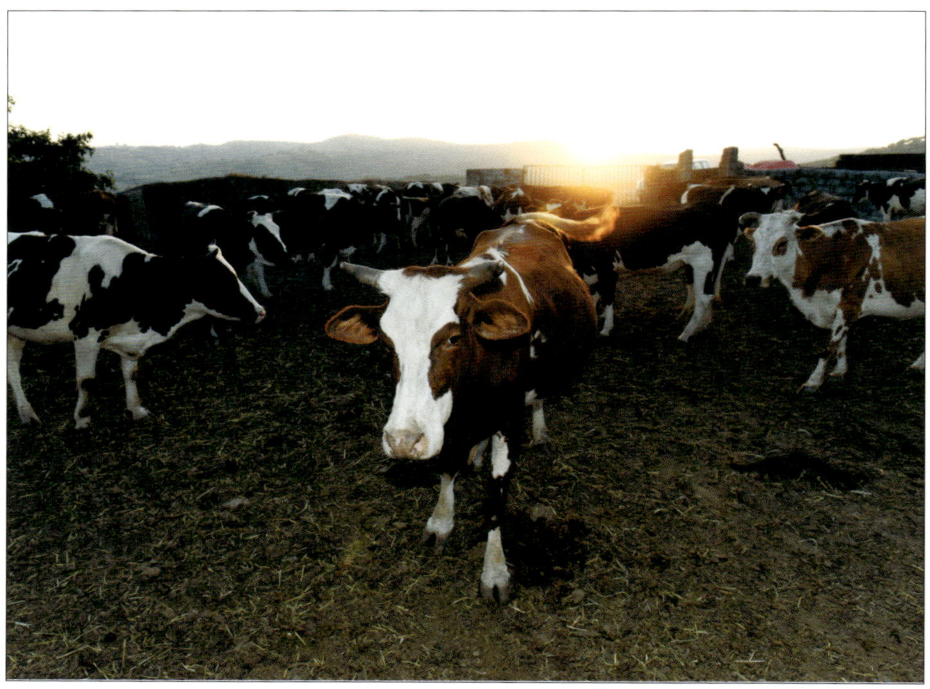

by labourers. They still go out each day to find pasture and in the monsoon the practice of night-time grazing, to avoid biting flies, is still followed. Small numbers of cattle are still moved to the Jarbib or the *qatn* during the monsoon and a number of cattle-holding families have established permanent settlements on the Jarbib, especially in the east. Elsewhere, particularly in the *qatn* cattle owners have acquired camels, principally for prestige. These remain on the Jabal throughout the year and after the monsoon are herded deep into the traditional cattle grazing areas of the *khatm*.

The response of camel herders to changing economic and social conditions since 1970 shows considerable variation but the migration to the Jarbib or *qatn* for the monsoon and subsequent return to the *khatm*, after the monsoon, remains the most important annual movement. However, the inevitable development of the Jarbib, especially close to Salalah, has meant that it is becoming increasingly difficult for herders to make this annual migration. During the monsoon, sprawling camel camps compete for space with residential areas and roads and the journey, often across multiple highways, is perilous for livestock.

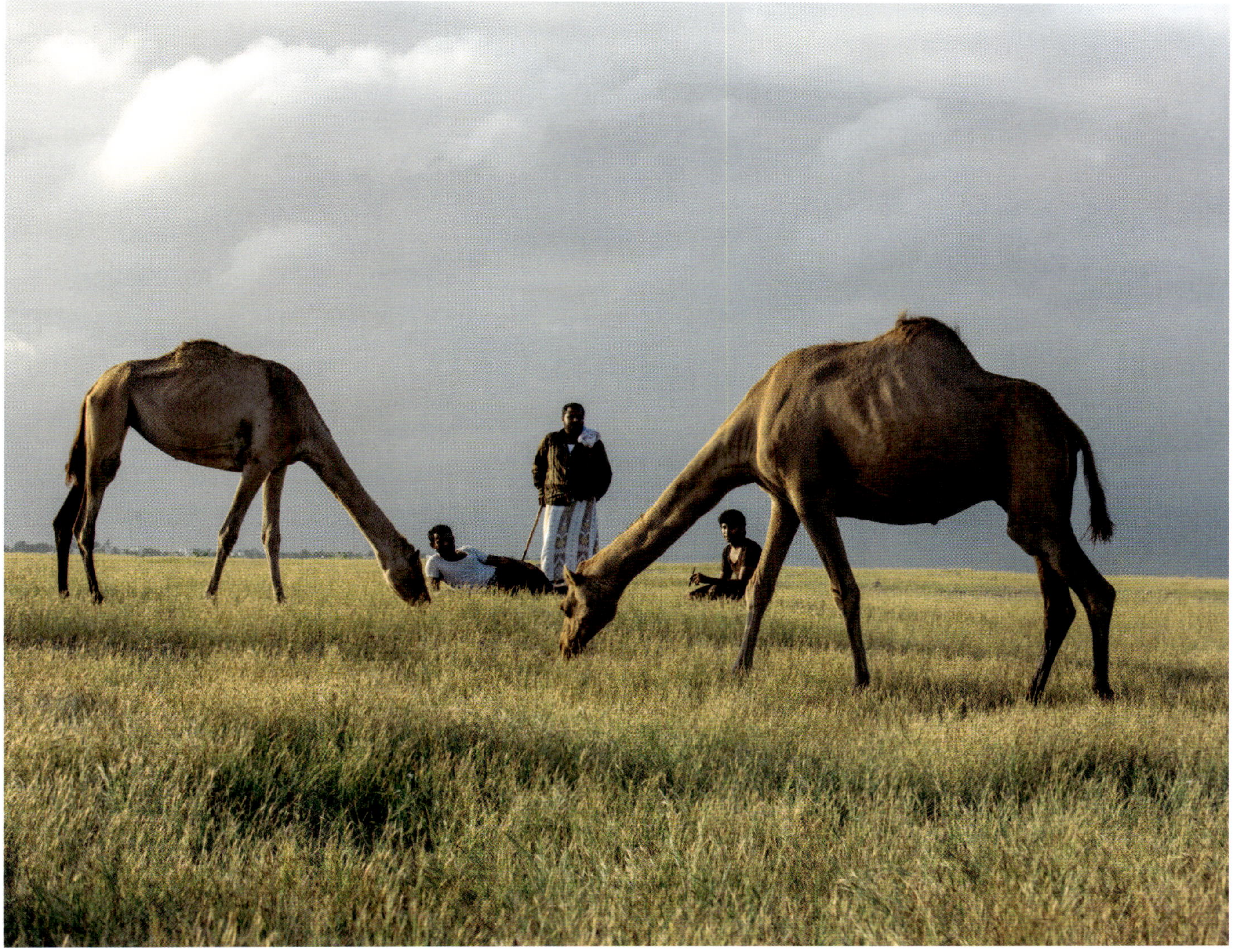

Pastoralism - Sustainability

Undoubtedly development after 1970 has greatly improved the lives of the people of Dhofar but it has also, inevitably, changed forever the ancient system of subsistence pastoralism. Where once the pastoralists were dependent on their livestock for survival, today the animals look to the herders for supplementary feed and piped water without which they cannot survive. Meanwhile the very large numbers threaten the integrity of the very rangelands where the pastoralist system developed more than 3,000 years ago.

For generations the herders have depended on their livestock for all aspects of their life and consequently have deep connections with them. There is certainly no need to remove all the livestock from the Jabal and indeed their trampling and fertilizing is, in moderation, essential to the health of the rangelands. Undoubtedly however, numbers need to be managed, especially on Jabal Al Qara and Jabal Al Qamar, and measures are needed to allow the rangelands to recover, such as resting the pastures for longer after the monsoon.

There is a reluctance to sell animals and the high value of livestock means that herders are unable to compete with cheap imported meat. The marketing chain might need to be improved to ensure that there is a demand for locally produced livestock and livestock products. Positive signs are provided by programmes that collect cow's milk from farms on Jabal Al Qara and by government plans for collection centres for both cow and camel milk. Ultimately it might be necessary to set up livestock farms outside the main Jabal, where animals are held for most of the year, but from where they can be herded on the pastures for a period of time after the monsoon but not throughout the year.

Crop Cultivation

Traditional Rain-Fed Agriculture on the Jabal

Rain fed agriculture (Ji. mišnu, Ar. *mashādīd*) has been practiced across Jabal Al Qara and Jabal Al Qamar during the monsoon season for millennia. Stone-walled enclosures that ranged from a few square metres to much larger stone-walled fields were planted at the beginning of the monsoon. While some were used for preserving tall-grass pasture most were used for a limited range of crops.[136]

Each season the enclosures were cleared, manured and sown with seed just before the onset of the monsoon. Once the monsoon clouds cleared the crops were harvested, usually between 15th September and 30th October.[137] Sorghum and two varieties of beans (mung bean *Vigna radiata*, and cowpea *Vigna unguiculata)* were the main crops with maize (*Zea mays*), cucumber (*Cucumis sativus)* and tobacco (*Nicotiana tabacum*) also commonly grown. Harvested grains were stored and either roasted whole or ground to be made into breads or various kinds of porridge.[129] Seeds were collected and stored for the next monsoon.

The *mashādīd* were usually found on intermediate elevations of the *khatm* that enjoy high precipitation and fine soil. The largest and greatest number are on Jabal Al Qara particularly on the eastern Jabal between Madinat Al Haq in the west and Tawi Aatayr in the east. On Jabal Al Qamar there are fine examples above Dalkut and close to Khadrafi.

After 1970 many of the *mashādīd* were abandoned, the main reason being increased access to cheaper vegetables grown on the Salalah plain.[138] Since that time the use of the *mashādīd* has been revived but practices have changed. The larger stone-walled fields that were once used for crops such as sorghum and cowpea are mainly used now for the production of hay from the naturally growing tall *Themeda* grasses. These continue to be rain-fed. Most of the smaller plots, however, are no longer supported solely by rainwater but are irrigated

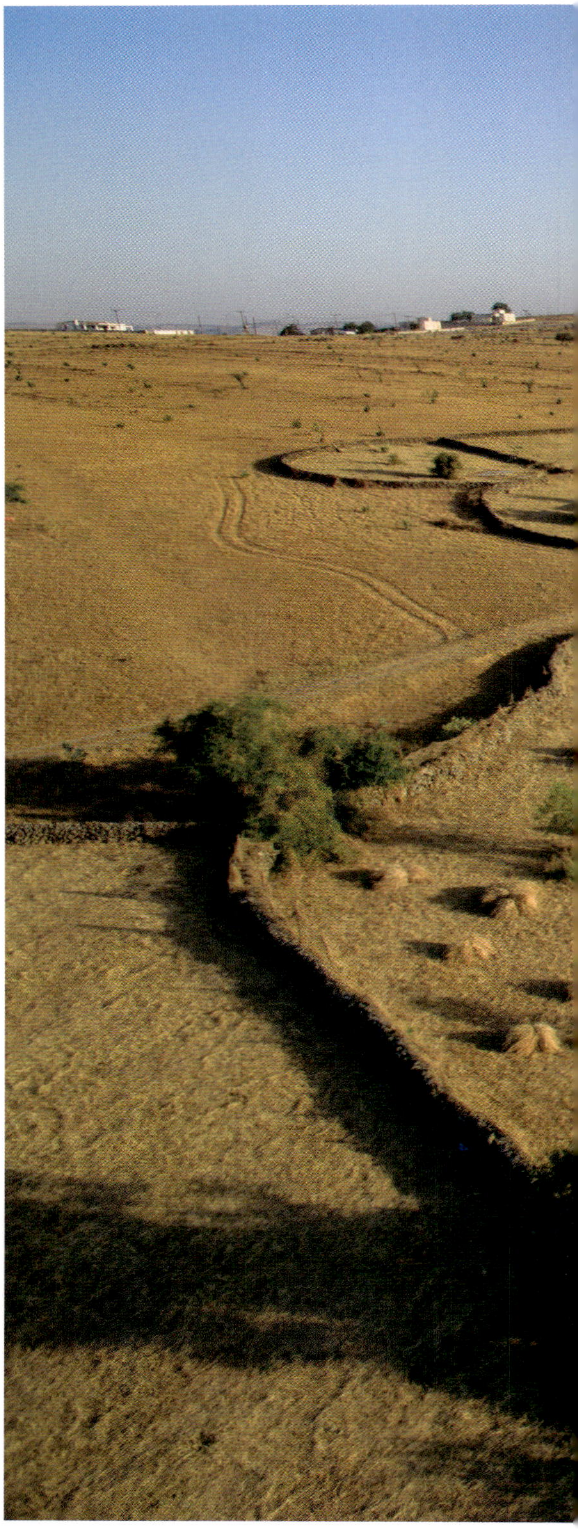

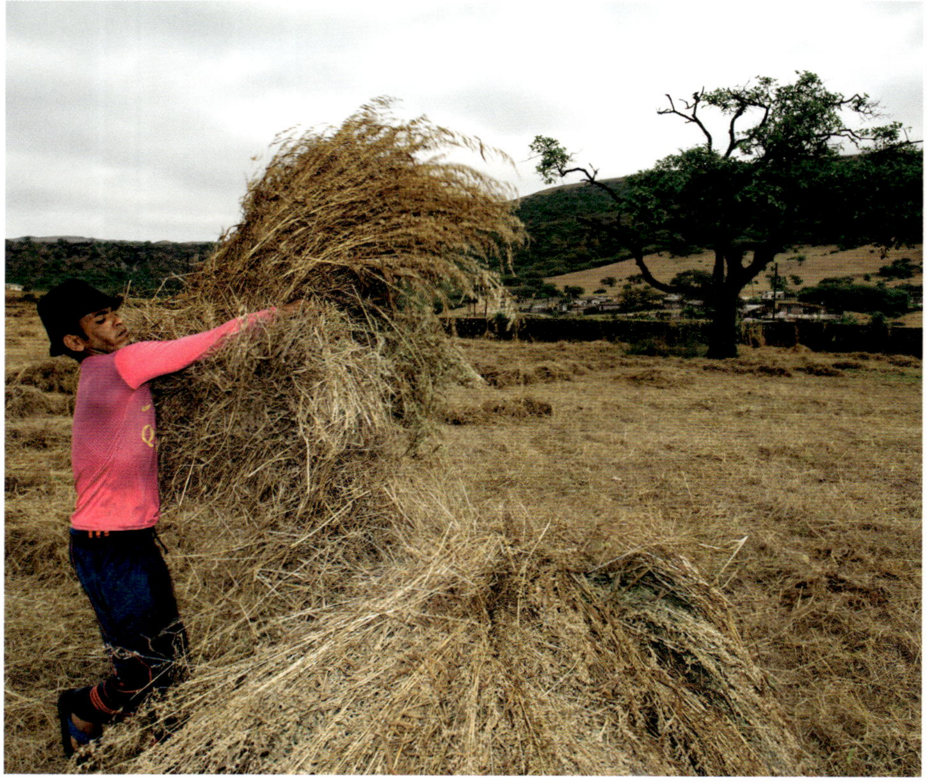

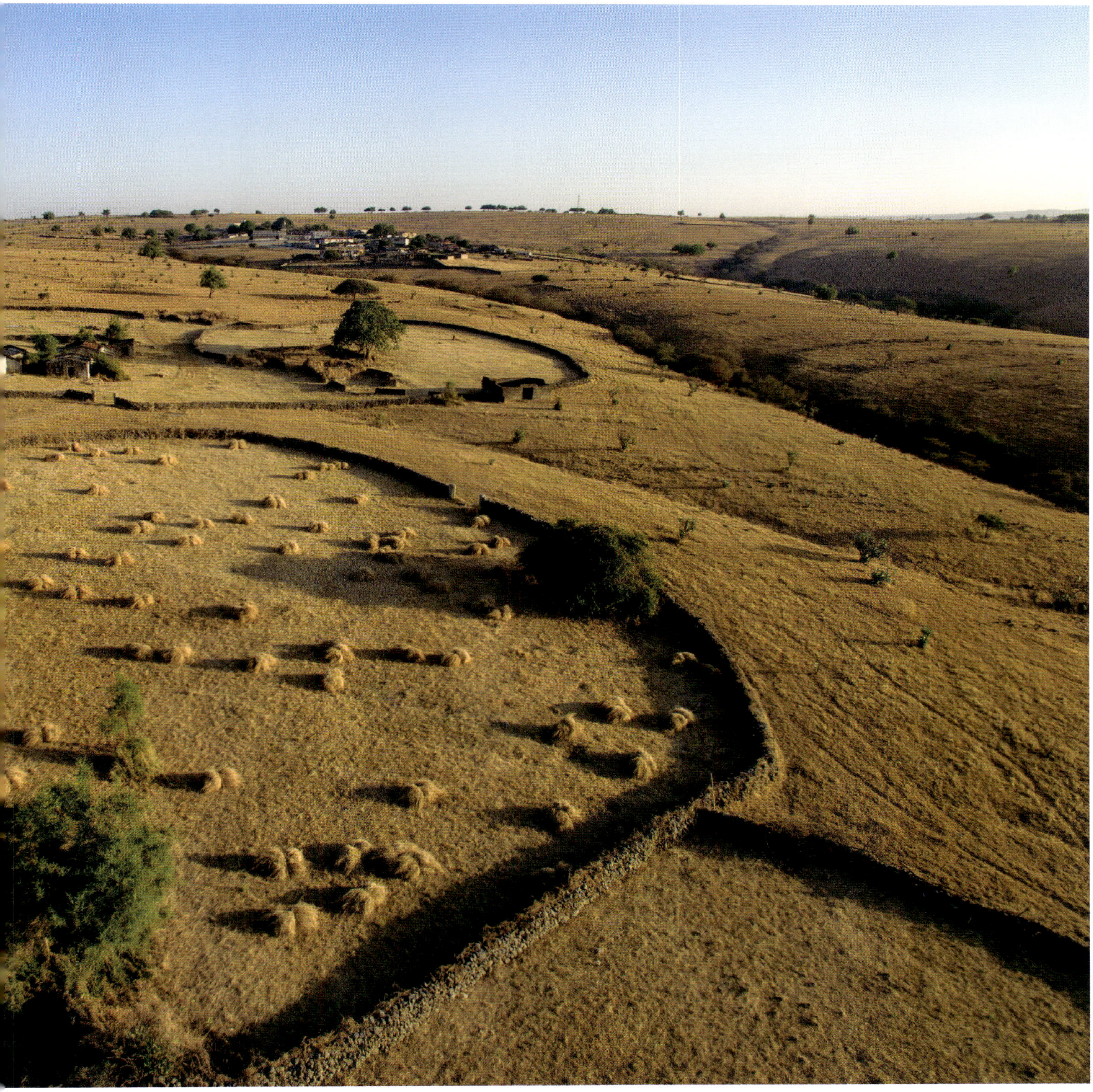

with piped groundwater. These plots comprise some of the old *mashādīd* but many new plots have been established since 1970, and these use piped water either from nearby boreholes or from springs at the foot of the *khatm*. Most of the plots are quite small, often resembling small gardens, and grow mixed vegetables and fruits, usually throughout the year. A number of the plots, some resembling small farms, have been established outside the monsoon

Once the monsoon has lifted, the tall-grass of the stone-walled fields turns golden-brown and the hand cut hay is stacked ***(opposite and above)***, ready to feed livestock when the monsoon pastures have been exhausted.

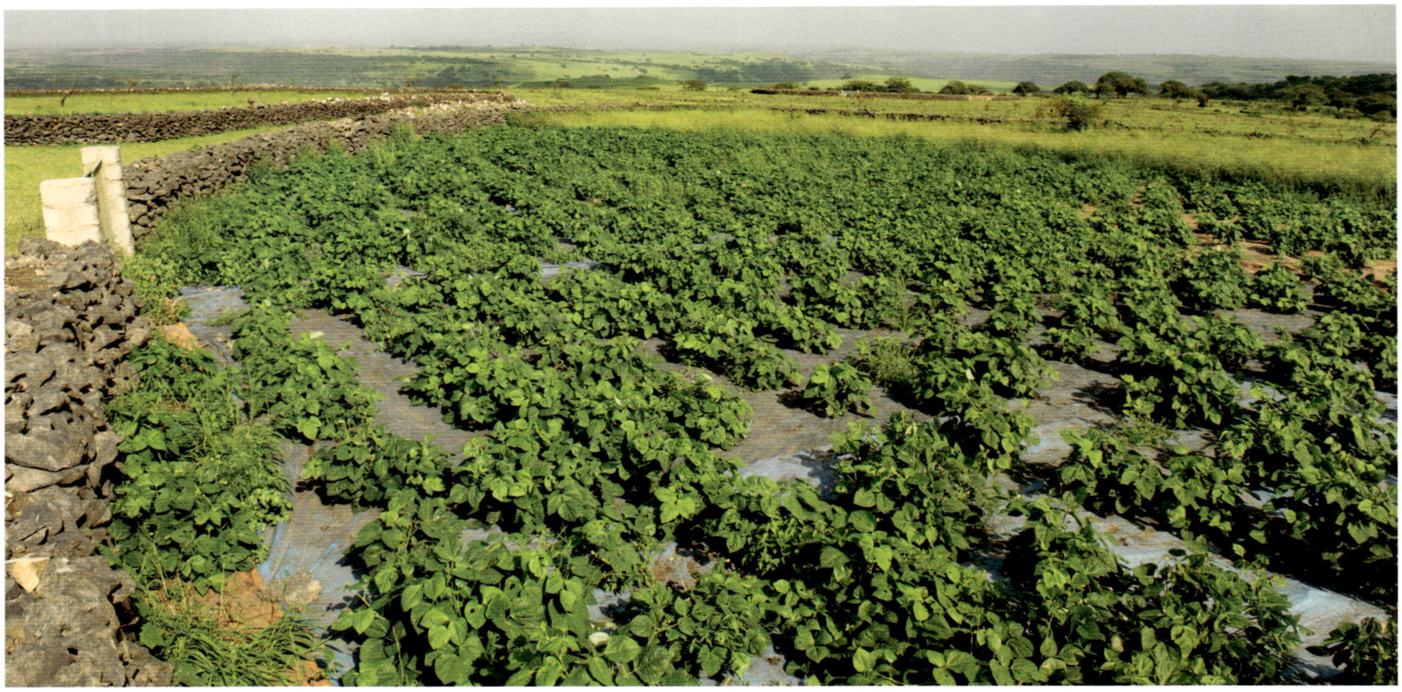

areas including for example north of Titam and in Wadi Al Mughsayl.

Fruit and vegetables grown on small agricultural plots and gardens include banana (*Musa spp.*), chickoo (*Manilkara zapota*), chilli pepper (*Capsicum* sp.), coconut palm (*Cocos nucifera*), cowpea, custard apple (*Annona reticulata*), guava (*Psidium guajava*), lemon (*Citrus limon*), lime (*Citrus aurantifolia*), luffa (*Luffa* sp.), maize, mango (*Mangifera indica*), orange (*Citrus sp.*), papaya (*Carica papaya*), pomegranate (*Punica granatum*), sorghum, sugar cane (*Saccharum* sp.) and tropical almond (*Terminalia catappa*).

Native plants grown on small agricultural plots and gardens include *Ṣġót*, *Commiphora* sp., fig, frankincense, tamarind (*Tamarindus indica*) and Christ's thorn.

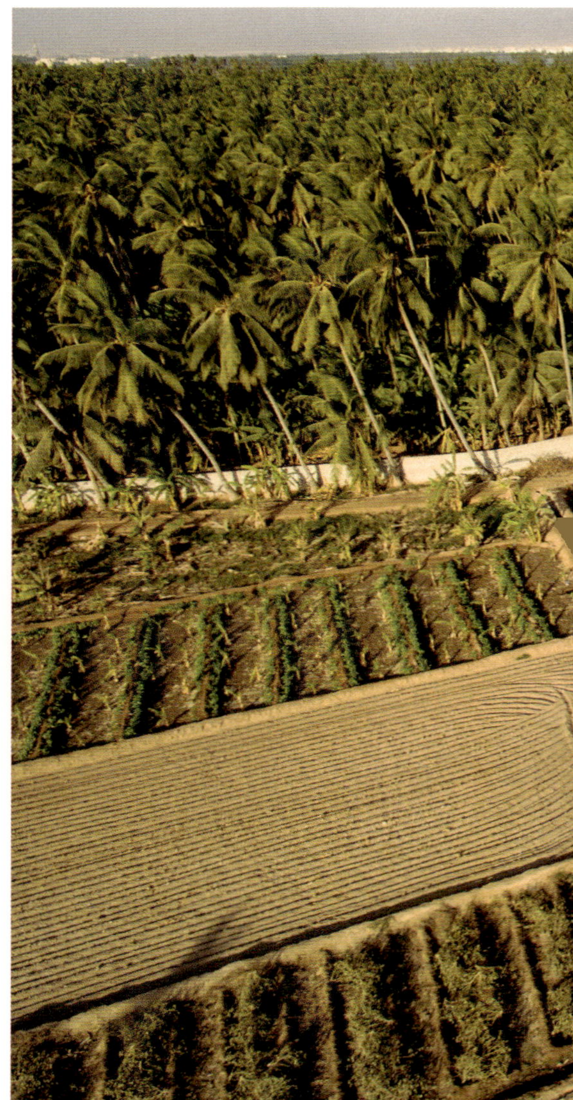

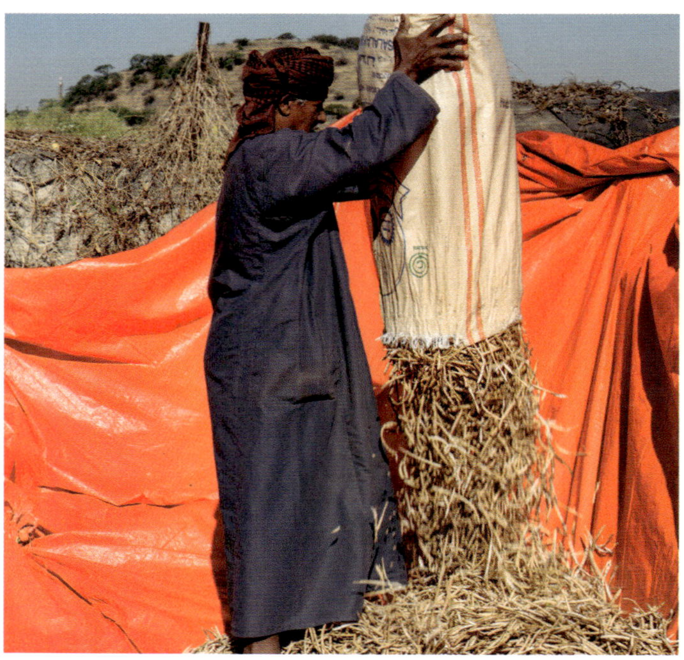

Stone-walled fields are also used for growing cowpeas ***(above)*** which are regarded as good feed ***(right)*** for milking cows.

Irrigated Agriculture on the Jarbib (Salalah Plain)

Irrigated agriculture, largely for subsistence, has been practiced in Salalah and Taqah for many centuries. Farms were mostly small, worked by the same families for generations and were dependent on hand dug wells from which the water was drawn by draught camels for flood irrigation. Travellers in the 19th century remarked on the very shallow water table and the importance of cotton (*Gossypium* spp.), coconut (*Cocus nucifera*) and coffee (*Coffea arabica*).[25]

Small numbers of camels, cattle, goats and sheep were raised by the settled peoples of Salalah and other coastal settlements for milk, meat and particularly in the case of camels as draught animals for ploughing or drawing water.

Water channels, known as *aflaj*, that carry water from springs are widespread in northern Oman but not found in Dhofar. However, in the 1930s three were built to carry additional water across the plain from springs at Ayn Jarziz, Ayn Razat and Ayn Sahalnawt. Later some of the draught camels were replaced by diesel pumps and in 1948 it was estimated that there were some 200 shallow wells on 500 hectares of cropped land.[127] Coconut was considered the principle crop

Where once cotton and coffee was grown, today the farms of Salalah produce many fruits and vegetables including cabbages, papaya, bananas and the ubiquitous coconut palm ***(below).***

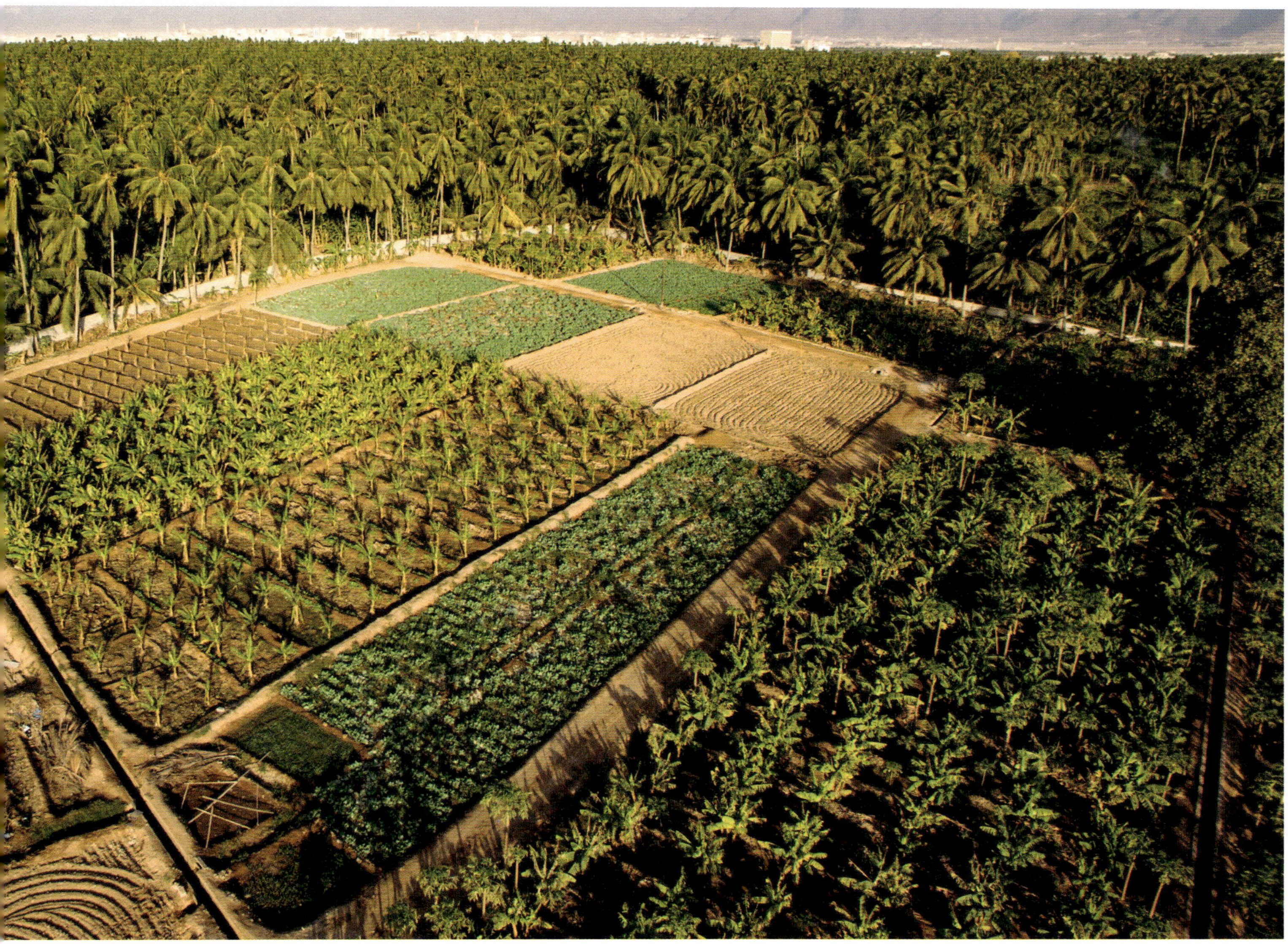

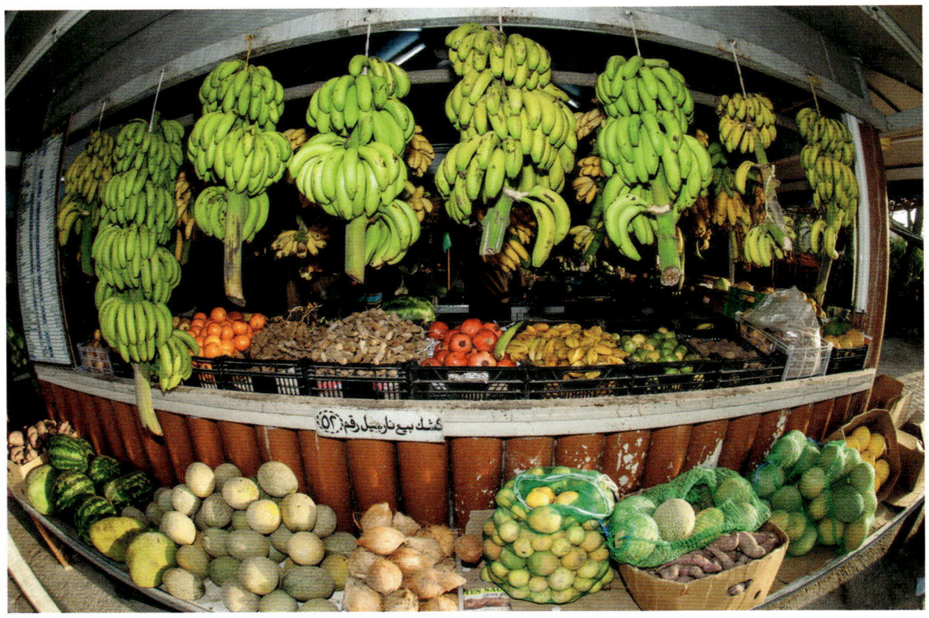

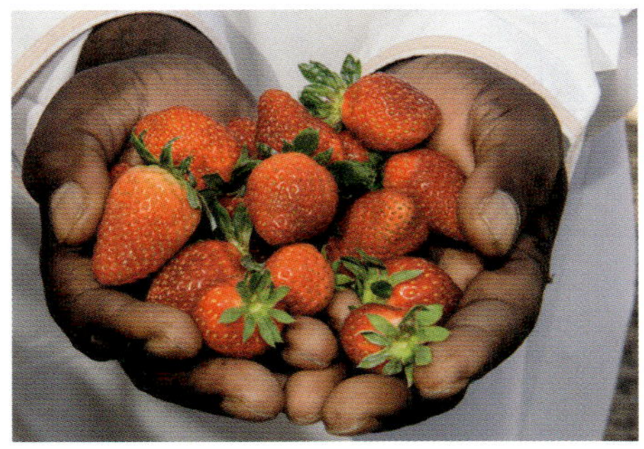

while cotton and coffee were no longer grown. Other important crops included cereals, especially different varieties of millet, while papaya, onion, pepper, cowpea, sweet potato (*Ipomoea batatas*), tomato (*Solanum lycopersicum*) and watermelon (*Citrullus lanatus*) were also grown.

After 1970 the growing of cereals largely ceased as corn and flour came onto the market and farmers shifted towards the growing of less labour intensive crops such as bananas and papaya and to the growing of fodder, particularly Rhodes grass. At that time there were about 700 hectares under cultivation close to Salalah but there afterwards followed a rapid increase in both small holdings and large farms. By 1986 the area under agriculture had risen to 2,230 hectares including 930 smallholdings and seven large farms of which at least two only grew Rhodes grass for large dairy units.[127] At Taqah the area under cultivation was 44 hectares, mainly tomatoes and fodder crops.

By the mid-1990s the cultivated area was about 3,000 hectares and included 796 farms, fewer than recorded in the 1980s, but the number of farms over 50 hectares had increased to nine, with four farms owning 41% of the total area.[139] Sixty percent of the land was either perennial fruit trees, banana and coconut being the most common, or fodder for livestock. Fodder was cut every 45 days with about eight crops each year. Most of the farm work was carried out by labourers with even the smallest farms employing at least one man.

Through the early 2000s Salalah grew quickly with little change in the area under agriculture. However, a few small areas were converted to non-agricultural use and in about 2013 a large block of about 260 hectares was taken out of agriculture for subsequent development. Consequently, by 2013 the area under agriculture had fallen to 2,683 hectares with fruit trees (50%), field crops (20%), fodder (15%) and vegetables (3%).[140]

Irrigated Agriculture in the Northern Najd

The northern Najd was well known for its harshness and at the height of summer even the tough nomadic pastoralists were forced back to the springs of the Najd and the Jabal. Apart from permanent springs at Ash Shisr and Muqshin, the only water was from very shallow wells dug by hand in wadis after a year when there had been good rainfall; water for drinking but certainly not for agriculture.

However, hidden deep below the arid surface of the Najd is an enormous store of fossil water left over from when the region was much wetter. In the 1950s and 1960s oil prospecting companies drilling for oil often found water, which, being under great pressure, came gushing to the surface from the aquifer deep below. These artesian wells were sometimes capped and at other times left flowing into the desert. The potential to use the water for agriculture was quickly grasped and by the early 1980s small private farms began to spring up close to the Salalah - Muscat highway and west to Ash Shisr. Two farms were established close to the artesian well at Dawkah and the first well at Ar Rakah was dug in 1983. By 1989 there were 42 farms producing Rhodes grass forage as well as a few date palms and vegetables, all for home consumption. At Ash Shisr there was estimated to be seven hectares under cultivation, again mainly Rhodes grass with date palms and some vegetables.

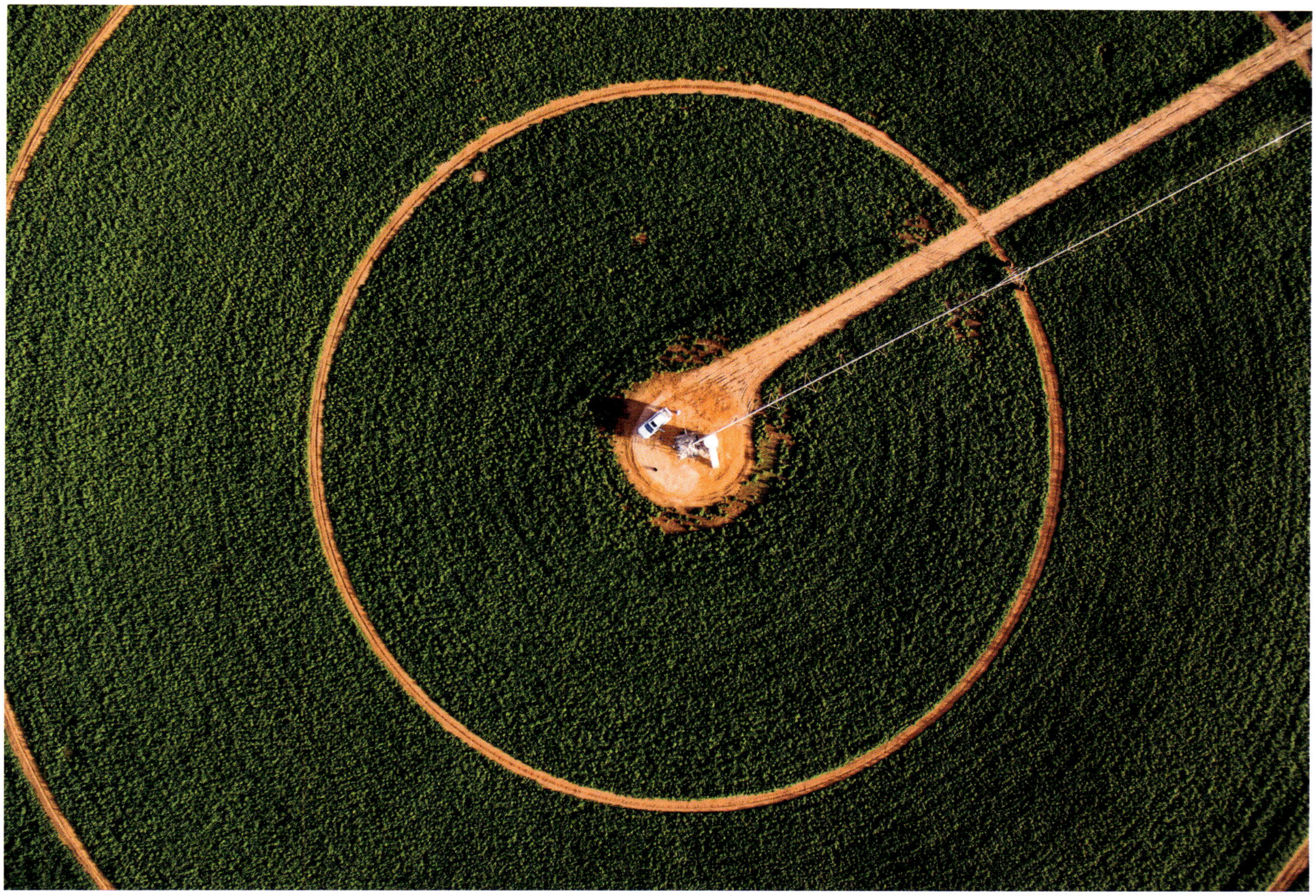

There was no machinery at this time and irrigation was by furrow.

In 1985 the Rahab experimental farm was set up near Marmul to investigate desert crop cultivation, soil management and the impact of agriculture on the ground water. Initially the farm cultivated 20 hectares of Rhodes grass, sold as fodder to local herders, and 15 hectares of other fodder crops and vegetables. Later it was expanded to 100 hectares with centre pivot irrigation; water being pumped from six wells sunk to 450-590 metres with the water table being 60 metres below ground.

In the early 1990s it was recognised that there was little opportunity to expand agriculture on the Salalah plain and the demand for fodder was growing enormously with much being brought in from outside the country. A study to develop irrigated agriculture began with an assessment of the suitability of the northern Najd, focusing on an area of 8,100 km² that included Dawkah, Ash Shisr, Hanfit and Qitbit. It found that in most areas the soils had poor structure, low nutrients and low organic matter and concluded that there was an area of 18,865 hectares that was moderately suitable and some 40 hectares that were highly suitable.[139]

A second phase of the Najd study was the setting up of the Najd Agriculture Research Station (NARS) that opened in 1994 at Al Nagha, just south of Dawkah. Its mission was to research best practice to achieve sustainable agriculture in the harsh conditions of the Najd. The team focused on the sustainable

The farms of Al Husaylah near Salalah produce a great range of fruits and vegetables ***(top left)*** while the farms of the northern Najd mainly grow Rhodes grass ***(above)*** though fruits such as strawberries ***(left bottom)*** are also cultivated.

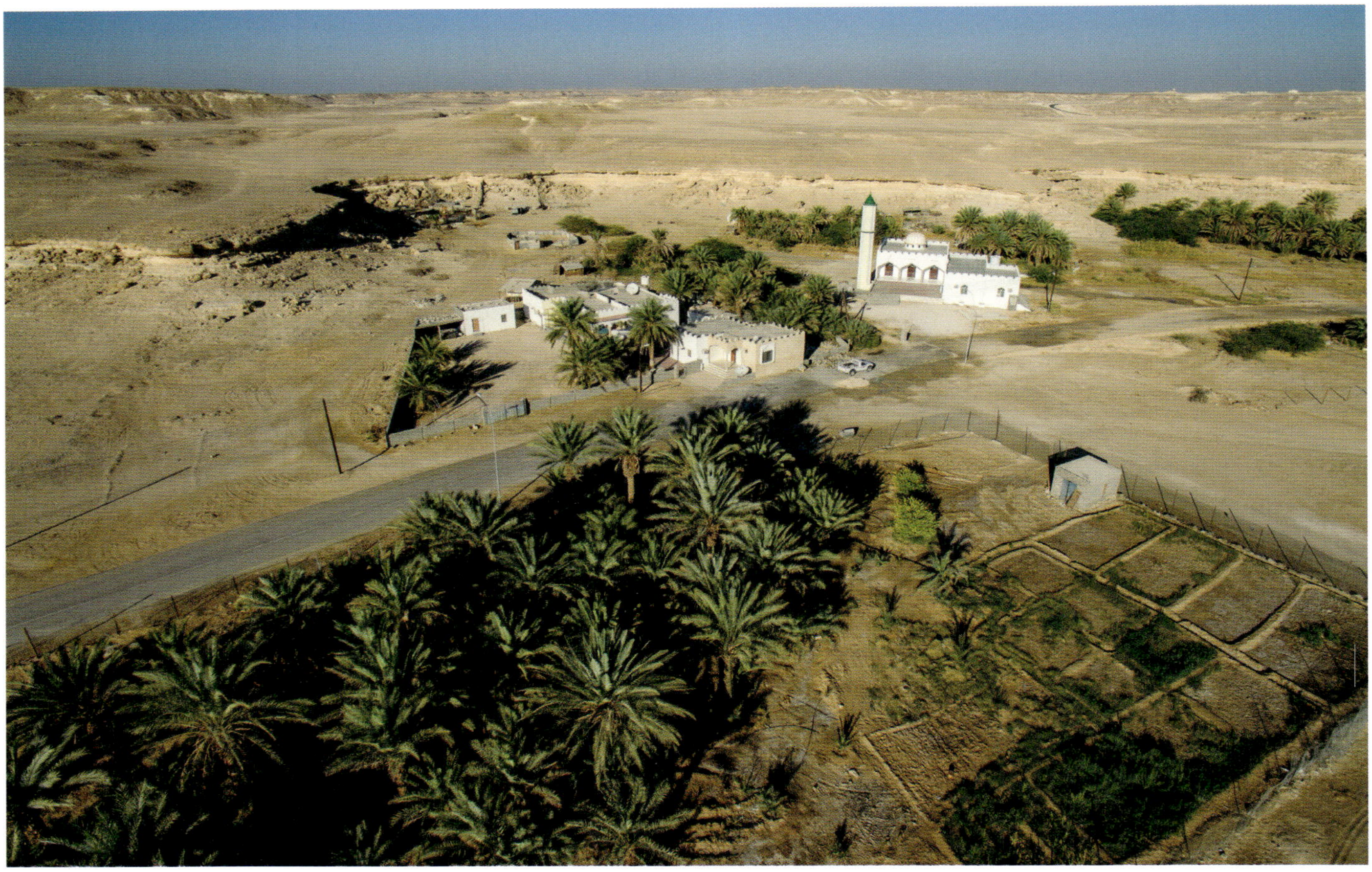

There are small farms and gardens scattered across the Najd, including at Muday *(above)*. In the northern Najd 55,000 date palms are grown at Rahab Farm ***(right top)*** while at Ar Rakah tomatoes are grown in a hydroponics system ***(right bottom).***

production of Rhodes grass fodder and set up centre pivot and linear movement irrigation systems. They experimented with irrigation, fertilizers, and pest control as well as best practices for seeding and harvesting. After two years of operation they achieved good yields of Rhodes grass, although they had to apply high levels of nitrogen, and they found some improvement in the organic matter content of the soil. However, they noted a continuous decline in the groundwater level.[139]

At the same time the growing of increasing amounts of fodder on the Al Batinah coastal plain of northern Oman had resulted in falling water tables and freshwater being replaced by salt water. It was decided to move fodder farms to the Najd and as a result the area under agriculture grew until, by 2013, there were nearly 4,000 hectares under production, growing forage crops (62%), vegetable crops (22%), date and fruit trees (15%) and field crops (1%).[140] The largest of the farms has 925 hectares under agriculture and uses 20 centre pivot systems; 19 for growing Rhodes grass and one for alfalfa. There are seven harvests of Rhodes grass each year and 12 of alfalfa; all is sold to feed livestock. The level of the groundwater is falling.

The Rahab Farm project, also in the Najd, closed in 2015 and the site is currently being used for 55,000 date palms as part of the Million Date Palm Project. Small farms have been developed in many wadis of the eastern Najd, such as Wadi Arah and close to many of the towns and villages, including Al Mazyunah and Muday, in the west. Elsewhere there are farms at Thumrayt and on the coast at Ash Shuwaymiyyah and

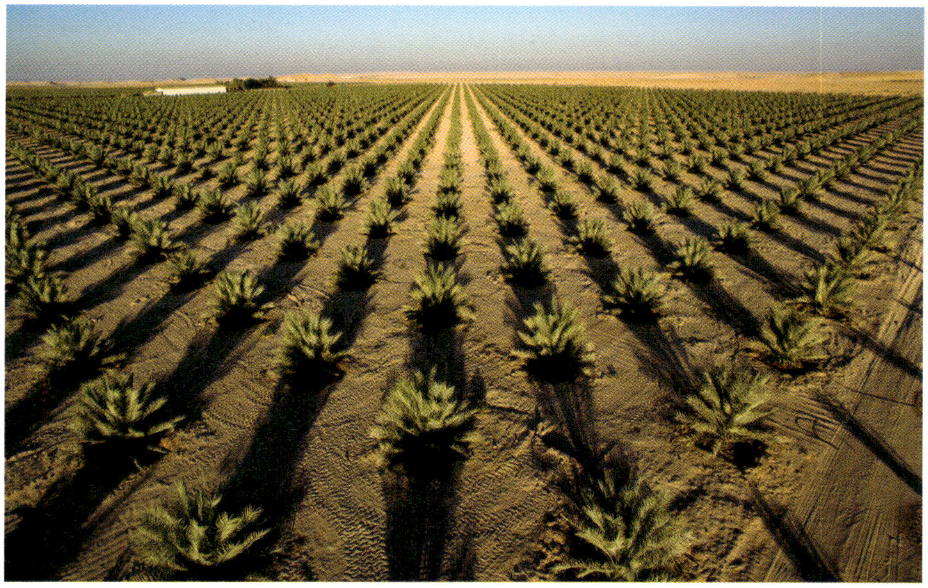

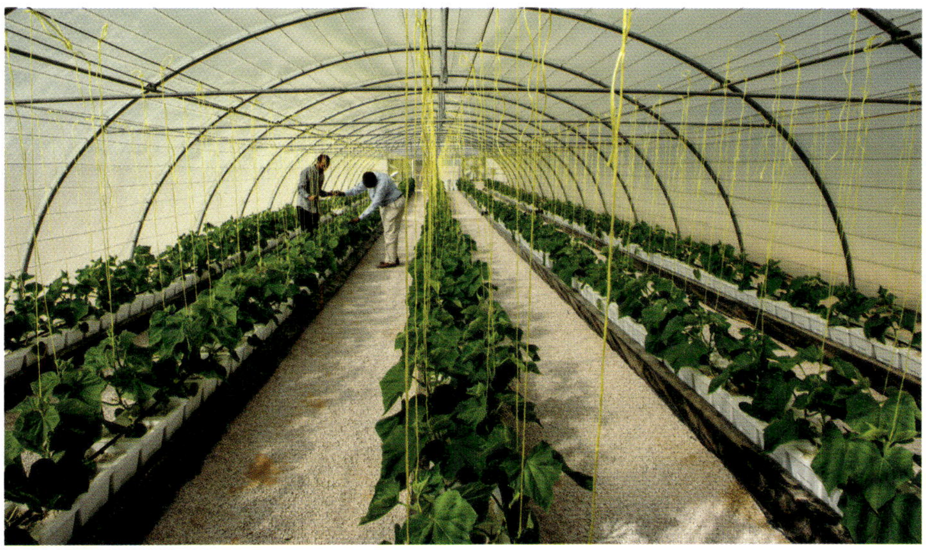

Sharbthat. These are mostly small farms using flood irrigation from springs and shallow wells.

Agriculture – Sustainability

The 'greening of the Najd' has opened up new areas of Oman to agriculture while also allowing fodder farms to be shifted away from the Al Batinah coastal plain of northern Oman and the Jarbib (Salalah plain) where a combination of rapid urban development and falling water tables with salt water intrusion has led to reduced areas suitable for agriculture. The growing of food crops has also helped Oman on its path towards food security and reduced dependence on external markets for fruit and vegetables, as well as for animal fodder.

However, there are still considerable challenges to ensure that agriculture on the Salalah plain and the Najd is sustainable. Currently the valuable fossil water of the Najd is being used at a greater rate than it can be replenished. Furthermore it is mostly being used to grow fodder for livestock that not only contributes little to the economy of Dhofar but is responsible for widespread overgrazing of the rangelands.

Hydroponics is used around the world and even on one farm at Ar Rakah in the northern Najd to grow fruit and vegetables. Plants are grown without soil and receive their nutrients from a water-based nutrient solution that can be strictly controlled and recycled. In recent years, in some countries where climatic conditions are less favourable for crops (dry areas, arid soils with low fertility), hydroponics is being used to grow animal fodder in special warehouses and growing rooms.[141] Hydroponics uses less space, little or no pesticides and most importantly a fraction of the water of conventional farming practices seen in the Najd.

Hydroponics for fodder production could be part of a solution to falling water tables. However, ultimately there needs to be a smaller and regulated livestock sector where livestock and livestock product availability is matched with demand. This will reduce the overgrazing of the rangelands and thus reliance on expensive supplements, leading to lower costs for herders, reduced fodder production and allowing more ground water to be used for the growing of food.

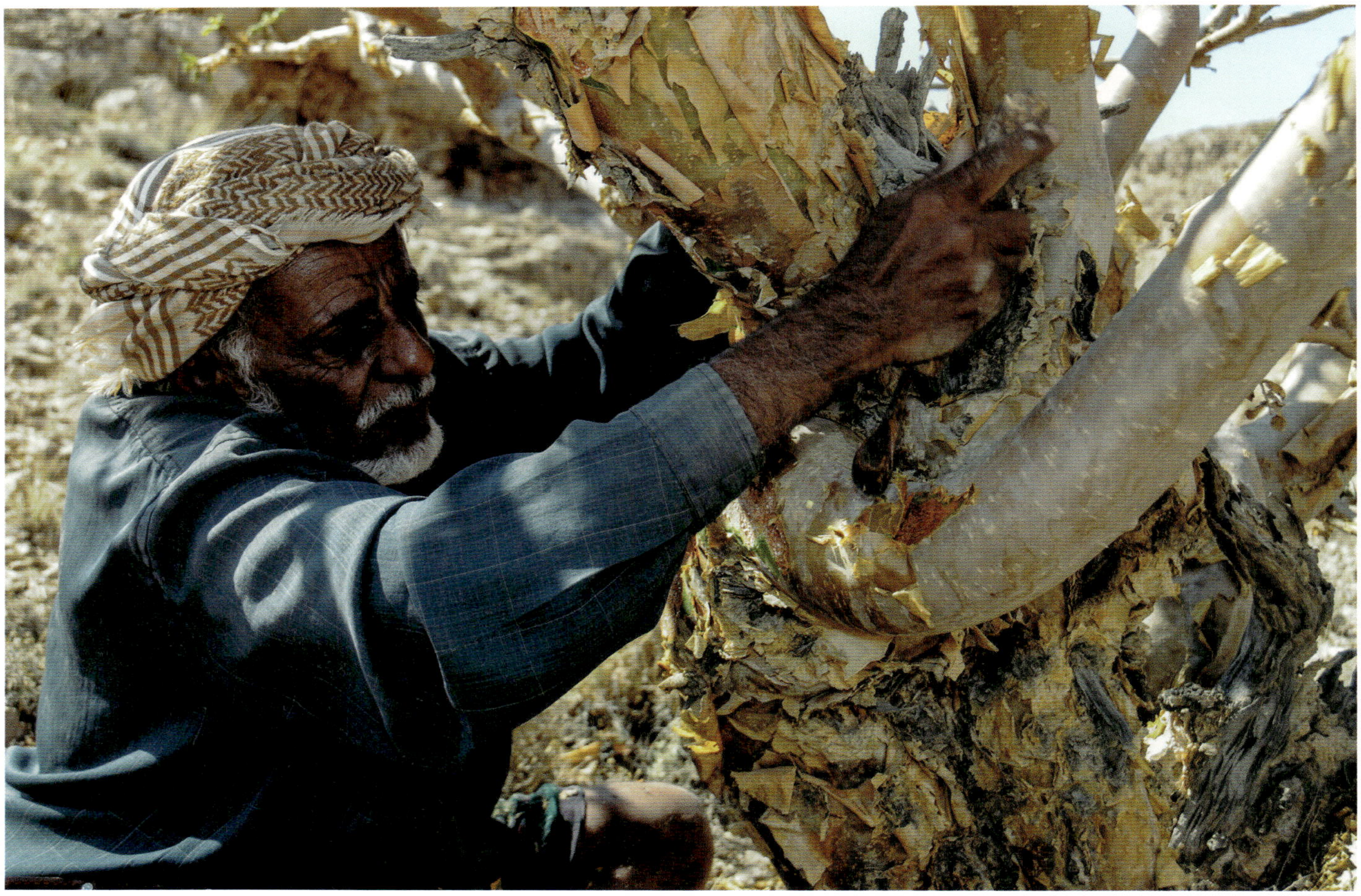

Frankincense harvesting

In the ancient world such was the importance of frankincense that more than 2,000 years ago the Roman Emperor Augustus Caesar dispatched his general Aelius Gallus to find and conquer the incense lands; he was not successful.[142]

The frankincense tree (*Boswellia sacra,* Ar. Shajarat al-*Lubān*, Ji. Meġerót) occurs in north and south-facing arid areas of all three Dhofar mountains. On Jabal Samhan it is found principally in the upper reaches of the dry northward-flowing wadis of the Najd or Fejr zone including Wadi Halit, Wadi Andhur and Wadi Arah. Here the trees produce the famous high quality *hojari* resin while further east in the wadis north of Hasik is found the illustrious *hasaki* resin. Frankincense is also found on the Salawt plain, including the area close to Sadah, and produces a lower quality resin known as *sahaali*.

On Jabal Al Qara frankincense occurs from Wadi Saalafan in the east to Wadi Gharah in the west, including Wadi Amat, Wadi Uyun, Wadi Hirayt, Wadi Dhahbun and of course Wadi Dawkah, part of which has been inscribed on the UNESCO World Heritage List as one of four components of the 'Land of Frankincense' site. Trees in this zone are famous for the high quality *najdi* resin. On the south side of the Jabal, frankincense is found in the arid area that marks the transition zone between Jabal Al Qara and Jabal Al Qamar. It extends from Wadi Ishat and Wadi Adawnab in the east though Wadi Al Mughsayl and Wadi Ashawq to Wadi Aful in the west. Here the frankincense resin is called *shazari*

On the north side of Jabal Samhan a frankincense harvester uses a traditional tool, called *manqaf* ***(above)***, to make the first cuts of the season. Once cut, the frankincense tree produces a gum known locally as *lubān* in Arabic and as *śáḥaz* in Jibbāli ***(right)***.

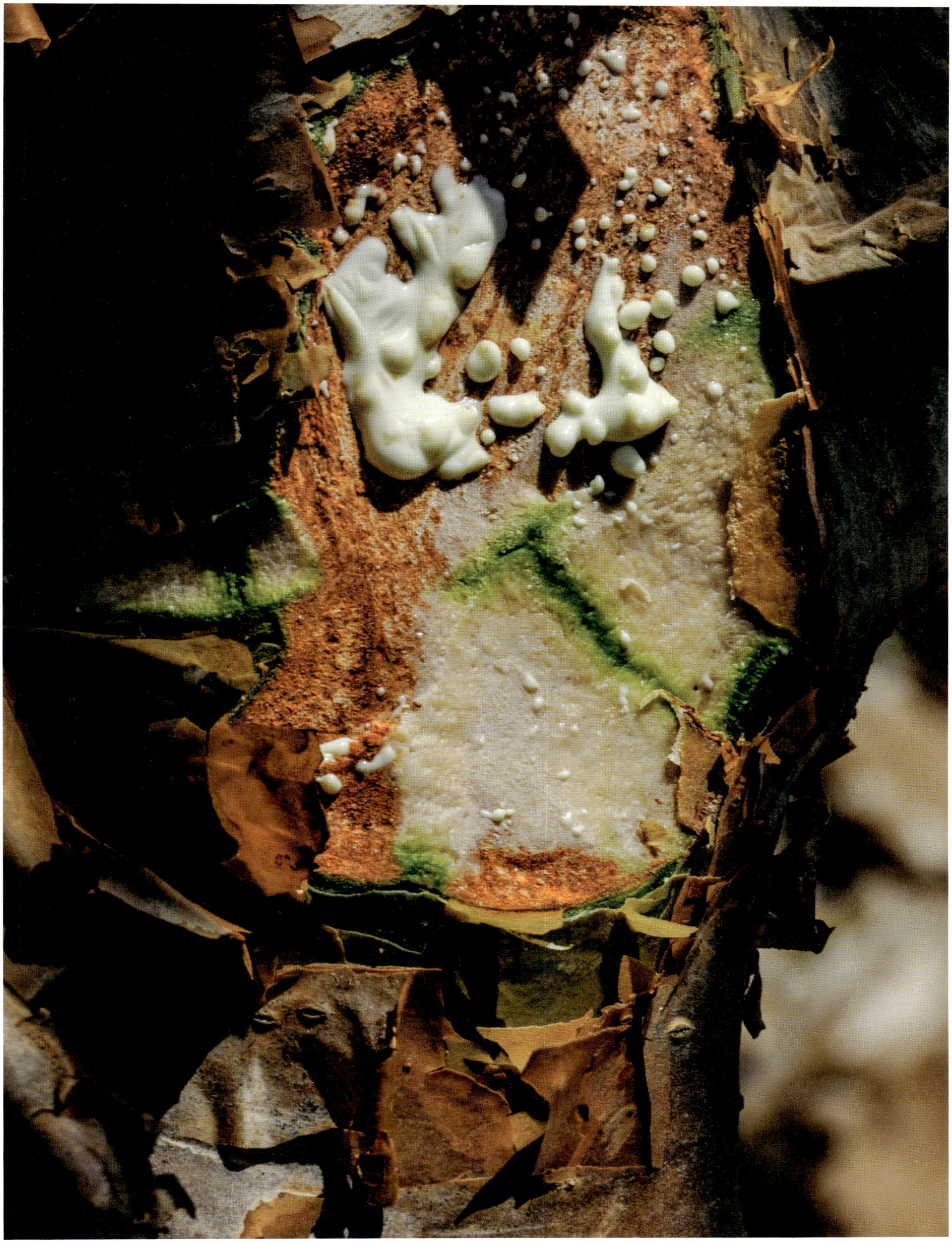

and is generally considered to be of a lower quality than the *najdi* and *hojari*.

On Jabal Al Qamar frankincense grows beyond the watershed, on the arid north facing slopes and wadi sides of Wadi Aydam and Wadi Sayq. Here the trees yield the *najdi* resin while the *sahaali* resin is collected from small stands of trees on the seaward facing slopes at Al Fazayih.

The frankincense groves were traditionally owned by the pastoralists of the Jabal although as Bertram Thomas observed in 1930, the herdsmen who owned the frankincense groves rented them to other clans in exchange for half the produce.[23] Other groves were owned or rented by merchants from coastal towns such as Sadah or Mirbat[143] and outsiders, including Somalis, were hired to cut the trees and harvest the resin, sometimes in return for livestock[126] or as is more common today, for cash or a share of the crop.[144]

In Jabal Samhan, the main harvest took place during the hottest period when other regions of Dhofar were experiencing the monsoon. This began with the first and careful cutting in late May and then over a period of about a month the incisions were revisited and cleaned before the resin flowed, marking the beginning of the main harvest. Harvesting took three to four months after which cutters and camels made their way to the coast arriving in a processional column.[143]

In the Najd the timing of the main harvest on the north side of the Jabal was likely similar to that for Jabal Samhan: June to October. However, the main harvest in the arid zone around Wadi Al Mughsayl was during the months of April, May and June that preceded the arrival of the monsoon.

Frankincense continues to be harvested today, much as it has been since the times of Ptolemy. However, an observed increase in the frequency of cutting and harvesting may well be endangering the trees and threatening the future of this ancient practice.[145]

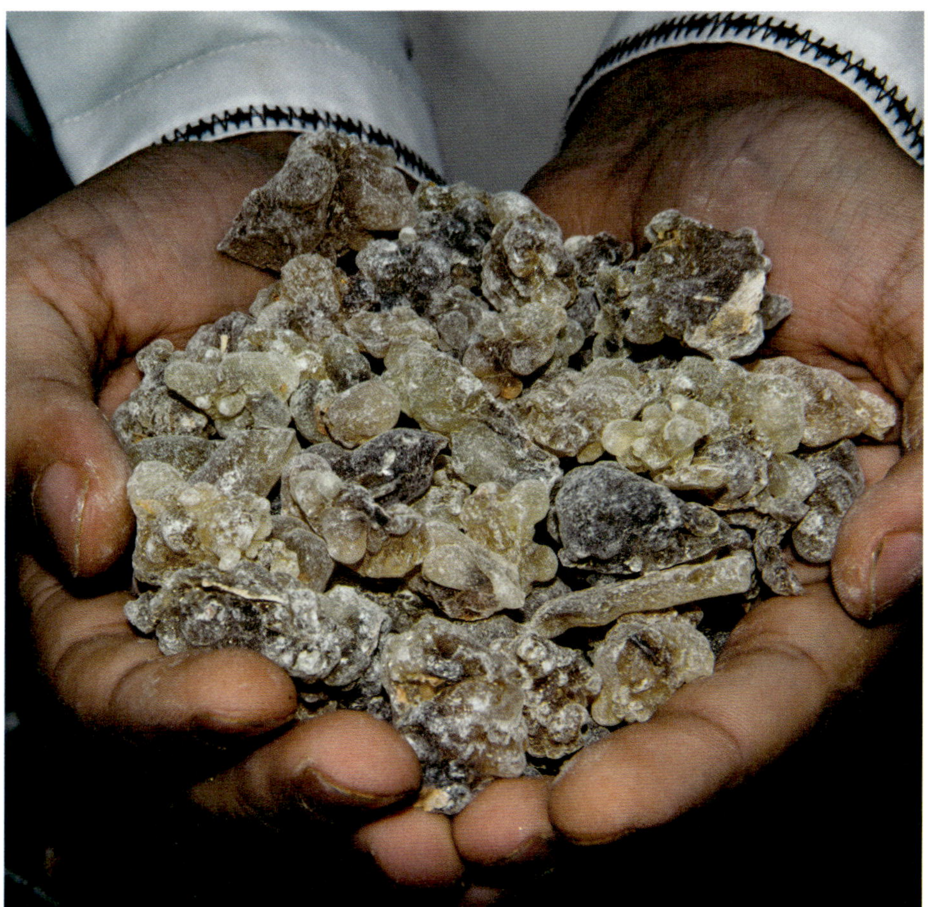

The frankincense gum is harvested when dry ***(left)*** and used in the home or distributed for sale.

Beekeeping, here on the southern escarpment of Jabal Samhan ***(right)***, is a relatively recent practice and only possible with the honey bee *(Apis mellifera jemenitica)*. However, honey is sometimes collected from wild colonies of both the honey bee and dwarf honey bee *(Apis florea)*.

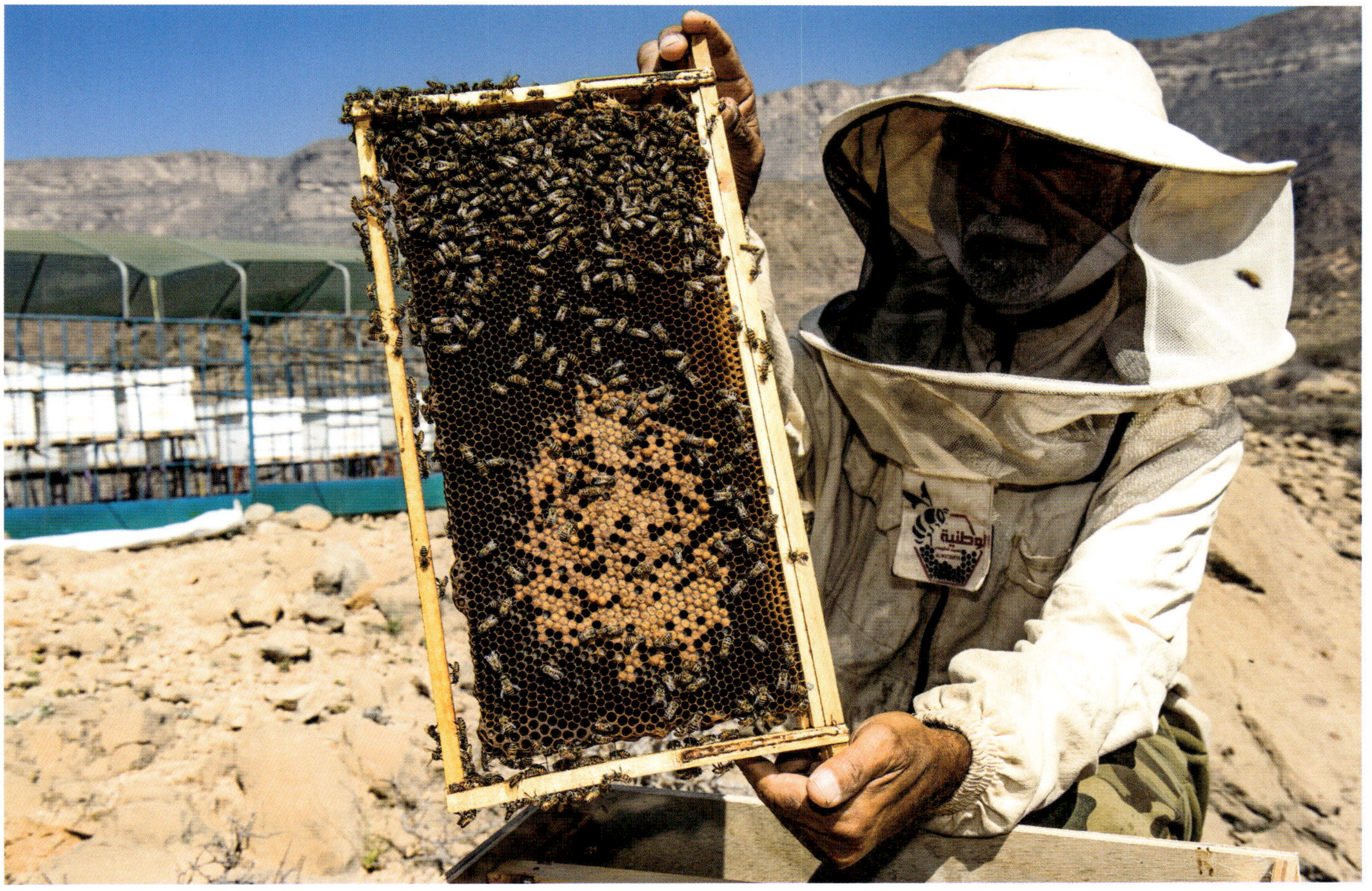

Beekeeping

Beekeeping was not practiced in Dhofar before 1970, although the wild honey bee (*Apis mellifera jemenitica*) does occur in the mountains, and pastoralists harvested the honey crop. Colonies are often found on cliff faces and these were usually removed by specialist honey hunters who descended by rope and removed the comb with a cleft stick, dropping the mixture of bees and honey into a leather bag. However, little thought was given to the survival of the colony or the damage done.[146]

Pilot beekeeping schemes, using modern (Langstroth) hives, commenced in the Jabal in 1979 and the prospects for beekeeping in Dhofar were considered good.[124] Local people first adopted beekeeping in the 1990s and by 2012 the agricultural census reported 23 beehives in the Wilayat of Taqah, 25 hives in the Wilayat of Dalkut and 1,685 hives in the Wilayat of Salalah; though most of the latter are thought to be on farms on the Salalah plain.[54] Reports of local people indicate that beekeeping is more widespread than the census data suggests, both on the lush woodlands and pastures of Jabal Al Qamar and Jabal Al Qara as well as on Jabal Samhan and in the southern Najd.

According to the beekeepers, the main season for honey production is after the *khareef* when many species of plant are in flower. The honey from this season is known as *al zuhur* from the Arabic word for flowers. Other seasons follow the flowering of Sidr (*Ziziphus spina-christi*) in November to February, frankincense in March to May and Ṯemmàr (*Acacia senegal*) and Simr (*Acacia tortilis*) in April to May.

One of the principal threats to the honey bee across the Arabian Peninsula is hybridisation with imported subspecies[147] such as those kept by beekeepers in Salalah and elsewhere. This has been recorded by local people who are also concerned about the movement of bees - something that carries an increased risk of disease. In recent years beekeepers from northern Oman have brought their bees south during the cool months of the monsoon, not to produce honey but to increase the number of their hives by swarming.

Fisheries

Before 1970

Before 1970 the sardine fishery was the largest fishery in Dhofar and was dominated by the Indian oil sardine (*Sardinella longiceps*). Landings reached a peak in December and January and while Taqah was considered to be the centre of sardine fishing, sardines were also fished by semi-nomadic pastoralists and settled coastal communities throughout Dhofar.

Sardines were caught by beach seine using dugout canoes or flat-bottomed small planked boats known as *sambuk* of about 7-9 metres length and 1.5 metres width. These were locally made of imported hardwood, mainly from India, and each was crewed by 11 men (10 oarsmen and one captain) with a single large net. The manufacture and repair of the nets was a hugely time consuming task and was done by the women year round. As the full nets were too heavy to pull ashore, they were usually emptied by men with smaller nets from the boats or, if inshore, by men wading out from the beach.[126]

Thousands of tons of sardines were landed and sun dried for 2-3 days in large drying areas where women turned the fish and kept scavenging birds at bay. Most was sold or bartered as fodder to cattle-owning pastoralists who faced dry season shortages while some was used as fertiliser. Sardines were also eaten locally and used in the production of oil that was then employed for the waterproofing of boats and as fuel in lamps.

Inshore fishing for other species also played an import role in the lives of coastal communities before 1970. Some had small wooden vessels but others relied on inflated goatskins on which they swam to set

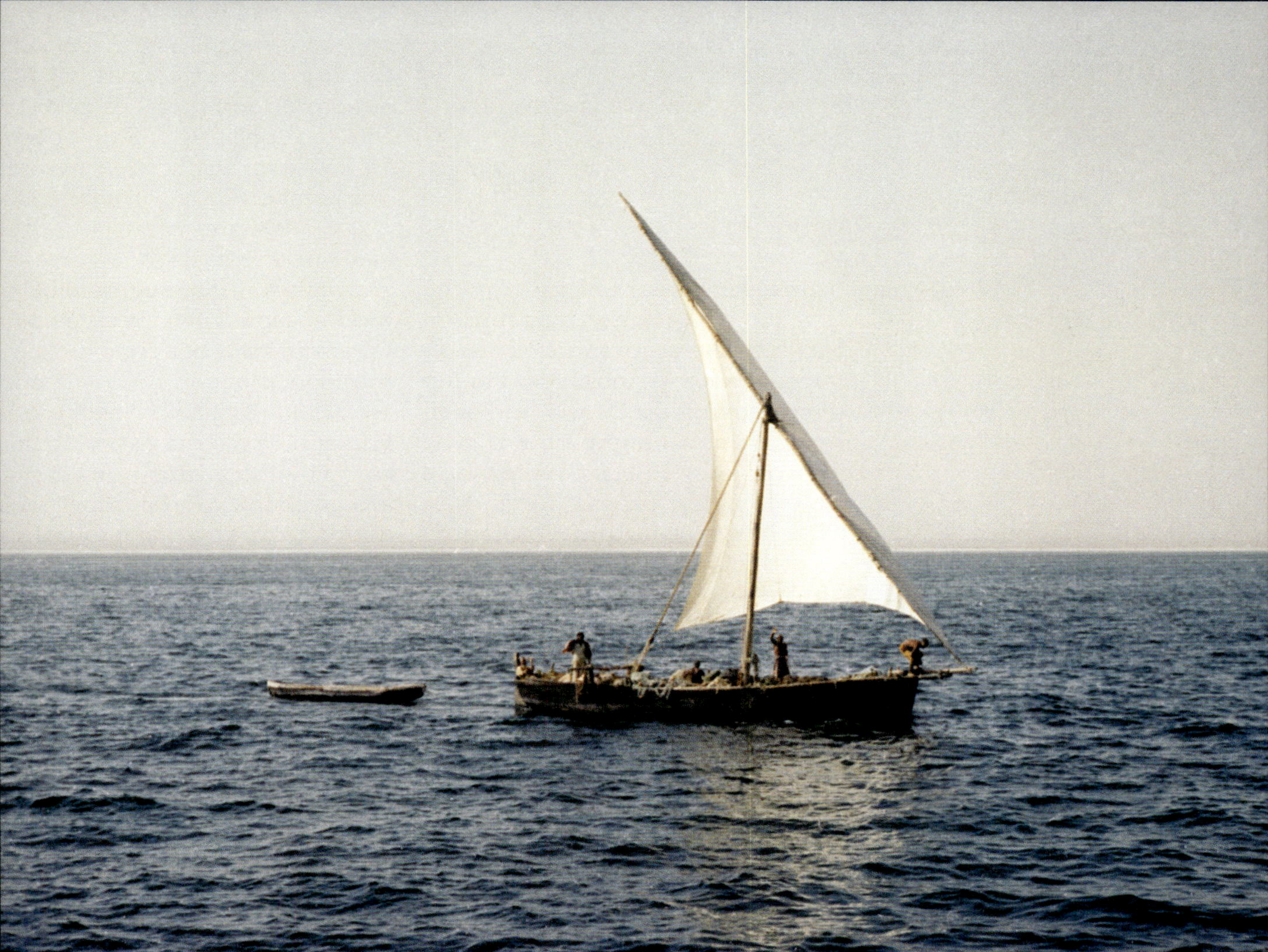

Before 1970 the *kambari* or *sambuk* ***(above)***, planked with mango wood and

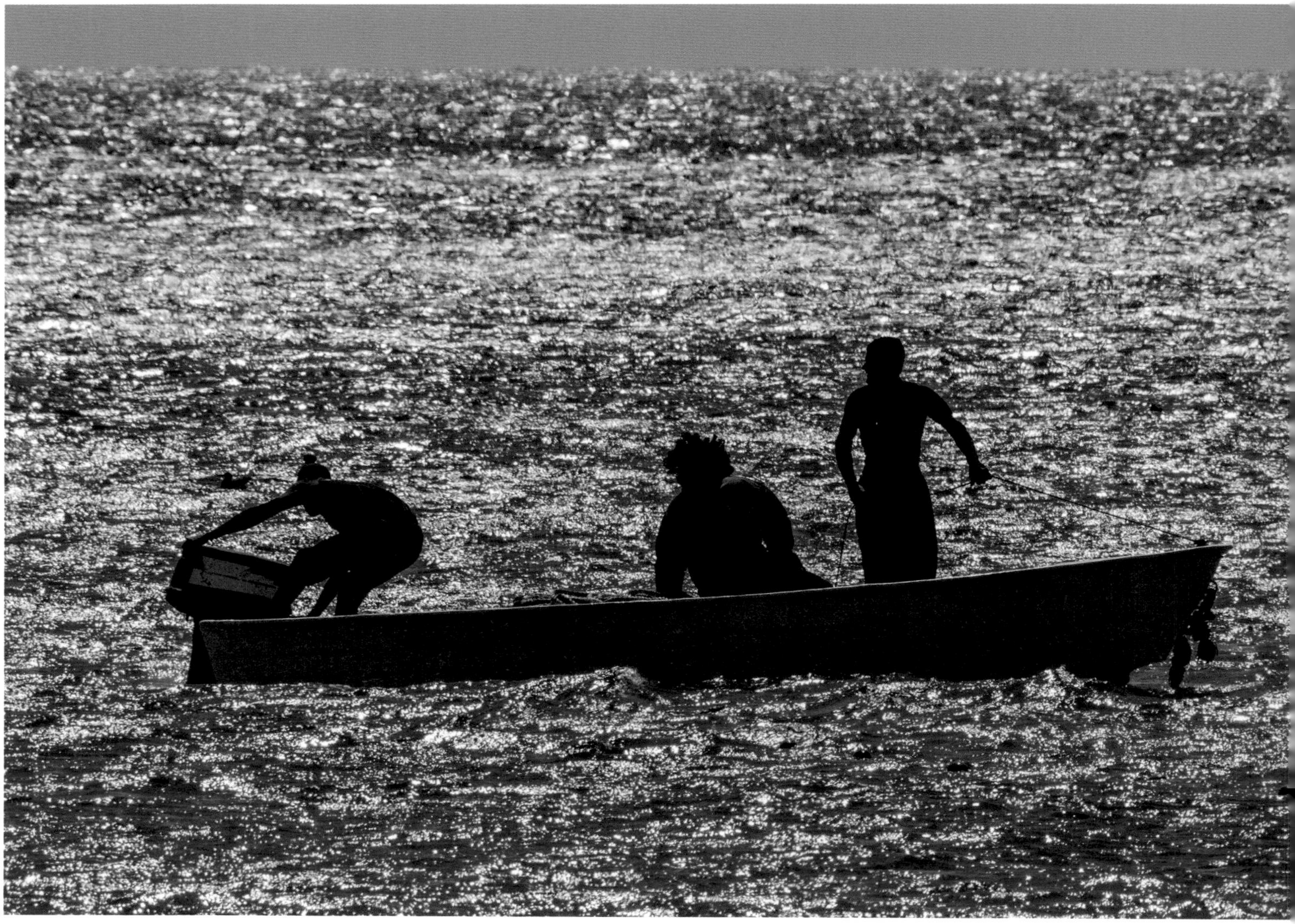

The sardine fishery is thriving, particularly between Salalah city and Taqah. Seine nets are laid by small fishing boats ***(above)*** and then pulled ashore by vehicles where the sardines are hauled to drying grounds just inland ***(opposite)***. Most sardines are used as livestock feed.

their nets, often at night when many species, including sharks, come close to shore to feed.[148] Sharks, together with species such as mackerel and tuna, were cleaned, cut into strips, salted and left to dry for several weeks. These were held in crude partially buried 'warehouses' before being collected by trading ships, usually from Sur, and thence to Yemen, East Africa and Zanzibar. Small sail boats owned by local fishermen plied the coastal route to Yemen. The importance of shark fin was noted as early as 1928 when Bertram Thomas recorded that the fins and tails of shark were sent to China, 'where they command a high price and make an epicurean soup.'[149] Dried fish, was also traded to the towns of Oman's northern interior such as Nizwa and Sinaw. Dried shark, in particular, was also an important part of the diet of the nomadic pastoralists as it did not perish and could be carried for many months.

Some coastal groups, including those of the Al Hallaniyyat Islands and Ash Shuwaymiyyah, were famous for their ability to hunt turtles while others hunted dolphins.[126] The variety of seafood taken is not only testimony to the skills of the local people but also a necessity of living in extremely harsh conditions.

After 1970

Once markets were opened in the early 1970s, fishermen, supported by government loans and subsidies, set about updating their gear. Aluminium and fibreglass boats replaced wooden ones, outboard engines replaced paddles, nylon nets replaced cotton and palm-leaf nets, and small ice-factories allowed the refrigeration of the fish.

Fishing became much easier and the fishermen adopted modern hook-and-line practices and started to use traps for pelagic fish such as seabream species, emperor (*Lethrinus* spp.) and porgy (*Diplodus* spp.). Small pelagic fish, including sardines (*Sardinella* spp.) and Indian mackerel (*Rastrelliger kanagurta*), are caught by hand-thrown cast nets and by large beach seines over 100m long that are set off sandy beaches by small skiffs and hauled ashore by four-wheel-drive vehicles. Larger pelagic fish such as tuna (*Thunnus* spp.) and groupers (e.g. *Epinephelus* spp.) are caught by gill or tangle nets, often set on the sea floor, and by trolling, where a baited fish hook or lure is towed behind a small skiff.

Fish production from the artisanal fishermen increased from the 1980s and overall has continued to increase through to the present day. Total landings for Dhofar in 1985 came to 18,707 metric tons compared with 43,132 metric tons for 2016.[150] However, this is not the case for all species, particularly for high value fish that were actively pursued as early as the 1970s. For example, yellowfin tuna (*Thunnus albacares*) landings have shown a steady decrease across the Sultanate, although some increase after 2015. Similarly catches of skipjack tuna (*Katsuwonus pelamis*) have declined sharply from high levels in the mid-1990s. Another much sought-after fish is kingfish (*Scomberomorus commerson*) and, after a steep drop in landings from the 1980s, reached very low

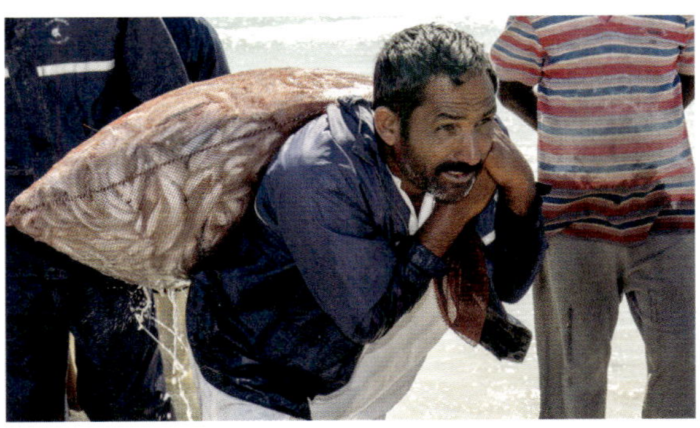

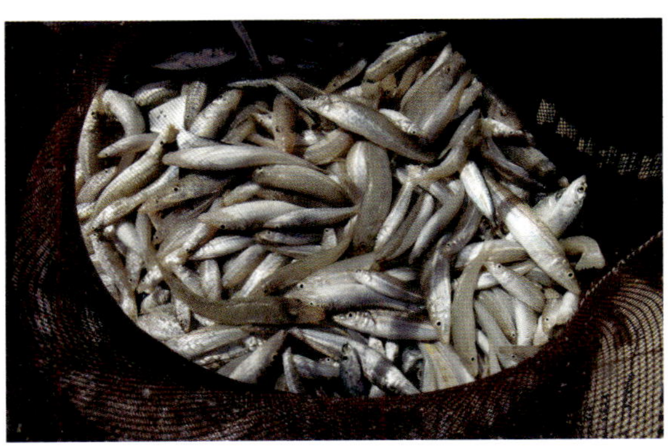

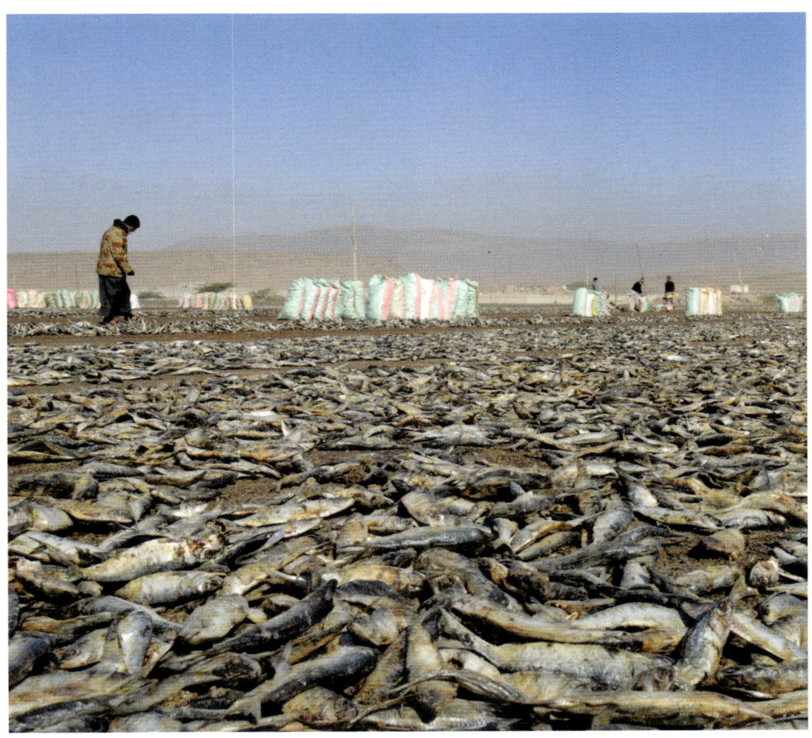

levels at the turn of the century before showing a slight recovery.

As some high-value fisheries deteriorated, fishermen switched their attention to other species and many of these have shown a steady increase in their catch. The landings of queen fish, barracuda and sailfish have all increased since 1990, though the sailfish catch declined after 2013. Mackerel landings have also increased while the number of groupers being landed has remained steady, albeit with a decline since 2011.

Sharks are heavily fished, for flesh and fins, with a steady increase in landings since 1990. Four species dominated landings in 2016: scalloped hammerhead (*Sphyrna lewini*), great hammerhead (*Sphyrna mokarran*), hardnose shark (*Carcharhinus macloti*), and graceful shark (*Carcharhinus amblyrhynchoides*).[150] All four species have dramatically declined across the region in the last few decades;[120] both hammerhead species face a high risk of extinction and are classified as Endangered on the IUCN Red List of Threatened Species, while both the hardnose shark and graceful shark are considered Near Threatened.

The sardine fishery remains one of the most important and although there seemed to be a decline in catch after 2000, reaching a low of 1,398 metric tons in 2012, it increased since that time to 7,811 metric tons in 2016. Annual fluctuation in catch has been attributed to a correlated fluctuation in spawning success, which in turn is strongly influenced by environmental parameters such as the strength of the annual

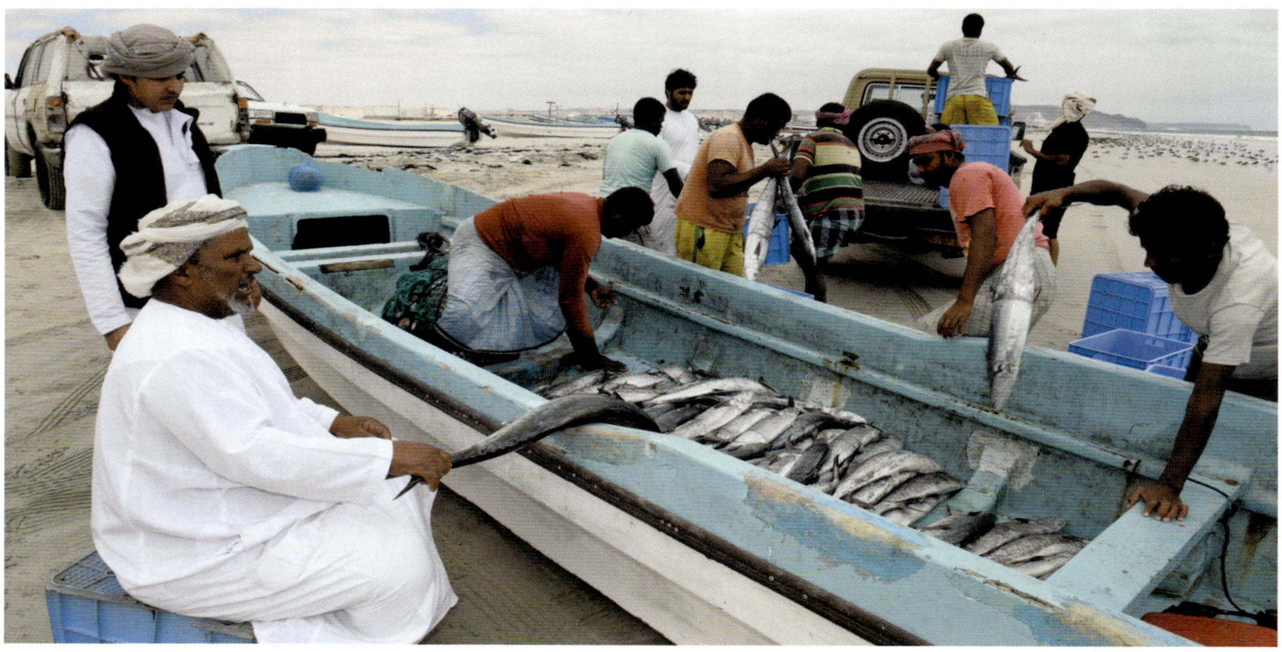

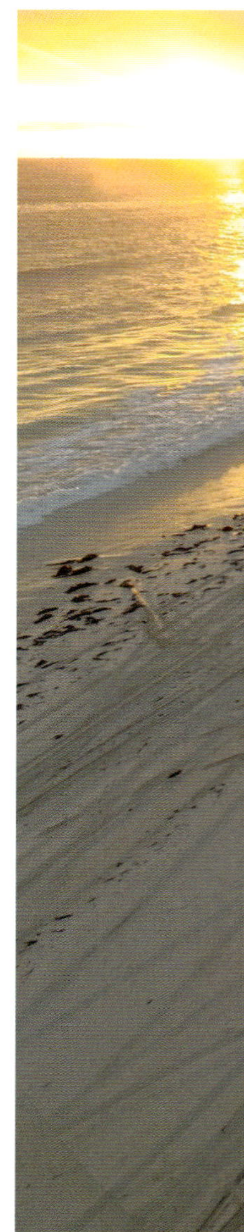

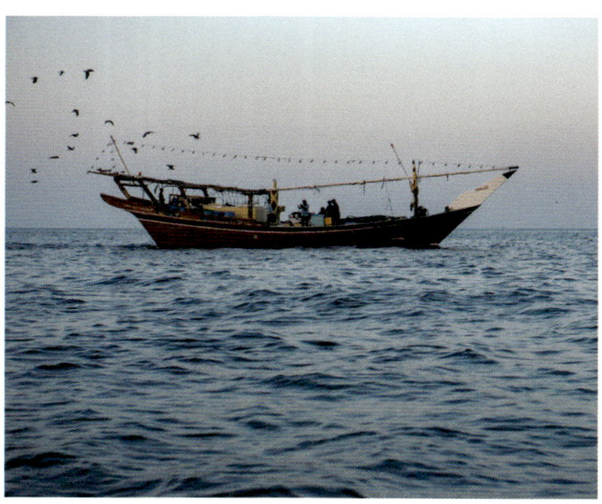

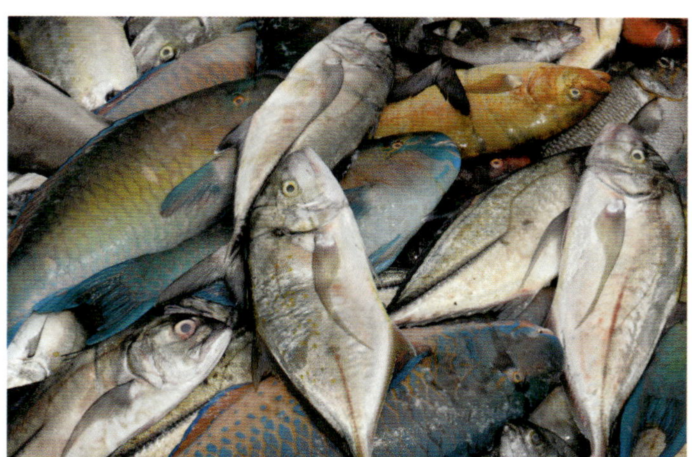

monsoon and the associated upwelling.

A further development after 1970 was the signing of agreements with foreign fishing companies that operated offshore vessels. There were trawlers that targeted pelagic fishes including croaker (*Johnius* spp.), seabream, ribbonfish (*Trichiurus lepturus*) and catfish (*Arius* spp.), and which were not allowed within 10 miles of the shoreline. Long-liner fleets fished yellowfin tuna, longtail tuna (*Thunnus tonggol*), sailfish (*Istiophorus platypterus*) and sharks and were to remain 20 miles offshore.[151] By the mid-1990s there were more than 100 vessels operating in Omani waters throughout the year and landing more than 30,000 metric tons of fish.[150] This was not sustainable and small-scale fishermen felt their livelihoods were threatened. Following a further increase in the number of vessels in the early 2000s the decision was taken in 2009 to ban all trawlers from 2011. This move was broadly welcomed.

The waters of the Al Hallaniyyat Islands bay support some of the largest fish stocks in Dhofar. These are fished by large fleets of inshore skiffs operating out of settlements such as Ash Shuwaymiyyah ***(left top)*** and Sharbthat ***(below)*** and by dhow fleets ***(left bottom)*** that come from much further afield.

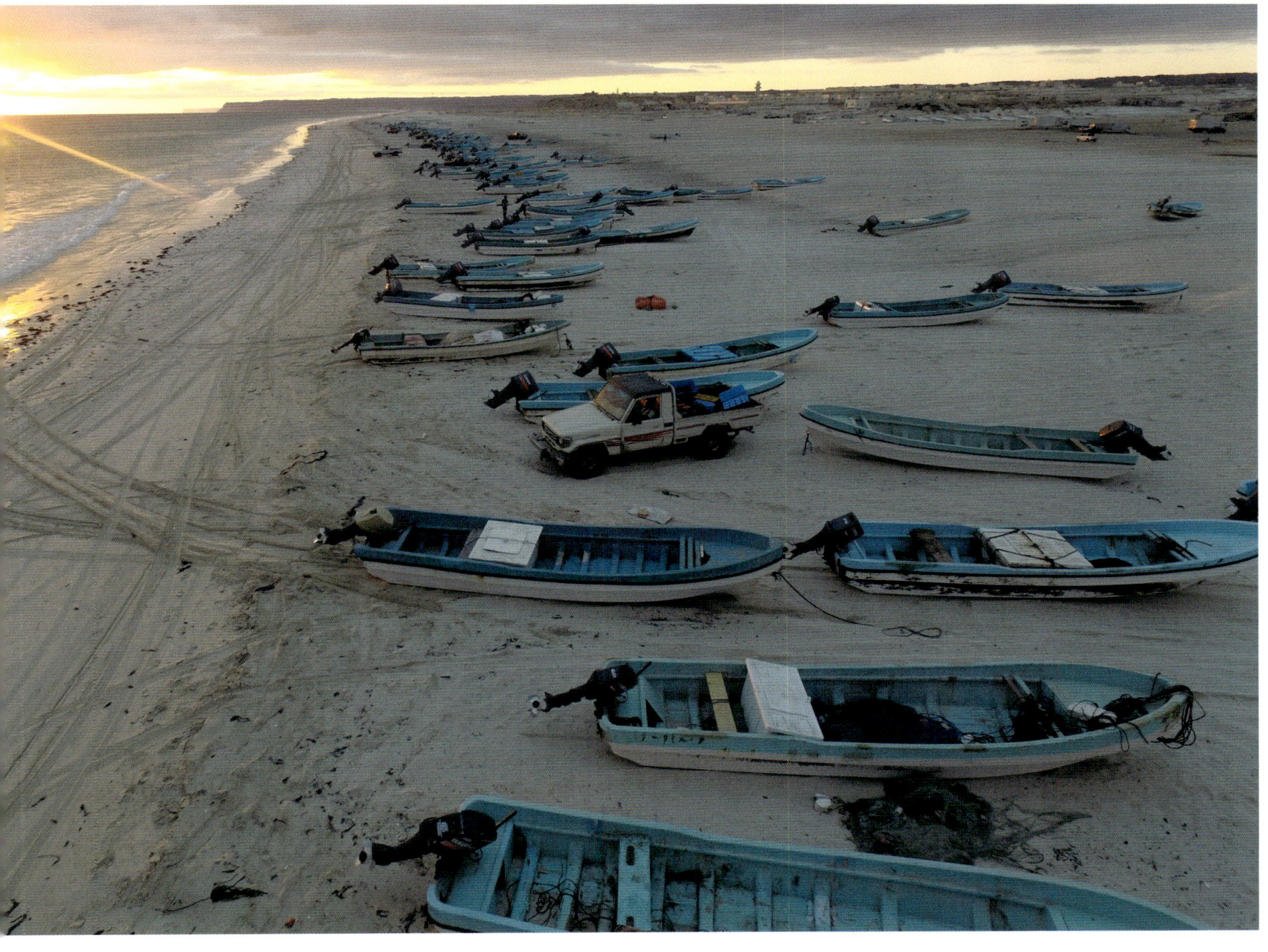

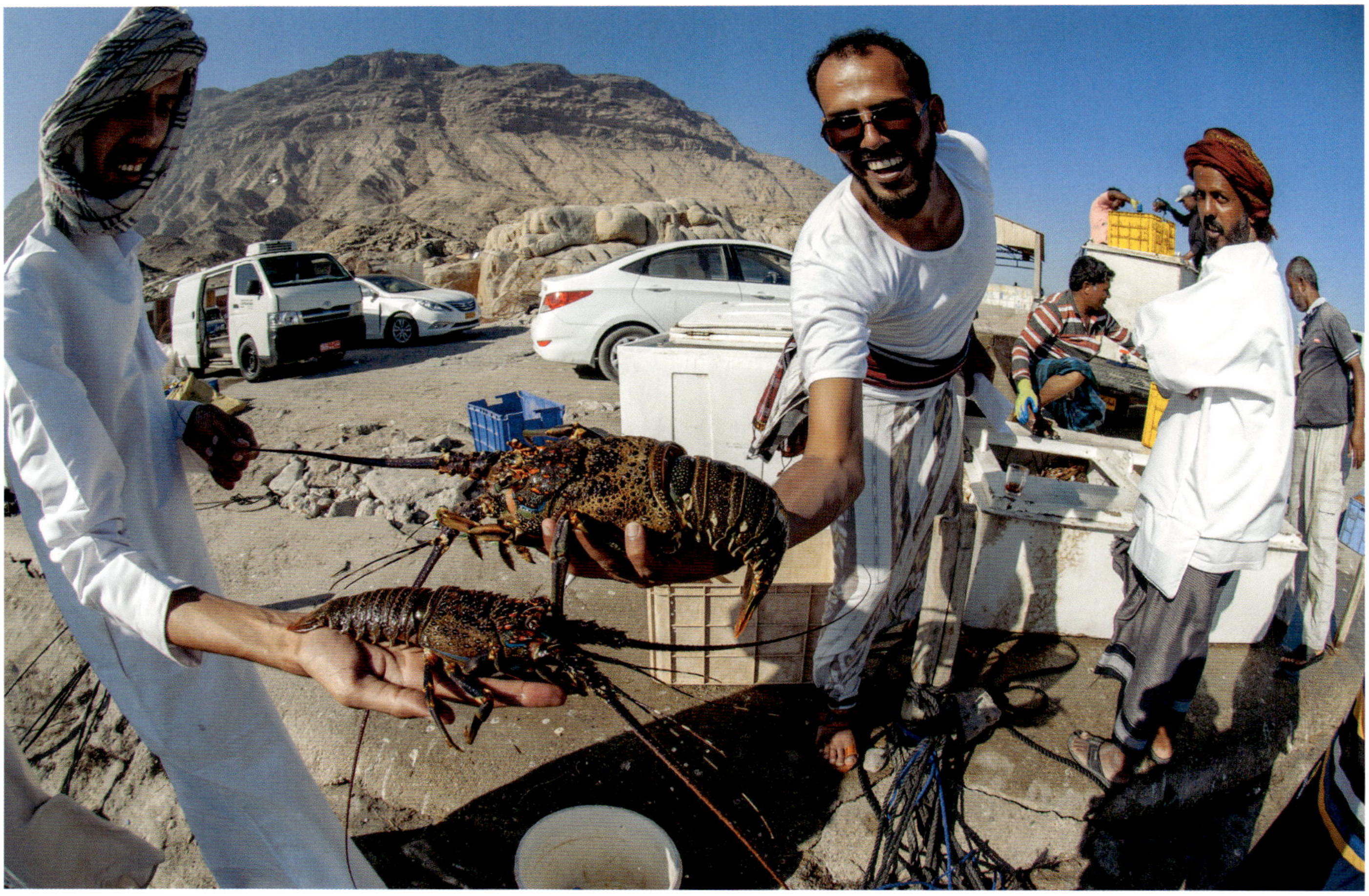

High-value seafood such as spiny lobster and abalone are in great demand and when the season is open there is intense activity in coastal towns such as Hadbin ***(above and right)***. Abalone is collected by free-divers who bring it ashore where the meat is removed, boiled and air dried before being sold ***(right)***.

Shellfish

Traditional coastal communities harvested shellfish including mussels, abalone, limpets, sea urchins and rock oysters, which were collected by women while sea cucumber, lobsters, crabs and cuttlefish were gathered by men.[148]

The spiny lobster (*Panulirus homarus*) was eaten for subsistence but it was not until the 1980s that its high value was recognised. At first they were captured by tangle nets and metal traps but since 1984 there was some uptake of plastic side-entry traps. The main fisheries were the rocky shores from Sharbthat south to Dalkut, including the Al Hallaniyyat Islands. However, because of the high value of this fishery, lobster catches quickly declined. In the mid-1980s measures reducing the fishing season to six months, to prevent the capture of small individuals and to ban the use of spear guns and nets, were already in place or being considered. However, these measures had limited impact and between 1986 and 2000 landings declined from 2000 to 500 tons.[152] The further shortening of the fishing season to 15 October – 15 December did arrest the decline somewhat but 2008 and 2009 saw the lowest yields on record, some 157 and a mere 19 tons respectfully. In 2010 the fishing season was set to March 1st - April 30th and by 2016 landings had recovered to nearly 500 tons.[150]

Abalone (*Haliotis mariae*), locally known as *sufaila*, is a marine gastropod that is endemic to the rocky southern coasts of Oman and Yemen and is not in evidence elsewhere. It is found

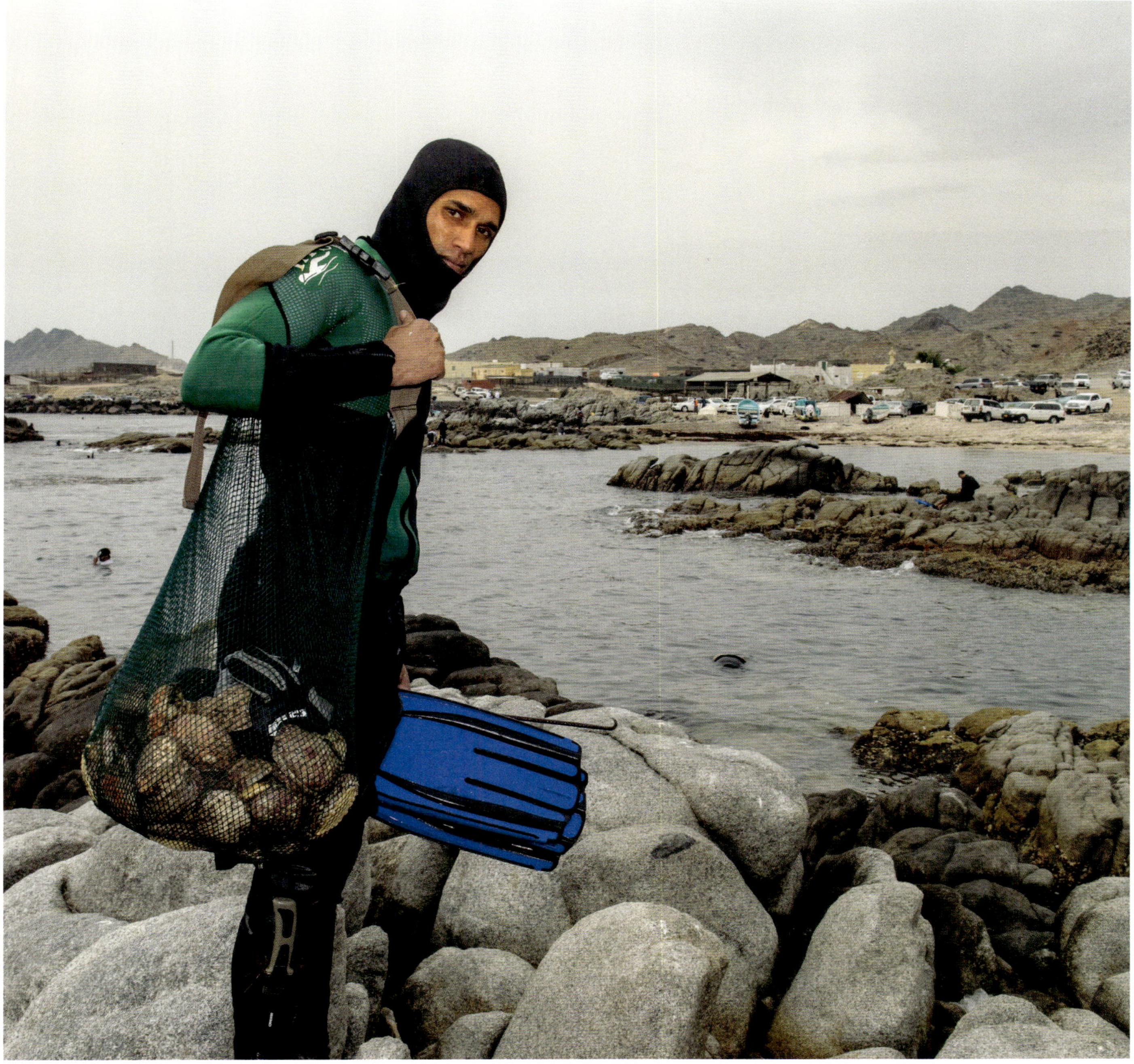

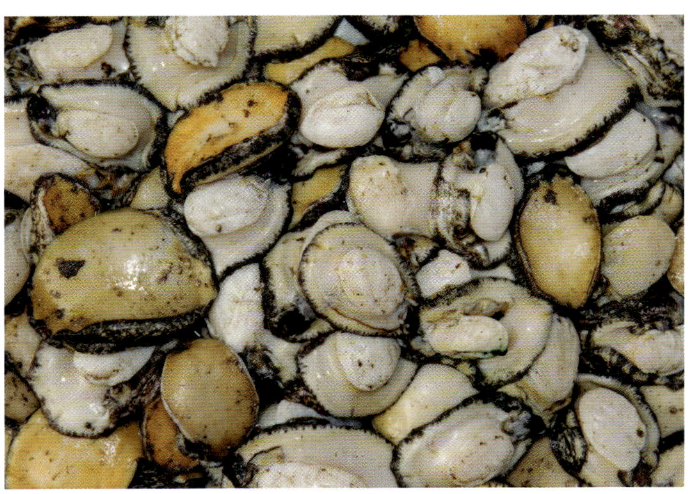

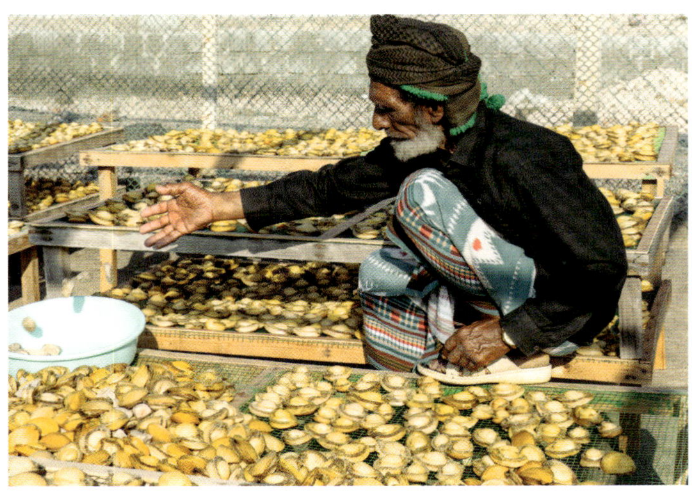

mainly between Mirbat and Hasik with greatest numbers close to Hadbin and Sadah and has been harvested by coastal communities for centuries. It was also found in the waters off Sharbthat but the population was destroyed by toxic algal blooms in 2006 and 2009.[153]

In the past abalone was one of the many shellfish eaten by coastal communities for whom gleaning was an important part of their subsistence lifestyle. The abalone could be reached by diving from the rocky shore. Abalone was also exploited for its very rare pearls and sold to merchants travelling to India and Africa. More recently, in the 1950s and 1960s, it was exported to Yemen, whence it was sent to fish markets in the Far East.[154]

After 1970 improvements made to the fisheries sector included making available modern masks to the free divers and this immediately led to increased landings of abalone. Diving either from the shore or from small skiffs, divers can use fins and wet suits but air tanks are not allowed. Each is armed with a net bag attached to their wetsuit and a special modified knife that is used to prise the shellfish from the rocks.

Although this is a male-dominated fishery women are able to gather abalone for a short period before the main season. Once it is brought ashore the abalone is sold fresh to dealers who remain in the main centres such as Hadbin and Sadah for the season. It is then boiled in huge pots over wood fires for about one and a half hours after which it is air-dried on caged wooden racks for approximately 10-14 days.

The divers are mostly from local communities and although diving on a rocky shoreline is dangerous work, often in rough seas and to depths of more than 10 metres, the rewards are great. In the early 1970s Dubai replaced Yemen as the main centre for the abalone trade and abalone from Oman was shipped from there to China and Hong Kong. Prices paid for abalone rose from one Omani Rial (RO) for 200 fresh abalone in 1970 to RO 1 for four abalone in 1980 and to RO 50 per kilogram in 1992. At that time an individual might harvest an average of 2.2 kilogram per day and the abalone

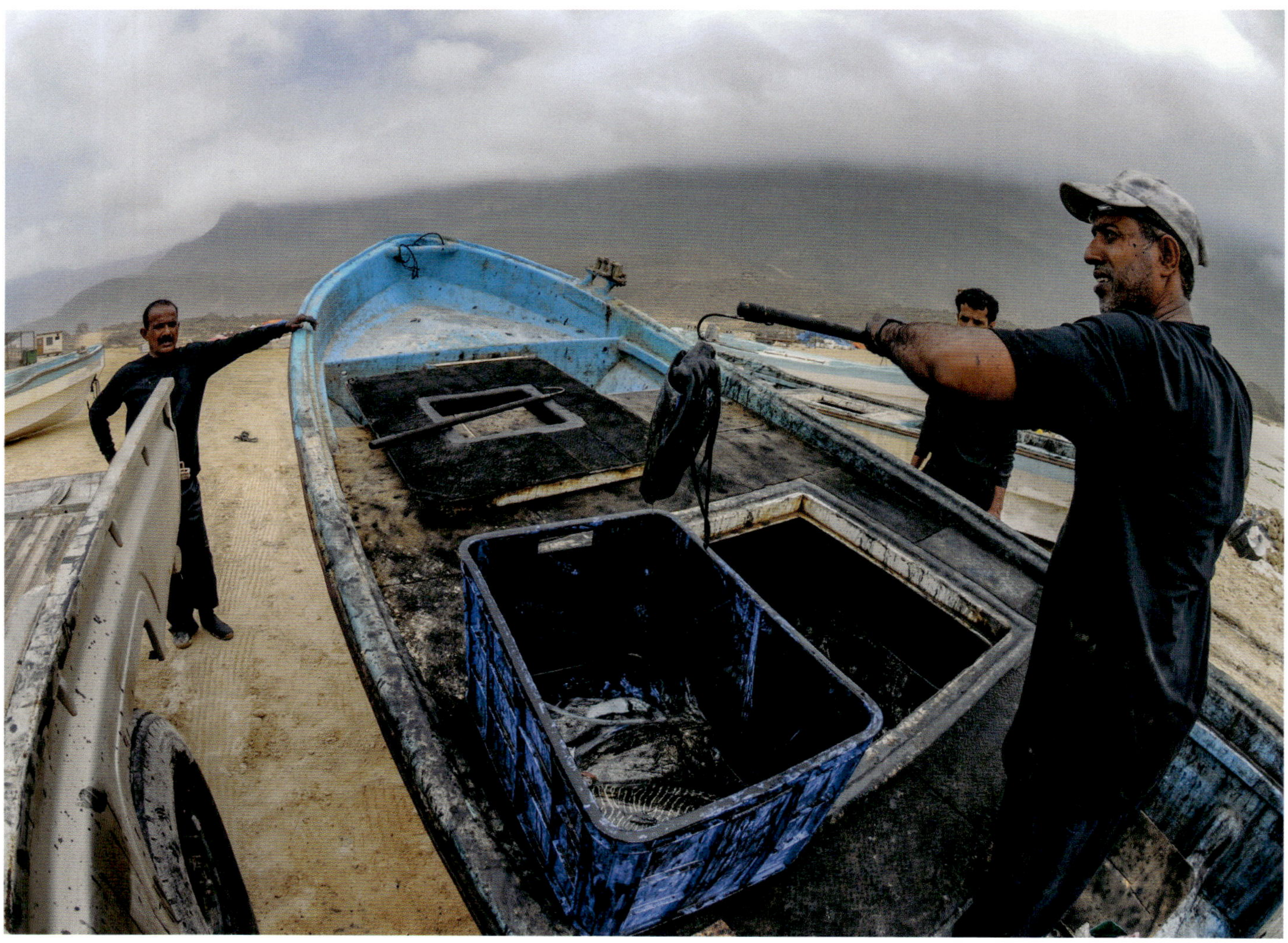

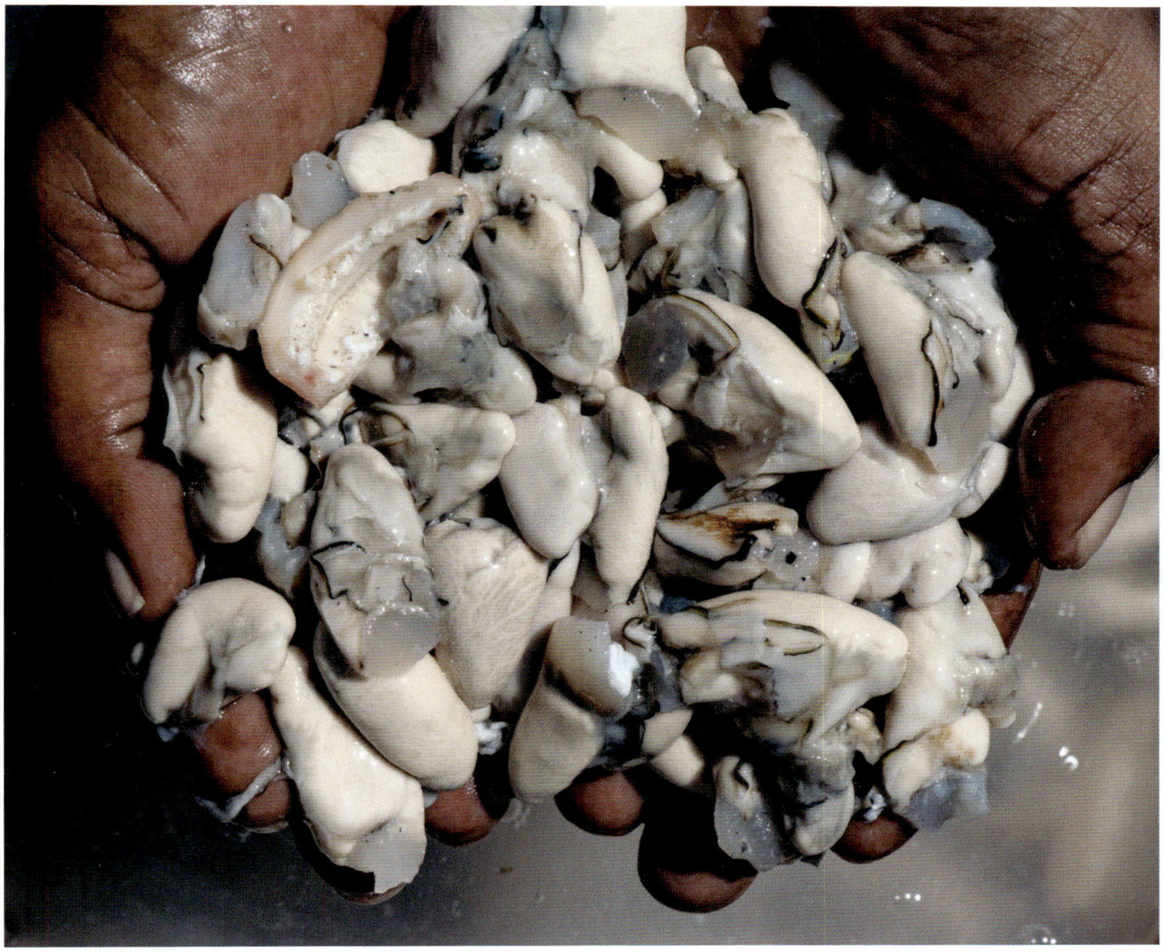

Pharoah cuttlefish *(below left)*, here being landed at Al Fazayih, command high prices while rock oyster or *zoka* *(left)* is a subsistence fishery largely limited to the rocky shores between Mirbat and Hadbin.

trade that year was worth about RO 2.5 million.[154]

However, already by 1987 there were signs that this lucrative trade was damaging the abalone populations. A closed season from 1 April to 1 October was introduced but had little effect and in 1991 the fishing season was restricted to November and December and a minimum size of 90 millimetres was set. Through the late 1990s and early 2000s yearly harvest averaged 46 tons, and in 1997 the price reached a maximum of RO 70 per kilogram. However, yields were still considered low and the fishery was close to collapse. The government responded by banning all fishing of abalone for three years. When fishing reopened in 2011 a record 149 tons was harvested, worth RO 7.5 million. However, in 2012 stocks dropped by 63% and fishing was again banned in 2013 and the fishing season was further restricted to just 12 days each winter. In spite of this and a further ban in 2015, the catch in 2016 was only 55 tons.[150] Consequently a further two-year ban was announced in 2017.

Abalone was successfully bred in a hatchery in Mirbat in the early 1990s and farming may represent the best way forward for this highly lucrative industry. It might also reduce pressure on the wild stock. Two projects to develop commercial abalone are being considered, one at Mirbat and one at Sharbthat.

The gathering of rock oyster (*Saccostrea cucullata*), known locally as *zoka*, on the rocky shores between Hasik and Mirbat is an old tradition that survives today and is carried out by women. Apart from some limited involvement in the fishing of abalone, this is the only fishery run by women, who gather and process the *zoka*. The main centres are Hasik and Sadah and while oysters are sold some are also retained for home consumption. Generally women collect oysters only close to their own settlements. It is not a high-value catch but can serve to supplement family income.[155]

Pharaoh cuttlefish *(Sepia pharaonis)* were not traditionally fished and were usually discarded by fishermen. Since the early 1990s landings have increased and as a fast growing species there may be opportunity for expansion. They are landed by trawlers and by local fishermen who use hand lines and traps.[156]

Fisheries – sustainability

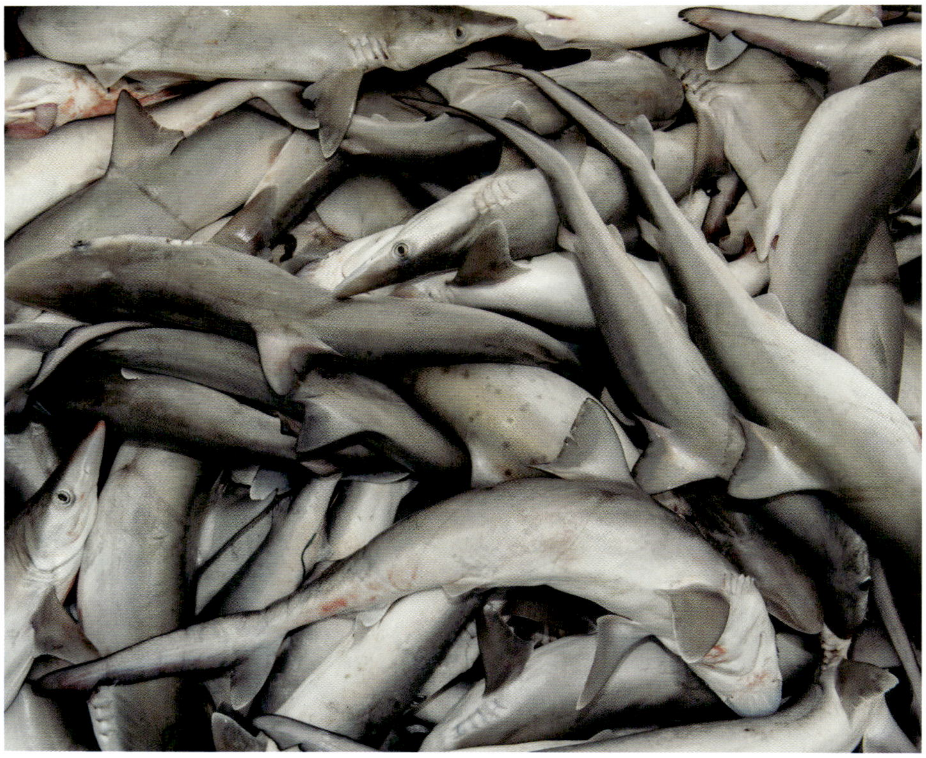

In less than 50 years Oman's fisheries have developed from being a largely subsistence industry to a high-value modern business, contributing significantly to employment in Oman, particularly outside the larger cities. As early as the 1980s, however, it became evident that some fisheries, including the spiny lobster, were already suffering from overfishing and by the 1990s there was evidence of a decline in high-value species such as kingfish. Between 1990 and 2000 yellow fin tuna, striped bonito, skipjack, kingfish and lobster catches all declined significantly. A study of Oman's fisheries from 1985-2007 led one scientist to conclude that Dhofar's fisheries at that time were unsustainable with declining catches and increasing number of vessels.[151]

The ban on international trawlers was a vital and important step to address declining landings but other challenges remain. Open access fisheries usually result in development of excess fisheries capacity and overfishing. For example the increasingly common practice of running nets between a series of *dhows*, creating of wall of net, is very destructive and results in huge and wasteful by-catch. A common step in sustainable fisheries is limited entry, where the number of licences of vessels is fixed and boats are licenced for particular fisheries. This might be done hand-in-hand with a system of quotas, whereby a total allowable catch is established, using scientific data about the health of fish stocks in a certain area. Catch shares are then licensed out, telling each fishing business or community how much of each species they are allowed to catch. Quotas make seafood more valuable, meaning a higher, more predictable profit, and also protect the environment.

Moving away from nets to other techniques such as traps and hook-and-line can allow the selective targeting of species. However, the recent explosion in the use of fish traps, known as *gargurs*, is a worrying development. Deployed in huge numbers, these non-selective traps can lead quickly to over-harvesting and also to 'ghost-fishing' whereby lost and abandoned traps continue to trap and kill fish. Fish traps, widely used in Oman, can be simply modified to prevent the capture of undersize fish and allow fish to escape from abandoned traps.[157]

Another opportunity is the establishment of local no-take zones or a marine sanctuary to help ensure sustainable catches in adjacent fisheries. The area of the Al Hallaniyyat Islands bay would make a globally important sanctuary; a place for sustainable fisheries and careful management of the unique marine biodiversity.

The recent pattern of local people moving away from fisheries to be replaced by non-native workers is a significant threat to the fisheries as they are more concerned with short-term rewards and thus likely to fish all species and at all times. Furthermore the loss of local people also means a loss of local knowledge and expertise that is essential for a sustainable fishery.

In the past the local tradition of *Senat Al-Bahar* (Code of the Sea) helped manage fisheries for local communities and in the case of the rock oyster it continues to do so today. A move towards community management might provide opportunities for those people who are very aware of the declining fish stocks but for whom open access provides no incentive to change their own behaviour.

Recreational fisheries and ecotourism are opportunities for fishermen to diversify their activities while using their skills and knowledge of the seas. The presence of game fish, especially the giant trevally (*Caranx ignobilis*) and permit fish (*Trachinotus africanus*), is a major attraction to recreational fishermen who in recent years have started to come to eastern Dhofar and the Al Hallaniyyat Islands. The activity is based on catch, tag and release, with the fish being returned to the sea. Game fishing can be profitable and contribute to the sustainable management of the fisheries. Similarly, scuba diving as well as whale and dolphin watching, if carefully managed, can be part of a sustainable fishery and present alternative economic opportunities for coastal communities.

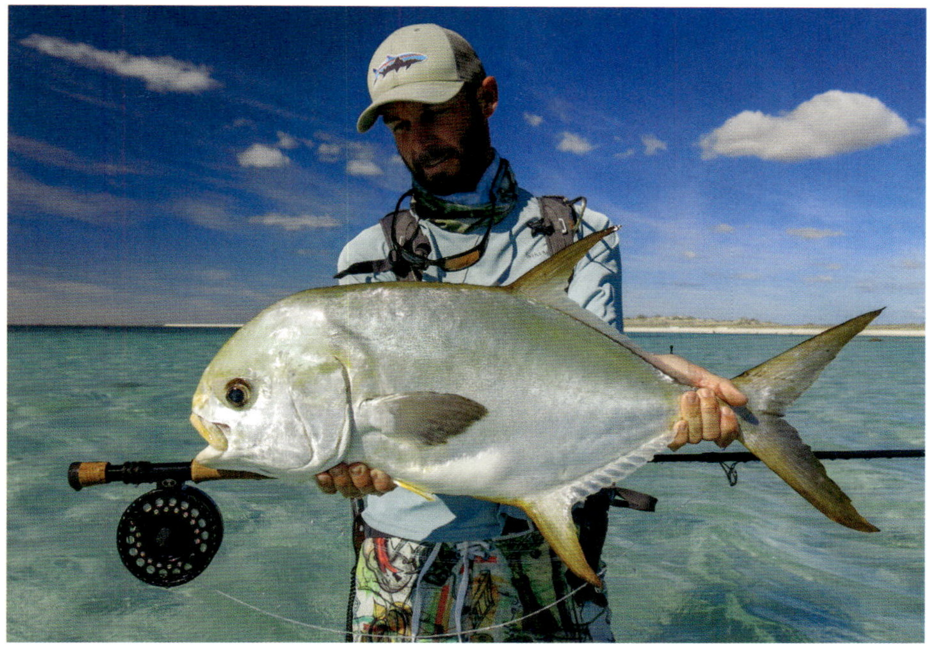

Careful management of fishing methods, such as the use of *gargur* traps ***(below)*** and measures to prevent over-harvesting of some species, such as sharks ***(opposite)***, can be combined with new opportunities such as game fishing ***(above)*** to create a sustainable fishing industry.

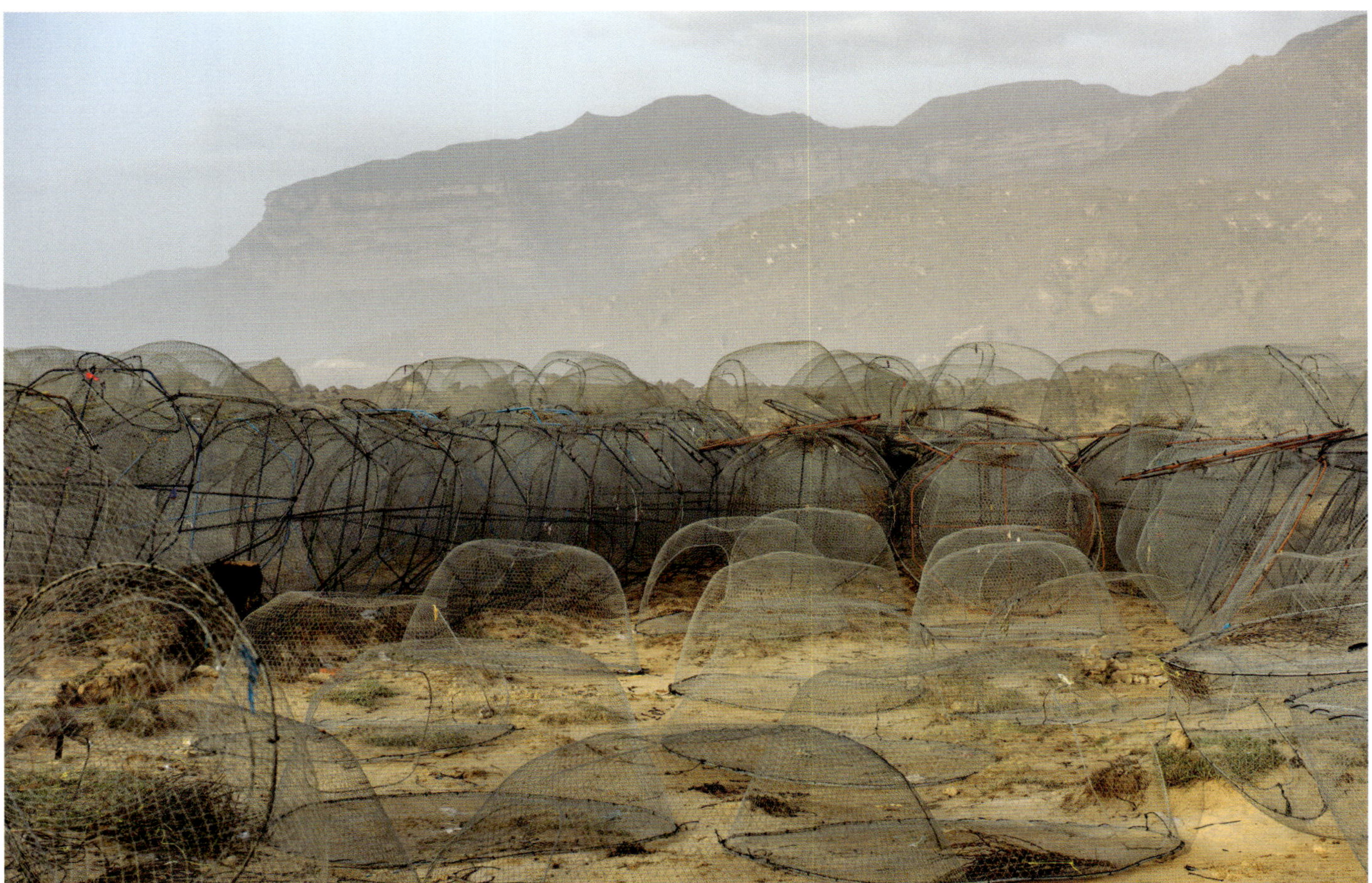

8 Sustainability

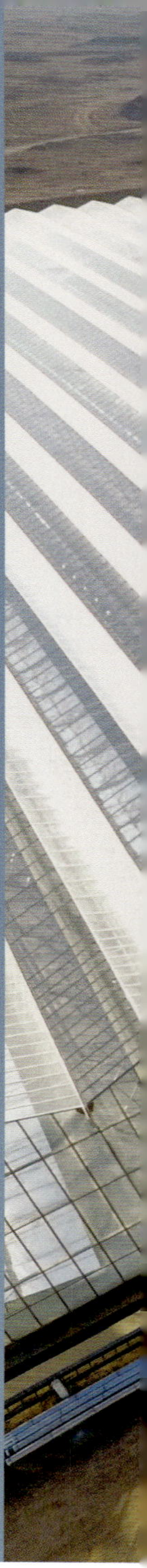

Introduction

Dhofar is celebrated for the diversity of its natural environments, that, from the cloud forest of the Jabal in the south to the Empty Quarter in the north, have supported human communities for at least 13,000 years. People fished the seas, gleaned the beaches, harvested frankincense, grew crops on the coastal plains, raised livestock on the Jabal and across the Najd, hunted wild animals and gathered plants for most day-to-day needs, including shelter, food, clothing and medicine. Recognising their own dependence on these natural resources, they took care not to over-utilise them.

Among the nomadic pastoralists of the Najd, areas were set aside to be used only at times of drought, and similarly on the Jabal, there were areas of grassland reserved for the months of the dry season when forage shortages were common. Elsewhere, camels on the Jabal were subject to strict control as to where and when they might graze.

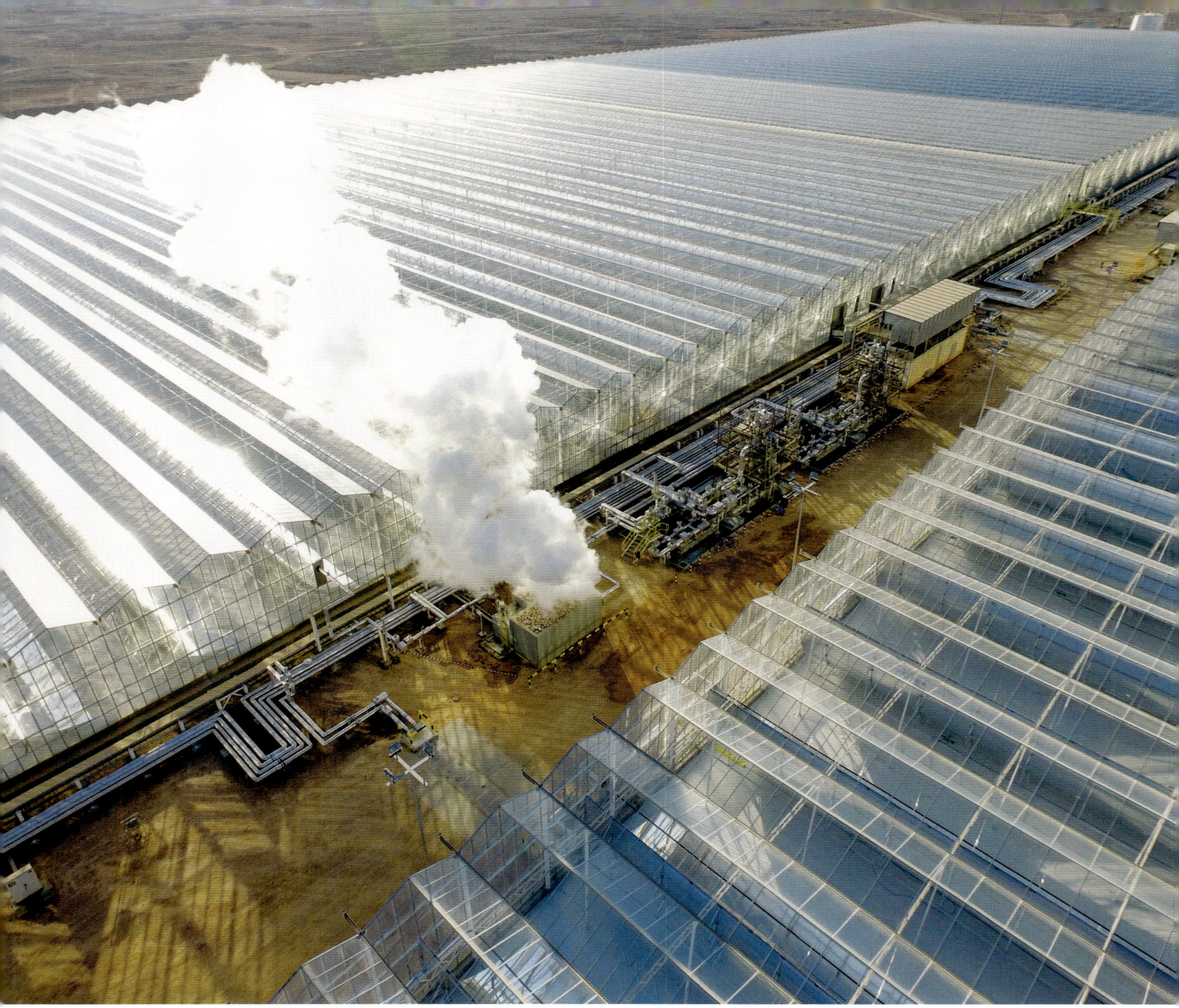

At the Amal Oilfield the Mirrah Solar Project uses solar energy instead of gas to generate steam that is injected into the oil-bearing rocks to help release oil, a process called enhanced oil recovery (EOR). Massive mirrors, housed in huge greenhouses, direct the sun's rays onto steel collecting tubes that heat up to 300°C, turning water to steam. A pilot project began operation in 2013 and saved the equivalent of an estimated million cubic meters of gas while reducing carbon footprint by 1,800 tons of CO_2. The Mirrah Solar Project will generate 6,000 tons of solar steam daily and save 5.6 trillion British Thermal Units (BTUs) of natural gas each year, enough to provide electricity to 209,000 people in Oman.

Similarly there were agreed practices for the lopping of trees; the branches of Ṣġót (*Anogeissus dhofarica*) could be partially cut to allow camels to browse but only just prior to the monsoon, when there would be vigorous new growth. For coastal and fishing communities, there was also a system of controls in place, locally known as *Senat Al-Bahar* (Code of the Sea), which served to manage fisheries and resolve disputes. Essentially, resources were managed by the various communities who established rules amongst themselves for sustainable use.

Since 1970, Dhofar's largely subsistence economy has been replaced by a modern market system and great oilfields, roads, power lines, quarries, towns and cities have transformed much of the region. Traditional use of many resources has ceased; for

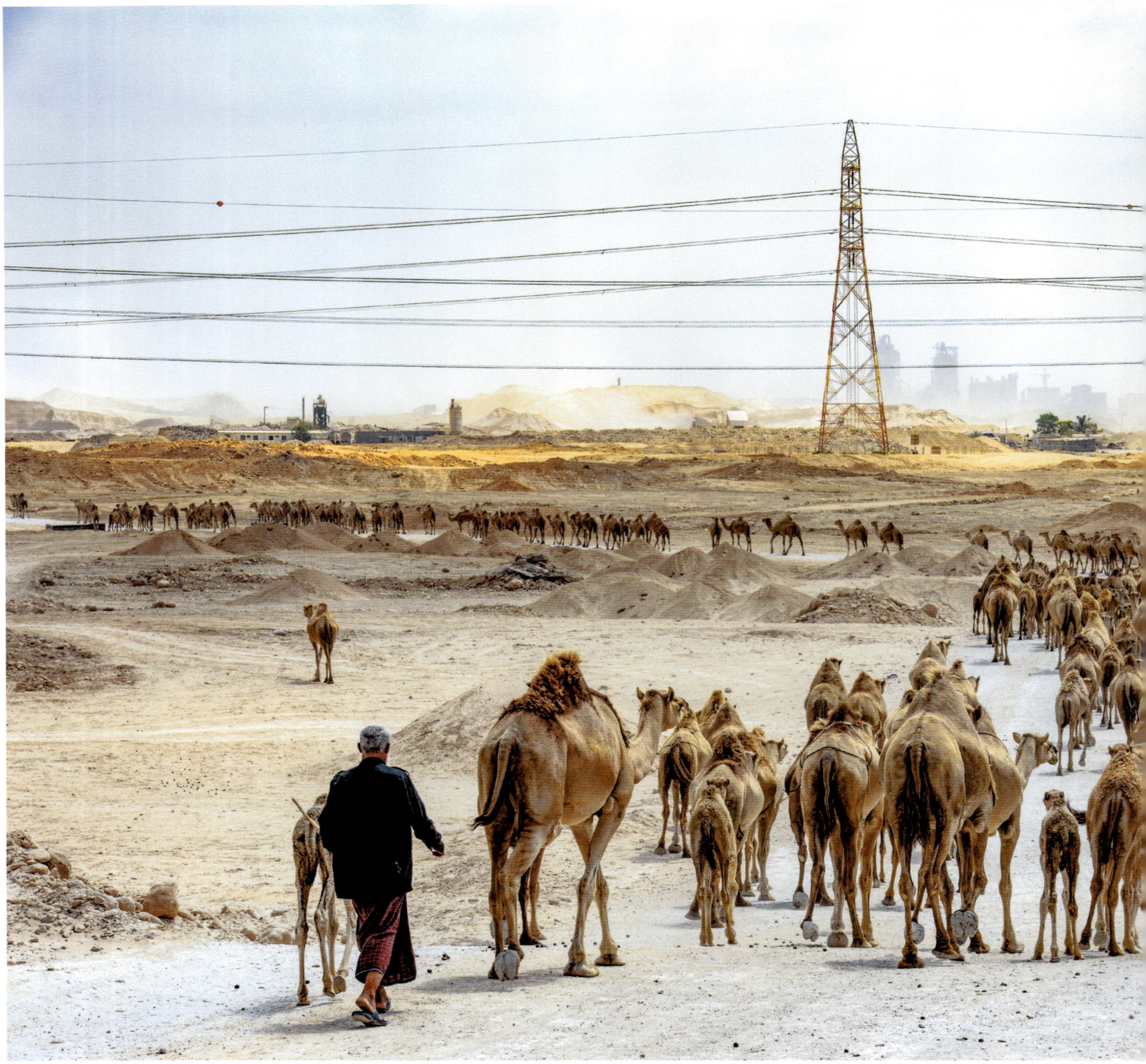

Sustainable development is a balance between social, environmental and economic objectives *(above)*.

example, modern medicines have replaced medicinal plants collected from the Jabal, concrete blocks for construction are now preferred over timber from the woodlands, gas and not wood is used for cooking, and fishermen focus more on lucrative, high-end species such as lobster, rather than gleaning the shoreline. Elsewhere, traditional practices of resource use remain but have been greatly modified; livestock is still herded but feed supplements have largely replaced natural forage and where once springs and shallow wells were the primary water source, today deep wells drilled into finite underground aquifers, and desalination, drawing water from

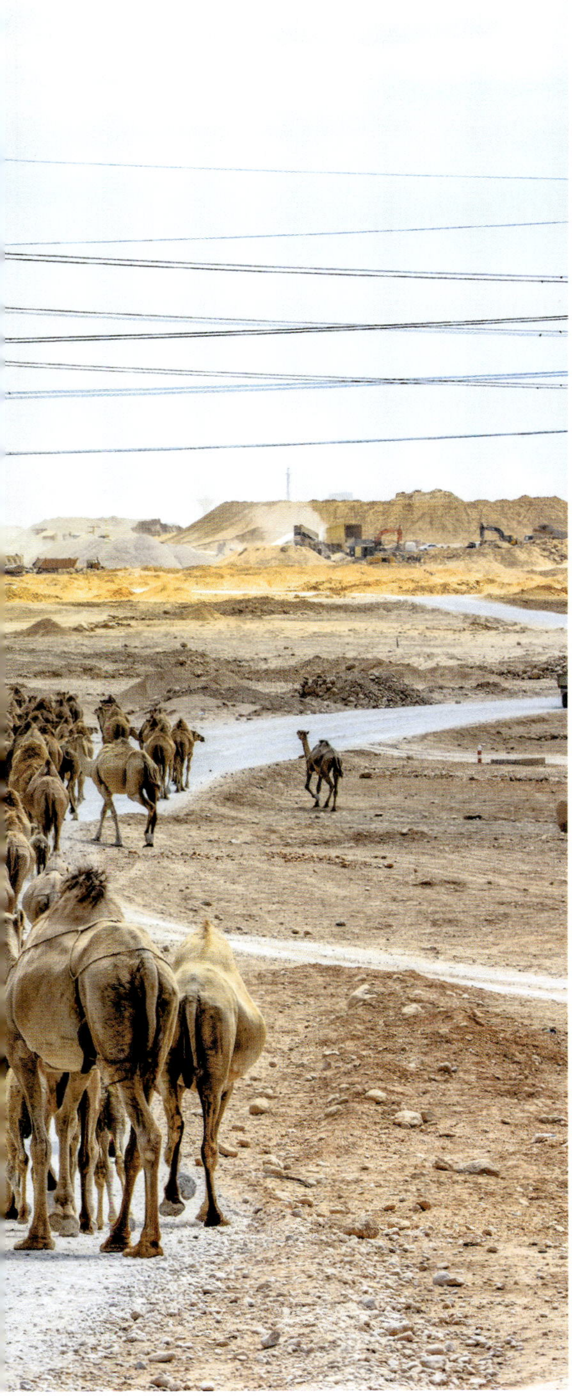

the sea, provide much of Dhofar's water.

Furthermore, new resources have come on stream, including oil and gas, which are the main drivers of Dhofar's modern economy. The mountains have yielded significant deposits of commercially valuable rock, including limestone, gypsum and marble. The diverse and beautiful landscapes are themselves a significant natural resource that attract tourists from across the globe.

Dhofar has prospered but in some sectors rapid development has put a strain on natural resources. This is particularly evident in livestock farming and fisheries where community management of resources has largely been abandoned and replaced by more or less open access, and consequently overuse, with often far reaching consequences. For example, the over-grazing of the rangelands by livestock not only threatens the diversity of flora and fauna but reduces the ability of the Jabal to capture monsoon rainfall that is vital for both surface and ground water supplies. In turn, as the Jabal pastures no longer provide sufficient pasture for the livestock, the precious and declining underground water reserves of the Najd are used to grow fodder when they might be used to grow fruit and vegetables. New ways to manage the livestock, especially on the Jabal, need to be found that reduce the pressure on the rangelands, bring economic benefits but also acknowledge the deep attachment pastoralists have for their livestock.

At sea, the banning of international trawlers has surely helped the fisheries but the continued indiscriminate use of nets, particularly gillnets, and more recently *gargur* traps has resulted in declines of the major fish species. It has also resulted in the loss of other 'non-target' fish species, as bycatch, alongside other marine life including whales, dolphins and sea turtles. As a solution, targeted fishing, licensing for particular species and the use of quotas might be considered alongside the creation of no-go zones or sanctuaries that allow fish stocks to recover. Ultimately fishermen may need to diversify their income and become involved in activities such as tag-release game fishing, diving and whale and dolphin watching, for which there are many opportunities, particularly close to the Al Hallaniyyat Islands.

The wonderfully rich flora and fauna of Dhofar has benefited from conservation programmes but has also felt the strain of development. A number of animals are threatened with extinction either as a result of direct persecution, over-harvesting (in the case of marine life) or more often as a consequence of habitat loss. Plants are endangered by overgrazing, construction of roads and other habitat loss. The development of a protected area on Jabal Al Qamar or Jabal Al Qara as well as the Jiddat Arkad would help safeguard unique plant and animal communities whose known habitat does not lie within Dhofar's existing nature reserves. Any measures to address overgrazing and the resulting desertification would benefit both plant and animal species and of course help improve the rangelands for livestock holders.

Dhofar's freshwater is arguably the most valuable of all its resources. In Salalah an integrated approach has managed the water resources effectively, although increased dependence on desalinisation of seawater is inevitable. Falling water tables

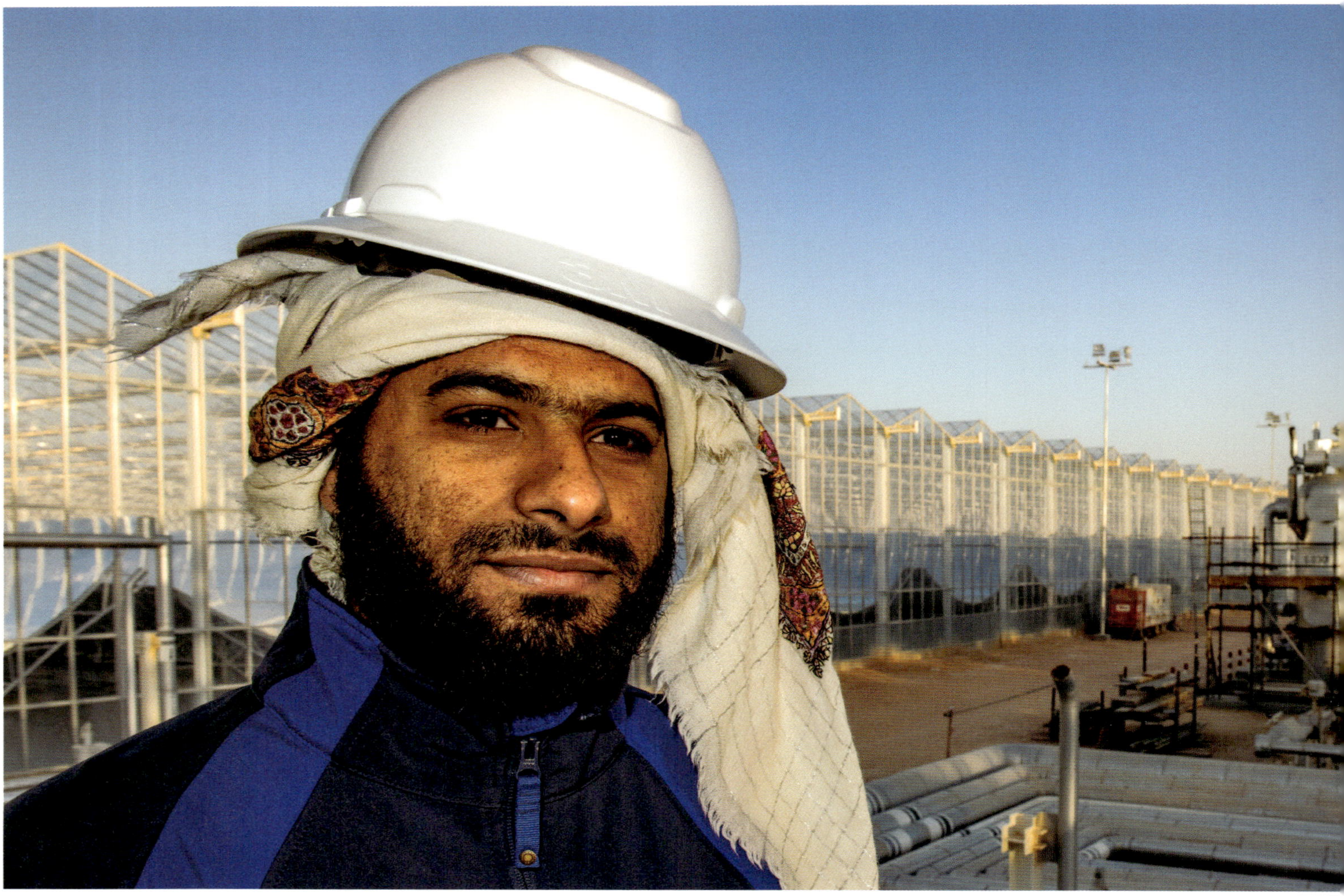

Dhofar has embraced modernity *(above)* while preserving traditions *(above right)* and traditional values.

in the Najd strongly indicate that the current practice of growing animal fodder is not sustainable and that alternative mechanisms for the management of Dhofar's livestock need to be found.

The overarching environmental challenge that faces Dhofar – and the rest of the world – is climate change, and this can be expected to impact all aspects of natural resource management. Temperatures are expected to increase and there is some indication from studies that the *khareef* might strengthen over coming years but also that climate change will bring an increased risk of severe weather events, such as Cyclone Mekunu, which hit Dhofar in May 2018. Climate change cannot be halted overnight but awareness can be raised and adaptation and resilience can be built into development plans.

The strain of development on natural resources has also provided positive opportunities. For example, the gradual exhaustion of oil reserves has made the development of renewable energy more attractive. Oman is diversifying away from reliance on oil and gas and its Vision 2020 policy set the goal of producing 10% of Oman's total electricity requirements from renewable energy sources by 2025. In 2016 Dhofar's first pilot solar energy project, at Al Mazyunah, generated nearly 550 MWh, reducing carbon emissions by 433

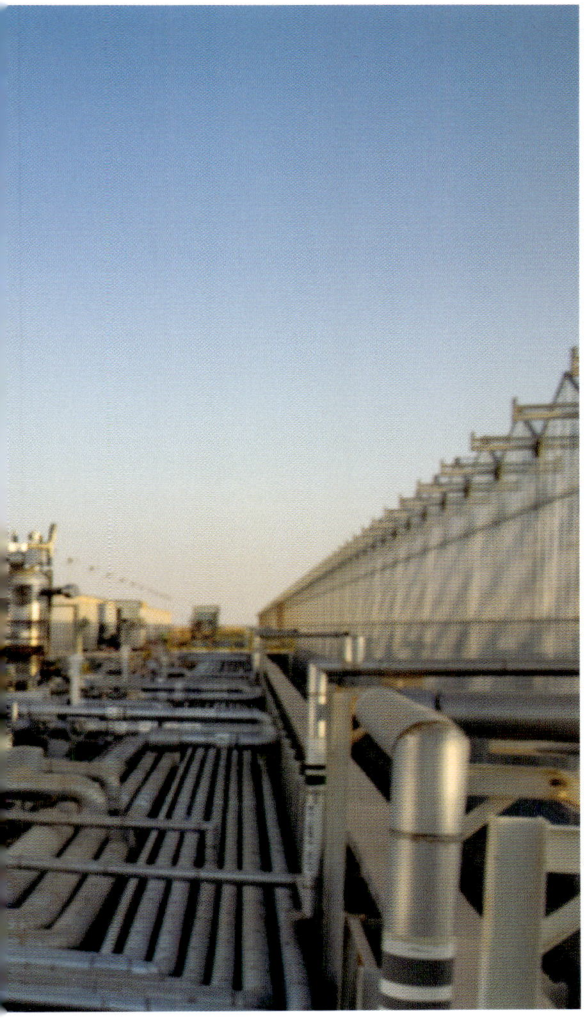

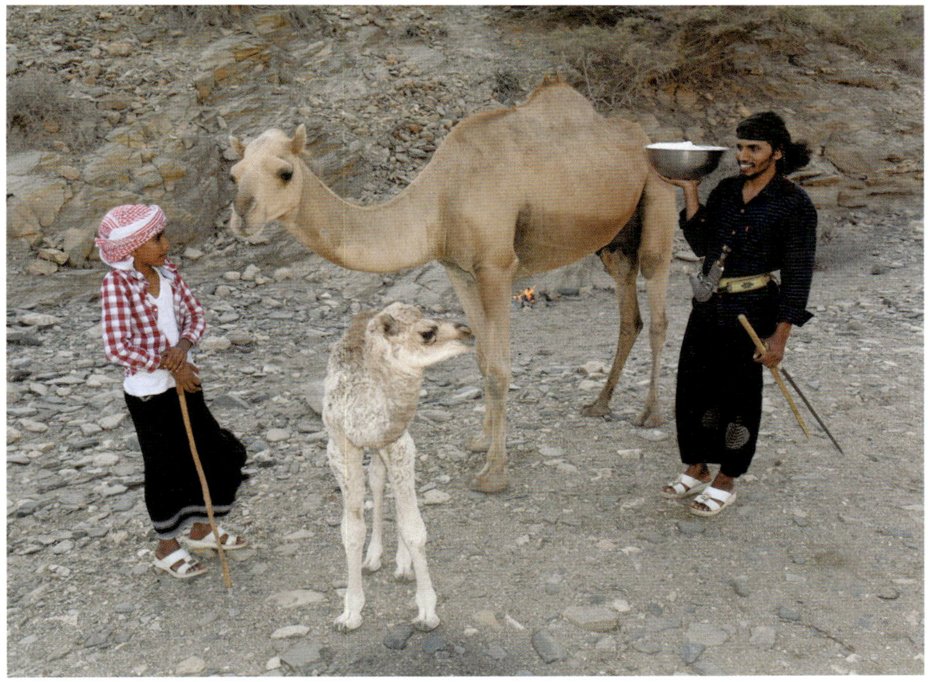

tons. Oman's first large-scale wind power project has been built at Harwil, northeast of Thumrayt in the Najd. The Dhofar Wind Farm Project comprises 13 huge turbines, each 150m in height, with a combined capacity of 50 MW, which will produce 160 GWh per year, sufficient to meet the needs of 16,000 homes.

Amongst the people of Dhofar there is an increasing awareness of the fragility of their natural resources and that some practices are not sustainable. In some areas, communities are trying to re-establish rules for resource use. For example to safeguard valuable grazing, communities are delaying the return of livestock to the Jabal pastures after the monsoon, giving grasses and other important plants longer to get established and grow. In other areas, barriers are being erected to prevent off-road driving that damages the rangelands, particularly during the *khareef* season. Along the southern coast, community volunteers have been patrolling to ensure there is no violation of the closed season for the fishing of abalone. Elsewhere, non-governmental agencies have supported programs for tree-planting.

Oman is currently implementing the National Program for Enhancing Economic Diversification (known as Tanfeedh), and has embarked on the Oman National Spatial Strategy to ensure a more balanced sustainable socio-economic and spatial development and is preparing its Vision 2040 to guide the country towards a sustainable and diversified economy. These initiatives are an opportunity to further improve the lives of the people of Dhofar as well as to ensure that the significant environmental challenges are taken into full account in plans for further development. Finally we should not forget the lessons learnt from previous generations who, understanding their own dependence on Dhofar's rich and diverse natural resources, took care not to overuse them.

Appendix: Mammals of Dhofar

Common name	Scientific name	Arabic (transliterated) name	Jibbāli	عربي
TERRESTRIAL MAMMALS				**الثدييات البرية**
Carnivores				**الثدييات اللاحمة**
African wildcat	Felis lybica lybica	Al Ket Al Barri	sinnort	القط البري
Arabian leopard	Panthera pardus nimr	An Nimr Al 'Arabi	'ḳéźer'	النمر العربي
Arabian wolf	Canis lupus arabs	Adh Dhib Al 'Arabi	^{c}ayléb / Koob	الذئب العربي
Blanford's fox	Vulpes cana	Ath Tha'alib Al Jabali / Tha'alab Blanford	ith^{c}él	الثعلب الجبلي أو ثعلب بلاندفورد
Caracal	Caracal caracal	Al Washaq	Khanjit / Khanshait	الوشق
Common genet	Genetta genetta	Ar Rubah	shīm	الرباح
Honey badger	Mellivora capensis	Gharir Al 'Asal	Kũr / Koor	غرير العسل
Red fox	Vulpes vulpes	Ath Tha'alib Al Ahmar	ith^{c}él	الثعلب الأحمر
Rüppell's sand fox	Vulpes rueppellii sabaea	Ath Tha'alab Ar Ramli	ith^{c}él	الثعلب الرملي
Sand cat	Felis margarita thinobia	Al Ket Ar Ramli	Sinort / Hur	القط الرملي
Striped hyaena	Hyaena hyaena	Adh Dhaba' Al Mukhatat	thīrīn	الضبع المخطط
White-tailed mongoose	Ichneumia albicauda	An Nams Abyada Aldhayl	khandhír	النمس أبيض الذيل
Herbivores				**الثدييات العاشبة**
Arabian gazelle	Gazella arabica	Al Ghazal Al 'Arabi	ṣa^{c}r	الغزال العربي
Arabian sand gazelle	Gazella marica	Al Ghazal Ar Ramli / Al Riym		الغزال الرملي أو الريم
Cape hare	Lepus capensis omanensis	Al Arnab Al Barri	^{ɔ}erni	الأرنب البري
Nubian ibex	Capra nubiana	Al Wa'al An Nubi	bo^{c}úź	الوعل النوبي
Rock hyrax	Procavia capensis	Al Wabar As sakhri	thòfen	الوبر الصخري
Insectivores				**الثدييات آكلات الحشرات**
Arabian shrew	Crocidura arabica	Az Zabab Al Arabi		الزباب العربي
Brandt's hedgehog	Pareachinus hypomelas	Al Qunfidh Al Aswad	qedwíw	القنفذ الأسود (قنفذ براندت)
Desert hedgehog	Paraechinus aethiopicus	Al Qunfidh	qedwíw	القنفذ الصحراوي
Dhofarian shrew	Crocidura dhofarensis	Az Zabab adh Dhofari		الزباب الظفاري
White-toothed pygmy shrew	Suncus etruscus	Az Zabab Al Qazam Dhul Al Asnan Al Bada		الزباب القزم ذو الأسنان البيضاء
Rodents				**القوارض**
African grass rat	Arvicanthis niloticus	Jird Al 'Ashab Al Afriqi		جرذ الأعشاب الأفريقي
Arabian jerboa	Jaculus loftusi	Al Jarbue Al Asgar		الجربوع الأصغر
Arabian spiny mouse	Acomys dimidiatus	Al Fa'r Ash Shuwki Al 'Arabi		الفأر الشوكي العربي
Black rat	Rattus rattus	Al Jaradh Al Aswad		الجرذ الأسود
Brown rat	Rattus norvegicus	Al Jaradh Al Boni		الجرذ البني
Bushy-tailed jird	Sekeetamys calurus	Fa'r Dhu Adh Dhayl Al Kathif		فأر ذو الذيل الكثيف
Cheesman's gerbil	Gerbillus cheesmani	Jarbue or Fa'r or Adl Cheesman		جربوع أو فأر أو عضل جيسمان
Dwarf gerbil	Gerbillus nanus	Jarbue / Fa'r / A'dl Baluchistan		الفأر الشوكي العربي
Golden spiny mouse	Acomys russatus	Al Fa'r Ash Shuwki Adh Dhahabi		الفأر الشوكي الذهبي
House mouse	Mus musculus	Fa'r Al Manzil		فأر المنزل
Indian crested porcupine	Hystrix indica	Ash Shiham / An Nayse	enṭeliṭ / Natlait	الشيهم الهندي المتوج

Sundevall's jird	Meriones crassus	Jird Sundevall		جرذ ساندفال
Wagner's gerbil	Gerbillus dasyurus	Jarbue / 'Adl Wagner		جربوع أو عضل واجنر
Bats				**الخفافيش**
African sheath-tailed bat	Coleura gallarum	Khafash Al Fakahat Al 'Afriqi Tabanay Al Lawn		خفاش الفاكهه الأفريقي تبني اللون
Arabian free-tailed bat	Nyctinomus thomasi	Khafash Afriqi Ghamdi Al Dhayl		خفاش أفريقي غمدي الذيل
Arabian mouse-tailed bat	Rhinopoma cystops	Al Khafash Al Misri Dhu Al Wajh A Mashqowq		الخفاش المعربي ذو الوجه المشقوق
Arabian trident bat	Asellia arabica	Khafash 'Arabi Thul'aathi An Natwat		خفاش عربي ثلاثي النتوءات
Botta's serotine	Eptesicus bottae	Khafash Bowta		خفاش بوتا
Desert pipistrelle	Hypsugo ariel	Watwat or Khafash As Sahra		وطواط أو خفاش الصحراء
Dhofarian pipistrelle	Pipistrellus dhofarensis	Al'watwat or Al Khafash Adh Dhafari		الوطواط أو الخفاش الظفاري
Egyptian fruit bat	Rousettus aegyptiacus	Khafash Al Fakaha Al Misri		خفاش الفاكهه المصري
Egyptian slit-faced bat	Nycteris thebaica	Al Khafash Al Misri F'ary Adh Dheel		الخفاش المصري فأري الذيل
Geoffroy's horseshoe bat	Rhinolophus clivosus	Khafash Hadwt Al Howasan		خفاش حدوة الحصان
Geoffroy's trident leaf-nosed bat	Asellia tridens	Al Khafash Thu Al Anf Al Waraqi Tha-lathi Al Tanwiy'at		الخفاش ذو الأنف الورقي ثلاثي النتوءات
Ghost bat	Otonycteris hemprichii jin	Al Khafash Ash Shabah		الخفاش الشبح
Naked-rumped tomb bat	Taphozous nudiventris	Khafash Al Maqaber Ari Al Batan		خفاش المقابر عاري البطن
Persian trident bat	Triaenops persicus	Khafash Iran Thul'aathi Al Natwat		خفاش إيران ثلاثي النتوءات
Sind serotine bat	Rhyneptesicus nasutus	Khafash Al Sund		خفاش السند
Straw-coloured fruit bat	Eidolon helvum	Khafash Al Fakahat Tabanay Al Lawn		خفاش الفاكهه تبني اللون
Tomb bat	Taphozous perforatus	Khafash Al Maqaber		خفاش المقابر
Yemeni trident leaf-nosed bat	Triaenops parvus	Al Khafash Al Yemeni Dhul Al Anaf Al Warqi Thu Al 'Aathi An Natwat		الخفاش اليمني ذو الأنف الورقي الثلاثي النتوءات
MARINE MAMMALS				**الثدييات البحرية**
Whales				**الحيتان**
Arabian Sea humpback whale	Megaptera novaeangliae	Al Hoowt Al Ahdab Al 'Arabi		الحوت الأحدب العربي
Bryde's whale	Balaenoptera edeni	Hoowt Birayd		حوت برايد
Cuvier's beaked whale	Ziphius cavirostris	Hoowt Kufiyiha Dhu Al Manqar		حوت كوفييه ذو المنقار
Dwarf sperm whale	Kogia sima	Hoowt Al 'Anabar Al Qazam		حوت العنبر القزم
False killer whale	Pseudorca crassidens	Al Hoowt Al Qatil Al Kadhib		الحوت القاتل الكاذب
Killer whale (Orca)	Orcinus orca	Al Hoowt Al Qatil		الحوت القاتل
Northern Indian Ocean blue whale	Balaenoptera musculus indica	Al Hoowt Al Az'raq		الحوت الأزرق
Short-finned pilot whale	Globicephala macrorhyn-chus	Hoowt Al Murshid Dhu Al Zaenif Al Qasira		حوت المرشد ذو الزعانف القصيرة
Sperm whale	Physeter macrocephalus	Hoowt Al 'Anabar		حوت العنبر
Dolphins				**الدلافين**
Common bottlenose dolphin	Tursiops truncatus	Dalfien Qarowory Al Anaf Ash Shayie		دلفين قاروري الأنف الشائع
Indian Ocean humpback dolphin	Sousa plumbea	Dalfien Al Maheed Al Hindi Al Ahdab		دلفين المحيط الهندي الأحدب
Indo-Pacific bottlenose dolphin	Tursiops aduncus	Dalfien Al Maheed Al Hindi - AlHadi Qarowory Al Anaf		دلفين المحيط الهندي - الهادي قاروري الأنف
Indo-Pacific common dolphin	Delphinus delphis tropi-calis	Ad Dalfien Ash Shayie Tawail Al Manqar		الدلفين الشائع طويل المنقار
Pantropical spotted dolphin	Stenella attenuata	Ad Dalfien Al Madari Al Mubaqa		الدلفين المداري المبقع
Risso's dolphin	Grampus griseus	Dalfien Risso		دلفين ريسو
Rough-toothed dolphin	Steno bredanensis	Ad Dalfien Dhul Al Asnan Al Khashana		الدلفين ذو الأسنان الخشنة
Spinner dolphin	Stenella longirostris	Ad Dalfien Al Dawaar		الدلفين الدوار
Striped dolphin	Stenella coeruleoalba	Ad Dalfien Al Mukhatat		الدلفين المخطط

References

1. Herodotus, Farnell, G.S. & Goff, M. (1991) Tales from Herodotus. Bristol: Bristol Classical Press.

2. Vine, P. (1995) Oman in History. London: Immel Publishing.

3. Bent, T. & Bent, M (1900). Southern Arabia. London: Smith Elder & Co.

4. Mercolli, I., Briner A., Frei, R., Schonberg, R., Naegler, T.M., Kramers, J. & Peters, T. (2006) Lithostratigraphy and Geochronology of the Neoproterozoic Crystalline Basement of Salalah, Dhofar, Sultanate of Oman. Precambrian Research 145, pp. 182–206.

5. Béchennec, F., J. Le Métour, J.-P. Platel & J. Roger (1993) Explanatory notes to the Geological map of the Sultanate of Oman, Scale 1:1,000,000. Directorate General of Minerals, Oman, Ministry of Petroleum and Minerals, 93 p.

6. McClure, H.A. (1988) Late Quaternary Paleogeography and Landscape Evolution of the Rub' Al Khali. In Potts, D.T. (ed) Araby The Blest: Studies in Arabian Archeology. Copenhagen: Museum Tusulanum Press, pp. 9-14.

7. Hilbert Y.H., Usik, V.I., Galletti, C.S., Morley, M.W., Parton, A, Clark-Balzan, L, Schwenninger J.-L., Linnenlucke, L.P., Roberts, R.G., Jacobs, Z. & Rose, J.I. (2016) Archaeological evidence for indigenous human occupation of Southern Arabia at the Pleistocene/ Holocene transition: The case of al-Hatab Dhofar, Southern Oman. Paléorient 41(2), pp. 31-49.

8. Zarins, J. (2001) The Land of Incense: Archaeological Work in the Governorate of Dhofar, Sultanate of Oman, 1990-1995. Muscat: Sultan Qaboos University.

9. Office of the Adviser to His Majesty The Sultan for Cultural Affairs (2013) Atlas of Archaeological Survey in Governorate of Dhofar. Muscat: Office of the Adviser to His Majesty The Sultan for Cultural Affairs.

10. Newton, L.S. & Zarins, J. (2010) Preliminary results of the Dhofar archaeological survey. Proceedings of the Seminar for Arabian Studies 40: 247-265.

11. NCSI (2018) Population Statistics. National Centre for Statistics & Information, 7 (2018).

12. Petraglia MD, Haslam M, Fuller DQ, Boivin N, Clarkson C. 2010. Out of Africa: new hypotheses and evidence for the dispersal of Homo sapiens along the Indian Ocean rim. Ann Hum Biol. 37:288–311.

13. Rose, J. I., Usik, V. I., Marks, A. E., Hilbert, Y. H., Galletti, C. S., Parton, A., Geiling, J.M., Černý, V., Morley, M. W. and Roberts, R. G. (2011) 'The Nubian Complex of Dhofar, Oman: An African Middle Stone Age Industry in Southern Arabia', PLoS ONE, 6(11). doi: 10.1371/journal.pone.0028239.

14. Rose, J. I., Hilbert Y.H., Usik, V.I., Marks, A.E, Jaboob, M. M. A., Černý, Crassard, R. & Preusser, F. (2018) 30,000-year-old geometric microliths from Oman reveal ice age refugium along southern route of human dispersal. Manuscript submitted for publication.

15. Rose, J. I. and Usik, V. I. (2009) 'The "Upper Paleolithic" of South Arabia', in Petraglia, M. D. and Rose, J. I. (eds) The evolution of human populations in Arabia: paleoenvironments, prehistory, and genetics. Dordrecht: Springer, pp. 169–185.

16. Interview with Dr J. Zarins, Nova Online, Sept. 1996.

17. https://whc.unesco.org/en/list/1010/d22documents/

18. Almathen, F., Charruau, P., Mohandesan, E., Mwacharo, J.M., Orozco-ter-Wengel, P., Pitt, D., Abdussamad, A.M., Uerpmann, M., Uerpmann, H.P., De Cupere, B., Magee, P., Alnaqeeb, M.A., Salim, B., Raziq, A., Dessie, T., Abdelhadi, O.M., Banabazi, M.H., Al-Eknah, M., Walzer, C., Faye, B., Hofreiter, M., Peters, J., Hanotte, O., & Burger, P.A. (2016) Ancient and modern DNA reveal dynamics of domestication and cross-continental dispersal of the dromedary. Proc Natl Acad Sci U S A. 2016; 113(24):6707-6712.

19. Manfred Boehme, Personal Communication, 30 March 2018.

20. Beckingham, C.F. (1948) The Kuria Muria Islands Geogrl. J. CX (1-3): 144.

21. Haines, S.B. (1845) Memoir of the South and East Coasts of Arabia. Part II. J. Roy. Geog. Soc. 15: 104-160 and map.

22. Miles, S.B. (1966) The Countries and Tribes of the Persian Gulf. Second edition. London: Frank Cass. 643 pp.

23. Thomas, B. (1932) Arabia Felix. London: Jonathan Cape.

24. Searle, M.P. (2014) Preserving Oman's geological heritage: proposal for establishment of World Heritage Sites, National GeoParks and Sites of Special Scientific Interest (SSSI). In: Rollinson, H. R., Searle, M. P., Abbasi, I. A., Al-Lazki, A. & Al Kindi, M.H. (eds.) Tectonic Evolution Of The Oman Mountains. London: Geological Society, Special Publications, 392, 9-44.

25. Ward, P. (1987) Travels in Oman. Cambridge: The Oleander Press.

26. Hanna, S. & Al-Belushi, M. (1996) Introduction to the Caves of Oman. Muscat: Sultan Qaboos University.

27. Thesiger, W. (1959) Arabian Sands. London:Longmans, Green & Co. Ltd.

28. Glennie, K.W. (2005) The Desert of Southeast Arabia. Bahrain: Gulf PetroLink.

29. http://timesofoman.com/article/104571

30. Vincent, P. (2008) Saudi Arabia: An Environmental Overview. London: Taylor & Francis.

31. Barlow M, Wheeler M, Lyon B, Cullen H. 2005. Modulation of daily precipitation over Southwest Asia by the Madden Julian Oscillation. Mon. Weather Rev. 133(12): 3579– 3594.

32. Fisher, M. & Membury, D.A. (1998) Climate. In Ghazanfar, S.A. & Fisher, M. (eds) Vegetation of the Arabian Peninsula. Netherlands: Kluwer Academic Publishers, pp. 5-38.

33. Data courtesy of Directorate General for Meteorology, Public Authority for Civil Aviation, Muscat, Oman.

34. Membery, D. Monsoon tropical cyclones: Part 1 (2001). Weather, 56: 431-438.

35. Membery, D. Monsoon tropical cyclones: Part 2 (2002). Weather, 57: 247-255.

36. Ministry of Regional Municipalities and Water Resources (2018)

37. http://www.ipcc.ch/ipccreports/tar/wg2/index.php?idp=29

38. Lelieveld, J., Proestos, Y., Hadjinicolaou, P. et al. Climatic Change (2016) 137: 245. https://doi.org/10.1007/s10584-016-1665-6

39. Alsarmi, S. and Washington, R. (2011) Recent Observed Climate Change over the Arabian Peninsula. Journal of Geophysical Research 116(D11):D11109. (http://doi.wiley.com/10.1029/2010JD015459).

40. Kwarteng, A.Y., Dorvlo, S, Vijaya G.T. (2009) Analysis of a 27-year rainfall data (1977–2003) in the Sultanate of Oman. Int J Climatol. 29: 605–617. https://doi.org/10.1002/joc.1727

41. Sousa, D., Small, C., Spalton, A. and A. Kwarteng, A. (2019) Coupled Spatio-temporal Characterization of Monsoon Cloud Cover and Vegetation Phenology.

42. Turner, A.G. & Annamalai, H. (2012)

Climate Change and the South Asian Summer Monsoon, Nature Climate Change, online publication June 24, DOI: 10.1038/NCLIMATE1495

43. http://blogs.ei.columbia.edu/2017/12/04/studying-bioluminescent-bloomsarabian-sea/

44. Barros, J. & Whitcombe, R. (1989) Fog and Rain Water Collection in Southern Region: 1989 Research Programme. Salalah: Planning Committee for Development & Environment in the Southern Region.

45. Hildebrandt, A. & Eltahir, E.A.B. (2006) Forest on the edge: Seasonal cloud forest in Oman creates its own ecological niche. Geophysical Research Letters, 33: 2-5. doi:10.1029/2006GL026022.

46. Shammas, M.I. (2007) Sustainable Management of the Salalah Coastal Aquifer in Oman using an Integrated Approach. PhD Thesis. Stockholm: Royal Institute of Technology.

47. T. Shoji, Personal Communication, 8 November 2017.

48. Schemenauer, R.S. & Cereceda, P. (1992) Water from fog-covered mountains. Waterlines, 10 (4): 10-13.

49. Müller, T. (2012) Recharge and residence times in an arid area aquifer. PhD Thesis. Dresden: Technische Universität.

50. MAF (2012) Oman Salinity Strategy. Main Report. Muscat: Ministry of Agriculture & Fisheries.

51. Travers Morgan (1996) Detail Land Use Study in Jabal Dhofar: Survey of Current Conditions. Final Report. Muscat: Supreme Committee for Town Planning.

52. Al Mukheini, A. & Roe, A. (2019) History [Southern Oman Mountains]. In: Al Zubair, M., Mershen,B., Al Saqri, S., Al Ghafri, A., Al Hosni, T., Al Nabhani, Y., Al Rajhi, A., Nasir, S., Patzelt, A., Spalton, A. & Anderson, A. The Mountains of Oman. An Illustrated Reference to Nature and Society. Hildesheim: Georg Olms AG.

53. PCDESR (1993) Khawrs and Springs of the Dhofar. Surveys and Monitoring Studies. Salalah: Planning Committee for the Development & Environmental in the Governorate of Dhofar.

54. Ministry of Agriculture and Fisheries (2014) Agricultural Census 2012/2013: Volume 3: Dhofar. Muscat: MAF.

55. Stephenson, M.T. (1992) Components of Produced Water: A Compilation of Results from Several Industry Studies, JPT, vol. 44, no. 5 (May 1992).

56. Hirayama, A., Maegaito, M., Kawaguchi, M, Ishikawa, A., Sueyoshi, M., AlBemani, A.S., M. Ahmed, Esechie, H., Al-Mazrui, S.A., Al-Haddabi, M.H. & AlKhanjari, S.S. (2002) Omani Oil Fields Produced Water: Treatment and Utilization. Proceedings of the 2002 SPE International Petroleum Conference and Exhibition in Mexico. Society of Petroleum Engineers.

57. PDO (2017) Sustainability Report 2017. Muscat: Petroleum Development Oman.

58. OPWP (2017) Seven Year Statement 2017-2023. (Vol. 11). Muscat: Oman Power and Water Procurement Co. (SOAC).

59. Shammas, M.I. & Jacks, G. (2007) Sea water intrusion in the Salalah plain aquifer, Oman. Environmental Geology, 53 (3): 575-587.

60. Turner, A.J., White, S., Smith, G., Al Ghafri, A., Aziz, A. & Al Suleimani, Z. (2005) Water efficiency - a sustainable way forward for Oman. Stockholm Water Symposium, Sweden, August 2005 in Stockholm Water Symposium, Workshop 5.

61. McDonnell, R. (2016) Groundwater Use and Policies in Oman. IVMI Project Report No. 14. Washington: International Water Management Institute.

62. Saber, M, Alhinai, S., Al Barwani, A., ALSaidi, A., Kantoush, S.A., Habib. E. & Borrok. D.M. (2007) Satellite-Based Estimates of Groundwater Storage Changes at the Najd Aquifers in Oman. In O. Abdalla et al. (eds.), Water Resources in Arid Areas: The Way Forward, Springer Water, DOI 10.1007/978-3-319-51856

63. A. Patzelt, personal communication, May 2018.

64. Patzelt, A. (2014) Oman Plant Red Data Book. Muscat: Oman Botanic Garden, Diwan of Royal Court.

65. Mosti, S., Raffaelli, M. & Tardelli, M. (2012) Contribution to the Flora of Central-Southern Dhofar (Sultanate of Oman). Webbia 67(1): 65-91.

66. Miller A.G. & Morris, M. (1988) Plants of Dhofar. The Office of The Adviser for Conservation of the Environment, Diwan of Royal Court, Sultanate of Oman.

67. Patzelt, A. (2004) Flora and vegetation of Juzur al Hallaniyyat (the Kuria Muria Islands) with a report of additional species. The Journal of Oman Studies 13: 139–153.

68. Gallagher, M.G. (2002) Observations on Juzur al Hallaniyyat (the Kuria Muria Islands) of Oman. The Journal of Oman Studies 12: 71-123.

69. Hildebrandt, A., Al Aufi, M., Amerjeed, M., Shammas, M. and Eltahir E.A.B. (2007) Ecohydrology of a seasonal cloud forest in Dhofar: 1. Field experiment, Water Resour. Res., 43, W10411, doi:10.1029/2006WR005261.

70. Patzelt, A. (2011) The Themeda quadrivalvis tall-grass savannah of Oman at the crossroad between Africa and Asia. Edinburgh Journal of Botany 68(2): 301-319.

71. Patzelt, A. (2015) Synopsis of the Flora and Vegetation of Oman, with Special Emphasis on Patterns of Plant Endemism. Abhandlungen der Braunschweigischen Wissenschaftlichen Gesellschaft, pp. 282–317.

72. Patzelt, A. (2019) Flora and Vegetation [Jabal Al Qamar]. In: Al Zubair, M., Mershen,B., Al Saqri, S., Al Ghafri, A., Al Hosni, T., Al Nabhani, Y., Al Rajhi, A., Nasir, S., Patzelt, A., Spalton, A. & Anderson, A. The Mountains of Oman. An Illustrated Reference to Nature and Society. Hildesheim: Georg Olms AG.

73. Al-Issai, G. (2019) Flora and Vegetation [Jabal Al Qara]. In: Al Zubair, M., Mershen,B., Al Saqri, S., Al Ghafri, A., Al Hosni, T., Al Nabhani, Y., Al Rajhi, A., Nasir, S., Patzelt, A., Spalton, A. & Anderson, A. The Mountains of Oman. An Illustrated Reference to Nature and Society. Hildesheim: Georg Olms AG.

74. Patzelt, A. (2019) Flora and Vegetation [Jabal Samhan]. In: Al Zubair, M., Mershen,B., Al Saqri, S., Al Ghafri, A., Al Hosni, T., Al Nabhani, Y., Al Rajhi, A., Nasir, S., Patzelt, A., Spalton, A. & Anderson, A. The Mountains of Oman. An Illustrated Reference to Nature and Society. Hildesheim: Georg Olms AG.

75. Brown, K. (1988) Ecophysiology of Prosopis cineraria in the Wahiba Sands, with reference to its reafforestation potential in Oman. In Dutton, R.W. (ed) The Journal of Oman Studies, Spec. Rep. No. 3. Muscat: Office of the Adviser for Conservation of the Environment, Diwan of Royal Court, pp. 257-270.

76. Bokrezion, H. (2008) The Ecological and Socio-economic Role of Prosopis juliflora in Eritrea. PhD Thesis. Johannes Gutenberg-Universität, Mainz.

77. Mahgoub O., Kadim I.T., Al Ajmi, D.S., Al Saqry, N.M., Al Abri, A.S., Richie, A.R., Al Halhali, A.S. & Forsberg, N.E. (2004) Use of local range tree (Prosopis spp.) pods in feeding sheep and goats in the Sultanate of Oman. In: Ben Salem H., Nefzaoui, A., Morand-Fehr, P. (eds.). Nutrition and feeding strategies of sheep and goats under harsh climates. Zaragoza: CIHEAM, pp. 191-195.

78. Alaamri, M.M.H. (2012) Distribution Boswellia sacra in Dhofar Mountains, Sultanate of Oman: Economic Value and Environmental Role. Journal of Life Sciences 6: 632-636.

79. Beyin, A. (2011) Upper Pleistocene Human Dispersals Out of Africa: A Review of the Current State of the Debate. International Journal of Evolutionary Biology. Article ID 615094, 17 pages doi:10.4061/2011/615094.

80. Spalton, A., & Al Hikmani, H. (2014)

The Arabian Leopards of Oman. London: Stacey International.

81. Stanley Price, M.R. (1989) Animal Reintroductions: the Arabian oryx in Oman. Cambridge: Cambridge University Press.

82. Al Hikmani, H., Zabanoot, S., Al Shahari, T., Zabanoot, N., Al Hikmani, K. & Spalton,(2015). Status of the Arabian Gazelle, Gazella arabica (Mammalia: Bovidae), in Dhofar, Oman. Zoology in the Middle East. http://dx.doi.org/10.1080/09397140.2015.1101905.

83. Benda, P., & Nasher, A.K. (2006) First record of Crocidura dhofarensis Hutterer et Harrison, 1988 (Mammalia: Soricidae) in Yemen. Journal of the National Museum, 175(1-2): 27-30.

84. Soto, E. & Pardiñas, U. (2015) First record of the bushy-tailed jird, Sekeetamys calurus (Thomas, 1892) (Rodentia: Muridae) in Oman. Mammalia, 80(5), pp. 563-566. Retrieved 9 May. 2018, from doi:10.1515/mammalia- 2015-0141.

85. Benda, P., Reiter, A., Uhrin, M. & Varadínová, Z. (2016) A New Species of Pipistrelle Bat (Chiroptera: Vespertilionidae) from Southern Arabia. Acta Chiropterologica, 18: 301 – 323. 10.3161/15081109ACC2016 .18.2.001.

86. Arlettaz, R., Dandliker, G., Kasybekov, E., Pillet, J.-M., Rybin, S. & Zima, J. (1995) Feeding habits of the long-eared desert bat, Otonycteris hemprichi (Chiroptera: Vespertilionidae). Journal of Mammalogy, 76: 873-876.

87. Mikhalev, Y. A. (1997) Humpback whales Megaptera novaeangliae in the Arabian Sea. Marine Ecology Progress Series, 149:13-21.

88. http://www.nmfs.noaa.gov/pr/species/mammals/whales/humpback-whale.html

89. Willson, A., Baldwin, R., Cerchio, S., Collins, T., Findlay, K., Gray, H., Godley, B., Al-Harthi, S., Kennedy, A., Minton, G., Sucunza, F., Zerbini, A. & Witt, M. (2016) Research update on satellite tagging studies of the Arabian Sea humpback whale in the Sultanate of Oman. Paper SC/66b/SH28 presented to the International Whaling Commission Scientific Committee, Slovenia, June 2016.

90. Minton, G., Collins, T.J.Q., Findlay, K.P., Ersts, P.J., Rosenbaum, H.C., Berggren, P. & Baldwin, R.M. (2011) Seasonal distribution, abundance, habitat use and population identity of humpback whales in Oman. Journal of Cetacean Research and Management, Special Issue on Southern Hemisphere Humpback Whales, 185– 198.

91. Cerchio, S., Willson, A., Muirhead, C., Minton, G., Collins, T., Baldwin, R., Sarrouf Willson, M., Al Harthi, S. (2017) Preliminary Report on Long-term Detection of Arabian Sea Humpback Whale Vocalizations off Oman. Paper SC/66b/SH32 presented to the International Whaling Commission Scientific Committee, Slovenia, May 2017.

92. Baldwin, R. (1999) A Review of Cetaceans from Waters off the Arabian Peninsula. In: Fisher, M., Ghazanfar, S. A. & Spalton, A. (eds.) The Natural History of Oman — a Festschrift for Michael Gallagher. Leiden: Backhuys, pp 161-189.

93. Minton, G., Collins, T. J. Q., Findlay, K. P. & Baldwin, R. (2010) Cetacean distribution in the coastal waters of the Sultanate of Oman. Journal of Cetacean Research and Management, 11: 301-313.

94. Baldwin, R.M., Collins, M., van Waerebeek, K. & Minton, G. (2004) The Indo-Pacific humpback dolphin of the Arabian region: a status review. Aquat. Mamm. 30(1): 111–24.

95. Eriksen, J. & Eriksen, H. (2004) Common Birds in Oman – an identification guide. Muscat: Al Roya Publishing.

96. K. Pedersen, personal communication, 10 May 2018.

97. Gallagher, M.G. (2002) Observations on Juzur al Hallaniyyat (the Kuria Muria Islands) of Oman. The Journal of Oman Studies 12: 71-123.

98. Arnold, E.N. (1980) The reptiles and amphibians of Dhofar, southern Arabia. In: Shaw Reade, S.N., Sale, R.B., Gallagher, M.D. & Daly, R.H. (eds.) The Scientific Results of the Oman Flora and Fauna Survey 1977. Journal of Oman Studies Special Report No 2: pp 347-385.

99. Carranza, S., Xipell M, Tarroso, P., Gardner, A., Arnold, E.N., Robinson, M.D., et al. (2018) Diversity, distribution and conservation of the terrestrial reptiles of Oman (Sauropsida, Squamata). PLoS ONE 13(2):e0190389. https://doi.org/10.1371/ journal.pone.0190389

100. Gardner, A. (2013) The Amphibians and Reptiles of Oman and the UAE. Frankfurt: Edition Chimaira.

101. IUCN (1989) Oman – Coastal Zone Management Plan Dhofar. Volume 2: Resource Atlas. Muscat: Ministry of Commerce & Industry.

102. Baldwin, R. & Al Kiyumi, A.A. (1999) The Ecology and Conservation Status of the Sea Turtles of Oman. In: Fisher, M., Ghazanfar, S. A. & Spalton, A. (eds.) The Natural History of Oman — a Festschrift for Michael Gallagher. Leiden: Backhuys, pp 89-98.

103. http://www.seaturtle.org/tracking/?pr oject_id=145

104. Schneider, T. & D. Ikemeyer (2016). Dragonflies of Oman - a revised illustrated checklist (Odonata). Entomologische Zeitschrift, Schwanfeld 126: 137–147.

105. T. Schneider, personal communication, 11 March 2017.

106. Ball, L. (2014) An investigation of odonate communities within Wadi Sayq, Dhofar Province, Oman (Insecta: Odonata). Check List 10: 857–863.

107. Larsen, T.B. (1980) Butterflies of Oman. London: Bartholomew Books.

108. Hausmann, A. (2009) New and interesting geometrid moths from Dhofar, southern Oman (Lepidoptera, Geometridae). Mitteilungen der Münchner Entomologischen Gesellschaft 099: 111-128.

109. Popov, G.B. (1980) Acridoidea of Eastern Arabia. In: Shaw Reade, S.N., Sale, R.B., Gallagher, M.D. & Daly, R.H. (eds.) The Scientific Results of the Oman Flora and Fauna Survey 1977. Journal of Oman Studies Special Report No 2: pp 113-148.

110. Ambrus, R. & Grosser, W. (2012) Contribution to the knowledge of longhorn beetles from Dhofar region in Sultanate of Oman (Coleoptera: Cerambycidae). Humanity Space International Almanac, 1 (2): 448-457.

111. Darlington, P.E.C. (1984) Termite Mounds as Indicators of Vegetation Change in Dhofar. A Report to the Adviser for Conservation of the Environment, Oman.

112. Guichard, K.M. (1980) A Preliminary Account of the Sphecid Wasps of Oman. In: Shaw Reade, S.N., Sale, R.B., Gallagher, M.D. & Daly, R.H. (eds.) The Scientific Results of the Oman Flora and Fauna Survey 1977. Journal of Oman Studies Special Report No 2: pp 223-232.

113. G Lowe, personal communication, March 16 2018.

114. Bosch, D & Bosch, E. (1982) Seashells of Oman. London: Longman Group, pp. 206.

115. Mordan, P.B. (1980) Land Mollusca of Dhofar. In: Shaw Reade, S.N., Sale, R.B., Gallagher, M.D. & Daly, R.H. (eds.) The Scientific Results of the Oman Flora and Fauna Survey 1977. Journal of Oman Studies Special Report No 2: pp 103-111.

116. Lyon, R. G., Geiger, M. F., & Freyhof, J. (2016): Garra sindhi, a new species from the Jebel Samhan Nature Reserve in Oman (Teleostei: Cyprinidae). Zootaxa 4154 (1): 079-088.

117. A Roe, personal communication, November 15 2018.

118. Randall, J.E. (1995) Coastal Fishes of Oman. Bathurst: Crawford House Publishing.

119. Al-Jufaili, S.M., Hermosa, G., Al-Shuaily, S.S. & Al Mujaini, A. (2010) Oman Fish Biodiversity. Journal of King Abdulaziz

University-Marine Sciences, 21 (1): 3-51.

120. Jabado, R.W., Kyne, P. M., Pollom, R. A., Ebert, D. A., Simpfendorfer, C. A., Ralph, G.M., & Dulvy, N.K. (eds.) (2017) The Conservation Status of Sharks, Rays, and Chimaeras in the Arabian Sea and Adjacent Waters. Abu Dhabi: Environment Agency and IUCN Species Survival Commission Shark Specialist Group.

121. IUCN 2017. The IUCN Red List of Threatened Species. Version 2017-3. <http://www.iucnredlist.org>.

122. Spalton, J.A. (2002) Canidae in the Sultanate of Oman. Canid News, 5, 1 [http//www.canids.org/canidnews/5/canids_in_oman.pdf, accessed 27 October 2017].

123. J. Zarins, personal communication, 2 May 2018.

124. Travers Morgan (1997) Detail Land Use Study in Jabal Dhofar: Policy Options and Proposals. Final Report. Muscat: Supreme Committee for Town Planning.

125. Chatty, D. (1991) Socio-economic aspects of traditional arid land management in the M. & Osman, A. (eds.) Pastoralists in Oman, Rome: FAO.

126. Janzen, J. (1986) Nomads in the Sultanate of Oman: Tradition and Development in Dhofar. Boulder and London: Westview Press.

127. Shankland Cox International (1986) *Economic Development Prospects for the Southern Region: Volume 2 Agriculture, Fisheries, Pastoralism and Livestock.* Salalah: Planning Committee for Development and Environment in the Southern Region.

128. Al Shahri, A. A. (1994) Ancient Inscriptions and Writings in Dhofar. United Arab Emirates: Al Ghurair Printing & Publishing House.

129. Morris, M. (1983) Life and Self-Sufficiency in the Mountain Region of Dhofar. Report presented at the Salalah Workshop on Environmental Aspects of Development in the Southern Region. Muscat: Diwan of Royal Court.

130. Ibrahim, A.S.A. (1988) Nomads in the Sultanate of Oman, Southern Region (Dhofar): Seasonal movement pattern: past and present, and the major changes affecting this pattern. Salalah: Planning Committee for Development & Environment in the Southern Region.

131. Morris, M. J. (1986) Pastoral Management Study 1986. Prospects for the Southern Region. Salalah: Technical Secretariat of Planning Committee for Development and Environment in the Southern Region.

132. Oates, P.M. and Mactaggart, R. (1985) Technical Working Paper No 2: Settlement, Grazing and Institutional Issues Concerning the Jerbeeb. Phase 1: Survey of Current Conditions. Salalah: Technical Secretariat of the Planning Committee for Development and Environment in the Southern Region.

133. Oates, P.M., Bashir, M.A. and Ahmed, A.S. (1987) Technical Working Paper No 5: Jabal al Qara: Settlements, Population and Livestock Ownership. Salalah: Technical Secretariat of the Planning Committee for Development and Environment in the Southern Region.

134. Japan International Cooperation Agency (1990) The Study on a Master Plan for Agricultural Development: Final Report. Volume 1. Japan: JICA.

135. Ministry of Environment and Climate Affairs (2002) Recommendations of the 2002 Desertification Workshop in Dhofar. Muscat: MECA [in Arabic, unpublished].

136. ElMahi, A.T. (2001) The traditional pastoral groups of Dhofar, Oman: a parallel for ancient cultural ecology. Proceeding of the Seminar for Arabian Studies, 31: 131-143.

137. Al Kathiri, A.M. (1996). Rainfed Agriculture (mashaadiid, mishnu) in Dhofar. Salalah: Ministry of Agriculture & Fisheries.

138. Sale, J.B. (1980) The Ecology of the Mountain Region of Dhofar. In: The Scientific Results of the Oman Flora and Fauna Survey 1977. Journal of Oman Studies Special Report No 2: pp 25-57.

139. Japan International Cooperation Agency (1997) The Study on Agricultural Development Project in the Najd Region: Final Report. Japan: JICA.

140. Ministry of Agriculture and Fisheries (2014) Agricultural Census 2012/2013: Volume 3: Dhofar. Muscat: MAF.

141. https://agronomag.com/hydroponicwarehouses-solution-desert-areas/

142. Groom, N. (1981) Frankincense and Myrrh. London: Butler & Tanner.

143. Morris, M. (1997) The Harvesting of Frankincense in Dhofar, Oman. In: Avanzini, A. (Ed.) Profumi d'Arabia: Atti del Convego. Roma: L'Erma di Bretschneider, pp. 231-247.

144. Highet, J. (2006) Frankincense: Oman's Gift to the World. Munich: Prestel Publishing.

145. Alaamri, M.M.H. (2012) Distribution Boswellia sacra in Dhofar Mountains, Sultanate of Oman: Economic Value and Environmental Role. Journal of Life Sciences 6: 632-636.

146. Boyles, P. (1983) Beekeeping in Dhofar – A Development Project Utilising the Existing Ecosystem. Report presented at the Salalah Workshop on Environmental Aspects of Development in the Southern Region. Muscat: Diwan of Royal Court.

147. Alattal, Y., Alghamdi, A. and Alsharhi, M. (2014) Population Structure of the Yemeni Honey Bee (Apis mellifera jemenitica) Entails an Urgent Conservation Strategy in Saudi Arabia. Journal of Entomology 11 (3):163-169.

148. Morris, M. (2019) Cultural Aspects [Central Oman Escarpments & Hills]. In: Al Zubair, M., Mershen,B., Al Saqri, S., Al Ghafri, A., Al Hosni, T., Al Nabhani, Y., Al Rajhi, A., Nasir, S., Patzelt, A., Spalton, A. & Anderson, A. The Mountains of Oman. An Illustrated Reference to Nature and Society. Hildesheim: Georg Olms AG.

149. Thomas, B. The South-Eastern Borderlands of Rub' Al Khali. The Geographical Journal 77 (1): 193-212.

150. Ministry of Agriculture and Fisheries (2016) Fisheries Statistics 2016. Muscat: MAF.

151. Al Habsi, M.S. and Mustapha, N.H.N. (2011) Fisheries Sustainability in Oman. Journal of Economics and Sustainable Development 2(7): 35-47.

152. Al-Marzouqi, A., Jayabalan, N. & Groenveld, J.C. (2007) An assessment of the Spiny Lobster Panulirus homarus Fishery in Oman – Another decline in the Western Indian Ocean? Western Indian Ocean J. Mar. Sci., 6(2): 159-174.

153. De Waal, S.W.P., Balkhair, M., Al-Mashiki, A., & Khoom, S. (2011) Habitat Preferences of Juvenile Abalone (Haliotis mariae) along the Dhofar Coast of Oman and Implications for Conservation. Agriculture and Marine Sciences, 17:45-52.

154. Al-Bahrani, K.M. (2008) Management of the Omani Abalone Haliotis mariae: An Integrated Policy. MSc Thesis. University of Rhode Island: Rhode Island.

155. Bose, S., Al-Kindy, F., Al-Balushi, A. & Rajab, M.M. (2013) Accounting the Unaccounted: A Case of Women's Participation in Shellfish Harvesting in the Sultanate of Oman. Gender Technology & Development, 17(31):31-53.

156. Al-Marzouqi, A. & Jayabalan, N. (2009) Biology and stock assessment of the pharaoh cuttlefish, Sepia pharaonic Ehrenberg, 1831 from the Arabian Sea off Oman. Indian Journal of Fisheries, 156(4): 231-239.

157. Al-Masroori, H.S., Al-Oufi, H. & McShane, P. (2009) Causes and Mitigations on Trap Ghost Fishing in Oman: Sciemntific Approach to Local Fishers' Perception. Journal of Fisheries and Aquatic Science, 4(3): 129-135.

Index

U

V

W

Y

Z

Acknowledgements

We are eternally grateful to the late Sultan Qaboos bin Said whose personal interest in the natural world guided Oman's active participation in biodiversity conservation and sustainable development. Furthermore we thank His Majesty Sultan Haitham bin Tarik for his commitment to continue on the path to environmental sustainability.

We gratefully acknowledge the support of His Excellency The Minister of the Diwan of Royal Court and his staff, in particular those of the Office for Conservation of the Environment.

We thank His Excellency the Secretary General of Royal Court Affairs and his staff, in particular staff of the Royal Farms and Gardens, Directorate General of Veterinary Services and the Directorate General of Transport.

The support of His Excellency the Minister of State and Governor of Dhofar and his staff is very much appreciated and in particular we would like to thank the Niab Wali of Juzur Al Hallaniyyat (Islands) and Niab Wali of Al Hashman for their generous hospitality.

Staff of the Ministry of Agriculture, Fisheries and Water Resources were very helpful and we wish to acknowledge the Marine Science & Fisheries Centre, and the Directorate General of Agriculture, Fisheries and Water Resources (Dhofar).

We are grateful to the Directorate General of Meteorology at the Public Authority for Civil Aviation for sharing weather data and in particular for providing images and information for Cyclone Mekunu.

Furthermore we thank Petroleum Development Oman (PDO) for facilitating a visit to Miraah Solar Project and to Nimr Reed Beds where we were kindly hosted by Bauer Nimr LLC.

We would also like to thank the following: Ali bin Salim Akaak, Rashid bin Abdulrab Al Batahari, Khalid bin Mohammed Al Hikmani, Omar bin Said Al Kathiri, Hassan bin Talib Al Lawati, Said bin Mohammed Al Mahri, Salim bin Mohammed Al Mashni, Zawan bint Jumaa Al Qassabi, Ali bin Ahmed Al Shahri, Ali bin Mohammed Al Shahri, Talal bin Said Al Shahri, Michael Butler, Yashwant Chauhan, Naseer bin Abdullah Jadad, Andy Kwartang, Gianna Minton, Annette Patzelt, Jeffrey Rose, Sue Ward, Robert Whitcombe, Andy Willson and Rams bin Mohammed Zabanoot.

Finally we would like to thank the people of Dhofar for their kindness and wonderful hospitality.

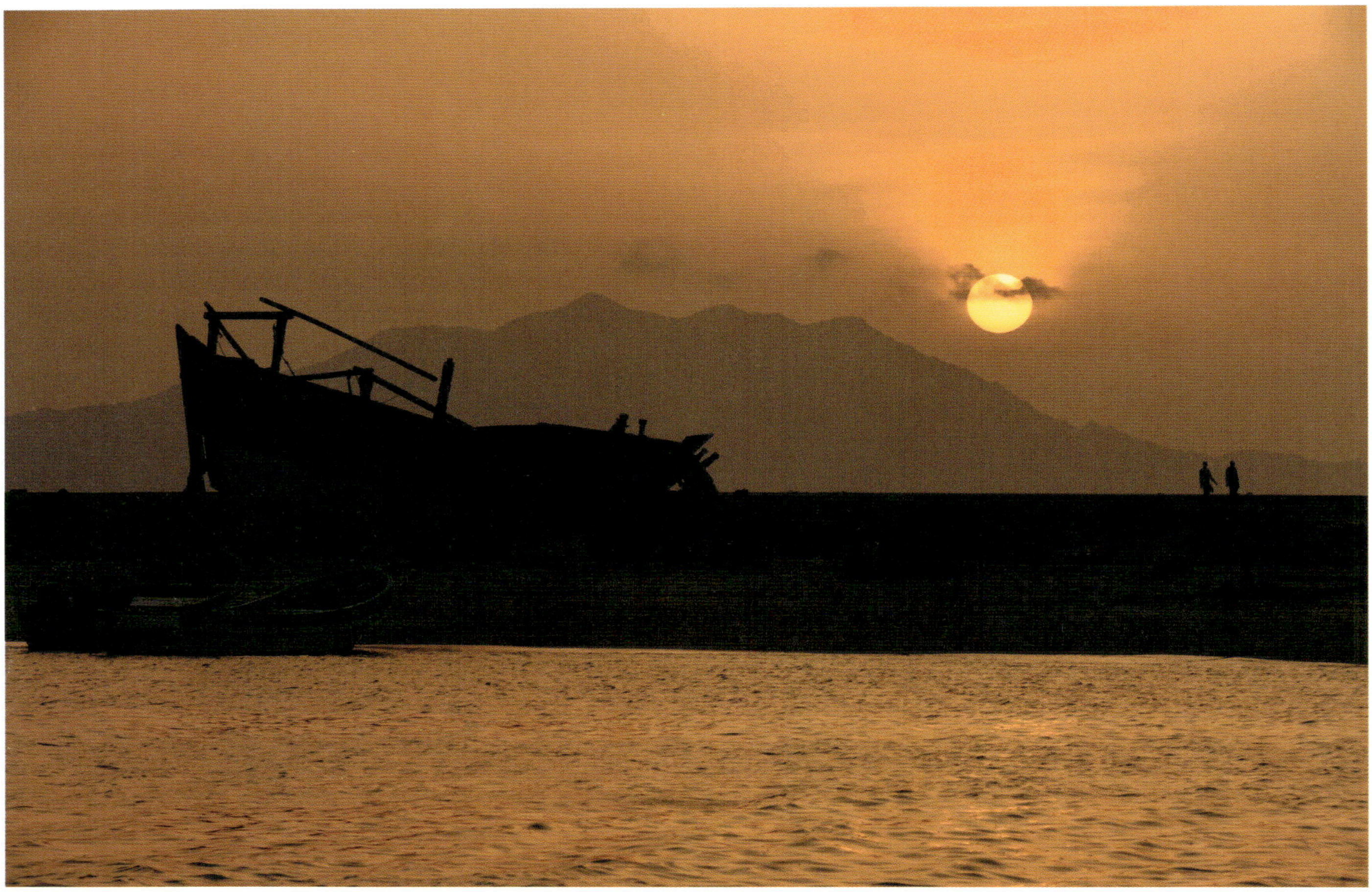